JAZZ

"You got to be in the sun to feel the sun.
It's that way with music, too."

—*Sidney Bechet*

JAZZ

Scott DeVeaux

University of Virginia

Gary Giddins

The Graduate Center, City University of New York

W. W. NORTON & COMPANY

NEW YORK ■ LONDON

W. W. Norton & Company has been independent since its founding in 1923, when William Warder Norton and Margaret D. Herter Norton first began publishing lectures delivered at the People's Institute, the adult education division of New York City's Cooper Union. The Nortons soon expanded their program beyond the Institute, publishing books by celebrated academics from America and abroad. By mid-century, the two major pillars of Norton's publishing program—trade books and college texts—were firmly established. In the 1950s, the Norton family transferred control of the company to its employees, and today—with a staff of 400 and a comparable number of trade, college, and professional titles published each year—W. W. Norton & Company stands as the largest and oldest publishing house owned wholly by its employees.

Editor: Maribeth Payne
Developmental editor: Susan Gaustad
Managing editor: Marian Johnson
Electronic media editor: Steve Hoge
Associate editor: Allison Courtney Fitch
Editorial assistant: Imogen Leigh Howes
Senior production manager: Jane Searle
Director of photography: Trish Marx
Photo researcher: Donna Ranieri
Design director: Rubina Yeh
Design and layout: Lissi Sigillo
Proofreader: Ben Reynolds
Music typesetter: David Budmen
Indexer: Marilyn Bliss
Composition by Matrix Publishing Services, Inc.
Manufacturing by Courier, Westford

Library of Congress Cataloging-in-Publication Data

DeVeaux, Scott Knowles.
    Jazz / Scott DeVeaux ; Gary Giddins. — 1st ed.
        p. cm.
    Includes bibliographical references and index.
    ISBN 978-0-393-97880-3 (pbk.)
    1. Jazz—History and criticism. I. Giddins, Gary. II. Title.
    ML3508.D47 2009
    781.65—dc22   2008046717

ISBN 978-0-393-97880-3

W. W. Norton & Company, Inc., 500 Fifth Avenue, New York, N.Y. 10110
www.wwnorton.com

W. W. Norton & Company Ltd., Castle House, 75/76 Wells Street, London W1T 3QT
1 2 3 4 5 6 7 8 9 0

To the women in my family: my grown-up daughters Amelia and Flora Thomson-DeVeaux; my newborn twins, Lena and Celia; and most of all, my wife, Nancy Hurrelbrinck.

—Scott DeVeaux

To Deborah Halper and Lea Giddins.

—Gary Giddins

CONTENTS

PART III

THE SWING ERA.. 164

PART V

THE AVANT-GARDE, FUSION, HISTORICISM, AND NOW

INTRODUCTION

One of the great things about studying jazz—beyond the excitement and variety of the music itself—is its relative historical newness. It may seem like an old story that predates rock and hip-hop and your grandparents. But following its contours today, in the early years of the twenty-first century, is like what it might have meant to study Shakespeare in 1650, when you could still meet people who saw the plays as originally produced and even worked or hung out with the guy who wrote them.

The pioneers of jazz, including its preeminent soloist (Louis Armstrong) and composer (Duke Ellington), worked into the 1970s and beyond. Innovators of later jazz styles and schools are with us now. Young musicians, creating tremendous excitement at this moment, will be acclaimed as tomorrow's masters.

In other words, the dust of history has by no means settled on jazz. The canon of masterpieces is open to interpretation and adjustment. In studying the jazz past, we are also helping to define it. That goes for students as well as teachers. *Jazz* is designed to impart a basic history of jazz—a narrative arc that traces its development from nineteenth-century musical precursors to the present. It requires no prior musical knowledge or ability, only a predisposition for the enjoyment of music and the imagination to feel its expressive power.

The Plan of the Book

Each part of *Jazz* opens with an introductory overview of the period and its music; a timeline, situating important jazz events within a broader context of cultural and political history; and dynamic photographs that capture the mood of the era.

PART I: MUSICAL ORIENTATION This first part introduces the vocabulary necessary for discussing the basic rudiments of music and demonstrates, by recorded examples, how those rudiments function in jazz. "Musical Elements and Instruments" analyzes timbre; rhythm, polyrhythm, and swing; melody and scales; harmony; and texture. "Jazz Form and Improvisation" delves into the area of formal structure, chiefly the twelve-bar blues and the thirty-two-bar **A A B A** popular song—forms that recur throughout jazz history. It provides a musician's-eye view of what happens on the bandstand, along with examples of essential jazz lingo, like trading fours, rhythm changes, grooves, and modal improvisation.

Admittedly, this is the most technical section of *Jazz*. But we have attempted to clarify these points on our website, with video and audio recordings by the Free Bridge Quintet, a band affiliated with the University of Virginia, which address each musical concept—from contrasting timbres of instruments to performance techniques to formal structures. When a head is accompanied by the audio icon, as below, that means you can go to the website (wwnorton.com/studyspace), click on the chapter (1 or 2), and then click on that head to hear and see examples of what the section describes—brass instruments, reed instruments, trumpet mutes, homophonic texture, major scales, harmonic progressions, and so on.

◀》 Grooves and Swing

◀》 Brass Instruments

We suggest that you absorb this material and listen to the examples with the expectation of returning to them periodically as you progress through *Jazz*.

The four main parts of *Jazz* cover the broad sweep of the music's history and its major figures, as illustrated by seventy-five recordings, analyzed in laymen's terms in Listening Guides. Again, you don't have to know how to read music to enjoy the guides—only how to read a clock.

PART II: EARLY JAZZ (1900–1930) After exploring the various roots of jazz (folk music, blues, minstrelsy, dance music, brass bands, ragtime), we focus on New Orleans, the birthplace of jazz, introducing its legendary (and unrecorded) founding father, Buddy Bolden, and the first artists to bring jazz to the North and, through records and tours, around the world: the Original Dixieland Jazz Band, King Oliver, Sidney Bechet, and Jelly Roll Morton. We follow them to Chicago and New York in the 1920s, the "Jazz Age," which saw the emergence of the first great jazz soloist, singer, recording artist, and performer, Louis Armstrong, as well as a generation of improvisers inspired by him, and the phenomenon of jazz-influenced, urban dance bands, crystallized in the early triumphs of Fletcher Henderson and Duke Ellington.

PART III: THE SWING ERA Within a decade of Armstrong's first recordings as a leader, his music became the foundation for the mainstream pop music of the United States and most of the world. In this section, we discuss the social, political, and economic contexts for the extraordinary crossover of a recently localized African American vogue into the commercial market. We examine key bandleaders like Benny Goodman, Jimmie Lunceford, and Artie Shaw, and, in particular, the titans of big-band swing, Ellington and Count Basie. We then look at individual performers who made up the great Swing Era bands, big and small: the soloists, vocalists, and rhythm section players who transformed jazz into an increasingly sophisticated music, setting the stage for the palace coup to follow.

PART IV: MODERN JAZZ During the hard times of Depression and war, the country had danced to swing. After the war, a sober reconsideration of America's standing in the world and its problems at home brought a dark turn to the arts. In an era of *noir* movies and action painting, jazz was transformed by bebop, the exhilarating virtuoso style pioneered by Charlie Parker and Dizzy Gillespie in the 1940s—a music that favored listening over dancing and required a deeper level of concentration from the audience. Bebop led to cool jazz and hard bop, movements that dominated the 1950s, and a renaissance in jazz composition, exemplified by Thelonious Monk, Charles Mingus, Gil Evans, and George Russell. Yet the central figure in the postbop era was Miles Davis, whose bands helped to launch other pioneers, including Sonny Rollins, Bill Evans, and John Coltrane.

PART V: THE AVANT-GARDE, FUSION, HISTORICISM, AND NOW In this last section, covering the second half of jazz's first century, we abandon the usual attempt to define the music in a decade-by-decade manner. By this time, jazz began to offer alternative narratives. If bebop was a radical response to swing, the avant-garde of the late 1950s and 1960s was an even more radical response to bop, opposing all the familiar conventions of jazz: instrumentation, form, dance-beat rhythm, and tonality. Bop remained the basic language of jazz while the avant-garde developed into an ongoing parallel stream, from the tumultuous "free jazz" of Ornette Coleman and Cecil Taylor, through the musician cooperatives (the AACM) and loft jazz events of the 1970s and 1980s, to the international avant-gardism that maintains a cult-like devotion today.

In contrary fashion, another school of jazz musicians combined jazz and contemporary rock to produce fusion. Most accounts of the fusion movement begin with the electric jazz-rock of the 1970s, but fusion has a much broader history than that, and helps us to understand several major developments in postwar jazz that are usually overlooked by jazz historians. These developments originated in the big bands yet offered listener-friendly alternatives to bop: singers (Frank Sinatra, Sarah Vaughan), rhythm and blues (Louis Jordan, Nat "King" Cole), soul jazz (Jimmy Smith), and Latin jazz (Cuban and Brazilian). Jazz-rock fusion extended that tradition, from the startling syntheses of Miles Davis and Weather Report to the more fluid mixture of twenty-first-century jazz and pop heard in jam bands (Medeski, Martin and Wood), acid jazz, hip-hop jazz, and smooth jazz.

Finally, we offer a historicist view of jazz history—predicated on jazz's evolving obsession with its own history, especially after the New Orleans revivalist movement of the 1930s. The historicist sensibility played a decisive role in advancing jazz education (this book is one consequence) and the presentation of jazz at festivals throughout the world—a phenomenon that continues to flourish. Historicism led to a long-delayed recognition of jazz by establishment organizations—cultural centers, academic programs, and the committees that confer awards and grants. The avant-garde plundered the past in its irreverent way (Anthony Braxton, Ronald Shannon Jackson), leading to a dramatically conservative response by Wynton Marsalis, who made possible Jazz at Lincoln Center. Today's jazz artists have little need to choose sides. We conclude with a representative figure in contemporary jazz, Jason Moran, who is equally at home with stride piano and hip-hop beats.

In addition: Within the chapters, key musical terms are highlighted in the text in boldface; these can also be found in the glossary at the back of the book. Throughout the text, new terms are occasionally defined in the margin, or old terms redefined. When one such term is accompanied by an audio icon, as below, that means you can hear an example of the concept being defined on the website.

🔊 **pentatonic scale** five-note
scale, as C D E G A

Each chapter ends with a list of suggestions for additional listening, including the date of the original recording and the most recent CD that features the recording. For three musicians whose careers span several parts, we provide a chronology at the end of his respective chapter—Louis Armstrong (Chapter 6), Duke Ellington (Chapter 8), and Miles Davis (Chapter 14). And each historical part (II–V) ends with a summary describing and outlining in detail the main style points of that era's music, along with lists of its major musicians.

In addition to the glossary, appendixes include an instrument-by-instrument list of many of the most significant jazz musicians of the last hundred years (with birth and death dates), a primer on musical notation, an essay on building a collection of jazz recordings, a filmography, and a bibliography.

The Art

We are very proud of the design of *Jazz*, and hope you will enjoy the two hundred black and white photographs—especially the work of the brilliant Herman Leonard, considered by many to be the greatest photographer ever to focus his camera on jazz. A protégé of Yousuf Karsh, Leonard is distinguished in his work by his total control of light. In the late 1940s, the peak of his jazz period, Leonard brought his equipment to clubs, blocked out the natural light, and created his own chiaroscuro effects, emphasizing the excitement of the music and the milieu—through reflected highlights and his signature use of cigarette smoke. Leonard's New Orleans studio was destroyed by Hurricane Katrina; he now lives and works in California. He shot most of the full-page photographs that introduce each chapter.

The color insert traces jazz in a different way: through the graphic styles of album covers, sheet music, and other desiderata. These evocative images illustrate the marketing of written and recorded jazz, from sheet music covers of the 1920s to CD covers of today.

The Recordings and Listening Guides

Jazz includes a four-CD set that provides a comprehensive overview of the music through seventy-eight selections, combining acknowledged classics (Miles Davis's "So What," Coleman Hawkins's "Body and Soul," Louis Armstrong's "West End Blues") with several unusual but illuminating tracks, ranging from a 1916 recording by Wilbur Sweatman to a pair of tracks by Jason Moran. Each selection is introduced by a passage in the text, designated with an icon (🔊), that sets the scene for the work. This is followed by a Listening Guide (carrying the same icon), in which significant musical moments are linked directly to CD timings along the left.

1. CD and track number are given at the upper-right-hand corner.

2. Below the title of the piece, you'll find basic information about the recording: the musicians, label (the original label is given first, followed by the most recent CD that features the recording), date of recording, and style and form of the piece.

3. The "What to listen for" box offers some key points to help orient your listening.

4. All boldface terms are included in the glossary at the back.

5. Occasionally a music example is provided to illustrate a distinctive melody or rhythm.

1.15 —①

🎧 snake rag ②

KING OLIVER'S CREOLE JAZZ BAND
King Oliver, Louis Armstrong, trumpets or cornets;
Honore Dutrey, trombone; Johnny Dodds, clarinet; Lil
Hardin, piano; Bud Scott, banjo; Baby Dodds, drums

- Label: OKeh 4933; *Off the Record: The Complete 1923 Jazz Band Recordings* (Archeophone ARCH OTR-MM6-C2)
- Date: 1923
- Style: New Orleans jazz
- Form: march/ragtime

What to listen for: ③

- march/ragtime form
- dramatic changes in texture from polyphony to monophony (breaks)
- breaks in **A** and **B** strains: descending chromatic line, trombone glissando
- modulation to a new key at the trio
- variety of breaks for the two cornets

INTRODUCTION (STRAIN A, abbreviated)

0:00   The band beings polyphonically, in **collective improvisation**. ④ Dodds on clarinet drops from a high note to play swirling patterns while Dutrey sticks to a slow, unsyncopated line on the trombone. The two cornets (Armstrong and Oliver) improvise on the main melody.

0:05   **Break**: the cornets play a "snake"—a steady descending line in harmony.

0:07   Using his slide, the trombone answers with simple, comic **glissandos**, followed by a pair of chords from the band.

STRAIN A

0:10   The first strain begins on the **I chord**. Oliver plays the lead cornet, with Armstrong barely audible behind him.

0:23   The band repeats the snake.

STRAIN B

0:28   The second strain begins on a different harmony (**V**).

0.35   In a two-bar **break,** Dutrey plays three upward trombone glissandos, the last accented by a cymbal crash.

0:42   The band repeats the snake.

STRAIN B

0:46   Strain **B** is repeated, with slight variation.

1:00   Snake.

STRAIN A

1:05   Strain **A** is repeated, with more variation.

1:18   Snake.

STRAIN C (TRIO)

1:23   With no transition, the tune suddenly **modulates** to a new key. This strain (trio) lasts twice as long as the previous two. Dutrey plays a trombone line with a distinctive rhythmic profile.

⑤

Online: StudySpace

Available at www.wwnorton.com/studyspace, this website offers some exciting features to enrich and reinforce your study of jazz.

■ Each chapter has its own content on the site (indicated by the Study-Space icon at the bottom right of every chapter's opening page). In Chapter 1, for example, you can click on any head that is accompanied by an audio icon in the book, to hear and see examples of what that section describes.

■ Interactive Listening Guides (iLGs): Each Listening Guide is also available in an easy-to-operate interactive form on the website (the four-CD set is required). Here you can instantly hear the points listed in the "What to listen for" feature. You can also test yourself with the listening quiz, which asks you to identify the instruments, performers, and structure of the piece.

■ Jazz Studio Audio/Video Podcasts: This set of audio and video demonstrations, prepared under the direction of Scott DeVeaux and recorded by John D'Earth and the Free Bridge Quintet, walks you through all the main musical concepts discussed in Chapters 1 and 2. The basic elements of music theory are brought to life through clear, simple examples. In addition, these superb musicians show how improvisation works in different tempos, grooves, and meters, and how the concepts specific to jazz (breaks, trading fours) are put into practice in a jam-session-style performance.

■ Author Insight Video Podcasts: Engaging interviews with Gary Giddins and Scott DeVeaux elaborate on important points made throughout the book.

■ Quizzes (by David Bubsey, East Tennessee State University): Test yourself with chapter and listening quizzes, many including audio excerpts from the four CDs.

■ Chapter Outlines help you review the material.

■ FlashCards and Audio Glossary will help you master the key jazz terms.

For Instructors

- Interactive Listening Guides (iLGs): These integrate text, visuals, and music into an easily navigable apparatus for lectures.

- Instructor's Resource Disc: Includes photographs from the book, PowerPoint lecture outlines, and Jazz Studio audio and video content.

- Instructor's Manual (by Howard Spring, University of Guelph): Provides chapter outlines, teaching strategies, sample course syllabi, suggestions for reading and viewing, and questions and prompts for class discussion and research papers. Download free from wwnorton.com.

- Test Bank in Microsoft Word and ExamView format (by John Murphy, University of North Texas): Offers over sixty multiple-choice, true/false, short-answer, and matching questions as well as essay prompts for each chapter, covering both text and repertory. Download free from wwnorton.com.

- Discography (by jazz critic Ted Panken): Provides recording information for all pieces mentioned in the book, and additional selections as well. Download free from wwnorton.com.

- Coursepacks for Blackboard, WebCT, and other course management systems: Include chapter quizzes, listening quizzes, additional listening assignments, study plans, and chapter outlines, all freely distributed. Your course can have an online presence in a matter of minutes.

Acknowledgments

Only two names are listed on the cover of *Jazz*, but this book could not exist without the contributions of many others. Chief among them is Norton editor Maribeth Payne, who shepherded the project through several years and over many obstacles. She brought the two writers together, and kept us fixated on the big picture, playing to our strengths individually and as a team. Every writer craves a good line editor and we are blessed with one of the best, Susan Gaustad, who shaved our excesses, pounced on our repetitions, and emended our solecisms. Quite simply: Without Maribeth and Susan, no *Jazz*.

Our work was also immeasurably aided by the rest of the staff at Norton: Courtney Fitch, ancillaries editor; Imogen Howes, editorial assistant; Jane Searle, senior production manager (responsible for, among other things, the quality reproduction of photos); Trish Marx, director of photography; Ben Reynolds, proofreader; and David Budmen, music typesetter. Their experience and unswerving attention to detail made the writing and production process much smoother. Steve Hoge, the media editor, has handled the complicated but exciting task of translating our on-the-page content for the digital world. Most of what you see up on the web—from online Listening Guides to audio/visual material—has been created under Steve's supervision. Lissi Sigillo is responsible for much of the physical look of the book—its layout, its sense of design, its logical flow. Tom Laskey of the Sony BMG Custom Marketing Group oversaw with grace and good humor copyright clearances for all recordings as well as the engineering and duplication of master discs.

Donna Ranieri gathered hundreds of illustrations, from which the final selection was made, tracking down images and photographers like Sherlock Holmes on the trail of a gigantic hound. The members of the Free Bridge Quintet—John D'earth, Jeff Decker, Pete Spaar, Robert Jospé, and Bob Hallahan—produced their splendid music with grace under pressure. We are especially grateful for John's contribution of original music used in our audio and video presentations. Ted Panken compiled an immense discography, checking information and availability of all the recordings mentioned in the text. We also deeply appreciate the work of several superb scholars: the musicologist Howard Spring, who wrote the Instructor's Manual; the ethnomusicologist John Murphy, who created the manual's Test Bank; and the quizzes devised by the trombonist (and musicologist) David Bubsey.

Finally, we are very grateful to the people who read and commented on the manuscript: Dwight Andrews, Emory University; David Bubsey, East Tennessee State University; John Fremgen, University of Texas at Austin; Charles Garrett, University of Michigan; David Joyner, Pacific Lutheran University; Jeffrey Magee, University of Illinois at Urbana-Champaign; Vincent Martucci, State University of New York at New Paltz; Mark Mazzatenta, University of North Carolina at Greensboro; Richard Mook, Arizona State University; John Murphy, University of North Texas; Cara Pollard, Texas Tech University; Emmett G. Price III, Northeastern University; Guthrie P. Ramsey Jr., University of Pennsylvania; Lindsey Sarjeant, Florida A&M University; David Schroeder, New York University; Howard Spring, University of Guelph; Patrick Warfield, Georgetown University; Christopher Washburne, Columbia University; and Carl Woideck, University of Oregon.

Scott DeVeaux
Gary Giddins
January 2009

JAZZ

Late 1800s–early 1900s

- Scott Joplin, John Philip Sousa, Fisk Jubilee Singers, Buddy Bolden, Manuel Perez, W. C. Handy.
- 1914–17, World War I: James Reese Europe, Vernon and Irene Castle.
- First recordings to show shift from ragtime to jazz: Wilbur Sweatman.
- Great Migration begins, including New Orleans musicians: Freddie Keppard, King Oliver, Jelly Roll Morton.
- 1917: First jazz recordings by Original Dixieland Jazz Band.

- 1919: Will Marion Cook takes band to Europe, including Sidney Bechet.
- 1919–20, white dance bands incorporate watered-down jazz elements: Art Hickman, Paul Whiteman.

1920s: Jazz Age

- Blues divas: Ma Rainey, Bessie Smith, Mamie Smith.
- New Orleans musicians record in Chicago and New York: Jelly Roll Morton, King Oliver, Sidney Bechet, New Orleans Rhythm Kings.
- Early big bands: Fletcher Henderson, Duke Ellington, Chick Webb.
- Stride piano: Earl Hines, James P. Johnson, Fats Waller.

Gertrude "Ma" Rainey was regarded as the "Mother of the Blues." She helped to introduce several important musicians on her recordings.

Oran "Hot Lips" Page, record producer Harry Lim, pianist Dave Bowman, bassist Clyde Newcombe, and Billie Holiday relax at a 1940s jam session.

In the prewar era, few musical events were more exciting than a "battle of the bands" waged before the most discerning of critics: dancers. Chick Webb led the home team at New York's Savoy Ballroom, and Fletcher Henderson was an especially notable three-time challenger—in 1927, 1928, and 1937.

simple: jazz is most rewarding to a listener conversant with its rules. By understanding what the musician is up against—in terms of structure; or the competing claims of melody, rhythm, and harmony; or the challenge in mastering a particular instrument—you are better able to empathize with and evaluate his or her work. Happily, this basic knowledge may be acquired with virtually no musical ability or training. Most jazz, as we will see, is based on two structures and is performed on a limited number of instruments. If you can feel "time," which is how jazz musicians refer to a rhythmic pulse, and can count to four (most jazz is based on patterns of four beats), you have already mastered its most essential principles.

- Virtuoso soloists: Bix Beiderbecke, Coleman Hawkins, Benny Carter.
- Tin Pan Alley songwriters: George Gershwin, Cole Porter, Irving Berlin, Richard Rodgers, Jerome Kern, Harold Arlen, Hoagy Carmichael.
- 1925: Harlem Renaissance begins.
- 1925–28: Louis Armstrong records with the Hot Five and Hot Seven.
- 1927: Duke Ellington triumphs at the Cotton Club.
- 1929: Great Depression begins.

1930s: Swing
- Boogie-woogie comes to Café Society: Pete Johnson, Big Joe Turner.

- 1935: Swing Era launched by Benny Goodman.
- Swing bands flourish around the country: Count Basie, Jimmy Lunceford, Artie Shaw, Glenn Miller, Cab Calloway, Duke Ellington, Andy Kirk (with Mary Lou Williams), Chick Webb.
- Jazz singing arrives: Armstrong, Bing Crosby, Billie Holiday, Ella Fitzgerald, Jimmy Rushing.
- Soloists become jazz stars: Armstrong, Hawkins, Fats Waller, Lester Young, Art Tatum, Django Reinhardt (first major European jazz figure), Roy Eldridge, Charlie Christian.
- Bass and drums come into their own: Jimmy Blanton, Milt Hinton, Jo Jones, Sid Catlett.
- 1939–45: World War II.

PART I

1944–49: Bebop
- Pioneeers: Charlie Parker, Dizzy Gillespie, Kenny Clarke, Thelonious Monk.
- First generation: Bud Powell, Dexter Gordon. Max Roach, Sarah Vaughan.

1950s: Cool jazz and hard bop
- Cool jazz: Miles Davis, Modern Jazz Quartet, Lennie Tristano, Gil Evans, Gerry Mulligan, Stan Getz, Dave Brubeck, George Russell.
- Hard bop: Max Roach, Art Blakey, Horace Silver, Charles Mingus, John Coltrane, Sonny Rollins, Clifford Brown, Wes Montgomery.
- 1950–53: Korean War.
- 1955–68: Civil Rights Movement.

1960s–1980s: Avant-Garde (or Free Jazz) and Loft Era
- 1960s avant-garde: Ornette Coleman, Cecil Taylor, Albert Ayler, Sonny Rollins, John Coltrane, Sun Ra, AACM, Anthony Braxton, Art Ensemble of Chicago, Andrew Hill.
- 1960s postbop: Miles Davis, Wayne Shorter, Joe Henderson.
- 1961–75: American involvement in Vietnam War.
- 1970s loft jazz: David Murray, Arthur Blythe, Leroy Jenkins, Henry Threadgill.
- 1989: Beginning of overthrow of Communist states.

Horace Silver, at piano, rehearses with his quintet: tenor saxophonist Junior Cook, trumpeter Louis Smith, bassist Gene Taylor, and drummer Louis Hayes, 1958.

Thelonious Monk (center) and Charlie Rouse (right) visit with the Prague Mime Troupe at the Village Gate in New York, 1963.

Wynton Marsalis in New Orleans, 1993.

Cab Calloway and two chorus girls at the Strand Theater in New York, 1940s.

Cecil Taylor was a controversial newcomer at the Newport Jazz Festival, 1957.

Fusion Narrative

- 1940s–1950s jazz-pop: Louis Jordan, Ray Charles, Jimmy Smith, Sarah Vaughan, Stan Getz, Frank Sinatra, Nat King Cole, Mongo Santamaria.
- 1969–70, beginning of jazz-rock: Miles Davis, Gil Evans, Tony Williams, Herbie Hancock.
- 1970s fusion: Chick Corea, John McLaughlin, Weather Report, Pat Metheny, Jaco Pastorius, Keith Jarrett, Oregon.
- 1980s "smooth jazz": Kenny G.
- 1990s hip-hop, acid jazz, jam bands: John Scofield, Medeski, Martin and Wood.

Historicist Narrative

- 1930s: New Orleans revival.
- 1950s: Festivals, academia.
- 1970s: Jazz as "tradition."
- CD reissues, repertory bands, jazz in film and documentaries.
- Neoclassical (or historicist) jazz: Wynton Marsalis, Anthony Braxton, Shannon Jackson, Harry Connick Jr., Diana Krall.
- Jason Moran and a new generation.

MUSICAL ELEMENTS AND INSTRUMENTS

EMPATHY, INDIVIDUALITY, AND TIMBRE

Empathy

Almost every jazz lover has had an experience like this one. You take your seat at a concert, as a quintet—trumpet player, saxophonist, pianist, bassist, and drummer—takes the stage. After a brief piano introduction, which sets the pace and feeling for the first piece, the trumpeter and saxophonist play a melody, supported by the accompaniment of piano, bass, and drums. The tune may or may not be familiar to you, but because it is played simultaneously by the two wind instruments and repeats certain melodic phrases, you can at least be sure that it is a written melody, or theme. Then the theme ends. As the trumpeter steps back, the saxophonist begins to improvise a solo. In a short while, you find yourself totally lost; while similar solos in previous concerts have caught and stimulated you right away, tonight it's all a tangle and you can't find a footing.

All music—all art, all entertainment—requires empathy, but jazz requires empathy of a particular sort. Jazz musicians are inventing a musical statement (improvising) in that space and in that moment. In order to share in their creativity, you have to follow the twists and turns of their musical ideas while simultaneously registering their interaction

Charlie Parker—blindingly fast virtuoso, bluesman, romantic ballad player—with his fellow 1949 Metronome All-Stars Lennie Tristano (piano), Eddie Safranski (bass), and Billy Bauer (guitar).

wwnorton.com/studyspace

with other musicians; only then can you evaluate whether a solo is a success—the soloist may be a spellbinder or a bore, inspired or aloof—and the band coherent. Sidney Bechet, the great soprano saxophonist of jazz's early years, once remarked, "You got to be in the sun to feel the sun. It's that way with music too."

The purpose of this book is to help put you in the sun as regards jazz, and one way to gain a deeper understanding is to learn some of the fundamental rules and techniques of music. Obviously, at a basic level you can simply listen to a performance and be amused, amazed, shaken, moved—you don't need anyone to tell you that you like it, or why. A great deal of jazz functions on just such a visceral level. Most fans can recall their first exposure to jazz, whether

While classical music is housed in permanent concert halls like Carnegie Hall, most jazz clubs have shorter life spans. Bop City opened in 1948 at Broadway and 49th Street in Manhattan, accommodating top-line acts, but was gone within a few years.

it was a performance in a nightclub or concert hall, or on a classic recording by Louis Armstrong, Billie Holiday, or John Coltrane. Often, just one encounter is enough to encourage a desire to hear more of that artist and other jazz artists—and, by extension, to learn more about the intricacies of this exciting and passionate art.

Yet only by pressing deeper into the music, to the point where you listen like a musician, can you penetrate the most rewarding mysteries of jazz. In this regard, music is no different from any other pursuit. As a child you went to the movies, and every movie was fun—a novelty, an outing, a new story with new people and situations. After you had seen many movies, you realized some were better than others and began to appreciate the unique talents of certain actors, directors, even film composers. Similarly, you may enjoy your first baseball game knowing only that one player pitches to another while teammates in the field strive to foil any hits. But soon you want more than that: a team to root for, understanding of rules, appreciation for tactics, statistics of varying relevance—all to intensify your involvement in the game. There are as many kinds of jazz fan as baseball fan, and as many stats.

Individuality: Timbre

Timbre refers to quality of sound, or tone color. All instruments, including the human voice, have distinct qualities—timbres—that set them apart, even when they play the same pitch. The gross differences are easy to hear: a violin sounds noticeably different from a trumpet. On a more subtle level, a tenor saxophone sounds different from an alto saxophone. We can readily hear the difference in most cases, and with an oscilloscope, which converts sound waves into visual graphs, we can see it as well.

An appreciation of timbre is basic to our ability to recognize voices as well as music. If a friend telephones, we recognize that person's identity by the timbre of his or her voice. In the same way, you can learn to pick out the differences in instruments—to be able to tell when a trombone is playing rather than a trumpet, for example. Timbre also has an aesthetic component. If two vocalists of the same age and background are equally adept at carrying a tune, hitting every note precisely, it's likely that the one with an appealing sound will please us more.

Further, timbre is something we control. Sometimes we deliberately manipulate our voices to whisper or shout, to command or console. At the same time, they reveal our emotions—fear, love, anger, exhaustion. Jazz musicians try to lend their instruments the same qualities of human speech, though this is not as easy with a piece of metal as it is with the larynx. Some horn players use **mutes**—physical devices inserted into the bell of the instrument to distort the sounds coming out. In performances by Duke Ellington from as early as the 1920s, trumpet and trombone players came up with an ingenious combination of mutes to produce unearthly, throat-growling sounds, as if they were vocalists singing *wa-wa* or *ya-ya*.

© JACK BRADLEY

Ruby Braff quiets his trumpet with the relatively rare bucket mute, a broad cylinder filled with absorbent material and held in place by steel springs projecting outward from the trumpet's bell. In this 1961 photo, Braff performs with tenor saxophonist Bud Freeman.

The use of unusual sounds for expressive purposes is known as **timbre variation.** This impulse undoubtedly came to jazz through African American folk culture, but it lies deep within the idea of all folk traditions. Jazz musicians, much more than their classical counterparts, use timbre to attain stylistic **individuality.** The tenor saxophonist Buddy Tate, known for his many years with the Count Basie Orchestra, once said that the first crucial step for young musicians is to find their own sound. That is a pretty radical notion. Tate didn't mean to suggest that an unfledged musician had to find a sound unlike anyone else's, just for the sake of novelty. Rather, the young musician needs to know *who* he is in order to find a sound he knows to be his own. The task is only partly a conscious one. Louis Armstrong had an ebullient personality that's reflected in his trumpet sound. Miles Davis had a more introverted personality that's reflected in his. This kind of individuality can't be taught.

THE ENSEMBLE

The usual way to classify instruments is by the way they make sounds. In jazz, the largest category consists of those that produce sound by moving air—all referred to in jazz (unlike classical music) as **wind instruments,** or **horns.** Other jazz instruments belong to different categories: the bass, for example, is a string instrument, while the drums are a form of percussion. The piano, which features strings hammered on by keys, falls in between.

We can also classify instruments by their musical use: players who improvise in the spotlight—the **soloists**—are distinct from their accompaniment, which is known as the **rhythm section.** In theory, the category of soloists is flexible: while wind instruments dominate, nothing prevents any instrument from taking a leading role. In "One Hour," by the Mound City Blue Blowers, we'll hear a solo played on a comb wrapped in tissue paper. The rhythm section is more fixed, restricted to instruments capable of supplying the basic elements of accompaniment: rhythm and harmony.

Louis Armstrong warms up on his trumpet while trombonist Tommy Dorsey and saxophonist Bud Freeman watch over his shoulder.

Winds

The physics of wind instruments is fairly simple. Blowing on or into a tube sets a column of air in vibration, producing a particular sound. (Most wind players produce a slight wobble in pitch, known as **vibrato**.) There are two options for modifying that sound. The first is changing the length of the tube. The second is blowing with increased intensity, which forces the vibration to suddenly jump to a new level, raising the pitch.

Both concepts can be demonstrated on the flute, perhaps the simplest wind instrument in Western music. The flute is blown sideways against a hole placed in the instrument's top, which has an edge that stops and divides the air so that some of it passes into the tube—an effect similar to blowing across the opening of a bottle. The player's fingers cover holes that run lengthwise along the flute. To change the length of the air column, you simply lift a finger to open one of the holes, shortening the vibrating column of air. In effect, the flute behaves as if it were an instrument of continuously changing length.

Increasing the speed of air is more dramatic: by changing the **embouchure**—the shaping and positioning of the lips and other facial muscles—and applying more pressure, an experienced player can push the pitch significantly higher than before (just how high depends on the instrument). This sets in motion an acoustic phenomenon known as the **overtone** series—higher pitches caused by secondary vibrations of the main sound wave.

BRASS INSTRUMENTS The term **brass** suggests that some instruments are defined by their shiny, metallic construction. But the crucial feature is how air is set into motion. Brass instruments use a cuplike **mouthpiece,** which cradles the performer's lips. The vibration of the lips, creating a kind of buzz, moves the column of air and produces tones.

Because brass instruments require an exceptional amount of pressure to get a sound, there are no external holes: fingers can't be counted on to completely seal them. Instead, most players use a clever technology developed in the nineteenth century. To the basic cylindrical tube, three **valves** (usually shaped like pistons) were added. These valves, on top of the instrument's middle section, are controls that shunt the air into a passageway of tubing of various lengths. By depressing different combinations of valves, the trumpet player alters the lengths, thereby producing most of the necessary tones. Changing the speed of air produces the rest. The musician is required to make two calculations before playing each note: the valve setting and the intensity of blowing.

Trumpet / cornet

The most common brass instrument is the **trumpet,** which has an unmistakable timbre: a brittle, crisp attack with brilliant overtones. Its vibrating tube is entirely cylindrical until it reaches the end, where it flares into the instrument's **bell.** Other instruments feature a tube that increases as it goes along, known as a conical bore. The **cornet** is a partially conical instrument, flaring toward the end; it's usually found in marching bands and was transplanted to early jazz bands. Another trumpet-like instrument, the **flugelhorn,** is entirely conical.

The similarity between the trumpet and the cornet causes much confusion in discussions of early jazz. The two instruments look and sound alike, but the cornet has an extra layer of tubing and a deeper mouthpiece, producing a slightly mellower timbre. They are so similar that it is often impossible to distinguish which one is heard on recordings made in the 1920s. Adding to the confusion is the inclination of some commentators and musicians to refer to the trumpet as a cornet, and vice versa. Although the cornet dominated jazz at first, by 1926 it began to lose favor to the trumpet, with its brighter, more piercing sound.

To vary their timbre, many trumpet players carry with them a small arsenal of mutes, each with its distinctive possibilities. The **straight mute** derives from the orchestra: inserted directly into the bell of the instrument, it quiets the sound without too much distortion. The **cup mute** adds an extension that more or less covers the bell, further attenuating the sound while rounding it out. The **Harmon mute** is a hollow mute with a hole in the center; originally the hole was filled with an adjustable sliding tube, suitable for comic effects, but most jazz musicians simply discarded the tube, creating a highly concentrated sound. Finally, the **plunger mute** is as simple as the name suggests: it is simply the bottom end of a sink plunger (minus the handle). By moving the plunger in various positions away from the bell, the player can adjust sound so expertly that it resembles human speech.

Mutes

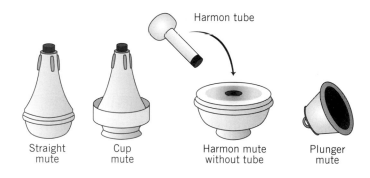

Harmon tube

Straight mute | Cup mute | Harmon mute without tube | Plunger mute

Often these mutes are used in combination. Bubber Miley, the cornetist with the early Duke Ellington band, developed an unearthly sound by modifying his trumpet, already muted with a tiny, straight **pixie** mute, with a plunger—all the while growling in his throat. A trumpet player can also vary his timbre by **half-valving:** depressing one or more of the valves only halfway. The restricted flow of air produces an uncertain pitch, often with a nasal sound. Yet another technique is the **shake,** a quick trill between two notes that mimics a wide vibrato.

The **trombone,** with its occasionally comical **slide,** appears to be an exception to the brass norm; but in fact the use of a slide to adjust the column of air was something of a warm-up for the valve system. Like the trumpet, the trombone has been part of jazz since the beginning. Given how difficult it is to play pitches by pumping a single slide, the achievement of virtuoso jazz trombonists is remarkable. On the other hand, the slide enables the player to glide seamlessly from one note to another, an effect known as a **glissando,** or **smear.**

Trombone

🔊 REED INSTRUMENTS With **reed** instruments, the whole procedure of setting air into vibration is reversed: instead of pressing lips against the mouthpiece, as with brass instruments, the mouthpiece is inserted between lips. The mouthpiece is rigid—made of ebonite, hard rubber, or metal—with an open back to which a thin cane reed is attached by a metal clamp. The player blows a stream of air into the narrow passageway between the limber reed and the hard part of the mouthpiece, causing the reed to vibrate and producing a sound less biting and more subtle than the brass instruments.

Virtually all jazz instruments use a **single reed**—double-reed instruments, such as the oboe and bassoon, are rarely heard except in large orchestrations. The reed is delicate, easily broken, and can be bought or custom-designed in gradations of thickness. The thicker it is, the harder it is to control. Musicians expressed amazement at Benny Goodman's clarinet reeds, which were so thick they were once described as "diving boards."

The particular sound on a reed instrument can be easily manipulated, resulting in a wide diversity of saxophone and clarinet sounds. A player usually presses the tongue lightly against the reed; the shape and quality of pitches is varied by pressing harder with lips or tongue or flicking the tongue against it to emphasize a note. Blowing intensely can result in complicated sounds, often containing more than one pitch: these are known as **multiphonics**, and are a valuable resource for avant-garde jazz.

Clarinet

The **clarinet** is a slim, cylindrical, ebony-colored wooden tube that produces a thin, occasionally shrill sound. A standard member of the New Orleans jazz ensemble, it achieved greater renown during the Swing Era of the 1930s, when two of the most popular bandleaders, Benny Goodman and Artie Shaw, offered an inadvertent clarinet rivalry that excited fans. The clarinet later declined in popularity, though some composers, most notably Duke Ellington, maintained its centrality to their music. Beginning in the early 1960s, thanks chiefly to Eric Dolphy, the **bass clarinet** (pitched lower than the regular clarinet) found acceptance by musicians and is still often heard.

Saxophone

The **saxophone** is the one wind instrument jazz can claim as its own. Adolphe Sax invented it in the 1840s in Paris as a family of instruments, deriving their individual names from parts in vocal choirs. The most common kinds of saxophone used in jazz are the **alto**, **tenor**, **soprano**, and **baritone saxophone**. Because Sax patterned his key system after the clarinet's, musicians already familiar with that instrument could readily master the saxophone.

After the Indiana-based Conn Company began to manufacture saxophones in the United States in 1904, American dance bands and vaudeville performers embraced the instrument as much for its comic potential as

During the Swing Era, Artie Shaw rivaled Benny Goodman for popularity on the clarinet. Here Shaw leads one of the few integrated small groups in 1945: Dodo Marmarosa (piano), Roy Eldridge (trumpet), Shaw, Barney Kessel (guitar), Morris Raymond (bass).

FRANK DRIGGS COLLECTION

musical versatility. The saxophone looked funny, with its gooseneck and curved bell, necessitated by the extended tubing. Some early masters of the instrument tongue-flicked the reed on every note, producing a droll, rigid virtuosity. As jazz musicians began to master it, they uncovered another quality—a cozy, seductive timbre that some moral guardians found dangerously sexy. A San Francisco newspaper editorial called it the "Siren of Satan" and demanded its banishment.

By 1930, thanks to such premier players as Sidney Bechet (soprano), Coleman Hawkins (tenor), Johnny Hodges and Benny Carter (alto), and Harry Carney (baritone), the saxophone had become the soul of American music: an all-purpose instrument able to play sweet or hot while suggesting tenderness or aggression. The tenor and alto are by far the most important solo saxophones. By contrast, the baritone is best known for anchoring big-band reed sections. The soprano virtually disappeared between 1930 and 1960, but became hugely fashionable in the 1970s, and has remained so: many established saxophonists **double** on it (play it in addition to their main instrument), and some have made it their primary instrument.

New Orleans virtuoso Sidney Bechet (center) was trained on the clarinet (several are lined up on the stage floor), but he soon switched to the soprano saxophone, a straight instrument that contrasts visually with the alto saxophone (held by Otto Hardwick, right) and the tenor (Frank "Big Boy" Goudie), all members of the Noble Sissle band, 1928.

Rhythm Section

The members of the rhythm section have changed over time, as jazz has changed, but they usually number three or four, and their functions have remained stable: to provide **harmony, bass,** and **percussion.**

HARMONY INSTRUMENTS Some instruments are naturally designed to play chords for the ensemble. These include the **vibraphone, organ, synthesizer, electric piano, guitar,** and, in the earliest years, **banjo.** The most important, though, is the **piano**—an instrument equally at home in the middle-class parlor and in the public sphere of nightclubs and dance halls. The acoustic piano (to distinguish it from its electric counterpart) had already gone through a full century of technological changes before the first jazz musicians discovered it. It's both a string instrument and a form of percussion: pianists use the wide range of the keyboard (over seven octaves) to imitate the sound of a full orchestra or pound on the keys like a drum.

In some bands, two instruments combine to play harmony—for example, piano and vibraphone or, more frequently, piano and guitar. Today we think of the guitar as a solo instrument, but before 1940 its function in jazz was chiefly harmonic and rhythmic. Many bands had four-man rhythm sections—piano, guitar, bass, drums—in which the guitar existed solely to strum chords, one for each beat of a measure. The pianist can, of course, accompany himself, playing chords with the left hand and improvising with the right.

BASS The bass is the rock on which the jazz ensemble is built. In a performance, we are naturally inclined to pay attention to the trumpet or saxophone soloist, while also registering the drums and pianist. The bass often gets lost in the undercurrent unless we focus on it. Musicians are always focused on it.

The bass has, roughly speaking, two crucial functions: playing notes that support the harmony, and providing a basic underlying rhythmic foundation.

The "All-American" rhythm section of the Count Basie band was light yet powerful. From left to right: Walter Page, bass; Jo Jones, drums; Freddie Green, guitar; and Basie, piano. The rest of the band, crowded into the tiny bandstand at New York's Famous Door in 1938, from front row to back: Herschel Evans, Earl Warren, Jack Washington, and Lester Young, saxophones; Buck Clayton (standing), Ed Lewis, Harry Edison, trumpets; Benny Morton, Dan Minor (hidden behind Clayton), Dicky Wells, trombones.

There are several instruments that can fill this role. The most common is the **string bass** (also known as double bass), the same instrument used in symphony orchestras. Classical musicians usually **bow** the bass, creating sound by drawing a horsehair bow across the strings. Jazz musicians also use the bow, but they prefer a technique known as **pizzicato**: plucking the strings with their fingers. The plucked string has a percussive power that is much better suited to jazz's rhythmic nature.

In the past half century, the string bass has often been supplanted by the **electric bass**—the same four-stringed guitar-like instrument found in popular music. It lacks the powerful natural resonance of the string bass (now often called "acoustic bass"), but has the advantages of loudness and portability. Some musicians, like Jaco Pastorius, have given it its own distinctive sound.

The role of bass can also be filled by the **tuba**, a low-pitched brass instrument with an intricate nest of tubing ending in an enormous bell. The tuba, which came to jazz from the marching band, was used in some early jazz groups because of its powerful volume, which musicians felt was needed as ballast for the other instruments in the band. In fact, though, the string bass can be played with enough volume; and these days, you almost never hear the bass without amplification (a **pickup**, or small microphone, on the bridge).

PERCUSSION The **drum kit**, or **drum set**, is a one-man percussion section within the rhythm section within the band. One seated individual operates the percussion instruments, using all four limbs to manipulate them with sticks (or brushes, mallets, or hands) and foot pedals. Another name is

trap set, or, as many musicians call them, **the traps** (short for "contraption"). Whatever you call it, this one-man band of percussion is, along with the saxophone, the most visually iconic of jazz's contributions to world music.

The drum set developed in the 1890s out of marching bands, which were then commonplace throughout the United States. In any parade, the most conspicuous drum is the huge **bass drum**, strapped to the player's chest and jutting out two to three feet, struck with mallets. Another musician plays the much smaller **snare drum**, hanging around the neck and named after the metal snare attached to the lower drumhead, which adds a penetrating, rattling sound to each stroke of the drumstick. A third musician holds two large **cymbals** with handles, and crashes them noisily together.

Some clever musical inventor made the drum set possible by equipping the bass drum with a **foot pedal** attached to a mallet; this got the bass drum off the musician's chest and freed up his hands. It was a logical step to add the snare drum, either on its own legs or attached to the rim of the bass drum, and a freely hanging cymbal, suspended from a stand or also attached to the bass drum. In effect, a new instrument and new kind of musician were born.

While every jazz drummer configures the drum set in his own manner, the basic arrangement is fairly stable. The drummer sits on a stool in the center of a semicircular assembly of drums and cymbals, with the bass drum front and center. The snare drum stands on an adjustable stand at knee-level. Spreading out from it are two or more middle-size drums without snares, called **tom-toms**. These drums are carefully tuned according to taste and come in various sizes.

A forest of cymbals provides a steely contrast to the drums below them. Two of them are suspended. The medium-size **ride cymbal** has a clear, focused timbre and is played more or less continuously—the band "rides" on its lithe rhythmic pulse. The slightly smaller **crash cymbal** has a splashy, indeterminate pitch, not unlike a small gong, and is used for dramatic punctuations. The third essential cymbal is actually a device with two cymbals, recalling the pair held by the musician in the marching band, but to entirely different effect. It's called the **high-hat** and consists of two shoulder-level (remember the drummer is seated) cymbals on an upright pole with a foot pedal at its base. The pedal brings the top cymbal crashing into the lower one with a distinct *chunk*.

Cymbals

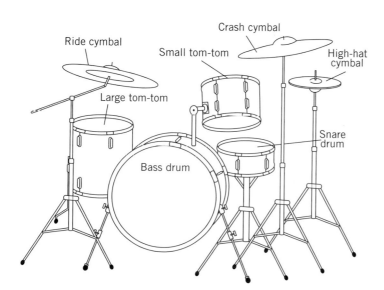

Ride cymbal
Crash cymbal
Small tom-tom
High-hat cymbal
Large tom-tom
Snare drum
Bass drum

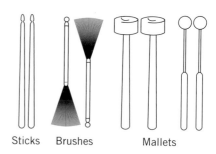

Sticks   Brushes   Mallets

Every drummer begins with the basic drum set, but finds a way to alter the sound to suit his particular personality. Jack DeJohnette's set-up is heavy on cymbals, ranging from the high-hat in the front to the ride in the back, with splash or crash cymbals in between.

Latin percussion

In all, a jazz drummer is responsible for at least a half-dozen instruments. Typically, he will use his right foot on the bass drum pedal, his left on the high-hat pedal, his right hand wielding a stick on the ride cymbal, and his left holding a stick to play the snare drum or tom-tom. This description applies to the playing of any conventional drum set in rock, soul, and most other genres of popular music. What distinguishes jazz drumming is the sheer virtuosity—the flexibility and subtlety—that keeps other musicians and the listener involved, a task very different from merely keeping the beat. The drummer is free to respond to whatever the soloist plays and is expected to be attentive and quick-witted enough to fill in the spaces (with a drum **fill**, or solo)—or to know when not to.

Drummers also contribute to the overall texture by altering timbre. Cymbals are often renovated to suit personal taste, sometimes with strips of tape on the underside to control the sizzle. The use of various sticks radically changes the sound of drumming. After wooden sticks, the most commonplace are **wire brushes**, used to strike or literally brush the drumheads with wire strands protruding from (usually) hollow handles. Early drummers realized that brushes, played hard or soft, produce a subtle, swishing sound ideal for gentle accompaniment. Mallets originally used to thump the giant bass drum are now preferred for conveying a soft, quiet rumble.

Some drummers don't play the traps at all. These are the masters of Latin percussion. **Congas** are tall drums of equal height but different diameters, with the smaller one assigned the lead role. The much smaller **bongos** have two drumheads, one larger than the other, compact enough to sit between the player's knees. The **timbales** consist of two drums mounted on a stand along with a cowbell and are played with sticks by a standing musician. Among other percussion instruments are shakers (the **maracas** is a gourd filled with beans) and scrapers (the **guiro** is a gourd with ridges). In recent decades, jazz bands often include a percussionist—someone who works with literally dozens of instruments: shakers, scrapers, bells, blocks, and noisemakers of every description. Percussion, like music, is a world without end.

Dynamics

In any ensemble, some instruments are inherently louder than others; a trumpet, for example, produces more volume than a flute. But each instrument has the ability to play loud and soft within its own range, another indispensable aid to expression. The terms used to indicate volume, or **dynamics,** come from the Italian; the most common are shown below, with their abbreviations. The piano, originally called the pianoforte, was named for its ability to play both soft (*piano*) and loud (*forte*), which earlier keyboard instruments like the harpsichord couldn't do.

pp	*p*	*mp*	*mf*	*f*	*ff*
pianissimo	piano	mezzo piano	mezzo forte	forte	fortissimo
softest			medium		loudest

© CHUCK STEWART

RHYTHM, METER, AND SWING

🔊 Rhythm

Rhythm in music is directly related to biology. The beating of our hearts and the intervals of our breathing are the foundations from which we developed dance and music. Heartbeats are relatively stable and articulate time with a steady *thump-thump-thump* of the pulse. This "pulse rhythm," moving at a given **tempo,** or speed, is the basic approach to rhythm used in jazz.

"Breath rhythm" is more elusive. Although we breathe continuously, we can speed it up or slow it down, or even (for a time) stop it altogether. In music, this can be called **free rhythm,** and it is often heard in an introduction, as in the opening of Louis Armstrong's "West End Blues" (0:00–0:12). This **cadenza**—a classical-music word for an unaccompanied passage of brilliant virtuosity—begins with a basic pulse, four even beats you could count as 1, 2, 3, 4. But as the phrase continues, nothing is that simple again. Although the passage is played with tremendous drive, we don't feel like tapping our feet. We are suspended in air until, finally, at 0:15, Armstrong returns to a steady, calm pulsation.

Sonny Rollins's "Autumn Nocturne," on the other hand, begins with an unaccompanied tenor saxophone solo that for nearly five minutes refuses to yield to any kind of regularity. The uneven, continually varying rhythms sound something like "speech rhythm." Through his saxophone, Rollins is talking to us. A still different technique occurs at the beginning of Art Tatum's "Over the Rainbow," where the familiar melody sometimes speeds up and sometimes slows down. This technique is known as **rubato,** from the Italian for "stolen": the performer "steals" from one part of the rhythmic flow to make another part longer. It is an elastic approach to rhythm used in jazz primarily to introduce tunes.

🔊 Meter

Listen now to "So What" beginning at 1:31, where the pulse rhythm is firmly in control. Try counting along with the music.

If you have tuned into the pulse, or beat, you probably have come up with a recurring pattern: either "1-2, 1-2" or "1-2-3-4, 1-2-3-4." Note that you do *not* count "1-2-3-4-5-6-7-8-9-10," and so on. That's because we *automatically* group pulses into patterns, and these patterns are called **meter.** In jazz and most other kinds of music, the most common is **duple meter,** which means that the beats are grouped into patterns of twos or fours: every **measure,** or **bar**—indicated in notation by vertical lines—has either two or four beats, as is the case with "So What." Counting with these groups in mind, you will be able to hear and feel the music through the meter.

Some pieces are in **triple meter**—groups of three, as in the 1-2-3, 1-2-3 rhythm of the waltz. In recent years, jazz musicians have adopted **irregular meters:** a pattern, for example, of 1-2-3, 1-2, | 1-2-3, 1-2 | 1-2-3, 1-2. We normally consider this a meter of five beats per measure, as in Dave Brubeck's performance of the Paul Desmond tune "Take Five." Many other metrical combinations are possible, adding together odd groups of twos and threes to

THE GRANGER COLLECTION, NEW YORK

The drum set is only the beginning of percussion in Latin music. Tito Puente, salsa bandleader, is shown in 1955 playing his favorite instrument, the timbales, a pair of high-pitched drums with a cowbell mounted overhead. Later in his career, Puente often played as many as eight timbales at once.

make complex meters of seven, nine, eleven, and so forth. Meter is thus an open-ended resource for creativity, one more way for jazz musicians to make their performances more rhythmically challenging.

Another rhythmic landmark is the **downbeat**—the place where we agree to begin our counting. Musicians typically make the downbeat clear through rhythmic accents, harmonic patterns, and the phrasing of their melodies. At the beginning of the trumpet solo on "So What" (1:31), Miles Davis plays two preliminary notes (the **upbeat**), and then places the third precisely on the downbeat, reinforced by accents on the cymbal and the bass. You can feel the meter kicking in at this point. Count along with him for a while, and you will immediately register the downbeat—the **1-2-3-4 | 1-2-3-4**—as second nature.

The distance between downbeats is a measure. In notation, musical time runs from left to right, and the bar lines parcel time out, measure by measure. We can think of a measure as a small cycle—a fixed unit of time that can be repeated endlessly. Cyclical time is the ideal structure for jazz. It is as flexible and open-ended as jazz performance itself.

In the Ghanaian performance that follows, the drum on the left (drum A) plays a fixed pattern, while the drum on the right (B) and the box drum in the center (C) interact in variable parts. The small tape recorder that captured these sounds in 1983 can be seen next to the box drum.

◀)) Polyrhythm, Call and Response, and Syncopation

The technical vocabulary presented to this point applies equally to standard European classical music. But jazz must also be understood as a music that derives, in a fundamental sense, from Africa. Within the repetitive cyclic structures of jazz, the music is organized by **rhythmic layers**: highly individualized parts that contrast with one another, even as they serve to create a unified whole. This simultaneous use of contrasting rhythms is known as **polyrhythm**, or **rhythmic contrast.** In a piece of African (and African American music), *there are always at least two different rhythmic layers going on at the same time.*

The most basic rhythms are the **foundation layers**—continuous, unchanging patterns whose very repetition provides a framework for the whole. Return to "So What" from 1:31 on. You should be able to pick out several rhythmic layers that are highly repetitive. In the lowest range, the bass plays a steady stream of evenly spaced notes. High above it, the drummer reinforces this pattern on the ride cymbal. These two layers are the foundation for jazz, and musicians responsible for them are said to be **"keeping time"**—a simple but essential part of good music-making. In "So What," the foundation layers are played by the lowest- and highest-sounding instruments, the extremes of **register**. In "A Sailboat in the Moonlight," a steady, dance-like pulse of two beats to the measure comes from the bass line, the pianist's left hand, and the cymbals.

In African music (and also Latin jazz), the foundation layer is often a complex rhythm known as a **time-line pattern**. In the excerpt of music from Ghana below, for example, it's impossible *not* to hear the time-line pattern, played continuously by the bells.

Another foundation layer is provided by a drum (A) playing a fixed pattern of two notes. Above the foundation, **variable layers** add contrasting parts; in African music, these are generally improvised. In the Ghanaian example, two other drums (B and C) supply these variable layers. When they play together (especially at the end of the excerpt), the music arises out of their complex interaction.

Another device you'll hear in the Ghanaian example is known as **call and response,** a pervasive principle in folk, pop, and art music. It's a kind of conversation: a statement by one musician (or group of musicians), the "call," is immediately answered by a counterstatement, the "response." Here, we can easily hear the call and response by a male singer and chorus, and, less easily, between drums A and B.

Call and response

LISTENING GUIDE

1.1

🎧 akuapim performance

GHANA FIELD RECORDING
- Date: 1983
- Style: African music
- Form: cyclic

What to listen for:
- time-line pattern of bells
- pair of notes played by drum A
- variable layers played by two other drums (B and C)
- interaction between fixed and variable layers
- call and response between male singer and chorus

0:00 The recording fades into a performance already in progress. The meter is duple: four beats to the cycle. There are two unchanging foundation layers: a time-line pattern played on a pair of metal bells, and a drum (A) sounding a pair of notes. Another drum (B) plays a pattern in a tight call and response with drum A. Above this, we hear a call and response between a male singer and a chorus.

0:13 While drum A remains stable, drum B begins to change, altering its rhythm and timbre.

0:27 Drum B switches to a polyrhythmic pattern, superimposing a meter of three over the basic duple meter.

0:38 A spoken phrase by the vocal leader signals the end to the call and response. He starts a new pattern.

0:50 A new drum (C) enters—a large wooden box with a resonating hole, hit on its sides with the hands and fist. In the background, someone claps the basic four beats. While drum B remains in its polyrhythmic pattern (in three), drum C plays complex phrases.

1:01 Drum B takes the lead by varying its part.

1:20 Drum B returns to the call and response with drum A heard at the beginning.

1:33 Drum C adds complex patterns.

1:48 As the excerpt fades out, drums B and C enter into a more intense conversation.

In jazz, good examples of call and response are easy to find. In the melody of "So What" (from 0:34), the two notes played first by piano and later by the horns answer the string bass's call. In "West End Blues" (1:24–1:53), Louis Armstrong creates new melodies by singing responses to Jimmy Strong's clarinet. Max Roach's drums react to Charlie Parker's opening melody in "Now's the Time" (0:05–0:19). Indeed, you could say that call and response is built in to the very fabric of jazz. Musicians are always listening carefully (in jazz slang, they have "big ears"), ready to respond to any rhythmic gesture at a moment's notice.

Jazz soloists supply the variable layers, but the rhythm section does as well. The pianist's chords sometimes fall on the beat (as they do, for example, in the first chorus of "West End Blues," 0:16–0:50), but just as often in between them. And while the drummer keeps time on the ride cymbal with his right hand, his other limbs are busy playing accents on the rest of the drum kit that comment on or contradict that pulse. As in the African example, these layers dance above the foundation, sometimes sticking close to the beat, at other times diverging sharply from it. This continuous commentary within the rhythm section is at the heart of improvisation in jazz.

Syncopation

Every time a strong accent contradicts the basic meter, **syncopation** occurs. In most classical music, syncopation is an occasional rhythmic disruption, a temporary "special effect" injected for variety. In jazz, syncopation is not an effect—it is the very air jazz breathes.

Consider, for example, what happens when you snap your fingers to "So What." More likely than not, your snap does *not* align with the downbeat. If you count along, the beats you emphasize are not **1**-2-**3**-4, but 1-**2**-3-**4**. This crucial layer in the music, known as the **backbeat**, offers a simple way for listeners to contribute. Whether we actually snap on the backbeat or silently respond to it in the course of listening, we add our own contrasting layer. We become part of the music.

◀) Grooves and Swing

If you combine the steady, four-beat rhythm in the bass and cymbal with a backbeat, you end up with a **groove**, the overall rhythmic framework within which rhythmic things happen. There are many different kinds of grooves. The one we've been describing is known generically as a **swing** groove, and it's basic to jazz.

Within the swing groove, jazz musicians use varied means to divide the main beat in an interesting way. If you listen closely to the passage in Miles Davis's solo on "So What" where he plays four quick notes in succession (1:45), you may notice that the notes are not the same length. Davis usually divides the beat by holding the first note of the beat slightly, compensating by compressing the second note. This practice is generally known as **swing eighth notes**—eighth notes being the division of a standard beat (a quarter note) into two parts.

We would normally write this passage as:

But in practice, it sounds more like this:

Such rhythmic nuances are usually not written out—partly to simplify the notation, but also because they are infinitely variable. Jazz musicians decide by feeling the rhythmic groove just how uneven they want their eighth notes to sound.

It is through such subtleties that musicians speak of **swinging**. This is a term that is impossible to define precisely: as Louis Armstrong is supposed to have said, "If you have to ask, you'll never know." But when all the rhythms interlock smoothly, something magical takes place and everyone in the vicinity (musicians, dancers, listeners) feels it. The band is swinging or is "in the groove" or "jumping" or "feeling it together." All those clichés mean basically the same thing. Swinging spreads sunlight on everyone it touches, beginning with the members of the band.

The score of a Beethoven symphony includes all the information a conductor needs to perform it with an orchestra. A score prepared for a jazz orchestra, on the other hand, may include the same kind of notation, but musicians unfamiliar with jazz practices, no matter how proficient, might play every note correctly and still turn out a plodding, unrecognizable performance. Similarly, if an operatic soprano who had never sung jazz sang "A Sailboat in the Moonlight," she might sing every note correctly yet capture nothing of Billie Holiday's lithe grace. This very problem, an inability to swing (and the impossibility of notating swing), has in fact befallen many gifted instrumentalists who have tried to play jazz and failed.

MELODY, SCALES, AND MODES

Pitch

A sound's **pitch** is determined by measuring its **frequency,** or vibrations per second. For example, the note that today's orchestras tune up to, A, is measured at 440 vibrations per second. As the vibrations increase, the sound goes higher; as they decrease, it goes lower.

Theoretically, the pitch spectrum is limitless. Fortunately, we can think of it in a much more finite manner. If a group of men and women were asked to sing an A, more than likely the notes they sing would *not* be the same: the women may be able to produce the precise pitch of A=440, but the men's deeper voices would automatically choose a corresponding note with half (220) or even a quarter (110) as many vibrations. These are all A's: the distance, or **interval,** between them is an **octave.** The octave has a simple mathematical ratio of 2:1 (which translates into 440:220).

Look at the piano keyboard in the diagram below. The key marked in the center is called "middle C" (256 vibrations per second). From C, count seven white notes from left to right: C, D, E, F, G, A, and B. The next note, again labeled C, is an octave higher, with exactly twice as many vibrations (512). If you look at the black keys, with their groups of twos and threes, you can see that a pattern is repeated over and over again. All we need to understand the world of pitch is to grasp the patterns that appear within the octave.

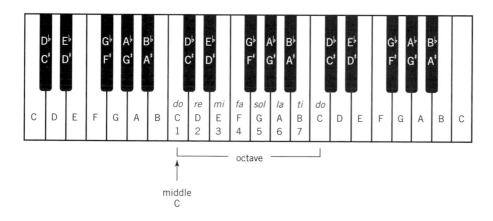

🔊 Scales or Modes

The basic unit of melody is the **scale**—a collection of pitches within the octave. The twelve notes in an octave (counting white and black keys) make up a scale by themselves, known as a **chromatic scale**, with the interval separating each note a **half step**. But it is hardly the most common scale.

Try singing the pitches from C to C, the white keys on the piano keyboard, on the following syllables: *do, re, mi, fa, sol, la, ti, do.* (The vast majority of people in Western culture can do this easily.) This scale, the most basic in Western music, is called the **major mode.** (For our purposes, "scale" and **Major mode** "mode" are synonyms.) Each note is a **degree** of the scale: *do* is the first degree, *re* the second degree, and so on.

A crucial aspect of this scale is that one pitch is more important than others. The first degree of the scale—C (*do*) in the C major scale—is particularly significant. Melodies may not necessarily begin on *do,* but they are very likely to end on it. Consider "Happy Birthday": if you sing the first phrase, "Hap-py birth-day to you," you end up floating in mid-air. That's because the last note, "you," falls on a note just short of *do.* The next phrase releases the tension, bringing the melody to its inexorable goal of *do* (on the second "you"). We call *do* the **tonic,** and music that insists on returning to the tonic (most of the music we listen to) is known as **tonal music.** The tension and release is like the use of gravity in dance. It is possible, through our muscles, to escape the pull of gravity, but we know that our return to earth is inevitable.

It doesn't matter what note you choose as the tonic. That's because scales represent *patterns* of pitches that can be moved (or **transposed**) up or down as you like. The pattern is made up of half and whole steps: C to D is a **whole step** because there's a key (black in this case) in between. D to E is another whole step, and E to F is a half step. The complete pattern for a major scale, easy to see starting on C, is W (whole step), W, H (half step), W, W, W, H.

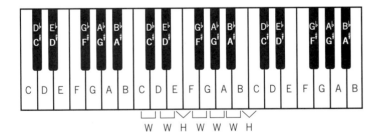

W = whole step
H = half step

The scale is named after its tonic: beginning on C produces C major, beginning on E♭ produces E♭ major. (The E♭ scale, following the same pattern, is E♭, F, G, A♭, B♭, C D, E♭.) Only C major stays on the white keys. For any other tonic, the patterns will inevitably involve the black keys, usually represented in written notation by **sharps** (♯) or **flats** (♭) at the beginning of a piece.

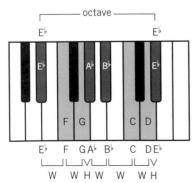

The converse of the major mode is the **minor mode**, with a different half-step/whole-step pattern. The most important difference is in the third degree of the scale. In minor, the interval between *do* and *mi* (known as a **third**) is a half step lower: instead of moving from C to E (on the white keys), we move from C to E♭. This difference may not seem like much, but it carries great emotional power, especially in classical music. In general, minor sounds sad, moody, angry, or even tragic, while major sounds happy, peaceful, or triumphant. You need only listen to pieces like the Fifth and Ninth Symphonies of Ludwig van Beethoven to hear the emotional upheaval that comes from minor mode being thunderously replaced by the major mode at the end.

Minor mode

Major and minor each include seven different pitches: the eighth note, the return of *do*, is the octave. (When we remember that *oct* is a Latin prefix meaning "eight"—as in "octopus" or "octagon"—the logic behind the term "octave" is finally clear.) These seven-note scales, called **diatonic scales**, are the basis of melodies in Western music.

Jazz musicians are also fond of using another scale, the **pentatonic**, a five-note scale that can evoke the simplicity of folk music. You can get a sense of its sound by rolling your hand along the black keys of the piano keyboard. Yet musicians also favor other diatonic scales, some of which come from European traditions but were abandoned long ago in favor of the major/minor dichotomy. These scales, or modes, have names that were originally derived from ancient Greek practice, such as Phrygian, Lydian, and Mixolydian. In fact, you've been listening to one already. "So What" features the **Dorian mode**, which you can hear by playing the *white* keys (not the major scale) on the piano running from D to D. The Dorian mode has a pattern that falls curiously between major and minor. Jazz thus blurs the major/minor dichotomy of classical music, creating many shades of emotional nuance.

Pentatonic scale

Dorian mode

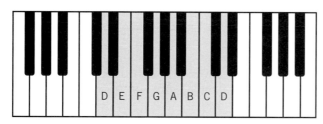

Dorian mode

Jazz musicians practice a wide variety of scales, many of which are intricate and bizarre. A scale made up entirely of whole steps may seem to have a certain logic, for example, but the sound it produces is deeply unsettling. Only well-trained musicians can sing the **whole-tone scale** with any accuracy. But in the hands of composers like Thelonious Monk and the classical composer Claude Debussy, it creates a musical effect that is easy to recognize. We don't need to follow musicians into these arcane nuances, but it helps to know that scales are an infinite resource.

◀)) **THE BLUES SCALE** The **blues scale** is not merely a collection of pitches, but an avenue into an African American cultural world. All American music—jazz, blues, gospel, pop, rhythm and blues, country and western, rock and roll, hip-hop—is influenced by its sound. We recognize the blues scale when we hear it. Defining it is more difficult.

The blues scale also falls somewhere in between major and minor. It's actually not so much a scale as a system for creating melody. It's impossible to pin down because it uses a different approach to **intonation**, which in

Western usage means "playing in tune." In the Western world of **fixed intonation**, where pitches are set at precise frequencies, performing slightly higher or lower is seen as a mistake—playing "out of tune." As with other cultures across the globe, African American culture takes a more relaxed approach. Certain notes are played with a great deal of flexibility, sliding through infinitesimal fractions of a half step (notes that are called **microtones**) for expressive purposes. We can call this system **variable intonation**. Closer to home, jazz musicians refer to **blue notes,** or **bent notes.** These notes are impossible to translate into Western notation. On the piano keyboard, we might say that they fall in between the cracks.

Some of the greatest blues musicians play instruments—guitar, bass, trumpet, trombone, clarinet, saxophone—that are capable of producing subtle gradations between proper notes. The piano has no way to vary pitch like this, but it *can* approximate the sound of the blue note by playing two neighboring keys at the same time. Normally, playing both the E♭ and E keys on the piano is a mistake. In jazz, this clash can spice up an improvisation; the pianist Thelonious Monk frequently used simulated blue notes to enliven his solos with expressive passion.

Blue notes occur only on certain degrees of the scale, such as the third, fifth, and seventh. If a jazz ensemble plays a piece in the key of C major and one of the musicians plays a blue third degree (the pitch E lowered a half step to E♭), the clash seems appealing, not harsh. In a sense, the blues is a mildly off-kilter way of looking at the world of music.

◉ LICKS, MOTIVES, AND RIFFS

All jazz soloists have their own way of communicating through melody. Their melodic **phrases** can be short or long. Listen to the beginning of Miles Davis's solo on "So What" (1:31–1:55). Most of the phrases are short and terse—a few notes surrounded by silence (or more precisely, by the rhythm section's response). This is Davis's melodic style, or **phrasing**. Compare it with that of Charlie Parker, from his solo on "Now's the Time" (0:35–1:03): his phrases are long, sinuous, and intense.

Some melodic phrases are simple and basic, part of the common lore of jazz. Known as **licks**, they are the foundation blocks of improvisation. Budding jazz musicians learn licks by listening closely to those of more experienced soloists. The fast lick in Parker's "Now's the Time" solo (0:46–0:47), for example, pops up in many of his other solos, including "Embraceable You" (1:07–1:10). A different lick turns up, with slight variations, in several different choruses of "Now's the Time" (0:56–0:58, 1:25–1:26, 1:38–1:39). Although it may be disconcerting to discover that even a brilliant player like Parker uses the same licks over and over, this is the way improvisation works. You might compare it to speech—another improvised act—where a relatively small vocabulary creates an infinity of sounds and meaning.

At the beginning of John Coltrane's solo in "Acknowledgement" (1:04), he plays a simple three-note **motive** (a small musical idea): jumping upward, then falling back a step (a).

Listen to how he varies that motive over the next several seconds. Another motive, a quick six-note fragment that first emerges at 1:16 (b), is used by Coltrane throughout the solo that follows. Later, listen to how he takes a four-note motive (c) (eventually sung to the words "A love supreme," the title of the album) on an extended chromatic journey through all the keys (4:55–5:50).

Finally, a **riff** is a *repeated* fragment of melody. In the main melody of "So What" (0:34–1:31), the bass plays a phrase that's answered by a two-note riff in the piano—barely long enough to count as a musical thought (but fitting the title: "So what!"). The horns then take it up, continuing the repetition. Another riff can be found in the opening melody of "Now's the Time" (0:05–0:35). Since any melody that repeats insistently is known as an **ostinato** (from the Italian for "stubborn"), each of these examples is an **ostinato riff**. Tunes such as Count Basie's "One O'Clock Jump" are practically made of riffs—sometimes in the background, sometimes as the main melody (2:10–2:57).

During his short career, John Coltrane became the most influential tenor saxophonist of his generation, while inspiring others to take up his secondary instrument, the soprano saxophone.

© CHUCK STEWART

◀)) HARMONY

Harmony—the simultaneous sounding of pitches—can be compared to the mixing of colors in painting. Combine red and yellow and you get a new shade, orange; combine three notes and you get a **chord**, a new sound, different from and richer than any of its component pitches. Unlike painting, however, where the original colors disappear into the new one, each individual tone in a chord is still distinct and audible.

The basic chord, combining three pitches, is the **triad**. The bottom note is the **root**, usually heard in the bass. The chord takes its name from its root: a C major chord consists of the notes C, E, and G; a D major triad consists of D, F♯, and A.

Jazz musicians can do whatever they want with harmony. There may be only three pitches in a C major chord, but those notes may be spread around as freely as the musician desires. The particular arrangements are known as **voicings**: pianists and guitarists have their own special way of spacing chords. And additional pitches can be placed in the upper reaches of the chord—for example, C, E, G, A, and D. These new, more elaborate harmonies are known as **extended chords**.

Jazz musicians play over a **harmonic progression**, a series of chords placed in a strict rhythmic sequence. As the term "progression" suggests, the movement from chord to chord conveys a feeling of moving forward. To understand this, we will have to place harmony in the same tonal framework we devised for melody.

Chords are classified by how they relate to basic diatonic scales. Thus, the chord built on the first degree (*do*) is given the Roman numeral I, and the chord built on the fifth degree (*sol*) is designated V. Moreover, just as the tonic (*do*) served as a center of gravity for melody, the I chord (or the **tonic triad**) is the focal point of harmony. The I chord is stable: it doesn't want to move. A chord with this stability is considered **consonant**. Other chords are unstable, or **dissonant**. The V chord—G, B, D in C major—also known as

Consonance/dissonance

the **dominant**, provides the classic example. When you add an extra note to it (called the **seventh**: G, B, D, F), it sounds as though the entire chord were begging to move, or **resolve**, to the tonic. This sense of forward movement—dissonant chords pulled as if by gravity toward consonant chords—provides the underlying rhythmic drive of a harmonic progression.

Jazz musicians are faced with whole networks of chords, usually notated in written music as strings of letters and numbers: in "A Sailboat in the Moonlight," for example, the chords for the first few measures are: G C B7 E7 A7 D7 G. The end of a phrase, where a chord progression comes to rest, is called a **cadence**.

Cadence

Let's return to the first line of "Happy Birthday" ("Happy birthday to you"), which ends on an inconclusive note (*ti*). That note would be harmonized with a V chord. Although it marks the end of the phrase, it sounds incomplete: the music couldn't end at this point. Such an ending is known as a **half cadence**. Just as commas and semicolons indicate intermediate stopping points in a sentence, the half cadence serves as a temporary resting place. And not surprisingly, the next phrase ends with the melody resting on *do* and the harmony on the tonic triad. This is a full stop, like the period at the end of a sentence: a **full cadence**.

To hear a half cadence and full cadence, listen once again to the opening of "A Sailboat in the Moonlight" (0:08–0:40). There are two long phrases, each beginning with the same melody on the tonic but veering off to different conclusions. The first ending, on a half cadence ("just for two," 0:23), sounds incomplete. The second phrase ("A soft breeze") begins like the first, but by 0:32 it moves inexorably toward a full cadence, with the melody and the harmony converging on the tonic. The first phrase poses a question that is answered by the second.

Harmonic substitutions

Jazz musicians don't stick with the chords written in a book. They have the right to make **harmonic substitutions**: replacing chords with ones they happen to like, inserting more to enliven a slow spot, making chords more complex, or even removing them to simplify the progression. These are things that can be done spontaneously, or they can be worked out in advance as part

The year before he released his landmark album *Kind of Blue* (1959), on which "So What" is featured, Miles Davis took his new band on the road. This picture shows five of its six members at the Newport Jazz Festival in July 1958: Bill Evans, Jimmy Cobb, Paul Chambers, Davis, and John Coltrane.

of an arrangement. One common way to increase the complexity of chords, besides extending them, is to base them on the chromatic scale (rather than a diatonic scale). Thus, when we speak of **chromatic harmony**, we are referring to harmony that sounds more complex.

Finally, it is worth noting that not all music operates according to the rules of tonal music outlined above. **Atonal** music recognizes no key center, and often doesn't acknowledge the triad as the basic form of chord. But most jazz doesn't reach all the way to atonality. There is plenty of music that loosens the grip of tonality, creating free-floating chord progressions but not entirely banishing their pull toward tonal centers. Jazz musicians have a word for it. When they play tonal harmonic progressions, they are playing **inside**; when they step outside of tonality, they are playing **outside**. This language at least suggests that a musician can easily move from one extreme to the other, even in the course of a solo.

TEXTURE

A piece's **texture** refers to the way it balances melody and harmony. There are three basic types: **homophony**, in which a melody is supported by harmonic accompaniment; **monophony**, in which a melody exists on its own, without harmonic accompaniment; and **polyphony**, in which two or more melodies of equal interest are played at the same time. (These terms don't include percussion.)

◀) Homophonic Texture

Most music in and out of jazz is homophonic. We are accustomed to hearing a strong main melody supported by a harmonic accompaniment. For example, when Charlie Parker improvises on "Now's the Time" (0:35–1:03), the pianist and bassist play the harmonies beneath him. While some of the things the pianist, and even the bassist, may play are also melodic, we never feel they are competing for attention with Parker's saxophone.

Homophony is usually performed with the melody and the harmony in separate musical layers: a guitar accompanying a singer, for example. But in one important sub-category of homophonic music, the melody and harmony exist in a single layer: two or more instruments play the same phrase with the same rhythmic patterns, but with different pitches filling out the harmony. You hear this sort of thing all the time in small vocal groups, like barbershop quartets. In jazz, this is called **block-chord** texture. Big bands depend on block chords; when the entire trumpet section plays, one trumpet will state the main melody, while the others play the same rhythm with harmonically complementary notes. Such passages are often called *soli*, since they sound like one improvised solo. For a brief example of block-chord texture, listen to the two-note harmonized figure played by the three wind instruments in the theme of "So What" (0:49).

Another sub-category is a **countermelody** (known in classical music as an **obbligato**). In this instance, the subordinate instruments have melodic interest of their own, though not strong enough to compete with the main melody. Near the beginning of "West End Blues" (0:16–0:50), the trombonist and clarinetist play independent melodic lines, but they merely supplement Louis

Block-chord texture

Countermelody

Armstrong's trumpet lead. A more typical example occurs in "A Sailboat in the Moonlight" (0:08–1:12). As vocalist, Billie Holiday clearly has the main melody. Yet Lester Young's tenor saxophone accompanies her throughout, creating melodic ideas so rich they race shoulder to shoulder with the singer. Still, Young knows his place, and only emerges with full volume in between Holiday's vocal phrases.

◀》 Monophonic Texture

When you sing in the shower, play a flute in the woods, or pick out a tune on the piano with one hand, you're creating monophony: a melody with no harmonic accompaniment. If 50,000 people sing "The Star-Spangled Banner" in a baseball stadium without a band, it's still monophonic texture.

Breaks/stop-time

In jazz, monophony usually occurs in brief moments of contrast. In early jazz, most bands included short two- or four-bar episodes in which the band abruptly stopped playing to let a single musician shine with a monophonic passage. These passages are known as **breaks**. We will hear many breaks in New Orleans jazz, but also in later jazz: musicians never tire of the challenge of filling a suddenly silent spot with their own music.

A different kind of monophonic texture occurs with **stop-time**. In some ways, stop-time produces a series of breaks. The band agrees to play a short chord at brief intervals—three times a bar, once every bar, or every other bar. The soloist then improvises with just these brief interruptions from the band prodding him on. Unlike the break, which rarely lasts more than two bars, stop-time is open-ended, lasting as long as the musicians want. (For an example, listen to George Russell's "Concerto for Billy the Kid" at 2:28–3:08.)

And monophonic texture is often used to begin or end a piece. Louis Armstrong begins "West End Blues" with what many regard as the single most significant monophonic outburst in jazz history—a radiant trumpet fanfare that keeps us on the edge of our seat until the rest of the band finally enters. In "Autumn Nocturne," Sonny Rollins extends his unaccompanied introduction long enough to make his audience scream with delight. In "Body and Soul," the monophonic texture comes toward the end: at 2:50, Coleman Hawkins lets the band drop out, leaving him with an unaccompanied line as a way of letting a heated performance cool down.

Polyphonic Texture

In polyphony, two or more simultaneous melody lines compete for our attention. Polyphony is a special province of classical music, where composers like Johann Sebastian Bach epitomize the art of **counterpoint** (the intertwining of several equal voices). Yet polyphony also occurs in jazz, which treats it more loosely. New Orleans jazz typically features polyphonic passages in which three instruments—trumpet, trombone, and clarinet—improvise simultaneously, with no one melody standing out.

Polyphony faded from jazz once New Orleans style was replaced by big-band swing, with its homophonic textures. Then in the 1950s, many musicians tried to revive this technique, often by imitating models from classical music. And in avant-garde jazz, musicians go to great lengths to institute equality between all members of the band. Some of these passages may sound like caterwauling as several musicians blow, holler, and screech at the same time, but they are also instances of pure polyphony.

Polyphony may look closely related to polyrhythm (both have the prefix *poly*, for "many"), and the two concepts do occasionally overlap. In New Orleans jazz, each separate melodic layer is also a separate rhythmic layer. But classical music includes many examples of polyphony without an African-based concept of polyrhythm. And though a great deal of jazz is polyrhythmic (in fact, virtually *no* jazz is not polyrhythmic), much of it is homophonic: solo plus accompaniment.

The basic musical elements introduced in this chapter will get you off to a good start in listening to jazz; the terms explained here will be used throughout the book to describe the music. Now we look at how these musical elements all come together in performance, in a miraculous combination of stable form and spontaneous improvisation.

JAZZ FORM AND IMPROVISATION

In jazz, unlike classical music, musical form is relatively straightforward. You don't have to be a musician to understand it. You only have to be able to hear four beats in a measure, count to thirty-two, and distinguish between basic melodies that are designated **A** and **B**. Obviously, it isn't necessary to know the difference between one song form and another to enjoy the flow of improvised ideas. After all, you have listened to some kind of music all your life without worrying about musical structure. But once you understand the basics of form, something magical happens that alters the *way* you hear. You'll find yourself listening with greater insight, riding alongside the musicians and observing the choices they make.

FORM

Jazz concepts of **form** are derived from African music, where improvisation happens within a **cycle**. In Africa, the cycle is rhythmic. In jazz, the cycle is known as the **chorus**, and it involves two dimensions: rhythm and harmony. Each tune is a fixed rhythmic length (twelve or sixteen measures, for example) and has its own harmonic progression. Moreover, the two are interlinked. Chord changes occur at specific times within the chorus.

Percy Heath, best known for his four decades with the Modern Jazz Quartet, also appeared on recordings and performances with Charlie Parker, Thelonious Monk, Miles Davis, and others.

wwnorton.com/studyspace

A harmonic progression can be any size. Some are very short. Consider this two-measure progression, often played by amateur pianists for fun.

Derived from the tune "Heart and Soul," this progression forms an endless cycle: the last chord in the sequence is a V chord, which demands a return to I. But the return to I is also the beginning of a *new* cycle, starting the process all over again. There is, in short, no comfortable way to end the progression, short of simply breaking away from the piano.

And as anyone who has played these chords knows, they make up one part of a piano duet, the province of the somewhat unfortunate pianist on the keyboard's left side. The more interesting part can be heard on the right side, where another person plays melodies that fit over the progression. The tune lasts until the melody player runs out of ideas or comes up with a satisfying conclusion.

Here, once again, we can see the African **principle of rhythmic contrast**. There are *two* distinct layers, one fixed and one variable. The chord progression (played on the left side) is the foundation, played in an unchanging and potentially endless circle of repetition. Above it there is a variable part, which can be constantly changing; indeed, it could be improvised. *Both* parts are necessary. By itself, the left-hand part is boring—endless repetition. Without its accompaniment, the right-hand part is incomplete—at times, no more than disjointed fragments of melody. The two layers combine to create music.

Although jazz choruses are, in theory, variable, in practice musicians tend to focus on a few forms. Of the two most common cycles, one is derived from the African American music known as the **blues** and the other from **popular song**.

BLUES FORM

Blues form has its origin in African American folk poetry. The blues features a distinctive, asymmetric three-line stanza, as in this excerpt from Bessie Smith's "Reckless Blues" (CD1, track 2):

> *When I wasn't nothing but a child,*
> *When I wasn't nothing but a child,*
> *All you men tried to drive me wild.*

Each line takes up four measures; or more precisely, two and a half measures for the singer, followed by one and a half measures of response by an instrumentalist (an example of call and response). Since three lines at four measures each add up to twelve measures, this form is generally known as the **twelve-bar blues**. Each twelve bars make up a single chorus.

Blues form is marked by a particular harmonic scheme, derived from folk practice. In its most basic form, it uses only three chords, beginning on the tonic, or I chord. The first big change comes at the beginning of the second line. Perhaps because this line is verbally identical to the first, its arrival is signaled by a shift to a

Of all the "classic" blues singers of the 1920s, Bessie Smith was the most powerful and subtle. Wrapped in her stage regalia, as in this 1923 shot, she billed herself as the "Empress of the Blues" in theaters and tent shows across the country.

FRANK DRIGGS COLLECTION

new chord: the IV chord, based on the scale's fourth degree. After two bars, it returns to the tonic. Finally, the third line is underscored with the V chord, the dominant, before also returning by line's end to I.

When I wasn't   nothing but a   child,
| I | I | I | I | |

When I wasn't nothing but a   child,
| IV | IV | I | I | |

All you men   tried to drive me   wild.
| V | V | I | I | |

This is the blues in its most basic form. But rarely is it ever performed so simply. Musicians use harmonic substitutions to add variety to the long stretches of unchanging harmony—for example, moving to IV in the second measure. In "Reckless Blues," the second measure adds a V chord (0:19–0:20), as does the sixth:

When I wasn't   nothing but a   child,
| I | I—V | I | I | |

When I wasn't   nothing but a   child,
| IV | IV—V | I | I | |

All you men   tried to drive me   wild.
| V | V | I | I | |

In Louis Armstrong's "West End Blues," the substitutions are more complicated and more spontaneous. One spot is especially notable: in the last two bars of each chorus, the musicians play a particularly complicated progression of chords known as a **turnaround**—to lead back to the I chord and the next chorus. The turnaround, also called a **turnback**, is the transitional passage between choruses or between the distinct parts of a chorus. In a twelve-bar blues, measures 11 and 12 constitute the turnaround.

Despite such intricacies, the piece follows the *same basic form,* which is not difficult to hear. Listen to several choruses, using the listening guide below to help keep your place in the harmonic progression.

"West End Blues" (CD1, track 3)

CHORUS I

0:16   The full ensemble begins with a I chord.

0:24   The ensemble adds a seventh to the chord, making it want to move on to IV.

0:27   The harmony moves to IV.

0:33   The harmony resolves back to I.

0:39   The band plays a V chord.

0:44   The harmony arrives on I, followed by a turnaround.

CHORUS 2 (TROMBONE ACCOMPANIED BY WOODBLOCKS)

0:50	I chord
1:02	IV chord
1:07	I chord
1:13	V chord
1:19	I chord and turnaround

CHORUS 3 (DUET BY CLARINET AND WORDLESS VOCAL)

1:24	I chord
1:36	IV chord
1:41	I chord
1:47	V chord
1:53	I chord and turnaround

CHORUS 4 (PIANO SOLO)

1:59	I chord
2:10	IV chord
2:16	I chord
2:21	V chord
2:27	I chord and turnaround

CHORUS 5

2:32	I chord
2:44	IV chord
2:50	I chord

CODA (tag ending)

2:56	V chord (piano, rubato)
3:12	I chord (full cadence)

The harmonic progression is only one dimension that jazz musicians can change. They can play a blues chorus in any rhythmic groove—swing, funk, or Latin—or at any tempo. Consider, for example, what a *fast* blues sounds like with "It's All Right, Baby," a live performance by blues singer "Big Joe" Turner and pianist Pete Johnson recorded at a Carnegie Hall concert. Here each chorus is compressed to only fifteen seconds. Although this performance is shorter than "West End Blues," it contains twice as many choruses. At this speed, you may want to focus less on the harmonic progression than on its overall rhythm.

"It's All Right, Baby" (CD1, track 4)

CHORUS 1

0:00	The singer (Big Joe Turner) is accompanied by piano (Pete Johnson): *"Well, it's all right then!"*

CHORUS 2

0:14   *"That's all right, baby."*

CHORUS 3

0:29   *"Well, you're so beautiful . . ."*

CHORUS 4

0:44   *"Baby, what's the matter now?"*

CHORUS 5

0:59   *"Roll 'em, boy."*

CHORUS 6

1:14   The piano takes two solos.

CHORUS 7

1:28

CHORUS 8

1:43   The singer returns (*"Yes, yes!"*) in call and response with the piano.

CHORUS 9

1:57   *"Well, all right, then!"*

CHORUS 10

2:12   *"Bye . . . bye!"*

CODA

2:24   *"Bye bye, baby, bye bye!"*

To hear the blues in a more modern style, listen to Charlie Parker's "Now's the Time" (0:05–0:35). It was recorded in 1953, twenty five years after "West End Blues" and fifteen years after "It's All Right, Baby." You can hear instantly the changes that have taken place: that sizzling cymbal in the first measure tells a very different story from the clip-clopping hand cymbals of 1928. Yet for all its volatility, its radically transformed rhythm, and its increase in dissonance and harmonic complexity, this is still a twelve-bar blues, relying on the same underlying pattern that guided Armstrong and Turner. Each musician takes a solo that fits precisely within the twelve-bar structure: Parker, the group's leader, has the longest solo at five choruses, followed by the pianist (two choruses) and the bass and drums (one chorus each.)

This performance suggests another question: if the blues harmonic progression is constant from piece to piece, what distinguishes one tune from another? In small-combo jazz, the answer is the **head**: a composed section fitting securely in the twelve-bar format. The head announces the form at the beginning of a tune, as well as the melody, and returns at the end, framing the performance. A head can be simple—a riff made up of only two notes, for example—or it can be more complicated. In "Now's the Time," the head is built on a simple six-note riff (0:05). Parker does a number of things to this riff: compressing it (0:08), adding dissonant notes (0:19), or abandoning it to insert a short improvised phrase (0:22).

Try to follow the blues structure in "Now's the Time." You may not be able to hear the basic harmonic progression as clearly, in part because the pianist plays the chords more irregularly, but also because there are so many distractions: the constantly changing rapid-fire solos, the loud interruptions by the drums. But it should be easy to hear the blues's rhythmic structure. See if you can *feel* where the next chorus is about to begin.

"Now's the Time" (CD1, track 5)

CHORUS 1

0:05   Charlie Parker (alto saxophone) plays the head.

CHORUS 2

0:20   Parker repeats the head with slight variations.

CHORUS 3

0:35   Parker takes a five-chorus solo.

CHORUS 4

0:49

CHORUS 5

1:03

CHORUS 6

1:18

CHORUS 7

1:32

CHORUS 8

1:46   The pianist, Al Haig, takes a two-chorus solo.

CHORUS 9

2:00

CHORUS 10

2:14   The bassist, Percy Heath, takes a one-chorus solo.

CHORUS 11

2:28   The drummer, Max Roach, takes a one-chorus solo.

CHORUS 12

2:42   Parker returns to the head.

Other examples of twelve-bar blues form in this book's music selections range from early New Orleans jazz to complex modernist pieces. To follow the form, look at the accompanying Listening Guides for these five recordings.

Count Basie, "One O'Clock Jump" (p. 207)
Jelly Roll Morton, "Dead Man Blues" (p. 95)
Dexter Gordon, "Long Tall Dexter" (p. 303)
Charles Mingus, "Boogie Stop Shuffle" (p. 357)
Ronald Shannon Jackson, "Now's the Time" (p. 532)

The blues may be interrupted by introductions or unexpected shifts to contrasting sections, yet the same basic form undergirds them all. The wide range of styles underscores the endless variety of the blues, which would later withstand various musical fashions to become the foundation form for rhythm and blues (in the 1940s) and rock and roll (in the 1950s). The blues remains a constant refrain in jazz and popular music.

THIRTY-TWO-BAR POP SONG FORM: A A B A

The other key structural form for jazz improvisation is the **thirty-two-bar A A B A** popular song. During the golden age of American popular songwriting, roughly from 1925 to 1960, tunes were written mostly by professional songwriters such as George Gershwin, Jerome Kern, Irving Berlin, Cole Porter, Richard Rodgers, Harold Arlen, Johnny Mercer, and many others, including such jazz compatriots as Duke Ellington and Fats Waller. The tunes often originated in scores for movies and Broadway shows and were widely dispersed over the radio and on sheet music.

These songs were often conceived in two sections: an introductory **verse**, which helped bridge the gap between spoken dialogue and song in musical theater; and the thirty-two-bar section known as the **refrain, or chorus**—the melody that made the song successful if, as the songwriters hoped, members of the audience left the theater humming it. Verses can still be found in the sheet music, but, with rare exceptions (some songs have famous verses that audiences expect to hear), were hardly ever performed outside the original theatrical context. Jazz musicians never played them: they preferred to concentrate on the refrain, turning it into a continuous repeating cycle, not unlike the African tradition.

The idea behind the form is simple. Compose an eight-bar phrase. Repeat it. Contrast it with a new eight-bar phrase (known as the **bridge**, or **release**), ending with a half cadence to drive the piece forward. Finally, repeat the original phrase one more time.

A	statement (8 bars)
A	repetition (8 bars)
B (bridge)	contrast (8 bars)
A	return (8 bars)

Note that this structure does *not* refer to the words, which can be written in any number of poetic forms. Instead, it refers to the melody and harmonic progression—the parts of the tune that most interest jazz musicians (including singers). Thus, even though the words change, the second and third **A**'s are musical repetitions of the first.

The **A A B A** pop song differs noticeably from the blues. Unlike the blues, it does not retain a basic chord progression—composers can choose any harmonies they like. It is, instead, a *pattern*: eight-bar phrases interrupted by the bridge. The first two **A** sections may not be exactly the same: one may end on a half cadence, while the second ends with a full cadence, as in "A Sailboat in the Moonlight."

Now listen to "Sailboat," an **A A B A** song sung in a classic performance by Billie Holiday. The thirty-two-bar form begins at 0:08, when Holiday enters after a four-bar introduction. Note that she doesn't sing during several bars: she leaves a two-bar space at the end, filled in by tenor saxophonist Lester Young (who has been quietly hovering behind her vocal line all along). You may also notice that Holiday doesn't sing the different **A** sections *exactly* the same: she adds subtle rhythmic variations as she goes along. Real melodic and harmonic contrast comes at the bridge (0:40).

Three musicians divide up the second chorus, with the pianist Jimmy Sherman playing the first two **A** sections, the trumpeter Buck Clayton the **B,** and Lester Young the final **A.** The reason for the brief solos was that a 78-rpm recording lasted only three minutes; for the same reason, the third chorus is abbreviated (**B A**), with Holiday entering on the bridge. Her rhythmic drive pulls all the other musicians along, leading to a grand climax.

"A Sailboat in the Moonlight" (CD1, track 6)

CHORUS 1 (BILLIE HOLIDAY, VOCAL)

A	0:08	*"A sailboat in the moonlight . . ."*
A	0:24	*"A soft breeze on a June night . . ."*
B	0:40	*"A chance to sail away . . ."*
A	0:57	*"The things, dear . . ."*

CHORUS 2

A	1:12	James Sherman, piano
A	1:28	
B	1:44	Buck Clayton, trumpet
A	2:00	Lester Young, tenor saxophone

CHORUS 3 (abbreviated)

B	2:16	*"A chance to sail away . . ."*
A	2:32	*"The things, dear . . ."*

From 1926 on, jazz musicians added their artistry to popular songs, as you will hear later in the book in such pieces as Lester Young's "Oh! Lady Be Good," Benny Goodman's "Dinah," Coleman Hawkins's "Body and Soul," and Art Tatum's "Over the Rainbow." In each case, familiarity with the melody gives the listener a convenient way to enter the performance. Once the cycle has been firmly established, the remainder of each tune fits securely into the thirty-two-bar **A A B A** form.

Musicians may sometimes adopt a popular song *without* the melody. Probably the most commonly used popular song in jazz is "I Got Rhythm,"

CBS/LANDOV

Singer Billie Holiday and tenor saxophonist Lester Young (to her right) were close colleagues from the 1930s, when they recorded tunes like "A Sailboat in the Moonlight." They hadn't seen each other in years when they appeared on a live television show in December 1957, along with tenor saxophonist Coleman Hawkins (in hat) and baritone saxophonist Gerry Mulligan. It was to be their last encounter.

written in 1930 by George Gershwin and his lyric-writing brother Ira for the Broadway show *Girl Crazy*. Jazz musicians loved the harmonic progression, but were disinclined to play the actual melody—the only part of the song (along with the lyrics) covered by copyright. They simply concentrated on the chords. Instead of "I Got Rhythm," they played what they referred to as **rhythm changes**—**changes** being a slang word for a harmonic progression. They also altered the form slightly: as composed by the Gershwins, "I Got Rhythm" includes a final two-bar tag, making thirty-four measures. These two bars were rejected by jazz musicians, who preferred the symmetry of the thirty-two-bar form. Having stripped the tune to its essentials, musicians fashioned thousands of melodies and altered the chord progressions to their taste. Some of these spin-offs, such as Duke Ellington's "Conga Brava" and Thelonious Monk's cleverly named "Rhythm-a-ning," became jazz standards in their own right.

Jazz musicians routinely use the **A A B A** form to create original compositions. One of the most famous is Miles Davis's "So What," one of hundreds of jazz-generated thirty-two-bar **A A B A** tunes that are known as jazz **standards**. The head, as we have seen, is a bass line in call and response with a simple two-note riff. Since the riff is short, to fill out eight-bars it must be repeated three times. Once you have adjusted to the eight-bar unit, the overall form becomes clear.

At the bridge, there is a subtle but significant difference: the riff moves up a half step to a new key. Listen for this **modulation**, as well as the return to the original key in the final **A** section. Once you learn to notice the half-step change, you should have no difficulty following the choruses of "So What" (the first five are given here).

Listen also to how Miles Davis on trumpet and John Coltrane on tenor saxophone negotiate the form according to their own style: Davis with simple, taut phrases, Coltrane with lengthy gusts of notes. You can usually hear the bridge, the only point of contrast, when the pianist plays the appropriate chord. Pay particular attention to the bridge of Davis's second chorus (2:56), when the trumpet signals the change with a sudden, forceful note.

"So What" (CD1, track 7)

CHORUS 1 (HEAD)
A	0:34
A	0:49
B	1:03
A	1:17

CHORUS 2 (MILES DAVIS, TRUMPET)
A	1:31
A	1:45
B	1:59
A	2:14

CHORUS 3
A	2:28
A	2:42
B	2:56
A	3:10

CHORUS 4 (JOHN COLTRANE, TENOR SAXOPHONE)
A	3:24
A	3:38
B	3:52
A	4:06

CHORUS 5
A	4:20
A	4:33
B	4:47
A	5:01

There are many other examples in this book of thirty-two-bar **A A B A** form, each with its own chord progression. Some borrow that progression from an existing tune: Charlie Parker's "Ko-Ko," for example, is based on the 1939 pop song "Cherokee." Consult the appropriate Listening Guide for more details.

"Blue Lou," Fletcher Henderson (p. 176)

"Tempus Fugue-It," Bud Powell (p. 299)

"Ko-Ko," Charlie Parker (p. 289)

"Walkin' and Swingin'," Andy Kirk with Mary Lou Williams (p. 202)

"Christopher Columbus," Fats Waller (p. 258)

"Dinah," Benny Goodman Quartet (p. 180)

A B A C (A A′) Form

Other tunes in this book could be diagrammed a different way: **A B A C,** or **A A′,** an elegant variation on **A A B A** form. While **A A B A** adds contrast (with the bridge) precisely halfway through the song, **A B A C** uses that same location to return to the opening melody.

A (8 bars)   statement

B (8 bars)   contrast

A (8 bars)   return of statement

C (8 bars)   conclusion

It's possible to think of this same form as two sixteen-bar sections, the first ending with a half cadence, and the second steering the harmony firmly home with a full cadence:

A (16 bars)   statement

A′ (16 bars)   statement with new conclusion

Tunes that fall into this form include standard pop songs like "Star Dust" and "Embraceable You," but also original compositions from early New Orleans jazz to the most modern styles. As with **A A B A,** the **A B A C** form is a template, filled in by different harmonic progressions; but you can always recognize it by its characteristic feature—the return of the opening melody halfway through the song.

"Singin' the Blues," Bix Beiderbecke (p. 153)

"Hotter Than That," Louis Armstrong (p. 146)

"One Hour," Mound City Blue Blowers (p. 156)

"Star Dust," Artie Shaw (p. 185)

"Embraceable You," Charlie Parker (p. 291)

"ESP," Miles Davis (p. 395)

"Twisted Blues," Wes Montgomery (p. 339)

◀ IMPROVISATION

How can music that's made up on the spot still make sense? How do musicians manage to keep together? In short, what is improvisation? To answer, we can start with the rhythm section, where each instrument fills multiple roles.

The bass has the most restricted role. Rhythmically, it is a foundation layer, keeping steady time in a swing groove with a continuous and even string of notes. Because this sound is the neutral backdrop against which every rhythmic gesture is heard, the bassist has little choice but to stick to the basic

Paul Chambers, seen here in 1956, was the foundation of the Miles Davis rhythm section in the 1950s, and a bassist in demand for hundreds of recording sessions.

pattern. But at the same time, the bass plays a crucial harmonic role. Each time a new chord appears on the **chart** (the musical score that serves as the basis for jazz performance), the bass is responsible for playing that chord's root. Thus, the bass has a daunting challenge: a steady and consistent beat, fitting into a harmonic puzzle. Today's bassists do this with ease. The sound of the bass line, marking four even beats to the bar, is known as a **walking bass**, and it is an essential ingredient for most jazz performances.

During Miles Davis's solo on "So What" (1:31–3:24), Paul Chambers's bass line lies underneath the solo, never calling attention to itself and never failing to fulfill its basic rhythmic and harmonic duties. Yet the line has a graceful melodic shape, controlled by Chambers's creative imagination. A good bass line is a subtle form of improvisation, constantly supporting and sometimes inspiring the soloist. An experienced bassist can choose from the available possibilities at a split second's notice.

Sometimes the bass line does *not* move: we call this a **pedal point**. The term derives from pipe organs, where the lowest pipes are sounded on a pedal keyboard played with the feet. During an improvisation, an organist can simply hold down a pedal for an extended period of time, allowing the chords to drift on top of this foundation. In jazz, pedal points can occur whenever the bass refuses to move. Listen, for instance, to how the bassist in Ronald Shannon Jackson's "Now's the Time" (1:47–1:55) freezes the harmony for a full eight bars.

The patterns bassists play in Latin or funk may be more syncopated and complex, while still serving as a rhythmic foundation. At the opening to Dizzy Gillespie's "Manteca" (0:00–0:30), the bassist repeats a short two-measure riff while the horns add sharply contrasting layers of polyrhythm. In John Coltrane's "Acknowledgement" (starting at 0:32), the bass is the only stable element in the ensemble. Few people notice the bass or give it credit, but it is the rock on which most of jazz stands.

The primary harmony instrument in the rhythm section—usually a piano, but sometimes guitar, organ, vibraphone, or electric keyboards—has a different role. Every chart specifies the chords that must be played, with a musical shorthand: Cmaj7, for example, means a C major triad with a major seventh, B, added. But exactly *how* the chords are to be played is left open. At any given moment, the pianist can play the chord in any **voicing** (arrangement) or add **extensions** (extra notes). He or she can also use **harmonic substitutions**—harmonies that replace the existing chord progression. Compare, for example, the first chorus of "West End Blues" (0:16–0:50) with the fourth chorus (1:59–2:32). In the first, the pianist, Earl Hines, sticks to the script, playing simple chords on the beat. By the fourth chorus, where he is the featured soloist, he replaces these chords with a dense harmonic thicket, carving his own path through the blues form with his knowledge of harmony.

Finally, while the bass is a rhythmic foundation, the piano, a variable layer, constantly changes its rhythms to enliven the groove. The pianist listens closely to the rhythmic gestures of the drummer while "feeding" chords to the soloist. This irregular, unpredictable manner of playing chords is known as **comping**—jazz slang that derives from the word "accompanying."

In a typical swing groove, the drummer will play a more or less constant pattern (known as the **ride pattern**) with his right hand, while accenting the

DUNCAN SCHEDT COLLECTION

Gene Krupa helped turn the drummer into a matinee idol with his exuberant performances with the Benny Goodman orchestra in the 1930s. This movie still is from the 1940s.

backbeat on the high-hat cymbal with his left foot. The right foot, controlling the bass drum pedal, plays thunderous accents (known during World War II as **dropping bombs**), while the left hand swoops over the rest of the drum kit, adding sharp responses on the snare drum, tom-tom, or crash cymbal. This is the default rhythm: when the drummer wants to add an improvised passage, or **fill**, he can use both feet and hands to create more complicated patterns. A good drummer can play in several rhythmic feelings, shifting from swing in one tune to funk, Latin, or a soft ballad in another.

Listening to the rhythm section is a delight in itself. You can concentrate on it as a team or in terms of each player, focusing on how he or she negotiates an individual role in a constantly changing context. Or you can watch interactions: seeing how the piano and bass work together, or the bass and drums. A good rhythm section makes the music move in countless ways.

Still, the main focus for a jazz performance lies with the soloist. How exactly does the saxophonist or trumpet player decide which notes to play? We can offer a few general paradigms.

◀🔊 Melodic Paraphrase

The simplest method takes a preexisting melody—a song known by millions or an original composition by a member of the band—and varies it. **Melodic paraphrase** typically adds notes and distorts the rhythm into something that swings, but does not destroy the source. Jazz musicians often use melodic paraphrase at the beginning and end of a performance.

In the 1930s and 1940s, people knew the melodies to countless pop songs by heart—as we might know our favorite hits of today. Few of us have that kind of knowledge of classic songs from the golden age. But listen to "Over the Rainbow"—a song that still lives on, thanks to *The Wizard of Oz*—as reimagined by pianist Art Tatum. Throughout the piece, Tatum makes sure you can hear the

FRANK DRIGGS COLLECTION

Art Tatum established the gold standard for jazz virtuosity as a piano recitalist, influencing generations of musicians with his startling harmonic substitutions. He's shown here at a celebrated jam session with clarinetist Barney Bigard, trombonist Jack Teagarden, and guitarist Al Casey at the Metropolitan Opera House, 1944.

melody. In the first chorus (0:07–1:17), he states the **A A B A** melody directly, making it easy to hear despite his intricate harmonies and brilliant runs. During chorus 2 (1:17–2:36), the tune recedes into the background but you can hear it at crucial points, such as the opening of the second **A** section (1:36) and the start of the bridge (1:55). Tatum is one of those rare jazz musicians who prefer to use the original melody to hold his improvisation together at all times.

Harmonic Improvisation

Most jazz improvisers, however, simply discard the original melody, preferring to rely on the chord progression, a technique known as **harmonic improvisation.** Each chord is made up of only a handful of notes. An E♭ triad, for example, features the chord tones E♭, G, and B♭. It excludes all the other notes, such as E, A, or B, which sound horribly dissonant when played next to an E♭ chord. In their earliest training, jazz musicians analyze the chords in a tune and learn to play the consonant chord tones in their improvisation, avoiding notes that sound "wrong." Every decision must be made quickly as one chord changes to another, because melody notes that were consonant with one chord can become painfully dissonant with the next. Thus, when chords move fast, as they do in John Coltrane's notorious "Giant Steps," playing becomes a superhuman task. It's like running the hurdles, with a new barrier for the runner to cross every few steps.

◀》 Modal Improvisation

Another technique, **modal improvisation,** takes a different approach. Instead of worrying about each chord, improvisers draw their melodies from a scale. Some modern pieces have been set up to do this deliberately. In "So What," improvisers are expected to create their melodies from the D Dorian scale, shifting up a half step on the bridge.

Musicians who want to sound bluesy simply play the blues scale, superimposing it over a passage as if it had no chords. In Charlie Parker's third chorus in "Now's the Time" (1:03–1:10), we hear a highly skilled harmonic improviser ignore the chords and play bluesy licks that contradict the underlying harmony—even though the tune itself is a blues. A similar sensibility can be heard in the last chorus of "West End Blues" (2:32–2:56), where Louis Armstrong follows Earl Hines's dense piano solo with a single spare note, followed by descending blues phrases. Modal improvisation makes it clear that for jazz musicians, simplicity is just as important as complexity.

IN PERFORMANCE

Jazz can be played by bands of any size, but—as in classical music, with its symphonic orchestras and chamber groups—there are two main kinds: **big bands** and **small combos**.

Big Bands

In the 1930s, dance orchestras usually employed about sixteen musicians. These orchestras began to fade after World War II, but there are nevertheless many big jazz bands still around. A few carry on the memory of now long-deceased bandleaders from the Swing Era. Newer ones, such as New York's Vanguard Jazz Orchestra (which plays on Monday nights at the Village Vanguard), perform a more modern repertory. The vast majority, however, are found at universities, where they serve as part of the curriculum for jazz programs. Because these bands are educational enterprises, and therefore not restricted by payroll, they often climb in size to twenty-five musicians.

Like symphony orchestras, big bands group musicians by instrument. There are sections of trumpets, saxophones (usually alto, tenor, and baritone, but also often including the clarinet), and trombones. Each group sits together behind music stands. The rhythm section generally consists of piano, bass, drums, and guitar (electric or acoustic).

Because of the size of the ensemble, big bands use **arrangements**—composed scores for the orchestra, with individual parts for each musician. These arrangements often feature the sections in block-chord texture. Improvisation happens only at special moments, when limited blocks of time (from four measures to several choruses) are set aside for a soloist. In this way, the big band balances between what is created in advance—the composition—and what is created during the performance.

Musicians in big bands are typically dressed up, often in uniform; they are seen not as individuals, but as members of "the band," though when an accomplished soloist is called on to improvise, it's his or her individuality that is most prized. The band is usually led by a conductor, if a student group, or a "front man" whose job is primarily to interact with the audience. Most bands are also comfortable playing for dancing, though many concert jazz bands perform exclusively for listening.

Small Combos

Jazz is usually played by a small group: a few horns (trumpet, tenor saxophone) plus rhythm section. Such a group will usually be named after an individual (e.g., the Dexter Gordon Quintet), and is typically found in nightclubs, where the size of the band fits the venue's closer quarters.

Small combos derive from the spatial limitations of small dance halls and the tradition of the **jam session**—an informal gathering at which musicians create music for their own enjoyment. The earliest jam sessions typically took place in out-of-the-way venues, far from the public eye. The music was meant as a form of recreation, but it also served an important function within the jazz community. Through open-ended improvisation, musicians could be heard—and judged.

By the 1940s, the jam session went public, becoming another way to hear jazz. Its atmosphere is different from that of a big band: it's as if you were overhearing the musicians playing for themselves. Dress is informal, as is stage behavior. Musicians may wander about as they please, or stand by nodding their heads in silent approval of someone else's solo.

The musical format is purposefully kept simple. The head is the only composed part of the performance, usually played at the beginning and the end.

The rest of the tune is improvised—as many choruses as the soloists want. A typical order of solos begins with the horn players, then proceeds through the rhythm section: piano (and/or guitar), bass, and drums. Under the bass solos, the accompaniment lightens: the drummer plays quietly and the piano plinks out a few chords.

Drum solos are a different matter. They can be completely open-ended, in which case the band waits for a signal to reenter the tune. Many drummers, though, prefer to play solos that fit within the cycle. If you listen closely, counting bars and paying attention to cues, you may be able to tell exactly when one chorus ends and another begins. The rest of the band is doing this, waiting for the right moment to enter precisely on time.

Because drum solos can be disruptive, jazz groups often prefer to trade short solos between the drums and the soloists. This is known as **trading fours**—"fours" meaning four-bar segments (though there is nothing sacred about the four-bar segments; musicians may trade longer solos or shorter ones). Trading fours, which can also take place between soloists, usually occurs toward the end of the performance, after the other solos have already been played.

The Role of the Audience

How should you react to what you hear? Compared with rock, jazz is quieter, but compared with classical music, it's rowdy. In a concert hall, you can tap your feet and bob your head in time with the music and applaud after each solo (which performers appreciate), although the present-day habit of

Jam sessions were informal assemblies, blending disparate musical personalities into harmony. In this session, held in a New York penthouse in 1939, Duke Ellington swaps his piano for gospel singer Sister Rosetta Tharpe's guitar. Behind them are Ellington soloists Rex Stewart (center, on cornet) and Johnny Hodges (far right), Kansas City–bred trumpeter Hot Lips Page (far left), and swing trombonist J. C. Higginbotham (to his right).

applauding every improvisation defeats the original idea of cheering only solos that are outstanding. There are no programs: musicians usually announce tunes and often decide what to play onstage.

In a club, the atmosphere is much more informal. Some clubs try to keep audiences quiet during a set; but in others, people may drink, eat, smoke (although tobacco is now barred from most jazz clubs in the United States), and even carry on conversations. It is important to remember that serious jazz clubs are de facto concert halls, and are not in the business of providing pleasant background music. For that, there's always the hotel lounge. Jazz attracts a diverse audience, from high school kids to senior citizens. All that unites them is the desire to listen, and the more listening experience you have, the more rewarding the shared experience will be.

FEATURED LISTENING

Louis Armstrong and His Hot Five

"West End Blues"
Armstrong, trumpet, vocal; Fred Robinson, trombone; Jimmy Strong, clarinet; Earl Hines, piano; Mancy Cara, banjo; Zutty Singleton, drums. OKeh 8597 (1928); *The Best of Louis Armstrong* (Columbia/Legacy 886972139524).

PART II

EARLY JAZZ (1900–1930)

Jazz developed as a convergence of multiple cultures. The most important factor was the importation of African slaves to a world dominated by warring European colonists—particularly the French, Spanish, and English. In striving to keep African musical traditions alive, the slaves eventually found ways to blend them with the abiding traditions of Europe, producing hybrid styles in North and South America unlike anything in the Old World. Miraculously, jazz and other forms of African American music, including spirituals, blues, and ragtime, overcame subjugation to assume dominant roles in American music.

The miracle crystallized in New Orleans, a port city that assimilated many musical influences; by the early twentieth century, it was home to a new blues-based, highly rhythmic, and improvisational way of playing music. New Orleans produced jazz's first great composers, bandleaders, instrumentalists, and teachers, as well as Louis Armstrong, the genius whose unique skills and temperament spurred the

1843
- Virginia Minstrels perform in New York: beginning of minstrelsy.

1861–65
- Civil War

1871
- Fisk Jubilee Singers begin performing.

1877
- Reconstruction ends.
- Thomas Edison invents the phonograph.

1878
- James Bland writes "Carry Me Back to Old Virginny."

1880
- John Philip Sousa takes over U.S. Marine Band, popularizing brass bands throughout the country.

1884
- Mark Twain's *The Adventures of Huckleberry Finn* published in England, in the U.S. a year later.

1886
- Statue of Liberty dedicated in New York harbor.

1893
- Chicago World's Fair; Scott Joplin performs on the Midway.

1894
- Jim Crow laws adopted in Southern states.

1896
- Ernest Hogan's "All Coons Look Alike to Me" published.
- Supreme Court, in *Plessy v. Ferguson,* allows "separate but equal" segregation of facilities.

1897
- First ragtime pieces published.

This late nineteenth-century poster of Primrose and West's Big Minstrels shows that the company offered two productions: black performers on the left, white performers on the right. Both would have appeared onstage in blackface.

Mamie Smith and Her Jazz Hounds, 1922. Note teenager Coleman Hawkins, on the right, playing an alto saxophone instead of his usual tenor.

Paul Whiteman, baton raised at the upper right, leads his elephantine orchestra on one of the elaborate sets built for the movie revue *The King of Jazz*, 1930.

acceptance of jazz around the world. Armstrong had been nurtured by a strong tradition, from the first important jazz musician, Buddy Bolden, to his own mentor, King Oliver, who summoned Armstrong to Chicago to join the Creole Jazz Band.

Armstrong transformed jazz from a provincial African American folk music into an art focused less on community tradition than on the achievements of exceptional individuals. Before Armstrong, jazz had won the hearts of classical composers who reckoned it as a resource for "serious" music. After him, a generation of instrumentalists and composers proved that jazz was more than a resource: it was an emotionally and intellectually complete art in its own right. This generation included the most prolific and characteristic of American composers, Duke Ellington, and such powerful performers as vocalist Bessie Smith, saxophonist Coleman Hawkins, and cornetist Bix Beiderbecke. By the early 1930s, jazz had traveled the world, making converts everywhere.

1898
- *Clorindy, or the Origin of the Cakewalk* popularizes the cakewalk.
- Spanish-American War

1899
- Joplin's "Maple Leaf Rag" published.

1900
- Sigmund Freud's *The Interpretation of Dreams* published.

1903
- Wright brothers make first flight at Kitty Hawk, North Carolina.
- W. E. B. DuBois's *The Souls of Black Folk* published.

1904
- Ma Rainey hears the blues for the first time in St. Louis.
- Saxophones first manufactured in U.S.

1905
- Buddy Bolden at his peak in New Orleans.
- Robert Abbott founds the *Chicago Defender*.
- Einstein proposes his theory of relativity.

1906
- San Francisco earthquake kills 700.

1907
- Pablo Picasso paints *Les demoiselles d'Avignon*.

1909
- Henry Ford establishes assembly line to produce Model Ts.
- National Association for the Advancement of Colored People (NAACP) founded.

1910
- Bert Williams becomes first black to star in Ziegfeld's Follies.

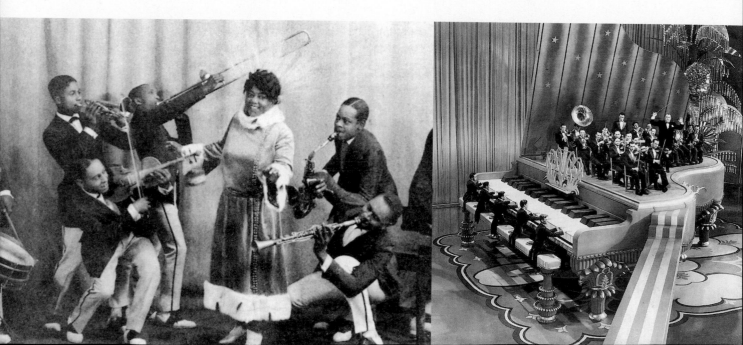

1910s
- Vernon and Irene Castle and James Reese Europe popularize dances like the turkey trot and cakewalk.

1912
- James Reese Europe performs in Carnegie Hall.
- W. C. Handy's "Memphis Blues" published.
- Sinking of the *Titanic*.

1913
- Igor Stravinsky's ballet *The Rite of Spring* premieres in Paris, causing a riot.

1914
- World War I begins in Europe.
- Charlie Chaplin makes his first short films.

1915
- D. W. Griffith's *Birth of a Nation* released, to cheers and protests.
- Franz Kafka's *The Metamorphosis* published.

1916
- Wilbur Sweatman records "Down Home Rag."

1917
- Original Dixieland Jazz Band makes first jazz recording; beginning of Jazz Age.
- U.S. enters World War I.
- Great Migration begins in earnest.
- Bolsheviks take power in the Russian Revolution.

1918
- World War I ends.

1919
- Prohibition (18th Amendment) becomes law.
- Chicago White Sox throw the World Series.

1920s
- Pianists (James P. Johnson, Fats Waller, Duke Ellington, Art Tatum) hit their stride in New York.

Two legends of New Orleans: trumpet player Freddy Keppard and soprano saxophonist Sidney Bechet, in Chicago, 1918.

The influential blues singer and guitarist Blind Willie McTell and his wife and occasional performing partner, Kate McTell, Atlanta, 1940.

Members of New York's music world gathered in Atlantic City, N.J., for the opening of the Vincent Youmans show *Great Day*: left to right, unknown, songwriter Harold Arlen, Fletcher Henderson (behind the wheel), trumpet player Bobby Stark, singer Lois Deppe, composer Will Marion Cook (standing), trumpet player Rex Stewart. Outside the Globe Theater, 1929.

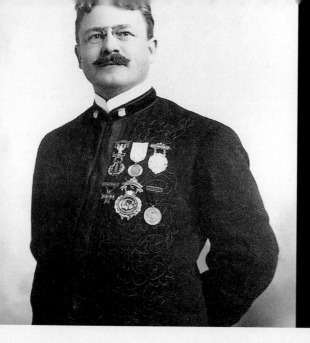

The midtown Cotton Club, 1938. Imagine a show featuring bandleader Cab Calloway and dancer Bill "Bojangles" Robinson, plus dinner, for $1.50.

John Philip Sousa brought military music to the concert stage.

1920
- Mamie Smith's "Crazy Blues" becomes first "race" recording hit.
- Paul Whiteman establishes his name with "Whispering."

1921
- First commercial radio broadcast.
- Eubie Blake and Noble Sissle's *Shuffle Along* premieres on Broadway.
- Arnold Schoenberg writes first twelve-tone piece of music.

1923
- First wave of black jazz recordings: King Oliver, Jelly Roll Morton, Bessie Smith.

1924
- Premiere of George Gershwin's *Rhapsody in Blue* at Paul Whiteman's "Experiment in Modern Music" concert.

- Fletcher Henderson Orchestra opens at the Roseland Ballroom, hiring Louis Armstrong.

1925
- Armstrong begins recording with his Hot Five.
- Development of electrical recording.
- *The New Negro* published, launching Harlem Renaissance.

1926
- Jelly Roll Morton and His Red Hot Peppers make electrical recordings.

1927
- Duke Ellington opens at the Cotton Club.
- Bix Beiderbecke records "Singin' the Blues."
- Bing Crosby introduced on Paul Whiteman recordings.
- *The Jazz Singer*, first talking picture, released.

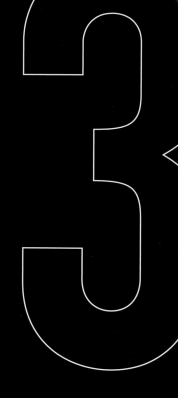

GEORGIA SEA ISLAND SINGERS
the buzzard lope

MISSISSIPPI FRED McDOWELL
soon one morning

BESSIE SMITH
reckless blues

JOHN PHILIP SOUSA
the stars and stripes forever

WILBUR SWEATMAN
down home rag

THE ROOTS
OF JAZZ

The first question we must address is: *what kind of music is jazz?* In 1987, the U.S. Congress passed a resolution declaring jazz a "valuable national American treasure," but the full text sums up the confusion sown by the music's contradictory qualities. Jazz is an "art form," brought to the American people through well-funded university courses and arts programs; but it is also a "people's music," a bubbling upward from the aspirations of ordinary folk. It's "an indigenous American music" but also international, having been "adopted by musicians around the world." Although jazz is a "unifying force" that erases ethnic gulfs, it is nevertheless a music that comes to us "through the African American experience."

There are three different categories that situate jazz within our society. The first is jazz as an **art form**. Jazz has been called "America's classical music," and it can now be found in the heart of the cultural establishment, whether in concert halls, television documentaries, or university curricula. While thinking of jazz as an art seems particularly appropriate for today, there has been reason to do so throughout its long history. Jazz has always been created by skillfully trained musicians, even if their training took place outside the academy. Their unique music demands and rewards the same respect and care traditionally brought to classical music.

African-Caribbean rhythms, imported into New Orleans as a result of the slave trade, played a powerful role in the birth of jazz. One of its later masters, the Cuban-born conguero **Chano Pozo** (seen here in 1949), gained prominence during the bebop era.

wwnorton.com/studyspace

At the same time, though, jazz is a **popular music**. It may seem an exaggeration to say so today, when jazz recordings comprise only 3 percent of the market. But jazz has always been a commodity, something bought and sold, whether in live performance or in the media—especially during the Swing Era of the 1930s, when vast audiences saw and heard Duke Ellington, Count Basie, and Benny Goodman on the radio, in the jukeboxes, or on movie screens. Even today, though, jazz musicians sell their services in the commercial marketplace. To understand this music, we must hear it as primarily commercial, its musicians constantly negotiating with the restless tastes of the American public.

Finally, we may also think of jazz as **folk music**. Not in the usual sense of music performed in rural isolation: jazz is distinctly urban, at home on the street corner and comfortable with modern technology. Yet on a basic level, the qualities that mark jazz as different from other musical genres stem directly from its folk origins. More often than not, those folk resources are African American.

Jazz and Ethnicity

We must therefore make the following simple but provocative assertion: *Jazz is an African American music.*

This is the kind of statement that seems designed to drive people crazy. Doesn't jazz belong to everybody? Calling it African American (or "black," or "Negro") suggests that only people who have been branded as such by American society can produce, or discern, jazz in any meaningful way. The rest, usually designated as "white" (although actually including the rest of humanity), have no real business being there. In fact, jazz musicians may be black, white, or any shade in between, just as they may be of any age or either gender, or from any part of the world. As Miles Davis once colorfully put it, if a jazz musician could play, he "didn't give a damn if he was green and had red breath."

So the first thing we must do is define our terms carefully. We usually take "African American" as an indication of **race**—the physical characteristics such as skin color that we inherit through our genes and dutifully report on census forms. But "African American" also tells us about **ethnicity**—how culture makes us who we are.

The difference is crucial. Race can't be changed. But because it is learned behavior, ethnicity can. We acquire it in our youth so unconsciously that our cultural habits become second nature. To learn another's culture can be more difficult, but the talented and determined can do it through diligent effort. And one of the most pleasant and expressive ways of sharing culture is through music. By listening to and loving jazz, the whole country, even the world, becomes more African American.

Jazz has a deep musical grammar that ultimately can be traced to Africa. As we saw in Chapters 1 and 2, African American music is characterized by **polyrhythm** within short, repeating rhythmic cycles. It relies heavily on **call and response**, the principle of interaction. Its melodies use **blue notes** to alter pitch, and its instrumentalists and vocalists use **timbre variation** as a fresh creative device. The music can melt away the boundaries separating music from dance and musician from audience.

None of these elements by itself is uniquely African. Call and response can be found everywhere, while polyrhythm crops up in such diverse places as Indonesia and India. But the particular *combination* of sounds that characterize jazz is uniquely African American. Moreover, the folk elements are not a fixed list of items that could be lost over the centuries, but flexible, living principles that can absorb and transform whatever music its performers encounter. To understand jazz, then, we must immerse ourselves first in its folk origins.

FOLK TRADITIONS

Black folk culture accomplished two things. First, it established an African American musical identity. This musical identity, having survived centuries of slavery, the tumultuous decades after the Civil War, and the transition from rural to urban in the early twentieth century, became a means of survival. Jazz musicians were able to draw on the folk tradition to ensure that the music they played was somehow congruent with what it meant to be "black."

At the same time, the popularity of black music transformed what had previously been white culture. Through music and dance, notions of "blackness" and "whiteness" became thoroughly mixed together. This result is what novelist and critic Albert Murray has called the "mulatto" nature of American culture.

The folk tradition included several different genres. One was the narrating of local history through lengthy songs known as **ballads**. The blasting of a railroad tunnel on the Virginia–West Virginia border, for example, resulted in "John Henry," in which the hard-muscled, steel-driving hero fights a losing battle against modern machinery. Other ballads, like "Staggerlee" and "Railroad Bill," celebrated the exploits of "bad men"—heroes of resistance who shrugged off society's constraints through their disrespectful and violent behavior. The taste for braggadocio and exaggeration, with its emphasis on sexual exploits and one-upmanship, is still part of African American culture: it can be heard today in hip-hop.

Ballads

Other kinds of secular music included **work songs**, which continued to thrive on the railroad, levee, or wherever else music was needed to pace manual labor. And in the lonely corner of the field where the now-freed slave continued to work, one could hear the **field holler**, an unaccompanied, rhythmically loose vocal line that expressed his loneliness and individuality.

Work songs/field hollers

A different folk tradition was the **spiritual**, which transformed call-and-response songs into religious poetry. This music was passed on in two ways. The Fisk Jubilee Singers, a vocal group from a new and impoverished black college, performed a polished, carefully arranged version of spirituals before the general public in 1871. But the music was also passed on orally from parents to children and transmuted through performance in storefront, "sanctified" Pentecostal churches. By the 1920s, it had turned into gospel music, a rich and vibrant tradition that still influences American music today. When early jazz musicians say they learned music in the church, we may assume they acquired the basic skills of musical interaction from this oral tradition.

Spirituals

🔊 "The Buzzard Lope" ("Throw Me Anywhere, Lord")

One place to look for African-influenced folk culture is on the sea islands of Georgia. Here, slaves brought directly from rice-growing West Africa worked the rice and cotton plantations; during the summer, when white residents fled inland to avoid malaria, there were only a few white overseers in charge. After Emancipation, the slaves, known as Gullahs, were left to eke out a living on their own. The result was a culture rich in African survivals, isolated from the mainland by swamps and salt marshes.

In the 1920s, bridges were built to the mainland, flooding Gullah culture with white capitalism. One woman, Lydia Parrish, a former Philadelphia Quaker who lived on St. Simons Island, studied the island's music carefully and took it upon herself to save it from extinction. She published her findings in 1942, in *Slaves Songs of the Georgia Sea Islands*. Earlier, she had used her resources to start a group eventually known as the Georgia Sea Island Singers. Folklorist Alan Lomax was brought to hear the singers by author Zora Neale Hurston in 1935. Twenty-five years later, he returned to the island with recording equipment, determined to preserve their sound.

"The Buzzard Lope" is a spiritual dance with African origins. On their death, slaves were often thrown into a field, where their bodies were devoured by buzzards. In the dance, singers gathered in a circle, leaving a piece of cloth in the center to represent the body. As they danced, individual singers would enter the ring, imitating a circling buzzard and snatching the carrion. The text is defiant: the superior power of "King Jesus" will protect the slaves, even under such horrible conditions.

The song is a call and response: the venerable folk singer Bessie Jones takes the lead, answered by a chorus of seven men. Each separate call and response makes one cycle, with the refrain (the same words) recurring in several of them. The singers clap two rhythms: a backbeat and the following (counted 3 + 3 + 2), providing a polyrhythmic background underneath the chorus:

$$
\begin{array}{c}

\end{array}
$$

3 + 3 + 2

But when Jones enters with her call slightly ahead of the beat, the clappers extend the polyrhythm (3 + 3 + 3 + 3 + 3):

3 + 3 + 3 + 3 + 3 (3)

Through intense repetition and syncopation, the music moves irresistibly forward until the singers abruptly cut it off.

🔊 **backbeat** in 4/4, the beats that fall on 2 and 4 (rather than 1 and 3)

LISTENING GUIDE

the buzzard lope (throw me anywhere, lord)

GEORGIA SEA ISLAND SINGERS

Bessie Jones, song leader; Joe Armstrong, Jerome Davis, John Davis, Peter Davis, Henry Morrison, Willis Proctor, Ben Ramsay, chorus

- Label: *Georgia Sea Island Songs* (New World Records, NW278); *Southern Journey*, vol. 13: *Earliest Times—Georgia Sea Island Songs for Everyday Living* (Rounder 1713)
- Date: 1960
- Style: African American folk
- Form: cyclic

> **What to listen for:**
> - cyclic structure
> - body percussion (hand claps, foot stomps)
> - polyrhythm
> - improvisation within the call and response

CYCLE 1 (REFRAIN)

0:00   Jones begins her first phrase with a rising melody, accompanied by a quiet foot stomp: *"Throw me anywhere, Lord."*

0:03   A chorus sings the **response**: a simple three-note melody, loosely harmonized: *"In that old field."* The hand clapping begins in earnest.

0:05   Jones repeats her call, this time with a falling phrase.

0:08   The response descends to a **full cadence**.

CYCLE 2

0:10   Jones sings the same melody to new text: *"Don't care where you throw me / Since my Jesus own me."*

0:12   The chorus sings the response, *"In that old field"* (which remains constant throughout the song).

CYCLE 3 (REFRAIN)

0:19   Jones returns to the refrain, this time varying the melody with a plaintive **blue note**. The hand claps follow the syncopated rhythm of her melody.

CYCLE 4

0:29   Jones sings a new couplet: *"You may beat and burn me / Since my Jesus save me."*

CYCLE 5 (REFRAIN)

0:38   Behind her, you can hear a bass humming a **dissonant** note.

CYCLE 6

0:47   As Jones adds new text, the rhythm becomes more driving: *"Don't care how you treat me / Since King Jesus meet me."*

CYCLE 7

0:56   New claps (recorded more distantly) are added to the overall texture: *"Don't care how you do me / Since King Jesus choose me."*

CYCLE 8 (REFRAIN)

1:05

CYCLE 9 (REFRAIN)

1:13   Jones changes the melody, moving it triumphantly upward. The performance begins to accelerate slightly.

CYCLE 10 (REFRAIN)

1:22   She repeats the refrain, keeping the new melodic variation.

CYCLE 11

1:31   The clapping becomes more intense. Jones drives the melody upward in response:
        "Don't care where you throw me / Since King Jesus own me."

CYCLE 12

1:40   *"Don't care how you treat me / Since King Jesus meet me."*

CYCLE 13

1:49   *"Don't care how you do me / Since King Jesus choose me."*

1:54   One member of the choir enters a beat early—perhaps by mistake, or perhaps as a
        signal to conclude.

1:57   Jones silences the hand clapping by sustaining her last note.

BLUES

At the dawn of the twentieth century, a new poetic genre, the **blues**, began to emerge, marked by its unusual three-line stanza. It took its name from the word that had been in use for centuries to describe an enervating depression: Thomas Jefferson, for example, once wrote that "we have something of the blue devils at times." Earlier forms of folk poetry usually fell into stanzas of two or four lines, but the blues took the two-line couplet and repeated the first line. The blues also became a musical form through its distinctive chord progression in the accompaniment to ballads such as "Frankie and Johnnie," a story of romantic betrayal from St. Louis that falls roughly into a twelve-bar pattern.

Unlike the ballad, which was a coherent, chronological account of an event usually told in the third person, the blues was personal, as though exploring the singer's solitary mind. This change in perspective matched the new mood of the time. As historian Lawrence Levine has observed, African American society had recently shifted from the communal confines of slave culture to the cold, terrifying realities of individualism. The blues was an apt and sobering metaphor for black people contemplating the true meanings of freedom.

Country Blues

The earliest blues combined old folk elements with new technology. Blues melodies borrowed their rhythmic flexibility from the field holler, prompting some musicians to observe that the blues was "as old as the hills." At the same time, they were accompanied by the guitar, which became widely available for the first time in the rural South in the late nineteenth century. Musicians used guitars as a blank slate for their creativity: they tuned them in unexpected ways and pressed knives, bottlenecks, and other implements against the strings to create haunting blue notes.

The early style was known as the **country blues** and was performed by solitary male musicians accompanying themselves on

Mississippi Fred McDowell's professional career did not begin until he was nearly sixty. A favorite of the blues revivalists, he regularly played on concert stages in the 1960s, inspiring artists like Bonnie Raitt to learn bottleneck guitar.

MICHAEL DOBO/MICHAEL OCHS ARCHIVES/GETTY IMAGES

guitar throughout the rural South, from the Carolinas to the Mississippi Delta into Texas. The form was loose and improvisatory, suiting the needs of the moment.

"Soon One Morning" ("Death Come a-Creepin' in My Room")

Mississippi Fred McDowell was actually from Tennessee, where he was born in 1904. In his thirties, he moved about forty miles south of Memphis to Como, Mississippi, where he worked on cotton farms and played guitar at country dances and juke joints. "I wasn't making money from music," he said. "Sometimes they'd pay me, and sometimes they wouldn't." In 1959, he was rediscovered by Alan Lomax, who recorded his music and launched his career as a professional blues artist. Like other musicians brought to public light during the folk revival that occurred in the 1960s, McDowell was cherished for his archaic acoustic guitar sound; but he also thought of himself as a modern artist. He liked playing electric guitar and was thrilled when the Rolling Stones recorded one of his songs on *Sticky Fingers* (1971).

"Soon One Morning" is not a blues: its poetic shape is a quatrain, not a three-line stanza. And though its text is religious, it is too solitary to be a spiritual. It falls somewhere in between, a spiritual reflection informed by blues musical habits. "It's just like if you're going to pray, and mean it, things will be in your mind," he explained. "Songs should tell the truth."

Here McDowell plays **bottleneck guitar**: he damps the strings with a glass slide placed over a finger, which gives him the freedom to slide from one note to the next. The effect is often noisy, as other strings will resonate alongside the desired melodic line. McDowell uses the guitar less as accompaniment than as a partner: "If you pay attention, what I sing, the guitar sings, too." When he seems unable to complete his phrases, the haunting guitar sound takes his place. It is literally an extension of his voice.

For rock musicians, country blues has a special authenticity. In fact, most of us know this rural style primarily because musicians like Eric Clapton and Mick Jagger listened to recordings by blues musicians from the Mississippi Delta—Son House, Charley Patton, and especially Robert Johnson, whose two-CD complete set sold more than half a million copies in 1990—and based their electrified bluesy sounds on this "down home" music.

LISTENING GUIDE

1.9

soon one morning (death come a-creepin' in my room)

MISSISSIPPI FRED McDOWELL, GUITAR, VOCAL
- Label: *Southern Journey 10: Yazoo Delta Blues and Spirituals* (Prestige 25010); *The Story of American Music* (Columbia/Legacy CK 61433-61437
- Date: 1959
- Style: African American folk music
- Form: four-line stanza (**A B A C; C** is the refrain)

What to listen for:
- cyclic structure
- body percussion (hand claps, foot stomps)
- polyrhythm
- improvisation within the call and response

INTRODUCTION

0:00   The recording starts abruptly, as if someone had just turned on a microphone. A preliminary note escapes from the guitar.

CHORUS 1

0:04   **A**   With a few louder notes, McDowell begins the first phrase of the four-phrase tune. His line includes **blue notes**, created by damping the strings with a glass slide. To keep time, he taps quietly but insistently on the downbeat, playing a single low guitar string on the upbeat.

0:13   **B**   The second phrase parallels the first, but starts on a higher pitch.

0:16   As the melody reaches its highest point, McDowell plays more intensely.

0:20   **A**   The third phrase also parallels the first, returning to a quieter volume.

0:27   **C**   The last phrase opens with a different rhythm.

0:32   The last note falls with an accent in the middle of a measure. It sounds as though McDowell has shortened the meter by two beats; but a few seconds later, he makes up the time by entering two beats early with his vocal.

CHORUS 2

0:35   **A**   McDowell sings the first line, **doubling** the melody on guitar: *"It was soon one morning, death come creepin' in [my room]."* In the middle of the word "morning," his voice trails off; the guitar finishes the phrase.

0:41   Again, he fades out before the end of the phrase, leaving the guitar to carry out the musical thought.

0:43   **B**

0:50   **A**   The third melodic phrase begins with the guitar; the voice enters a few seconds later.

0:57   **C**   The last line is a **refrain**, with these words heard in every stanza: *"Oh my Lord, oh my Lord, what shall I do to be [saved]?"*

CHORUS 3

1:05   **A**   On the next stanza, McDowell's words are almost too faint to be intelligible: *"Well hurry, children, hurry, hurry when my Lord calls."*

1:12   **B**

1:19   **A**

1:26   **C**   He sings the refrain, fading off on the last word.

CHORUS 4

1:34   **A**   McDowell moves his guitar accompaniment down an octave, to a lower **register**. *"I'm gonna stand right here, I'm gonna wait until Jesus [comes]."*

1:41   **B**

1:48   **A**

1:54   **C**

CHORUS 5

2:00   **A**   Over a sharply chopped **backbeat**, the guitar takes a solo chorus.

2:08   **B**   McDowell's playing causes other strings to resonate, creating a complex, clanging timbre.

2:14   **A**   The tempo begins to increase noticeably.

2:20   **C**

CHORUS 6

2:26   **A**   McDowell returns to the opening stanza: *"Well, soon one morning, death come creepin' in [my room]."*

2:32   **B**

| 2:38 | **A** | The guitar takes the remainder of the stanza by itself. |
| 2:44 | **C** | |

CHORUS 7
2:50	**A**	The last chorus again features solo guitar, with the melody down an octave.
2:56	**B**	
3:01	**A**	
3:07	**C**	
3:10		The guitar stops, ending the piece.

Vaudeville ("Classic") Blues

Jazz musicians began to encounter the blues when it crossed the boundary line into popular music. The transition began virtually as soon as the country blues caught the ear of curious professionals. Gertrude Pritchett, a black stage singer who later became better known as "Ma" Rainey (1886–1939), heard it from a young woman in St. Louis around 1904. Asked about her peculiar style of music, she told Rainey, "It's the blues." The new style went into Rainey's repertory, and she went on to fame as one of the most popular singers of **vaudeville,** or **classic, blues**—a theatrical form featuring female singers, accompanied by a small band, on the stages of black vaudeville circuits in the 1910s and 1920s.

Known as the "Mother of the Blues," Rainey was a short woman with a powerful voice that could be heard in the back rows of crowded theaters or in the unfriendly acoustics of outdoor tent shows. In the hands of artists like Rainey, the blues became more codified, falling into strict twelve-bar stanzas with written harmonic progressions. Many soon-to-be jazz musicians entered show business with singers like Rainey, learning through trial and error how best to match their horns to the singers' distinctive bluesy strains.

Around the same time Ma Rainey first heard the blues, a wandering cornet-playing band musician named W. C. Handy encountered what he later described as "the weirdest music I had ever heard" in a Mississippi railroad station: a guitarist repeating the same line of poetry endlessly ("goin' where the Southern cross' the dog") while scraping blue notes out of the strings with a knife. Struck by how eagerly Southern audiences responded to this sound (see box below), Handy studied the music carefully. Using his command of music notation, he began writing it down for his own dance ensemble to play. Soon Handy—later known as the "Father of the Blues"—began publishing a string of new blues-related popular songs, including "Memphis Blues"(1912), "Beale Street Blues" (1917), and the biggest hit of the time, "St. Louis Blues" (1914). One discographer estimates that "St. Louis Blues" was recorded 135 times in the thirty years that followed—more than any other tune.

Ma Rainey

Ma Rainey, the "Mother of the Blues," in 1924, with blues musician "Georgia Tom," also known as Thomas Dorsey. By 1932, Dorsey had composed "Precious Lord" and turned his back on secular music, becoming the father of gospel music.

FRANK DRIGGS COLLECTION

Recordings

By the 1910s, the blues was hot commercial property. Pop-song publishers broke through with blues hits, and recording companies followed almost immediately after. At first, their audience was white, as were their performers: vaudeville stars who specialized in mimicking black people (as well as white immigrant groups, like the Irish and Dutch). But in 1920, Perry Bradford, an African American songwriter and tune plugger, convinced OKeh Records to try a black artist, Mamie Smith. As sales of her recording "Crazy Blues" soared into the hundreds of thousands, recording companies realized that African Americans constituted a new market.

By the 1920s, black people were crowding into Northern cities. Although eager to claim themselves as newly urbanized, they were still hungry for music that proclaimed their folk roots. The blues—a genre that had itself crossed over from folk to popular—became *their* music. To satisfy their tastes (and to augment profits), record companies offered a new product: "race records," black music created for black people.

Race records

Although the idea sounds offensive today, the term was meant as respectful: African American newspapers frequently described their own people as "the race." Modern sensibilities are more justifiably shocked by the treatment of black performers by white-owned record companies. Singers did not receive copyright royalty, just a modest performer's fee. They were also pressured by executives to record *only* the blues, turning it into a kind of musical ghetto. But the recordings sold, stimulating a small boom in the musical economy and leaving us a wealth of sound documents that reveal what the blues was like in the 1920s.

Bessie Smith beams in her only film appearance, *St. Louis Blues* (1929). When her dance partner (played by Jimmy Mordecai) abandons her for another, she pours out her heart in a performance of the title tune, composed in 1914 by W. C. Handy.

■ BESSIE SMITH (1894–1937)

The most popular blues artist of the era was Bessie Smith. Known as the "Empress of the Blues," she was an extraordinarily powerful singer who had learned how to project her voice in crowded halls in an era before microphones. Yet she was also a sensitive singer who adapted beautifully to the recording studio. In a career lasting only fourteen years, Smith made nearly two hundred recordings, establishing her style once and for all as *the* standard for singing the blues.

Born in Chattanooga, Tennessee, Smith began her career as a stage professional, singing and dancing in black theaters in the Theater Owners Booking Association (better known as TOBA), the vaudeville circuit for African American performers. Because of the treatment they experienced on the road, performers joked that TOBA stood for Tough on Black Asses. She became a favorite in theaters and tent shows, while offstage she liked to drink and even fight; as one musician remembered, "She could cuss worse than a sailor."

Her recording career as a blues singer began with OKeh Records in 1923. Some of her accompanists were already familiar with the blues: Louis Armstrong, for example, had grown up hearing prostitutes singing it in New

Orleans saloons. For others, recording with Bessie Smith amounted to a crash course in the music, with accompanists scurrying to match the nuances of her phrasing and tone. Jazz musicians enjoyed working with her, and she in turn enjoyed the 1920s in style, wearing necklaces of gold coins and underscoring her status as a recording diva by bursting onstage through a replica of one of her recordings.

Smith's career peaked in 1929, the same year she made her only film appearance as a downhearted lover in the seventeen-minute short *St. Louis Blues*. Thereafter, the Depression curtailed her earnings and forced her to make far fewer recordings. By the mid-1930s, feeling her blues style had slid from fashion, she tried to update her sound by recording with modern swing musicians. But her comeback was not to be. In 1937, as she rode to a gig on the back roads of the Mississippi Delta, her car plowed into the back of a truck. Smith's arm was torn loose and she went into shock. By the time she reached a hospital, she had lost too much blood to survive. Her record producer, John Hammond, angrily wrote an account that is still recounted today (and dramatized in Edward Albee's 1961 play *The Death of Bessie Smith*): that Smith was taken first to a white hospital, where she died shortly after being refused admission. This was untrue: no one in Mississippi would have thought of taking a black woman to a white facility. Hammond may have altered the story, but the message—that her death was attributable to the casual violence that was the fabric of life for black musicians in the Deep South—rang true for many people.

🎧 "Reckless Blues"

The trumpet player Louis Armstrong was not Smith's favorite accompanist: she preferred the cornetist Joe Smith (no relation), who allowed that the great singer deserved a more subservient and discreet accompanist. But on "Reckless Blues," Armstrong shows how thoroughly the language of the blues had expanded by 1925 under the influence of singers like Smith.

"Reckless Blues" is a duet for two great artists, each striving for our attention. Backed by Fred Longshaw's stolid chords on reed organ—as unswinging a background as we could imagine—Smith is in command from the start, singing each line of the stanza with simplicity and control. As the "responder" to her "call," Armstrong is alert to every gesture, filling in even the tiny spaces she leaves in the middle of a line. His sound is affected by two mutes: a straight mute to reduce the sound and a plunger to produce *wa-wa* effects. With each stanza, their intensity continues to grow. Smith's lines stick to the melodic outline she starts with, but become richer in timbre and more unpredictable in rhythm.

Eyewitness to History

Cornetist W. C. Handy (1873–1958) described hearing something like the blues early in the twentieth century while playing with a nine-piece band at a dance in Cleveland, Mississippi. As he remembered it, one night a local black band was allowed to play:

They were led by a long-legged chocolate boy and their band consisted of just three pieces, a battered guitar, a mandolin and a worn-out bass. The music they made was pretty well in keeping with their looks. They struck up one of those over-and-over strains that seem to have no very clear beginning and certainly no ending at all. The strumming attained a disturbing monotony, but on and on it went, a kind of stuff that has long been associated with cane rows and levee camps. Thump-thump-thump went their feet on the floor. Their eyes rolled. Their shoulders swayed. And through it all that little agonizing strain persisted. It was not really annoying or unpleasant. Perhaps "haunting" is a better word, but I commenced to wonder if anybody besides small town rounders and their running mates would go for it.

The answer was not long in coming. A rain of silver dollars began to fall around the outlandish, stomping feet. The dancers went wild. Dollars, quarters, halves—the shower grew heavier and continued so long I strained my neck to get a better look. There before the boys lay more money than my nine musicians were being paid for the entire engagement. Then I saw the beauty of primitive music. They had the stuff the people wanted. It touched the spot. Their music wanted polishing, but it contained the essence. Folks would pay money for it. . . .

That night a composer was born, an *American* composer.

reckless blues

1.2

BESSIE SMITH

Bessie Smith, vocal; Louis Armstrong, trumpet; Fred Longshaw, reed organ

- Label: Columbia 14056-D; *St. Louis Blues*, vol. 2: *1924–1925* (Naxos 8.120691)
- Date: 1925
- Style: vaudeville blues
- Form: 12-bar blues

What to listen for:
- vaudeville (or classic) blues singing
- clear twelve-bar blues form
- call and response between Smith and Armstrong
- trumpet adopting blues singing style

INTRODUCTION

0:00 Over Longshaw's organ, Armstrong plays an extended blues line, his timbre distorted by a plunger mute. Throughout the piece, Longshaw remains in the background, playing a stable series of chords.

CHORUS 1

0:14 *"When I wasn't nothing but a child,"*
Smith begins her first blues chorus with a descending melody.

0:17 She pauses briefly, leaving room for a quick Armstrong response.

0:28 *"When I wasn't nothing but a child,"*

0:35 The end of the line is marked by a brief melodic idea, falling and rising through the **blue third**, seeming to underscore her girlish sauciness.

0:42 *"All you men tried to drive me wild."*

CHORUS 2

0:56 *"Now I am growing old,"*
Smith's melody follows the same basic pattern as chorus 1. On the word "now," her line is **melismatic**—several notes for a single syllable.

1:04 Armstrong's response begins with a striking **blue note.**

1:10 *"Now I am growing old,"*
Smith holds out the second "now" with a single note, quavering slightly at the end.

1:23 *"And I've got what it takes to get all of you men told."*

CHORUS 3

1:37 *"My mama says I'm reckless, my daddy says I'm wild,"*
As if responding to the emotional quality of the lyrics, Smith bursts in a few beats early.

1:50 *"My mama says I'm reckless, my daddy says I'm wild,"*
Her line is intensely **syncopated**, dragging against the beat.

1:58 Armstrong lets a blue note fall agonizingly for three seconds.

2:04 *"I ain't good looking but I'm somebody's angel child."*

CHORUS 4

2:18 *"Daddy, mama wants some loving, Daddy, mama wants some hugging,"*
Smith interrupts the usual three-line stanza with a repeated call to "Daddy."
Armstrong's response mimics the word with a two-note pattern.

2:33 *"Darn it pretty papa, mama wants some loving I vow,"*
Smith's emotions are signaled by changes in timbre.

2:40 Mirroring Smith, Armstrong's response is also more emotionally involved.

2:46 *"Darn it pretty papa, mama wants some loving right now."*

CODA

2:54 In the last two measures, Armstrong and Longshaw signal the end by slowing down slightly. Longshaw's last tonic chord adds a blue seventh note.

POPULAR MUSIC

Minstrelsy

If the blues was created by the black community for its own enjoyment, a surprising number of black musicians moved toward a different audience: the larger and more affluent audience of white Americans. "Mighty seldom I played for colored," remembered one violinist. "They didn't have nothing to hire you with." Virtually from the beginning, black people realized they could perform their "blackness" for money. This happened, for example, in racially mixed areas on the Lower East Side of Manhattan, where in the early nineteenth century loose-limbed black men entranced white onlookers by dancing on a shingle placed on the ground. A few black performers managed to earn a living this way: on one of his American tours, English novelist Charles Dickens acclaimed William Henry Lane, also known as Master Juba, as "the greatest dancer known."

The deep imbalance of power between the races, however, made it difficult for black performers to succeed. Instead, popular culture was shaped in the other direction. Attentive white performers studied black performers: they adopted black comedy and dance and accompanied themselves on banjo (an African instrument) and "the bones" (a primitive form of homemade percussion), creating in the process a new form of entertainment.

In New York in 1843, a quartet of white musicians called the Virginia Minstrels (after an Austrian group that had recently visited the city) presented an evening's entertainment that claimed to depict the culture of plantation slaves. They performed in blackface—a mask of burnt cork, with grotesquely exaggerated eyes and mouths. Their success was astonishing, prompting numerous imitators. Within a decade, the "minstrel show" had become the most popular form of theater in the country.

Minstrels pushed concepts of blackness into the bizarre. As "Ethiopian delineators," their "hair" (mops of unruly curls) was wild and woolly, their stage clothes tattered and outrageously designed. To be sure, one of the main minstrel types, named Zip Coon, was an overdressed dandy whose foppish behavior savagely parodied upper-class whites. But the most memorable characterizations were based on a poisonous racial contempt. Happy-go-lucky plantation "darkies" combined savvy musical talent with foolish, childlike behavior that no adult could take seriously. The best known of these was a dancing crippled stablehand known as Jim Crow. This character was so thoroughly identified with racial exploitation that the name "Jim Crow" became a shorthand for the entire system of segregation that flourished in Southern states after the Civil War.

Jim Crow

There is no doubt that white audiences enjoyed the black culture presented in the minstrel show. But their admiration was stained with indelible stereotypes. Consider the phrase "natural rhythm," a backhanded compliment paid black musicians. While on the surface it expresses delight in black rhythmic qualities, "natural" suggests that for blacks, rhythm is not a learned talent but something genetically given—and therefore unearned. And along with "natural rhythm" came many less desirable qualities: thieving, lying, and sheer idiocy. No matter how musically gifted, black people, like *idiot savants*, did not understand what they were doing, and were incapable of behaving otherwise.

THE GRANGER COLLECTION, NEW YORK

Long after minstrel stage shows had passed into memory, minstrelsy's grotesque smile still remained in films like the 1939 *Swanee River*, a fictional biography of Stephen Foster, featuring Al Jolson in blackface.

BLACK PERFORMERS After Emancipation, minstrel troupes began featuring black performers, who accepted roles demanded by the white audience, disguising their wide range of complexions with blackface makeup. Even under these conditions, some black minstrel stars—like Billy Kersands, a comedian whose facial muscles were so malleable that he could hold a cup and saucer in his mouth—rose to the top of show business. James Bland, a Howard-educated performer and songwriter, wrote a sentimental ballad, "Carry Me Back to Old Virginny," that served as the state song of Virginia until 1997, when the song's racial dialect ("There's where the old darkey's heart am long'd to go") finally prompted its removal.

By the time jazz made its first inroads into American popular culture, the minstrel show was on its last legs. Performers such as the richly comic Bert Williams and the brilliant tap dancer Bill "Bojangles" Robinson moved their acts to the vaudeville stage. Yet the basic business of the minstrel show—the stereotypical representation of blackness—remained central to show business. In the first sound film, *The Jazz Singer* (1927), white entertainer Al Jolson proved his devotion to American popular culture (and distance from his Jewish past) by belting out "Mammy" in blackface. Up through the 1940s, film actors such as Mickey Rooney, Bing Crosby, and Judy Garland occasionally performed in blackface, and on radio white actors used "blackvoice" dialect to bring minstrel stereotypes into the present, as with the hit show "Amos 'n' Andy." Minstrelsy had become such a traditional show-biz staple that by now entertainers were using it without paying attention to its racial slurs.

Thus, any time a black performer stepped onto a public stage, audiences expected an enactment of black stereotypes. This did not affect most jazz musicians, whose job was simply to provide music. But those who were seen as entertainers had to know how to act. Louis Armstrong routinely mugged his way through ridiculous roles: in one 1930s short subject, he appears in "heaven," wearing a leopard skin, standing in soap bubbles, and singing "Shine," a song about racial stereotypes. This may strike us as outrageous, but blacks of the time thoroughly enjoyed Armstrong's inventive humor, knowing that the sound of his trumpet and the witty authority of his vocal delivery dispelled racist absurdity, turning it into something approaching an act of defiance. If stereotypes could not be exploded, they could be undermined from within.

Dance Music

The very first slave musicians knew they had a knack for inspiring movement with their music. Black fiddlers roamed across the South, relying on their musical abilities for money as well as physical freedom. Most were anonymous artisans. Some, like the character Fiddler from Alex Haley's 1976 novel *Roots*, saved their earnings in order to buy their freedom. A few became celebrities. In early nineteenth-century Philadelphia, the free black bandleader and composer Frank Johnson used his knowledge of African American music to "distort a sentimental, simple, and beautiful song into a reel, jig, or country-dance." Among his accomplishments was a tour of London, where he earned a silver bugle by performing for Queen Victoria.

Careers like Johnson's were rare. But at a time when most black people were pushed toward manual labor, music was one of the few skilled professions open to them. Like a butler, cook, or maid, a black musician hired to play tunes for dancing became a domestic servant, wearing livery (or the conventional black tuxedo) as a symbol of his role. His position in society was elegant and profitable, if clearly subservient. This situation held until the beginning of the twentieth century, when a revolution shook the world of dance.

THE DANCING CRAZE In late nineteenth-century America, respectable people danced at balls restricted by invitation to a small, exclusive social circle. Their favorite dances, like the quadrille and the lancer, were formal and elaborate. The waltz placed couples in close physical contact, but the speed of the dance countered what was considered its brazen intimacy.

All that began to change early in the twentieth century. When restaurants and cabarets threw open their dance floors to middle-class couples, a slew of new dances entered the mainstream. Sometimes known as "animal dances" (the "turkey trot," "bunny hug," and "grizzly bear"), these dances were more uninhibited and physical, requiring vigorous movement from the hips and lower body. Dancing, previously for the young and single, was now taken up by married couples as well. Women shed their corsets, finding dance a means of physical exercise and personal expression. New technologies played a role: the phonograph made it possible for people to learn these snappy new dances in the privacy of their living rooms.

■ THE CASTLES and JAMES REESE EUROPE (1881–1919)

The dances that entranced white America were often African American in origin. The Charleston, for example, derived its name and its syncopations from the highly Africanized islands of South Carolina. These dances were introduced to middle-class audiences by experts such as Vernon and Irene Castle, who offered graceful interpretations that carefully removed lower-class excesses. In an interview, Irene Castle explained the origins of the "shimmie shake" (with a casual racism that was typical for its time):

> We get our new dances from the Barbary Coast [a well-known red-light district in San Francisco]. Of course, they reach New York in a very primitive condition, and have to be considerably toned down before they can be used in the drawing-room. There is one just arrived now—it is still very, very crude—and it is called "Shaking the Shimmy." It's a nigger dance, of course, and it appears to be a slow walk with a frequent twitching of the shoulders. The teachers may try and make something of it.

While the Castles transformed such dances into cool, middle-class elegance, the subversive, syncopated music was inescapably black. This music was known as **ragtime** (see below). When it was played, it seemed to affect its listeners physically. "When a good orchestra plays a 'rag,'" Vernon Castle said, "one has simply *got* to move."

With her bobbed hair and flowing gown, Irene Castle (shown here with her husband Vernon in 1914, the year they introduced the fox-trot in Irving Berlin's *Watch Your Step*) symbolized the new freedoms available to women at the dawn of the twentieth century.

FRANK DRIGGS COLLECTION

The Castles' ragtime was performed by the black bandleader James Reese Europe. Born in Alabama, Europe moved to New York at age twenty-two to play for and conduct black musical theater. By the 1910s, he had shifted his focus to dance music. Most of the good dance jobs in New York were held by white orchestras playing gypsy music. Because Europe wanted to use black musicians, he created the Clef Club—part talent agency, part orchestra. In 1912, as the dance/ragtime craze was nearing its peak, the Clef Club showed its strength with a massive concert in Carnegie Hall. This was not a jazz band: the 125-piece orchestra was made up primarily of string instruments, such as the mandolin and the harp-guitar. Playing arrangements that highlighted "Negro" syncopation, the Clef Club orchestra reaffirmed the black musician's place at the center of the dance world. Europe himself caught the ear of the Castles and formed his own society orchestra to back them.

When the United States entered World War I, Europe joined the military, eager to show that black men were willing to die for their country. He fought bravely in the trenches and formed the 369th Infantry Band, known as the

Hellfighters

"Hellfighters," which he persuaded dozens of his best musicians (including clarinet players from Puerto Rico) to join. Today, recordings of the Hellfighters sound closer to jazz (though Europe frowned on improvisation), if only because the military band favors the brass and reed instruments we have come to expect. Sadly, though, Europe did not live to see jazz come to flower. In 1919, shortly after his triumphant return to New York, he was stabbed in the neck by a disgruntled drummer, dying at age thirty-eight.

Europe left two different kinds of dance bands in his wake. One was the small combo, an inexpensive group ideally suited for jazz through its size and flexibility. The other kind was the large dance orchestra, exemplified by Europe's groups and bands such as Will Marion Cook's Southern Syncopated Orchestra and Tim Brymn's Black Devil Orchestra, which impressed audiences with their full orchestral sound. Ultimately, both kinds of bands would prove important for jazz: the large orchestras became the model for the swing bands of the 1930s, while the small combo was the basis for early New Orleans jazz as well as the modern bebop style.

FRANK DRIGGS COLLECTION

James Reese Europe (far left) was a stellar musician, conductor, arranger, and administrator. In World War I, he also proved to be a brave soldier, fighting in the trenches of France. Here he conducts his 369th Infantry Band, known as the Hellfighters, in Paris, 1919.

ART MUSIC

Having learned during slavery that literacy was a kind of power—why else would it be systematically denied to them?—musically inclined African Americans were drawn to the mysteries of notation and theory. In the all-black schools and universities that sprouted throughout the South after Emancipation, music became a central part of formal education. Some, like educator Booker T. Washington, disdained the usefulness of musical skills: visiting a poor family, he was disgusted to find that people who dined with a single eating utensil had spent their meager income on an expensive reed organ. But many aspiring African Americans saw music as an inextricable part of becoming middle class.

Through public education, children learned to play classical instruments like the violin. A few became skilled performers, such as Joseph Douglass, grandson of the abolitionist Frederick Douglass and a brilliant violinist. Soprano Sisserietta Jones was so renowned that she billed herself professionally as "the Black Patti" (after the popular Italian opera star Adelina Patti). Yet even such talented performers as these could not support themselves professionally. White audiences refused to hear them, and black audiences were simply not affluent enough to support them. Barred from opera houses, Jones had to tour with a troupe, known as Black Patti's Troubadours, her operatic performances stuck in the middle of minstrel entertainment.

As classically trained youngsters became old enough to worry about employment, jazz absorbed their talents. Violin and cello were traded in for commercially useful instruments like saxophone or string bass. Other instruments like the trumpet and trombone absorbed new techniques from the bandstand. Still, classical education brought standards of execution and music theory into jazz, and musicians brought up in the concert tradition carried with them a social ambition that led them to dream of becoming something more in the world.

Brass Bands

If the symphony orchestra was a remote goal for classically trained musicians, the brass band provided a more practical alternative. An import from Britain, the brass band was originally a military institution that in peacetime became a local "people's" orchestra. New brass instruments like the sousaphone were designed for ease in marching, while reed instruments like the clarinet and flute were often added to make the overall sound more fluid and flexible.

The sousaphone was inspired by John Philip Sousa (1854–1932), a conductor and composer whose name was synonymous with brass band excellence. Sousa took over the U.S. Marine Band in 1880 and transformed it into a top-notch concert orchestra, mounting ambitious programs that featured European music as well as his own concert marches. In 1892, he formed his first ensemble. For the next forty years, the Sousa Band toured across the world, bringing to concert band music the highest level of virtuosity and precision in performance.

John Philip Sousa

Below Sousa lay thousands of bands, ranging in size from large professional bands (often led by former Sousa soloists) to small, local amateur groups. Indeed, it was said that "a town without its brass band is as much in need of sympathy as a church without a choir." Staffed by townspeople who had mastered just as much notation as was necessary, local bands played for dances and concerts as well as parades. On such occasions, the local butcher, policeman, and lawyer traded their work clothes for uniforms, with the band's name proudly displayed on the front of their caps. We can imagine them in a small town on a summer's evening, delighting a crowd from a gazebo on the city square.

BRASS BANDS AND JAZZ Not surprisingly, towns with a significant African American population had their own brass bands, just as eager to display their skills as their white counterparts. For black musicians, bands provided a friendly, supportive environment in which to create music. They were also social organizations, offering insurance to members and a decent, brass-led burial at life's end. As the dance craze gathered steam, brass bands boiled down to small dance ensembles, led by a violinist but featuring wind instruments central to jazz: cornet, clarinet, and trombone. Cymbals, bass drum, and snare drum were combined into the modern drum set. Marches, in duple meter—sometimes a straight 2/4, at other times a jauntier meter with the beat divided into triplets, known as 6/8—were also used for dancing. The lively rhythms of Sousa's "The Washington Post," written in 1889, accompanied the two-step, a popular dance that had just been introduced.

March form

The band's most important contribution to jazz, though, came with the structure known as **march form**. The defining unit of a march is a sixteen-bar section known as a **strain**—so called because of its dominant melody, or "strain," but equally identifiable by its chord progression. Marches feature a steady succession of strains, each usually repeated before passing on to the next. A typical march with four strains could be diagrammed as **A A B B C C D D** or **A A B B A C C D D** (with the return of **A** offering a hint of closure). There is no attempt to round things off at the end by returning to the beginning.

The third strain (**C**), known as the **trio**, stands out particularly. For one thing, it modulates to a new key (the subdominant, or IV), sometimes with the aid of a short introductory passage, and is often twice as long, lasting thirty-two instead of sixteen bars. Composers might also change dynamics, texture, or orchestration. Many marches concentrate on the trio at the end, repeating it several times after dramatic disorienting interludes. A good example of this procedure is Sousa's most famous march, "The Stars and Stripes Forever."

🔊 "The Stars and Stripes Forever"

Sousa wrote this march on Christmas Day of 1896, supposedly to commemorate the recent death of his manager, David Blakley. It immediately became one of his most popular compositions, a brilliant display of patriotism that is forever commingled with America's entry into world affairs in the Spanish-American War of 1898. Sousa performed the march in virtually every concert.

"The Stars and Stripes Forever" is a good example of march form. It begins with a forceful four-bar introduction, followed by two sixteen-bar strains, each repeated. The third strain, or trio, at first offers a peaceful respite: a pleasant, hummable melody in a new key. Sousa later set it to the words "Hurrah for the flag of the free!"; but it is better known by another patriotic sentiment, "Hurray for the red, white, and blue!" or the sillier "Be kind to your web-footed friends." The trio is twice interrupted by a tumultuous passage, one of the most dramatic that Sousa ever wrote. After twenty-four bars, this interlude leads back to the trio again, this time with countermelodies: first a sparkling part for piccolo, then a triumphant one for the trombone section.

the stars and stripes forever

GUNTHER SCHULLER AND THE INCREDIBLE COLUMBIA ALL-STAR BAND
- Label: *Footlifters: A Century of American Marches* (Columbia M 33513; Sony SK94887)
- Date: composed 1896
- Style: concert march
- Form: march (**A A B B C C C**)

What to listen for:
- march form: three strains, each repeated, with interludes
- cadences: half-cadence for strain **A**, full cadence for strain **B**
- contrasting trio (**C**) in a new key
- countermelodies in trio

INTRODUCTION (4 bars)

0:00   The band opens at full volume, moving forcefully to a **half cadence**.

STRAIN A (16 bars)

0:03   Strain **A** begins with a brisk tune in E♭ major played by the cornets and clarinets. The melody is accompanied by percussion (snare drum and cymbals).

0:10   Halfway through, the tune becomes quiet, occasionally interrupted by short bursts from the lower instruments.

0:16   The strain ends on a half cadence.

STRAIN A

0:17   Strain **A** is repeated.

STRAIN B (16 bars)

0:30   The melody of strain **B** features a steady rhythm, accented by **offbeat** "hiccups" from the flutes.

0:43   The strain ends on a **full cadence.**

STRAIN B

0:44   Strain **B** is repeated.

STRAIN C (TRIO) (32 bars)

0:58   The winds serenely play the trio's melody, now in a new key (A♭ major). Accompanying them are the cornets and horns, playing rhythmic background chords. The trio is 32 bars, twice as long as the previous strains.

1:12   The melody repeats, moving through more distant harmonies before finally ending on a full cadence.

INTERLUDE (24 bars)

1:25   The lower brass instruments (trombones and horns) enter with a tumultuous descending melody, suddenly pulling us out of the key.

1:28   The melody is repeated at a higher pitch.

1:32   Dissonant **chromatic** chords dissolve into a descending chromatic scale.

1:36   The chords are repeated at a higher pitch.

1:39   The harmony begins to settle on the **dominant.**

1:43   A descending chromatic scale leads to a repetition of the trio.

STRAIN C

1:46   The trio is repeated with a **countermelody:** an elaborate line, decorated with trills, played by the piccolo flute.

INTERLUDE

2:14   The interlude is repeated.

STRAIN C

2:36   A final repetition of the trio with a new trombone countermelody, played at full volume.
        The drums and cymbals strongly mark each beat.

RAGTIME

In the long run, jazz embodied the collision of African American music with the white mainstream, absorbing and combining the disparate strains of folk music, popular music, and art music. But in the years before 1917, a different genre accomplished the same thing: it was known as **ragtime**.

The term probably came from "ragged time," a colorful description of African American polyrhythm. At the time of the Civil War, "ragged time" would have been heard on the banjo, the black instrument *par excellence*. But over the next half century, black performers found their way to the piano. The very symbol of middle-class gentility, the piano was also sturdy enough to find a place in the lower-class saloons catering to black people. Musicians who stumbled onto this instrument found that the same polyrhythms that enlivened banjo playing fit naturally under a pianist's fingers. The left hand kept a steady, two-beat rhythmic foundation: low bass notes alternating with higher chords. Against this background, the right hand was free to add contrasting rhythms that contradicted the duple meter. To "rag" a piece meant to subject it to this process of rhythmic complication.

Like other terms from popular culture (blues, swing, rock, hip-hop), ragtime meant different things to different people. For some, it was a type of popular song; for others, a dance; for still others, a piano style. Together, these definitions tell us something about how ragtime saturated American pop music at the turn of the century.

In the late 1890s, black performers danced the cakewalk dressed in high fashion, encouraging white audiences to follow their step. This sheet music cover undercuts their elegance, however, through minstrel-style exaggeration and derisory language.

Coon Songs

One of the earliest commercial forms of ragtime was the **coon song,** which yoked polyrhythmic accompaniments to racial stereotypes. These songs ("coon" was a derisory nickname for blacks) were a late product of the minstrel show. Sold as sheet music with covers and titles that seem shocking today, they occupied a questionable part of the popular song business, one devoted to racial caricature (other targets were the Irish and the Chinese). One of the most popular, "All Coons Look Alike to Me," was written by Ernest Hogan, a black minstrel-show star, who simply changed the title of a prostitute's song, "All Pimps Look Alike to Me." While the song's rhythms convey the excitement of ragtime, its subject matter was so offensive that whistling the melody within sight of black men was enough to start a fight. Coon songs were so reckless in their stereotypes that by 1905, the popular song industry felt the need to retreat, toning them down and calling them "ragtime songs" instead.

The Cakewalk

One of the dances ragtime appeared in was the **cakewalk,** a comic dance supposedly dating from the time of slavery. On the plantation, the story goes, slaves would amuse themselves (and their white masters) by imitating the ballroom finery of a formal dance. The cakewalk satisfied both sides: blacks felt they were parodying their masters' ridiculous dance steps, while whites enjoyed the blacks' lively, exaggerated movements. On the minstrel stage, it was an "exhibition dance," a high-strutting two-step with elaborate costumes and twirling canes. The most outrageous dancers won a cake.

By the turn of the century, the cakewalk was opened to public competition and the prize became a week's theatrical booking. Its syncopated rhythms charmed people of all social origins, including high-class aristocrats at home and abroad. In France, Claude Debussy immortalized the dance in a piano piece entitled "Golliwog's Cakewalk." Through the cakewalk, white people became comfortable with ragtime syncopations and began the long process of adapting black dance as their own.

■ RAGTIME PIECES AND SCOTT JOPLIN (1868–1917)

Ragtime was also a piano style that survives today as published sheet music. The first "rags," translations of improvised piano technique into written form, appeared in 1897. These pieces adopted march form, fitting rhythmic contrast into a succession of separate strains; indeed, from this point forward, we will refer to march form as **march/ragtime form.** Over the next two decades, thousands of rags were published–some written by piano virtuosos who adapted their extraordinary technique to the level of the ordinary pianist, others painstakingly notated by "folk" composers from the hinterland. The best known of these composers was Scott Joplin.

The few photographs that survive of ragtime composer Scott Joplin show him as impeccably dressed and intently serious.

Joplin was born in the backwaters of East Texas. A child of Reconstruction, he believed in the power of literacy to lift black people out of poverty. In Texarkana (situated on the Texas-Arkansas border), he received a sound musical education from a sympathetic German music teacher, who offered him free piano lessons and inspired him with excerpts from German operas. (Joplin eventually returned the compliment with his opera *Treemonisha*, for which—like Richard Wagner—he wrote both the words and music.) As a teenager, Joplin left home to become a professional pianist, touring up and down the Mississippi River. In 1893, he performed at the Midway, the rowdy entertainment venue adjacent to the World's Columbia Exposition (or World's Fair) in Chicago.

The following year, Joplin settled in Sedalia, Missouri, a small but bustling railroad town. He took a leading role in the musical affairs of the local black community, organizing a brass band (for which he played cornet) and studying music theory at the local black college. He also began composing. In 1899, he published the "Maple Leaf Rag" (named after a local saloon), a piece that wedded African American polyrhythm to the harmonies and structure of a concert march. Joplin was shrewd enough to insist on royalty payments for the piece rather than the usual flat fee, so that when the song eventually sold hundreds of thousands of copies, the income supported him for the rest of his career.

As his career advanced, Joplin moved to St. Louis and later to New York City. He published several dozen rags (now available in a complete edition) as well as a ballet. He is probably best known today for "The Entertainer" (1903), a lively tribute to the musical stage that brought him posthumous fame in the 1970s through the movie *The Sting*. The last part of his life was devoted to *Treemonisha*, a semi-autobiographical opera in which an impoverished Texas town is saved from superstition by an enlightened, educated young woman.

Joplin did not live to witness the Jazz Age. Having caught syphilis as a youth, he deteriorated slowly and painfully, spending his last few years in a mental home. By the time he died in 1917, recordings had already displaced sheet music as the most effective way to convey ragtime. We celebrate Joplin today not as a jazz musician but as a composer: in record stores, he is one of the few African American names in the classical section.

Behind Joplin lay hundreds of pianists whose names are known to us largely through oral history: Joe Jordan, Tom Turpin, Blind Boone, Louis Chauvin. Most were unrecognized virtuosos, capable of improvising confidently within the confines of ragtime harmony and competing against each other in contests of skill. A single recording made in Savannah, Georgia, captured the brilliant playing of Sugar Underwood, but the music of others was performed and forgotten, since few knew how to notate it.

■ THE PATH TO JAZZ: WILBUR SWEATMAN (1882–1961)

Ragtime became jazz when a new generation of musicians began to use recordings, rather than written notation, to represent their music. One of these was Wilbur Sweatman, whose career parallels the tumultuous changes of the ragtime era. Sweatman began playing clarinet in minstrel-show and circus bands until his exuberant showmanship catapulted him onto the theatrical stage in the 1910s. His particular gimmick involved playing three clarinets simultaneously—a bizarre, visually stunning trick that was not imitated in jazz until the blind Rahsaan Roland Kirk did it again in the 1950s. Musicians admired his knowledge of music and professional brilliance. Garvin Bushell, an early jazz reed player, once said, "Sweatman was my idol. I just listened to him talk and looked at him like he was God."

Originally, Sweatman was a ragtime composer. His best-known piece was "Down Home Rag" (1911), a multistrain piece in march/ragtime form built around a type of polyrhythm known as **secondary ragtime**. While the meter of the piece is duple, the main melody insistently repeats a pattern of three notes, implying a cross-rhythm. (This device is a kind of "novelty ragtime," a rhythmically tricky subcategory carried on by pianists such as Zez Confrey and George Gershwin.) The piece was moderately successful and was recorded as early as 1913 by James Reese Europe's Society Orchestra, a string-based ensemble that played it as written.

When Sweatman decided to record it himself in 1916, his performance hinted at a new era of bluesy improvisation. He chose Emerson Records, a small recording company that used an alternative (and soon-to-be-obsolete) technology for cutting grooves into a disc or cylinder. Emerson's recordings were playable only on a handful of machines, which became virtually impossible to find once larger companies like Victor had established a different recording technique. Accordingly, Sweatman's version of "Down Home Rag" is not well known. That's a shame, since his performance is crucial evidence for the transition between ragtime and jazz.

⊙ "Down Home Rag"

"Down Home Rag" has four strains. The first two (**A** and **B**) are nearly identical: they share a chord progression and end with the same fragment of melody. As we might expect, the trio (strain **C**) offers contrast by modulating to a nearby key; this trio, however, is the same length as the other strains. In between repetitions of **C**, the fourth strain (**D**) moves to the minor mode.

Throughout, Sweatman is the main focus of attention, performing his composed melodies with enthusiasm. But especially when repeating a strain, he is just as likely to take off in unpredictable directions. It may be too much to call what he plays "improvising": as with many early jazz artists, his variations have a limited range. Still, the swooping blue notes and the piercing timbre of his clarinet suggest what many ragtime musicians may have been doing in actual performance.

FRANK DRIGGS COLLECTION

Multi-instrumentalist Wilbur Sweatman was a star when he performed at the Lafayette Theater in Harlem in 1923. Accompanying him is the young Duke Ellington, who had recently moved to New York from his hometown, Washington, D.C.

LISTENING GUIDE

⊚ down home rag

WILBUR SWEATMAN

Wilbur Sweatman, clarinet, with the Emerson Trio
(piano, clarinet, and trombone)

- Label: Emerson 2377-1, 7161; *Recorded in New York, 1916–1935* (Jazz Oracle 8046)
- Date: 1916
- Style: ragtime/early jazz
- Form: march/ragtime

What to listen for:

- march/ragtime form (A A B B′ A C C′ D D′ C C′)
- contrasting trio (**C**) in a new key
- "secondary ragtime" (implied meter of three over meter of two)
- Sweatman's ragtime/jazz improvisation on clarinet
- blue notes

INTRODUCTION

0:00   The entire band plays an introductory figure, ending with a half cadence.

STRAIN A

0:04   On clarinet, Sweatman plays the main melody, with a second clarinet distantly in the background. It features a kind of polyrhythm known as **secondary ragtime**: against the duple meter, Sweatman's line implies a meter of three.

Behind Sweatman, the trombone plays a composed **countermelody**.

STRAIN A

0:12   Strain **A** is repeated.

STRAIN B

0:20   Sweatman plays a new melody over the same chord progression.

0:26   The last two bars of strain **B** are identical to those of strain **A**.

STRAIN B′

0:28   Sweatman plays a variation on the melody of **B**, which at times features **blue notes** (0:31, 0:35).

STRAIN A

0:36   After a brief pause, the band repeats strain **A**.

TRANSITION

0:44   In a four-bar chordal passage, the band **modulates** to a new key.

STRAIN C (TRIO)

0:48   Sweatman plays a new melody, constantly returning to the same high note. Once again, the trombone plays a countermelody.

STRAIN C′

0:56   While the background clarinet continues with the melody, Sweatman plays a variation, again featuring blue notes.

STRAIN D

1:05   The new strain changes mode from major to **minor**.

STRAIN D'

1:12   Sweatman's variation again features secondary ragtime.

STRAIN C'

1:20   Returning to major mode, Sweatman plays his blue note variation (heard at 1:00).

STRAIN C'

1:28   The band repeats the strain.

CODA

1:36   A single additional note ends the piece.

THE STAGE IS SET

By the time America was poised to enter World War I, the basic elements for jazz were in place. For several decades, popular entertainment had been deeply affected by the rhythms and sounds of African American music. To be sure, this was a time of intense racism, some would say the worst the nation has ever suffered. Yet through the persistence of folk practices ultimately deriving from Africa, black music continued to define American musical identity. Dance music and popular song moved to the insistent, syncopated beat of ragtime. A new genre, the blues, connected ancient traditions of African American singing with the modern commercial realities of vaudeville and recording. The country was ready for a new phenomenon, soon to be labeled "jazz." It arrived from a remote, dilapidated, and somewhat exotic Southern city: New Orleans.

ADDITIONAL LISTENING

Eubie Blake	"Stars and Stripes Forever" (1969); *The Eighty-Six Years of Eubie Blake* (CBS C2S847/22223)
Scott Joplin	"Maple Leaf Rag" (1916); *Ragtime Piano Roll, 90th Anniversary Edition* (Milan Records MIL36293.2)
Sugar Underwood	"Dew Drop Alley" (1927); *Maple Leaf Rag: Ragtime in Rural America* (New World NW235)
Bessie Smith	"In the House Blues" (1931); *Bessie Smith: Greatest Hits* (Fabulous 824046200428)
James Reese Europe	"Too Much Mustard" (1913); *Too Much Mustard* (Saydisc 221)
Gunther Schuller	"The Entertainer" (1973); *The Red Back Book* (Columbia LP)

ORIGINAL DIXIELAND JAZZ BAND
dixie jass band one-step

JELLY ROLL MORTON
dead man blues

JELLY ROLL MORTON
doctor jazz

KING OLIVER
snake rag

RED ONION JAZZ BABIES (SIDNEY BECHET)
cake walking babies (from home)

NEW ORLEANS

Jazz was born from a rich and complicated African American experience, drawing on musical traditions from Africa and Europe (as we saw in Chapter 3) and the Caribbean, along with those that took root in the United States. Imagine jazz as a river, like the Mississippi, fed by numerous tributaries such as blues, ragtime, and marching band music, and you will gain a sense of its nationwide scope.

In its earliest days, jazz was also local. It was a performing tradition unique to the port city of New Orleans, and took its distinctive character from the ever-changing social conditions of that metropolitan area. This first style, usually known as **New Orleans jazz**, was distinctive enough to attract the attention of the rest of the country, who, after 1917, clamored for musicians like King Oliver, Jelly Roll Morton, and Louis Armstrong to play the new music. New Orleans jazz became the foundation of the jazz tradition.

New Orleans jazz derived from marching bands and dance music, but it transformed them through a highly unusual polyphonic texture known as **collective improvisation**. In a typical performance, melodic lines created by a handful of wind instruments (cornet, clarinet, and trombone) combined and interacted with chaotic rhythmic complexity over a firmly stated dance beat. This was a style drawing on such time-honored African American folk principles as polyrhythm, vocalized timbres, and repetitive, cyclic structures.

Jelly Roll Morton, the seminal New Orleans pianist, composer, and bandleader, at a 1926 recording session.

wwnorton.com/studyspace

The complex racial history of New Orleans is important to our story as well. As we will see, black people pouring into New Orleans from nearby plantations encountered a racially mixed group known as the Creoles, who tied their sense of social superiority to musical standards drawn from European culture. Jazz resulted from a struggle between the two groups and drew its strengths from its own mixture of European and African traditions. At the same time, jazz represents a triumph for African American musicians who refused to be cowed by pressures to conform to European gentility and insisted on the importance of their own homegrown musical principles.

EARLY NEW ORLEANS

Southeastern Louisiana slips into the Gulf of Mexico like a well-curved shoe. New Orleans has always been the principal city on the shoe's tongue, cradled in a crescent-shaped bend of the Mississippi River, which flows down through the sole and empties into the Gulf. To the north, New Orleans faces Lake Pontchartrain, the largest inlet in the South, some forty miles wide.

This watery setting not only allowed the city to grow as a major port before the railroad replaced shipping as the primary vehicle for trade, but gave New Orleans a distinct cultural character, blending elements of American commerce with those of a Caribbean island. Founded by France in 1718 and then relinquished as unprofitable to Spain in 1763, New Orleans was reclaimed for the French in 1803 by Napoleon, who almost immediately sold it to the United States as part of the Louisiana Purchase. Many people continued to speak French and Spanish, infusing the city with traditions of European Catholicism and culture. During a time when the South was almost entirely agricultural, it was the largest city of the region. While Atlanta, its nearest rival, was little more than an undeveloped railroad junction, New Orleans rapidly expanded as a lively, advanced urban center with a distinct architectural look, discrete neighborhoods, and a level of sophistication associated with European capitals.

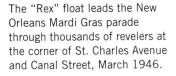

The "Rex" float leads the New Orleans Mardi Gras parade through thousands of revelers at the corner of St. Charles Avenue and Canal Street, March 1946.

ASSOCIATED PRESS

From the early eighteenth century, New Orleans was a hub for the high-life. While grand opera struggled to gain a foothold in New York and Boston, it thrived in New Orleans. Yet these same opera lovers also celebrated the coming of Lent with Mardi Gras, an uninhibited revelry resembling the carnivals in Latin countries but unlike anything else in the United States. New Orleans loved dances and parades, and offered balls and citywide celebrations to suit everyone—rich and poor, cultured and debauched.

The city's attitudes toward race, unsurprisingly, differed from general practices in Protestant North America, especially during the time of slavery. Elsewhere in the United States, the slaves were forced to discard their connection to Africa and accept most aspects of Western society—they were required to learn English, for example, and become Christian (and therefore Protestant). The goal was a more efficient interaction between slaves and masters, who often worked together on small landholdings. New Orleans, however, was oriented toward the Caribbean and South America. In places like Cuba and Brazil, where the slave trade remained constant until well into the nineteenth century, Africans were allowed to retain their own languages, beliefs, and customs. And those retentions carried over to New Orleans, where nearly half the population was black, whether slave or free. When Haiti declared its independence through revolution in 1804, white masters and their slaves fled to New Orleans. In this growing metropolis at the edge of the Caribbean slave world, old-world religious rites (voodoo) and musical traditions thrived.

Congo Square

Nowhere was the conservation of African musical and dance practices more apparent than in a large field behind the French Quarter, popularly known as Congo Square. The square, used in the eighteenth century as a market for merchants of every stripe, eventually became the site of a whites-only circus, complete with carousel. In protest, the free black community set up its own market across the way, and by 1817 slaves and free blacks were permitted to congregate there to dance and play music on Sunday afternoons.

Whites were shocked by what they saw: intricate vocal choirs, massed groups of musicians playing drums, stringed gourds, and other homemade instruments; dances that ranged from the rhythmic slapping patterns called "juba" to the slow sensual gyrations known as "bamboula." Benjamin Latrobe, writing in 1819, described one such slow dance: two women, each holding the end of an outstretched kerchief, swayed slowly to the rhythm, "hardly moving their feet or bodies."

The Congo Square events ended before the Civil War, probably in the mid-1840s, by which time few young slaves had personal recollections of Africa. The important thing is that they were permitted to continue as long as they did—a consequence, argues writer Jerah Johnson, of a large African population, abiding tolerance on the part of the French, the proximity of the Caribbean, and the remoteness from other major cities in the United States. Here, African music enjoyed an untrammeled exposure that assured it a role in the developing culture of New Orleans.

Creoles of Color

The same tolerance that allowed the Congo Square exhibitions influenced racial dynamics in New Orleans both before and after the Civil War. North of the Gulf of Mexico, race was divided into two distinct legal spheres—black and white. Anyone within the wide spectrum of browns, tans, and beiges (possessing the proverbial "single drop" of black blood) was technically considered "black," whether slave or free, and forced to live on that side of the racial division. The Caribbean world took a more pragmatic view. While continuing to enforce a barbarous society in which whites owned blacks, it acknowledged a mulatto culture and allowed that culture intermediary social status, to the benefit of free blacks with lighter skins.

New Orleans adhered to that mulatto conception of race, producing a caste of "mixed-race" Negroes known as Creoles of Color. (The full description was *les gens de couleur libres*, or free people of color.) These Creoles—usually the result of black and French or black and Spanish alliances—evolved into a significant social group, accorded many legal and social liberties. By 1860, they had acquired civic power and are thought to have owned about $15 million in New Orleans property. Some even participated in the slave trade. Most Creoles had French surnames, spoke French as well as English, attended Catholic churches, enjoyed a decent education, and worked at skilled trades—cigar-making, cobbling, carpentry—that Creoles, as a group, virtually monopolized.

Their superior standing began to dissipate after the Civil War, when Reconstruction brought an increasingly intolerant racism. In 1894, Louisiana and other Southern states adopted the so-called Jim Crow laws, which imposed and enforced a rigid color line. Two years later, the U.S. Supreme Court issued its infamous verdict in *Plessy v. Ferguson*, deciding against a light-skinned man (one-eighth black and seven-eighths white) who had insisted on his right to ride a streetcar in the area reserved for whites. When he lost that case, which essentially legalized segregation, the Creoles lost the last threads of their shabby aristocracy.

A MEETING OF MUSICAL STYLES

Creoles and Uptown Negroes

As their social standing fell, the Creoles, who had not lost their pride, attempted to reserve a geographical separateness from the "corn and field Negroes" pouring into New Orleans from the countryside. For a time, the dividing line was Canal Street, a large thoroughfare that begins at the Mississippi Riverfront and provides a western border for the French Quarter, home to most of the Creoles. On the other side of Canal, moving upward on the river, was the area known as Uptown, which included some of the grimmest neighborhoods in the United States. Each side had its own musical tradition; yet as Jim Crow forced the integration between Creoles and "black blacks," the two traditions collided.

The Uptown Negroes, largely uneducated and unskilled, played a loud, upbeat, impassioned music combining elements of late-nineteenth-century marching band, ragtime, and folk music with an ad-libbed and often idiosyncratic vitality. Many could not read music, and "faked" their performances by relying on an oral tradition that employed variable intonation (blue notes), rhythmic contrast, and improvisation. To Creoles, who were educated in the European manner and favored a more genteel approach, they failed to meet the minimum standards of professional musicianship.

rhythmic contrast the simultaneous use of contrasting rhythms (polyrhythm)

As long as the Creoles remained on top, socially and musically, they landed the better-paying jobs, and were able to augment their incomes through teaching. However, their students numbered black Uptown players as well as downtown Creoles, and the bringing together of these two groups ultimately favored the Uptown musicians, who were onto something new: an artistry relying on improvisation, quick thinking, the ability to blend with other improvising musicians, and a rhythmic sharpness that appealed to dancers and listeners. For its part, Creole music contributed French quadrilles, Spanish habaneras, and an insistence on high professional standards.

Manuel Perez, the influential parade band leader and trumpeter, at home in New Orleans, 1939.

■ MANUEL PEREZ (1878–1946)

We can see a microcosm of the Creole role by looking at one of the more notable careers that figured in this cultural mix. Manuel Perez was born in New Orleans, attended a French-speaking grammar school, trained as a cigar maker (his father's profession), and studied classical music, focusing on the cornet. He soon established a local reputation, and throughout his teen years played with marching bands, dance bands, and ragtime bands, all requiring written music.

For thirty years, beginning at the dawn of the new century, Perez worked with and led the Onward Brass Band, an ensemble with as many as a dozen musicians and a great favorite at picnics along Lake Pontchartrain as well as at the downtown dance halls. He also led small groups, including one that played on riverboats. Dozens of musicians came under his influence, whether they worked with him or took individual lessons (for which he is said to have refused payment)—among them, clarinetists Albert Nicholas and Barney Bigard, trumpeter Natty Dominique, and drummer Paul Barbarin. The jazz guitarist Danny Barker remembered Perez as "the idol of the downtown Creole colored people. To them, nobody could master the cornet like Mr. Perez." Jelly Roll Morton considered him the finest trumpeter in New Orleans (until the advent of a young jazz player, Freddie Keppard), but noted that he was a Creole from a good family and played "strictly rag time"—syncopated music, but with no improvisation.

Perez himself realized that improvisation, as practiced by the Uptown musicians, was essential for a successful band in the 1910s, and he hired Joe Oliver (the future King Oliver) as his band's improviser. Despite his prodigious technique, though, Perez found it increasingly difficult to find work for his kind of parade music, and in 1937 he returned full-time to cigar making until his death nine years later. He had lived to see the kind of parade music at which he excelled reduced to a tourist attraction and jazz itself transfigured into a worldwide phenomenon no one in 1910 could have imagined. Significantly, Manny Perez was born fifteen months after an Uptown cornetist and bandleader named Charles Joseph Bolden.

■ BUDDY BOLDEN (1877–1931) and the Birth of Jazz

In the realm of jazz myths, no one stands taller or blows louder than King Buddy Bolden. Some frequently reported "facts" about Bolden are simply untrue: that he attended the exhibitions in Congo Square (they ceased thirty years before he was born), that he owned a barbershop (he worked as a plasterer until he turned to music), and that he edited a scandal sheet called *The Cricket* (no such journal ever existed). What remains, however, is a myth that connects Bolden's superlative musicianship with the racial realities of turn-of-the-century New Orleans. Bolden is generally acknowledged as the first important musician in jazz, and his rise to fame marks the triumph of African American culture.

Charles "Buddy" Bolden was born in New Orleans, and took up the cornet in his middle or late teens. He began working at parades and other functions in 1895, and turned to music full time in 1901 or 1902. Fighting alcoholism and depression, he suffered a mental breakdown in 1906, and was incarcerated in the state hospital for the insane, where he remained until his death in 1931. His career as musician and bandleader lasted no more than eleven years, in which time he earned the respect of almost every black and Creole musician in the city (few whites were aware of him), as well as a large public following.

Bolden's Style

The most frequent boasts concerning Bolden's prowess relate to the loudness of his playing and the snake-charmer seductiveness of his approach to slow blues. Jelly Roll Morton claimed that "on a still night," Bolden's cornet could be heard as far away as twelve miles, the distance between the Mississippi Riverfront and Lake Pontchartrain. On the stillest of nights, that would not be possible. Yet it is a fact that Bolden would sometimes step outside of halls in which his band was employed and play a few phrases to attract customers. He often played in Johnson Park, a fenced picnic and baseball grounds directly across the road from the theatrical complex in Lincoln Park, where his primary Creole rival, the Joseph Robichaux Orchestra, often performed. By blowing his horn in the direction of Lincoln Park, he attracted audiences who preferred his livelier, raunchier brand of music.

Jazz begins here. The only known photograph of the Buddy Bolden Band, c. 1905: Jimmy Johnson, bass; Bolden, cornet; Willie Cornish, valve trombone; William Warner, clarinet; Jefferson Mumford, guitar; Frank Lewis, clarinet.

The unmistakable implication of these stories is that Bolden was not only loud, but also distinctive in timbre and attack. Other musicians of his generation, like Manny Perez, were remembered for their overall musicianship, the bright clarity of their sound. Only Bolden is consistently recalled in terms of a personal style—establishing him as the first figure whose individuality was a decisive element, the first for whom the "how you do it" is more important than the "what you do." That made him the first jazz celebrity: the father figure on which the New Orleans story (and by extension, the jazz story) is grounded. Combine that distinction with the brevity of his career, the excesses he indulged, his competitive spirit and Pied Piper charisma, and we have a template for American jazz and popular music legends, from Bix Beiderbecke, Charlie Parker, and John Coltrane to Elvis Presley, Jimi Hendrix, and Kurt Cobain.

Bolden and Jazz

Did Bolden invent jazz? We can't know for certain, but a qualified yes seems reasonable. He was the only musician in that era who was commonly regarded as an innovator of a new way of playing that evolved into jazz. Eyewitnesses to the musical life of New Orleans at the dawn of the twentieth century fail to cite a precursor to Bolden, or a significant rival to him during his glory days. Even the incurably boastful Jelly Roll Morton recalled Bolden, respectfully, as a stand-alone figure of mythic resonance.

By all accounts, Bolden was the kind of artist on whom little is lost, and he arrived at the right time, amid a musical cornucopia in which schooled and unschooled musicians worked together to provide a broad range of functional music—for picnics, concerts, dances, funerals, parades, and publicity events. Bolden, who could read music (he had studied with a neighbor), played in every kind of setting. The demand for music was so great that, perhaps inevitably, musicians devised ways to perform away from written scores.

In this respect, it's worth looking at a notorious illustration that appeared on the cover of the weekly newspaper the *New Orleans Mascot* in November 1890, five years before Bolden ever performed in public. It depicts four Negro musicians, three playing brass instruments and one a bass drum, all wearing top hats and producing a raucous music that has the power to send the white citizens into a panic, cupping their ears, swooning in pain, imploring the band to stop, or fainting dead away. The musicians have no music stands. Is the band playing something we might recognize as jazz? We can never know, but three things are clear: the musicians are Uptown blacks, not trained Creoles; the music is unusual enough to provoke outrage and confusion; and it is performed without sheet music.

Whatever the illustrator's musicians played added to the unique mix of New Orleans music at the turn of the century. The musicians who worked in

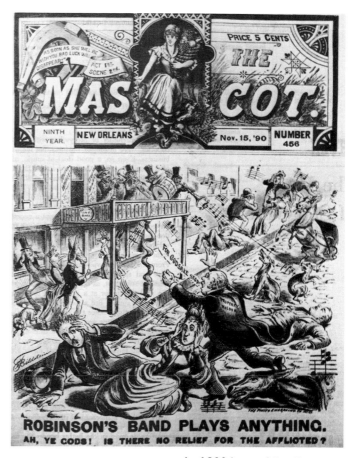

An 1890 issue of the *New Orleans Mascot* depicts white citizens pleading for mercy as a black band, hired to advertise a museum, performs some kind of new, raucous music without the aid of sheet music.

New Orleans Mascot

parades (brass bands) by day and in saloons and dance halls by night had to master the technical know-how required for the former as well as the looser, bluesier ad-lib style necessary for the latter.

Of the musicians who did both, Bolden was the one everyone talked about and remembered. Pops Foster, a jazz bassist, saw him once as a young man and characterized his blues repertory as "stink" music, emphasizing its funky or low-down quality. George Baquet, a Creole clarinetist, recalled seeing Bolden once at the Odd Fellows and Masonic Hall—a "plenty tough" place where customers kept their hats on and interacted with the music through encouraging shouts or sexually provocative dancing. Suddenly Bolden stomped his foot, marked a few beats by banging his cornet on the floor, and began playing the rowdy ballad "Make Me a Pallet on the Floor":

> Everybody got up quick, the whole place rose and yelled out, "Oh, Mr. Bolden, play it for us, Buddy, play it!" I never heard anything like that before. I'd played "legitimate" stuff. But this! It was somethin' that pulled me! They got me up on the stand that night, and I was playing with them. After that, I didn't play "legitimate" so much.

Another tune frequently associated with Bolden was called "Funky Butt" or, more politely, "Buddy Bolden's Blues," a melody adapted by Bolden at an insinuatingly slow tempo, almost a crawl, inviting improvised (often risqué) lyrics with plenty of space for bluesy cornet effects. Other pieces Bolden played that have remained a part of jazz include "Tiger Rag," "Didn't He Ramble," "Panama," "Careless Love," and "Bucket's Got a Hole in It." He also played spirituals ("Ride On, King Jesus," "Go Down, Moses"), sentimental pop fare ("Home, Sweet Home"), and waltzes. A trombonist of the period, Bill Matthews, suggested the diversity of Bolden's repertory:

> He was one of the sweetest trumpet players on waltzes and things like that and on those old slow blues, that boy could make the women jump out the window. On those old, slow, low down blues, he had a moan in his cornet that went all through you, just like you were in church or something. Everybody was crazy about Bolden when he'd blow a waltz, schottische, or old low down blues.

Bolden headed several bands, depending on the kind of music required. His best-known jazz ensemble, in place by 1905, consisted of his cornet, a valve trombonist, two clarinetists, a guitarist, a bassist, and a drummer. On occasion, he added a second cornet. Some said this was because he was drinking and needed a reliable back-up player; whatever the motivation, Bolden's use of two cornets would enjoy a historic payoff (as we will see) in King Oliver's Creole Jazz Band. By the time Oliver began to establish himself, Bolden had been hospitalized as alcoholic and schizophrenic. When he died in 1931, jazz was on the verge of international acclaim, but King Bolden probably did not know it. Except in New Orleans where old-timers still reminisced, he had long since been forgotten.

NEW ORLEANS STYLE

In the decade from Bolden's heyday until the popularization of jazz in 1917, New Orleans musicians continued to develop their own distinctive style. We have no precise idea what their music sounded like, since no recordings survive from this period. But by extrapolating backward from later recordings, and by drawing information from photographs and interviews, it's possible to offer a a general portrait of New Orleans–style jazz.

Instrumentation

The instruments for New Orleans bands derived from two sources. Brass band societies, which often spawned smaller dance groups, gave the music its melody instruments: trumpet (or cornet), trombone, and clarinet. Together, these instruments are known as the **front line**, from their position at the head of a marching band. (The fans who followed a band wherever they marched were known as the "second line.") The parading percussion—bass drum, snares, cymbals—were adapted into the modern drum set. The other source was the string ensemble, which featured violin, banjo, mandolin, and other instruments. From this group, jazz borrowed the guitar and bass for its rhythm section. The piano—often not present in early groups—was added later from the generation of solo ragtime pianists.

Originally, the earliest New Orleans bands also included a lead violinist, whose job was to play the melody straight, without improvisation or ornamentation. Against this, the cornet probably improvised a syncopated, or "ragged," version of the melody. But by the time recording came around in 1917, the cornet had simply displaced the violinist, offering the tune in a more compact, improvised form.

Above the cornet, the clarinet played a countermelody—an improvised accompaniment (mostly in eighth notes) that danced around and between the sharply articulated cornet notes. In the beginning, the clarinet part was often drawn directly from published arrangements; a famous line from the march "High Society," played by many New Orleans clarinetists, was adapted from the written piccolo part. Eventually, clarinet players learned to create their own lines, drawing notes from the underlying chord progression.

Similarly, the trombone originally played parts written for cello or baritone horn, but soon managed to create its own simple lines alongside the cornet. The trombone plays fewer notes than the clarinet, and many of them are exaggerated slurs or **glissandos** (sliding from one note to the next), created by the trombone slide. (This was sometimes called **tailgate trombone**, or **smear**: when bands toured the streets of New Orleans in a horse-drawn wagon to publicize a gig, the trombone often performed with its slide stuck over the tailgate.)

Improvisation

By the time their sound was first captured on recordings, New Orleans bands had already attained their own distinctive style. There was no obvious star or stand-out soloist.

Storyville

Storyville—better known as "The District" to New Orleans locals—was a zone of legalized prostitution named for alderman Sidney Story, who wrote the bill that brought it into existence. Some of the women working in Storyville were housed in the elaborate mansions of successful madams, often depicted proudly in city postcards; but many others labored in brutal and disease-ridden shacks.

A pernicious myth links jazz to Storyville. According to this legend, jazz musicians were happily employed by brothels until 1917, when the murder of four sailors on shore leave caused the federal government to shut the district down. But except for a few pianists, jazz musicians didn't play in bordellos. Many worked in cabarets within Storyville's precincts, but they found much of their work in parks, excursions, parades, advertising wagons, riverboats, and dances throughout the city. The dismantling of Storyville had little effect on the exodus of jazz musicians from New Orleans, which had begun as early as 1907. As guitarist Danny Barker remarked, "You never had to figure on getting work in the district, so it wasn't so important when it closed."

Still, it would be a mistake to altogether dismiss Storyville as a factor in the development of New Orleans jazz. The very funkiness of its saloons undoubtedly contributed to the adoption of rhythmic blues as a central part of the repertory, along with expressive techniques that emphasized the music's seductive earthiness. The achingly slow "snake-hips" dancing encouraged by Bolden and the "talkative" timbre variation introduced by King Oliver on cornet (see p. 99) probably found more traction in this environment than at other social events. In rough precincts like Storyville, where white social arbiters did not breathe down their necks, musicians could explore their bonds with dancers and listeners, and let loose with the kind of artistic transgression typical of outcast communities.

Robert S. Abbott founded the influential *Chicago Defender* in 1905, and helped fuel the "Great Migration" of Southern blacks to the North.

Instead, the three instruments in the front line (cornet, clarinet, trombone) improvised simultaneously in a dense, polyphonic texture. This way of playing, known today as **collective improvisation,** is perhaps the most distinctive feature of New Orleans jazz. Each instrument occupies its own musical space (the clarinet is on top, the cornet in the middle, and the trombone at the bottom), rhythm (the clarinet is the fastest, the trombone slowest), and timbre.

Collective improvisation is not the only texture in New Orleans jazz. During the trio section of a piece, for example, the band often plays in block-chord texture, or more rarely, a single horn over accompaniment. Breaks (where a single horn improvises unaccompanied) and stop-time (where the band leaves space for a soloist by playing a series of brief, sharp chords) are common. Still, soloing as we currently think of it is rare: it tended to occur primarily when one horn continued while the others rested their "chops."

Behind the horns, the rhythm section played with a steady, unrelenting pulse. This is often something we can't hear on the earliest recordings, because percussion (especially the drum set) interfered with the primitive recording equipment. But a steady, four-beat accompaniment was the particular rhythmic foundation on which collective improvisation relied.

Form

For the most part, New Orleans jazz continued to use the multistrain forms of ragtime. This meant that performances were not based on simple, repetitive cyclic structures—or at least not completely so. At the beginning of a performance, each strain would be repeated only once before moving to a new strain with its own harmonic progression. The trio offered a point of contrast: modulating to a new key, and often insisting on a new dynamic level (as mentioned earlier) or a new kind of texture. Only toward the end, when the band had hit a groove and didn't want to stop, would strains begin to be repeated with various embellishments, until the leader called a halt.

Some of the tunes played by New Orleans bands fit a new structure, the twelve-bar blues. But many of these were arranged so that they still fit the general appearance of a ragtime tune, as we will see in Jelly Roll Morton's "Dead Man Blues." This model offers a broad description of New Orleans jazz. We will hear how it actually worked when we listen to the various bands that emerged from New Orleans during the Jazz Age.

THE GREAT MIGRATION

Jazz began to leave New Orleans in the years of the Great Migration, perhaps the largest movement of people in the history of the United States. It started in the late nineteenth century, when former slaves began to drift away from their agricultural labors toward cities like New Orleans, but with the coming of World War I the movement became a torrent, depositing African Americans further northward in new ghettos in Chicago and New York.

It's not hard to understand why black Americans would want to leave the South. Very few owned land. Under the system of sharecropping, black farmers would work a plot of land, relying on the white landowners for plow, seed, housing, and provisions. At year's end, the two sides would "share" the proceeds. In reality, whites manipulated the accounting to leave black families permanently in debt. Meanwhile, blacks were continually reminded of their second-class status. They were forced to use segregated transportation, waiting rooms, water fountains, lavatories, doorways, stairways, and theaters, as well as schools, housing, and every other aspect of life. Politically powerless, they were subject to white laws. Outside the law, the iniquity extended to murder.

We can never know exactly how many blacks were beaten, tortured, and killed in the years between Reconstruction and World War II, but more than 3,400 lynchings are documented, and thousands of other African Americans simply disappeared. No one was arrested for these crimes, despite photographic evidence of participants (including postcards made as souvenirs). The federal government refused to intervene with legislation. The nation's first anti-lynch activist, Ida B. Wells-Barnett, herself the daughter of slaves, estimated in 1900 that as many as 10,000 blacks had been murdered in the latter part of the nineteenth century alone.

The issue was decided by economics. With the United States' entrance into World War I in 1917, coming on the heels of Henry Ford's automobile assembly line, the labor market in the Northern industrial cities exploded. The war snatched millions of men away from the workforce, and put a hold on immigration. The manpower shortage was so severe that railroads paid fares to encourage blacks to move. Newspapers like the black-owned *Chicago Defender* encouraged Southerners to leave, and even listed contact numbers of people in churches and other organizations who would provide financial help. Agricultural interests in the South tried to stop the exodus through intimidation and such tactics as delaying travelers until their trains left or disregarding prepaid tickets. But they could not combat the lure of decent wages and a more humane way of life.

Chicago Defender

An inscribed 1913 portrait of trumpet player Freddie Keppard, one of the first musicians to take a New Orleans ensemble to Chicago and Los Angeles.

■ FREDDIE KEPPARD (1890–1933)

Foremost among pioneers seeking to escape the South were entertainers—in black minstrel troupes, tent shows, bands, and the formal tours of vaudeville. One of the most important of the New Orleans musicians to travel widely was the cornet player Freddie Keppard.

A hard-drinking, overweight, and temperametal man, Keppard was the star attraction of the Creole Jazz Band, a New Orleans band that played in vaudeville theaters in Los Angeles, Chicago, New York, and places in-between—all before 1917. Keppard's historical importance thus lies in his impact in bringing New Orleans jazz to the rest of the country. By the time he finally made some recordings in the 1920s, he had apparently lost much of his technique; but those who heard him in his prime hailed him as the dominant figure to follow Buddy Bolden. Sidney Bechet said, "He played practically the same way as Buddy Bolden, but he played, he *really* played!"

Keppard was said to play with a handkerchief over his hand so other musicians couldn't see his fingering, and refused a historic

opportunity to record in 1916: some say he didn't want to make his music available for others to steal, others say he didn't like the money. Consequently, the distinction of making the first jazz records went to a white New Orleans group: the Original Dixieland Jazz Band.

◼ ORIGINAL DIXIELAND JAZZ BAND

Spell it Jass, Jas, Jaz or Jazz—nothing can spoil a Jass band. Some say the Jass band originated in Chicago. Chicago says it comes from San Francisco—San Francisco being away off across the continent. Anyway a Jass band is the newest thing in the cabarets, adding greatly to the hilarity thereof.

Reading this excerpt from the Victor Talking Machine Company's publicity sheet for the all-white Original Dixieland Jazz Band (ODJB), we may surmise that "jazz"—at the dawn of the "Jazz Age"—was often misspelled, that many people did not know the location of San Francisco, and that no one had heard about New Orleans, though all five members of the ODJB were natives of that city. The reason for the company's interest was that the band had come to New York to play at Reisenweber's Restaurant in January 1917, causing a sensation. It was the talk of the town, and the record industry wanted some of the action.

Columbia Records was first off the bench, but required the band to record a test of two pop songs, which the label then rejected as cacophony and refused to release. Within weeks, Victor signed the band and produced a double-sided blockbuster: "Livery Stable Blues" / "Dixie Jass Band One-Step." Columbia then rushed its "test" into stores, and sold hundreds of thousands of copies. To most listeners, the ODJB had no precedent. Many ragtime records had preceded those of the ODJB (from as far back as 1897), and elements of jazz can be detected in records made between 1914 and 1916 by such African American performers as comic monologist Bert Williams, bandleader James Reese Europe, and clarinetist Wilbur Sweatman, as well as the white "Mammy singer" Al Jolson. But those elements—robust rhythms or embellishments beyond written ragtime—merely hint at the real thing. The ODJB *was* the real thing, a musical eruption and something genuinely new to the market.

The Original Dixieland Jazz Band popularized jazz (word and music) in Chicago and New York, and made the first jazz recording in 1917: Henry Ragas, Larry Shields, Eddie Edwards, Nick LaRocca, and Tony Sbarbaro.

So great was the band's initial popularity that it established the word "jazz" as part of the international vocabulary—a term, like "okay," that requires no translation anywhere in the world. Some older musicians would continue to call their music ragtime or New Orleans music, but the die had been cast. Within five years, dozens of bands had appropriated the word. (Originally, it was "jass," but the spelling was changed after vandals repeatedly crossed out the j on billboards and posters.) Hotels throughout Europe began to hire what they called jazz bands (basically any kind of dance ensemble that had drums and at least one reed instrument). The 1920s would always be remembered as the **Jazz Age**.

Origins

A vital aspect of New Orleans at the turn of the century was that many neighborhoods were integrated. White musicians were attracted to ragtime and to jazz, although they don't seem to have had much influence on the initial progress of New Orleans jazz. There were important white ragtime players, songwriters, and teachers who likely influenced black jazz musicians in terms of repertory, harmony, and instrumental technique, but they don't figure in written or oral accounts of the evolution of jazz. The widely imitated five-piece instrumentation of the Original Dixieland Jazz Band, for example, originated with Freddie Keppard.

Yet the white New Orleans jazz tradition is significant in its own right. The commonly accepted father of white jazz was a parade drummer named George "Papa Jack" Laine, who led the Reliance Band in the late nineteenth and early twentieth centuries. Unlike Bolden, who was four years his junior, Papa Jack discouraged improvisation; nevertheless, he trained many young men who took jazz north, including trombonists Tom Brown (who brought the first white jazz band to Chicago in 1915) and George Brunies (who made his name with the New Orleans Rhythm Kings, an important and influential white band), as well as most members of the ODJB. By the time the ODJB began to play in New York, its personnel consisted of cornetist Nick LaRocca, trombonist Eddie Edwards, clarinetist Larry Shields, pianist Henry Ragas, and drummer Tony Sbarbaro.

Papa Jack Laine

Influence

The ODJB has taken a bad rap in jazz history. True, its individual musicians were not especially talented, and the band freely indulged in vaudeville antics (such as barnyard imitations on "Livery Stable Blues"), but so did Jelly Roll Morton, and it seems unfair to single out the ODJB for courting the audience or attempting comedy. Compared with later records by King Oliver, the New Orleans Rhythm Kings, and Morton, the ODJB often sounds hokey and insincere. An embittered LaRocca did not help the band's reputation by making racist and self-serving remarks in later years. Still, the ODJB played a spirited, unpretentious music, and served jazz well in several ways: its tunes became Dixieland standards; its name signaled a break with a musical past called ragtime; and a visit the band made to Europe in 1919 helped make jazz international. After its European tour, however, the band lost its verve, and finally called it quits in 1922, just in time for Jelly Roll Morton and King Oliver to redefine New Orleans jazz for all time.

"Dixie Jass Band One-Step"

"Dixie Jass Band One-Step," an enduringly popular Dixieland theme, retains ragtime's multistrain form; at the same time, the musicians burst through with their embellishments—especially the clarinetist and the drummer, and especially in the third strain (or trio). From the opening, which juxtaposes sharp **staccato** (detached) chords with collective improvisation, to its triumphant conclusion, this music is very well organized, even as it suggests the feeling of carefree spontaneity.

The trio is the most famous part of the piece, borrowed from one of the leading rags of the day ("That Teasin' Rag," written by pianist Joe Jordan in

1909) and sometimes played alone. It's a thirty-two-bar chorus, played three times. But because the chorus is made up of two similar sixteen-bar sections, we get a sense that the ensemble is playing the same melody six times, and growing increasingly rowdy with each repeat. In 1917, this outpouring of energy, underscored by repetition, had no precedence in recorded music—and it struck listeners as either exciting and optimistic or unruly and subversive. The Victor engineers did a remarkable job in capturing the sounds of the instruments, including the drummer's cymbal and woodblocks. The instrumentation allows us to hear polyphonic details as clarinet and trombone swirl around the cornet lead.

1.12

🎧 dixie jass band one-step

ORIGINAL DIXIELAND JAZZ BAND

Nick LaRocca, cornet; Eddie Edwards, trombone; Larry Shields, clarinet; Henry Ragas, piano; Tony Sbarbaro, drums

- Label: Victor 18255; *75th Anniversary* (Bluebird/ RCA 61098-2)
- Date: 1917
- Style: New Orleans jazz
- Form: march/ragtime

What to listen for:

- rehearsed collective improvisation
- march/ragtime form, with modulations between the different strains
- raucous clarinet playing, using glissandos
- 32-bar **C** strain (trio), which grows rowdier and more percussive with each repeat

STRAIN A

0:00	**a**	The band opens with forceful **tonic** chords, surrounded by a brief silence.
0:03		A dramatic outburst (a loud trombone **glissando**, a clarinet shriek) is followed by a cymbal crash.
0:04		The band breaks into a short polyphonic passage of **collective improvisation**.
0:08	**a**	The material from 0:00 to 0:08 is repeated.

STRAIN B

0:16	**b**	A clarinet **break** introduces the next strain, which **modulates** to a new key.
0:18		The band follows with a longer passage of collective improvisation.
0:23	**b'**	The clarinet break returns, followed again by collective improvisation.
0:28		The strain comes to a **full cadence** on the tonic.

STRAIN A

| 0:31 | | Strain **A** is repeated. |

STRAIN B

| 0:46 | | Strain **B** is repeated. |

STRAIN C (TRIO)

1:01	**c**	The trio modulates to yet another key. While the trumpet plays the main melody, the clarinet plays a faster **countermelody** and the trombone adds glissandos.
1:09		The drummer adds strong **counterrhythms** on a woodblock (one of the few parts on the drum set easily captured by acoustic recording equipment).
1:16		The clarinet marks the first sixteen bars with a high note.
1:17	**c'**	
1:25		As we approach the final cadence, the harmonies begin to change.

1:31		A loud, raucous note on the cornet signals a repetition of the trio.
STRAIN C		
1:33	**c**	As the band repeats the trio, the drummer increases the intensity of the polyrhythm.
1:48	**c′**	
1:53		The drummer plays two powerful strokes on the bass drum.
1:56		The clarinet's line often sounds like a shriek.
2:02		Another repetition is signaled by the cornet's note, played alongside a clarinet squeal.
STRAIN C		
2:03	**c**	The band plays the trio one last time.
2:18	**c′**	The drummer signals the second half by hitting the bass drum, followed by a cymbal crash.
2:26		The drummer finally uses the full drum set, adding military-style rolls on the snare drum and driving the band toward the conclusion.
CODA		
2:34		The band adds a four-note **coda**, a common Jazz Age ending.

■ JELLY ROLL MORTON (1890–1941)

The development of jazz may be viewed as an ongoing alliance between improvisers and composers: soloists who spontaneously create music and writers who organize frameworks for them. They influence each other, much as Creoles and Uptown blacks did. So it's fitting that the first great jazz composer was a Creole who endured expulsion from his family in order to learn from and eventually work with the kind of musicians epitomized by Buddy Bolden. Jelly Roll Morton's genius is extensively documented on recordings: his legacy is not a matter of speculation, unlike Bolden's—though it, too, is encrusted in myths, chiefly of Morton's own devising.

One of the most colorful characters in American music, Morton worked as a bordello pianist, pimp, pool hall hustler, and comedian before establishing himself as a fastidious musician and recording artist—a pianist, singer, composer, arranger, and music theorist. He was also a diamond-tooth dandy, insufferable braggart, occultist, and memoirist. Morton engraved his most infamous boast on his business card: "Originator of JAZZ - STOMP - SWING." He claimed that he had invented jazz in 1902, giving his own date of birth as 1885. In fact, New Orleans baptismal records indicate that he was born Ferdinand Joseph Lamothe in 1890. His proud family traced its lineage back to Haiti, and he apparently inherited a strain of arrogance and standoffishness as well as a lifelong fear of voodoo: in his later years, he paid much of his earnings to a practitioner in hope of lifting a curse.

Morton recognized early on that a French surname would be a liability on the show business circuit, so he changed his to an anglicized version of his stepfather's name, Mouton, claiming that he didn't want to be called "Frenchy." A born hustler, he talked himself in and out of work, alienating many in the jazz world of the 1920s, including Duke Ellington, who dismissed him as a boaster. If Morton didn't exactly invent jazz, he certainly helped to define it, propelling the New Orleans style forward at a time when no one knew precisely what jazz was.

Morton studied guitar and trombone before focusing on piano at age ten. His family disowned him when he began sneaking out to the honky-tonks in Storyville to hear the vibrant new music. He ran errands for a singer-pianist named Mamie Desdumes just to learn her trademark blues, and he credited his education in the district for his ability to live in style when he left New Orleans and traveled through Memphis, Jacksonville, St. Louis, Kansas City, Chicago, and California, assimilating new musical approaches and combining them with the dances (habaneras, quadrilles), operas, military music, and jazz he had learned at home.

In Chicago

Morton was thirty-two when he settled in Chicago, in 1922. He made his first records a year later, derivative exercises overwhelmed by loud woodblocks. In July 1923, however, he spent two afternoons at the ramshackle Gennett Records studio in Richmond, Indiana (see box), recording with a talented white hometown band called the New Orleans Rhythm Kings—this was the first significant integrated recording session in jazz history. There, Morton introduced a few of his tunes, the best of which show how he took the multiple-themes structure and syncopated rhythms of ragtime to a new level, emphasizing a foot-tapping beat (he called it a *stomp*) and tricky syncopations. Among them are "King Porter Stomp," which has four sections, the last of which became a major anthem of the Swing Era.

FRANK DRIGGS COLLECTION

In Chicago, 1926, Jelly Roll Morton created his most enduring work and a pinnacle in the New Orleans style with a recording unit he called the Red Hot Peppers.

The Red Hot Peppers

Over the next few years, Morton became a successful songwriter, earning royalties from sheet music sales or selling the rights altogether. Hoping to increase interest in his published tunes, Morton's publisher helped convince the Victor Talking Machine Company to offer him a contract. He began recording with ensembles of seven and eight players in the fall of 1926, at the very moment that Victor switched from acoustic to electrical recording (see p. 100), giving his recordings a vivid fidelity. Morton called his group the Red Hot Peppers, and Victor advertised it as "the Number One Hot Band," although it existed solely to record. To many, the Peppers sessions represent the pinnacle of the New Orleans tradition, an ideal balance between composition and improvisation.

"Dead Man Blues"

"Dead Man Blues" is Morton's interpretation of the New Orleans burial ritual, which he traced back to Scripture: rejoice at the death, and cry at the birth. It begins with a scene-setting dialogue in the style of black minstrelsy, a comedic way of announcing Morton's intention to invoke a New Orleans funeral. This leads to the first chorus—each chorus is a twelve-bar blues—in which the musicians collectively embellish a melody in familiar New Orleans style: you can almost see the Grand Marshal leading the mourners, gracefully prancing with his parasol. This particular performance (an alternate take) was not chosen by Morton to be released commercially, probably because of the unmistakable gaffes made by the cornetist later in the performance. On this take, however, we can hear the nimble elegance in the collective improvisation that the band failed to capture the second time around.

Morton organized his music scrupulously, going so far as to notate the parts for bass (bass lines are usually improvised, rarely composed), and making the most of his musicians. We are always conscious of each instrument: the tailgate smears of the trombone, the snap of the trumpet, the pretty harmonizing of the clarinets, the clanging rhythm of the banjo. For those who think of New Orleans–style jazz as genial chaos, with simultaneously improvised melody lines tumbling untidily on top of one another, Morton's music may come as a revelation.

While "Dead Man Blues" is a twelve-bar blues, it's also organized like a tune in march/ragtime form: choruses 1 and 2 correspond to the first strain (**A**), choruses 3 and 4 to the second (**B**). The fifth chorus serves as the trio, a section of the piece for which Morton often reserved his most melodic ideas. For this recording session, he hired two extra clarinetists to blend with Omer Simeon in playing block-chord harmonies. In the sixth chorus, Morton introduces another of his trademark devices to increase the power of the performance: against the clarinetists' lissome melody, we hear a countermelody played by the trombonist (Kid Ory, whom we will encounter again), his bluesy phrases adding a touch of drama.

LISTENING GUIDE

1.13

 dead man blues

JELLY ROLL MORTON AND HIS RED HOT PEPPERS (ALTERNATE TAKE)

Jelly Roll Morton, piano; George Mitchell, cornet; Kid Ory, trombone; Omer Simeon, Barney Bigard, Darnell Howard, clarinets; Johnny St. Cyr, banjo; John Lindsay, bass; Andrew Hilaire, drums

- Label: Victor 20252; *Birth of the Hot* (RCA/Bluebird 66641)
- Date: 1926
- Style: New Orleans jazz
- Form: 12-bar blues

What to listen for:
- vaudeville humor, references to New Orleans funerals at beginning
- collective improvisation alternating with clarinet and cornet solos
- clarinet trio at chorus 5, with countermelody in trombone at chorus 6

SPOKEN DIALOGUE

0:00 Morton and St. Cyr act out a vaudeville scene, with exaggerated minstrel accents, to prepare us for a New Orleans funeral.

Morton: "*What's that I hear at twelve o'clock in the daytime? Church bells ringing?*"
St. Cyr: "*Oh, man, you don't hear no church bells ringing twelve o'clock in the day.*"
Morton: "*Don't tell me—somebody must be dead!*"
St. Cyr: "*Ain't nobody dead. Somebody must be dead drunk.*"
Morton: "*Don't tell me, I think there's a fyoo-neral!*"
St. Cyr: "*Well, looky here! I believe I do hear a funeral! I believe I hear that tram-bone blowin'!*"

INTRODUCTION

0:18 A trombone **glissando** introduces a somber march, played by the band in **block-chord** texture. The tune comes from the beginning of the traditional hymn "Flee as a Bird to the Mountain," usually performed during the procession to the cemetery.

CHORUS 1

0:33 Suddenly, as if the funeral ceremony were over, the band swings into a faster tempo. The texture is **polyphonic**, with each instrument contributing its individual melodic line to the **collective improvisation**.

The bass plays a variety of patterns: the relaxed two-beat pattern at the opening adjusts at times to four beats to the bar (0:41) or even eight beats to the bar (0:48).

CHORUS 2

0:55 Simeon plays a clarinet solo marked by **variable intonation** (or **blue notes**). Underneath, Morton plays a delicate **counterpoint** on the piano.

CHORUS 3

1:18 Mitchell's cornet solo begins roughly, marred by several obvious errors (1:19, 1:27).

1:25 Morton continues to play underneath.

CHORUS 4

1:40 As Mitchell continues his solo, he plays with more accuracy and confidence.

CHORUS 5 (TRIO)

2:03 Two other clarinets (Bigard and Howard) join Simeon, playing a simple melody in block-chord texture. The rhythm section responds to each line with a loud accent.

CHORUS 6

2:26 As the clarinets repeat their block-chord line, Ory adds a subtle bluesy **countermelody**.

2:47 The trumpet and trombone enter loudly to signal the beginning of the next chorus.

CHORUS 7

2:48 The band improvises polyphonically in a climactic chorus of collective improvisation.

CODA

3:11 In a witty coda, Morton brings back the clarinet trio, only to cut it short with a final accent by the rhythm section.

⊙"Doctor Jazz"

The surprisingly raucous "Doctor Jazz," recorded in late 1926, exemplifies the kind of vitality that distinguished American music to the rest of the world—a nearly bumptious optimism found not only in jazz but also in pop music, from the theatrical bravura of songs like the Gershwins' "I Got Rhythm" to the big-beat mayhem of rock and roll. Morton engages the wilder side of New Orleans jazz, and yet the piece is carefully put together. The structure is a thirty-two-bar **A B A C** song (by King Oliver, with whom Morton often performed), providing an ideal map for Morton to use to navigate between New Orleans jazz and popular song.

Morton employs several jazz techniques to vary the texture and heighten the drama, including stop-time and breaks. "Even if a tune hasn't got a break in it," he advised, "it's always necessary to arrange some kind of spot to make a break." One of the most unusual aspects of the performance is that it begins with the last eight bars of the tune—and a stop-time passage to boot. Stop-time usually appears in the middle of a performance to increase interest; here, Morton grabs you by the lapels with his first blunt chord.

The two most memorable passages are the simplest and most obvious. The second chorus opens with the clarinetist (Simeon) holding a single note for eight bars. In Chapter 2, we heard a similar approach in Louis Armstrong's "West End Blues" (recorded two years later), where the steadiness of a single note makes us more conscious of the moving harmonies over which it floats; in this instance, we can follow Morton signaling the changes on piano.

That chorus is a hard act to follow, but Morton finds a way. In the only vocal he recorded at the Red Hot Peppers sessions, he blurts the first syllable—it's not a note so much as a holler, demanding attention. He then keeps us in thrall with his rhythmic displacements (note his phrasing of the line "Ah, the more I get, the more I want it seems"), emphasizing unexpected syllables and exaggerating his vibrato.

LISTENING GUIDE

1.14

⊙ doctor jazz

JELLY ROLL MORTON AND HIS RED HOT PEPPERS
George Mitchell, trumpet; Kid Ory, trombone; Omer Simeon, clarinet; Jelly Roll Morton, piano; Johnny St. Cyr, guitar; John Lindsay, bass; Andrew Hilaire, drums

- Label: Victor 20415; *Jelly Roll Morton Centennial: His Complete Victor Recordings* (RCA 078635236125)
- Date: 1926
- Style: New Orleans jazz
- Form: 32-bar popular song (**A B A C**)

What to listen for:

- stop-time at the very beginning and in last eight bars (**C**) of each chorus (except for chorus 1)
- ingenious use of collective improvisation and breaks within the tune
- chorus 2: single held note in clarinet, cut off by cymbal
- chorus 3: Morton as singer, emphasizing unexpected syllables
- a build in intensity toward the end

INTRODUCTION

0:00		The band begins with the last eight bars of the tune, performed in **stop-time**: short chords by in the band set up two-bar **breaks** for the clarinet.
0:03		The clarinet plays a **blue note.**
0:05		The band responds with **collective improvisation**.

CHORUS 1

0:09	**A**	The overall texture is **polyphonic**. The muted trumpet paraphrases the melody, while the clarinet improvises beneath him.
0:13		The trombone enters with a melody that responds to the trumpet's statement.
0:19	**B**	The trombone's improvised line forms a **counterpoint** to the trumpet's melody.
0:29	**A**	
0:38	**C**	

CHORUS 2

0:47	**A**	For a full eight bars, Simeon holds a single, unchanging high pitch on clarinet. Underneath, we can hear Morton improvising freely on the harmonies.
0:57	**B**	A cymbal crash cuts Simeon short, returning him to normal improvising.
1:07	**A**	Again, the clarinet holds a single note.
1:12		After another cymbal crash, Simeon slowly descends, following a change in harmony.
1:16	**C**	The band stops playing at the beginning of the measure, leaving the clarinet free to improvise over the guitar's chords.
1:22		At the chorus's end, Simeon retreats to his high note.
1:24		Morton begins to sing, his voice breaking on the opening word, "*Oh!*"

CHORUS 3

1:25	**A**	"*Oh, hello, Central, give me Doctor Jazz! He's got what I need, I'll say he has.*" Each phrase of Morton's melody is followed by the trumpet and clarinet in collective improvisation.
1:35	**B**	"*Oh, when the world goes round, and I've got the blues,* *He's the man that makes me get out a-both my pair of shoes!*"
1:44	**A**	"*Ah, the more I get, the more I want it seems.* *I page ol' Doctor Jazz in my dreams.*" Morton begins each phrase with a powerful growl.
1:54	**C**	"*When I'm in trouble, bound and mixed, he's the guy that gets me fixed.* *Hello, Central, give me Doctor Jazz!*" In this stop-time passage, the voice is accompanied only by the steady pulse on the bass drum.

CHORUS 4

2:03	**A**	A brief phrase of clarinet melody is followed by a composed-out response, featuring the trombone and trumpet playing in harmony.
2:13	**B**	Morton plays a brief (eight bars) piano solo.
2:22	**A**	Simeon's clarinet solo is interrupted by two breaks for St. Cyr's guitar.
2:31	**C**	Stop-time, featuring first Mitchell's trumpet, then Ory's trombone.

CHORUS 5

2:41	**A**	For the final chorus, the band plays polyphonically in collective improvisation.
2:51	**B**	
3:00	**A**	The polyphonic texture is interrupted twice by Simeon's clarinet breaks.
3:09	**C**	The stop-time breaks highlight short **staccato** chords by Morton.

CODA

3:19		The band plays collective improvisation for another two measures.

Last Years

"Dead Man Blues" and "Doctor Jazz" suggest the opposing sides of Morton's music: a gift for lyricism and a penchant for anarchy. He harnessed the potentially chaotic energy of collective improvisation to meet his own exacting standards, with great originality, nuance, and humor. He accomplished this in an era when critical and racial disdain were ever present. As Louis Armstrong once remarked, "No matter how much his diamond sparkled, he still had to eat in the kitchen, the same as we blacks." What Morton's music embodies above all is the raw, restless social energy of the early years of the century, when jazz was a new hustle and the rules had to be made before they could be broken.

By the 1930s, Morton's music was dismissed as hopelessly outdated. In 1938, in a series of Library of Congress interviews with folklorist Alan Lomax, he narrated his life, sitting at the piano and playing examples of the musical points he wished to make. When he died in 1941, a revival of interest in New Orleans jazz was just beginning to build. In retrospect, he was acclaimed as one of the guiding figures of early jazz—indeed, as its finest composer.

■ KING OLIVER (1885–1938)

If New Orleans jazz started out, in the Buddy Bolden era, as a local gumbo flavored by the great variety of music available in that city, by 1922 the gumbo was traveled and seasoned. Instrumental mastery had increased, hundreds of new pieces had been written, and the New Orleans style assimilated flavors of the cities in which it prospered. Jazz had become a fad in the late teens, tricked up with comical routines and instrumental gimmicks. In refusing to cheapen or remodel his music, Joseph "King" Oliver brought New Orleans jazz to an enduring plateau.

King Oliver's Jazz Band promotes its latest OKeh Record in Chicago, 1923. Oliver stands tall at the center. Louis Armstrong, with one leg over the sign, sits beside pianist Lil Hardin, soon to be his wife.

FRANK DRIGGS COLLECTION

Gennett Records

Gennett, the company that recorded King Oliver's Creole Jazz Band, Jelly Roll Morton, and the New Orleans Rhythm Kings, was a small label owned by a firm that manufactured pianos. Gennett had been recording jazz since 1919, but only white bands and not very good ones. With Oliver and Morton, it recognized the commercial potential of music aimed at black audiences. Other labels formed subsidiaries to promote "race records" (see Chapter 3), but not Gennett, which saw no reason to segregate its product.

The Gennett studio was an unprepossessing sight. The squat rectangular building was built a few feet from railroad tracks, which meant frequent disruptions as trains bustled through Richmond. The recording space was a room lined with wood planks. From one wall, a megaphone-shaped horn, about eighteen inches in diameter, jutted out through a black curtain. The musicians had to figure out a way to position themselves around the horn so that the music—traveling through the horn into a stylus (an engraving phonograph needle in the adjoining room), which transmitted the sound onto a lateral disc—would be well balanced. In other words, the only "mixing" (manipulating the sounds of various instruments) they could do was in deciding where to stand. This was the acoustic method of recording. No other method was available in 1923, which is the main reason Oliver's Creole Jazz Band records have always been more difficult to listen to than Morton's electrically recorded 1926 sessions for Victor. In 2006, however, recording engineers working with state-of-the-art transfer techniques brought unsuspected detail and vibrancy to these recordings, which were released as *King Oliver Off the Record: The Complete 1923 Jazz Band Recordings*.

Born in an unknown area of Louisiana, Oliver moved to New Orleans in early childhood with his mother, a cook. He did yard work and other menial jobs before turning to music (relatively late in life) around 1905, the peak of Buddy Bolden's reign; after briefly taking up the trombone, he focused on the cornet. He served a long apprenticeship in various brass bands and saloon groups, finally achieving local renown in an orchestra led by trombonist Kid Ory, who billed him as King Oliver in 1917, cementing his place as Bolden's heir. Other trumpeters, notably Freddie Keppard, had called themselves King, but the royal moniker stuck only to Oliver.

He presented quite a sight. Self-conscious about his blind and protruding left eye, the result of a childhood accident (some people called him Popeye), Oliver played seated or leaning against a wall, sporting a derby rakishly angled to cover the affliction, and used an arsenal of objects as mutes to vary his timbre. He would insert or hang over the bell of his horn a rubber plunger, pop bottle, bucket, glass, doorknob, or hat. "He could make his horn sound like a holy-roller meeting," said Mutt Carey, a New Orleans trumpet player who imitated him. Oliver's love of muting devices had an immense influence on jazz, and eventually led to the manufacture of professional mutes. Richard M. Jones, a pianist who later became an important record producer, recalled Oliver's resourcefulness one night when his band was playing at a Storyville dance hall called Abadie's and his rival, Freddie Keppard, had drawn a larger crowd across the street at Pete Lala's:

I was sitting at the piano and Joe Oliver came over to me and commanded in a nervous harsh voice "Get in B-flat." He didn't even mention a tune, just "Get in B-flat." I did, and Joe walked out on the sidewalk, lifted his horn to his lips, and blew the most beautiful stuff I ever heard. People started pouring out of the other spots to see who was blowing all that horn. Before long our place was full and Joe came in, smiling, and said "Now that SOB won't bother me no more." From then on, our place was full every night.

King Oliver's Creole Jazz Band

The similarity of this story to those told of Bolden is a reminder of the small community in which jazz continued to mature. In his early years, Oliver, again like Bolden, organized different bands as required for specific occasions, from casual socials in the black community to formal affairs at New Orleans's Tulane University. He could be brusque and ill-tempered, but he was regarded as honest and loyal, and musicians liked working with him. In 1918, Oliver moved to Chicago (he played in the band that cheered the White Sox at the fixed 1919 World Series) and after several years on the road returned there in 1922 to play at Lincoln Gardens, a swanky, black-owned nightclub on the Southside (Chicago's black district).

With one exception, Oliver recruited musicians for his new band who had traveled north from New Orleans: trombonist Honore Dutrey, clarinetist Johnny Dodds, drummer Warren "Baby" Dodds (Johnny's brother), and bassist and banjoist Bill Johnson (who had founded the Original Creole Jazz Band, which hired Oliver when he first arrived in Chicago). The ringer was pianist Lil Hardin, from Memphis by way of Fisk University in Nashville. The band was an immediate success, but Oliver felt it was missing something. Suffering from pyorrhea, a disease of the gums, he wanted a second cornetist to punch up the front line and spell him when his embouchure failed him. Weeks into the job, he cabled New Orleans for twenty-year-old Louis Armstrong to join him. Oliver had mentored Louis, who later remembered him as a man who "would stop and show the kids in New Orleans anything they want to know about their music."

Armstrong

With Armstrong on board, respectfully playing second cornet, the great ensemble was now complete: King Oliver's Creole Jazz Band attracted black and white musicians alike, who stopped by when their own engagements were finished. They had never heard anything like it. Nor had they seen a dance hall like Lincoln Gardens, one of the largest nightclubs (it could accommodate a thousand dancers) in the Midwest. A mirrored ball refracted the light over dozens of tables ringing the dance floor, where fans and musicians sat riveted by the band's collective power.

Unlike Morton's Red Hot Peppers band, which existed only in the recording studio, Oliver's Creole Jazz Band played for audiences, including many people who, like him, had moved to Chicago from the South. Oliver had to

A typical set-up for an early acoustic recording: Rosario Bourdon, a major figure in the development of the Victor Talking Machine Company, conducts its ensemble at the RCA-Victor Studios in Camden, N.J., 1928. The musicians play into a horn attached to a recording apparatus in the adjoining room. Note the cellist's custom-built high chair.

be responsive to the moods and desires of dancers and listeners alike. Despite its name, his band embodied the ascendancy of the Uptown improvised style over the Creole written style. They performed an unmistakably collective music, its most salient characteristic a polyphonic (or many-voiced) attack—similar to the style established, albeit more superficially, by the Original Dixieland Jazz Band.

Gennett recordings

In April 1923, King Oliver's Creole Jazz Band loaded its instruments into a couple of Model T Fords and traveled the short trip to Richmond, Indiana, to make its first recordings with Gennett Records. On these recordings, Oliver used two-bar breaks, stop-time choruses, and other devices to vary the texture, but the most memorable moments occur when the entire ensemble builds its head of steam. At first, it may be hard to distinguish between the front-line instruments, but as your ears become accustomed to the sound, you begin to isolate the separate voices—the piping clarinet, the trombone skirting the edges, the two cornets buoying each other. Yet the important thing is not the discrete components, but the marvel of a music in which each instrument contributes to the whole as judiciously as if a master composer had plotted every move, instead of leaving the musicians to spontaneously interact.

A useful introduction to the Oliver Gennetts is his trademark number, "Dippermouth Blues," in part because so much of it is given to solos. After the ensemble plays the theme (a twelve-bar blues), clarinetist Johnny Dodds improvises two choruses over stop-time rhythm played by the rest of the band. Armstrong follows with an open-horn chorus, which serves to introduce Oliver's unmistakably muted sound as he steps forward to play a solo of three choruses. (Of course, it's not really a solo; the other instruments are playing alongside him in polyphonic texture, but they lower their volume to favor Oliver's improvisation.) The vocal timbre he gets from the mute makes his short phrases particularly pungent—they were widely imitated by other trumpeters; during the Swing Era, Fletcher Henderson orchestrated Oliver's solo as "Sugar Foot Stomp." "Snake Rag" is a more typical performance in that the ensemble is the star performer.

🔊 "Snake Rag"

As its title suggests, "Snake Rag" is a rag, following the march/ragtime structure of several disparate strains. (Note: Oliver recorded this piece twice, for Gennett in April 1923 and for OKeh Records two months later; we have chosen the more accomplished OKeh performance.) This sly piece, disrupted by an unusual series of two-part bluesy breaks, takes its name from Oliver's slang for complicated chromatic lines: he called them "snakes," and the snake here is the descending scale played, unaccompanied, by the dual cornets of Oliver and Armstrong at the end of the **A** and **B** strains. The last strain, or trio, is twice as long: thirty-two bars instead of sixteen. The fact that it is played three times in succession contributes to the buildup in excitement and tension. Yet notice how steady the underlying pulse remains.

chromatic moving by half step

During the trio, Oliver and Armstrong play quite different two-bar breaks, accompanied by the trombone. These breaks preserve an aspect of the band's presentation at Lincoln Gardens that had become a signature routine, and a mystery to musicians in the audience. They couldn't figure out how the two cornetists managed to harmonize perfectly on apparently ad-libbed passages. Armstrong later explained that seconds before each break, Oliver would mime the fingering of the upcoming part on his cornet, which cued him as to which break they would play. The two examples on this recording are exceptionally bluesy, and we can imagine the audience cheering them on.

LISTENING GUIDE

1.15

🔊 snake rag

KING OLIVER'S CREOLE JAZZ BAND
King Oliver, Louis Armstrong, trumpets or cornets; Honore Dutrey, trombone; Johnny Dodds, clarinet; Lil Hardin, piano; Bud Scott, banjo; Baby Dodds, drums

- Label: OKeh 4933; *Off the Record: The Complete 1923 Jazz Band Recordings* (Archeophone ARCH OTR-MM6-C2)
- Date: 1923
- Style: New Orleans jazz
- Form: march/ragtime

What to listen for:
- march/ragtime form
- dramatic changes in texture from polyphony to monophony (breaks)
- breaks in **A** and **B** strains: descending chromatic line, trombone glissando
- modulation to a new key at the trio
- variety of breaks for the two cornets

INTRODUCTION (STRAIN A, abbreviated)

0:00 The band beings polyphonically, in **collective improvisation.** Dodds on clarinet drops from a high note to play swirling patterns while Dutrey sticks to a slow, unsyncopated line on the trombone. The two cornets (Armstrong and Oliver) improvise on the main melody.

0:05 **Break:** the cornets play a "snake"—a steady descending line in harmony.

0:07 Using his slide, the trombone answers with simple, comic **glissandos,** followed by a pair of chords from the band.

STRAIN A

0:09 The first strain begins on the **I chord.** Oliver plays the lead cornet, with Armstrong barely audible behind him.

0:22 The band repeats the snake.

STRAIN B

0:26 The second strain begins on a different harmony (**V**).

0:33 In a two-bar **break,** Dutrey plays three upward trombone glissandos, the last accented by a cymbal crash.

0:40 The band repeats the snake.

STRAIN B

0:46 Strain **B** is repeated, with slight variation.

0:59 Snake.

STRAIN A

1:03 Strain **A** is repeated, with more variation.

1:17 Snake.

STRAIN C (TRIO)

1:21   With no transition, the tune suddenly **modulates** to a new key. This strain (trio) lasts twice as long as the previous two. Dutrey plays a trombone line with a distinctive rhythmic profile.

1:37   Dodds fills a break with a descending clarinet line.

STRAIN C

1:58   Strain **C** is repeated, with considerable variation.

2:13   During a break, Oliver and Armstrong play a bluesy and complex riff.

2:32   Break: St. Cyr sings out in full voice, *"Oh, sweet mama!"*

STRAIN C

2:34   On this third appearance of strain **C**, the collective improvisation becomes freer and more intense.

2:50   For the final break, the cornets play a new passage, ending with a lengthy **blue note**.

CODA

3:10   The band tacks on an additional two measures before the cymbal finally cuts them off.

Last Years

As influential as his music proved to be—as we will see, Louis Armstrong, Bix Beiderbecke, and Duke Ellington all borrowed from him—Oliver enjoyed only a brief time in the sun. As his gums continued to worsen, he tried to modernize the New Orleans sound with larger ensembles, such as the ten-piece Dixie Syncopators (which included three saxophones), but the arrangements failed to find a place in the market. Increasingly, he had to delegate the trumpet solos to younger musicians. By 1935, he couldn't play at all; plagued by illness and bad business decisions, he settled in Savannah, Georgia, where he worked as a pool-room janitor and ran a fruit stand. He was broke but not broken when Armstrong ran in to him, in 1938:

> He was standing there in his shirtsleeves. No tears. Just glad to see us. Just another day. He had that spirit. I gave him about $150 I had in my pocket, and Luis Russell and Red Allen, Pops Foster, Albert Nicholas, Paul Barbarin—they all used to be his boys—they gave him what they had. And that night we played a dance, and we look over and there's Joe standing in the wings. He was sharp like the old Joe Oliver of 1915. . . . And pretty soon he died—most people said it was a heart attack. I think it was a broken heart.

■ SIDNEY BECHET (1897–1959)

It can be argued that Sidney Bechet, who played both clarinet and soprano saxophone, was the first great soloist in jazz history. During the early years of jazz, when the saxophone was on the margins of this music, playing sweet sounds in a dance orchestra or virtuoso novelties on vaudeville bills, Bechet turned the instrument into one of its leading voices. He was a moody, impassioned man whose tendency toward violence occasionally landed him in jail; but his emotions were imparted to the very sound of his instrument. He was one of the music's first global stars: he spent a good deal of the Jazz Age overseas, and was one of the first Americans to perform in the Soviet Union in the 1920s.

Bechet was born in New Orleans to a musical Creole family. Although primarily self-taught on the clarinet, he was also instructed by a few renowned Creole teachers, including George Baquet, who heard him playing on a street corner and took him under his wing. As a young man, Bechet played in every important marching band in the city, occasionally doubling on cornet. In 1916, he left to travel with touring bands; one took him up to Chicago, where, three years later, he attracted the attention of Will Marion Cook (1869–1944). A classically trained violinist and conductor (and protégé of composer Antonin Dvořák), Cook made his name as a songwriter and composer. In later years, he organized the first concerts in New York devoted exclusively to black composers, including jazz musicians. When they met, Cook was about to take his Southern Syncopated Orchestra to London, and he recruited Bechet—a momentous decision on two counts.

Will Marion Cook and London

In London, Bechet purchased a straight (no bell curve) soprano saxophone, the instrument with which he ultimately made his mark. He also played clarinet in several prestigious halls with Cook's orchestra (they played for King George V), inspiring the first serious essay written about jazz. The writer was a famous conductor, Ernest Ansermet, and his lengthy review singled out "an extraordinary clarinet virtuoso who is, so it seems, the first of his race to have composed perfectly formed blues on the clarinet." He concluded:

> I wish to set down the name of this artist; as for myself, I shall never forget it—it is Sidney Bechet. When one has tried so often to rediscover in the past one of those figures to whom we owe the advent of our art,—those men of the 17th and 18th centuries, for example, who made expressive works of dance airs, clearing the way for Haydn and Mozart who mark, not the starting point, but the first milestone—what a moving thing it is to meet this very black, fat boy with white teeth and that narrow forehead, who is very glad one likes what he does, but who can say nothing of his art, save that he follows his "own way," and when one thinks that his "own way" is perhaps the highway the whole world will travel tomorrow.

Bechet's fellow musicians were also in awe of him. At one performance, Cook's wife, Abby Mitchell, sang an aria from Puccini's *Madame Butterfly*, and Bechet, without warning (and drawing on his own Creole love for opera), left his seat, walked over to her, and improvised an accompaniment. He expected to be rebuked or fired, but after she finished, Mitchell embraced him with tears in her eyes and said, "Ah, Sidney, only you could have done it like that."

By the time Cook left England, Europe had taken American Negro music to its heart, an affection that would continue throughout the twentieth century. Bechet liked the way he was treated there and, with a contingent of musicians from the Southern Syncopated, decided to stay. He played in both Paris and London, clearing the way for an invasion of black entertainers, but his involvement in a violent argument in London ended with his deportation.

Bechet on Soprano Saxophone

Bechet returned to New York in 1921, and a few years later was hired by yet another important musical figure, though he was virtually unknown at the time. Duke Ellington later wrote of that encounter, "It was a completely new sound and conception to me." He was referring to Bechet's mastery of the soprano saxophone, a difficult instrument to play in tune, but one with a commanding, even piercing sound. The volatile Bechet did not like playing second fiddle to anyone; in jazz, that meant playing clarinet in support of the cornet. With the soprano saxophone, he could dominate any ensemble. What's more, he had begun to think of himself not as a member of a fixed group but as a virtuoso soloist—a new category of which he was perhaps the prime example.

Clarence Williams

Unsuited to the rigors of a big band, Bechet soon parted with Ellington and reunited with an old buddy from New Orleans—the pianist, song publisher, and record producer Clarence Williams (1893–1965), who asked him to participate in a series of recordings billed as Clarence Williams's Blue Five. These records document, for the first time, Bechet's unparalleled stylistic maturity. On the first recordings, Williams paired Bechet with an uninspired cornetist, and Bechet ran roughshod over him. But in 1924, Williams hired Louis Armstrong, recently departed from King Oliver's Creole Jazz Band and already the most admired, in-demand black musician in New York. Bechet rose to the challenge. On their dynamic recording "Cake Walking Babies (from Home)," Bechet is more than a match for Armstrong. He proved to be the only musician of that era who could stand head to head with the younger man—occasionally, as in this instance, standing a bit taller.

"Cake Walking Babies (from Home)"

Recorded in New York, where jazz and Tin Pan Alley pop songs first became inextricably entwined, "Cake Walking Babies (from Home)" combines New Orleans jazz polyphony with the popular music of the day. The title refers to the cakewalk, one of the first dances to cross over from black to white society (see Chapter 3). As a song publisher who put his name on songs he may or may not have worked on, Clarence Williams saw records as a way to boost sheet music sales, and usually included vocal choruses on his recordings to promote words and music. The vocal chorus of "Cake Walking Babies" underscores the high-stepping cheerfulness of this forty-bar song (singer Alberta Hunter went on to enjoy a long career as an entertainer, mixing blues and standards).

The rest of the performance offers a different kind of excitement, as cornet and soprano saxophone transform the usual New Orleans front line into a battle of wits. The first chorus begins with the usual collective improvisation. Bechet seems to anticipate Armstrong's every rest, filling those spaces with melodic figures. This chorus is followed by a statement of the sixteen-bar verse—a seldom-heard contrasting melody used as a way of introducing the chorus. The vocal (second) chorus is accompanied only by banjo and piano, and is lively if dated: it's hard to imagine a singer today performing in this style, whereas the bravura interpretations by Armstrong and Bechet, especially in choruses 3 and 4 (the last two), would be impressive in any day.

1.16

 ## cake walking babies (from home)

THE RED ONION JAZZ BABIES

Louis Armstrong, cornet; Charlie Irvis, trombone;
Sidney Bechet, soprano saxophone; Lil Armstrong,
piano; Buddy Christian, banjo; Clarence Todd and
Alberta Hunter, vocals

- Label: Gennett 5627; *Louis Armstrong and King Oliver* (Milestone MCD-47017-2)
- Date: 1924
- Style: New Orleans jazz
- Form: verse/chorus; chorus is 40-bar popular song
  (**A B A′ C A″**)

> ### What to listen for:
> - **New Orleans–style collective improvisation**
> - a "duel" between two great jazz soloists, Armstrong and Bechet, especially in choruses 3 and 4
> - triplets in the Bechet breaks

CHORUS 1

0:00	**A**	The three horns (Armstrong on cornet, Bechet on soprano saxophone, Irvis on trombone) play in **collective improvisation**. While Armstrong plays the melodic lead, Bechet competes for attention with his aggressive, fluid improvisation.
0:08	**B**	
0:17	**A′**	
0:25	**C**	Armstrong closely paraphrases the original melody (which we will hear in its entirety at 1:00).
0:34	**A″**	

VERSE

0:42	Armstrong and Bechet loosely paraphrase the original melody; the trombone adds a lively response.
0:47	While Armstrong sticks close to the tune, Bechet improvises with more freedom.

CHORUS 2 (SONG)

0:59	**A**	Hunter sings the song, harmonized by Todd (his extra lyrics are in parentheses); the two are accompanied by banjo and piano. *"Here they come (oh, here we come!), those strutting syncopators! Going some (oh, going some!), look at those demonstrators!"*
1:08	**B**	*"Talk of [the] town, Green and Brown, picking 'em up and laying 'em down!"*
1:16	**A′**	*"Prancing fools (oh, prancing fools!), that's what we like to call 'em, They're in a class all alone!"*
1:24	**C**	*"The only way for them to lose is to cheat 'em, You may tie 'em, but you'll never beat 'em!"*
1:33	**A″**	*"Strut that stuff, they don't do nothing different, Cake walking babies from home!"*
1:39		Underneath the vocalists' last notes, the horns begin playing.

CHORUS 3

1:41	**A**	The instruments resume their collective improvisation. Armstrong plays more freely and with greater intensity. Bechet's timbre is hard and penetrating.
1:49	**B**	
1:56		Bechet plays a two-bar break in **triplets**, a rhythm that srongly divides the beat into threes.

Soprano saxophone

1:58	A'	
2:06	C	**Stop-time**: Armstrong improvises a complex syncopated line in his upper register.
2:14		At the end of the passage, Armstrong plays his last note with a growl.
2:15	A"	
2:22		The horns sustain a long note, a signal that another chorus is coming.

CHORUS 4

2:24	A	The two soloists differ dramatically in style: Armstrong plays sparsely, with intense syncopation, while Bechet smoothes out into lengthy strings of eighth notes.
2:32	B	
2:38		Irvis plays a gruff trombone solo during the break.
2:40	A'	
2:49	C	Stop-time: Bechet begins with a rough series of slurs and improvises a rhythm that shifts unpredictably between triplets and jazzy syncopation.
2:58	A"	To signal the end of the piece, both Armstrong and Bechet play repeated riffs.

Last Years

In 1925, Bechet returned to Europe with a musical called *Revue Negre,* starring singer and dancer Josephine Baker. He played in Berlin, Amsterdam, and Moscow, where he met up with his most important partner, Louisiana-born trumpet player Tommy Ladnier. Together, in New York in the early 1930s, the two formed the New Orleans Feetwarmers, and made records that confirmed Bechet's unique style. Bechet continued to make dozens of memorable recordings ("Summertime" and "Blue Horizon" are high-water marks of a New Orleans revival that took place in the 1940s), demonstrating a broad repertory, advanced sense of harmony, and adventurous spirit. In 1932, his "Shag" was the first jazz original based on the chords to "I Got Rhythm," and in 1941, "The Sheik of Araby" employed overdubbing (recording over an existing recording) to allow him to play all the parts—clarinet, soprano saxophone, tenor saxophone, bass, and drums.

Bechet's dominance of the soprano saxophone was so complete that he remained its chief exponent until his death in 1959. By then, he had become one of the most beloved musicians in Europe, especially France, where he settled in 1951. His records graced every café jukebox in France (one of his compositions, "Petite Fleur," became a national phenomenon), and a memorial bust was unveiled in Nice.

NEW ORLEANS STYLE TODAY

New Orleans jazz has never disappeared, though generations of modern jazz enthusiasts have done their best to ignore it. The tradition is kept alive, quite naturally, at New Orleans's Preservation Hall, a popular tourist attraction located in a small eighteenth-century building in the French Quarter, a few blocks from the Mississippi River. Bands and societies devoted to New Orleans or Dixieland jazz can be found all over the world, from New Jersey to Brazil, Denmark, and Japan. It has become a kind of feel-good folk music, often played by amateurs. No matter where it is played, the repertory, instrumentation, polyphonic front line, and marchlike rhythm section remain essentially the same. So does the attitude, which ranges from happiness to exultation, and is usually nostalgic though rarely sentimental. Dixieland musicians often wear straw hats and sleeve garters as if to announce that they are part of a musical tradition sufficient unto itself, a thing apart from the evolution of jazz and complete in its own right.

ADDITIONAL LISTENING	
Bunk Johnson	"C. C. Rider" (1944); *King of the Blues* (American Music Records AMCD-1)
Jelly Roll Morton	"Buddy Bolden's Blues" (1938); *Library of Congress Recordings*, vol. 2 (Rounder)
	"King Porter Stomp" (1926); *Doctor Jazz: Jelly Roll Morton, His Greatest Recordings* (ASV/Living Era)
	"I Thought I Heard Buddy Bolden Say" (1939); *Classics 1930–1939* (Classics 654)
King Oliver	"Dippermouth Blues," "High Society" (1923); *Off the Record: The Complete 1923 Jazz Band Recordings* (Off the Record OTR-MM6)
Sidney Bechet	"Maple Leaf Rag" (1932); *Maple Leaf Rag / Sidney's Blues* (Membran/Cja 221983)
	"Summertime" (1939); *The Best of Sidney Bechet* (Blue Note B2-28891)
	"Make Me a Pallet on the Floor" (1940); *Sleepy Time Down South* (Classics 619)
	"Weary Blues" (1945); *Sidney Bechet: 1945–1946* (Classics 954)
Original Dixieland Jazz Band	"Tiger Rag," "Livery Stable Blues" (1917); *The 75th Anniversary* (Legacy)
Freddie Keppard	"Stock Yards Strut" (1926); *The Complete Set, 1923-1926* (Retrieval 79017)

PAUL WHITEMAN
changes

FLETCHER HENDERSON
copenhagen

JAMES P. JOHNSON
you've got to be modernistic

DUKE ELLINGTON
black and tan fantasy

NEW YORK IN THE 1920S

ARABIAN NIGHTS

New York City, particularly the borough of Manhattan, has served as the focus for jazz's maturity and evolution from the late 1920s to the present. But it never quite carried the mythological resonance of places that enjoyed intense associations with specific eras in jazz. The parishes of New Orleans, as we have seen, sparked the first great fomenting of jazz; then Chicago proved to be the primary magnet that drew Southern musicians to the North. The wide-open nightlife of Kansas City would inspire countless musicians in the 1930s, and the laid-back temper of Los Angeles would take up the "cool" style of the 1950s. In the end, however, no matter where they came from, no matter how much local renown they achieved, nearly all the great jazz musicians had to make their way to New York to cement a genuine, enduring success.

New York's centrality may be explained in part by cultural inertia, as each generation of musicians there lured the next. Yet as we look more closely at the development of jazz in New York, especially the early years, we find three interlocking spheres of influence.

COMMERCIAL The entertainment *infrastructure*—concert halls, theaters, museums, galleries, radio and television, newspapers and magazines, book publishers, and record la-

Duke Ellington conducts his orchestra from the piano at the Olympia Theater in Paris, 1958.

wwnorton.com/studyspace

bels, not to mention managers, agents, bookers, and publicists—of the country took root in New York in the closing years of the nineteenth century and never left. New York media spoke for the nation, and as jazz became a commercial entity, it needed access to that media and to the stimulating atmosphere forged by a powerful industry designed to match performers with audiences.

SOCIOLOGICAL The years of the Great Migration from South to North coincided with a massive East-to-West emigration from Europe to the United States. Jazz is unusual as an art form in that a majority of its performers belong to ethnic minorities. Most of the major figures in jazz history who were not African American derived from immigrant families that originated in Italy, Ireland, Germany, and Russia. Middle European Jews, whose music involved a blues-like use of the pentatonic scale and a feel for improvisation, were especially drawn to jazz. This confluence of ethnicities proved particularly profound in New York, which in the 1920s accounted for America's largest urban communities of blacks and Jews. An alliance between black musicians and Jewish songwriters replicated, in part, the give-and-take between New Orleans blacks and Creoles, and helped to define jazz for three decades.

pentatonic scale five-note scale, as C D E G A

MUSICAL It is often said that in encompassing all of jazz, New York produced no specific style of its own. This isn't entirely true. Stride piano, which we will examine in this chapter, originated on the Eastern Seaboard and flowered in New York in the 1920s and 1930s; New York's receptivity then advanced the innovations of modern jazz (or bebop) in the 1940s and avant-garde (or free) jazz in the 1950s and 1960s. The city's most significant contribution to jazz, though, was the development of large bands and orchestrations: the influx of jazz musicians in the 1920s from New Orleans, Chicago, and elsewhere overlapped with the growing enthusiasm for ballroom dancing, generating a demand for elegant orchestras. These were jazz's first important big bands, and they would later fuel the Swing Era.

Small wonder that when a young, untested, and unknown Duke Ellington arrived in New York for the first time in 1923 and surveyed the bright lights that extended from one end of Manhattan to the other, he exclaimed, "Why, it is just like the Arabian Nights!" The possibilities were limitless, and the soundtrack was jazz—or soon would be.

1920s TRANSFORMATIONS

Recordings, Radio, and the Movies

The twentieth century unfurled in an unceasing progression of technological marvels, from the airplane to cellphones. In the field of entertainment, three periods stand out: the 1920s, for radical transformations in recordings, radio, and movies; the 1940s, for television; and the 1980s, for digitalization. All three media in the first period, the one that concerns us here, had been introduced in the later part of the nineteenth century, but were refined in the 1920s in ways that changed the way Americans lived their lives.

In 1925, the development of electrical recording as a replacement for the primitive technology of acoustical recording meant that records, formerly inadequate for reproducing certain instruments and vocal ranges, now boasted a stunning fidelity that especially benefited jazz, with its drums and cymbals and intricately entwined wind instruments. The recording industry, in a slump since 1920, came back to life with dramatically reduced prices in phonographs and discs.

Radio, which had been little more than a hobby for most people, blighted by static and requiring headphones, sprang to life as a broadcast medium in 1921 (KDKA in Pittsburgh), achieving a lifelike clarity with the invention of the carbon microphone and, subsequently, the much-improved condenser microphone. The first radio network, the National Broadcasting Company, debuted in 1926, followed a year later by the Columbia Broadcasting System, uniting the nation with unparalleled powers of communication. The advances in radio and recording gave entertainment seekers a kind of permission to stay at home—a permission that quickly became a national habit, as people grew emotionally attached to broadcasts or obsessed with collecting records. The cinema responded to these technological challenges with an innovation of its own. In 1927, Warner Bros. introduced the first feature film with synchronized sound—an adaptation of a Broadway play significantly, if deceptively, called *The Jazz Singer.*

Historically, music had evolved at a pace no faster than human travel. A symphony by Mozart, written in Vienna, might not reach England for months or years; the music of New Orleans could spread only as fast as the musicians moved from one place to another. The rapid growth in radio and records meant that a recording manufactured in New York could reach California the same day over the air and within a week through the mail. Speed affected everything. Earlier, a vaudeville comedian might work up an evening of jokes that he could deliver for an entire year, in one city after another. Now, on radio, those jokes were depleted in one night. Similarly, pop songs and musical styles wore out faster than ever before, like hemlines and hairdos.

Prohibition

As technology encouraged people to stay at home, nightlife received an unintended boost. In 1920, a Republican Congress passed—over President Wilson's veto—the Eighteenth Amendment to the Constitution, prohibiting the manufacture, transporting, and sale of alcohol. Under Prohibition, it was legal to drink and even purchase alcoholic beverages, but since no one could legally sell (or manufacture) it, the amendment's principal effect was to create a vast web of organized crime, catering to a generation that often drank to excess simply to prove that the government could not dictate its level of intoxication.

By 1921, the country was pockmarked with tens of thousands of speakeasies (illicit saloons). Their gangster owners competed for customers by hiring the most talented musicians, singers, comedians, and dancers around. In mob-controlled cities like Chicago, Kansas City, and New York, many of these nightspots stayed open through breakfast, and jazz was perfectly suited to an industry that required music to flow as liberally as beer. All the composers in town could not have written enough music to fill the order, but improvisers could spin an infinite number of variations on blues and pop songs. Musicians follow the lure of work, and—until it was repealed in 1932—Prohibition provided a lot of work.

In the 1920s, Fletcher Henderson led the orchestra at the Roseland Ballroom, one of the most gloried dance halls in America, at Broadway and 51st in New York.

DANCE BANDS

A cursory look at early jazz suggests a long dry spell between the 1917 triumph by the Original Dixieland Jazz Band and the classic recordings of King Oliver and others in 1923. Yet the interim was a period of great ferment, especially in New York, where jazz came face to face with a melting pot of musical styles: Tin Pan Alley popular songs (see p. 125), ragtime, New Orleans jazz, marching bands (especially popular after 1918, in the aftermath of World War I), and vaudeville, which featured anything that could keep an audience attentive during a fifteen-minute act—including comical saxophones, blues divas, and self-styled jazz or ragtime dancers. Jazz musicians freely borrowed and transformed elements from every type of music. Jazz also found its way into elaborate ballrooms and concert halls. Two leading figures in this process came east from San Francisco: Art Hickman and Paul Whiteman.

■ ART HICKMAN (1886–1930)

Art Hickman, a pianist, drummer, and songwriter, encountered jazz in the honky-tonks of the Barbary Coast in San Francisco, where he believed jazz originated: "Negroes playing it. Eye shades, sleeves up, cigars in mouth. Gin and liquor and smoke and filth. But music!" In 1913, Hickman organized a dance band in San Francisco, which soon included two saxophonists. Though he did not harmonize them in the manner of a reed section (where two or more reed instruments play in harmony), he did assign them prominent roles, creating a smoother sound than the brass-heavy ensembles associated with New Orleans jazz and marching bands. The saxophones gave an appealing character to a band that otherwise consisted of trumpet, trombone, violin, and a rigid rhythm section with two or three banjos (a remnant from minstrelsy). Hickman's success served to establish saxophones as an abiding component in the jazz ensemble.

In 1919, the Victor Talking Machine Company brought Hickman's band to New York with great fanfare, partly as an antidote to the boisterousness of the Original Dixieland Jazz Band. But Hickman disliked the city and hurried back to San Francisco, leaving room for a successor—a far more formidable figure.

■ PAUL WHITEMAN (1890–1967): A Short-Lived Monarchy

It may be difficult now to appreciate how incredibly popular bandleader Paul Whiteman was in the 1920s. Tall and corpulent, with a round and much caricatured face, he was the first pop-music superstar of the twentieth century, a phenomenon at home and abroad—as famous as Charlie Chaplin and Mickey Mouse.

Whiteman, more than anyone else, embodied the struggle over what kind of music *jazz* would ultimately be. Would it be a scrappy, no-holds-barred improvisational music built on the raw emotions and techniques of the New Orleans style, or a quasi-symphonic adaptation, with only vestigial elements to suggest the source of inspiration? Was jazz merely a *resource,* a primitive music from which art music could be developed, or was it an art in itself? By the late 1920s, almost everyone, including Whiteman, recognized jazz as an independent phenomenon, destined to follow its own rules and go its own way. Yet the question had been passionately argued.

Born in Denver, Whiteman was the son of an influential music teacher, Wilberforce J. Whiteman, who despised jazz and Paul's association with it. (Ironically, his students included two major figures of the Swing Era, Jimmie Lunceford and Andy Kirk, whom we will meet in Chapters 7–8.) Paul studied viola and joined the Denver Symphony Orchestra while in his teens. He began to attract attention when, after moving to San Francisco to play in the San Francisco Symphony Orchestra, he organized a Barbary Coast ragtime outfit in his off hours. He formed his first ballroom band in 1919, achieving success in Los Angeles, Atlantic City, and finally New York, where he became an immediate favorite at the ritzy Palais Royal.

Up to this point, Whiteman had been thoroughly outshone by Hickman. The tables turned in 1920, when Victor released Whiteman's first recordings, "Whispering" and "Japanese Sandman," which sold well over a million copies. Whiteman and Hickman had begun with similar instrumentation in their bands, but Whiteman built a much larger one, producing a more lavish and flexible sound, with considerable help from composer-arranger Ferde Grofé. Whiteman himself rarely played viola anymore, but he conducted with graceful pomp, demonstrated an appealing personality, and made news by articulating his argument on behalf of American music.

Symphonic Jazz

In 1924, Whitman formalized his argument with a concert at New York's Aeolian Hall that became a fabled event in twentieth-century musical history. In this concert, called "An Experiment in Modern Music," Whiteman attempted to prove his contention that a new classicism was taking root in lowborn jazz. He opened with a crude performance of the Original Dixieland Jazz Band's "Livery Stable Blues," played for laughs as an example of jazz in its "true naked form," and closed with a new work he had commissioned from the ingenious Broadway songwriter George Gershwin (1898–1937), *Rhapsody in Blue,* performed with the composer at the piano. No jazz was heard in the interim, but the response to the concert was so fervent that Whiteman was promoted as the "King of Jazz" and honored as the originator of **symphonic jazz,** a phrase he coined.

Bandleader Paul Whiteman sought to legitimize American music in a 1924 concert at Aeolian Hall that introduced George Gershwin's jazz-influenced concert piece *Rhapsody in Blue,* performed with the composer at the piano.

PAUL WHITEMAN
AND HIS
Palais Royal Orchestra
WILL OFFER
An Experiment in Modern Music

Zez Confrey
and
George Gershwin

New Typically American Compositions by Victor Herbert, George Gershwin and Zez Confrey will be played for the first time.

AEOLIAN CONCERT HALL
Tuesday, Feb. 12th $\binom{\text{LINCOLN'S}}{\text{BIRTHDAY}}$ at 3 P. M.

Tickets now on Sale, 55c. to $2.20

Victor Records   Chickering Pianos   Buescher Instruments

Early fusion

Symphonic jazz represented a **fusion** of musical styles (the first of several in jazz history)—in this instance, between Negro folk art and the high-culture paradigm of European classical music. Speaking to a distinctly urban sensibility, it attempted to incorporate the hurry and clatter of the big city in an age of skyscrapers, technology, and fast living. It was also an attempt to democratize high art by giving it an American twist. Much as Joseph Haydn had found profundity in simple folk songs in the late eighteenth century, Claude Debussy and Igor Stravinsky sought inspiration from ragtime in the early twentieth. With symphonic jazz, which was already under way before Whiteman's concert, a new group of classically trained composers in both Europe and America hoped to redefine modern music by accenting African American elements.

Such symphonic works as French composer Darius Milhaud's *La creation du monde* (1923), American composer George Antheil's *Jazz Symphony* (1925), John Alden Carpenter's *Skyscrapers* (1926), and Grofé's *Metropolis* (1928) all depicted the frenzy of the modern city, specifically New York. Gershwin went so far as to replicate the sound of automobile horns in his 1928 *An American in Paris*. Symphonic jazz lost steam during the Depression (1929–41); in the 1950s, it was revived as Third Stream music, combining techniques of postwar jazz and classical music.

Crosby, Challis, and the New Guard

The media did not notice that in the year of Whiteman's Aeolian Hall triumph, a relatively unknown Louis Armstrong had arrived in New York to take a seat in Fletcher Henderson's orchestra. Whiteman, however, did notice, and in 1926 he decided it was time for the King of Jazz to hire a few jazz musicians. Initially, he wanted to recruit black musicians, but his management convinced him that he couldn't get away with a racially integrated band: he would lose bookings, and the black musicians would be barred from most ho-

Bing Crosby, advertised on a Broadway billboard, brought jazz rhythms and inflections to popular ballads, revolutionizing radio and breaking the all-time house record at the Paramount Theater in New York, 1931.

tels and restaurants. Whiteman countered that no one could stop him from hiring black arrangers; he traded orchestrations with Henderson and added African American composer William Grant Still to his staff.

Whiteman's first important jazz hire came from vaudeville: singer Bing Crosby (1903–1977) and his pianist and harmonizing partner Al Rinker. Never before had a popular bandleader hired a full-time singer; in the past, instrumentalists had assumed the vocal chores. During his first week with the Whiteman organization, in Chicago in 1926, Crosby heard Louis Armstrong, and was astonished by Armstrong's ability to combine a powerful art with bawdy comedy, ranging from risqué jokes to parodies of a Southern preacher. Crosby became the most popular singer in the first half of the twentieth century, a decisive force on records and radio and in the movies. An important aspect of his accomplishment was that he helped make Armstrong's musical approach accessible to the white mainstream public, by adapting rhythmic and improvisational elements of Armstrong's singing style to his own. In turn, Crosby inspired Armstrong to add romantic ballads to his repertory. They often recorded the same songs within weeks of each other.

Whiteman then signed up the most admired young white jazz instrumentalists in the country, including Bix Beiderbecke, Frank Trumbauer, and Eddie Lang (see Chapter 6). An especially influential new recruit was the highly original arranger Bill Challis, who had an uncanny ability to combine every aspect of Whiteman's band—jazz, pop, and classical elements alike. Thanks to Challis and the other new additions, Whiteman released innovative jazz records in the years 1927–29, until financial considerations exacerbated by the Depression obliged him to return to a more profitable pop format.

◉ "Changes"

In 1927, the Whiteman band served as a microcosm of the three-way battle involving jazz, symphonic jazz, and pop. Bill Challis favored Crosby and the jazz players, but when the band's old (symphonic) guard complained of neglect, he found ways to bring everyone into the mix. His arrangement of Walter Donaldson's "Changes" opens with strings, incorporates pop and jazz singing, and climaxes with a roaring Bix Beiderbecke solo, the sound of his cornet tightened by a straight mute inserted into the bell of his horn.

The title itself is significant, suggesting changes in the band, changes in taste as ballroom music assimilated the vitality of jazz, and changes in improvisation techniques as harmonic progressions (noted in the lyrics) took the place of polyphonic elaborations of the melody. The title also signifies broader cultural changes that were transforming the United States. In the several months before the recording was made, Charles Lindbergh had flown the Atlantic Ocean, Babe Ruth had hit sixty home runs, and talking pictures had premiered. The national mood was optimistic, as reflected in songs like "Good News," "Hallelujah," "'S Wonderful," "Smile," "There'll Be Some Changes Made," and many others.

Challis emphasizes changes between new and old with contrasting rhythms and vocal groups. Rhythmically, a **Charleston beat** (two emphatic beats followed by a rest; see Listening Guide), usually enunciated by the trumpets, alternates with the more even rhythms stated by the violins. The performance never sticks to any one sound, preferring to cut back and forth between strings, brasses, saxophones, and voices, with solo spots interspersed.

Note that although six vocalists are listed among the personnel, they never sing in tandem. Three of them, representing Whiteman's old guard, were full-time instrumentalists (trombonist Jack Fulton and violinists Charles Gaylord and Austin Young) who were occasionally deputized to sing pop refrains. Shortly after Crosby and Rinker joined Whiteman, they recruited singer-pianist Harry Barris to form a novel group called the Rhythm Boys. Of the singers, Crosby was by far the most gifted. Accordingly, Challis divided the vocal chorus into sections, employing both vocal trios and Crosby as soloist. The chorus begins with the old guard ("Beautiful changes"), then—with Barris signaling the change by imitating a cymbal ("pah")—switches to the Rhythm Boys, who blend high-pitched harmonies and a unified **scat** break (wordless vocalizing). This is followed by the old guard setting up a solo by Crosby, who mimics a trombone slide on the words "weatherman" and "Dixieland." Crosby's solo leads to the record's flash point: Beiderbecke's improvisation.

LISTENING GUIDE

1.17

🎧 changes

PAUL WHITEMAN

Paul Whiteman, director; Henry Busse, Charlie Margulis, trumpets; Bix Beiderbecke, cornet; Frank Trumbauer, C-melody saxophone; Wilbur Hall, Tommy Dorsey, trombones; Chester Hazlett, Hal McLean, clarinets, alto saxophones; Jimmy Dorsey, Nye Mayhew, Charles Strickfaden, clarinets, alto and baritone saxophones; Kurt Dieterle, Mischa Russell, Mario Perry, Matt Malneck, violins; Harry Perrella, piano; Mike Pingitore, banjo; Mike Trafficante, brass bass; Steve Brown, string bass; Harold McDonald, drums; Bing Crosby, Al Rinker, Harry Barris, Jack Fulton, Charles Gaylord, Austin Young, vocals

- Label: Victor 21103; *Paul Whiteman and His Dance Band* (Naxos 8.120511)
- Date: 1927
- Style: early New York big band
- Form: 32-bar popular song (**A B C A'**), with interlude and verses

What to listen for:
- full instrumentation of a large commercial dance band, including strings
- **Charleston rhythm**
- vocalists: "sweet" trio vs. "jazz" trio (with scat-singing)
- Beiderbecke's "hot" cornet solo

INTRODUCTION

0:00   The brass section rises through unstable **chromatic** harmonies until it finally settles on a **consonant** chord.

SONG (D♭ major)

0:10 **A** The saxophones play the melody, decorated above by short, syncopated trumpet chords and supported by the strings. Underneath, the banjo and piano play four beats to the bar, while the bas plays two beats.

0:19 **B** The melody shifts to the violins.

0:28 **C** The trumpets play a jaunty **Charleston rhythm,**

answered first by the saxophones, then by the strings.

0:38   **A′**   The saxophones return to the opening melody, which moves toward a **full cadence.**

INTERLUDE

0:45   The rhythmic accompaniment temporarily stops. Over changing orchestral textures (including a violin solo), the piece **modulates** to a new key.

VERSE 1 (16-bar A A B A)

0:52   **A**   The trumpets and strings return to the Charleston rhythm, underscored by the trombones' offbeat accents. The phrase begins in **minor** but ends in **major.**

0:56   **A**

1:01   **B**   For the bridge, the saxophones quietly sustain chords.

1:05   **A**

SONG (E♭ major)

1:10   **A**   *"Beautiful changes in different keys, beautiful changes and harmonies."*
The "sweet" vocal trio harmonizes the melody in **block-chord** harmony, accompanied by the rhythm section (string bass, banjo, drums).

1:19   **B**   *"He starts in C, then changes to D. He's foolin' around most any old key."*
The harmonies shift away from the tonic, matching the intent of the words.

1:28   **Break:** Barris introduces the "jazz" vocal trio (Rhythm Boys) by imitating a quiet cymbal stroke ("pah").

1:29   **C**   *"Watch that—hear that minor strain! Ba-dum, ba-dum,"*
The Rhythm Boys adapt to the new style by singing a more detached and "cooler" series of chords.

1:35   *"Bada(ba)da-lada(bada-lada)-la-dum!"*
During a break, the vocalists imitate scat-singing, changing the dynamics to match the rhythm.

1:38   **A′**   *"There's so many babies that he can squeeze, and he's always changing those keys!"*
The first trio returns to set up Crosby's solo.

1:46   The voices retreat to background chords.

VERSE 2

1:47   *"First, he changes into B, changes into C, changes into D, changes into E,*
As easy as the weatherman! Now, he's getting kinda cold, getting kinda hot,
Listen, I forgot, since he was a tot, he's been the talk of Dixieland!"
Crosby sings the verse with ease, ending each phrase with a rich, resonant timbre.

SONG

2:05   **A**   While the voices continue their background harmony, Beiderbecke takes a cornet solo with a sharp, focused sound. Underneath him, the bass switches to a four-beat **walking bass.**

2:14   **B**

2:24   **C**   The full band returns with the Charleston rhythm.

2:33   **A′**   In full block-chord texture, the band plays a written-out version of the melody with syncopations.

CODA

2:40   The tempo moves to **free rhythm.** Over sustained chords, a saxophone plays a short solo.

2:49   As the chords dissipate, all that's left is the sound of a bell.

■ FLETCHER HENDERSON (1897–1952)

Like every other bandleader in New York, black and white, Fletcher Henderson initially looked to Whiteman for inspiration, seeking to emulate his opulent sound and diverse repertory as well as his public success. Yet he would ultimately take big-band music down a very different, far more influential route as he developed into an outstanding arranger.

An unassuming, soft-spoken man who initially had no particular allegiance to jazz, Henderson, like Paul Whiteman, grew up in a middle-class home with parents who disdained jazz. Born in Cuthbert, Georgia, he studied classical music with his mother but seemed determined to follow in the footsteps of his father, a mathematics and Latin teacher, when he graduated from Atlanta University with a chemistry degree. Soon after traveling to New York in 1920 for postgraduate study, he switched from chemistry to music, overcoming his class resistance to the blues by learning how to play piano well enough to record dates with singers Ethel Waters and Bessie Smith. From there, he went on to organize dance bands for nightclubs and ballrooms.

In 1924, Henderson began a lengthy engagement at the luxurious Roseland Ballroom at 51st Street and Broadway, New York's preeminent dance palace. As a black musician working in midtown venues with exclusively white clienteles, Henderson offered polished and conventional dance music: fox-trots, tangos, and waltzes. At the same time, he had access to the best black musicians, including an attention-getting young saxophonist named Coleman Hawkins (see Chapter 6), and, like Whiteman, felt a desire to keep up with the ever-changing dance scene.

Fletcher Henderson, seated at the piano, organized the first great black orchestra in New York and introduced many major jazz musicians. The 1924 edition of his band included tenor saxophonist Coleman Hawkins (third from left) and trumpet player Louis Armstrong (sixth from left).

Henderson's band grew in confidence, stature, and size over the next several years. By 1926, it was widely regarded as the best jazz orchestra anywhere, a standing it began to lose in 1927, with the rise of Duke Ellington and other bandleaders who elaborated on the approach pioneered by Henderson and his chief arranger, Don Redman. Although Henderson never achieved a popular renown equal to that of Ellington, Count Basie, Benny Goodman, and other big-band stars, his influence among musicians increased during the 1930s, as he produced a stream of compositions and arrangements that helped to define big-band music in the Swing Era.

■ DON REDMAN (1900–1964)

At first, Henderson relied primarily on **stock arrangements**, anonymous versions of standard popular songs made available by publishing companies, which tended toward basic harmonies with no jazz content. As his pioneering arranger Don Redman began revising them, making increasingly radical changes, the arrangements took on a distinct and exciting character. Duke Ellington would later recall that when he came to Manhattan with the dream of creating an orchestra, "[Fletcher's] was the band I always wanted mine to sound like."

Redman, a child prodigy from West Virginia, who received a degree in music from Storer College at age twenty, played all the reed instruments and composed songs and instrumental novelties, often characterized by his wry sense of humor. His most famous work, "Chant of the Weed," was a hymn to marijuana. Redman's great achievement as arranger was to treat the band as a large unit made up of four interactive sections: reeds (saxophones and clarinets), trumpets, trombones, and rhythm section. Over the decade 1924–34, the orchestra grew to an average of fifteen musicians: typically three trumpets, two to three trombones, up to five reeds, and four rhythm (piano, bass or tuba, banjo or guitar, drums). This basic big-band instrumentation, notwithstanding numerous variations, remains unchanged even now.

Redman and Henderson closely studied jazz records coming out of Chicago, and adapted these tunes to a more orchestral approach. Redman especially liked the New Orleans custom of short breaks, which allowed him to constantly vary the texture of a piece. Yet he avoided the anarchy of New Orleans style: when he used polyphony, it was usually not collectively improvised but composed in advance. His principal organizing technique, derived from the church, was a call-and-response interchange, pitting, say, the saxophone section against the trumpets. His best arrangements retained the vitality of a small jazz band, but were scrupulously prepared.

Enter Armstrong

When Henderson decided to add a third trumpet player in 1924, he looked for the hottest soloist he could find. After several long-distance discussions with Lil Hardin Armstrong, Louis's wife, he convinced her to persuade her husband to take his offer. At first, Henderson's well-paid, spiffily dressed musicians didn't know what to make of a country boy like Louis. Customers were also confused: the first time Armstrong stood up to play a solo at Roseland, the audience was too startled to applaud. But Armstrong brought with him essential ingredients that the band lacked: the bracing authority of swing, the power of blues, and the improvisational logic of a born storyteller.

The standard had been raised, and no one understood that better than Redman, who later acknowledged that he changed his orchestration style to accommodate Armstrong's daring. In recordings like "Copenhagen" and "Sugar Foot Stomp" (an ingenious adaptation of King Oliver's "Dippermouth Blues," with Armstrong playing Oliver's solo), Redman's writing began to take on a commanding directness and sharper rhythmic gait. Nor was his fanciful use of breaks and popular melodies lost on Armstrong, who employed them in the Hot Five sessions he initiated after his year with Henderson (see Chapter 6). Redman's writing not only launched big-band jazz, but also served to link Oliver's Creole Jazz Band (1923) and Armstrong's seminal Hot Five (1925).

🔊 "Copenhagen"

Several historic threads come together in Fletcher Henderson's 1924 recording of "Copenhagen," a multistrain composition by a Midwestern bandleader (Charlie Davis), named not for the capital of Denmark but after a favorite brand of snuff. The Wolverines, a scrappy little band featuring Bix Beiderbecke, had recorded it in May, and its publisher issued a stock arrangement of the song. To this Don Redman added his own variations, employing aspects of New Orleans jazz (orchestrated polyphony), block-chord harmonies (standard for large dance orchestras), brief breaks, hot solos, old-fashioned, two-beat dance rhythms, and sectional call and response. The piece combines twelve-bar blues with sixteen-bar ragtime strains.

Louis Armstrong's jolting blues chorus is an undoubted highlight in a performance also notable for the spirit of the ensemble and of individual contributions such as Charlie Green's trombone smears and Buster Bailey's whirling clarinet. Bailey joined Henderson around the same time as Armstrong (1924), extending the New Orleans tradition of clarinet obbligato into big-band jazz a decade before, as we will see, the clarinet came to symbolize the Swing Era. Note the contrasting trios featuring three clarinets in the **B** strain and three trumpets in the **D** strain, and compare the notated polyphony in the **A** strain with the improvised polyphony (played against block-chord trumpets) in the **E** strain. The harmonically surprising finish inclined listeners to shake their heads in wonder and move the needle back to the beginning.

🔊 **block-chord harmonies** two or more instruments playing the same phrase and rhythm, in harmony

🔊 **obbligato** an independent countermelody, less important than main melody

---

LISTENING GUIDE

1.18

🔊 copenhagen

FLETCHER HENDERSON

Fletcher Henderson, piano; Elmer Chambers, Howard Scott, Louis Armstrong, trumpets; Charlie Green, trombone; Buster Bailey, clarinet; Don Redman, clarinet and alto saxophone; Coleman Hawkins, clarinet and tenor saxophone; Charlie Dixon, banjo; Ralph Escudero, tuba; Kaiser Marshall, drums

- Label: Vocalion 14926; *Fletcher Henderson* (Columbia Legacy/Sony 61447)
- Date: 1924
- Style: early big band
- Form: march/ragtime

What to listen for:

- 16-bar ragtime strains alternating with 12-bar blues
- sectional arranging: clarinet trios (**B** strain) and trumpet trios (**D**)
- an early Armstrong solo
- trombone and clarinet glissandos
- notated polyphony (**A**) vs. improvised polyphony (**E**)
- unexpected ending

STRAIN A (16 bars)

0:00 The saxophones and trumpets move up and down through the **chromatic scale** in **block-chord** harmony.

0:04 Led by a trombone, the entire band responds with a cleverly written-out imitation of **collective improvisation.**

0:09 The opening passage is now given to clarinets playing in their lowest register. The response, once again, is scored collective improvisation.

STRAIN B (12-bar blues)

0:17 A high-pitched clarinet trio plays a bluesy melody. Underneath, the rhythm section (piano, banjo, drums, tuba) plays a lively two-beat accompaniment, with the drummer and banjo player adding a strong **backbeat.**

STRAIN B

0:29 A repetition of the previous twelve bars.

STRAIN B

0:42 Armstrong plays a well-rehearsed solo (the same solo can be heard on another take). His playing is hard-driving, with a swing rhythm and a bluesy sensibility.

STRAIN C (16 bars)

0:54 The full band plays a series of syncopated block chords, punctuated by cymbal crashes. Again, the response is scored polyphony.

1:02 The previous eight-bar section is repeated.

STRAIN D (16 bars)

1:11 A trio of trumpets plays a melody in a simple three-note rhythm.

1:17 During a two-bar **break,** the trumpets are interrupted by the clarinet trio performing a disorienting, rising **glissando**.

STRAIN A

1:28 The opening of strain **A** is played by the clarinet trio in its highest register.

1:36 The same passage is played by the saxophones.

STRAIN E (12-bar blues)

1:44 The trombone plays an introductory melody.

1:48 While the trumpets play in block-chord harmony, the clarinet and trombone improvise in New Orleans style.

STRAIN E

1:57 The repetition of strain **E** has a looser, more improvised feeling: the trombone plays with more glissando, while the clarinet sustains its high pitch for four measures.

STRAIN F (16 bars)

2:09 As the trumpet trio plays block-chord harmonies, the clarinet improvises busily underneath.

2:16 The break is divided between the banjo and the tenor saxophone.

CODA

2:26 The band returns to strain **A**.

2:34 Without pause, the band suddenly shifts to the beginning of strain **C**.

2:38 A high-pitched clarinet trio reintroduces strain **A**.

2:45 The band moves to block chords that descend precipitously outside the piece's tonality. With this bizarre gesture, the piece abruptly ends.

Later Years

Throughout his career, Henderson continued to provide a showcase for the finest black musicians in New York. A short list of major jazz figures who worked with him includes, in addition to the remarkable trinity of Armstrong, Hawkins, and Redman and those already mentioned, trumpet players Rex Stewart, Tommy Ladnier, Henry "Red" Allen, Roy Eldridge; trombonists Jimmy Harrison, Benny Morton, J. C. Higginbotham, Dicky Wells; clarinetists and saxophonists Benny Carter (also a major composer-arranger), Lester Young, Ben Webster, Chu Berry, Russell Procope, Omer Simeon; bassists John Kirby, Israel Crosby; drummers Kaiser Marshall, Sidney Catlett; and arranger Horace Henderson (his brother). No other big-band leader can lay claim to such a roll. We will encounter Henderson again as an accidental architect of the Benny Goodman Orchestra.

Don Redman left Henderson's band in 1927 to become director of Mc-Kinney's Cotton Pickers, an inventive big band in which he proved himself a charming vocalist—speaking his interpretations with a light, high-pitched voice—and a productive composer. He wrote pop standards ("Cherry," "Gee Baby, Ain't I Good to You," "How'm I Doin'?") and blues ("Save It, Pretty Mama"), as well as instrumental masterpieces like "Chant of the Weed" (1931). As a freelance arranger, he wrote for Armstrong, Whiteman, Jimmy Dorsey, Jimmie Lunceford, and many others, but by the middle 1930s his style was considered passé and he began to recede from jazz. In 1951, Redman became music director for the singer-actor-comedienne Pearl Bailey, an association that lasted more than a decade and took him far from his roots as a jazz visionary yet kept him firmly in the lap of New York entertainment.

THE ALLEY AND THE STAGE

Like New Orleans with its parishes and Chicago with its Southside and Northside, the island of Manhattan consists of diverse neighborhoods ruled by racial and ethnic divisions. In the 1920s, the downtown section, below 14th Street, encompassed the Lower East Side, a populous Jewish area (home to the Yiddish theater), as well as Little Italy and Chinatown; and the West Side, with its business district (Wall Street) and an enclave that attracted artists and bohemians, Greenwich Village. Downtown Manhattan included hundreds of working-class saloons and theaters that presented every kind of entertainment, from vaudeville bills to bar pianists, singers, and small bands, creating variations on ragtime, opera, and pop songs and often combining them with European folk traditions. One of the most important of the ethnic importations came to be known as **klezmer,** a Jewish dance music (named after the Hebrew phrase for "musical vessel") that shared several elements with jazz, such as bluesy-sounding melodies that were often embellished through improvisation.

In New York's midtown section, the wealthy homes and establishments on the East Side were divided from mostly white ghettos on the West Side (such as Hell's Kitchen). Running down the middle, north to south, was and is Broadway, where theaters, cabarets, and dance halls (like the Roseland Ballroom) offered a constant, ravenous market for new songs and entertainers. On Broadway, you could see plays, musicals, ballet, opera, revues, movies, vaudeville, and every other kind of show business. More than a dozen newspapers competed in reporting on the nightlife of the "guys and dolls" (in columnist Damon Runyon's phrase) who frolicked in the most fabled playground of the Jazz Age.

Tin Pan Alley

Midtown was also the home of Tin Pan Alley, the first songwriting factory of its kind. The name has come to represent the popular music written for the stage and cinema from the 1890s through the 1950s, when rock and roll began to change the business. Originally, it was the nickname for buildings on 28th Street between Broadway and Sixth Avenue, where many music publishers had their offices and passers-by could hear the cacophony of a dozen or more competing pianos—songwriters demonstrating their wares. The Alley introduced the idea of the professional songwriter, who wrote specific kinds of songs to order—ballads, novelties, patriotic anthems, rhythm songs, and so forth—as commissioned by performers or to meet a public demand. In the 1920s, for example, thanks to the enormous popularity of Al Jolson, there was an appetite for Southern-themed (or "Mammy") songs, which were dutifully turned out by songsmiths who had never been south of 14th Street.

George Gershwin, seen here c. 1928, wrote pop songs for Broadway, concert works for symphony orchestra, and the opera *Porgy and Bess*, incarnating the influence of jazz on all forms of American music.

By the middle 1920s, the most sophisticated generation of songwriters ever assembled was in place. Rejecting the sentimental formulas that had dominated the Alley during the previous thirty years, they wrote music and words that were original, intelligent, expressive, and frequently beautiful, with harmonic underpinnings that gave them a particularly modern and enduring appeal. The songs this generation wrote remain the core of the classic American songbook, and were vital to the development of jazz. The songwriters, influenced by jazz rhythms and blues scales, came of age with Armstrong-inspired improvisers who required new and more intricate material than the blues and ragtime strains that had served their predecessors. The two groups were ideally matched: a composer like George Gershwin actively tried to capture the jazz spirit, and an improviser like Coleman Hawkins found inspiration in Gershwin's melodies and harmonies.

Among the most masterly and prolific of the new Tin Pan Alley songwriters were Irving Berlin and Cole Porter, who were unusual in writing both words and music. For the most part, pop songs were the work of teams. In the 1920s, those teams included the composers Gershwin, Jerome Kern, Harold Arlen, Richard Rodgers, Vincent Youmans, and Hoagy Carmichael, and the lyricists Ira Gershwin, Lorenz Hart, Oscar Hammerstein II, E. Y. Harburg, and Dorothy Fields.

Blacks on the Great White Way

Although whites, and especially Jews, dominated the Alley, black songwriters made important contributions from the start. W. C. Handy was one of the most successful songwriters in the early years (his 1914 "St. Louis Blues" remains one of the most recorded songs of all time), and any account of the major songwriters in the 1920s would have to include composers Duke Ellington and Fats Waller and lyricist Andy Razaf. Yet while white entertainers

Bert Williams, the most successful black entertainer in history until his death in 1922, was forced to perform in blackface, but he broke down several racial barriers: he appeared on Broadway and became the first major Victor recording artist, in 1901.

The public never saw Williams looking as he does in the publicity shot; he deeply resented having to perform exclusively in blackface.

BOTH: FRANK DRIGGS COLLECTION

often performed songs by black songwriters, black artists were segregated from theatrical revues and struggled for recognition on the Great White Way—as Broadway, with its glittery marquee lights, was known. Their struggle had had its ups and downs since the beginning of the century.

During Reconstruction and after, a stage show with a black cast usually meant minstrels, which obliged its performers to enact the same stereotypes and wear the same costumes and makeup (burnt cork, white gloves, frizzy wigs) as white entertainers who pretended to be black. Then in 1898, Will Marion Cook (a composer and violinist whom we encountered in Chapter 4) presented *Clorindy, or the Origin of the Cakewalk*, the first black production to play a major Broadway theater (the Casino Roof Garden); that show went far in breaking with minstrelsy, in songs like "On Emancipation Day." More important, *Clorindy* popularized the cakewalk and was the first musical to incorporate ragtime melodies and rhythms.

During the next decade, black musicals were often seen on Broadway. Cook also wrote the music—and poet Paul Lawrence Dunbar the lyrics—for the smash hit *In Dahomey* (1903), starring the legendary team of Bert Williams and George Walker. The beloved Williams went on to enjoy an astonishing career as the first African American to sign an exclusive recording contract (with Victor, in 1901), the first to star in the Ziegfeld Follies (1910–19), and the first featured in a movie (1910).

Despite Williams's popularity, many white producers and performers resented the success of blacks on Broadway, and by 1910 the bubble had burst. The black presence all but disappeared, until Eubie Blake and Noble Sissle produced their blockbuster of 1921, *Shuffle Along*, launching a renaissance of sophisticated black entertainments. A new generation of African American songwriters, publishers, and performers now flourished, including, for the first time, sexy women who had been liberated from any hint of the Aunt Jemima stereotype—among them Ethel Waters, Florence Mills, Nina Mae McKinney, and Josephine Baker, a chorus girl who later became a sensation in Paris (sometimes accompanied by Sidney Bechet, as we saw in Chapter 4).

Black Songwriters

In 1923, Clarence Williams, the New Orleans pianist and songwriter who produced the Blue Five recordings with Sidney Bechet (see Chapter 4), moved to New York, where his song-publishing company encouraged black composers to write a stream of new tunes for black musical revues and white vaudeville stars who needed "rhythmical" numbers. Black songwriters responded by turning out some of the best-known classics in the American songbook; among them were Spencer Williams ("I Ain't Got Nobody," "Basin Street Blues," "I Found a New Baby"), Maceo Pinkard ("Sweet Georgia Brown," "Sugar"), Henry Creamer and Turner Layton ("Way Down Yonder in New Orleans," "After You've Gone"), Shelton Brooks ("The Darktown Strutters' Ball," "Some of These Days"), Chris Smith ("Ballin' the Jack," "Cake Walking Babies [from Home]"), James P. Johnson ("If I Could Be with You One Hour Tonight," "Charleston"), and Noble Sissle and Eubie Blake ("Memories of You," "I'm Just Wild About Harry"), in addition to Ellington and Waller.

THE HARLEM RENAISSANCE

While blacks managed to make their mark on Broadway and Tin Pan Alley, they positively dominated uptown Manhattan, or Harlem, which became an entertainment haven, with its dozens of nightclubs and theaters. Until the close of the nineteenth century, the largest African American community in New York had lived in Greenwich Village (where Fats Waller was born). As whites moved in and landlords raised the rents, blacks were driven into the worst sections of Hell's Kitchen and similar districts. In those years, Harlem, a vast and, until the advent of mass transportation, isolated settlement stretching from 110th Street to 155th Street, was mostly white and upper class; regal townhouses still stand on 139th Street, known as Striver's Row. By 1915, most Harlemites were lower- and middle-class Jews, Germans, and Italians, with blacks occupying a few pockets.

Yet a gradual demographic change had begun in 1904, when the Afro-American Realty Company organized a campaign—not unlike the *Chicago Defender*'s crusade to bring Southern blacks to Chicago—to lure African Americans to Harlem. The movement accelerated over the next fifteen years, producing a massive migration involving especially large numbers of Southern and West Indian Negroes. The simultaneous exodus of whites resulted in a nearly complete racial reversal. By 1920, central Harlem had become what poet and memoirist James Weldon Johnson described as "not merely a Negro colony or community, [but] a city within a city, the greatest Negro city in the world." In 1925, philosopher and critic Alain Locke edited a book of essays called *The New Negro*, one of the most influential manifestos ever published in the United States and the foundation for what would become known as the **Harlem Renaissance**. Locke's anthology argued that African American artists represented a political and cultural force in literature, art, dance, theater, and music.

The New Negro

The leaders of this renaissance had an ambiguous relationship to jazz, which too often reminded them of coarse stereotypes they preferred to leave behind. In one *New Negro* essay, "Jazz at Home," J. A. Rogers celebrated jazz as "a balm for modern ennui" and a "revolt of the emotions against repression," but argued that jazz's "great future" lay with bandleaders (including Will Marion Cook, Paul Whiteman, and Fletcher Henderson) who "sublimated" those emotions and displayed "none of the vulgarities and crudities of the lowly origin." By contrast, the influential white critic and Harlem nightclub habitué Carl Van Vechten romanticized the more squalid aspects of the "city within a city" in a best-selling novel, *Nigger Heaven* (1926), which made uptown an attraction for thousands of downtown whites.

Unhappily, the very forces that turned Harlem into a cultural carnival also turned it into a slum and a profit center for organized crime. The crammed residents, unable to spread out to racially restricted neighborhoods, fell victim to landlords who increased the rents while partitioning apartments into ever-smaller units. As an added insult, mobsters financed ornate nightclubs—including the Cotton Club, which featured top black performers and sexy floor shows—that refused entrance to black patrons. In these Harlem getaways, the New Negro was banned from witnessing the fruits of his own renaissance.

STRIDE

Fittingly, the city that established orchestral jazz also encouraged the ripening of the most orchestral brand of jazz piano, initially known as "Harlem style" but eventually recognized internationally as **stride piano**. Here was an exciting, virtuoso way of playing piano that directly reflected the musical vigor of New York. Imagine ragtime taken for a ride down Tin Pan Alley and then revved up to reflect the metropolitan noise and bustle. Where ragtime was graceful, polished, and measured, stride was impetuous, flashy, and loud. Where ragtime produced a contained repertory, stride was open to anything. The evolution from one to the other occurred gradually.

Like ragtime, stride began as a composed music made up of multiple strains. Then, just as ragtimers had competed in contests of virtuosity, the East Coast stride players began to add their own flourishes and rhythms, eventually developing an offshoot that was livelier, faster, and more propulsive. Perhaps the most remarkable parallel between ragtime and stride is that each style gave birth to the foremost African American composers of its time. Ragtime's pedigree from Scott Joplin to Jelly Roll Morton was more than equaled by stride pianists of the 1920s who, through their disciples, shaped jazz piano and jazz composition for decades to come—a lineage that includes James P. Johnson, Fats Waller, Duke Ellington, Art Tatum, and Thelonious Monk.

Piano Power

The name "stride" describes the motion of the pianist's left hand, striding back and forth from low in the bass clef to the octave below middle C. On the first and third beats, the pianist plays either a single low note or a chord, usually involving a tenth—an octave plus a third (for example, a low C together with an E, ten white keys higher counting the first C). Tenths require large hands, so resourceful pianists without the necessary reach perfected "broken tenths": the notes played in rapid succession instead of simultaneously. On the second and fourth beats, the pianist plays a three- or four-note chord in the upper part of the bass clef.

The masters of stride created intricate harmonic and rhythmic patterns that kept the left hand from becoming a mechanical rhythm device. They also developed tricks for the right hand that allowed it to embellish melodies with luscious glissandos, producing a richer texture than traditional ragtime. Many stride pianists studied classical music, and incorporated keyboard techniques of the nineteenth-century European virtuosos, particularly Franz Liszt and Frédéric Chopin. They were obliged to keep up with the latest tunes, which also brought a modern harmonic richness to their music.

Stride pianists found they could earn a livelihood by hiring out for Harlem "rent parties." These get-togethers, a social phenomenon of the 1920s, arose from people's need to meet ever-higher rents. Friends and neighbors would congregate for food and music, making contributions to a communal kitty. As the average living room could not accommodate a band, the pianist had to be loud and steady enough to suit dancers and be heard over the volume of conversation. Inevitably, stride pianists achieved a high social standing. They competed with each other pianistically and also in personal style—with tailored suits, rakish derbies, expensive cigars, and colorful personalities.

James P. Johnson, the most influential of the pioneering stride pianists and a Broadway composer whose songs include the 1920s anthem "Charleston," at a 1930s jam session.

■ JAMES P. JOHNSON (1894–1955)

James P. Johnson is widely known as the "Father of Stride Piano." With his rhythmic brio and improvisational variations, Johnson perfected the East Coast style as a progressive leap from its ragtime roots. Almost every major jazz pianist who came along in the 1920s and 1930s—not just Waller, Tatum, and Ellington, but also Earl Hines, Count Basie, and Teddy Wilson—learned from him. Although he never achieved the fame of his protégés, many stride revivalists continue to regard him as the most creative artist in the idiom.

Johnson was born in New Brunswick, New Jersey, where his mother sang in the Methodist Church and taught him songs at the piano. He later credited the **ring-shout dances** (the earliest known African American performing tradition, combining religious songs and West African dances) and brass bands he heard as a child as important influences. After the family moved to New York in 1908, he studied classical piano and encountered like-minded ragtimers—especially Eubie Blake and Luckey Roberts, who was regarded by his colleagues as the best pianist in New York.

Johnson and the others found jobs playing in Jungle's Casino, a Hell's Kitchen dive where black laborers from the Carolinas danced to piano music and managed to impart Southern melodies to Johnson's receptive ears. Beginning in 1918, he punched out a series of influential piano rolls, including an early version of "Carolina Shout," which became an anthem and a test piece—a kind of "Maple Leaf Rag" for New York's piano elite. As ragtime had become popular through widely distributed sheet music, stride found a smaller but dedicated audience through piano rolls (see box on p. 130). Some pianists, including Ellington and Waller, learned to imitate Johnson's vibrant attack by slowing down a roll of "Carolina Shout" on a player piano and placing their fingers on the depressed keys.

In 1921, Johnson initiated a series of sensational recordings, including a definitive "Carolina Shout," "Keep Off the Grass," "Worried and Lonesome

The Player Piano

Patented in 1897, the player piano (or pianola) became a hugely popular entertainment apparatus in middle- and upper-class American homes of the 1920s. It served two functions: as a regular piano, and as a piano capable of mechanically playing music inscribed on piano rolls. These were rolls of paper perforated with tiny squares representing the notes; as the squares rolled over a "tracker bar," they triggered a suction device that, in turn, controlled a lever of the keyboard. Piano rolls could be purchased like recordings, and were often made by celebrated musicians—Igor Stravinsky wrote an etude for pianola, and pianists as prominent as Scott Joplin, Sergei Rachmaninoff, George Gershwin, and Fats Waller introduced original music on rolls. As there was no limit to the number of squares that could be cut into a roll, some pianists (notably Gershwin) would secretly cut the same roll twice, adding accompanying notes the second time. (This practice stymied customers trying to learn how to play a piece by imitating such a roll. They would complain that Gershwin must have had four hands; turns out, he did.)

The player piano operated as a teaching tool: you could play the roll at any speed, and slow it down enough to study the depressed keys. As accompaniment for a sing-along, it was arguably the world's first method of karaoke. The increased availability of radio and records in the later 1920s sped the player piano into obsolescence. Some rolls, however, have been collected on CDs, and although they have a mechanical, steely sound, they are as close as we can get to the actual playing of otherwise unrecorded artists like Joplin.

Blues," and other piano milestones. His career took a whole new direction in 1922, when he was appointed music director of the revue *Plantation Days*, which traveled to London. A year later, he and lyricist Cecil Mack wrote the score for the Broadway smash *Runnin' Wild*, which toured the country. Two of its songs became standards: "Old Fashioned Love," which, thanks to a Bob Wills recording in the 1930s, became a country-music favorite; and "Charleston," perhaps the most widely recognized melody of the 1920s.

While continuing to write songs, produce shows, and play piano (he recorded often as a sideman), Johnson also composed classical pieces that combined nostalgic folk melodies with his own urbane techniques—notably *Yamekraw: Negro Rhapsody*, which W. C. Handy debuted at Carnegie Hall in 1928. He followed this work with *Harlem Symphony* and *Symphony in Brown* in the 1930s and *De-Organizer*, written with the poet Langston Hughes, in 1940. Illness slowed him down, and a stroke incapacitated him in 1951, a time when pianists Thelonious Monk and Erroll Garner were extending the Johnson style into modern jazz.

"You've Got to Be Modernistic"

The transition from ragtime to stride, from formal composition to jazz variations, is illuminated in Johnson's dazzling 1930 recording of "You've Got to Be Modernistic." Consider two aspects of its "modernism." First, the introduction and first two strains are ornamented by advanced harmonies, drawing on the whole-tone scale, that keep the listener in a state of perpetual surprise. Second, Johnson switches midway from the formalism of ragtime to the theme and variations of jazz. The structure consists of three sixteen-bar strains (with a four-bar interlude), but with the introduction of strain **C**, the piece then romps through seven choruses of variations with no reprise of strain **A** or **B.**

whole-tone scale six-note scale, each note a whole step from the next

Interestingly, the **C** strain, unlike the virtuosic **A** and **B** strains, has the most traditional melody. It begins with a two-bar riff (which Johnson later set to the words "You've got to be modernistic!"), yet suggests a simple Scott

Joplin–style ragtime harmony in measures 7 and 8. Johnson, for all his flashing speed and hairpin changes, always exercises a composer's control. Each strain is so distinct from the others (and in the **C** series, one chorus accents blue notes, another bass notes, another an insistent triple-chord pattern) that the listener is never lulled by repetition or familiarity. The entire performance is a well-ordered whirlwind.

LISTENING GUIDE

1.19

🎧 you've got to be modernistic

JAMES P. JOHNSON, PIANO
- Label: Brunswick 4762; *Snowy Morning Blues* (GRP GRD-604)
- Date: 1930
- Style: Harlem stride
- Form: march/ragtime (**A B A C**)

What to listen for:
- stride piano accompaniment: a steady alternation of bass note and chord
- whole-tone harmonies in introduction, strain **A**, and interlude
- Trio (**C**) played seven times, with jazzy riffs
- pianistic blue notes

INTRODUCTION

0:00   After an opening left-hand chord, Johnson's right hand plays a series of descending **whole-tone** chords (triads derived from the whole-tone scale).

STRAIN A

0:04   Johnson plays the main melody in **stride** style, with the left hand alternating between bass notes and chords.

0:07   The end of the first phrase is marked by a syncopation in the left hand.

0:10   The melody leads to a **chromatic** passage featuring whole-tone harmonies.

0:12   The opening melody is repeated.

0:16   A rising series of whole-tone chords resolves in a **full cadence.**

STRAIN A

0:20   Following march/ragtime form, Johnson repeats the strain.

0:29   He shifts the pattern in his left hand, playing the bass note one beat early and temporarily disrupting the accompaniment with a polyrhythm.

STRAIN B

0:35   The next strain begins with left-hand bass notes alternating with right-hand chords. The pattern descends chromatically.

STRAIN B

0:50   Johnson repeats the strain an octave higher, adding a bluesy figure.

STRAIN A

1:05   The right hand is even higher, near the top of the piano keyboard.

INTERLUDE

1:20   To **modulate** to a new key, Johnson brings back the whole-tone harmonies and texture of the introduction.

STRAIN C (TRIO)

1:24   The trio is built around repetitions of a short riff.

STRAIN C

1:39 As before, the repetition is played an octave higher. The end of the riff pattern is reduced to an emphatic **blue note,** achieved by playing two adjacent notes at the same time.

STRAIN C

1:54 The melody is now in the bass line, with the left hand playing each note twice.

2:01 The rhythmic pattern in the left hand intensifies to three notes in a row.

STRAIN C

2:09 The right hand plays widespread chords in a **polyrhythm** against the basic meter.

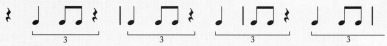

2:17 Here (and again at 2:23), Johnson disrupts the accompaniment by shifting the position of the bass note.

STRAIN C

2:24 Against the same harmonic background, Johnson improvises a new riff.

STRAIN C

2:39 Johnson begins his riff pattern with a held-out chord.

2:45 For two measures, the right and left hands play together rhythmically.

2:47 The riff pattern shifts to the downbeat, changing the groove.

STRAIN C

2:54 Johnson plays his right-hand chords in a quick three-note repetition (similar to what we heard in the left hand at 2:03).

3:07 With a few short chords, he brings the piece to an end.

■ DUKE ELLINGTON BEGINS (1899–1974)

As the most important composer that jazz—and arguably the United States—has produced, Duke Ellington played a vital role in every decade of its development, from the 1920s until his death in 1974. To this day, his music is more widely performed than that of any other jazz composer. Ellington achieved distinction in many roles: composer, arranger, songwriter, bandleader, pianist, producer. He wrote music of every kind, including pop songs and blues; ballets and opera; theater, film, and television scores; suites, concertos, and symphonies; music for personal homages and public dedications; and, most significantly, thousands of instrumental miniatures. All of his music contains strong elements of jazz, even where there is no improvisation. He made thousands of recordings, more than any other composer or bandleader, some inadvertently (he rarely discouraged fans with tape recorders) and others privately and at his own expense, to be released posthumously.

Ellington's early breakthrough, in the late 1920s and early 1930s, defined four aspects of New York's musical culture. The first three were strictly musical. (1) He clarified the nature of big-band jazz, demonstrating potential beyond Whiteman's imagination or Henderson's achievement. (2) He solidified the influence of stride piano as a jazz factor, employing it not only as a pianist himself but also as a foundation in orchestrations. (3) He proved that the most individual and adventurous of jazz writing could also be applied to popular songs.

The fourth area concerned his persona and proved no less vital to the standing of jazz and especially its relationship to the Harlem Renaissance. Ellington, a handsome, well-mannered, articulate, and serious man, violated the assumptions about jazz as a low and unlettered music. A largely self-taught artist, Ellington earned his regal nickname with an innate dignity that musicians, black and white, were eager to embrace. He routinely disconcerted critics, but never lost the adoration and respect of fellow artists. In his refusal to accept racial limitations, he became an authentic hero to black communities across the country for nearly half a century.

Edward Kennedy Ellington was born in Washington, D.C., to a middle-class family who encouraged his talent for music and art. He is said to have acquired his nickname as a child, by virtue of his proud bearing. In school (Armstrong High School, as it happens), Ellington's painting won him a scholarship to study art at the Pratt Institute. Instead, he pursued and studied the stride pianists who visited the capital. His first composition, "Soda Fountain Rag," written at fourteen, mimicked James P. Johnson's "Carolina Shout."

As a high school senior, Ellington organized a five-piece band and found enough work to encourage him to try his luck in New York, in 1923. There, at the Hollywood Club, which after two incidents of insurance-motivated arson returned as the Kentucky Club, he began to enlarge the band, focusing on growling, vocalized brasses and finding a creative ally in Bubber Miley, an innovative trumpet player from South Carolina who enlarged on King Oliver's expressive muting effects. Ellington called his new band the Washingtonians,

Duke Ellington—composer, arranger, orchestra leader, pianist—is regarded by many as the most accomplished figure in American music. Gifted musicians devoted their lives to his band, including guitarist Fred Guy (at front), baritone saxophonist Harry Carney (to his left), alto saxophonist Johnny Hodges (far right in middle row), and clarinetist Barney Bigard (to his left, here playing saxophone). Ellington is pictured at the piano and on the bass drum played by Sonny Greer, 1938.

and made a few records between 1924 and 1926, although they show little distinction.

By late 1926, Ellington began to reveal a style of his own, influenced by Miley, whose almost macabre, bluesy mewling—quite unlike Armstrong's open-horn majesty—was ideally suited to Ellington's theatrical bent. In crafting pieces with and for Miley, Ellington ignored Don Redman's method of contrasting reeds and brasses, and combined his instruments to create odd voicings, thereby creating a new sound in American music. As presented in his first major works, "East St. Louis Toodle-O" (Ellington's version of a ragtime dance), "Black and Tan Fantasy," and two vividly different approaches to the blues, "The Blues I Love to Sing" and "Creole Love Call" (in which he used wordless singing as he would an instrument), the overall effect was mysterious, audacious, and carnal.

The Cotton Club

Ellington's career took a giant leap on December 4, 1927, when he opened at Harlem's Cotton Club. Although this segregated citadel was thought to represent the height of New York sophistication, it actually exploited tired minstrel clichés. The bandstand design replicated a Southern mansion with large white columns and a painted backdrop of weeping willows and slave quarters. A mixture of Southern Negro and African motifs (featuring capering light-skinned women) encouraged frank sexuality. For Ellington, though, the whole experience was enlightening. He learned much about show business by working with other composers (including the great songwriter Harold Arlen), choreographers, directors, set designers, and dancers.

As the headliner for the next three years, Ellington became a major celebrity in New York and—through the Cotton Club's radio transmissions—the country. His reputation quickly spread to Europe. The club's erotic revues had inspired him to perfect a wry, insinuating music in which canny instrumental voices were blended into an intimate and seductive musical tableau. Inevitably, it was described as "jungle music," a phrase Ellington found amusing. In truth, he was up to something quite radical.

Duke Ellington, Cab Calloway, and other legendary black performers established themselves onstage at the world-famous, mob-run Cotton Club, but they were not allowed to enter the front door or sit at the tables, which were reserved for whites.

Ellington was finding legitimate musical subjects in racial pride, quite different from Tin Pan Alley's coon and Mammy songs, and sexual desire, quite different from Tin Pan Alley's depictions of romantic innocence. He was not a Broadway composer who borrowed from jazz, like Gershwin, but a true jazz composer—with enormous vitality and wit, and a gift for sensuous melodies, richly textured harmonies, and rollicking rhythms that reflected his love of stride piano. As the band grew in size, it gathered a cast of **Ellingtonians** (see Chapter 8), musicians who stayed with him for years, decades, and in some instances entire careers—stylists such as alto saxophonist Johnny Hodges, baritone saxophonist Harry Carney, trumpeter (and Miley's successor) Cootie Williams, trombonist Joe "Tricky Sam" Nanton, clarinetist Barney Bigard, and bassist Wellman Braud. Upon leaving the Cotton Club in 1931, the fifteen-piece band now known as Duke Ellington and His Famous Orchestra traveled the world, and in the process defined the future of jazz with a 1932 song title: "It Don't Mean a Thing (if It Ain't Got That Swing)."

"Black and Tan Fantasy"

A great deal of Ellington's music is **programmatic**, attempting to describe specific places, people, or events. As a rule, programmatic music is most successful when it can be appreciated with no knowledge of the subject. For example, it is not necessary to know that Beethoven set out to depict a pastoral scene, complete with sudden storm, in his Sixth Symphony to appreciate the logic and beauty of his music. This is also true of Ellington's arresting "Black and Tan Fantasy"; still, its tongue-in-cheek attitude is more compelling if we understand his satirical point.

Unlike the Cotton Club, which refused to admit blacks, other Harlem clubs catered exclusively to African Americans. And some, which were regarded as a pinnacle of liberality, invited members of both races; these were known as the "black and tan" clubs. Ellington's piece has been interpreted as a response to the idea that these small, overlooked speakeasies absolved a racially divided society. "Black and Tan Fantasy" contrasts a characteristic twelve-bar blues by Miley with a flouncy sixteen-bar melody by Ellington. Miley's theme, the black part of the equation, was based on a spiritual he had learned from his mother. Ellington's, the tan part, draws on the ragtime traditions that lingered in the 1920s. As the two strains merge in a climactic evocation of Chopin's famous "Funeral March" theme, the piece buries the illusions of an era. While the black and tans disappeared, the "Fantasy" remained a steady and much revised number in Ellington's book—an American classic.

1.20

 # black and tan fantasy

DUKE ELLINGTON AND HIS ORCHESTRA

Duke Ellington, piano; Bubber Miley, Louis Metcalf, trumpets; Joe "Tricky Sam" Nanton, trombone; Otto Hardwick, Rudy Jackson, and Harry Carney, saxophones; Fred Guy, banjo; Wellman Braud, bass; Sonny Greer, drums

- Label: Victor 21137; *The Best of the Duke Ellington Centennial Edition* (RCA 63459)
- Date: 1927
- Style: early New York big band
- Form: 12-bar blues (with a contrasting 16-bar interlude)

> **What to listen for:**
> - the growling timbre of Ellington's horns
> - clash between blues harmony and contrasting pop-song material
> - the expressive use of mutes by Miley (trumpet) and Nanton (trombone) in their solos
> - Ellington's stride piano

CHORUS 1 (12-bar blues)

0:00 Over a steady beat in the rhythm section, Miley (trumpet) and Nanton (trombone) play a simple, bluesy melody in the **minor mode.** The unusual sound they elicit from their tightly muted horns is an excellent example of **timbre variation.**

0:25 A cymbal crash signals the appearance of new material.

INTERLUDE (16 bars)

0:26 The harmonic progression suddenly changes with an unexpected chord that eventually turns to the **major mode.** The melody is played by Hardwick (alto saxophone) in a "sweet" style, with thick vibrato, a sultry tone, and exaggerated **glissandos.**

0:38 During a two-measure **break,** the band plays a **turnaround**—a complicated bit of chromatic harmony designed to connect one section with the next.

0:42 Repeat of the opening melody.

0:54 The horns play a series of chords, then stop. The drummer plays several strokes on the cymbal, muting the vibration with his free hand.

CHORUS 2

0:58 Over a major-mode blues progression, Miley takes a solo. For the first four bars, he restricts himself to a high, tightly muted note.

1:06 Miley plays expressive bluesy phrases, constantly changing the position of his **plunger mute** over the **pixie mute** to produce new sounds that seem eerily vocal (*wa-wa*).

CHORUS 3

1:23 Miley begins with a pair of phrases reaching upward to an expressive **blue note.**

1:25 The cymbal responds, as if in sympathy.

1:26 In the next phrase, Miley thickens the timbre by growling into his horn.

CHORUS 4

1:47 The band drops out while Ellington plays a cleverly arranged **stride piano** solo.

1:51 The left hand plays in **broken octaves:** the lower note of each octave anticipates the beat.

1:58 Ellington plays a striking **harmonic substitution.**

CHORUS 5

2:11 Nanton begins his solo on tightly muted trombone.

2:15 He loosens the plunger mute, increasing the volume and heightening the intensity of the unusual timbre.

2:27 Nanton precedes his last phrase with a bizarre gesture, sounding somewhere between insane laughter and a donkey's whinny.

CHORUS 6

2:36   Miley returns for an explosive bluesy statement, featuring quick repeated notes. Each phrase is answered by a sharp accent from the rhythm section.

2:50   As the harmony changes, the band enters, reinforcing Miley's moan.

CODA

2:57   With Miley in the lead, the band ends by quoting Chopin's "Funeral March"—returning the piece to the minor mode.

Perhaps the quickest way to appreciate the amazing progress jazz made in the 1920s is to listen to "Black and Tan Fantasy" back-to-back with Jelly Roll Morton's "Dead Man Blues," which also involves a satiric fantasy that invokes death and was recorded the previous year. The differences between them exceed their key musical techniques—Morton's polyphony and Ellington's call and response. Far more significant is the difference in perspective. Morton's piece looked back, celebrating the traditions from which he sprang. Ellington's looked at the present in a provocative way that promised a vital future.

In the music of Ellington and other composers and instrumentalists who achieved success in the jazz world of Prohibition New York, we hear little deference to jazz's Southern roots. Their music channeled the city's cosmopolitanism: it's smart, urban, fast moving, glittery, independent, and motivated. In liberating jazz from its roots, the Ellington generation is ready to take on everything the entertainment business and the world can throw at it. This sense of a second youth, of a new start, became a motive in the development of jazz, as each subsequent generation strove to remake it in its own image.

ADDITIONAL LISTENING

George Gershwin / Paul Whiteman	*Rhapsody in Blue* (1927) (Pristine Classical, MP3)
Bert Williams	"Nobody" (1906); *The Early Years: 1901–1909* (Archeophone 5004)
Art Hickman	"Rose Room" (1919); *Art Hickman's Orchestra: The San Francisco Sound*, vol 1 (Archeophone 6003)
Paul Whiteman	"Whispering" (1920); *Paul Whiteman: Greatest Hits* (Collector's Choice)
	"From Monday On" (1928); *Bix Restored*, vol. 2 (Origin Jazz Library BXCD 04-06)
Fletcher Henderson	"Dicty Blues" (1923); *Fletcher Henderson: 1923* (Classics 697)
	"King Porter Stomp" (1928); *Fletcher Henderson* (Columbia/Legacy 074646144725)
James P. Johnson	"Carolina Shout" (1921), "Keep Off the Grass" (1921), "Worried and Lonesome Blues" (1923); *James P. Johnson, 1921–1928* (Classics 658)
	"Charleston" (1924); *Carolina Shout* (Biograph BCD 105)
Duke Ellington	"East St. Louis Toodle-oo" (1926); *Early Ellington: The Complete Brunswick and Vocalion Recordings, 1926-1931* (GRP)
	"Creole Love Call" (1927); *Best of the Duke Ellington Centennial Edition: The Complete RCA Victor Recordings, 1927–1973* (RCA-Victor 63459)

LOUIS ARMSTRONG
hotter than that

LOUIS ARMSTRONG/EARL HINES
weather bird

BIX BEIDERBECKE/FRANK TRUMBAUER
singin' the blues

MOUND CITY BLUE BLOWERS (COLEMAN HAWKINS)
one hour

LOUIS ARMSTRONG AND THE FIRST GREAT SOLOISTS

■ LOUIS ARMSTRONG (1901–1971)

Louis Armstrong is the single most important figure in the development of jazz. His ascension in the 1920s transformed the social music of New Orleans into an art that, in the words of composer Gunther Schuller, "had the potential capacity to compete with the highest order of previously known musical expression," one in which musicians of every geographical and racial background could find their own voice. He remains the only major figure in Western music to influence the music of his era equally as an instrumentalist and a singer. Within a decade, he codified the standards of jazz, and his influence did not stop there. It penetrated every arena of Western music: symphonic trumpet players worked to adapt his bright vibrato, and popular and country performers adapted his phrasing, spontaneity, and natural sound.

Armstrong was also one of the most popular musicians of the twentieth century—the man who, more than anyone else, conveyed the feeling and pleasure of jazz to audiences throughout the world. The matter of his popularity is important, because it had cultural and political ramifications beyond music. Though raised in unimaginable poverty and racial segregation, he was able to present his music in a generous way that exhilarated

Louis Armstrong, described by Bing Crosby as "the beginning and the end of music in America," radiated an energy that seemed to transcend his artistry. Paris, 1960.

wwnorton.com/studyspace

and welcomed new listeners. At a time when jazz was denounced from political and religious pulpits as primitive, unskilled, immoral, and even degenerate, Armstrong used his outsize personality to soothe fears and neutralize dissent. America had never experienced anything like him. He seemed to combine nineteenth-century minstrel humor and a nearly obsequious desire to please with an art so thunderously personal and powerful that audiences of every stripe were drawn to him. By the 1950s, he was accepted as a national "ambassador of good will"—of America's most admirable qualities. For Duke Ellington, he was "the epitome of the kind of American who goes beyond the rules, a truly good and original man."

Primary Innovations

Before Armstrong, jazz was generally perceived as an urban folk music that had more in common with ragtime and military bands than with the driving rhythms we now associate with jazz or swing dance music. It was ensemble music, tailored for social functions ranging from dances to funerals, employing a fixed repertory and a communal aesthetic. Without Armstrong, it would surely have developed great soloists (it had already produced at least one in Sidney Bechet), but its progress as a distinctive art—a way of playing music grounded in improvisation—would have been slower and less decisive. His influence may be measured, in large part, by his innovations in five areas.

BLUES Armstrong emphatically established the blues scale and blues feeling as jazz's harmonic foundation at a time when significant jazz figures, especially those on the Eastern Seaboard, thought the blues might be a mere fashion, like ragtime. In 1924, when he first worked in New York, many jazz composers were under the sway of the arrangers who scored Broadway shows and commercial dance bands. The emotional power of Armstrong's music countered that trend like a powerful tonic.

IMPROVISATION Armstrong established jazz as music that prizes individual expression. His creative spirit proved too mighty for the strictures of the traditional New Orleans ensemble. His records proved that improvised music could have the weight and durability of written music. But his increasing technical finesse always remained bound to his emotional honesty. To compete on Armstrong's level, a musician had to do more than master an instrument; he had to make the instrument an extension of his self.

SINGING As a boy, Armstrong mastered scat-singing—using nonsense syllables instead of words, with the same improvisational brio and expressive candor as an instrumentalist. Until 1926, however, when he recorded "Heebie Jeebies," few people had heard a scat vocal. That recording delighted musicians, who imitated him shamelessly. In effect, he had introduced a true jazz vocal style, dependent on mastery of pitch and time as well as fast reflexes and imagination. He soon proved as agile with written lyrics as with scat phrases. Almost instantly, Armstrong's influence was heard in the work of singers as diverse as Bing Crosby and Billie Holiday.

REPERTORY In the 1930s, New Orleans "purists" argued that jazz musicians should confine themselves to original New Orleans jazz themes, and avoid popular tunes as lacking in authenticity. Yet many traditional jazz pieces had themselves been adapted from pop tunes, hymns, blues, and classical works heard in the South. Armstrong resolved the debate by creating masterworks based on Tin Pan Alley songs. He showed that pop music could broaden jazz's potential both musically and commercially. His ability to recompose melodies was later summed up in the title of a Swing Era hit by the Jimmie Lunceford Orchestra: "'Tain't What You Do (It's the Way That You Do It)" (see Chapter 7).

RHYTHM Perhaps Armstrong's greatest contribution was to teach us to swing. He introduced a new rhythmic energy that would eventually become second nature to people the world over. As the most celebrated Negro artist in Western music history to that point, born just two generations after slavery, he incarnated the promise of a new age in which American music would rival that of Europe and Russia. And he did so in a peculiarly American way, defying conventional notions of art, artistry, and artists: his approach to rhythm exemplified the contagiously joyous, bawdy, accessible, human nature of his music.

Early Years

The miracle of Armstrong's achievement is that it was forged from such bleak beginnings. Unlike his predecessors in the Great Migration, Louis Armstrong, the first major jazz figure born in the twentieth century, did not peak during the Jazz Age (1920s) and then fade away. He helped to spearhead the Swing Era of the 1930s; and although, like most of his generation, he was disconcerted by modern jazz (bebop) and the jazz-blues synthesis (rhythm and blues) that followed, he persevered beyond those developments with increasing success. He scored his last major hit record ("Hello, Dolly!") at the height of the Beatles frenzy in the 1960s.

Armstrong was born, on August 4, 1901, to an unwed teenager (no older than sixteen) and a laborer who abandoned them, in an area of New Orleans

Armstrong, known in childhood by several nicknames, including Little Louis, Dippermouth, and Satchelmouth, sits at the very center of the brass band at the New Orleans Colored Waif's Home, where he was incarcerated in 1913.

Louis first experienced the world beyond Louisiana when he worked in Fate Marable's orchestra on the excursion boat *S.S. Capitol*, 1920: Henry Kimball, bass: Boyd Atkins, violin; Marable, piano; Johnny St. Cyr, banjo; David Jones and Norman Mason, saxophones; Armstrong, cornet; George Brashear, trombone; Baby Dodds, drums. Note the sign warning patrons not to stand "in front of orchestra."

FRANK DRIGGS COLLECTION

so devastated by violence, crime, and prostitution that its residents called it "the Battlefield." Mayann, as he called his mother, was physically fragile but strong-minded, and she instilled in her son a sense of worthiness and stoic pride. Armstrong, a prolific writer all his life, wrote of her in his autobiography *Satchmo: My Life in New Orleans*: "She never envied no one, or anything they may have. I guess I inherited that part of life from Mayann."

At age seven Louis was already working, delivering coal to prostitutes by night and helping with a rag-and-bone cart by day, blowing a tinhorn to announce the cart's arrival. He organized a quartet to sing for pennies on street corners (the Singing Fools), and received his first cornet from the immigrant Jewish family that owned the rag-and-bone business; the first tune he learned to play, he recalled, was "Home, Sweet Home." In the early hours of New Year's Day, 1913, Louis was apprehended for shooting blanks in the air and was sent to the New Orleans Colored Waif's Home for Boys for eighteen months. There, he received rudimentary musical instruction from the home's bandmaster, Peter Davis, who initially refused to work with a boy of Louis's rough background. During his incarceration, as Davis's position softened, Louis progressed from tambourine to bugle to cornet. Ultimately, Davis made him leader of the institution's band. After his discharge, Louis apprenticed with his idol, Joe Oliver, running errands in return for lessons.

RIVERBOAT YEARS Things began to move quickly for Armstrong in 1918, when he married a violently possessive prostitute (the first of his four wives); adopted the son of a young cousin who had been raped by a white man; and worked saloons and parades, often leading his own trio (with bass and drums) in mostly blues numbers. His career began in earnest that same year with two jobs. When Oliver left for Chicago, he suggested that Louis replace him in the band he had co-led with trombonist Kid Ory. A short time later, Louis was recruited to play on Mississippi riverboat excursions. In order to prove himself eighteen and thus legally responsible, he applied for a draft card, backdating his birth to 1900—July 4, 1900, a patriotic date that became famously associated with him, and the only birthday he ever acknowledged.

Armstrong spent three years on riverboats operated by the Streckfus Steamboat Line, working under the leadership of Fate Marable, a stern taskmaster known for his powerful playing of the calliope—a difficult instrument consisting of organ pipes powered by steam from the ship's boiler. Audible from a great distance, the calliope announced a steamboat coming to port. This was a decisive engagement for Louis on several counts: he greatly improved his ability to read a music score; he learned to adapt the expressive music of New Orleans to written arrangements; he absorbed a variety of songs beyond the New Orleans repertory; he saw another part of the world and experienced a different kind of audience (exclusively white, except for the one night a week reserved for black customers); and he grew accustomed to the rigors of traveling from one engagement to another, establishing a lifelong pattern.

With Oliver in Chicago

One restriction, though, galled him: Marable's refusal to let him sing. Partly for that reason, Armstrong quit in September 1921, and returned to Ory's band. During this period, his reputation spread throughout the region. The celebrated New York singer and actress Ethel Waters toured New Orleans with her then little-known pianist, Fletcher Henderson, and attempted to lure him to New York. But Armstrong resolved not to leave his hometown unless Joe Oliver himself sent for him. That summons arrived in August 1922, in the form of a wire inviting him to become a member of Oliver's Creole Jazz Band at Lincoln Gardens, on Chicago's Southside.

In Oliver's band, Armstrong usually played second trumpet, though he occasionally played lead, as on the recording of "Dippermouth Blues." The trumpet breaks he harmonized with Oliver astonished musicians, as did the brilliance of his timbre—evident on the Creole Jazz Band recordings of "Chimes Blues" and "Froggie Moore." In Oliver's pianist, Armstrong found his second wife. Memphis-born Lil Hardin, a product of the middle class, encouraged Louis to leave Oliver and establish himself as a leader. He resisted at first, but in 1924, when Fletcher Henderson, now leading a much-admired orchestra in New York, offered him a seat in the band, he accepted.

With Henderson in New York

Armstrong spent little more than a year in New York, which turned out to be a crucial period for him and for jazz. In a time of strict segregation, Henderson's dance band hired the best black musicians of the day—much as his counterpart and friend Paul Whiteman did with white musicians. Henderson's men, street-smart, well dressed, and self-assured, initially viewed Armstrong as a rube, a newcomer from the country who had made a modest name for himself in Chicago playing in a style that was already deemed old-fashioned. The mockery ceased when they heard him play the trumpet. Armstrong's authority and originality, his profound feeling for the blues, and his irresistible, heart-pounding rhythmic drive affected everyone who heard him.

Armstrong also became a favorite of record producers. Blues divas had become immensely popular after Mamie Smith scored a hit with "Crazy Blues" in 1920 (see Chapter 3), and Armstrong was the accompanist of choice. He recorded with Bessie Smith ("Everything I did with her, I *like*,"

CLARENCE WILLIAMS

The Foremost "Blues" Specialist of the Race

"**B**LUES" lovers of the Race, be thankful for Clarence Williams! This smilin', happy young man has undoubtedly done more for the present wide-spread enjoyment of "blues" music than any other one member of the Race. He is unquestionably the foremost "blues" pianist of the Race. He is widely known as the composer of a great many sensational "blues" hits. He is nationally known as the head and owner of the largest and liveliest colored "blues" music publishing house in America. A leader in practically every branch of "blues" music, he is putting musical happiness and entertainment in your homes.

When OKeh released the first and original Race record, it opened up a new field of endeavor to musically inclined members of the Race. And now, today, OKeh offers the talents of the best known and most popular Race artists in the country. We are especially proud of the fact that Clarence Williams, the foremost "blues" specialist of the Race, records exclusively for OKeh Records.

Clarence Williams, an influential and incredibly prolific music publisher, recording director, composer, and pianist, was billed by OKeh Records as a "Race" man, 1924.

he recalled), Ma Rainey, Sippie Wallace, Bertha Hill, and others. In that same year (1924), he participated with Sidney Bechet in a series of recordings organized by Clarence Williams—Clarence Williams's Blue Five sessions—which combined the breezy entertainment of Southern vaudeville with the sweeping exuberance of a lean New Orleans–style ensemble.

During his fourteen months with Henderson, Armstrong recorded more than three dozen numbers with the band (including an orchestration of Oliver's "Dippermouth Blues" called "Sugar Foot Strut"). With Armstrong on board, the band played with a more prominent beat, while embracing the blues and longer solos. Each of the band's fine musicians sought in his own way to reproduce something of Armstrong's clarion attack, exciting rhythms, and diverse emotions. Every bandleader wanted a soloist in Armstrong's mold, from Paul Whiteman to Duke Ellington.

Armstrong's association with Henderson ended, in part, because of disagreement (again) over one of his talents. Like Louis's boss on the Mississippi riverboat, Henderson would not let him sing—beyond a brief scat break on one record ("Everybody Loves My Baby"). Louis, confident of a vocal ability that everyone else denounced because of his gravelly timbre, angrily returned to Chicago in late 1925.

The Hot Five

Back in Chicago, Armstrong earned his living playing in a pit orchestra that accompanied silent movies, offering overtures and quasi-jazz numbers during intermission. But before the year 1925 was out, OKeh Records invited him to make his first records as a leader. Other than his wife Lil, he surrounded himself with New Orleanians, three musicians he had already worked with: clarinetist Johnny Dodds and banjoist Johnny St. Cyr in Oliver's band, and trombonist Kid Ory in New Orleans. Louis called his band the Hot Five, and unlike Oliver's Creole Jazz Band, it existed only to record.

It would be difficult to overstate the impact of the Hot Five and Hot Seven (the same instrumentation plus tuba and drums) recordings, made between 1925 and 1928—sixty-five titles in all, not including similar sessions in which Armstrong appeared as a **sideman**—that is, a supporting player on recordings that featured vocalists or other bandleaders. Here at last we witness jazz's rapid evolution from a group concept dominated by polyphony to a showcase for soloists and individual expression. The modest embellishments we heard in Oliver and Morton performances give way here to daring improvisations; two- and four-bar breaks are extended to solos of a full chorus or more; and the multiple strains of ragtime are winnowed down to the single-theme choruses of popular song and blues. Each of these elements can be found in other recordings of the day, but the force of Armstrong's creativity and instrumental control—the incredible vitality and spirit—impart the sensation of a great art coming into flower.

"Hotter Than That"

This 1927 Hot Five recording is an illuminating example of the way Armstrong revolutionized the New Orleans tradition. The thirty-two-bar chorus is based on the chords of the main strain of "Tiger Rag," a New Orleans jazz tune, popularized in 1918 by the Original Dixieland Jazz Band, though no one knows who wrote it. An unusual aspect of this performance is the addition of a guest, the pioneer guitarist Lonnie Johnson. Johnson, a native of New Orleans, apprenticed on riverboats and went on to enjoy two dramatically different careers: as one of the first jazz guitar soloists in the 1920s and as a popular blues singer-guitarist of the 1940s and after. His very presence reminds us that long after New Orleans generated jazz, the city also provided sustenance for rhythm and blues and rock and roll.

The banjoist in the Hot Five, Johnny St. Cyr, doesn't play on "Hotter Than That," so that the dialogue between Armstrong and Johnson is emphasized. Armstrong plays the first chorus, which is entirely improvised: there is no written theme to set up the improvisations, only a harmonic underpinning borrowed from "Tiger Rag." The third chorus features one of his most memorable scat-singing vocals. Listen to what follows the mid-chorus break, where Armstrong sings counterrhythms of enormous complexity. Try counting four beats to a measure here, and you may find yourself losing your moorings, because his phrases are in opposition to the ground beat—a technique used by later musicians, such as Miles Davis.

The most influential small band in jazz history, Louis Armstrong and His Hot Five, existed only to make records: Armstrong, trumpet; Johnny St. Cyr, banjo; Johnny Dodds, clarinet and saxophone; Kid Ory, trombone; Lil Hardin Armstrong, piano. Chicago, 1926.

1.21

 **hotter than that**

LOUIS ARMSTRONG AND HIS HOT FIVE

Louis Armstrong, trumpet; Kid Ory, trombone; Johnny Dodds, clarinet; Lil Hardin Armstrong, piano; Lonnie Johnson, guitar

- Label: OKeh 8535; *Louis Armstrong: Portrait of the Artist as a Young Man* (Sony/Legacy 57175)
- Date: 1927
- Style: New Orleans Jazz
- Form: 32-bar popular song (**A B A C**)

What to listen for:
- polyphonic collective improvisation vs. homophonic solos
- Armstrong's soloing and scat-singing
- his intense improvised polyrhythms
- dialogue between voice and guitar

INTRODUCTION

0:00   The band begins with **collective improvisation**, with Armstrong's trumpet clearly in front. The remaining instruments provide support: the trombone plays simple single-note figures, while the clarinet is distantly in the background. The harmonies are those of the last eight bars of the chorus.

CHORUS 1

0:09 **A** Armstrong begins his improvisation. Many of his notes are **ghosted**—played so lightly that they're almost inaudible.

0:18 **B**

0:25   Trumpet **break**.

0:27 **A** Coming out of the break, Armstrong places accents on the **backbeat**, before finishing with a quick **triplet** figure.

0:36 **C** Armstrong emphasizes a high note with a **shake**—an extra vibrato at the end.

0:43   During a two-measure break, Dodds begins his clarinet solo.

CHORUS 2

0:45 **A** Dodds plays his solo in the clarinet's upper register. Beneath him, Hardin plays rhythmic piano fills.

0:54 **B**

1:02   Dodds's clarinet break ends on a **blue note**.

1:03 **A**

1:12 **C**

1:19   A scat-singing break introduces the next solo, by Armstrong.

CHORUS 3

1:21 **A** Armstrong begins his solo by singing on-the-beat quarter notes, backed by the guitar's bluesy improvised lines. The timbre of his voice is rough but pleasant.

1:30 **B** As his melodic ideas take flight, he stretches the beat in unpredictable ways.

1:36   Scat-singing break.

1:39 **A** Armstrong ingeniously uses melody, rhythm, and scat syllables to create a strong sense of polyrhythm.

1:47 **C**

INTERLUDE

1:55   In a loose extension of the previous chorus, Armstrong exchanges intimate, bluesy moans with Johnson's guitar.

2:13   Hardin on piano calls the band together with four bars of **octaves**.

CHORUS 4

2:17	**A**	Ory takes a sharply accented trombone solo, which echoes the beginning of Armstrong's scat solo.
2:26	**B**	
2:33		Trumpet break: Armstrong interrupts Ory's solo with a rocket-like string of quick notes, ending with a high B♭.
2:35	**A**	Collective improvisation, with Armstrong hitting his high note again and again in a short, syncopated riff.
2:43	**C**	The last eight bars are in **stop-time**: Armstrong generates tension by playing unpredictable short lines.

CODA

2:50	Johnson and Armstrong exchange brief solos.
2:56	Johnson's line ends on a dissonant **diminished-seventh chord**, which leaves the harmony suspended.

■ ENTER EARL HINES (1903–1983)

In 1926, Armstrong was hired as featured soloist with the Carroll Dickerson Orchestra, at the Sunset Café in Chicago. For the first time, his name was up in lights, as "the world's greatest trumpet player." Young white musicians, including Bing Crosby, cornetist Bix Beiderbecke, and clarinetist Benny Goodman, flocked to hear him. Throughout that year and the next, Armstrong produced such benchmark recordings as "Potato Head Blues," "Wild Man Blues," "Willie the Weeper" (famous for its climax propelled by the drums of Baby Dodds), and "Struttin' with Some Barbecue." But something just as special was also developing at the Sunset. While on tour earlier, Dickerson had recruited a young pianist from Pittsburgh, Earl Hines, an utterly original stylist who subverted the techniques on which other jazz pianists relied.

Earl Hines earned the nickname Fatha for the originality of his piano style, making him an ideal partner for Armstrong. Chicago, 1926.

Hines was content neither to play on-the-beat background chords, in the manner of Lil Armstrong, nor to confine himself to the propulsive rhythms of stride or boogie-woogie (a Midwestern phenomenon in which the pianist's left hand plays eight beats to every bar; see Chapter 8). He preferred to combine those approaches, with the result that his idiosyncratic style seemed to play games with the rhythm. Above all, he was determined to use the piano much as Armstrong used the trumpet, as a solo instrument improvising single-note melodies. To make them audible, he developed an ability to improvise in octaves (instead of hitting an A, he hit two As an octave apart) and **tremolos** (the speedy alternation of two or more notes, creating a pianistic version of the brass man's vibrato).

Hines and Armstrong hit it off immediately. As Hines recalled, "I was amazed to find a trumpeter like Louis who was playing everything that I was trying to do on the piano. So, there were the two of us expressing the same spirit." For the 1928 Hot Five recordings, Armstrong changed the personnel to employ the younger musicians he worked with in Dickerson's band at the Sunset Café and New York's Savoy Ballroom. (The Savoy posters advertised: "SPECIAL ATTRACTION. THE GREAT LOUIS ARMSTRONG IN PER-SON!" To capitalize on his success in New York, many of the 1928 recordings were released as Louis Armstrong and His Savoy Ballroom Five.) On occasion, he recruited guests—notably Fletcher Henderson's arranger and saxophonist, Don Redman.

The new recordings, regarded as an advance on their sensational predecessors, included the seminal "West End Blues," "Basin Street Blues," "St. James Infirmary," and "Tight Like That." With these records, the polyphonic New Orleans ensemble all but disappeared, replaced by the mixture of solos and homophonic section work that continues to dominate jazz today. The best example of the interplay between Armstrong and Hines came about at the end of one of the sessions, when the ensemble had finished for the day. The two men improvised a duet on an old Armstrong rag they had played in concert, "Weather Bird." Worried that fans of the Hot Five would object, the record company did not release it until 1930.

"Weather Bird"

"Weather Bird" has a dizzying stop-and-go momentum, punched up with humor, competitive daring, and an unanticipated beauty. Armstrong wrote "Weather Bird" for King Oliver and recorded it with him in 1923. Unlike his other compositions, it uses the traditional ragtime structure of three sixteen-bar strains. On Oliver's record, the piece is played as a ragtime march, with a stop-time section and brief breaks (including one by the twin trumpets); there is no sustained improvisation.

Armstrong and Hines follow the same format, but turn the piece into a friendly battle, packed with broken rhythms, shifty jabs and feints, until the grand finale: a sixteen-bar coda, during which they exchange phrases with a mocking "where-are-we-going-with-this" wariness, resolved by Armstrong's exquisitely timed ascending scale, cradled by Hines's concluding chords.

LISTENING GUIDE

1.22

weather bird

LOUIS ARMSTRONG AND EARL HINES

Louis Armstrong, trumpet; Earl Hines, piano

- Label: OKeh 41454; *Louis Armstrong: Portrait of the Artist as a Young Man* (Sony/Legacy 57175)
- Date: 1928
- Style: early jazz
- Form: march/ragtime

What to listen for:

- improvised call and response between trumpet and piano
- great soloists pushing each other to their limits
- cadence figure at the end of each strain
- unpredictable rhythms
- exchange between soloists in the coda, figuring out how to end the piece

INTRODUCTION

0:00   Armstrong plays the opening melody on trumpet, discreetly backed by Hines's piano.

STRAIN A

0:04   Armstrong displays his command of **dynamics**. Some notes are played at full volume; others (**ghosted**) are so soft that they virtually disappear. Underneath him, Hines plays surprising syncopations, undermining the steady rhythm: he has no intention of playing the well-behaved accompanist. His style is not ragtime or stride, but a more idiosyncratic mixture.

0:13   The strain comes to rest on a **half cadence**.

0:18   The harmonies begin a drive to a **full cadence**. (We will call this passage, already heard in the introduction, the *cadence figure*.)

STRAIN B

0:23   A new strain, marked by a striking melodic phrase. Armstrong primarily sticks to the original tune, leaving room for Hines to improvise.

0:28   Armstrong plays a static ragtime polyrhythm, against which Hines adds his own melodies and rhythms.

0:33   At times, they seem to read each other's minds: Armstrong plays a short phrase that Hines instantly echoes; a few seconds later, when Armstrong briefly rests, Hines pounces in with a dramatic flourish.

0:39   Armstrong ends his line with the last few notes of the *cadence figure*.

STRAIN B

0:41   Hines begins to solo in **stride** piano style.

0:49   At the place where a break would normally occur in early jazz, he suddenly shifts to a new pianistic texture. For the next several measures, his playing is highly polyrhythmic and unpredictable.

0:56   As the strain ends, he returns to a more normal texture, clearly playing the *cadence figure*.

STRAIN A

1:00   Armstrong repeats the melody for strain **A**, embellishing it, and then abandoning it for outright improvisation.

1:07   He begins a phrase with a vivid high note and a flurry of eighth notes.

1:14   He returns to the *cadence figure*.

INTERLUDE

1:18   A transitional passage: Armstrong and Hines begin with simple syncopated figures, but rapidly increase the rhythmic intensity to unnerving levels.

STRAIN C (TRIO)

1:23   Unusually, the trio doesn't modulate: it's in the same key as the first two strains. Hines plays a piano solo.

1:32   Hines pushes his improvisation so far that it outraces even his own abilities: we can occasionally hear mistakes.

1:37   At the end of the strain, he dissolves tension by returning to a variation of the *cadence figure*.

STRAIN C

1:41   The strain begins with a **break** for Armstrong.

1:44   The two men test each other's mettle, phrasing both *on* and *off* the beat, in a kind of **call-and-response** match.

1:51   During a break, Armstrong ascends to a new high note.

1:58   He returns to the *cadence figure*.

STRAIN C

2:00   The call-and-response roles are reversed: Hines begins with a break, Armstrong responding.

| 2:10 | During an oddly impromptu break, Hines plays a disorienting rhythm ending on an aggressively **dissonant** note, resolved—at the last second—with a **consonance**. |
| 2:14 | Armstrong plays the *cadence figure* with an interesting rhythmic twist. |

CODA

2:18	Once again, Armstrong begins with a break.
2:20	Hines responds with dissonant harmonies, suggesting that he wishes to end the piece.
2:22	Armstrong answers, matching the dissonance in his melodic line.
2:25	Hines moves toward a final cadence. The exchanges become shorter, as the two musicians try to figure out where to go.
2:32	Suddenly, Armstrong begins a new phrase, ascending slowly but with steady acceleration, virtually eliminating all previous sense of meter.
2:36	In response to Armstrong's high note, Hines adds the concluding harmonies.

THE ARMSTRONG IMPACT: A GENERATION OF SOLOISTS

Before Armstrong came along, most jazz groups reflected primarily the concepts of their leaders (Jelly Roll Morton and King Oliver) or took an ensemble approach (Original Dixieland Jazz Band). Armstrong's brilliance as a soloist blew the old polyphonic ensemble apart, inspiring countless young musicians to study jazz as a new kind of musical expression that allowed a relatively unfettered improvisational freedom.

Armstrong seemed to be offering jazz as a gift to anyone who could feel and master it, of any region or race. By the end of the 1920s, the fad of naming jazz bands after New Orleans had virtually disappeared. And the arrival, in those same years, of gifted and original white musicians underscored the reality that jazz had the potential to become an idiom of universal acceptance. Armstrong put it this way: "Jazz is only what you are."

We have seen, in Earl Hines, the example of an outstanding musician whose thinking correlated with that of Armstrong, who adapted a "trumpet-style" attack to the piano. By 1929, dozens of forceful musical personalities, some of them older and more experienced than Armstrong, were following suit. They forged a music in which the soloist emerged as prince of the realm—in which the best composers were, in part, those who made the most creative use of those soloists. Two examples of the great early soloists were Bix Beiderbecke and Coleman Hawkins.

■ BIX BEIDERBECKE (1903–1931)

Leon Beiderbecke, known throughout his life as Bix (a corruption of his middle name, Bismark), was born in Davenport, Iowa. His mother played church organ and encouraged her son to pick out melodies on the family piano. Bix took a few lessons but relied chiefly on his exceptional musical ear. The piano influenced his harmonic thinking as he started on cornet (here, he was entirely self-taught), and he never abandoned it: he auditioned for the musicians' union as a pianist and composed his most ambitious music for piano, specifically four short pieces that have been much adapted and orchestrated.

Beiderbecke belonged to the first generation of musicians who learned about jazz from recordings. This kind of introduction had an immediate threefold influence. First, young people were exposed to jazz without having to live in a particular area or sneak into off-limits places (saloons) where it was performed. Second, owning recordings encouraged, through repeated plays, study and memorization. Third, records freed the imagination of young listeners to interpret jazz as they pleased, without the constricting influence of tradition. In the era before network radio (before 1926), the recording of a New Orleans jazz ensemble brought a distant world into many non-Southern towns, including the stolid German-American community of Davenport.

Bix was fourteen when the Original Dixieland Jazz Band issued its first records, and they affected him deeply—much to the vexation of his parents, whose abhorrence of jazz and Beiderbecke's association with it never abated. He taught himself cornet by mimicking and harmonizing with recorded music. Live jazz played by Southern black musicians also came his way, thanks to the Streckfus steamers that regularly docked at Davenport, one of the northernmost ports on the Mississippi River. He may well have heard Armstrong at one of the riverboat musicians' jam sessions.

Bix Beiderbecke, seen here in 1923, was the first major white jazz star and the first to acquire a mythological aura after his early death.

While Bix was haunting jazz clubs, he neglected his schoolwork and even suffered a humiliating run-in with the police. As a result, in 1921 his parents sent him to Lake Forrest Academy in Illinois, a move that Bix experienced with anguish as an exile from his family, but one that put him within train-hopping distance of Chicago. Soon he was making regular visits to Lincoln Gardens and other Chicago nightclubs, soaking up the music of King Oliver, Louis Armstrong, the New Orleans Rhythm Kings, and others. More truancies led to his expulsion from Lake Forrest, and in 1923 he joined the Wolverines—the first band of Northern whites formed in imitation of New Orleans ensembles. A year later, they recorded for Gennett; their thirteen numbers, often awkwardly played, would be forgotten today except for the clarity and supple drive of Beiderbecke's cornet, which suggests at times a highly individual, almost detached temper.

Chicago Style

Late in 1924, Beiderbecke also recorded with the Sioux City Six, alongside C-melody saxophonist Frank Trumbauer (1901–1956)—the beginning of a lifelong association. The C-melody saxophone enjoyed popularity in the early years of the twentieth century because of its strong supple sound—suggesting a cross between an alto and a tenor—and because it's in the key of C, the same as the piano. It never made much headway in jazz; Trumbauer was its only important exponent. In the 1920s, he presided over the most admired white small-group jazz records of the day, and his sweet-without-being-corny timbre, lyricism, phrasing, and songlike use of smears and glides (or *portamentos*) introduced a delicacy to the jazz saxophone that made an indelible impression on several major black saxophonists, most notably Lester Young and Benny Carter.

Frank Trumbauer

Beiderbecke and Trumbauer became the figureheads for a generation of white jazz musicians (almost all born between 1904 and 1909) often referred

Austin High Gang

to as the Austin High Gang, after those who had attended Chicago's Austin High School: pianist Joe Sullivan, drummer Dave Tough, tenor saxophonist Bud Freeman, cornetist Jimmy McPartland, and clarinetist Frank Teschemacher. Their associates, white musicians who had either grown up in Chicago or, like Beiderbecke, gravitated there from other points in the Midwest, included clarinetists Benny Goodman, Pee Wee Russell, and Don Murray, guitarist Eddie Condon, bass saxophonist Adrian Rollini, drummer Gene Krupa, and singer Red McKenzie. Collectively, they created the **Chicago style**, which began by imitating New Orleans bands and evolved into a more slapdash, aggressively rhythmic school that combined expansive solos with polyphonic theme statements.

While some black musicians came from homes where the saxophone was considered "the devil's instrument" and the blues decried as vulgar, the majority were committed professionals, devoted to perfecting their art and honing their careers. The neighborhoods in which they flourished (New Orleans, Chicago's Southside, and New York's Harlem) gave them little reason to think of themselves as youthful rebels. But for white musicians of Bix's generation to align themselves with African Americans and their music was a daring act, almost a gauntlet thrown down to their disapproving parents. As Eddie Condon, the most verbal and obstinate proponent of the Chicago school (sometimes referred to as Condon style jazz) boasted, they were out to rile "the Republicans." He proudly recalled of an early performance: "One of the ladies told me it was just like having the Indians in town again."

Beiderbecke's flamelike career, cut short at twenty-eight from the effects of alcoholism, strengthened their rebellious conviction, despite the financial security Bix had achieved in his last years as featured soloist in Paul Whiteman's orchestra (see "Changes" in Chapter 5). Largely unknown to the public during his life, his gentle genius accrued in death the lineaments of martyrdom.

Bix recorded between 1924 and 1930, and the high-water mark of his legacy is a series of sessions made in 1927 with Trumbauer (they were initially released as Frankie Trumbauer & His Orchestra) and the influential, innovative guitarist Eddie Lang. "Singin' the Blues," one of the most imitated records of all time, is generally considered their masterpiece.

◉ "Singin' the Blues"

Three things to keep in mind while listening to this recording: (1) the source material is a popular song, introduced in 1920; (2) the song is never actually played as written except in the eight-bar ensemble passage following the cornet solo; (3) the tempo and feeling of the performance are indicative of a ballad. These aspects were considered novel in 1927, when jazz musicians rarely drew on Tin Pan Alley songs, when improvisers embellished the written melody instead of displacing it with original variations, and when contemplative tempos were usually reserved for the blues.

This performance is dominated by full-chorus solos by Trumbauer and Beiderbecke, accompanied by Eddie Lang, whose firm second- and fourth-beat accents and fluid, responsive arpeggios give it much of its propulsion and charm. Trumbauer's virtues are beautifully displayed in this, his most famous solo. Beiderbecke's performance is even more celebrated. We can immediately feel the quality of his playing that so startled his contemporaries. Jazz is a music of individuality and, therefore, of sensibility. Beiderbecke introduced

arpeggio chord in which each note is played one at a time

a new sensibility, quite different from the extroverted Armstrong. There is a shy politeness to Bix's playing, as he rings each note with the precision of a percussionist hitting chimes. He plots his variations with great care—as Lang does his accompaniment, playing with greater harmonic daring to match Bix's melodies.

🎧 singin' the blues

1.23

FRANKIE TRUMBAUER AND HIS ORCHESTRA
Frankie Trumbauer, C-melody saxophone; Bix Beiderbecke, cornet; Bill Rank, trombone; Jimmy Dorsey, clarinet; Doc Ryker, alto saxophone; Paul Mertz, piano; Eddie Lang, guitar; Chauncey Morehouse, drums

- Label: OKeh 40772; *Bix Beiderbecke,* vol. 1: *Singin' the Blues* (Sony/BMG 723808)
- Date: 1927
- Style: Chicago-style jazz
- Form: 32-bar popular song (**A B A' C**)

What to listen for:
- chorus 1: Trumbauer's fluid solo on C-melody saxophone, answered by Lang's inventive guitar
- chorus 2: Beiderbecke's introverted, delicate cornet solo
- Chicago-style collective improvisation and solos

INTRODUCTION

0:00   In a passage arranged by Bill Challis, the horns enter in **block-chord** texture, accompanied by fills on the cymbals.

CHORUS 1

0:07 **A**   Trumbauer begins his solo on C-melody saxophone, swooping up to his first note, accompanied by Lang on guitar (with the pianist distantly in the background).

0:16   Lang's accompaniment occasionally provides improvised **countermelodies**.

0:21 **B**   Trumbauer's high note is preceded by a lengthy scooped entrance.

0:31   A two-measure **break** features Trumbauer's subtle phrases. The break ends with guitar chords and a cymbal crash.

0:35 **A'**

0:41   A passage by Trumbauer in rapid triplets is neatly extended by Lang's guitar.

0:49 **C**

0:59   Trumbauer's concluding break is fast and unpredictable.

CHORUS 2

1:03 **A**   Beiderbecke enters on cornet. He plays with a cool, introverted feeling, pulling back in volume at the end of each phrase.

1:17 **B**   His melody features the hint of a **blue note**.

1:28   On his break, Beiderbecke improvises a fast passage that ends with delicately played repeated notes.

1:31 **A'**   He suddenly erupts into a dramatic upward rip. This heated emotion quickly subsides, as if he were letting off a bit of steam.

1:46 **C**

1:52   To bring his solo to a close, he hints at bluesy playing.

CHORUS 3

2:00 **A**   The band states the original melody of the song, disguised by a mild version of New Orleans polyphony. The drummer adds accents on the cymbals.

2:15 **B**   Dorsey's clarinet solo loosely suggests Beiderbecke's restrained style.

2:26		Dorsey's break ends almost in a whisper.
2:29	**A'**	The band returns with collective improvisation, with Beiderbecke's cornet on top.
2:44	**C**	
2:46		A one-measure break features Lang playing a rapid upward **arpeggio** on guitar.
2:51		Beiderbecke begins his last line with another aggressive rip, followed by short riffs on a repeated note.
2:58		A cymbal stroke brings the piece to a close.

FRANK DRIGGS COLLECTION

Coleman Hawkins, shown here in 1949, was known for his powerful timbre and rhapsodic improvisational style. He established the tenor saxophone as the most iconic instrument in jazz.

The two long solos on "Singin' the Blues" instantly entered the lexicon of jazz, and have since been endlessly studied and imitated. Fletcher Henderson recorded a version in which his reed saxophone section played the Trumbauer solo and cornetist Rex Stewart played Bix's improvisation, as though they were composed pieces of music, which in this instance they were (by virtue of being transcribed and played from a written score). These solos are also believed to be the first to which lyrics were written (a process known as "vocalese" when it became popular in the 1950s). In 1935, Marion Harris made a very fine recording singing both Beiderbecke and Trumbauer.

■ COLEMAN HAWKINS (1904–1969)

In contrast with Beiderbecke's meteoric career, Coleman Hawkins's spanned five decades of jazz history, at the end of which he had become one of its universally admired patriarchs. We will encounter him later, as we explore the 1930s and 1940s.

Hawkins, born in St. Joseph, Missouri, began learning piano at age five from his mother, a teacher and organist. He also studied cello, and added the C-melody saxophone at nine; as a teenager, he played both instruments professionally at Kansas City dances. In 1922, Hawkins joined with Mamie Smith and Her Jazzhounds; that summer he also took up the tenor saxophone. Touring with Smith, he traveled from Kansas City to Chicago and eventually to both coasts, electing to stay in New York to freelance with top musicians, including ragtime clarinetist Wilbur Sweatman. When Fletcher Henderson heard Hawkins with Sweatman's band, he engaged him for a record session and then for a spot in his new orchestra. Hawkins stayed with Henderson for eleven years, establishing himself as the leading figure on tenor saxophone.

From the beginning, he demonstrated tremendous authority, bringing to the saxophone qualities more often associated with the cello: wide vibrato, dynamics, and a huge sound. What he lacked in swing, blues sensibility, and emotional clarity became clear to him when Henderson hired Louis Armstrong in 1924. Like everyone else in the band, Hawkins was stunned by the power of Armstrong's music. During the next few years, he strove to adapt Armstrong's style to the tenor saxophone. An early indication of his increasing maturity was an explosive solo on Henderson's 1926 record "Stampede," a great success among musicians and often cited by the next generation of tenor saxophonists as a decisive influence on their education.

Hawkins's masterpiece, "Body and Soul" (1939), has been called the greatest of all jazz solos (we will hear it in Chapter 9), but it was a decade in the making. The performance we examine here, "One Hour," was a benchmark in that process. Up to this point (1929), Hawkins's playing had conspicuously lacked a **legato**, or smooth attack. His phrasing had consisted of clearly articulated notes, even at very fast tempos. An essential component of swing was missing: relaxation. Nor was there any romance in his music. Playing more legato meant learning how to soften the gruff edges of his timbre and move from one note to another with a fluid, more gracefully expressive manner. In "One Hour," Hawkins accomplished this, and unveiled a radically new approach to the tenor saxophone—one that transcended the smooth melodicism of Trumbauer with nearly rapturous power.

⊚ "One Hour"

"One Hour" was recorded at an integrated session—a circumstance that in 1929 was very infrequent in recordings and unheard-of in live performance. Hawkins and bassist Pops Foster are the black musicians in a white band led by Red McKenzie, who created studio groups under the rubric Mound City Blue Blowers. Except for trombonist-arranger Glenn Miller, all the white musicians were closely identified with the Chicago style, though you wouldn't know it from this performance.

The piece consists of a series of improvised variations on the popular song "If I Could Be with You One Hour Tonight," composed by James P. Johnson (whom we encountered in Chapter 5), with lyrics by Henry Creamer. The song was published in 1926, but did not become a hit until 1930, when Louis Armstrong, pop singer Ruth Etting, and McKinney's Cotton Pickers (a popular big band arranged by Don Redman) each recorded it—the latter achieving a No. 1 hit. In other words, when "One Hour" was made, few people had ever heard the actual melody on which it is based.

The structure is that of a sixteen-bar song, following the **A B A C** format; each segment is four bars rather than the usual eight. Unlike the original song, however, this version adds two measures to each **C** section, in what amounts to a soloist's coda, extending each chorus to eighteen measures. The first chorus, by leader Red McKenzie, has a dated, pleading quality, very much of its time, emphasized by the raspy sound of his instrument, the pocket comb (wrapped in tissue to simulate a kazoo).

But the spotlight belongs to Coleman Hawkins, who plays with a romantic expressiveness new to jazz. Hawkins's style is strongly influenced by Louis Armstrong: we can easily imagine the trumpeter playing many of Hawkins's phrases, though not with his rhapsodic attack. Perhaps the most obvious aspect of his improvisation is the calm authority with which it is played. He has everything under control: a richly virile timbre; superb intonation; rhythmic, melodic, and harmonic variety underscored by his use of long, expressive phrases. Hawkins carries the listener along with force, logic, and character.

Pee Wee Russell, a highly original clarinetist who strenuously resisted being stereotyped as a Chicago-style musician, follows with a gripping solo. The Armstrong influence is especially clear in Russell's clipped percussive notes at the beginning, each carefully articulated and colored while providing affecting contrast to Hawkins's lavish melodies. Finally, Glenn Miller's comparatively conventional and restrained trombone solo offers, in turn, a sharp contrast to Hawkins's romanticism and Russell's idiosyncratic ideas.

LISTENING GUIDE

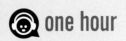 **one hour**

1.24

**MOUND CITY BLUE BLOWERS
(WITH COLEMAN HAWKINS)**
Red McKenzie, pocket comb; Coleman Hawkins,
tenor saxophone; Glenn Miller, trombone; Pee Wee
Russell, clarinet; Eddie Condon, banjo; Jack Bland,
guitar; Pops Foster, bass; Gene Krupa, drums
- Label: Victor V-38100; *Mound City Blue Blowers
  Hot Comb & Tin Can* (Vintage 0151)
- Date: 1929
- Style: early jazz
- Form: 18-bar popular song (**A B A C,** with two bars
  added to the **C** section)

....
What to listen for:
- romantic expressiveness of Hawkins's tenor
  saxophone
- supporting solos by McKenzie, Russell, and
  Miller
- blue notes and timbre variation in Russell's
  clarinet solo
- collective improvisation at the end
....

INTRODUCTION (6 bars)

0:00		Hawkins begins on his own, the band quickly entering to support him. His playing is rhapsodic and rhythmically unpredictable.

CHORUS 1

0:17	**A**	McKenzie enters playing the pocket comb. His melodies feature sweeping bluesy phrases with **variable intonation**, a wide **vibrato**, and throaty timbre. Behind him, the horns play simple chords, outlining the song's harmonic progression.
0:22		The bass enters, adding a firmer rhythmic foundation. McKenzie plays a kind of **melodic paraphrase**, coming close to the original tune without quite stating it.
0:28	**B**	
0:39	**A**	
0:50	**C**	
1:04		Hawkins enters a bar early, on a repeated note.

CHORUS 2

1:06	**A**	Hawkins begins with a pair of gently matched phrases, fitting the original melody's mood but with notes of his own.
1:16	**B**	Hawkins imitates Armstrong's style by hardening his tone to play more vigorous **double-time** figures.
1:27	**A**	
1:32		He returns to a more rhapsodic rhythmic style.
1:37	**C**	Once again, he hardens his tone, aiming for a climax on his highest note.

CHORUS 3

1:53	**A**	Russell begins his clarinet solo. His first phrase is slow and tentative, but gains intensity when it reaches a **blue note**.
2:03	**B**	
2:13	**A**	
2:16		He colors certain notes with a distinctive growl.
2:24	**C**	
2:29		Russell's solo concludes with a series of blue notes.

CHORUS 4

2:40	**A**	Miller takes a trombone solo. His playing is simple, building on the mood of Russell's solo but gradually becoming more lyrical.
2:50	**B**	
3:01	**A**	
3:11	**C**	As the piece nears the end, all the musicians enter in **collective improvisation**.

SATCHMO'S WORLD

Louis Armstrong's Chicago recordings, made in the late 1920s, emancipated jazz from the conventions of an inherited, ritualized tradition, and paved the way for a new music. His records sold well by the standards of "race" labels, distributed to targeted urban communities, but caused barely a ripple in comparison with the popular white musicians of the day—such as Paul Whiteman and singers Al Jolson and Gene Austin. Musicians, however, eagerly awaited every new Armstrong release, and his reputation in jazz circles grew with each one. This equation was reversed in the 1930s: as the mainstream audience discovered him, Armstrong became one of the world's most successful recording artists, while musicians looked to younger players for new directions.

To World War II

After the last of the Hot Five sessions in 1928, Armstrong went on the road with Carroll Dickerson, performing in Detroit and at Harlem's Savoy Ballroom. His next record date, in March 1929, was a double milestone. It included the first integrated jazz ensemble that was generally acknowledged as such: the band released only one track—an impromptu blues, "Knockin' a Jug"—but its personnel (three blacks, three whites) symbolized the fact that jazz had crossed the racial divide and had produced a new crop of musicians who had the technical and creative abilities to function as soloists. The three white participants, as we will see, would each enjoy important careers: guitarist Eddie Lang (featured in "Singin' the Blues"), trombonist Jack Teagarden, and pianist Joe Sullivan.

At the same recording session, Armstrong **fronted** (a front man is the nominal star of a band, but not really its leader or music director) a completely different integrated, ten-piece orchestra, under the musical direction of Luis Russell, a Panamanian-born pianist, arranger, and bandleader who as a teenager had won a $3,000 lottery and used the prize to move to New Orleans. This band not only mingled black and white, but also encompassed a broad geographical sweep, with musicians from South America, New Orleans, Georgia, Alabama, Indiana, and Boston. They were not chosen for that reason, nor were their diverse backgrounds widely known. But for those paying attention, the lesson was clear: jazz had a global, pan-racial future. The orchestra recorded two numbers that day: a traditional New Orleans anthem, "Mahogany Hall Stomp," on which Armstrong improvised a very untraditional three-chorus solo; and "I Can't Give You Anything but Love," a New York show tune by the team of Jimmy McHugh and Dorothy Fields. This was the record that proved how effective a singer Armstrong could be with pop material and how completely he could reinvent it as jazz.

Luis Russell

There was no stopping him now. Weeks later, in July 1929, he achieved a major hit with Fats Waller's song "Ain't Misbehavin'," which he performed that summer on Broadway in more than 200 performances of the revue *Hot Chocolates*. Also that July, he recorded another Waller song, "(What Did I Do to Be So) Black and Blue," altering it in his interpretation from a torch song to a statement of social protest. During the next few years (1930–33), Armstrong recorded every kind of song, from "St. Louis Blues" and "Tiger Rag" to "Star Dust" and "Song of the Islands." New York celebrities feted him with a banquet, while younger musicians and fans, black and white, imitated everything he did. The clarinetist Mezz Mezzrow recalled people copying his trademark white handkerchiefs, his slouch, his slang, his growl, and his fondness for marijuana: "All the raggedy kids, especially those who became vipers [pot smokers], were so inspired with self-respect after digging how neat and natty Louis was, they started to dress up real good."

Europe/films After long engagements in Los Angeles, New York, and Chicago and tours that took in most of the Midwest and Northeast, Armstrong sailed for Europe in 1932, triumphing in London and Paris. The reviewers were ecstatic. One British journalist mispronounced one of Louis's nicknames (Satchelmouth) as "Satchmo," and the name stuck for good. He returned to Europe to even greater acclaim in 1933 and 1934—thousands greeted him at the train station in Copenhagen. By this time, he had begun to star in short films. The films invariably employed demeaning stereotypes, but Armstrong transcended them, virtually winking at the audience. He became a hero in the black community—a great artist who subverted the clichés of minstrelsy.

The years 1935 and 1936 found Armstrong taking the steps that allowed him to conquer the American mainstream audience. The Swing Era had been launched, and the whole country wanted to dance to big-band jazz. Armstrong signed a long-term contract to front Luis Russell's Orchestra, in effect making it his own. He took on a powerful manager, Joe Glaser, whose control of Louis's career began with a lucrative Decca Records contract that lasted nearly twenty years. Armstrong published his first (heavily ghostwritten) autobiography, *Swing That Music*, and received star billing for a cameo appearance in a Bing Crosby movie, *Pennies from Heaven*. He released dozens of hit records, appeared in other movies, and became the first black performer to host a nationally sponsored radio show.

In this period (the mid-1930s), Armstrong's voice developed into a surprisingly mellow tenor, and he was widely acclaimed as one of the great singers in jazz or popular music. His trumpet playing achieved an astonishing brilliance, famous for intricate high-note flourishes and melody statements that imparted unsuspected depths to familiar songs. Among his great big-band recordings are a glittering remake of "Struttin' with Some Barbecue," "Swing That Music," "Jubilee," "Love Walked In," "Ev'ntide," "I Double Dare You," and "Skeleton in the Closet." There was no place to go but down.

After fronting a big band for more than fifteen years, Louis Armstrong returned to a small group with his aptly named All Stars: Sidney Catlett, drums; Barney Bigard, clarinet; Armstrong, trumpet; Earl Hines, piano; Jack Teagarden, trombone; and Arvell Shaw, bass, at the Blue Note in Chicago, 1948.

FRANK DRIGGS COLLECTION

The All Stars

Things began to sour during World War II (1939–45). Tastes were changing, and some thought that Armstrong's orchestra had lost its spark—that he was bored and simply going through the motions. The younger audience had discovered rhythm and blues, and many forward-looking musicians were entranced by new jazz styles, later known as bebop or cool jazz, and shunned the good-natured, old-fashioned show business presentation Armstrong had come to represent. His career was in a slump when, in 1946, he appeared in a Hollywood travesty, *New*

Orleans (he later observed, "The things those Hollywood people make us do are always a sham"), which had the beneficial result of encouraging him to return to a small-band format for the first time in seventeen years. Then triumphs at New York's Carnegie Hall and Town Hall in 1947 led to the formation of an integrated sextet billed as Louis Armstrong and His All Stars, the unit he would lead for the rest of his life.

In its early years, the All Stars really *were* stars, including his old friend trombonist Jack Teagarden, clarinetist Barney Bigard (formerly of Duke Ellington's Orchestra), drummer Sid Catlett (an audience favorite who had played in the big bands of Fletcher Henderson, Benny Goodman, and others), and his old partner Earl Hines. Armstrong continued to make movies and hit records throughout the 1950s, regularly appearing on television, traveling constantly, and earning his reputation as America's ambassador of good will. In the latter part of that decade, however, he found himself at the center of a political storm.

© HERB SNITZER

The public rarely saw the private side of Armstrong, shown here at rest during a road tour in 1960. Note the Star of David, a gift from the Jewish family who befriended him as a small boy (the owners of the rag-and-bone business), and the skin graft on his upper lip, necessitated by his flair for high notes. The cigarette is just that—not his favorite natural herb, which he also smoked daily.

Africa and Arkansas

In 1956, CBS News arranged for Armstrong to visit Africa as part of a documentary film it was preparing about him. When he arrived in Accra, in Ghana, thousands stormed the tarmac to see him. After lunching one day with Prime Minister Kwame Nkrumah, an old fan of his, Nkrumah escorted him to the stadium, where he performed for an audience of 100,000; CBS cameras captured Nkrumah in tears as Armstrong sang "(What Did I Do to Be So) Black and Blue." The experience was no less emotional for Armstrong, who remarked, "After all, my ancestors came from here and I still have African blood in me." Inspired by Ghana's independence, he faced a quandary on his return home: how to deal with the fight for civil rights in his own country. Armstrong insisted on touring the South with an integrated band or not at all, even when the audiences were segregated (with blacks in the balcony). Early in 1957, racists dynamited one such concert in Knoxville, Tennessee. Armstrong managed to avert panic by reassuring the audience, "That's all right folks, it's just the phone."

His humor failed him that September, though, when Arkansas governor Orval Faubus ordered the National Guard to block the admission of black students to Little Rock's Central High School. "The way they are treating my people in the South, the government can go to hell," he told a reporter. Meanwhile, the U.S. government, determined to capitalize on Armstrong's African success, planned to send him to the Soviet Union as part of the 1950s cultural exchange program. But Armstrong balked: "The people over there ask me what's wrong with my country, what am I supposed to say?" When President Eisenhower called in federal troops to Arkansas, Armstrong sent him a supportive telegram. The FBI investigated him, and even black entertainers criticized him for speaking out.

At the same time, black spokesmen characterized him as an Uncle Tom, confusing his persona as an entertainer with minstrel stereotypes. His demeanor ("aggressively happy," in writer Truman Capote's words) made them uncomfortable. He was now a confusing figure: irresistible as an entertainer and artist, even to many of his detractors, but an embarrassing vestige of the era when black performers grinned and shuffled. By the mid-1960s, the controversy had passed, especially when young cutting-edge jazz musicians rediscovered him and spoke of his genius. The totally surprising success of "Hello, Dolly!" in 1964 triggered one of the great reassessments in entertainment history: although Armstrong had never stopped touring, recording, and broadcasting, he was once again beloved by all. In his last years, he devoted much of his energy to writing his memoirs, detailing the grueling hardships of his youth in New Orleans. His death, on July 6, 1971, was mourned the world over. Incredibly, seventeen years later, Satchmo had the best-selling record in the country, with the rediscovery (thanks to a film score) of the previously ignored "What a Wonderful World."

JAZZ PERSONALIZED

The arc of Armstrong's life was, in many ways, the arc of jazz. In 1929, Armstrong achieved the beginnings of a mainstream acceptance, while such musicians as Bix Beiderbecke and Coleman Hawkins underscored the importance of individual expression and the emotional potential of a music just coming into its own. In the 1930s, a generation of musicians would personalize jazz, removing most of its ties to New Orleans and the Chicago and New York of the 1920s—to the degree that many old-timers scarcely recognized it. In the process of modernization, these younger players achieved something that now seems unbelievable . They transformed jazz into the world's best-known popular music. The change was so dramatic that many fans and musicians refused to call it jazz: they called it swing.

ADDITIONAL LISTENING	
Louis Armstrong	"Potato Head Blues," "Struttin' with Some Barbecue," "St. James Infirmary" (1928); *The Complete Hot Five and Hot Seven Recordings* (Columbia/Legacy)
	"Basin Street Blues" (1928); *Louis Armstrong, 1928–1931* (Nimbus 6002)
	"Tight Like That" (1928); *The Essential Louis Armstrong* (Columbia/Legacy)
	"I Can't Give You Anything but Love" (1929); *Louis Armstrong: King Louis* (Proper Box 93)
	"(What Did I Do to Be So) Black and Blue" (1929); *Hot Fives & Sevens* (JSP 100)
Bix Beiderbecke	"I'm Comin' Virginia," "In a Mist" (1927); *Bix Restored*, vol. 1 (Origin Jazz Library)
Coleman Hawkins	"The Stampede" (1926); *Coleman Hawkins* (Verve 2000)
	"Heartbreak Blues" (1933); *Coleman Hawkins, 1929–1934* (Classics 587)
	"Hocus Pocus" (1934); *Fletcher Henderson and His Orchestra (1927–1936)* (RCA Victor)

LOUIS ARMSTRONG CHRONOLOGY		
1901	Born August 4 in New Orleans.	
1913	Sent to New Orleans Colored Waif's Home; joins band.	Learns New Orleans style.
1918–21	Mississippi riverboats, Fate Marable.	
1922	Chicago: King Oliver's Creole Jazz Band.	2nd cornet, New Orleans style.
1923	Recordings with King Oliver.	
1924–25	New York: Fletcher Henderson; recordings with Clarence Williams's Blue Five (Sidney Bechet), Bessie Smith.	Soloist, big-band.
1925	Back to Chicago.	
1925–28	Hot Five/Hot Seven recordings.	Combines solo improvisation with New Orleans style.
1926	Featured soloist, Carroll Dickerson, Sunset Café.	Soloist in live performance.
1928	Recordings with Earl Hines.	
1929	New York: fronts big band (Luis Russell).	
1932–34	Tours of Europe.	
1935	Signs with Joe Glaser; major recording artist.	Swing Era band.
1947	Abandons big band; forms Armstrong's All Stars.	Return to New Orleans style.
1957	Little Rock controversy.	
1964	No.1 hit: "Hello, Dolly!"	
1971	Dies July 6 in New York City.	

PART II SUMMARY

PRECURSORS TO JAZZ

Jazz embodied the collision of African American music with the white mainstream, combining elements of folk music, popular music, and art music.

Folk music techniques that made their way into jazz include polyrhythm, call and response, cyclic form, blue notes (variable intonation), and timbre variation. "Classic" or "vaudeville" blues solidified the 12-bar blues form.

Popular music influences include minstrelsy and dance music.

Art music was represented by brass bands, which contributed instrumentation—cornet, clarinet, trombone, percussion—and march/ragtime form: 16-bar strains (usually **A A B B A C C D D**), with the **C** strain (trio) twice as long and in a different key.

Before 1917, the music that combined all these elements was ragtime: in popular songs ("coon" songs), dances (the cakewalk), and a piano style organized in march-like strains, with a steady two-beat rhythm in the left hand and contrasting rhythms in the right.

Major musicians

- Blues: Ma Rainey, Bessie Smith
- Dance: Vernon and Irene Castle, James Reese Europe
- Ragtime: Scott Joplin (piano), Wilbur Sweatman (clarinet)

In New Orleans, ragtime, blues, march music, and social dance combined in their turn to produce the music we know as jazz. The transformation was already complete as musicians began to make recordings.

NEW ORLEANS STYLE

Texture

- largely polyphonic
- occasional homophonic passages
- breaks: monophonic

Instrumentation

- cornet/trumpet, clarinet, trombone ("front line")
- rhythm section: string bass or tuba, acoustic guitar, piano, drums

Form

- march/ragtime
- 12-bar blues
- occasional 32-bar popular song (**A B A C**)

Special techniques

- collective improvisation (polyphonic)
- stop-time
- breaks

Major New Orleans bands

- Buddy Bolden
- Original Dixieland Jazz Band
- Creole Jazz Band (to 1916: Freddie Keppard)
- King Oliver's Creole Jazz Band
- Jelly Roll Morton and His Red Hot Peppers

Major New Orleans musicians

Cornet/trumpet

- Buddy Bolden
- Freddie Keppard
- Nick LaRocca
- Joseph "King" Oliver
- Louis Armstrong

Clarinet

- George Bacquet
- Johnny Dodds
- Sidney Bechet (and soprano saxophone)

Piano

- Jelly Roll Morton

BIG BANDS BEFORE 1930

The 1920s saw a migration of jazz musicians from New Orleans, Chicago, and elsewhere to New York, the center of the entertainment infrastructure. Here, the growing enthusiasm for ballroom dancing led to the establishment of the first important big bands. New York also encouraged the ripening of the most orchestral brand of jazz piano, stride.

Texture
- homophonic

Instrumentation
- sections of trumpets, trombones, saxophones/clarinets
- rhythm section: tuba, banjo, piano, drums

Form
- 32-bar popular song (**A A B A, A B A C**)
- 12-bar blues
- occasional march/ragtime

Special techniques
- two-beat groove
- block-chord texture

Major early big bands
- Paul Whiteman
- Fletcher Henderson
- Duke Ellington
- McKinney's Cotton Pickers (Don Redman)

Early stride pianists
- James P. Johnson
- Eubie Blake
- Luckey Roberts

Ellingtonians (early)
Saxophone
- Johnny Hodges (alto)
- Harry Carney (baritone)

Clarinet
- Barney Bigard

Trumpet
- Bubber Miley
- Cootie Williams

Trombone
- Joe "Tricky Sam" Nanton

Bass
- Wellman Braud

Piano
- Duke Ellington

LOUIS ARMSTRONG

Guided by Armstrong's vitality and contagious spirit, jazz evolved from ensemble music characterized by polyphony to music that featured soloists and daring improvisation; the multiple strains of ragtime become single-themed choruses of popular songs and blues; two- and four-bar breaks become solos of a full chorus or more.

In addition, Armstrong
- established the blues as jazz's melodic and spiritual foundation;
- introduced scat-singing;
- created brilliant improvisations on popular songs;
- introduced a new rhythmic energy: swing.

Armstrong-influenced soloists
Saxophone
- Frank Trumbauer (C-melody)
- Coleman Hawkins (tenor)

Clarinet
- Pee Wee Russell

Trumpet/cornet
- Bix Beiderbecke

THE SWING ERA

t took ten years for jazz to develop from an often disdained urban phenomenon, played mostly by young male musicians for black audiences, into a national obsession that crossed geographical, generational, gender, and racial borders. Louis Armstrong inaugurated his Hot Five recordings in November 1925; Benny Goodman inadvertently launched the Swing Era in August 1935. In the decade that followed, *jazz* was used almost exclusively to describe traditional New Orleans music. The new word was *swing,* which encompassed "hot" orchestras, like those of Duke Ellington and Count Basie, and "sweet" bands, like those of Sammy Kaye and Hal Kemp, which had virtually nothing to do with jazz. Many bands played both hot and sweet in attempting to create stylish dance music that combined elements of jazz with lush instrumentation and pop songs.

The swing bands revived a music industry considered moribund in the dark days of the Depression, and lifted the country's spirits during the darker days of World War II. Even the Nazis, who spurned jazz as a symptom of American de-

1920s
- Territory dance bands proliferate across country.

1922
- James Joyce's *Ulysses* published.
- T. S. Eliot's *The Wasteland* published.

1925
- The Ku Klux Klan marches in Washington, D.C.
- John Scopes convicted in Tennessee for teaching evolution.
- F. Scott Fitzgerald's *The Great Gatsby* published.
- Ernest Hemingway's *In Our Time* published.

1926
- Savoy Ballroom opens in New York.
- First national radio network (NBC).

1927
- Charles Lindbergh flies solo across the Atlantic.

1928
- Mickey Mouse makes first screen appearance.

1929
- *St. Louis Blues*, featuring Bessie Smith, released.
- Stock market crashes, Great Depression begins.
- William Faulkner's *The Sound and the Fury* published.

1930s
- Guitar replaces banjo, string bass replaces tuba in jazz bands.
- Stride and boogie-woogie piano styles at their peak.

1930
- George Gershwin composes "I Got Rhythm."
- Warner Bros. launches gangster film cycle with *Little Caesar.*

1931
- Cab Calloway records "Minnie the Moocher."
- Universal launches horror film cycle with *Frankenstein* and *Dracula.*

Roy Eldridge, a terror on the trumpet, respectfully known as Little Jazz or just plain Jazz, poses in front of the Savoy Ballroom in the 1930s.

Rosie the Riveter was a familiar symbol for feminine power during World War II.

The phenomenal popularity of Benny Goodman's dance band launched the Swing Era. New York, 1937–38.

Mary Lou Williams, "the lady who swings the band," was the chief arranger and pianist for Andy Kirk's Clouds of Joy. Cleveland, 1937.

broadcasts in occupied countries. In the United States, swing created new styles in slang, dress, and especially dance—an energetic, athletic "jitterbugging" that kept ballrooms jumping from coast to coast. Millions of fans debated the merits of bands and knew the names of key soloists: in that era, jazz and pop were largely inseparable.

Yet there was more to swing than big bands and riotous dancing. A new virtuosity had taken hold—a technical bravura that advanced the harmonic and rhythmic underpinnings of jazz, spurring innovations that would last long after the Swing Era had faded. Jazz singing came into its own, the guitar found a new voice through electronic amplification, and orchestrating became an art in its own right. If jazz of the 1920s, created in times of plenty, illuminated a defiant individualism, the Swing Era responded to years of hardship and war with a collective spirit that expressed a carefree, even blissful optimism.

1932
- Duke Ellington records "It Don't Mean a Thing (if It Ain't Got That Swing)."
- Unemployment in the U.S. reaches 14 million.
- Franklin D. Roosevelt elected president.

1932–34
- Louis Armstrong tours Europe.

1933
- Billie Holiday makes first recordings.
- Ellington tours Europe.
- Recording industry at nadir: only 4 million records sold.
- Prohibition repealed.
- Adolf Hitler becomes chancellor of Germany.

1934
- Fats Waller makes first recordings.
- Jimmie Lunceford band performs at the Cotton Club.

- The Quintette du Hot Club de France (with Django Reinhardt) performs in Paris.
- Ella Fitzgerald wins talent competition at the Apollo Theater in New York.
- *Le jazz hot*, *Down Beat* founded.
- Dust Bowl begins (lasting till 1939).
- Frank Capra's *It Happened One Night* released.

1935
- Benny Goodman band, at the Palomar Ballroom in California, launches Swing Era; Goodman begins recording with integrated trio.
- Billie Holiday records with top musicians, including Teddy Wilson.
- Ella Fitzgerald records with Chick Webb.
- George Gershwin's opera *Porgy and Bess* opens in New York.
- Popular Front formed.

PART III

1936
- Count Basie takes band to New York.
- Lester Young records "Oh! Lady Be Good."
- Gibson Company produces first electric guitar.
- Jazz clubs thrive on New York's 52nd Street.
- Jesse Owens wins four gold medals at Berlin Olympics.
- *Life* magazine founded.
- Charlie Chaplin's *Modern Times* released.
- Fred Astaire/Ginger Rogers film *Swing Time* released.

1936–39
- Spanish Civil War

1937
- Mary Lou Williams and Andy Kirk band in New York.
- Count Basie band performs at Savoy, records "One O'Clock Jump."
- Hindenburg explodes in New Jersey.

- Pablo Picasso paints *Guernica*.
- *Snow White and the Seven Dwarfs* released.
- Oscar Hammerstein/Jerome Kern musical *Show Boat* opens in New York.

1938
- Benny Goodman concert at Carnegie Hall (January).
- "From Spirituals to Swing" concert at Carnegie Hall (December).
- Ella Fitzgerald records "A-Tisket, a-Tasket."
- Billy Strayhorn joins Duke Ellington.
- Germany annexes Austria.
- Orson Welles's radio broadcast "The War of the Worlds" creates national panic.

1939
- Coleman Hawkins records "Body and Soul."
- Billie Holiday records "Strange Fruit."
- Glenn Miller records "In the Mood."

The Original Blue Devils defined Kansas City jazz. Lester Young stands to the left and Buster Smith to the right of leader Alvin Burroughs, 1932.

The most famous dance hall in America: the Savoy Ballroom on Lenox Avenue, Harlem, 1940.

The best dancers at the Savoy Ballroom could have doubled as acrobats.

Ella Fitzgerald, "the first lady of song," brought the stars out, including Swedish clarinetist Stan Hasselgård (behind Ellington), Duke Ellington, Benny Goodman, and music publisher Jack Robbins. New York, 1949.

Fats Waller and His Rhythm (including saxophonist Gene Sedric and trumpet player Herman Autrey) recording with the Deep River Boys at the RCA-Victor studios in New York, 1942.

- Lester Young records "Lester Leaps In" with Count Basie.
- Benny Goodman hires Charlie Christian.
- World War II begins in Europe.
- John Steinbeck's *The Grapes of Wrath* published.
- *Gone with the Wind*, *The Wizard of Oz*, *Young Mr. Lincoln* released.

1940
- Cootie Williams leaves Duke Ellington's band.
- Ellington records "Concerto for Cootie," "Conga Brava," "Ko-Ko."
- Winston Churchill becomes prime minister of Britain.
- The Blitz: bombing of England.

1941
- Ellington records "Take the 'A' Train."
- Japan bombs Pearl Harbor, U.S. enters war.
- *Citizen Kane*, *The Maltese Falcon* released.

1942
- Glenn Miller forms Air Force band.
- Bing Crosby records "White Christmas."

1943
- Ellington performs *Black, Brown, and Beige* at Carnegie Hall.

1944
- Glenn Miller's plane disappears over English Channel.
- Allies invade Normandy, France (D-Day).

1945
- U.S. drops atomic bombs on Hiroshima and Nagasaki; World War II ends.
- Franklin D. Roosevelt dies, Harry S. Truman becomes president.

FLETCHER HENDERSON
blue lou

BENNY GOODMAN
dinah

ARTIE SHAW
stardust

JIMMIE LUNCEFORD
'taint what you do
(it's the way that you do it)

SWING BANDS

In the 1930s, jazz was known as **swing**. We call this period the Swing Era, to distinguish it from the jazz of the 1920s. It was mostly **big-band** music, performed by large dance orchestras divided into sections of trumpets, saxophones, and trombones, as well as rhythm. Although swing was a new music to the casual consumer, it retained the basic elements of jazz we have already seen: polyrhythm, blues phrasing, timbre variation. And though it used written music more than previous forms of jazz, swing continued to balance composition against spontaneous improvisation.

The size of the bands transformed dance music into an orchestral music, thus realizing some of the aspirations of symphonic jazz; but the style was not complex. Swing offered a smooth, readily digestible sound, displacing the knotty polyphony of New Orleans jazz with clear homophonic textures, simple bluesy riffs, strong dance grooves, and well-defined melodies. It was a thoroughly commercial phenomenon. Like film, radio, and popular song, swing was central to a nationwide system of mass entertainment.

The Depression

Swing was bounded by two crucial events in American culture. The first is the Great Depression, which began with the stock market crash of October 1929 and deepened slowly and inexorably toward its nadir in the early 1930s. The crisis ruined the banking

Buddy Rich, one of the flashiest drummers of the Swing Era, caught here in the middle of a solo, 1954.

wwnorton.com/studyspace

By the early 1930s, all Americans had to scrounge for meals. New York soup kitchen, 1931.

system, cast millions into unemployment, and shifted America's political landscape. African Americans were a crucial part of a new coalition—including organized labor, Southern whites, Catholics, and the dispossessed poor—that swept the Democratic candidate, Franklin Roosevelt, to the presidency in 1932. Roosevelt swiftly launched a new government policy known as the New Deal, a blizzard of programs that stretched the nation's political and economic resources to help the needy and unemployed. His actions were popular enough to warrant him a record four terms in office; but for all his efforts, recovery was still slow and laborious. Not until the end of the decade, when the shadow of war jolted America into industrial action, did the Depression finally lift.

Swing came of age during the Depression, but it hardly caught the era's deep anxiety. Like movies, swing was a counterstatement to reality—an upbeat, slickly packaged commodity to distract people from their daily cares—and one that produced many great artists. But while movies fed its audience fantasies in dark, enclosed spaces, swing inspired action. It was a teenager's music, the first in our nation's history, loud and brash and demanding exuberant dance steps. Its improvisatory flair and buoyant energy encouraged America to recover from the country's economic disasters. Just as Roosevelt conquered hard times through the ingenuity of his New Deal programs, so too did swing make average Americans feel alive, alert, and engaged.

World War II

The second crucial event defining the Swing Era was World War II (1939–45), a global conflict that transformed America into a powerhouse of unprecedented strength. With the bombing of Pearl Harbor in 1941, all the country's resources—its industries, resources, manpower, even entertainment—were drawn into the worldwide fight against fascism.

For four long years, while the country was on edge, shifting unsteadily from steely grimness to giddy recklessness, swing drew eager and anxious patrons to ballrooms and theaters. Its rhythms permeated the lives of millions, inspiring workers in defense factories while giving soldiers abroad a taste of home. For many people, swing exemplified what Americans were fighting for: compared with authoritarian Nazi Germany, the casual, participatory quality of swing, yoking together people from different backgrounds, was a rousing statement of democracy.

At the war's end, thousands of servicemen returned home to their families and jobs, shutting down the hyperactive dancing culture that had formed the basis for hundreds of large swing orchestras. It was the end of an era—and with the explosion of the atomic bomb, the beginning of a new one.

Swing and Race

Swing was situated on the fault line of race. It emerged out of African American culture, its dance steps worked out on the floor of black ballrooms and its arrangements mimicking the black church in call-and-response patterns. Its success boosted the careers of hundreds of musicians, and pushed a handful of black bandleaders (Ellington, Armstrong) into the realm of stardom. Much of white America was dancing to an African American beat.

But swing did not dissolve racial barriers. The white audience was enthusiastic about the music, but indifferent as to its origins. Most of them probably did not know that the hit tune "Stompin' at the Savoy" referred to Harlem, or that their "jive" talk was black slang. Behind the scenes, racial bigotry was as alive as ever. Black and white musicians played together backstage in jam sessions, but racially mixed bands were not tolerated. As most of the money from swing went into white pockets, many black musicians felt that the music had been "stolen" from them—a feeling that would later help fuel the musical revolution known as bebop.

Swing and Economics

The Depression nearly destroyed the recording companies. At a time when people could barely afford food and rent, the price of a record was too much to bear. Besides, why spend money on records when music was available over the radio for free? Sales of records plunged—from over 100 million in 1929 to only 4 million in 1933. Familiar jazz labels like Gennett, OKeh, and Columbia went bankrupt or were bought up by speculators.

Things began to improve a few years later, thanks to the invention of the jukebox, a garish record-selecting machine that filled restaurants or bars with music for a mere nickel. By the late 1930s, recordings were dominated by two labels owned by the main radio networks: Columbia (bought by CBS) and Victor (by NBC). A third company, Decca, muscled in with the brilliant marketing strategy of slashing record prices in half. These three companies, known as "the majors," produced about 90 percent of the recordings all Americans listened to.

Similar patterns of concentration could be found in other media. Millions of families listened to regular broadcasts of "Amos 'n' Andy" or "The Burns and Allen Show" over national radio networks. The studio system in Hollywood produced an endless stream of elaborate films to thousands of movie theaters. In the days before television, movies commanded a large and loyal audience: by 1939, two-thirds of the public went to the movies at least once a week. Popular songs were at their peak: every week Tin Pan Alley published new tunes written by the likes of Gershwin, Kern, Arlen, Rodgers, Berlin, or Porter, available as sheet music and performed by innumerable singers and orchestras. Moreover, all of these

Voices

Roy Eldridge, one of the top trumpet players of the Swing Era (see Chapter 9), was a black soloist in otherwise white bands led by Gene Krupa and Artie Shaw. Years later, he explained why he would never cross racial barriers again:

We arrived in one town and the rest of the band checks in. I can't get into their hotel, so I keep my bags and start riding around looking for another place, where someone's supposed to have made a reservation for us . . . then the clerk, when he sees that I'm the Mr. Eldridge the reservation was made for, suddenly discovers that one of their regular tenants just arrived and took the last available room. . . .

One night the tension got so bad I flipped. I could feel it right up to my neck while I was playing "Rockin' Chair"; I started trembling, ran off the stand, and threw up. They carried me to the doctor's. I had a hundred-and-five fever; my nerves were shot. . . .

Later on, when I was with Artie Shaw, I went to a place where we were supposed to play a dance, and they wouldn't even let me in the place. "This is a white dance," they said, and there was my name right outside, Roy "Little Jazz" Eldridge. . . .

Man, when you're on the stage, you're great, but as soon as you come off, you're nothing. It's not worth the glory, not worth the money, not worth anything. Never again!

Two dancers in the midst of executing a daring "air step" at the Savoy Ballroom in Harlem, during the early 1940s.

entertainment branches intersected. The pop song industry depended on radio to broadcast its tunes, and often premiered them in movies. Movie stars drifted back and forth between Hollywood sets and radio studios.

Swing was thus part of a single popular entertainment network. Everyone listened to the same radio shows, watched the same movies, heard the same popular songs. A tune might be blasted over a local restaurant's jukebox or in a late-night radio broadcast, in the soundtrack of a movie or performed live on the movie theater's stage. The topmost rank of dance bands was national in scope. People heard them on radio or recordings and clamored to see them in person.

For some, this sameness was a loss; they compared it with fascism, the fervor of the swing "jitterbugs" resembling "the abandon of a crowd of Storm Troopers demanding their Fuehrer." Today, we're less likely to invoke Hitler than to complain that swing was swamped by commercialism. The hard-core swing outfits featured in the next few chapters were a crucial part of the scene, but difficult to sort out from the other bands—the "sweet" or "sweet-swing" bands that occasionally played a hot dance number but primarily focused on pop song and old-fashioned dance music. Indeed, some "big-band music" can in fact be thought of less as jazz than as pop with occasional jazz interpolations.

Nevertheless, the commercial excitement made jazz possible. Musicians poured into the field from all over: from Georgia (Fletcher Henderson), Washington, D.C. (Duke Ellington), Iowa (Glenn Miller), and New Jersey (Count Basie). As competition for the best jobs increased, musical standards rose precipitously. Musicians were now expected to play their instrument flawlessly, to sight-read efficiently, and to improvise. Dance bands offered steady work at a respectable salary, making music one of the few skilled crafts open to African Americans.

SWING AND DANCE

At the core of swing style was its groove: a steady, unaccented four-beats-to-the-bar foundation, perfect for dancing. This was neither revolutionary nor new: one could hear the same groove in recordings by Louis Armstrong, or emerging from passages by Jelly Roll Morton's Red Hot Peppers. But in the early 1930s—the same time that Duke Ellington immortalized it in the title "It Don't Mean a Thing (If It Ain't Got That Swing")—the four-beat groove became firmly established as the standard for hot dance music.

The Savoy

The swing dance style emerged from New York's Savoy Ballroom, which opened for business in 1926. The Savoy was an enormous space, filling an entire block in Harlem. Like many new dance halls, it offered a luxurious environment for a modest fee. Entering up the marble staircase, dancers saw "fancy wall decorations all over, thick patterned carpets on the floor, soft benches for sitting, round tables for drinking, and a heavy brass railing all around the long, polished dance floor." Two bands were hired on a given night, alternating sets on opposite sides of the hall. Harlem was proud of the Savoy, and opened its doors to white visitors from downtown and around the world; but unlike the Cotton Club, its primary constituency was the black neighborhood surrounding it.

In the Savoy, social dancing was an intense, communal activity. Thousands of dancers packed the hall. In the Cat's Corner, a special place next to the bandstand, the best dancers would execute their steps: the Charleston, the black bottom, or the fox-trot. Since the most ambitious often rehearsed their steps in the afternoon while the band was practicing, musicians and dancers could communicate closely on issues of tempo and groove. "For the dancer, you know what will please him," remembered trombonist Dicky Wells. "It has got to be something that will fit around him and with his step. When you see a dancer take his girl, and then drop her hands and walk off, something isn't right. Most likely the rhythm's wrong. But when you get that beat he's right in there saying: 'Play that again!'"

The Savoy dance style came to be known as the Lindy Hop—named after Charles Lindbergh, whose dramatic flight across the Atlantic in 1927 startled the nation. The steady four-four beat opened up new possibilities. A good dancer, one professional recounted, "takes the unvarying accent, and dances *against* it." The new dance was more "African": lower to the ground, demanding flexibility in the knee and hip joints. There was also greater room for improvisation. While the fox-trot or waltz insisted that couples remain linked arm-in-arm, the Lindy Hop featured "breakaways" where the partners could separate at arm's length to execute their own steps. The best dancers began adding new acrobatic variations, including "air steps," in which the female was thrown heedlessly (but always with grace) over her partner's shoulders. White observers were amazed. Author Carl Van Vechten, who watched safely from the side, described its movements as "epileptic," but added that "to observe the Lindy Hop being performed at first induces gooseflesh, and second, intense excitement, akin to religious mania."

The Rhythm Section

To help bands adjust to the new groove, major changes were made in the rhythm section. While the bass drum continued to play a rock-solid four-beat pulse, the tuba, commonly used in large dance bands of the 1920s, was replaced by the string bass. During the early years of recording, the tuba was able to project a clear, huffing sound. But the string bass had always been a specialty of New Orleans, and many players, including Wellman Braud with Duke Ellington's band, showed that the instrument had a special percussive flavor when the strings were given a pizzicato "slap" (plucked rather than bowed). Change came gradually in the late 1920s, once word had gotten around about how well the string bass worked; many tuba players realized that they'd better switch instruments or lose their jobs.

The banjo, with its loud and raucous tone, was replaced with the guitar, which provided a more subtle and secure pulsation (*chunk-chunk*) in the foundation rhythm. As the saying went, the guitar was more *felt* than heard. Listeners felt the combined sound of bass, guitar, and drums as a sonic force that pushed through cavernous dance halls. "If you were on the first floor, and the dance hall was upstairs," Count Basie remembered, "that was what you would hear, that steady *rump, rump, rump, rump* in that medium tempo."

Arranging

To fit the new groove, dance-band arranging became more inventive. To some extent, this was a belated influence of Louis Armstrong, whose rhythms continued to be absorbed by soloists and arrangers through the 1930s. Arrangers learned to write elaborate lines for an entire section, harmonized in block chords, called *soli*. They were conversant with chromatic (complex) harmony and knew how to make the most of their flexible orchestra.

Arrangements could also arise spontaneously out of oral practice. This approach was especially popular in Kansas City, as we will see in Chapter 8. But even in New York, where bands prided themselves on their musical literacy, musicians could take improvised riffs and harmonize them on the spot. The result, known as a **head arrangement**, was a flexible, unwritten arrangement created by the entire band. One musician compared it to child's play—"a lot of kids playing in the mud, having a big time."

FLETCHER HENDERSON Both kinds of arrangements, written and unwritten, could be heard in the hundreds of recordings made in the 1930s by Fletcher Henderson. For flashy pieces, Henderson relied on experienced arrangers, from his brother Horace to Don Redman and Benny Carter. But his biggest hits emerged from the bandstand. One, as we saw in Chapter 5, was "Sugar Foot Stomp," derived in the early 1920s from the King Oliver tune "Dippermouth Blues" and still in the repertory. By the 1930s, it had evolved into a thoroughly up-to-date dance tune, with a faster tempo to match the tastes

Fletcher Henderson, whose arrangements featuring call-and-response riffs helped to launch the Swing Era, gathered some of his all-stars for a reunion performance at Café Society, 1941. Left to right: J. C. Higginbotham, Buster Bailey, Sandy Williams (behind Bailey), Henderson (at piano), "Big Sid" Catlett, John Kirby, Henry Red Allen, Benny Carter, Russell Procope.

of the dancers. Another hit was "King Porter Stomp," a ragtime piece by Jelly Roll Morton that became radically simplified, shedding its two-beat clumsiness and march/ragtime form as it went.

Many of these pieces were ultimately written down by Henderson, who became his band's chief arranger. His genius for rhythmic swing and melodic simplicity was so effective that his music became the standard for numerous swing arrangers. Henderson was fond of short, memorable riffs—simple, bluesy phrases—in call and response: saxophones responding to trumpets, for example. In some passages, he distorted the melody into ingenious new rhythmic shapes, often in staccato (detached) bursts that opened up space for the rhythm section. Henderson was shrewd and efficient. He wrote only a few choice choruses, leaving the remainder of the arrangement open for solos accompanied by discreet, long-held chords or short riffs. As each piece headed toward its climax, the band erupted in an ecstatic wail.

◉ "Blue Lou"

The early Henderson band was dramatically effective in person: "We used to rock the walls," remembered Coleman Hawkins. But it was notoriously imperfect in the studio. Some of the best-known records from the early 1930s sounded, according to Hawkins, "like cats and dogs fighting." By 1936, the band had perfected its public presentation, and is in particularly splendid form on "Blue Lou."

The piece was composed by Edgar Sampson, a saxophonist and arranger with the Chick Webb band who also wrote for Henderson and later for Benny Goodman (among his tunes are "Stompin' at the Savoy" and "Don't Be That Way"). It was arranged in the Henderson style by Fletcher's brother Horace, who oriented it toward the band's chief soloists: the brilliant trumpeter Roy Eldridge and one of Coleman Hawkins's most gifted followers on tenor saxophone, Chu Berry (see Chapter 9).

Like many swing tunes, "Blue Lou" is built around a simple idea. The tune is in major, but the opening riff—a descending two-note figure— introduces a flatted scale degree from the minor mode. That peculiarity gives the piece its tension, and gives musically astute soloists an idea to use in their harmonic improvisation. Listen, for example, to the opening of Chu Berry's solo, which mimics the opening riff, and to the last eight bars of Roy Eldridge's solo, where the dissonant flatted note is blasted at the top of his range.

flatted scale degree note played a half step lower

Although "Blue Lou" begins with a relaxed two-beat feeling, the four-four dance groove gradually takes over. The first chorus introduces the original tune (note how the tune is expanded in the second **A** section into an elaborate *soli*), while the fourth (and last) chorus deforms it through ecstatic starts and stops. But the piece doesn't end there: with half a minute to go, there is a sudden modulation to the unusual key of A major (notoriously difficult for brass instruments). The new sixteen-bar section doesn't last long, but its presence suggests that this arrangement may have been flexible. Perhaps the drum stroke that precedes the modulation was a cue to follow if the band wanted to keep dancers on the floor. Eldridge's solo at the end sounds as though it could have gone on forever.

LISTENING GUIDE

2.1

 blue lou

FLETCHER HENDERSON AND HIS ORCHESTRA

Dick Vance, Joe Thomas, Roy Eldridge, trumpets; Fernando Arbello, Ed Cuffee, trombones; Buster Bailey, Scoops Carey, alto saxophones; Elmer Williams, Chu Berry, tenor saxophones; Horace Henderson, piano; Bob Lessey, guitar; John Kirby, bass; Sidney Catlett, drums

- Label: Vocalion/OKeh 3211; *Fletcher Henderson: 1924–1936* (Giants of Jazz 634479088476)
- Date: 1936
- Style: big-band swing
- Form: 32-bar popular song (**A A B A**)

What to listen for:

- two-note riff at beginning, echoed in trumpet (chorus 2) and tenor saxophone (chorus 3) solos
- *soli* by saxophones in chorus 1 and by trumpets in chorus 4
- modulation to new key and new 16-bar tune at chorus 5

CHORUS 1

0:00	**A**	The tune begins immediately with the saxophones playing a simple yet dissonant two-note riff, colored with a note borrowed from the **minor mode**.
0:01		The saxophone section is immediately answered by the brass, with short chords.
0:05		The saxophones continue with a *soli*—a simple syncopated melody.
0:09	**A**	The chord progression is repeated, but the saxophones now play a complicated *soli* in the style of an improvisation.
0:19	**B**	On the bridge, the tune **modulates** to a new key. The saxophone section plays another simple riff, answered by brief chords from the brass.
0:29	**A**	Return of the opening two-note riff.

CHORUS 2

0:38	**A**	Eldridge takes a dominating trumpet solo, jumping quickly from his lower to his highest register. Behind him, the saxophone section plays jumpy background riffs or sustained chords.
0:48	**A**	
0:57	**B**	On muted trombone, Cuffee plays a **melodic paraphrase** of chorus 1's bridge.
1:06	**A**	Searching for a dramatic reentry, Eldridge begins in his highest register, playing the first few dissonant notes slightly out of tune.

CHORUS 3

1:16	**A**	Berry, on tenor saxophone, begins his solo with the opening two-note riff. Underneath him, the brass section swells in volume on background harmonies.
1:25	**A**	
1:35	**B**	As Berry increases in intensity, the bass finally begins playing a **walking-bass** line.
1:44	**A**	

CHORUS 4

1:53	**A**	The brass section plays a simpler *soli*, with short **staccato** notes, opening up a lot of space.
2:03	**A**	
2:12	**B**	Berry returns to take an eight-bar solo, accompanied only by the rhythm section.
2:22	**A**	As if interrupting, the trumpets reenter on a new variation (of the original two-note riff).

CHORUS 5 (NEW TUNE: 16-bar A A)

2:31	**A**	Signaled by a drum shot, the tune suddenly modulates to a new key, A major, offering a new melody over a new harmonic progression. The bass returns to a (mostly) two-beat feel.
2:41	**A**	

CODA

2:50		The band repeats a short, four-measure harmonic figure.
2:54		As the figure is taken up by the saxophones, Eldridge takes a muted solo.
3:03		Eldridge's solo is cut short by a brief cadence figure, ending the piece.

BREAKTHROUGH

In the early 1930s, the music industry resembled the nation by being firmly divided by race. In economic terms, segregation clearly worked to the advantage of white musicians. In the South, where Jim Crow rules still required black people to use "colored" water fountains and duck off the sidewalk to make room for whites, black musicians walked a tightrope, working their gigs at night while hoping not to draw attention from drunk, racist mobs or surly law enforcement officials. In the North, the rules were more relaxed, but the best jobs—major hotel ballrooms, radio shows—were restricted to whites on the grounds that Southern customers might be offended by the sight or sound of a black band.

For a time, black musicians, who had never challenged the stereotype that insisted their music was naturally "hot," kept jazz as their racial specialty. To survive in the world of dance music, black bands had in fact to be versatile: capable of performing all kinds of dance styles, including the waltz and the mambo as well as swing. The best bands played both sides of the fence. A small but significant number of bandleaders, including Duke Ellington, pursued their careers even as the Depression discouraged most of their colleagues.

But white musicians were keenly interested in jazz. We have already encountered Chicago's Austin High Gang (Chapter 6). In the 1920s, future swing bandleaders Artie Shaw, Glenn Miller, and Tommy and Jimmy Dorsey increasingly gravitated toward jazz, mastering it and even adding their own innovations. Some were hired by Paul Whiteman to play hot solos, while still others made small-group jazz with bands like Red Nichols and His Five Pennies. Most found jobs playing demanding if uninspiring arrangements in white dance bands and radio orchestras while dreaming of the chance to play some "real" jazz late at night in a jam session. All that changed with the surprising breakthrough of the orchestra led by Benny Goodman.

■ BENNY GOODMAN (1909–1986)

Goodman grew up in the slums of Chicago, where his father, a recent immigrant from Warsaw, worked in the stockyards. The boy showed a prodigious talent on the clarinet, which gave him a way out of menial labor. He was accepted into the band at the Hull House, a settlement house founded by Jane Addams to provide educational and cultural opportunities to the city's poor, and acquired a solid training from Franz Schoepp, the clarinetist from the

Chicago Symphony. At the same time, he heard the jazz that was buzzing around him and modeled his improvisation on its clarinetists, both white (Leon Rappolo) and black (Jimmie Noone). By the 1920s, he was a bluesy and elegant soloist, distinguishing himself in white bands that had an inclination toward jazz, like Ben Pollack's.

Goodman's tastes led him to create a band that would bridge the gap between the jazz he loved and the realities of commercialism. Taking advice from vocalist Mildred Bailey, who advised him to "get a Harlem book" of arrangements, he hired some of the best underemployed black arrangers he could find: Benny Carter, Edgar Sampson, and Fletcher Henderson, who was struggling to hold his own band together and eager for extra cash.

"Let's Dance!"

In 1935, Goodman's band was featured as the "hot" orchestra on a national radio program, "Let's Dance!" and went on a national tour. Their reception in places like Salt Lake City and Denver was so discouraging that Goodman felt ready to quit. But in August, at the Palomar ballroom in Los Angeles, where the late-night broadcasts had been inadvertently positioned in prime time for California listeners, everything changed: Goodman's swing repertory suddenly found its audience. Through their vigorous, almost violent enthusiasm for this new Harlem-based sound, white teenagers awakened the music industry and launched the swing revolution.

Goodman's success electrified the country. White fans celebrated him as a hero, much as they would Elvis Presley two decades later. The more extreme enthusiasts, known as "jitterbugs," adopted black dancing and "jive" slang, driving their parents and even musicians over the edge. In theaters, fans eager to see Goodman clogged traffic in lines that stretched for blocks; inside, they danced in the aisles. It was enough to make some people feel that the bounds of civilization had begun to part.

But in the end, America accepted his music gracefully. Goodman's band blended his swing rhythms with up-to-date arrangements of current pop

The quartet led by Benny Goodman brought racial integration to the public and invaluable opportunities to its members. Within a few years, each musician—pianist Teddy Wilson, vibraphonist Lionel Hampton, and drummer Gene Krupa—had become a band-leader. New York's Paramount Theater, 1937.

FRANK DRIGGS COLLECTION

songs. The first chorus would be recognizable enough to satisfy Tin Pan Alley, even as the rest transported its listeners into jazz. As historian James Maher remembered: "These were our songs. They were part of the daily ordinary. And this I think is what took Benny Goodman over the gap, out of jazz into the American parlor. He arrived with 'Blue Skies.' . . . I mean, everybody knew Irving Berlin! So we were home free." Goodman managed to both satisfy the jitterbugs and make swing acceptable to the cultured middle classes. One of his memorable acts was to bring jazz to New York's Carnegie Hall, a citadel of musical respectability, in January 1938. The musicians may have felt out of place (like a "whore in church," as Harry James described it), but the band's rousing success there cemented jazz's place in contemporary American culture.

Teddy Wilson, the cool and elegant pianist with the Benny Goodman Quartet, briefly led his own big band in the late 1930s.

The Goodman Trio and Quartet

Goodman was also a pioneer through launching various small groups that helped cast jazz as a kind of chamber music— relaxed and spontaneous, yet highly polished and refined. These groups revived an interest in small-combo improvisation that had faded since the rise of the big bands. They were even more remarkable in being among the few interracial groups in jazz.

Goodman first heard pianist Teddy Wilson on passing through Chicago from California in 1935. The son of an English professor at Tuskegee Institute, Wilson grew up studying piano and violin. His role model was Earl Hines, whom he admired for his superb stride technique. But where Hines was breathtakingly risky in his improvisation, Wilson's style was smooth and carefully polished, cool and controlled even at high speed. When Goodman jammed with Wilson at an after-hours private party, he was thrilled by the pianist's panache, but also dismayed at the unspeakable risk of forming a mixed-race trio with his white drummer, Gene Krupa. Fortunately, recordings by the trio sold well, inspiring Goodman to present the trio not as full members of the band, but as "special guests." Within a few years, Goodman's "band-within-the-band" had been widely imitated in the industry by Cab Calloway (the Cab Jivers), Artie Shaw (the Gramercy Five), Tommy Dorsey (the Clambake Seven), and Woody Herman (the Woodchoppers).

Teddy Wilson

Gene Krupa

The trio expanded to a quartet when Goodman added Lionel Hampton in 1936. Hampton was originally a drummer who had played with Louis Armstrong's big band in the early 1930s. While with Armstrong, he stumbled over the vibraphone in a recording studio, a then-new instrument that used rotating discs and amplification to enhance the sound of a metal xylophone. Within a few years, he shifted to the vibes as his main instrument. Unlike Wilson, a shy man who rarely changed his facial expression while playing, Hampton was a tireless entertainer who used his whole body to communicate with audiences. "I have always been Mr. Showmanship," he later wrote. "There was a long, honorable tradition of clowning in black performing that I wanted to carry on." Hampton's extroverted energy, combined with the sweaty glamour of drummer Gene Krupa, was a crucial part of the quartet's popular appeal. After leaving Goodman in the early 1940s to form his own band, Hampton carried his reckless energy into rhythm and blues, ultimately linking jazz with rock and roll.

Lionel Hampton

"Dinah"

"Dinah," a thirty-two-bar **A A B A** pop song composed in 1925, first became popular in Goodman's teenage years. Such tunes normally had a short shelf life, lasting no more than six months. But jazz musicians were attracted to its harmonic structure, which was similar to that of "I Got Rhythm": an opening section firmly in the tonic, followed by a bridge with more elaborate harmonic movement. "Dinah" became an "evergreen"—or to use more modern language, a **standard**: a permanent addition to the jazz repertory.

In the Goodman Quartet's 1936 recording, the mood is exuberant and playful, even bewildering: during Lionel Hampton's introduction, it's virtually impossible to hear where the downbeat is. The four musicians play in an informal jam-session spirit, exercising their freedom to listen and interact spontaneously. In the first **A** section, Goodman plays the melody with delicacy and circumspection; but in the bridge, he obliterates it in a lengthy string of fast notes. When Hampton plays in the second chorus, he shifts between simple riff figures and complicated harmonic substitutions of his own devising.

As befits a jam session, the performance heats up over time. Krupa begins with a steady two-beat foundation, but soon barges in with his snare drum and tom-tom accents. Goodman's later improvisations have little to do with the original melody. In his brief solo spot, Wilson shows the kind of delicate filigree he could weave around the harmonies of the bridge. At the end, the three soloists coincide in a kind of ecstatic polyphony. It's not chaotic, however, and the ending is tightly controlled.

LISTENING GUIDE

2.2

dinah

BENNY GOODMAN QUARTET

Benny Goodman, clarinet; Lionel Hampton, vibraphone; Teddy Wilson, piano; Gene Krupa, drums

- Label: Victor 25398; *The Legendary Small Groups* (RCA/Bluebird 090266-39942-0)
- Date: 1936
- Style: small combo swing
- Form: 32-bar popular song (**A A B A**)

What to listen for:

- Goodman's melodic paraphrase of this jam-session standard
- exuberant solo improvisation (choruses 2–4)
- polyphonic improvisation (chorus 5)
- tightly controlled ending

INTRODUCTION

0:00		Hampton begins at a brisk tempo, playing a short introductory passage on the vibes.
0:02		Krupa enters, accompanying Hampton on the drums.

CHORUS 1

0:04	**A**	The rest of the band enters. Goodman takes the lead on the clarinet, delicately paraphrasing the original melody. Behind him, Krupa thumps a two-beat pattern on the bass drum.
0:12	**A**	Wilson quietly plays a contrasting accompaniment.

| 0:20 | B | As Goodman begins to improvise, Wilson plays a simpler **stride** accompaniment. |
| 0:28 | A | Goodman returns to the original melody. |

CHORUS 2

0:36	A	Reacting to Hampton's solo on the vibes, Krupa plays **polyrhythms** on the tom-tom drums.
0:43	A	As Hampton warms up, his line becomes a long, continuous string of even eighth notes, occasionally punctuated by Krupa's quick drum strokes.
0:51	B	
0:59	A	

CHORUS 3

1:07	A	Hampton divides a **cross-rhythm** between his two hands.
1:13		Krupa plays a disorienting snare-drum accent just before his bass drum stroke.
1:15	A	
1:22	B	
1:30	A	To conclude his solo, Hampton plays a few simple notes polyrhythmically.
1:36		Goodman sneaks in at the end of Hampton's solo with a scooped blue note.

CHORUS 4

1:37	A	
1:40		Goodman follows his opening bluesy phrase with another line that continues, unbroken, until halfway through the next **A** section.
1:45	A	
1:50		The next phrase begins with another piercing, descending **blue note**.
1:53	B	Wilson plays a discreet solo over the bridge.
1:58		At the end of the bridge, Wilson embellishes the chord progression with a **harmonic substitution**.
2:00	A	With a strikingly high entrance, Goodman concludes his solo.

CHORUS 5

2:08	A	The three soloists play together: Wilson's riffs are responded to by Goodman, who paraphrases parts of "Dinah" before abandoning the melody in improvisation.
2:16	A	
2:23	B	**Break:** Hampton plays an unaccompanied solo, interrupted every two beats by a brief chord from Wilson.
2:29		Krupa reenters, followed by Goodman.
2:31	A	The entire band plays an untrammeled polyphonic conclusion.
2:38		The piece ends discreetly with a bass drum thump.

JOHN HAMMOND
AND OTHER JAZZ ENTHUSIASTS

The interracial Goodman Quartet was encouraged by John Hammond (1910–1987), the most influential entrepreneur and activist of his period. A list of artists whose careers he helped would include Bessie Smith, Fletcher Henderson, Goodman, Billie Holiday, and Count Basie—and in a later generation, Bob Dylan, Aretha Franklin, and Bruce Springsteen. Hammond was no musician (although he was an amateur violinist for a while), but his in-

FRANK DRIGGS COLLECTION

Benny Goodman (wearing a sweater vest) converses with his bespectacled guitarist, Charlie Christian, during a 1940 recording session for Columbia Records. John Hammond is visible in profile in the left corner.

tense commitment and political convictions made him a crucial figure in jazz history.

Born into a wealthy New York family (his mother was connected to the Vanderbilts), Hammond grew up in an atmosphere of privilege on the Upper East Side. As a youth, he turned his back on the "sweet" sounds of popular music. Instead, he used his weekly violin lesson as an excuse to explore the music that excited him in Harlem's theaters and nightclubs. He attended Yale, but dropped out and, supported by a generous trust fund, plunged into the world of music. He became a jazz reporter, a producer of recordings, and the music's insistent political voice.

Hammond developed two passions. The first was a love of black jazz and folk music, which to him seemed infinitely superior to any other kind. "There was no white pianist to compare with Fats Waller," he once said, "no white band as good as Fletcher Henderson's, no blues singer like Bessie Smith." The second was a hatred of racial injustice. Although raised on prejudice typical of his time (his mother once explained to him that black people were "different" because "their skulls harden when they are twelve"), he became outraged by inequality. His battles to help black people in cases like the Scottsboro Nine (nine black Alabama youths falsely accused of raping two white women in 1931) aligned him with struggles on the far left. Typically, he never joined the Communist Party, but he did join the NAACP.

Hammond used a long-running association with Columbia Records to champion the music he loved. He became a ubiquitous figure in nightclubs, standing out with his conservative crewcut and uninhibited behavior. "Hammond in action is the embodiment of the popular conception of the jitterbug," the *New Yorker* reported. "When the music jumps, he begins to move his head, his feet, and sometimes his whole body. His eyebrows go up, his mouth opens wide and reveals a set of even, gleaming teeth, and a long-drawn-out 'Yeah' slides out of his throat." He was responsible for hundreds of recording dates, having shepherded his latest discoveries into the studio. Some black musicians did not relish his overbearing insistence. Duke Ellington, for example, broke publicly with him after Hammond complained in 1935 that Ellington's longer pieces were "vapid and without the slightest semblance of guts." But few nonmusicians came close to Hammond in shaping the course of jazz.

Early Jazz Fans

Hammond was by no means the only enthusiast. The Swing Era saw the emergence of jazz record collectors—young men of privileged backgrounds who combed through discarded vinyl at flea markets and junk shops looking for forgotten old recordings. To distinguish one recording from another, they duly noted all the pertinent information: personnel, dates, matrix numbers (the codes inscribed on the disc that identify a particular master disc, or matrix), release numbers. These data formed the beginnings of the science of record classification, or **discography**.

"Hot Clubs" were formed in towns throughout the country, bringing together fans and sponsoring public jam sessions. To suit their reading tastes, new mass-market magazines like *Downbeat* and *Metronome* and smaller fan-based journals like *Jazz Information* emerged. From their pages came the first American jazz critics (Leonard Feather, George Simon).

While jazz enthusiasts were excited that their favorite music had achieved popular success, their attitude toward swing was mixed. Many were uneasy about "commercialism"—the tainting of the music through the marketplace. They also felt that the "real" jazz was beyond most people's ken. Joining their ranks was like joining a cult. "Sooner or later, you became acquainted with other zealots who I call 'jazzniks,'" said one observer. "And they of course are instantly telling you that all the people you like and admire, they all stink. They don't play jazz." Ironically, it was the commercial success of jazz in swing that fostered a counterfaith: that jazz was an "anticommercial" music.

MAJOR SWING BANDS

As the dance business boomed, the number of new bands exploded. By 1940, there were hundreds of bands—some leaning toward conventional dance music (the "sweet-swing" bands), others specializing in hard-driving swing. Benny Goodman's own band was a seedbed for bandleaders: they emerged from his trumpet section (Harry James and Bunny Berigan), saxophone section (Vido Musso and Toots Mondello), and quartet (Wilson, Krupa, and Hampton). Early jazz heroes like Louis Armstrong and Earl Hines switched to big bands. For the rest of this chapter, we will consider just a few of the numerous swing headliners.

■ ARTIE SHAW (1910–2004)

Like Benny Goodman, Artie Shaw was a child of the ghetto. Born Arthur Arshawsky on the Lower East Side of Manhattan, he was the son of recent Jewish immigrants who used his skill on saxophone and clarinet to rise in the world of dance orchestras. By 1931, he was studying with Harlem pianist Willie "the Lion" Smith and listening to Armstrong, pianist Earl Hines, and clarinetist Jimmie Noone in the nightclubs of Chicago, which he whimsically called "one of the foremost jazz conservatories in the world." By browsing in record stores, he also became fascinated with music by Igor Stravinsky, Claude Debussy, and other "guys with screwy-sounding names" who were creating dissonant modern classical music.

During the early 1930s, Shaw lived a double life. He had completely fallen in love with jazz, and spent his time jamming regularly in Harlem with "the Lion" and others. "I was actually living the life of a Negro musician," he wrote later, "adopting Negro values and attitudes; and accepting the Negro out-group point of view not only about music but life in general." At the same time, he made ends meet with a job in a radio orchestra, playing what he disdained as "soap and cereal programs" in an all-white band.

Shaw never expected to accomplish much in music. His fondest hope was to earn a few thousand dollars so that he could quit and write a book. But to his surprise, he became astronomically successful after the band he had formed in 1938 sold millions of copies of its hit record "Begin the Beguine." Being a major celebrity couldn't have been all that bad: Shaw's eight marriages, some to movie stars (Lana Turner, Ava Gardner), along with his matinee idol looks, kept him on the pages of Hollywood magazines. Yet the commotion of stardom conflicted with his values. He exploded with resentment against the jitterbugging fans who screamed with wild enthusiasm and demanded to hear his hits again and again, played exactly like the record: "They won't even let me play without interrupting me!" he once complained. He railed against the promoters and other hangers-on, eager for a share of Shaw's $30,000 weekly earnings.

Periodically, Shaw dissolved his band to brood in silence, only to return to even greater acclaim. Finally, in 1954, he retired from playing altogether.

⏺ "Star Dust"

Shaw's various bands reflected his restless temperament. At times he wanted to satisfy his fans' desire for "the loudest band in the whole goddamn world." Other bands attempted to bridge the gap between the worlds of jazz and classical music. His first claim to fame came in 1936 when he wrote, for the musicians' community, a piece for clarinet, string quartet (two violins, viola, cello), and rhythm. In 1940, now a celebrity, he enriched his swing band with

Artie Shaw, who dropped his civilian life to join the service during World War II, crowds his Navy Band onto the deck of the *U.S.S. Saratoga*, 1944.

a nine-piece string section, intelligently used by arranger Lennie Hayton.

"Star Dust," which dates from this period, is a restrained and lyrical performance, focusing on the haunting melody written by pianist and composer Hoagy Carmichael in 1927. The soloists treat the tune with love and respect. In the opening chorus, trumpeter Billy Butterfield uses a rich vibrato (reminiscent of Harry James, who led one of the most popular dance bands at the time) to paraphrase the melody openly. Subsequent soloists explore the tune's mood of romantic sentiment in their own creations. Jack Jenney's brief but melting trombone solo is a highlight: note his gentle but expressive leap up an octave into the trombone's upper register. So is Shaw's. He was a brilliant technician on the clarinet, fluid and supple as an improviser. This solo is finely sculpted, suggesting the reach of a great violinist when it climaxes in the stratosphere on a high A.

LISTENING GUIDE

 star dust

2.3

ARTIE SHAW AND HIS ORCHESTRA
Artie Shaw, clarinet; George Wendt, J. Cathcart, Billy Butterfield, trumpets; Jack Jenney, Vernon Brown, trombones; Bud Bassey, Neely Plumb, alto saxophones; Les Robinson, Jerry Jerome, tenor saxophones; Johnny Guarnieri, piano; Al Hendrickson, guitar; Jud DeNaut, bass; Nick Fatool, drums; T. Boardman, T. Klages, B. Bower, Bob Morrow, Al Beller, E. Lamas, violins; A. Harshman, K. Collins, violas; F. Goerner, cello

- Label: Victor 27230; *Artie Shaw: Greatest Hits* (RCA 68494)
- Date: 1940
- Style: big-band swing
- Form: 32-bar popular song (**A B A C**)

> **What to listen for:**
> - big-band instrumentation (with strings)
> - Shaw's virtuosic paraphrase of the tune
> - Jenney's trombone solo

INTRODUCTION

| 0:00 | | Tentatively holding out each note, an unaccompanied trumpet soloist (Butterfield) plays the first few notes of the tune. |

CHORUS 1

0:05	**A**	With a gentle slide, he signals the band to enter. Underneath, the saxophone section plays long-held chords in a slow, measured tempo.
0:14		Immediately after a dramatic chord change, the string section emerges from the background.
0:27	**B**	
0:49	**A**	The string section plays an elaborate variation on the main melody.
1:10	**C**	The trumpet returns on a high note, while the accompaniment returns a few seconds later (1:14).
1:21		For the final statement of the tune, the entire band enters.

INTERLUDE

| 1:29 | | The band **modulates** for the next chorus. |

CHORUS 2

1:40	**A**	Shaw enters for his clarinet solo, with a highly decorated version of the melody that moves into **double-time.**
2:02	**B**	As Shaw begins exploring the chords through **harmonic improvisation,** his line becomes a string of eighth notes.
2:13		Shaw's line climaxes on a dramatic high note.
2:25	**A**	Jenney enters on trombone, playing a beautiful solo with subtle ornaments.
2:47	**C**	With the strings hovering in the background, the band takes over the melody. The drummer underscores the excitement with cymbals.
2:57		The last phrase is signaled by a sharp, syncopated accent.
3:01		**Break:** the band drops out, leaving Shaw to conclude the melody unaccompanied.

CODA

3:04	Shaw continues his line, improvising harmonically.
3:07	On a rising series of chords, the band reenters.
3:13	The string section emerges with its own **dissonant** harmonic progression, which finally resolves (by 3:18) to the **tonic** chord.
3:19	Final cadence.
3:23	Over a held chord, the strings have the last word, adding a decorative skein of dissonant chords.

■ JIMMIE LUNCEFORD (1902–1947)

Jimmie Lunceford fit few swing stereotypes. He was not a star performer. As a youth, he studied saxophone as well as guitar and trombone, but in his maturity he never played his favorite instrument, the alto saxophone, with his band. He was instead a stern taskmaster and disciplinarian who brought an air of the school classroom with him onto the bandstand.

Lunceford held impressive educational credentials. After taking courses at City College in New York, he graduated from Fisk University in Nashville in 1926 and took a job as a music instructor at a Memphis high school. He saw music as a tremendous engine for social and economic uplift, and turned his students into a dance band, the Chickasaw Syncopators. From this initial group came his longtime drummer, Jimmy Crawford. The Syncopators soon became a professional orchestra, augmented by friends from Fisk such as alto saxophonist Willie Smith (the band's main soloist) and pianist Ed Wilcox. The band got its break in 1934 when invited to play at the Cotton Club in New York, one of the few places where a black band could broadcast in prime time. With his music pouring out over the airwaves from the Cotton Club, Lunceford became a mainstay of the Swing Era, recording dozens of records for Decca and Columbia and continually touring the United States.

A light-skinned, athletic man, Lunceford felt at ease in positions of authority. Nicknamed "the Professor," he drilled his band like a martinet, insisting on impeccable appearance ("he checked their socks," one bandleader remembered) and exacting musicianship through endless rehearsals. He refused to accept sloppy behavior, demanding that his musicians adhere to the three P's: punctuality, precision, and presentation. The result was a band that embodied the best in black middle-class respect, with Lunceford at its center.

"Until I met Jimmie, I'd never met anybody of whom I felt any intellectual fear," his arranger Sy Oliver recalled. "The musicians don't all realize it, but that man raised them. He changed their lives."

With the gradual decline of vaudeville, dance bands were often thrust onto the stage in its stead, and fortunately the Lunceford band was eager to put on a show. Audiences were treated not only to excellent swing music, but also humorous novelties ("I'm Nuts About Screwy Music," "The Merry-Go-Round Broke Down"), unusual repertory ("Organ Grinder's Swing") and bizarre physical antics. Trombonist Eddie Durham described a show at the Apollo Theater:

> They would come out and play a dance routine. The Shim Sham Shimmy was popular then and six of the guys would come down and dance to it—like a tap dance, crossing their feet and sliding. Then Willie Smith would put his bonnet on and sing a sort of nursery rhythm. [Trumpeter] Eddie Tompkins hit the high notes and did a Louis Armstrong deal. Then they had a Guy Lombardo bit and a Paul Whiteman bit—see, they imitated bands. The lights would go down next and they'd all lay down their horns and come out to sing as a glee club . . . The next number, they'd be throwing their horns and hats up to the ceiling. That was all novelty, and I liked it.

The band's downfall can be traced to racial discrimination and Lunceford's overeager work habits. He kept his band on the road, on a grueling, continuous tour in worn-out buses. The sheer volume of touring was unbelievable: to give one example, the band played in Providence, Rhode Island, on one night; in Martinsburg, West Virginia, the next; and the following night in Clemson, South Carolina.

The genial Jimmie Lunceford wields his baton at the Fiesta Danceteria in New York, 1940. At the microphone is Trummy Young, a trombonist who also sang on tunes like "'Tain't What You Do (It's the Way That You Do It)."

"'Tain't What You Do (It's the Way That You Do It)"

Sy Oliver   Melvin "Sy" Oliver, a trumpet player from Ohio, was already an experienced arranger by the time he first encountered the fledgling Lunceford band in 1933. He was ready to quit music to return to school, but the Lunceford band's flawless sight-reading of his arrangements made him change his mind. Until he was finally hired away in 1939 by Tommy Dorsey's more affluent orchestra, Oliver wrote dozens of witty, inventive charts that were a mainstay of Lunceford's repertory, turning unlikely tunes like "The Organ Grinder's Swing" and "Put on Your Old Grey Bonnet" into swing masterpieces.

On "'Tain't What You Do (It's the Way That You Do It)," Oliver's co-composer was James "Trummy" Young, a skillful trombone soloist who occasionally sang for the group. Like Ellington's "It Don't Mean a Thing (if It Ain't Got That Swing)," this song offers a sly observation from the African American perspective, in which verbal arts transform style into meaning. As James Weldon Johnson once noted in 1912, a black preacher's eloquence "consists more in the manner of saying than in what is said." "'Tain't What You Do" simply puts this idea into the musical vernacular.

Young is not much of a vocalist. But his hip, understated delivery, with its subtle swoops and sideways slips into speech, matches the intent of the words. Set against him is the unvarnished sound of band members intoning the opening phrase. The rest of Oliver's arrangement uses improvised solos by alto saxophonist Willie Smith and simple but cleverly arranged riffs to suggest that the Lunceford band has been abiding by this bit of family wisdom all along.

LISTENING GUIDE

2.4

 'Tain't What You Do (It's the Way That You Do It)

JIMMIE LUNCEFORD
Eddie Tomkins, Paul Webster, trumpets; Sy Oliver, trumpet and arranger; Elmer Crumbley, Russell Bowles, trombones; Trummy Young, trombone and vocal; Willie Smith, Earl Carruthers, Dan Grisson, alto saxophones; Joe Thomas, tenor saxophone; Edwin Wilcox, piano; Al Norris, guitar; Moses Allen, bass; Jimmy Crawford, drums

- Label: Vocalion/OKeh 4582; *Lunceford Special* (Columbia 65647)
- Date: 1939
- Style: swing
- Form: 32-bar popular song (**A A B A**)

What to listen for:
- simple, bluesy melody sung by Young
- solos by Smith (alto saxophone) and Crawford (drums)
- call-and-response riffs

CHORUS 1

0:00   **A**   After a short drum upbeat, the tune begins in the saxophones, accompanied by the hollow sound of bass drum strokes alternating with tom-tom strokes. The melody is simple, beginning with a syncopated repetition of a single note.

0:07		The saxophones gradually increase in volume.
0:09		On one note, the saxophones briefly erupt into **block-chord** harmony.
0:11		The saxophone melody is answered by the brass.
0:13	**A**	The same melody is now heard with a more conventional accompaniment: a swing drum beat, a walking-bass line that moves down the major scale, and detached syncopated chords in the brass.
0:24	**B**	The brass take over, starting the melody from a new note and descending through a bluesy dissonance.
0:28		The melody is extended by Smith's alto saxophone improvisation.
0:32		Smith interrupts again with a falling **blue note**.
0:37	**A**	The melody is divided between saxophones and brass, alternating with their own soli in **call and response**.
0:46		To emphasize the last bluesy phrase, all the horns combine on a single line.

INTERLUDE

0:48		The band plays a series of chords headed toward the dominant, ultimately ending on a **half cadence**.
0:59		A drum roll introduces the vocal.

VERSE

1:00		Young steps forward to sing the tune. His wispy, understated vocal line is un-accompanied, punctuated occasionally by short chords in the bass and piano. *"When I was a kid, about half-past three, my daddy said, 'Son, come here to me.' Says, 'Things may come, things may go, but this is one thing you ought to know.'"*

CHORUS 2

1:13	**A**	The piece **modulates** upward to a new key. The melody is sung by the band, with Young answering in call and response, his voice dropping off to a speech tone by the end of the phrase. Underneath, the rhythm section provides steady rhythmic and harmonic accompaniment while the piano **comps** and adds fills. *"'Tain't what you do, it's the way 't-cha you do it. [repeats two times] That's what gets results! Mama, mama!"*
1:24	**A**	*"'Tain't what you do, it's the time that 'cha do it. [repeats two times] That's what gets results! Oh. . . ."*
1:36	**B**	Over the bridge, the band sings the entire line, leaving Young with humorous responses. *"You can try hard, don't mean a thing! Don't mean a thing! Take it easy. . . . Greasssy! Then your jive will swing! Oh, it . . ."*
1:48	**A**	*"'Tain't what you do, it's the place that 'cha do it. [repeats two times] That's what gets results!"*
1:58		As Smith enters a bar early on a blue note, the tune modulates upward yet again.

CHORUS 3 (extended)

2:00	**A**	Smith takes a solo while the trumpet section plays a riff, using **plungers** to alter their timbre.
2:11	**A**	The trombones slide from one chord to another, answered by the saxophones with a paraphrase of the main melody. The trumpets continue their riff, making it denser and more syncopated.
2:23	**A**	The band builds intensity by repeating the **A** section one more time.
2:35	**B**	Over this extended bridge, Crawford takes a drum solo, playing primarily on his tom-toms. Barely audible underneath, the guitar and bass continue to provide the harmony.
2:40		Crawford complicates the groove with sharp syncopated accents on the bass drum and cymbals.
2:45		As Crawford finishes his solo, the band enters on a dominant chord, holding it for two additional measures.

2:49	**A**	Chord in the trombones is followed by a high-pitched chord in the trumpets and a unison line for the saxophones.
2:59		As the tune ends, the trumpets finish on the tonic chord.
CODA		
3:01		Crawford follows a pair of cymbal strokes with a bass drum stroke.

■ GLENN MILLER (1904–1944)

As America entered the war, its most popular bandleader was Glenn Miller, an owl-eyed trombonist who brought swing firmly into mainstream entertainment. It was decidedly not Miller's intention to join the jazz canon. "I haven't [got] a great jazz band," he once explained to an interviewer, "and I don't want one." Instead, the unmistakable sound of his arrangements, with their lush blend of clarinet and saxophones, aimed straight at the white middle class, who heard his music as the embodiment of the Swing Era.

Miller grew up in a Midwestern household where he absorbed his parents' habits of discipline and self-control. As a teenager, he developed a taste for jazzy dance music, prompting him to drop out of college to become a musician. Throughout the 1920s, he was an ambitious young sideman, sharpening his skills as a soloist and arranger in some of the same dance bands as his colleague Benny Goodman. Yet by the time Goodman became a celebrity in 1935, Miller was still working behind the scenes, coaching lesser-known bands toward the big time.

When he started his own dance band in 1938, Miller refused the path laid out by Goodman. He knew what his audiences wanted: simple, clear

Glenn Miller, who led the most popular swing band of the early 1940s, combined conventional dance music with hit swing standards like "Chattanooga Choo Choo" and "In the Mood."

melodies, a smooth, danceable rhythm, and above all, a unique sound. To achieve the latter, he topped his saxophone section with a wide, pulsating clarinet (played by Willie Schwartz), creating a warm, mellifluous timbre that became his calling card. The sound can be heard on Miller's theme song, the lushly romantic "Moonlight Serenade," as well as on numerous other hit recordings ("A String of Pearls," "In the Mood") that dominated the industry's record charts in the early 1940s. Indeed, Miller's tunes were so popular that early in 1942, when shellac was limited by Japanese advances in Asia, record companies scaled back production of all other recordings so that they could supply millions of copies of "Chattanooga Choo Choo."

That same year, Miller became the best-known swing bandleader to offer his services to the armed forces. The enormous Glenn Miller Army Air Force Band featured forty-two musicians and combined strings and brass. Like Paul Whiteman before him, Miller included jazz as part of an eclectic mixture that offered something for everybody. Tragically, Miller disappeared in December 1944 when his plane flew over the English Channel and never landed. It took decades to discover that he died by accident: a U.S. bomber, returning from a mission, threw its unexploded munitions overboard, only to hit Miller's unseen airplane underneath.

■ CAB CALLOWAY (1907–1994)

Cab Calloway was a curiously ambivalent icon of black culture during the Swing Era. To whites, he offered an entrée into the black ghetto: through his singing, with its suggestive use of slang, they could catch a glimpse of an alluring world of illicit drugs and sex. To blacks, he represented hope: he showed how a man with talent and ambition could rise to the top of the music business. He wowed the cats in New York's Harlem with his stylish, zoot-suited flair, but he also impressed the black establishment with his unmistakable accoutrements of success.

Calloway grew up in Baltimore in the black middle class. He studied classical singing and diligently polished his enunciation. But in the evenings, unbeknownst to his teacher (or to his mother, who expected her son to become a lawyer like his father), he discovered the joys of singing jazz. For a time he worked as a professional basketball player, but he gave that up for the world of entertainment, where he put his athletic ability to use in exuberant dancing. One musician remembers him winning over his audience by leaping over chairs and turning somersaults—all while singing.

In the late 1920s, Calloway formed his own band, the Alabamians, which he took to New York's Savoy Ballroom; but the corny music they played there was washed away by a young band from Kansas City, the Missourians. Then in 1930, when the Missourians themselves needed a singer and leader, Calloway accepted, changing their name to Cab Calloway and His Orchestra. He was ready to debut with the band at a new Harlem nightspot called the Plantation Club, only to find it destroyed just before opening night by hoodlums from the Cotton Club who were not eager for competition. But once again his luck turned when, later that year, the Cotton Club invited him to replace Duke Ellington as the house band.

On the Cotton Club's staff were songwriter Harold Arlen and lyricist Ted Koehler, who crafted new songs to match Calloway's exuberant personality with imaginary scenes from Harlem. In "Kickin' the Gong Around" (a thinly-veiled reference to opium), the mysterious Smokey Joe searches for his drug-addict girlfriend, Minnie. Calloway took that scenario a step further in "Minnie the Moocher," enriching the moody, minor-mode song with rhyming slang from Harlem to turn Minnie into a powerful central character (the "toughest frail" with "a heart as big as a whale"). His performances of "Minnie" were always climaxed by his scat-singing—plangent wails of "hi-de-ho," echoed by both band and audience.

Calloway was a superb singer, his voice ranging from a deep baritone to a high tenor. He was also a shrewd businessman who continually improved his band with the best musicians money could buy. He was unafraid to take his black band down South, where their New York hipness often attracted the hostile attention of racists ("We were not docile Negroes," he said). Calloway knew what it took to survive. "The only difference between a black and a white entertainer," he proclaimed, "is that my ass has been kicked a little more and a lot harder because it's black." His band traveled in style, in its own Pullman car, with Calloway's lime-green Lincoln stashed in its cargo. "Cab was like a breath of fresh air," his bassist Milt Hinton remembered. "He said, 'I feel obligated to try to show these people that there's a better way of life— that entertainment is higher than this.'"

By the late 1930s, Calloway was deeply immersed in jazz. He hired the best upcoming soloists, including Chu Berry on tenor saxophone, Cozy Cole on drums, and the young Dizzy Gillespie, who tormented Calloway with his experimental modernist playing and zany antics. Soon after Calloway's band (like other swing bands) folded in the late 1940s, he moved into solo singing. Perhaps his most celebrated role was as the ne'er-do-well Sportin' Life in a 1950 production of Gershwin's *Porgy and Bess*—a fitting twist if, as some have said, Gershwin devised the part after watching Calloway at the Cotton Club. For people of a younger generation, he's probably best known for his appearance in the 1980 movie *The Blues Brothers*. Even at age seventy-three, every step he took was full of class.

BEYOND THE FORMULAS

As a commercial product, swing necessarily tended toward certain formulas, of which the Fletcher Henderson arranging style (riffs in call and response) was the most obvious. Anyone could imitate this style, it was said, and many did.

Yet at the same time, swing allowed for individual creativity of a high order. In the next chapter, we consider the music of two bandleaders who were especially bold and influential in bending the rules of swing to their own advantage: the Kansas City swing style of Count Basie and the mature compositions of Duke Ellington.

ADDITIONAL LISTENING

Fletcher Henderson	"New King Porter Stomp" (1932); *Fletcher Henderson, 1924–1936* (Giants of Jazz 074646144725) "Sugar Foot Stomp" (1925); *Fletcher Henderson* (Columbia/Legacy 074646144725)
Benny Goodman	"Blue Skies," "Stomping at the Savoy" (1938); *Benny Goodman Live at Carnegie Hall 1938* (Columbia/Legacy 65143)
Artie Shaw	"Nightmare" (1937), "Begin the Beguine" (1938); *Begin the Beguine* (RCA Bluebird 078635627428)
Jimmie Lunceford	"The Organ Grinder's Swing" (1936), "For Dancers Only" (1937), "Annie Laurie" (1937); *It's the Way That You Swing It: The Hits of Jimmie Lunceford* (Jasmine 391)
Glenn Miller	"In the Mood" (1939); *The Best of Glenn Miller* (RCA/Legacy 886972136424) "Moonlight Serenade" (1938); *The Essential Glenn Miller* (Bluebird/Legacy)
Cab Calloway	"Minnie the Moocher" (1931); *Hits of the 1930s*, vol. 2: *1931–1933* (Naxos)

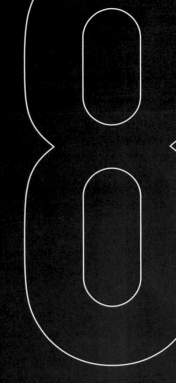

PETE JOHNSON/BIG JOE TURNER
it's all right, baby

ANDY KIRK/MARY LOU WILLIAMS
walkin' and swingin'

COUNT BASIE
one o'clock jump

DUKE ELLINGTON
mood indigo

DUKE ELLINGTON
conga brava

DUKE ELLINGTON
blood count

COUNT BASIE
AND DUKE ELLINGTON

Two swing bandleaders tower over their contemporaries, as their aristocratic nicknames suggest: William "Count" Basic and Edward Kennedy "Duke" Ellington. In the latter part of the chapter, we will pick up the trail of Ellington's long career where we left it in Chapter 5, at the Cotton Club in the 1920s. But we begin with Kansas City and the Southwest, where the startling, hard-driving swing of Count Basie took root.

THE SOUTHWEST

Although swing was a national music, disseminated by recordings and radio across the country, one region was strong enough to pull that national sound in a new direction. It was known as the Southwest—not, as we would have it today, the desert regions north of Mexico, but the area south and west of the Mississippi, including Missouri, Oklahoma, and Texas—and its urban headquarters lay in Kansas City.

African Americans had known about the Southwest since the end of the Civil War, when, seeking economic opportunity and social freedom, they began heading toward what they would call "the territory." Some founded all-black towns, such as Nicode-

Count Basie accomplished the most with the least effort. Here we see his good humor in action, at the Newport Jazz Festival, 1955.

wwnorton.com/studyspace

mus, Kansas, and Boley, Oklahoma. Others simply searched for jobs requiring unskilled manual labor. Working on the river, on the railroad, in turpentine factories, or in mines couldn't have been easy, but there was a satisfaction in avoiding the stifling agricultural work of Mississippi, Arkansas, and Georgia.

From the Margins to the Center: Boogie-Woogie

One way to judge the impact of the Southwest on national music is by tracing the path of **boogie-woogie**, a blues piano style. Where precisely boogie-woogie came from is impossible to know, but one early nickname—"fast Western"—suggests the Southwest, while other bits of oral evidence point to east Texas and Louisiana. The style spread rapidly during the 1920s, following the urbanizing trend of the Great Migration and securing a home in the major Midwestern cities of Kansas City and Chicago.

As with ragtime, boogie-woogie was built on a firm rhythmic foundation in the left hand. But unlike ragtime, which turned the four-beat measure into a two-beat feeling by alternating bass notes and chords, boogie-woogie doubled the pace with fierce, rhythmic **ostinatos** (insistently repeated melodies). Known as "chains" after their repetitive quality, these ostinato patterns divide each beat in two, so that the four-beat measure now has an eight-beat feeling. Heavily percussive, this torrent of sound in the left hand was the main feature of the music. Against it, the right hand was free to play bluesy patterns in percussive cross-rhythms.

cross-rhythm rhythm that conflicts with the underlying meter

Boogie-woogie was a social music—tumultuous and inexpensive, perfect for dancing and blues singing. In the countryside, it emerged from logging and turpentine camps where men listened to music in rough outbuildings known as "barrelhouses." In cities, boogie-woogie was played in speakeasies where hard-working pianists played through the night for a few dollars plus tips. Much as stride served as an ideal accompaniment at rent parties in New York (see Chapter 5), boogie-woogie provided the preferred rhythmic punch in the Midwest. Like its later progeny, rock and roll, its thunderous sound cut through the tumult, spurring dancers onto the floor.

In the 1920s, boogie-woogie found its way onto recordings. "Honky Tonk Train Blues" (1927), by Meade Lux Lewis, imitated the bustle of railroad travel through consistently overlapping ostinato patterns. The 1928 "Pine Top's Boogie Woogie," by Clarence "Pine Top" Smith, featured the pianist shouting as if to control an imaginary Saturday night crowd. The style probably found its name from the dance that Smith introduces at one point: "When I say 'hold yourself,' I want all of you to get ready to stop! And when I say 'stop,' don't move! And when I say 'get it,' I want all of you to do a boogie-woogie!"

■ PETE JOHNSON (1904–1967) and BIG JOE TURNER (1911–1985)

One place to hear boogie-woogie in Kansas City was in the Sunset Café at 18th Street and Highland, where the star attractions were vocalist Big Joe Turner and pianist Pete Johnson. Johnson had worked as a manual laborer (shining shoes, working in a slaughterhouse) before discovering that the piano could offer better money for less work. He met Turner at a speakeasy called the Backbiter's Club, where he earned three dollars (plus tips) working literally all night. Johnson was a versatile pianist, playing ragtime and pop songs, but he became famous for a hard-driving, percussive blues that seemed never to end. Big Joe Turner, a young man with an intensely powerful voice, worked across the room as the bartender serving beer for fifteen cents in tin cans. Turner would sing from behind the bar, and occasionally step outside to the sidewalk to sing down the street—a method of luring in customers he referred to as "calling the children home," much as Buddy Bolden and King Oliver had done in New Orleans.

In the wake of John Hammond's "From Spirituals to Swing" concert, Café Society offered its New York patrons the finest in boogie-woogie: Meade Lux Lewis, Big Joe Turner (with his face turned), Albert Ammons, Pete Johnson, 1939.

Once the music started, it was hard to stop. John Hammond, who visited Kansas City for the first time in 1936, recalled slow tunes that would last for more than half an hour. Faster tunes were shorter ("only" twenty minutes), but they generated an intensity that was palpable. One overheated reporter wrote that "the colored patrons got excited and threw themselves on the floor, completely hysterical by the rhythm and atmosphere." The same energy twenty years later would translate into the teenage hysteria of early rock and roll. Turner, who contributed to rock with his unexpected 1954 hit "Shake, Rattle, and Roll," commented drily: "We was doin' rock and roll before anyone ever heard of it."

Boogie-Woogie Revival

In the early 1930s, boogie-woogie struggled to survive. It was too rhythmically complicated to transfer to the printed page, and record companies were cutting back sharply on black dance music. Individual performers drifted by the wayside. Pine Top Smith was killed in 1929 by a stray bullet in a Chicago nightclub. Jimmy Yancey, a former vaudevillian who became one of the most successful boogie-woogie players, worked as a groundskeeper at the White Sox's Comiskey Park in Chicago. Other musicians, like Lewis and Albert Ammons, worked as cab drivers.

In the course of the 1930s, however, boogie-woogie made a sudden turnaround when it became a craze with the more affluent white public. This startling comeback can be credited to the folk revival, which began as a self-conscious attempt to publicize black folk traditions, and its central figure, once again John Hammond. Having seen black dance music marketed successfully as "swing," Hammond decided to go further: why not show the world how swing was based on neglected traditions, such as blues and gospel? He scoured the countryside looking for performers and brought them together for a 1938 concert, "From Spirituals to Swing," held in New York's most prestigious venue, Carnegie Hall. There, well-dressed patrons heard the familiar sounds of swing juxtaposed with the harmonica playing of Sonny Terry, Chicago blues by singer Big Bill Broonzy, and religious music by the Golden Gate Quartet and Sister Rosetta Tharpe. Hammond also made sure that New York heard the finest boogie-woogie—Meade Lux Lewis and

Albert Ammons from Chicago, and Pete Johnson accompanying Big Joe Turner. The concert program encouraged the audience to "forget you are in Carnegie Hall" by relaxing into the spirit of Kansas City.

Soon boogie-woogie became mainstream as pianists everywhere were expected to learn its thumping rhythmic ostinatos. Even popular song was affected: in a tune popularized during World War II by the Andrews Sisters, a trumpet player from Chicago is drafted and finds he can't play in his favorite "eight to the bar" groove until the army provides him with a bass and guitar. "He makes the company jump when he plays reveille," the Andrews Sisters sang. "He's the boogie-woogie bugle boy of Company B." The formerly underground music of black Kansas City and Chicago became the soundtrack for America.

"It's All Right, Baby"

Turner and Johnson were not new to New York: Hammond had brought them East in 1936, hoping to drum up excitement for their music. But at the "From Spirituals to Swing" concert, they faced the daunting challenge of compressing their loose, casual backroom flavor into a tight three minutes. Fortunately, they had done that two years earlier with a recording of "Roll 'Em Pete," a number roughly recast as "It's All Right, Baby" when it was performed at Carnegie Hall.

Turner models perfect blues behavior from the outset. After a long, languorous bluesy phrase ("Well, it's all . . . right . . . then!"), he shouts encouragement to Johnson and keeps lively time with his feet while delivering simple three-line blues stanzas. After several choruses of Johnson's percussive playing, Turner's words melt down to simple shouts, serving as calls to Johnson's inventive responses. It sounds like Sunset Café craziness—until the business-like, abrupt ending makes it clear that the professionals were fully in charge all along.

LISTENING GUIDE

it's all right, baby

1.4

BIG JOE TURNER AND PETE JOHNSON

Big Joe Turner, vocal; Pete Johnson, piano

- Label: *From Spirituals to Swing: 1938 & 1939 Carnegie Hall Concerts* (Vanguard 169-171-2)
- Date: 1938
- Style: boogie-woogie
- Form: 12-bar blues

What to listen for:

- solid, rocking rhythm
- Kansas City–style boogie-woogie piano: 12-bar blues, left-hand ostinato
- powerful and varied blues singing
- call and response between voice and piano

CHORUS 1

0:00   Johnson opens with a dramatic series of repeated chords on the piano.

0:05   (sung) *"Well, it's all . . . right . . . then!"*
       As the harmony shifts to IV, Johnson begins a boogie-woogie **ostinato.** Turner enters with a broad, sweeping phrase.

0:09   (spoken) *"Yeah, papa."*
       While commenting on Johnson's solid groove, Turner adds an additional rhythmic layer
       by tapping his feet.

CHORUS 2

0:14   *"That's all right, baby, that's all right for you.*
       [Unintelligible] for you, babe, that's the way you do."
       Turner sings his first full chorus, full of subtle variations in rhythm. His first line begins
       on the offbeat, then shifts to the **downbeat**. Johnson's left hand continues the ostinato,
       while the right hand retreats to simple lower-register chords.

0:27   Johnson responds to Turner's melodies with a low melodic riff.

CHORUS 3

0:29   *"Well, you're so beautiful, but you've got to die someday.*
       All I want [is] a little lovin' just before you pass away."
       At the end of his first line, Turner escapes into an expressive **blue note**.

CHORUS 4

0:44   *"Baby, what's the matter now? Tryin' to quit me, babe, where you don't know how."*
       Behind Turner's vocal, Johnson begins playing short riffs.

CHORUS 5

0:59   *"Roll 'em, boy . . . let 'em jump for joy. Yeah, man, happy as a baby boy.*
       Well, just got another brand-new choo-choo toy."
       Turner jumps in ahead of the bar line. In response, Johnson plays a familiar boogie-
       woogie riff.

1:12   (spoken) *"Ah, pick it, papa!"*

CHORUS 6

1:14   Spurred by Turner's foot stomp and hand clap on the **backbeat**, Johnson begins his two-
       chorus solo.

1:16   (spoken) *"Yeah, yeah!"*

1:24   (spoken) *"Way down, way down!"*

CHORUS 7

1:28   Johnson suddenly plays a high-pitched series of repeated notes at the top of the
       keyboard.

1:35   As Johnson returns to the middle register, Turner chuckles appreciatively.

1:39   (spoken) *"Solid, pops, solid!"*

CHORUS 8

1:43   *"Yes, yes! Yes, I know!"*
       Turner's simple phrase becomes a call, prompting a response from Johnson's piano.

1:45   Each time Turner repeats his phrase, he varies it in pitch and rhythm.

CHORUS 9

1:57   *"Well, all right, then!"*
       Without taking a breath, Turner launches into a new phrase, again answered by
       Johnson.

CHORUS 10

2:12   *"Bye . . . bye!"*
       Turner transforms his two-syllable phrase into a lengthy, expressive arc that spans sev-
       eral measures.

CODA

2:24   *"Bye-bye, baby, bye-bye!"*
       Johnson suddenly cuts off the boogie-woogie ostinato. With a few simple gestures,
       Johnson and Turner dismantle the rhythmic momentum and bring the performance to a
       close. Thunderous applause follows.

TERRITORY BANDS

During the 1920s and early 1930s, there were thousands of dance bands scattered across America. Known as **territory bands**, these bands worked a geographic area no more than a day's drive from their headquarters. Some "territories" were close to the center of the music business in New York, while others ranged from the Southeast to the upper Midwest (where the polkas of Lawrence Welk were the favorite) to Northern California. Some were white, others were black. Some specialized in "hot" swing while others purveyed more genteel music. A surprising number, including the Melodears, the Prairie View Co-Eds, and the International Sweethearts of Rhythm, were all-female. A few were even religious, like the mysteriously bearded and gentile House of David band, sponsored by a commune in Michigan. Bands often sported names that had little contact with reality: Art Bronson's Bostonians, for example, were based in Salinas, Kansas. Only a few territory bands ever set foot in a recording studio.

■ ANDY KIRK (1898–1992) and MARY LOU WILLIAMS (1910–1981)

The Twelve Clouds of Joy, led by tuba player Andy Kirk, lived a typical life for a territory band during the Depression—constant touring, no access to recording studios, and the constant threat of financial failure. During the early 1930s, when future star saxophonists Ben Webster, Lester Young, and Buddy Tate passed through the band, the Twelve Clouds of Joy endured night after night in small Midwestern towns. Sometimes they were paid in fried chicken; other times, they stole corn and roasted the kernels.

In 1936, Kirk finally caught his break. The band had signed a contract with Decca Records, which expected its black bands to specialize in the blues.

After leaving the Andy Kirk band, Mary Lou Williams, seen here in 1949, led her own band for several years at Café Society.

DUNCAN SCHIEDT COLLECTION

Kirk convinced them to record a ballad he had heard on the streets of Kansas City played by three kids with ukuleles, known informally as the "Slave Song" (after a chorus that began "I'll slave for you"). Kirk copyrighted the song with the changed title "Until the Real Thing Comes Along," listing himself as composer. When the record became a hit, Kirk and the Clouds of Joy were launched into the big time.

The musical genius of the group was the pianist and arranger, Mary Lou Williams. She had grown up in Pittsburgh, where she learned to play piano by listening to local great Earl Hines and records by Jelly Roll Morton and James P. Johnson. Her brilliance was evident by age fourteen, when she left home to join a vaudeville show; but a few years later, she married John Williams, who joined the Kirk band as a saxophonist. She remained backstage, occasionally earning some dollars by driving the bus and styling hair, until 1929, when one day the band's pianist didn't show up for a recording session. Williams volunteered to sit in, having already learned the band's repertory by ear (she had perfect pitch and an uncanny memory). She was hired on the spot, and soon became one of the few female instrumentalists to star in swing. As one of her arrangements put it, she was "the lady who swings the band."

At first, Williams couldn't read music (like many women, she had received little formal training) and relied instead on her exceptional aural skills to negotiate difficult musical situations. For her first arrangements for the band, she sang the instruments' lines to Kirk, who hastily put them into musical notation. But she quickly learned her music theory. "She'd be sitting up at the foot of the bed, legs crossed like an Indian," Kirk recounts, "just writing and writing."

As pianist, Williams was a powerful force. "I listened to how a pianist pushed, like Count Basie," she said, "and *I* pushed." She once proudly claimed that she played "heavy, like a man"—an assessment that probably says more about her social upbringing than about her playing. Today, we are more likely to celebrate Williams as a female pioneer who showed that power and taste transcend gender.

"Walkin' and Swingin'"

"Walkin' and Swingin'" was written by Mary Lou Williams in 1936, shortly after the agent Joe Glaser had taken control of the Twelve Clouds of Joy's bookings and brought them to Decca Records. Although Williams's arrangement earned her only a few dollars—a small bonus to her salary as pianist—she was satisfied that the piece furthered her own reputation as a performer and arranger, as well as that of her small swing band.

The opening may remind you of Fletcher Henderson's "Blue Lou": both tunes begin with a dissonance from the minor mode that resolves to the major. Yet the arrangements are distinctly different—partly because of individual style, but also because Kirk's band was small, only a dozen musicians (as its name suggests). While most arrangers depended on four or five saxophones to fill out their harmonies, Kirk's band had only three. Williams's solution was ingenious: she asked one of the trumpet players to "talk into a hat"—to use a metal derby mute—to help it blend with the saxophones. The mood is sly and conversational, as if the collective voice of the band had continually new things to say.

One of Williams's musical ideas will appear later in this book (Chapter 13) in a more modern style. The riff from the end of the second chorus (1:12) was appropriated by her friend Thelonious Monk for his tune "Rhythm-a-ning," which wasn't recorded until 1957.

Mary Lou Williams's career was not restricted to the Swing Era. In 1942, tiring of continuous band travel, she left Andy Kirk's band and took a spot at the Café Society in New York. She also became more active as a composer, recording elaborate pieces such as *Zodiac Suite* (1945). Her interest in complex chromatic harmonies (she called them "zombie chords") pulled her into the bebop revolution of the 1940s, where she assumed a position of leadership. Her apartment on Hamilton Terrace in Harlem became a gathering place for such musicians as Dizzy Gillespie, Kenny Clarke, Bud Powell, and especially Thelonious Monk, whom she took on as a protégé.

In the 1950s, Williams underwent a dramatic conversion to Roman Catholicism, and renounced music in favor of charitable work. When she resurfaced in the 1960s, it was as a teacher of jazz history. Her concerts often featured lengthy pieces designed to show the evolution of the music from ragtime to the most dissonant modern jazz. She remained fearless, even recording a duo album with avant-garde composer and pianist Cecil Taylor. Toward the end of her life, she took a position as professor in the Music Department at Duke University, instilling in her students a vision of jazz as a continuous tradition and illustrating her points with rich, sonorous chords on the piano.

2.5

🎧 walkin' and swingin'

ANDY KIRK AND HIS TWELVE CLOUDS OF JOY
Harry "Big Jim" Lawson, Paul King, Earl Thompson, trumpets; Ted Donnelly, Henry Wells, trombones; John Williams, John Harrington, alto saxophones; Dick Wilson, tenor saxophone; Mary Lou Williams, piano; Ted Robinson, guitar; Booker Collins, bass; Ben Thigpen, drums

- Label: Decca 809; *Andy Kirk & The 12 Clouds of Joy* (ASV/Living Era 5108)
- Date: 1936
- Style: big-band swing
- Form: 32-bar popular song (**A A B A**)

What to listen for:

- swing groove (two-beat bass line, switching to four-beat)
- ingenious *soli* by saxophone/trumpet section in chorus 2
- Williams's intricate solo, featuring blue notes

CHORUS 1

0:00	**A**	The saxophones begin a long, swooping melody, supported by a **seesawing riff** in the brass. The bass plays a two-beat pattern (although we still feel the overall four-beat framework).
0:08		After the saxophone melody finishes, the brass section emerges with a brief figure on the **offbeats**.
0:10	**A**	
0:20	**B**	The piece **modulates** to a new key. The brass take the lead, with the saxophones quietly in the background.
0:30	**A**	The tune modulates back to the original key.

INTERLUDE

0:38		The saxophones, topped by a solo trumpet, extend the seesawing riff to a **full cadence**.

CHORUS 2

0:43	**A**	The piece modulates again, this time to yet a different key. The saxophone/ trumpet combination plays a chorus-long passage in block-chord texture (*soli*). By subtly changing dynamics and rhythm, the band suggests an improvising soloist.
0:52	**A**	As it passes over the same chord progression, the band plays shorter, more propulsive figures.
1:02	**B**	Again the tune modulates, with the written-out *soli* line rising and falling over the chords.
1:12	**A**	The *soli* settles into a simple, on-the-beat riff.

CHORUS 3

1:21	**A**	Williams begins her piano solo, interspersing punchy percussive phrases with delicate, intricate runs.

1:31	A	She simulates a **blue note** by crushing two notes together.
1:41	B	Wilson plays a tenor saxophone solo, accompanied by background riffs.
1:50	A	Williams returns to continue her solo.
1:56		She plays a riff that sounds like an improvisation. But when the band immediately repeats it (in a two-bar **break**), we realize that the entire passage is part of Williams's arrangement.

CHORUS 4 (abbreviated)

2:00	A	In a climactic chorus, the saxophones return to their seesawing riff while the bass switches to a four-beat pattern. Above them, the brass punctuate strongly on the offbeat.
2:08	A	In the next section (which arrives two bars early), a simple brass riff is answered by the saxophones.
2:17	B	As the arrangement reaches its climax, saxophones scurry beneath a brass high note.
2:28	A	The brass play a new two-note riff, answered by the saxophones.
2:35		The two-note riff falls to a final cadence.

Women in Jazz

Perhaps no symbol from World War II has as much modern impact as Rosie the Riveter, her arms flexed in determination to let the world know that women were capable of working on the factory floor for their nation's defense. The war years similarly opened the door for women musicians. They had played jazz and dance music all along, but with able-bodied young men joining the service, their services were suddenly needed to fill empty slots in hundreds of Swing Era dance bands.

Most women in show business were dancers or singers, showing off their bodies in luxurious or skimpy clothing. To play an instrument in public, however, women had to overcome the prejudice of men who did not want to see them doing this. One exception was the piano, so firmly associated with the feminine family parlor that Jelly Roll Morton worried that playing it might make him a "sissy." We have already encountered two pianists, Lil Hardin and Mary Lou Williams. Many others earned the respect of their local jazz community: Julia Lee and Countess Margaret in Kansas City, Lovie Austin (Williams's first inspiration) in Chicago, Mamie Desdoumes in New Orleans. The flute and harp carried similar feminine associations, but had little impact on jazz.

A woman on the stage, people reasoned, was not fit for middle-class society. Some women simply toughed it out. While touring with the Count Basie band, Billie Holiday ruined her stockings by playing craps on the floor of the bus. Vocalist Anita O'Day, tired of the expense of maintaining several fancy evening gowns and wanting to be treated simply as a musician, ordered the same band jacket that the men wore. This prompted accusations of lesbianism, leading O'Day to wonder, "What does a jacket or shirt have to do with anyone's sex life?"

A few women made names for themselves as instrumentalists in male bands: trumpeter Billie Rodgers, vibraphonist Marjorie Hymans, trombonist Melba Liston. But others found it much simpler to band together in an all-female group, which could protect each woman's reputation by traveling under strict supervision. Some of these groups, their names advertising their gender (the International Sweethearts of Rhythm, the Harlem Playgirls, the Darlings of Rhythm), were among the hardest-swinging territory bands of the day.

Ultimately, the pressures of the road proved too much for most women, whose careers were cut short by family duties, marriage, or social convention. Still, the war years had shown that swing was not a male thing and that there was nothing unfeminine about playing jazz.

Count Basie could look suave and elegant, as in this 1939 portrait. Yet to his musicians he was "ol' Base," an unpretentious bandleader who made sure the music never traveled far from its core elements—the blues and the dance groove.

■ COUNT BASIE (1904–1984)

It would probably surprise most jazz fans to discover that the most famous bandleader form Kansas City, William "Count" Basie, actually grew up on the New Jersey shore. His home was in Red Bank, not far from New York City, and his parents were working class: his father was a groundskeeper, his mother took in laundry. After dropping out of junior high school, he became a musician simply for the love of it—"playing music has never really been work," he once said. He learned his trade in New York, studying the work of the stride masters while trying to avoid direct competition with pianists like James P. Johnson, who were far above him in ability. When the chance came to leave town as the accompanist for a touring vaudeville show, he grabbed it.

Not until the mid-1920s did Basie find himself in the Southwest, when his vaudeville act fell through and left him high and dry in Oklahoma City. One morning, from his hotel window, he heard a new type of jazz played by a territory band called the Blue Devils, who were using the back of a truck as a bandstand. "I had never heard anything like that band in my life," he remembered. "Everybody seemed to be having so much fun just being up there playing together. . . . There was such a team spirit among those guys, and it came out in the music, and as you stood there looking and listening you just couldn't help wishing that you were a part of it."

Basie soon became an irregular member of the Blue Devils, which was nominally led by the bassist Walter Page. Like many other groups of the time, it was a "commonwealth" band, distributing its funds evenly among its members and relying on group consensus for decisions. This informality ultimately spelled disaster. As one band member remembered, "Whenever we wanted to do something, accept a job, we have to sit down and have a discussion. . . . Seven would vote for it and six would vote against it." The band finally dissolved in 1933 when funds ran out altogether in Bluefield, West Virginia.

Benny Moten ▶ By this time, Basie and Page had already been scooped up by the most prosperous band in the Kansas City region, led by Benny Moten (1894–1935). Moten was a skilled ragtime pianist but an even more successful businessman. In Kansas City, he dealt shrewdly with the powerful city organization led by Tom Pendergast (see box), whose *laissez-faire* attitude toward illegal activities such as gambling and selling alcohol made for a boisterous night life. According to trumpet player Oran "Hot Lips" Page, Moten's proposition to his musicians was simple: "If we would provide the music, he would provide the jobs."

In 1935, Benny Moten's career came to an unexpected end when he entered a hospital for a tonsillectomy. Fearing anesthesia, he insisted on using Novocain—a therapy that proved tragically insufficient. While lying on the operating table, he suddenly felt the surgeon's knife and jumped, jolting the doctor's arm. He bled to death from a severed artery.

Moten's demise, while devastating, ended up being Basie's gain. He retreated to the Reno Club in Kansas City, where he gathered together many of the Moten musicians. This tiny, L-shaped saloon was so small that Walter Page often had to sit on a stool outside and lean in the window. Basie's band was also small, with only nine pieces—three trumpets, three saxophones, and three in the rhythm section—and managed to create music without written arrangements. "I don't think we had over four or five sheets of music up there," Basie recalled. "We had our own thing, and we could always play some more blues and call it something."

Head Arrangements and Jam Sessions

The unwritten arrangements that the Basie band created were known as **head arrangements,** so called because the music, created collectively, was stored in the heads of the musicians who played it. Head arrangements typified the casual but creative atmosphere of the jam session in Kansas City. A club like the Sunset Café would typically hire only a piano and drums, expecting the rest of the music to be created by musicians who would drop by in the course of an evening. Tunes lasted as long as the musicians wanted. "It wasn't unusual for one number to go on about an hour or an hour and a half," the drummer Jo Jones recalled. "Nobody got tired. They didn't tell me at that time they used to change drummers, so I just sat there and played the whole time for pure joy."

Although only one soloist played at a time, the mood of the jam session was collective, with horn players waiting their turn to join in. If one musician played a riff, others nearby would harmonize it, searching for notes to fit the riff in block-chord texture. According to bassist Gene Ramey, this skill derived from black folk traditions. It reminded him of "revival meetings, where the preacher and the people are singing, and there's happenings all around." The more musicians, the more notes were needed: a saxophonist might add extra extended notes to standard chords (sixths, ninths) to avoid "stepping on" someone else's line (that is, to avoid playing the same basic chord tone). At the same time, since this spontaneous music was created by professionals, it had a slick, orchestral polish. All that was needed to transfer it to the dance band was a group of musicians capable of remembering what they had played.

The Benny Moten band, behind the Old Folks' Home in Kansas City. Moten died unexpectedly in 1935, leaving his best talent to be gathered in by Count Basie. This version of the band included Jimmy Rushing (far left), Basie (left, head on hand), Bennie's brother Bus (standing on bench), with Eddie Durham to his immediate right, and Moten (far right).

Kansas City

"Everything's up to date in Kansas City!" As Rodgers and Hammerstein made clear in their 1943 musical *Oklahoma!*, Kansas City had a certain flair other places lacked. Known as "Paris of the plains" for its role as a world market for cattle, it developed during the Depression the additional, somewhat unsavory, reputation as a "wide open" town.

In the 1920s and 1930s, Kansas City was controlled by the political boss, Tom Pendergast. Technically, Pendergast was only a city alderman, but behind the scenes he ran a political machine that turned the city into a haven for gambling and alcohol. Even though Prohibition was the law until 1933, violators were rarely convicted; saloons stayed open all night. Although Pendergast, like his rival, the Louisiana governor Huey Long, offered a kind of populism for "the poor, the black, the Italian, the immigrant," ultimately his high-handed rule brought him down. His years of power ended when he was convicted in 1939 for income tax evasion—the same charge that ended Al Capone's career in Chicago.

Under Pendergast's rule, a free-wheeling jazz thrived in Kansas City's black neighborhood. The music was saturated in the blues—streamlined, urbanized, and hip. Black musicians didn't escape racial prejudice in Kansas City (it "might as well as been Gulfport, Mississippi," one performer remembered), but they could always find work. The corner of Twelfth Street and Vine (to quote another popular song) was not prosperous, but it was perhaps the hippest place to be on a Saturday night.

For dance bands, head arrangements offered special flexibility. Some became fixed arrangements, written down to preserve the order of riffs. But in the heat of performance, musicians could extend the tune to unimaginable lengths. New riffs could be created to match the dancers' ingenuity. "When you play a battle of music, it's the head arrangements that you could play for about ten minutes and get the dancers going," remembered Teddy Wilson, whose music-reading dance band could not keep up with Kansas City-style spontaneity. Once the Basie band began playing "One O'Clock Jump," the contest was over: "That was the end of the dance!"

🎧 "One O'Clock Jump"

"One O'Clock Jump" was a fluid arrangement of the twelve-bar blues that had evolved gradually for more than a decade before finally being recorded. Many of its riff tunes were collected over time by Basie longtimers like saxophonist Buster Smith, trumpeter Hot Lips Page, and trombonist Eddie Durham. The main theme itself (not played until the ninth chorus) can be heard in the 1920s Don Redman arrangement "Six or Seven Times." Originality was hardly the issue: like the blues itself, these riffs were assumed to be public property.

There was little else holding the piece together. The band knew it as "Blue Balls," a slightly indecent title they never expected to make public. When the tune was finally performed on the radio, commercial pressures ("You can't call it *that!*") forced a change. "One O'Clock Jump" presumably commemorates the hour of the morning it was first broadcast. Simple but tremendously effective, it became Basie's first hit.

Basie begins with a piano solo that locks the rhythm section into its groove. He often insisted on starting off on his own, playing several choruses until the tempo felt right— "just like you were mixing mash and yeast to make whiskey," his trumpet player Harry "Sweets" Edison once said, "and you keep tasting it." A sudden modulation switches from Basie's favorite key (F major) to the distant key the horn players preferred (D-flat major). The arrangement is primarily a string of solos, featuring the best of the Basie band with riff accompaniment. Then comes what might be called a "rhythm section solo" (chorus 7): Basie is the main voice, but his minimal jabs divert our attention to the light, clear sound of what was often considered the best rhythm section of the Swing Era.

The last three choruses consist of interlocking riffs. This version is the commercial recording, a 78-rpm disc limited by technology to three minutes. Some radio broadcasts extended the piece for several minutes; musicians have said it could go on for half an hour. The maximum length, one supposes, depended on the fortitude of the musicians. Like African music, it could be extended to suit any occasion.

2.6

 **one o'clock jump**

COUNT BASIE AND HIS ORCHESTRA

Count Basie, piano; Buck Clayton, Ed Lewis, Bobby Moore, trumpets; George Hunt, Dan Minor, trombones; Earl Warren, alto saxophone; Jack Washington, baritone saxophone; Herschel Evans, Lester Young, tenor saxophones; Freddie Green, guitar; Walter Page, bass; Jo Jones, drums

- Label: Decca 1363; *The Complete Decca Recordings* (GRP 36112)
- Date: 1937
- Style: Kansas City swing
- Form: 12-bar blues

What to listen for:

- Kansas City–style head arrangement
- string of solos, accompanied by riffs
- steady rhythm section, highlighted in chorus 7
- Young's solo in chorus 5 (including false fingerings)

INTRODUCTION

0:00   Basie begins with a **vamp**—a short, repeated figure in the left hand. Other members of the rhythm section enter gingerly, as if feeling Basie's tempo and groove.

CHORUS 1

0:11   With the rhythm section now in full gear, Basie begins his solo with a clear melodic statement. His left hand, playing a spare and tentative **stride** accompaniment, blends in with the consistent on-beat attacks of the guitar, bass, and drums.

CHORUS 2

0:28   Basie suddenly attacks the piano in octaves, ending his phrases with a **tremolo** (a rapid shaking of the notes in a chord).

0:43   Closing off the introduction, Basie quickly **modulates** to a new key.

CHORUS 3

0:45   On the tenor saxophone, Evans plays a stately chorus with full **vibrato**. Behind him, the muted trumpets play a simple, two-note harmonized riff.

CHORUS 4

1:02   Hunt (trombone) takes over smoothly for the next chorus, accompanied by a background riff by the saxophones. The drummer moves the pulse to the high-hat cymbal.

1:15   The trombonist uses his slide to create **blue notes**.

CHORUS 5

1:19   Young (tenor saxophone) begins his chorus with **false fingerings**—playing the same note with different fingerings to create new timbres.

1:21   To match Young's sound, the drummer adjusts his pattern to an accent on the bass drum every other measure.

1:32   At the end of the chorus, the drummer plays the **backbeat**.

CHORUS 6

1:36   On trumpet, Clayton starts his solo with a simple riff (resembling the beginning of "When the Saints Go Marching In"). Behind him, the saxophones play a long descending riff. The drummer returns to playing the high-hat cymbal with occasional snare drum accents.

CHORUS 7

1:53   Basie plays sparely, accompanied only by the rhythm section. Each of his chords has a distinctive sound: high-pitched, spanning slightly over an octave. The bass, drums, and guitar play unflaggingly.

2:02   For a few measures, the bass plays slightly sharp (above pitch).

CHORUS 8

2:10 The band reenters with overlapping riffs: a simple melody, played by the saxophones, is interwoven with three trumpet chords. Both are answered by a trombone chord.

CHORUS 9

2:27 The riffs remain the same except for the saxophonists', who play the melody usually recognized as the theme to "One O'Clock Jump."

CHORUS 10

2:43 The saxophones change to a simple, unharmonized riff. The drummer reinforces the trombone chord with a sharp accent on the snare drum.

2:57 With a short series of chords, the saxophones signal the end.

The Basie Band

In Kansas City, Basie's world was limited to the ten-block black neighborhood in which he lived and worked (at the Reno Club). As critic Gerald Early notes, he "did not aspire to live in an integrated world." Then one night in 1936, John Hammond happened to hear the band on the shortwave radio built into his car (from the peripatetic local radio station W9XBY) and soon thereafter made the trip to Kansas City to hear for himself. Entranced with the band's loose, easy swing, he decided to bring Basie into the commercial mainstream.

For Basie's musicians, moving from the Reno Club was not easy. Some of their instruments were held together with rubber bands and string. Some members left, while others were added to raise their number to the industry standard of fifteen. On the road to New York, when asked to play conventional dance music ("I don't think I even knew what a goddamn tango was," Basie remembered), the band floundered. "By the time you read this," a Chicago newspaper reported, "they will be on their way back to Kansas City." To Hammond's dismay, Basie had already signed an exploitative recording contract with Decca. But over the long road trip, Basie worked out the musical kinks. In 1937, having made it to New York, the band began practicing in earnest in the basement of Harlem's Woodside Hotel, developing their own repertory. As Basie later remembered:

> It was like the Blue Devils. We always had somebody in those sections who was a leader, who could start something and get those ensembles going. I mean while somebody would be soloing in the reed section, the brasses would have something going in the background, and the reed section would have something to go with that. And while the brass section had something going, somebody in the reed section might be playing a solo. . . .
>
> That's where we were at. That's the way it went down. Those guys knew just where to come in and they came in. And the thing about it that was so fantastic was this: *Once those guys played something, they could damn near play it exactly the same the next night.* . . . And a lot of times the heads that we made down there in that basement were a lot better than things that were written out.

Basie was no arranger, but he worked closely with trombonist Eddie Durham to cast these collectively created charts into permanent form. He also edited many an elaborate chart that fell into his hands down to a clean, uncluttered piece, in accordance with the twentieth-century maxim "less is more." The result was not technically dazzling—few Kansas City arrangements are swing landmarks—but Basie made history by insisting on simplicity and refusing to interfere with the groove. His own piano technique simply melted away: a full-blown stride artist, he ended by becoming the most laconic pianist ever. Yet every note he played contributed to the band's swing. "The Count don't do much," one band member explained, "but he does it better than anyone else."

The most crucial characteristic of Kansas City jazz was its distinctive dance groove of four beats to the bar, and at its core was Walter Page, a large man nicknamed "Big 'Un" who made dancers happy by evening out the beat. The drummer, Jo Jones—like Page, a veteran of the Blue Devils—played with extraordinary lightness and a keen sense of ensemble. Guitarist Freddie Green was added in 1937, recommended by John Hammond, who had spotted him at a Greenwich Village club. "He had unusually long fingers, a steady stroke, and unobtrusively held the whole rhythm section together," Hammond remembered. "He was the antithesis of the sort of stiff, chugging guitarist Benny Goodman liked." The propulsive lightness of what became known as the "All-American Rhythm Section" was perhaps the band's most far-reaching innovation. "When you listen to that Basie section," bassist Gene Ramey remembered, "the drums didn't sound any louder than the guitar, the piano—it was all balanced. . . . It showed the rhythm section was 'teaming.'"

Rhythm section

The Apollo Theater demanded the most of any band performing there, including the Count Basie band. Beneath drummer Jo Jones (on platform), Lester Young matches the exuberance of his playing by raising his tenor saxophone to its limit.

Soloists   Basie's soloists initially included Blue Devils veteran Hot Lips Page, but in 1936 Page decided to strike out on his own as a solo trumpet player and singer. His replacement was the debonair trumpeter Buck Clayton, a handsome man who brought years of versatility and experience, including a stint in Shanghai in the 1920s. A year later, Clayton was joined by Harry Edison, nicknamed "Sweets" in ironic tribute to his caustic tone and witty, low-register solos, often distorted with the derby mute. The trombone section included Eddie Durham, who was also one of the earliest electric guitarists; and Dickie Wells, whose solos are often identifiable by tone alone.

One reason the Basie band became famous was because of its dueling tenor saxophonists. The elusive Lester Young, perhaps the band's most famous soloist, will be discussed in Chapter 9. His dueling partner was Herschel Evans, a powerful saxophonist from Denton, Texas, who embodied a full, rich approach to the tenor known as "Texas style." Basie typically featured Evans in slow blues tunes and melodramatic ballads like "Blue and Sentimental," recorded just months before Evans unexpectedly died from a heart condition at age twenty-nine. Evans and Young could not have presented a stronger contrast. Although their personal relationship was reportedly warm and cordial, they sat on opposite sides of the saxophone section and played as though they were in open competition, with crowds cheering each soloist. This two-tenor rivalry (with Buddy Tate taking Evans's place in 1939) was widely imitated by other swing bandleaders.

Basie's vocalist was Jimmy Rushing, a rotund man known as "Mr. Five by Five" in honor of his nearly circular measurements. Rushing graced many recordings with his high, penetrating baritone. While he was best known for his urbane interpretations of the blues, he was a versatile performer who was equally comfortable with the many varieties of pop songs of the day.

Later Basie

Basie's highly influential initial period lasted from his recording debut in 1936 to the late 1940s. Like other swing bandleaders, Basie struggled after World War II and finally broke up the band, reducing his musical entourage to a septet in 1950. Several years later, when he decided to revive his big band, only Freddie Green was left from the original crew. The rest of the musicians were drawn from the large number of excellent studio musicians available. This group, known as the "New Testament" Basie band in theological deference to its predecessor, was a decidedly different outfit. The head arrangements were gone, replaced by sturdy written arrangements. The new musicians were capable of switching between "mainstream" swing and new currents in modern jazz, but all were accustomed to a written repertory. Basie accepted this with good grace: "You know, don't you," he once said, "that if the lights go out on this band, the music will stop!"

Fortunately, the written arrangements were excellent. Basie hired some of the best arrangers in the business, like Neal Hefti (also known for composing film and TV scores) and Thad Jones, allowing his band to be used as a showcase for their talents. On the 1957 *Atomic Mr. Basie* (featuring an alarming atomic explosion on its cover), the band shows its versatility in switching from up-tempo swing charts to Hefti's "Lil Darling," perhaps the slowest swing ever recorded.

For a later generation, Basie came to exemplify the swing sound. He was the ideal choice for singers such as Frank Sinatra, Tony Bennett, and Billy Eckstine, who wanted to spark their mainstream pop with the hardest-swinging jazz available. For thirty years, Basie toured the world as a roving ambassador of swing. At the end, he sat in a wheelchair, supervising his band and continuing to play spare piano. It was the twilight of a splendid career.

■ DUKE ELLINGTON

When we last left Duke Ellington, he had led his band into Harlem's swank Cotton Club in the late 1920s. From this point on, his scope was national. Before 1935, when the entire country became swing-conscious, Ellington had displaced Fletcher Henderson as the most prominent black dance band in the business. His niche was unique: his was not merely a fine orchestra, but a showcase for unusual and inimitable compositions.

All told, Ellington's career spanned half a century. When swing bands began to disappear after World War II, Ellington kept his musicians together by subsidizing them with his own money. He spent the rest of his life as a self-described "itinerant song and dance man," shuttling between sumptuous concert halls and international festivals on the one hand and county fairs and 4-H clubs on the other. Yet we define him today by the scope of his compositions, which stand as some of the greatest accomplishments in the American arts.

Ellington the Composer

Ellington would not have been comfortable being classified as a "jazz composer." For one thing, he disliked the word "jazz," which he sensed tended to marginalize the creativity of black musicians. Sometimes he claimed that he wrote "Negro folk music." He once described Ella Fitzgerald as "beyond category," a term that applies equally well to himself.

DUNCAN SCHIEDT COLLECTION

In 1929, few knew that the young bandleader Duke Ellington took his composing seriously. Yet we can feel here the focused intent he brought to the challenges of organizing his band's sound.

Cootie Williams, brought on board in the early 1930s to replace Bubber Miley, was one of Ellington's favorite musicians, using a plunger mute over a pixie mute to create otherworldly sounds. He's seen here with the Benny Goodman Orchestra, 1940.

European classical music has taught us to think of composers as working in isolation, scribbling music on manuscript paper for others to perform. Ellington *could* work this way. Whenever he traveled, he carried with him a pad of paper and a pencil in his pocket. At odd moments throughout the day, and in the unlikeliest places (often on the train), he jotted down ideas as they came to him.

But the real business of composition—turning his musical ideas into actual pieces—was social. Ellington liked collaborating with his musicians. Rather than present them with a score, he would invite the band to work with him: explaining the mental picture that inspired it, playing parts, and assigning musicians roles. Writer Richard Boyer, who traveled with the band in 1944, described such moments as a "creative free-for-all" that sounded "like a political convention" or "a zoo at feeding time": "Perhaps a musician will get up and say, 'No, Duke! It just can't be that way!' and demonstrate on his instrument his conception of the phrase or bar under consideration. Often, too, this idea may outrage a colleague, who replies on *his* instrument with *his* conception, and the two players argue back and forth not with words but with blasts from trumpet or trombone."

Ellington's muse was inspired by this ongoing ruckus, which made his orchestral parts a copyist's nightmare. Dizzy Gillespie, who joined the band briefly in the 1940s, recalled the complicated jumble of his trumpet parts. "I'm supposed to remember that you jump from 'A' to the first three bars of 'Z,' and then jump back to 'Q,' play eight bars of that, then jump over to the next part, and then play the solo." Another musician, a bassist, found his entire part for a piece scrawled on a cocktail napkin. No permanent record survives for Ellington's music, which was reconceived whenever new soloists entered the band. There is a set of scores at the Smithsonian Institution, derived from recordings and manuscripts, that combine carefully notated Ellingtonian harmonies with vague verbal directions (for example, "Tricky ad lib," meant for Tricky Sam Nanton to take a solo). They were presented to Ellington on his sixtieth birthday; the composer thanked everyone, but forgot to take the scores home. He knew his music could not be contained by notation.

It's not surprising, therefore, that Ellington as composer has been frequently misunderstood. The most notorious case came in 1965 when the music committee for the Pulitzer Prize nominated him for an honorary lifetime award but was overruled by the Pulitzer board. The sixty-six-year-old composer responded: "Fate is being kind to me. Fate doesn't want me to be too famous too young."

The simplest way to understand Ellington's compositions is to compare them with other art forms. As a former graphic artist, for example, he continued to think of music in visual terms. "There's always a mental picture," he said. "In the old days, when a guy made a lick, he'd say what it reminded him of. I remember ole Bubber Miley taking a lick and saying, 'That reminds me of Miss Jones singin' in church.' That's the way I was raised up in music." Ellington employed the individual sounds, or colors, of his musicians like paints on a palette. His co-composer Billy Strayhorn explained: "Each member of his band is to him a distinctive tone color and set of emotions, which he mixed with others equally distinctive to produce a third thing, which I like to call the Ellington Effect." And like the director of a summer stock ensemble, Ellington worked interactively with a stable cast of characters, relying on his instincts to make the most out their quirky contributions. His powers of charm and flattery made it easy for him to draw other people's energies into his imaginative vision.

Fortunately, Ellington's legacy has been brilliantly captured on recordings. Unlike swing bands that sounded much better live than on record, Ellington was "at the height of his creative powers" in a recording studio. For the first half of his career, he squeezed hundreds of recordings into the three-minute limit dictated by the 78-rpm format. His first attempts at longer pieces were spread out awkwardly over several discs, but eventually technology caught up with him. By the 1950s, the LP recording made it easy for him to conceive his music in broader terms. Through these recordings, Ellington's compositions continue to enchant us today, more than a generation after the last of them was created.

Dramatis Fedilae

In his autobiography, *Music Is My Mistress,* Ellington identified his co-creators as "dramatis fedilae"—the "cats" in the band. His music was inseparable from the musicians who created it.

Most swing bands organized musicians by sections: saxophones, trombones, and trumpets tended to play together, producing a uniform wall of sound. Arrangers treated musicians interchangeably, expecting their creations to be played by virtually any combination of competent professionals. Ellington was the grand exception to this rule. In the Cotton Club, where musical effects resonated with scenery and imagery, he had learned how to use orchestral sounds creatively. Moreover, he knew that "sound," in jazz, was individual. His music was, literally, inimitable because the sonorities he relied on derived from musicians he worked with year in and year out. "You can't write music right," he once said, "unless you know how the man that'll play it plays poker."

By 1935, Ellington had already gathered the personality quirks that stimulated his imagination: brass players who specialized in bizarre timbres, saxophonists with heartbreaking ones, and radically different trombonists who could nevertheless blend together beautifully. For these voices, Ellington created pieces that set them off as a fine jeweler sets off his special stones.

We have already met some of Ellington's earliest musical compatriots—trumpet player Bubber Miley, trombonist Tricky Sam Nanton, and drummer Sonny Greer. Some of his longest-serving musicians dated from these years. The baritone saxophonist Harry Carney joined Ellington in 1927 at such a callow age that the band nicknamed him "Youth"—a name he kept for the forty-seven more years he remained with the band. (Carney died four months after Ellington—some said of bereavement.) His deep, rich sonority was an integral part of Ellington's sound, floating to wherever it was needed. Miles Davis once said, "If he wasn't in the band, the band wouldn't be Duke."

Harry Carney

Other musicians lasted far less long. Bubber Miley in some ways epitomized Ellington's musical values—his motto was "If it ain't got swing, it ain't worth playin'"—but his behavior was impossible. After drinking too much, he would crawl under the piano to go to sleep. Ellington let him go in 1929, hiring Cootie Williams in his place. True to form, Ellington did not tell

Cootie Williams

Williams what to do. He simply let the new musician listen carefully and realize, after playing in the trumpet section for a while, that something was missing—and that it was up to him to provide it. Williams laughed when he first heard Tricky Sam Nanton's yowling trombone, but soon took on the esoteric art of mutes to create his own bizarre sounds. Ellington described his growling solos as having "a sort of majestic folk quality." But Williams continued to play open horn as well. "Those were my two ways of being," he once said. "Both expressed the truth."

Sometimes musicians were drawn in for their musical style. Playing with Sidney Bechet in the mid-1920s gave Ellington a taste for the elegant simplicity and earthy quality of the New Orleans clarinet. His love of that "all **Barney Bigard** ▸ wood" sound led him to lure Barney Bigard, a sometime tenor saxophonist, back to his original instrument. Bigard had learned to play the clarinet in New Orleans through an old-fashioned system of fingering that was harder to play but was thought to offer a richer, more open timbre. His imagination became part of Ellington's artistic vision.

🎧 "Mood Indigo"

According to Ellington, his 1930 tune "Mood Indigo" was inspired by a plaintive scene. While having his back rubbed in between shows, he described it to a newspaper reporter:

> "It's just a little story about a little girl and a little boy. They're about eight and the little girl loves the little boy. They never speak of it, of course, but she just likes the way he wears his hat. Every day he comes by her house at a certain time and she sits in her window and waits." Duke's voice dropped solemnly. The masseur, sensing the climax, eased up, and Duke said evenly, "Then one day he doesn't come." There was silence until Duke added: "'Mood Indigo' just tells how she feels."

That was the explanation given to casual observers. In fact, the melody for "Mood Indigo" came to Ellington from Barney Bigard (who had probably acquired it from his New Orleans teacher, Lorenzo Tio). But Ellington made it his own through his disturbingly original arrangement. The instrumentation at the beginning suggests New Orleans jazz—clarinet, trumpet, and trombone—but the sound is as different as night from day. The brass players (Nanton and Williams) are distant and deliberately muted, holding their sound in check, while the clarinet, instead of being the highest instrument, is plunged into its deep and rich lower register.

Also according to Ellington, this unusual combination was an adjustment to technology. In the recording studio, a faulty microphone reacted strangely to the sound of his horns, producing an illusory pitch that ruined several takes. Eventually, Ellington decided to work with what he had, and adjusted the horns so that the microphone's errant tone became "centralized" in the overall sound. However it was achieved, the opening bars of "Mood Indigo" are unearthly and inexplicable, and probably the source of conductor-pianist André Previn's famous comment: "Duke merely lifts a finger, three horns make a sound, and I don't know what it is!"

2.7

 mood indigo

DUKE ELLINGTON AND HIS ORCHESTRA

Duke Ellington, piano; Arthur Whetsol, Freddy Jenkins, Cootie Williams, trumpets; Joe "Tricky Sam" Nanton, Juan Tizol, trombones; Johnny Hodges, alto saxophone and clarinet; Harry Carney, baritone saxophone and clarinet; Barney Bigard, clarinet; Fred Guy, banjo; Wellman Braud, bass; Sonny Greer, drums

- Label: Victor 22587-A; *The Best of Duke Ellington* (RCA/Legacy 886972136523)
- Date: 1930
- Style: early big band
- Form: 16-bar popular song

What to listen for:

- unusual instrumentation: muted brass and low-register clarinet (chorus 1), clarinet trio (chorus 2)
- a quiet mood of melancholy: low dynamics and blue notes
- Bigard's expressive clarinet solo in chorus 3

CHORUS 1 (16 bars)

0:00 Williams, Nanton, and Bigard play their three horns (trumpet, trombone, and clarinet) in **block-chord** texture, but the trumpet and trombone are on top, heavily muted, while the clarinet is in its lowest register. Guy plays a steady, thrumming beat on the banjo.

0:15 To connect from one harmony to another, Ellington plays a **chromatic scale** on the piano.

0:22 Nanton's trombone, producing unearthly sounds from a combination of straight pixie mute, plunger mute, and throat growls, can be briefly heard on its own.

INTERLUDE

0:43 On piano, Ellington provides breathing space between the first two choruses.

CHORUS 2

0:54 Williams (trumpet) continues reharmonizing the theme, this time supported by a clarinet trio (with Hodges and Carney joining Bigard on clarinet).

1:15 Williams ascends to a long-sustained top note, leaving room for the clarinets to take the lead.

1:36 A brief flourish by the brass signals the next chorus.

CHORUS 3

1:37 Bigard plays a new melody on clarinet, over a background of sustained brass chords. While the banjo continues its steady thrumming, the bass often doubles its pace to eight beats to the bar.

2:04 For several bars, Bigard chooses pitches that clash with Ellington's elusive harmony.

CHORUS 4

2:20 The final chorus reprises the unusual instrumentation of the opening chorus.

3:01 The banjo finally comes to a rest on a **tremolo** chord, punctuated by a single piano note.

■ JOHNNY HODGES (1906–1970) and the Trombones

No Ellington voice was more important than the alto saxophonist Johnny Hodges, who joined the group in 1928 and remained, off and on, for over forty years. Ellington had been searching for a saxophonist with the visceral punch and stylish elegance of Sidney Bechet, and in Hodges he found someone who had already taken Bechet as his model. He immediately became one of Ellington's main soloists, sometimes projecting a bluesy toughness, other times a gentle lyricism. As the years went on, his romantic voice flourished. He used agonizingly slow glissandos created from his embouchure (a technique known as "lipping up"), and a full sound that reminded Charlie Parker of the operatic soprano Lily Pons. We will hear more from Hodges on "Blood Count" later.

Lawrence Brown

Ellington's new trombonists were an interesting pair. Lawrence Brown was a dignified man from a minister's family in Kansas who joined the band in California in 1932. He originally wanted to be a doctor, which made his presence in the livelier setting of a swing band surprising. In his playing, he translated the rich orchestral sound of the cello to the trombone, with delicate solos and intricate inner lines.

Juan Tizol

Alongside him was a Puerto Rican virtuoso, Juan Tizol, who played a trombone equipped with valves, like a trumpet, rather than a slide. Tizol, who joined the band in 1929, carved out a niche for himself as the band's "legitimate" (or classical) trombone player, incapable of improvising but perfect for realizing a written part with a beautiful, polished tone. He was also one of the few people Ellington trusted to copy out parts for the rest of the band. As a Hispanic, Tizol was one of the few white men in the 1930s and 1940s to play with a black band. Among the tunes to which he contributed were exotic evocations like "Caravan" and "Conga Brava" (see below), through which Ellington updated the Cotton Club's "jungle" sound to new, more modern circumstances.

In the Swing Era

Ellington only gradually learned how to become a celebrity. In 1933, he took his band to England and France, where knowledgeable critics and adulatory fans who compared his music to Shakespeare made him realize how much larger his ambitions could be. Back home, he divided his time between theaters and the more ordinary experience of providing a groove for dancing. "It's a primitive instinct, this dancing business," he told an interviewer, "but it also signifies happiness, and I like to see happy people." From dancing came a maxim that he presciently turned into a song in 1932: "It don't mean a thing if it ain't got that swing."

Ellington soon developed the persona that would become familiar to millions: the flashy, natty suits, the wide, welcoming grin, the extravagant style of speaking that made him an aristocrat of the swing world. In the film *Symphony in Black* (1935), Ellington plays himself: an urban sophisticate writing and conducting a score about black manual labor and rural worship (illustrated in the film with graphic, if highly stylized, images). Backstage, a more private Ellington was so relaxed and at ease that his band nickname was Dumpy. His lassitude in the midst of the day-by-day hustle of running a dance band caused his road manager to complain, "This band has no boss."

"Race man"

Boss or no boss, Ellington sensed the responsibilities that came with being a black celebrity. He became a "race man," a spokesperson for black America, and whenever possible reminded his audiences about race consciousness. In 1941, he insisted that the black man was the country's "creative voice": "It was a happy day in America when the first unhappy slave was landed on its shores. There, in our tortured induction into this 'land of liberty,' we built its most graceful civilization. Its wealth, its flowering fields and handsome homes; its pretty traditions; its guarded leisure and its music, were all our creations." Black audiences everywhere understood this message. When his band toured the country, passing through cities and small towns with their splendid uniforms and evocative sounds, they were "news from the great wide world." Author Ralph Ellison, who heard him in Oklahoma, asked: "Where in the white community, in *any* white community, could there have been found images, examples such as these? Who were so worldly, who so elegant, and who so mockingly creative?"

Ellington's passion for racial justice led him into a musical, *Jump for Joy*, which opened in Los Angeles in 1941. The show was designed to "take Uncle Tom out of the theater, eliminate the stereotyped image that had been exploited by Hollywood and Broadway, and say things that would make the audience think." Among its tunes—one, in fact, so provocative that it was excised from performance—was "I've Got a Passport from Georgia (and I'm Going to the U.S.A.)."

Jump for Joy never made it to Broadway, but with *Black, Brown, and Beige*, Ellington made an orchestral statement that was just as persuasive. This forty-eight-minute piece, premiered at his first concert at Carnegie Hall in 1943, conveyed in tones the history of the American Negro. Unfortunately for Ellington, the piece did not have the effect he had hoped. Jazz fans found his symphonic rhetoric pretentious, while classical critics declined to hear it as a serious work. "I guess *serious* is a confusing word," Ellington mused. "We take our American music seriously."

But the 1940s were nevertheless a particularly rich era for Ellington. Indeed, most critics consider this period the peak of Ellington's long career. With Ben Webster (see Chapter 9), he acquired a hard-blowing tenor saxophonist in the Coleman Hawkins vein. Playing by ear, Webster added new notes to the chords, extending them into more dissonant territory and enriching Ellington's harmonic palette.

A trio of Ellington's musicians on a city street in the early 1930s. Alto saxophonist Johnny Hodges (left), guitarist Fred Guy, and clarinetist Barney Bigard, a New Orleans Creole so pale that he once petitioned the Los Angeles musicians' union (unsuccessfully) to admit him as white.

◉ "Conga Brava"

By 1940, the Cotton Club was safely in Ellington's past. But the habits of mind that had been formed there—"exotic" evocations of distant lands, unusual timbres—continued to affect new compositions. "Conga Brava" is an excellent example. It was probably a successor to an earlier piece, "Caravan," co-written with Juan Tizol. The opening melody—undoubtedly Tizol's contribution—is admirably suited to his trombone, played here with unfailing classical excellence evocative of Romantic opera. ("I don't feel the pop tunes," Tizol once said, "but I feel 'La Gioconda' and 'La Bohème.' I like pure romantic flavor.") This opening mood, however, is complicated seconds later by Barney Bigard's elaborate improvised curlicues and snarling commentary by Cootie Williams, Rex Stewart, and Joe Nanton. Ellington covers a staggering amount of territory in his customary three minutes, from a Kansas City–style blowing session for Ben Webster to a stunning virtuosic *soli* for the brass. Ultimately, though, all these moments are folded back into the mood of the opening. It's as though Ellington has taken us on a short but eventful trip, eventually escorting us gently home.

2.8

 conga brava

DUKE ELLINGTON AND HIS ORCHESTRA
Duke Ellington, piano; Wallace Jones, Rex Stewart, Cootie Williams, trumpets; Joe "Tricky Sam" Nanton, Lawrence Brown, Juan Tizol, trombones; Johnny Hodges, Otto Hardwick, alto saxophones; Ben Webster, tenor saxophone; Harry Carney, baritone saxophone; Barney Bigard, clarinet; Fred Guy, banjo; Jimmy Blanton, bass; Sonny Greer, drums
- Label: Victor 26577; *Never No Lament: The Blanton-Webster Band* (Bluebird 50857)
- Date: 1940
- Style: big-band jazz
- Form: extended popular song (**A A B A**)

What to listen for:
- big-band instrumentation
- **contributions by Ellington soloists: Tizol, Webster, Bigard, Stewart, Williams, Nanton**
- **unusual timbres (muted brass)**
- **smooth shifts between Latin and swing grooves**
- **dramatic changes in texture from solos to virtuosic block-chord passages**

INTRODUCTION

0:00	The rhythm section establishes a Latin groove, contrasting a syncopated bass line with an **ostinato** pattern by Ellington on piano. Greer (drums) plays a disorienting accent on the fourth beat of the measure.

CHORUS 1

0:04	**A** (20 bars)	Tizol enters with a long, lingering melody on the valve trombone. Ellington continues his ostinato, adjusting it up and down to suit the harmonies.
0:21		Tizol holds out the last note of his melody. Underneath, Bigard enters with a clarinet **countermelody**.
0:24	**A** (20 bars)	Tizol repeats his long melody. In place of Ellington's ostinato, a trio of muted brass (Williams, Nanton, Stewart) accompanies him with snarling, syncopated chords.
0:41		Bigard reenters underneath Tizol's last note; the brass chords continue.
0:44	**B** (8 bars)	The groove shifts from Latin to straightforward swing. Over a new harmonic progression, Bigard's low-register solo competes for our attention with the brass chords.
0:52	**A'** (6 bars)	The band as a whole enters in a brief passage in **block-chord** texture, ending on the dominant chord.

CHORUS 2

0:59	**A** (20 bars)	Firmly within the swing groove, Webster enters on tenor saxophone for a "blowing chorus" accompanied by the rhythm section. The harmonic progression is the same as in chorus 1.
1:13		In bars 15 and 16, Ellington marks the closing of the first section with two simple chords.
1:17		The bass drops down to the lower octave.
1:19	**A** (20 bars)	Webster continues his solo.
1:33		Ellington again plays his two simple chords.
1:36		In his last phrase, Webster increases the volume and intensity of his playing.
1:39	**B** (8 bars)	The muted brass trio returns in block-chord texture.
1:47	**A** (20 bars)	The saxophones enter in rich harmonies, reestablishing the opening melody. The drums stay within the swing groove, but recall the Latin opening by again accenting the fourth beat of the measure.

| 1:51 | | Against the melody, Stewart (trumpet) improvises a countermelody. |
| 2:05 | | Ellington briefly reprises his ostinato figure. |

INTERLUDE (based on A)

2:07		The brass enters with a rhythmically brilliant **soli.** Greer (drums) answers each of the first two phrases with an accent on the fourth beat.
2:17		A repeat of the *soli.*
2:22		Halfway through, the harmony heads toward a cadence, ending with a dominant chord.

INTRODUCTION

| 2:28 | | A sudden drop in volume signals the return of the Latin groove. |

CHORUS 3 (abbreviated)

| 2:32 | **A** | Tizol (trombone) plays the opening melody, once again accompanied only by the rhythm section. |

CODA

| 2:52 | | Over the opening vamp, the band fades out. |

The Later Years

After a long period on top, Ellington was overdue for a decline. The strain of continuous touring over twenty years had exhausted his musicians; one trumpet player claimed that he slept for nearly a year after leaving the band. More tellingly, Ellington suffered his first on-the-job death when Tricky Sam Nanton was felled by a stroke in 1946. Other musicians left to cash in on their growing reputations. In the mid-1940s, Ellington had to scramble to replace longtimers Webster, Tizol, and Stewart. In 1951, the loss was even greater when his chief alto saxophonist Johnny Hodges departed, partly out of irritation with Ellington's habit of appropriating musical ideas (during a tune he felt was actually his own, Hodges used to mimic counting out money onstage), taking with him Lawrence Brown and Sonny Greer.

The business landscape was changing as well. Scores of theaters were demolished or renovated. Radio no longer broadcasted live music, thus removing one of the few ways black bands could be heard nationwide (film was a remote shot, as was the new medium of television). With the rise of modern jazz (discussed in Chapter 11), Ellington's music no longer seemed central. He kept his band together with his income from songwriting (he was an early member in ASCAP, the performing rights organization). He left Columbia Records for Capitol Records, where he recorded one last hit song, "Satin Doll." He played music for ice skaters, wrote mambos, and waited.

The turnaround came in 1956. His band had been invited to the third Newport Jazz Festival, one of the first of the new summer extravaganzas that helped to transform jazz listening (see Chapter 18). Ellington came on late at night, after waiting for what seemed an eternity ("What are we—the animal act, acrobats?" he complained). The band broke into a two-part piece from 1937, "Diminuendo and Crescendo in Blue." In between the parts, there was an open-ended interval on the twelve-bar blues. Paul Gonsalves, Ellington's

Newport, 1956

new tenor saxophonist, began playing, and as his intensity grew, Ellington kept the solo going. A blonde woman in the crowd began dancing, and the audience went wild. Gonsalves played for a full twenty-seven blues choruses. The whole proceeding, preserved on tape, was later issued as *Ellington at Newport* and quickly became his best-selling album. Ellington made the cover of *Time* magazine. A new era had begun.

In his last twenty years, Ellington took advantage of the space afforded by new LP recordings to write lengthy pieces. Most were suites—collections of pieces loosely organized around a theme—written for a Shakespeare festival (*Such Sweet Thunder*), a State Department–sponsored tour (*The Far East Suite*), a television program (*A Drum Is a Woman*), or a visit with the Queen of England (*The Queen's Suite*). Ellington also worked as a film composer (*Anatomy of a Murder, Paris Blues)*, and joined forces with modernists, recording albums with John Coltrane, Charles Mingus, and Max Roach.

■ BILLY STRAYHORN (1915–1967)

Ellington's partner in all this late activity was Billy Strayhorn, his co-composer. Strayhorn was a diminutive, introverted intellectual, who declined the limelight. Born in Pittsburgh, he was initially drawn to classical music. By the time he graduated from high school, he had already composed and performed a concerto for piano and percussion. But because black careers in classical music were decidedly limited, he moved instead into popular music where his creativity could be given free rein. One of his most accomplished

Duke Ellington used his wiles to convince his musicians to do exactly what he wanted, but he treated Billy Strayhorn (right), a brilliant composer who was an essential figure in the post-1930s Ellington band, with unwavering friendship and respect. This picture dates from 1960, when they were in Paris to score the film *Paris Blues*.

early tunes, "Lush Life," reflected both his love of densely chromatic music and his sense of isolation as a black man who refused to compromise his homosexuality.

Strayhorn joined Ellington in 1938 after meeting him backstage in Pittsburgh and serenading him with different versions of "Sophisticated Lady"—one replicating Ellington's mannerisms, the other adding his own variations. Ellington, who was comfortable enough to recognize new talent without feeling threatened, invited him to join him in New York. Strayhorn's first tune with Ellington was based on the directions Ellington gave him to his apartment: when you get to Manhattan, take the A train (rather than the D train, which headed off to the Bronx) to reach Harlem. "Take the 'A' Train" relied heavily on swing conventions, but its harmonic ingenuity and the sureness of its orchestral textures provided the band with a new classic. When the radio networks refused to accept ASCAP's demands for higher rates, thus barring ASCAP-member Ellington's compositions from the air for most of 1941, "'A' Train" became the band's new theme.

Nicknamed "Swee' Pea" (after the baby in the comic strip "Popeye"), Strayhorn steadily rose in stature through the 1950s and 1960s. The two composers worked so closely together, sharing insights and completing one another's phrases, that it is often impossible to separate their work. Numerous pieces, such as the larger suites from the 1950s, carry both their names in the composers' credits. A significant number are clearly Strayhorn's alone: "Satin Doll" (perhaps Ellington's last pop hit in 1954), "Chelsea Bridge," "A Flower Is a Lovesome Thing," "Day Dream," and the haunting "Blood Count."

🎧 "Blood Count"

As Billy Strayhorn turned fifty, he developed cancer of the esophagus. Two years later, his health had declined so severely that he was in around-the-clock treatment in a New York hospital. There, confined to bed, he continued to work on music. One of the tunes was originally entitled "Blue Cloud"; but as Strayhorn became mesmerized by his declining vital signs, it ultimately became "Blood Count." It was his last composition. "That was the last thing he had to say," a close friend remembered. "And it wasn't 'Good-bye' or 'Thank you' or anything phony like that. It was 'This is how I feel . . . like it or leave it.'" Shortly afterward, Strayhorn slipped into oblivion. The band recorded the piece three months later, as part of an emotional tribute to Strayhorn entitled . . . *and His Mother Called Him Bill.*

The tune begins with harmonic ambiguity, more than usual for Strayhorn. We don't know where we are or where we're heading. In this bleak territory, Johnny Hodges, one of Strayhorn's favorite voices (listen to the lushly romantic "Chelsea Bridge"), plays the lead melody with his characteristic subtle timbres, sweet vibrato, and unnerving glissandos. The piece proceeds with quiet resignation, first through D minor, then D major, until the second bridge (in chorus 2), when it erupts in a violent *crescendo*. It's as if the normally serene Hodges, overwhelmed by the resentment and impatience Strayhorn had encoded in the chromatic harmonies, suddenly explodes into an outpouring of grief, pressing against the physical limitations of his alto saxophone.

crescendo growing louder

The moment of anger subsides. As the piece draws to a close, we can hear one of Strayhorn's dramatic farewell gestures. Over a coursing pedal point, the harmonies drop chromatically, one by one, toward the tonic. It's a bittersweet climax to a bittersweet tribute. The original LP recording ended with an almost unbearably private moment: while the band files out of the recording studio, Ellington sits at the piano, playing one of Strayhorn's tunes, "Lotus Blossom," over and over, hushing the departing musicians through his devotion. In the album's notes, Ellington offered this eulogy:

> His greatest virtue, I think, was his honesty—not only to others but to himself.... He demanded freedom of expression and lived in what we consider the most important of moral freedoms: freedom from hate, unconditionally; freedom from all self-pity (even throughout all the pain and bad news); freedom from fear of possibly doing something that might help another more than it might help himself; and freedom from the kind of pride that could make a man feel he was better than his brother or neighbor.

LISTENING GUIDE

2.9

🎧 blood count

DUKE ELLINGTON AND HIS ORCHESTRA
Duke Ellington, piano; Cat Anderson, Mercer Ellington, Herbie Jones, Cootie Williams, trumpets; Lawrence Brown, Buster Cooper, trombones; Chuck Connors, bass trombone; Johnny Hodges, Russell Procope, Jimmy Hamilton, alto saxophones; Paul Gonsalves, tenor saxophone; Harry Carney, baritone saxophone; Aaron Bell, bass; Steve Little, drums

- Label: RCA LSP-3906; . . . and His Mother Called Him Bill (Bluebird/RCA 63744)
- Date: 1967
- Style: big band
- Form: 32-bar popular song (**A A′ B A′**)

What to listen for:
- harmonic ambiguity, resigned mood
- unusual brass timbres
- a dramatic explosion by Hodges in chorus 2
- rising and falling chromatic harmonies

CHORUS 1 (32 bars)

0:00	**A**	Hodges (alto saxophone) begins playing melodic fragments over ambiguous harmonies. The band accompanies with slow, sustained harmonies and occasional **chromatic** lines. The bass plays two beats to the bar. The drums add color with the cymbals, with occasional accents on the tom-toms.
0:17		The harmony settles into a new key area in the **minor mode**, with the bass holding a pedal point. The saxophones increase tension with a gradually rising chromatic line. Hodges repeats a short, quick motive.
0:34	**A′**	A return to the opening melody.
0:50		The harmony is now in the **major mode**.
1:08	**B**	The new melodic phrase starts on a high pitch, descending sharply to a **blue note**.
1:16		By manipulating his embouchure, Hodges slides up to the high note.
1:33		The harmony rises chromatically.
1:41	**A′**	Hodges returns to the opening melody, expressing his emotions through swelling dynamics.
1:58		As the harmony settles into the major mode, the mood is hushed and expectant.
2:12		Driven by a drum roll, the band rises suddenly in a dramatic **crescendo**.

CHORUS 2 (abbreviated)

2:15	**B**	The band has the melody. Hodges improvises furiously in response.
2:31		As the intensity of his line increases, Hodges's tone thickens. Some of his individual notes are almost forced out, like barks.
2:39		Over a chromatic rise in harmony, he plays a violent two-note rising motive.
2:45		At the end of the phrase, the dynamics begin to abate.
2:48	**A′**	In a return to the opening, Hodges now sounds resigned, reflective.

CODA

3:20	The music continues quietly in the same vein.
3:37	The harmony has reached the dominant, preparing for the final cadence. Over a **pedal point**, the harmony falls chromatically. Hodges plays simple, mournful figures with a quiet, bluesy feeling.
3:45	The bass finally reaches the tonic, but the baritone saxophone continues to hold its note until the end.
3:47	The brass section, tightly muted, continues the chromatic falling chords.
3:52	Hodges uses variable intonation to color his melodies.
4:01	In his last phrase, Hodges plays a phrase from the opening of the tune, leaving us feeling unsettled.

STANDING OUT

Although the orchestral "big bands" dominated swing, every solo a musician in a swing band took reflected not just the aesthetics of the bandleader or arranger (as with the "Ellingtonians"), but the personality of the musician who created it. Dedicated swing fans relished these soloists' work and understood exactly how each musician fit into the jazz tradition.

There were swing musicians—most notably stride pianists—who by virtue of their instrument fit uneasily into the big-band framework. Still others had careers so complicated that they could not be comfortably assigned to any one band: a few became independent, earning a living by playing in small combos, much as bebop musicians would do in the later 1940s. We will consider all of these soloists—horn players, pianists, singers, members of the rhythm section—in the next two chapters.

DUKE ELLINGTON CHRONOLOGY		
1899	Born April 29 in Washington, D.C.	
1923	Arrives in New York.	
1927	Opens at the Cotton Club.	"Black and Tan Fantasy"
1929	Bubber Miley leaves, replaced by Cootie Williams.	
1930		"Mood Indigo"
1932		"It Don't Mean a Thing (if It Ain't Got That Swing)," "Sophisticated Lady"
1933	Tours Europe.	
1938	Billy Strayhorn joins the band.	
1939	Jimmy Blanton and Ben Webster join the band.	
1940		"Conga Brava"
1941		*Jump for Joy* (musical)
1943	Performs at Carnegie Hall.	*Black, Brown, and Beige*
1951	Johnny Hodges leaves to form his own band.	
1955	Hodges returns.	
1956	Triumph at the Newport Jazz Festival.	*Such Sweet Thunder*
1965	Offer of Pulitzer Prize overruled.	
1966		*Far East Suite*
1967	Strayhorn dies.	"Blood Count"
1974	Ellington dies, May 24, in New York City.	

ADDITIONAL LISTENING

Clarence "Pine Top" Smith	"Pine Top's Boogie Woogie" (1928); *The Many Faces of Boogie-Woogie* (Avid 553)
The Blue Devils	"Squabblin'" (1929); *Kansas City Jazz: 1924–1942* (Fremeaux FA5095)
Andy Kirk (with Mary Lou Williams)	"The Lady Who Swings the Band" (1936); *Mary's Idea* (GRP, GRD 622, 1993)
Mary Lou Williams	"Little Joe from Chicago" (1939); *Boogie Woogie and Blues Piano* (Mosaic Select 030)
Bennie Moten	"Toby" (1932); *Moten Swing* (Living Era 5578)
Count Basie	"Every Tub," "Blue and Sentimental," "Doggin' Around," "Jumpin' at the Woodside" (1938); *The Complete Decca Recordings* (Decca Jazz 3–611)
	"Lil' Darling" (1957); *The Complete Atomic Basie* (Blue Note 28635)
Duke Ellington	"It Don't Mean a Thing (if It Ain't Got That Swing)" (1932); *The Best of Duke Ellington* (RCA/Legacy 886972136523)
	"Ko-Ko" (1940), "Concerto for Cootie" (1940), "Chelsea Bridge" (1941); *Never No Lament: The Blanton-Webster Band* (Bluebird 50857)
	Black, Brown, and Beige (1943); *The Carnegie Hall Concerts: January 1943* (Prestige 34004)
	"Diminuendo and Crescendo in Blue" (1956); *Ellington at Newport 1956: Complete* (Columbia/Legacy C2K64932)
	"The Star-Crossed Lovers" (1957); *Such Sweet Thunder* (Columbia/Legacy CK65568)

COLEMAN HAWKINS
body and soul

COUNT BASIE/LESTER YOUNG
oh! lady be good

BENNY CARTER/DJANGO REINHARDT
i'm coming, virginia

BILLIE HOLIDAY
a sailboat in the moonlight

ELLA FITZGERALD
blue skies

SWING ERA SOLOISTS

JAMMIN' THE BLUES

During the Swing Era, the leading bands were almost as well known for their star performers as for their overall styles. These soloists, like actors in a play, were assigned specific parts, which rarely allotted them as much as a full chorus and often no more than eight measures. As a result, they developed styles so distinct that fans tuning into radio broadcasts could quickly identify them by their timbres, melodic phrases, and rhythmic attacks. When these performers stood up to play in a ballroom, dancers crowded the bandstand to listen and cheer.

Still, soloists were merely components in a larger unit, shining only as bright as the leader permitted. They might quit or be lured away, traded (like athletes) or fired, but the band went on. The most controversial instance of a soloist leaving a band occurred in 1940, when trumpeter Cootie Williams departed Duke Ellington's orchestra for Benny Goodman's sextet. The musical world was astonished because of Williams's long and vital association with Ellington's music. Bandleader Raymond Scott commemorated the incident with his composition "When Cootie Left the Duke." After Count Basie lost several prominent soloists, including saxophonist Lester Young, he vowed to focus on ar-

Billie Holiday, the quintessential jazz vocalist, has an angel over her shoulder, partly obscured by smoke at this 1949 recording session.

wwnorton.com/studyspace

227

rangements instead of individual players. Arrangements, unlike people, would always remain under the leader's thumb.

For obvious reasons, soloists were dissatisfied by the restrictions imposed on them. One way they worked off their frustrations was in jam sessions, usually played after hours. In the 1940s, when the wartime draft depleted the ranks of many orchestras, staged jam sessions became popular with the public. Soloists also found relief in small-group bands, which many successful orchestra leaders—Goodman, Ellington, and Basie among them—formed as supplementary units.

The smaller groups had a social as well as musical impact on jazz and popular entertainment. Goodman, as we saw in Chapter 7, used his trio and quartet (with Teddy Wilson on piano and Lionel Hampton on vibraphone) to racially integrate his concerts and recording sessions. Although in a sense the big bands had been integrated when white leaders hired black arrangers and composers, it was a radical step to offer a racially mixed group onstage. Blacks and whites had long jammed together in after-hours venues, but few mainstream audiences had ever seen an integrated band.

Smaller units also favored musical experimentation. Ellington crafted some of his most challenging pieces for seven-piece bands that recorded under the nominal leadership of whichever soloist was featured. Artie Shaw used a harpsichord for his Gramercy Five records. As we saw earlier, some bandleaders gave their secondary bands distinct names: Woody Herman had his Woodchoppers, for example, and Bob Crosby his Bobcats. John Hammond assembled all-star groups for recording sessions (most famously those built around singer Billie Holiday) by combining key members of various orchestras. These makeshift studio groups achieved an informal, spontaneous flavor recalling the free spirit of 1920s recordings by Louis Armstrong and Bix Beiderbecke.

The increasing popularity of soloists portended a new respect for jazz musicians. As free agents, they enjoyed diverse professional opportunities—working on records, in pit bands, and even in movie and radio studios, though most of those well-paid positions were reserved for white musicians. Beginning in the 1930s, fans voted for their favorite bands, soloists, and singers in magazine polls. The friendly and not-so-friendly rivalries helped to spur a rapid development in musical technique. If we compare, say, Louis Armstrong's 1928 "West End Blues" and Benny Carter's 1938 "I'm Coming, Virginia" (discussed below), we hear startling developments in harmony, rhythm, and technical agility. Armstrong established free reign for the individual soloist; within a few years of "West End Blues," jazz was inundated by gifted musicians, each attempting to forge a personal approach to his or her instrument and to jazz itself.

In 1944, as the Swing Era ground to a standstill, impresario Norman Granz hired photographer Gjon Mili to direct a classic ten-minute film, *Jammin' the Blues*, which featured soloists who had become famous for their work with Count Basie, Lionel Hampton, and other bandleaders. Fastidiously directed, this film captured the idea of what its narrator calls "a midnight symphony," an informal letting-go by musicians in an environment free of written scores and other constraints. It foreshadowed the turnaround in jazz that took place in the postwar years, as small groups and extended improvisations replaced the checks and balances of big bands.

■ COLEMAN HAWKINS

No one exemplifies the rise of the Swing Era soloist better than Coleman Hawkins. We have already seen (in Chapter 6) how he adapted Armstrong's ideas during his years with Fletcher Henderson, eventually producing a legato style that, in performances like "One Hour," refined the jazz ballad. But Hawkins's overall impact went way beyond that performance and era. The jazz singer Jon Hendricks once introduced him to a concert audience as "the man for whom Adolphe Sax invented the horn," an engaging way of saying that beyond dominating the instrument for many years, Hawkins established its legitimacy in contemporary music.

Father of the Tenor

In his later years, Hawkins modestly claimed, "People always say I invented the jazz tenor—it isn't true. . . . Why, gangs of tenors would be coming into New York all the time from bands on the road." The saxophone had been around for sixty years before Hawkins's birth, occasionally used in symphonic music by Hector Berlioz, Georges Bizet, and Maurice Ravel, among others. But when Hawkins began playing, it was best known as a starchy novelty instrument. Its most famous proponent was vaudevillian Rudy Wiedoeft, whose tongue would snap against the reed to articulate or pop each note, producing a brisk, staccato, comical music; this way of playing was considered technically "correct." The titles of his compositions—"Saxophobia," "Sax-O-Phun"—indicate the limits of his ambition.

The first important saxophonists in jazz focused on soprano (Sidney Bechet) and C-melody (Frank Trumbauer), but those instruments disappeared or declined in popularity as Hawkins established the tenor as the embodiment of jazz—much as the guitar came to signify rock and roll. Imbuing the tenor saxophone with individuality, passion, dignity, and romance, Hawkins expunged its association with comic antics. He made the goose-necked horn look cool, virile, and even dangerous. Thanks to Hawkins, the tenor rivaled and sometimes usurped the trumpet as jazz's most iconographic instrument.

The Way of the Arpeggio

Musicians called him Hawk or Bean (as in "He's got a lot on the bean," a synonym for "egghead"). During his eleven years with the Henderson band (1923–34), Hawkins had few rivals and no peers. His style was now considered the "correct" one, characterized by heavy vibrato, powerful timbre, emotional zeal, and a harmonic ingenuity that fascinated musicians. His great musical innovation, beyond remaking the tenor saxophone in his own image, was to change the emphasis in jazz improvisation from embellishing the melody to creating variations based on the song's harmonies.

Hawkins mastered chords and the way they relate to each other by developing a style based on arpeggios. In an **arpeggio**, a chord's notes are played

Coleman Hawkins, nicknamed Bean (as in "He's got a lot on the bean"), performed with characteristic passion at the second annual Newport Jazz Festival, 1955.

successively, one at a time. They can be played in any order: a C7 chord, for example, may be arpeggiated as C, E, G, B-flat or in reverse or in another sequence entirely. Hawkins found myriad ways to maneuver through chords by breaking them down into these component notes, which he shaped into powerfully rhythmic melodies.

This was a major breakthrough, prefiguring the modern jazz movement (or bebop) of the middle and late 1940s. In the course of breaking down chords, Hawkins frequently added harmonic substitutions—chords richer and more intricate than those the composer had provided. These interpolated chords increased the variety of his inventions and spurred his melodic imagination. The broken chords of arpeggios don't mean much unless they form melodies that enchant the listener.

Hawkins's mastery of chords steadily deepened during his years with Henderson. One example is his composition "Queer Notions," recorded by Henderson's band in 1933, which employs augmented chords (in which an interval has been made larger by a half step) and the whole-tone scale. During this same period, Hawkins recorded many sessions as a sideman and, in 1933, organized his own recording unit, with New Orleans trumpeter Henry "Red" Allen, who similarly gravitated toward sophisticated harmonic ideas—a good example is their "Heartbreak Blues."

Across the Atlantic

In 1934, Hawkins signed with British bandleader Jack Hylton to tour England. He set sail expecting to stay for six months, but, bowled over by the size and enthusiasm of crowds that greeted him at every stop, ended up living in Europe for the next five years. During this time, he performed and recorded in London, Paris, the Hague, Zurich, and elsewhere, establishing an international paradigm for the tenor saxophone and jazz. While he was gone, a serious rival appeared in Lester Young, who offered an almost diametrically opposed approach that attracted many adherents. Hawkins kept up with the American scene and the newer crop of tenor saxophonists through recordings; he expressed particular admiration for Ben Webster.

In July 1939, weeks before Germany invaded Poland, Hawkins had no choice but to return to the United States, where observers wondered if he could retain his standing as the No. 1 tenor saxophonist. In September, he appeared on a Lionel Hampton session alongside two tenors who had been influenced by him, Webster and Chu Berry (who had recently enjoyed success with his version of "Body and Soul"), as well as an unknown trumpet player, Dizzy Gillespie. This session was a warm-up for Hawkins.

☉"Body and Soul"

A month later, Hawkins conducted his own session, which unexpectedly turned out to be one of jazz's seismic events. The idea was to showcase the nine-piece band he commanded at a New York nightclub, Kelly's Stables. The band spent most of the session nailing down three complicated arrangements Hawkins had prepared; but the record label needed a fourth side in order to release two discs. The producer cajoled him into playing an ad-lib rendition of a song he had performed at the nightclub, "Body and Soul." Hawkins wasn't happy about it, but he agreed to play it once, without rehearsal.

Hawkins's "Body and Soul" is a pinnacle in jazz improvisation. Recorded entirely off the cuff, it has the weight and logic of formal composition and the tension and energy of spontaneous invention. John Green had composed the thirty-two-bar **A A B A** melody for a Broadway revue (*Three's a Crowd*) in 1930, and it quickly became a favorite among "torch singers"—women who specialized in heart-on-sleeve laments. Louis Armstrong adapted the tune as a jazz piece, and memorable renditions followed by Benny Goodman, guitarist Django Reinhardt, and Chu Berry. Hawkins's version confirmed it as a jazz and pop standard, and made it an everlasting challenge to other tenor saxophonists.

After the piano introduction by Gene Rodgers, the performance is all Hawkins for two choruses and a coda. He begins briskly, his tone smooth as worn felt. Then, after two measures, something unusual happens: "Body and Soul" disappears. More dramatically than on "One Hour," Hawkins heads into new territory, extending his initial phrase into an original melodic arc. His spiraling phrases, representing a zenith of the arpeggio style, advance with assurance and deliberation, building tension. Hawkins later described the climactic passages as a kind of sexual release. This record proved to be a critical milestone and a tremendous commercial success.

LISTENING GUIDE

2.10

 body and soul

COLEMAN HAWKINS

Tommy Lindsay, Joe Guy, trumpets; Earl Hardy, trombone; Jackie Fields, Eustis Moore, alto saxophones; Coleman Hawkins, tenor saxophone; Gene Rodgers, piano; William Oscar Smith, bass; Arthur Herbert, drums

- Label: Bluebird B-10253; *Body & Soul: The Complete Victor Recordings, 1939–1956* (Definitive 33782)
- Date: 1939
- Style: small group swing
- Form: 32-bar popular song (**A A B A**)

What to listen for:

- Hawkins's melodic paraphrase (at beginning) *and* harmonic improvisation
- a gradual build from the romantic opening to the exciting leaps at the climax
- double-time passages (played at twice the speed of the ground rhythm)
- chromatic harmony

INTRODUCTION

0:00		Rodgers (piano) plays a four-bar introduction in D♭ major.
0:09		Hawkins begins his solo with three introductory notes.

CHORUS 1

0:10	**A**	Hawkins plays a decorated version of the original melody of "Body and Soul"—the opening phrases (in the lower register) with a breathy tone and somewhat behind the beat. Behind him, the piano keeps time by playing on every beat, with the bass tending to play every other beat.
0:15		The drums' cymbals enter, lightly emphasizing the backbeat.
0:31	**A**	Hawkins's phrases curve upward as they begin to escape the gravity of the original melody.
0:51	**B**	A **modulation** leads to the bridge, in the distant key of D major.

| 1:08 | | Through a **chromatic** chord sequence, the tune modulates back to Dᵇ major. |
| 1:11 | **A** | Hawkins's improvisation is now securely in **double-time**, moving in 16th notes, twice as fast as the accompaniment. |

CHORUS 2

1:32	**A**	The horns enter, playing a solid chordal background behind Hawkins's solo.
1:35		Hawkins begins adding even faster figures (32nd notes).
1:47		The improvised line uses **sequences**: short melodic patterns repeated on different pitches.
1:52	**A**	
2:00		An intense, piercing entry in the upper register (over a **diminished-seventh chord**).
2:13	**B**	During the second bridge, the horns drop out, leaving Hawkins accompanied only by the rhythm section.
2:33	**A**	The horns reenter; with a series of ascending leaps, Hawkins's solo suddenly reaches its climax.
2:39		His highest note of the solo.

CODA

| 2:48 | | During the last two bars of the second chorus, Hawkins allows both the horn and rhythm sections to dissipate. He continues to play with no accompaniment, his line dropping in register and volume. |
| 2:56 | | He holds his final note, signaling the end to the rest of the band, which enters (somewhat untidily) on the tonic chord. |

Hawkins's recording of "Body and Soul" scored on the pop charts for six weeks in the beginning of 1940—audiences demanded he play it at virtually every appearance. Significantly, they clamored not for the original song, but for his recorded improvisation. In later years, he performed the 1939 solo as if it were the written theme, following it with additional variations. Jazz singer Eddie Jefferson put lyrics to his solo, and Benny Carter arranged it for a band. In 1948, Hawkins adapted the song's harmonic framework for a piece he called "Picasso," the first jazz work conceived entirely for unaccompanied tenor saxophone. Just about every important tenor saxophonist in jazz eventually took a shot at "Body and Soul," from Lester Young and Ben Webster to Sonny Rollins and John Coltrane to David Murray and Joshua Redman. Charlie Parker memorized the solo, quoting from it on his first radio broadcasts.

The idea of improvising on the harmonic foundation of songs greatly influenced the development of modern jazz. Adventurous musicians like Parker, Dizzy Gillespie, and Thelonious Monk were encouraged to forge their own paths. Hawkins himself, however, continued to work in the swing style with which he felt most comfortable, though he often played with young modernists.

THE HAWKINS SCHOOL

Hawkins's impact on jazz was not unlike that of Louis Armstrong. His solos on Fletcher Henderson records so mesmerized musicians around the country that many who had taken up the C-melody saxophone after hearing Frank Trumbauer switched to the tenor. Hawkins's combustible riff-laden solo on Henderson's "The Stampede" (1926) was especially influential: for the first time, the tenor leaped from the band, punching and feinting with the dynamism of a trumpet. During the next decade, Hawkins's primacy was nearly absolute, except in Kansas City and the Southwest, where an indigenous tenor saxophone style took root, exemplified by Lester Young. But even Young acknowledged Hawkins's preeminence.

As we learned in Chapter 6, Hawkins himself had apprenticed in the Southwest, before traveling to New York in 1922 with blues singer Mamie Smith. These circumstances led the critic Martin Williams to wonder whether the "so-called Southwest tenor style" was, in fact, first "expounded by Coleman Hawkins in a New York recording studio." One highly individual proponent of Hawkins's model was Bud Freeman, a member of the Austin High Gang in Chicago who, spurred by Hawkins's tonal projection, fashioned a smoother timbre. A few others developed even more dramatic extensions.

■ BEN WEBSTER (1909–1973)

Born in Kansas City, Ben Webster studied violin and piano before taking up the tenor. His mentors included Budd Johnson, who later emerged as a tenor star and arranger with Earl Hines's big band, and Lester Young, whose father gave Ben his first important band job. It's a measure of Hawkins's power that Webster chose him as his muse—knowing his music only from 78-rpm records—over Young, with whom he traveled. Webster arrived in New York in 1932 as a member of Benny Moten's orchestra, and worked with several key bandleaders—including Andy Kirk, Fletcher Henderson, Cab Calloway, and Teddy Wilson—before Duke Ellington recruited him; with Ellington, he made his name.

The Duke Ellington Orchestra had the most illustrious reed and brass sections in jazz history, especially after Ellington recruited tenor saxophonist Ben Webster. Top row: Rex Stewart, trumpet; Ray Nance, violin and trumpet; Wallace Jones, trumpet; Sonny Greer (top, partly obscured), drums; Joe Nanton, Juan Tizol, Lawrence Brown, trombones. Bottom row: Barney Bigard, clarinet; Johnny Hodges, Otto Hardwick, alto saxophones; Ben Webster, tenor; Harry Carney, baritone. Onstage at Sioux Falls, South Dakota, 1939.

In later years, Webster frequently accompanied singers and achieved distinction as a ballad player. This surprised those who remembered him as the tempestuous soloist of Ellington's "Cotton Tail." (Musicians even nicknamed him the Brute for his rambunctious playing and capricious temper.) Trumpeter and memoirist Rex Stewart, who worked alongside Webster in both the Henderson and Ellington bands, wrote of him, "During his early period, he blew with unrestrained savagery, buzzing and growling through chord changes like a prehistoric monster challenging a foe. With the passage of time, this fire has given way to tender, introspective declamations of maturing and reflective beauty."

Webster's gruff yet empathic style established him as one of the three great pillars of prewar tenor saxophone, along with Hawkins and Young. Of the three, Webster ripened the most in later years; his playing in the 1950s and 1960s is arguably more distinctive and satisfying than the innovative triumphs of his youth. Ironically, the 1960s enshrined the kind of musical volatility Webster had left behind; his mature, mellow style—marked by an idiosyncratic embouchure technique involving audibly heavy breathing—fell out of favor. In search of work, Webster moved to Europe, where he spent his last nine years.

Roy Eldridge (trumpet) and Chu Berry (tenor saxophone) were among the most exciting soloists of the Swing Era, and close friends who appeared together on recording sessions and with the Fletcher Henderson band. In this picture, they were just getting started as members of Teddy Hill's Orchestra, in 1935.

■ CHU BERRY (1908–1941)

Leon "Chu" Berry, born in West Virginia and educated at West Virginia State University, began on alto saxophone and switched to tenor in 1929. A year later, he traveled with a band to New York and soon became a musical mainstay, working and recording with such important musicians as Benny Carter and Charlie Johnson (a little-remembered bandleader who led a very popular group at Small's Paradise in Harlem). As Hawkins toured Europe, Berry took his spot as Henderson's tenor soloist from 1935 to 1937. His work on "Blue Lou" (Chapter 7) is characteristic of his rhythmic drive and weighty timbre; his second bridge (in the fourth chorus, at 2:13) is an especially good example of his ability to remain melodically relaxed at a speedy tempo—an aspect of his playing that impressed the young Charlie Parker. Berry achieved his greatest success in 1937 when he joined the Cab Calloway band, a tenure tragically cut short by his death in an automobile accident, at thirty-three.

■ ROY ELDRIDGE (1911–1989)

Roy Eldridge, who plays the exciting first solo and climax on "Blue Lou," was an outstanding virtuoso. He inherited Armstrong's mantle as the most original and influential trumpeter of the Swing Era, and set the stage for the ascension of Dizzy Gillespie (who called him "the messiah of our generation"). Born in Pittsburgh, Eldridge joined a carnival at sixteen: "I got that job," he recalled, "because I could play Coleman Hawkins's chorus on 'Stampede' on the trumpet, which was unheard of then." He created his singular style in part by looking to tenor saxophonists, not trumpet players, for inspiration.

After working throughout the Midwest, Eldridge moved to New York in 1930. Within two years, his competitive spirit and short size earned him the nickname Little Jazz; among musicians, he was known simply as Jazz. He closely studied Armstrong, but his primary stimulation continued to come from saxophonists. One admirer was Hawkins. "He told me he liked my playing from some records he heard in Europe," Eldridge said. "He was saying, 'Man, this cat ain't playing harsh like the rest of them cats. He's kind of playing more or less like a saxophone, lot of legato things, playing changes.' But he didn't realize that I was playing some of his stuff, and Pres's [Lester Young's] and Chu's."

Eldridge joined Henderson in 1935, and left a year later to form his own eight-piece group. A fierce battler at jam sessions, he possessed an extraordinary harmonic and dramatic talent that stimulated musicians of every generation, and his penchant for raising the roof with high-note climaxes thrilled jazz fans. His timbre was unmistakably personal, bright yet coated with grit, as effective on ballads as on showstoppers—making him a natural for backing singers, including Ella Fitzgerald and Billie Holiday.

In the 1940s, Eldridge became a focal point in the battle for integration, as the first black musician to sit in a white orchestra, the Gene Krupa band. During his stay with Krupa (1941–43; see box in Chapter 7), he achieved success as a singer (his sexy duet with white singer Anita O'Day, "Let Me Off Uptown," was a breakthrough in its own right) and recorded classic trumpet solos, including what many consider his masterpiece, "Rockin' Chair." He also played with Artie Shaw's band (in 1944) and participated in the after-hours Harlem sessions that contributed to the birth of bebop. Eldridge moved to Paris in 1950 for a year, where he was revered. Later, he continued to perform with musicians of both the swing and bop eras.

■ THE LESTORIAN MODE (1909—1959)

Lester Young's tenor saxophone style was initially considered so radical that he was hooted out of the Henderson band. Born in Mississippi, Young grew up in New Orleans, where his father, W. H. Young, trained him and his siblings to play a variety of instruments, with the intention of forming the Young Family Band. This band, in which Lester played violin, drums, trumpet, and several kinds of saxophone, toured tent shows in the summer and wintered in Minneapolis. An ardent admirer of Frank Trumbauer, whose records he carried everywhere, Lester sought to reproduce Trumbauer's lighter, vibratoless sound on tenor; according to Ben Webster, he developed a distinctive tenor saxophone timbre as early as 1929.

Lester Young, nicknamed Pres (as in president of all saxophonists) by Billie Holiday, epitomized cool in his music, his lingo, and even the angle at which he held the tenor saxophone. A New York club, 1948.

After leaving the family band in 1927, Young traveled the Midwest, performing with King Oliver, Benny Moten, the Blue Devils, and others. In 1933, he settled in Kansas City, where he was quickly accepted. When Fletcher Henderson's band came to town in December of that year, Young and Hawkins squared off at a legendary jam session involving several tenor saxophonists (including Ben Webster) and lasting all night and into the morning. By all accounts, Young emerged the victor.

When Hawkins departed for Europe in 1934, Henderson convinced Young to come to New York. He didn't last long there, however: the other musicians in Henderson's band ridiculed his light sound and introverted personal style, and Henderson's wife even made him listen to Hawkins's records, insisting he learn to play like the older man. Henderson reluctantly let him go, after lecturing his musicians that Lester played better than any of them, and he worked his way back to Kansas City as a member of Andy Kirk's band. Safe at home, he returned to Count Basie, with whom he had previously played. Basie's sizzling, rangy swing was an ideal platform for Young; unlike Henderson's ornate arrangements, Basie's were streamlined and blues-driven. His soloists were encouraged to improvise at length, accompanied by the rhythm section and ad-libbed head arrangements.

In that atmosphere, Young created a free-floating style, wheeling and diving like a gull, banking with low, funky riffs that pleased dancers and listeners alike. Stan Getz, one of countless young musicians who began by imitating Young, called his style of playing the Lestorian Mode: a fount of ideas expressing a new freedom in jazz.

Lester's Style

Young's way of improvising on a song differed from Hawkins's in almost every particular. Where Hawkins arpeggiated each chord in a harmonic progression, Young created melodic phrases that touched down on some chords and ignored others. Given, for example, an eight-measure passage with a dozen or so chords, Young would improvise a melody that fit the overall harmonic framework without detailing every harmony. He also had a more liberal attitude toward dissonance and rhythm. One of his favorite gambits was to repeat a note while slightly altering its pitch, making it slightly flat. And while Hawkins's phrases were tied to the beat, Young's phrases sometimes disregarded the beat, creating an uninhibited counterrhythm.

In 1936, Basie brought his band to Chicago and New York. This time the world was ready for Lester, though he would always remain something of an outsider. More than any other musician, Young introduced the idea of "cool," in musical style and personal affect. Shy and diffident, he stood aloof from most conventions. "I'm looking for something soft," he said. "I can't stand that loud noise. It's got to be sweetness, you dig? Sweetness can be funky, filthy or anything."

Young famously wore a broad-brimmed porkpie hat—a kind of Western fedora with a flat top—and narrow knit ties. When he played, he held the saxophone aloft and at a horizontal angle, almost like a flute. He spoke a colorful, obscure slang of his own invention, some of which became a part of jazz diction, including his nicknames for musicians. He called Billie Holiday, for example, Lady Day. She returned the favor by naming him Pres (as in president of all saxophonists), an honorific that stuck.

Many of the musicians who went on to pioneer modern jazz worshipped Young, learning his solos and imitating his look. White saxophonists (like Stan Getz, Zoot Sims, and Al Cohn) focused on his lyricism and feathery timbre in the upper register. Black saxophonists (like Dexter Gordon, Wardell Gray, and Illinois Jacquet) preferred his blues riffs and darker timbre in the middle and lower register. Dexter Gordon once observed, "Zoot and I worked in a club in Hollywood. He was playing Lester and I was playing Lester, but there was always a difference." Young's riffs were so pleasing and varied that they managed to spur the Swing Era, bebop, *and* rhythm and blues.

🔊 "Oh! Lady Be Good"

In "Oh! Lady Be Good," we can hear the youthful zest of Lester Young's style at its peak—indeed, this two-chorus solo is often cited as his finest work on records. All the attributes he brought to jazz are apparent, from the initial entrance followed by a rest and a long, rolling phrase to the slurred (connected) notes, polyrhythms, staccato single notes, pitch variation, and unfailing swing that make this improvisation a riveting experience. The song, by George and Ira Gershwin, originated in their score for the 1924 Broadway musical *Lady Be Good*. Count Basie plays the melody; Young leaves it behind, inventing melodies that float over the song's chords.

"Jones-Smith Incorporated" is a pseudonym created by John Hammond, who arranged for Basie to enlarge his nine-piece Kansas City group and take it east (see Chapter 8). Before Hammond actually met with Basie, an executive from Decca Records visited Kansas City and (implying he was Hammond's associate) signed him to a brutal contract that allowed for no royalties. Hammond couldn't legally record Basie until the Decca contract was fulfilled, but he was determined to do so anyway. One morning in Chicago, after the band had played through the night, he recorded a Basie quintet. To release the records, Hammond took the names of trumpeter Carl "Tatti" Smith and drummer Jo Jones and made up a new group.

🔊 oh! lady be good

2.11

JONES-SMITH INCORPORATED
Carl Smith, trumpet; Lester Young, tenor saxophone; Count Basie, piano; Walter Page. bass; Jo Jones, drums

- Label: Vocalion 3459; *Lester Young* (Verve 549082)
- Date: 1936
- Style: Kansas City swing
- Form: 32-bar popular song (**A A B A**)

What to listen for:

- Young's two-chorus solo: unpredictable rhythms, relaxed and bluesy
- Jones's cool, quiet drumming (with the beat on the high-hat cymbal)

CHORUS 1

0:00	A	Basie begins by stating the melody to the song with his right hand. Behind him, Jones on drums plays quietly on the high-hat cymbal.
0:10	A	At times, Basie begins to show traces of a **stride** foundation in his left hand.
0:20	B	
0:29		The drums begin to build intensity by playing a **backbeat**.
0:30	A	

CHORUS 2

0:40	A	Young enters with a three-note statement, accompanied by a drum accent. His phrases are inflected with notes from the blues. Behind him, Basie plays chords on the beat.
0:51	A	
0:59		In one of the phrases, Young bends one of his pitches.
1:01	B	He begins to build intensity by starting phrases with accented, scooped notes.
1:11	A	He creates **polyrhythms** out of a single note.
1:16		Another striking use of variable intonation.

CHORUS 3

1:21	A	Young's second chorus begins higher in pitch and adds faster rhythmic values.
1:24		On bass, Page relaxes from four beats to two beats to the measure.
1:32	A	Beginning with a scooped note, Young creates polyrhythms from a short phrase. Page returns to four beats to the measure.
1:42	B	At the bridge, Young plays a descending phrase that becomes polyrhythmic through off-center repetition; the drummer responds with a drum roll.
1:48		Young reaches the high point of his solo.
1:52	A	He starts the last section with a dramatic **syncopation**, followed by another off-center repetition.
2:00		Young's last phrase bids us a bluesy farewell.

CHORUS 4

2:03	A	Smith begins his trumpet solo. Behind him, Young starts playing a background riff figure.
2:13	A	
2:23	B	Smith's solo and Young's syncopated riff tangle in a complex polyrhythmic interaction.
2:34	A	

CHORUS 5 (abbreviated)

| 2:44 | B | While the drums drop out, the bass line quietly rises to a higher register. Basie plays a simple piano solo. |
| 2:54 | A | With a sudden increase in volume, the two horns and the drums reenter for a climactic final chorus. |

Goodbye Pork Pie Hat

As an artist, Young represented a blend of tenderness and exuberant nonconformity. Yet his personal story suggests the cautionary tale of an artist too fragile for life's hard knocks. Young remained with Basie until 1940, during which time he also appeared on a series of records with Billie Holiday (discussed below). Feeling hampered by Basie's increasingly intricate arrangements, however, he decided to set out on his own. He led his own small groups, toured army camps with the Al Sears band, and briefly reunited with Basie. Then his life changed irrevocably when he was drafted, in October 1944—he was starring in *Jammin' the Blues* when he received the summons.

After admitting to officers that he smoked marijuana, and additionally nettling them with his perplexing lingo, Young was subjected to a ninety-five-minute trial and sentenced to a year of hard labor at a debilitation barracks (D. B.) in Georgia. Although he announced his return to civilian life nine months later with his triumphant 1945 recording "D. B. Blues," he never completely recovered from the incarceration and soon surrendered to alcoholism. His playing in later years was occasionally spirited and inventive, but the spark had dimmed: his timbre became drier, his interpretations eccentric, his youthful radiance replaced by a candid, vulnerable lyricism. Charles Mingus's tribute "Goodbye Pork Pie Hat" expresses the feeling of loss that accompanied Young's death, at forty-nine.

JAZZ OVERSEAS

Having spread out from New Orleans and the South to Chicago, New York, Kansas City, California, and other parts of the United States, jazz leaped the oceans as quickly as recordings could carry it. Adherents listened to and learned to play jazz in Europe, Asia, South America, Australia, and Africa. Jazz thus returned to the nations whose emigrants had first transported the musical ingredients that African Americans fused into a unique New World music.

Two contrary factors stimulated jazz's growth abroad. First, it was recognized as a serious, exhilarating new art—"a new reason for living," in the words of French critic Boris Vian. When Armstrong, Ellington, Fats Waller, and Hawkins appeared in France, England, Holland, and Denmark, they received the kind of respect due artists, and many black musicians, singers, and dancers followed their lead. Racism continued to rear its head, but it was not supported by laws that defined its victims as second-class citizens. In France, Negro entertainers were considered chic: stereotypes redounded in their favor.

The second factor tried to quash the first. In some areas—the Soviet Union, Nazi Germany—jazz was illegal, and thus came to represent rebellion and liberty. Music that prized personal expression as its highest aesthetic goal could not help but exemplify the lure of freedom and democracy. In these societies, jazz flourished underground. (This remained true into the 1980s, when Czechoslovakia banned the Prague Jazz Section and jazz musicians in East Berlin performed in hiding.) In the 1930s, Soviet jazz fans nursed their devotion at the risk of imprisonment. When Benny Goodman toured Moscow in the 1950s, he was amazed to discover that he had thousands of Russian fans who referred to his records by catalog numbers—a practice once intended to fool spies.

The Nazis banned jazz as decadent, the product of barbaric blacks and Jews. Then as the world moved toward war, German leaders were obliged to face the fact that in the countries they occupied, citizens were far more likely to listen to the local radio stations, which played jazz constantly, than to German broadcasts. Instead of combating the jazz craze, they tried to join it, as German musicians recorded (unintentionally hilarious) imitations of American swing hits. After the war, liberated cities like Paris, Copenhagen, and Amsterdam treated jazz musicians as heroes. A ballad by French guitarist Django Reinhardt (discussed below), "Nuages," had become an anthem of the resistance. Conversely, jazz temporarily lost its popularity in those same cities, in part because many people associated it with the horrific days of the occupation.

At a 1948 recording session, Lester Young was beckoned from his instrument and music. He put his cigarette on a Coke bottle and hung his famous porkpie hat on his saxophone case. Photographer Herman Leonard took one look and recognized an iconic still life—and created a classic of jazz photography.

World Jazz

Wherever jazz landed, it developed a bond with local musical practices. Argentina's tango, Brazil's samba, and Cuba's clave influenced jazz and were influenced by it in turn. Jazz similarly mixed with the music of Africa, Japan, Finland, and Hawaii, generating new compounds. American jazz musicians remained stars in all these places, but local musicians also achieved fame. In 1971, Duke Ellington, who had already composed *The Far East Suite*, *The Queen's Suite* (honoring Great Britain), and *The Latin American Suite*, among other geographically inspired works, introduced *The Afro-Eurasian Eclipse*, pointing out that as various cultures lose their provincial identities, "it's most improbable that anyone will ever know exactly who is enjoying the shadow of whom."

FRANK DRIGGS COLLECTION

Django Reinhardt, the Belgian Gypsy who proved that Europeans could not only master but also innovate jazz, acquired his first Gibson electric guitar, shown here in 1946, while visiting New York as a guest of Duke Ellington.

■ DJANGO REINHARDT (1910–1953)

Only one European jazz artist is universally conceded a seat at the table of prime movers—those figures who decisively changed the way jazz is played. Django Reinhardt was born in a Gypsy caravan that was passing through Belgium. He and his two younger siblings (one of whom, Joseph, also became a guitarist) grew up in a settlement near Paris. Their father, an itinerant entertainer, abandoned the family when Django was five, and their mother supported them by weaving baskets and making bracelets from artillery shells found in World War I battlefields.

Django learned violin and banjo from relatives before taking up guitar, which he began playing professionally at twelve. A habitué of music halls, where he usually worked as an accompanist, he mastered waltzes and traditional themes as well as pop tunes. Then in 1928, shortly before he turned nineteen, Reinhardt was struck by a tragedy that would have ended the ambitions of most musicians: his caravan caught fire, and he was stuck inside. His left hand, which held tight the blanket that saved him, suffered severe burns and mutilation—the fourth and fifth fingers were paralyzed, folded inward like a claw. Determined to continue with the guitar nevertheless, he developed a way of playing single notes and chords with only two fingers and his thumb; at the same time, he had to learn to arch his hand so that the paralyzed fingers did not get in the way.

Within a few years, Reinhardt created new fingerings to play chords while perfecting rapid-fire single-note improvisations that ranged over the entire length of the fret board. His right hand picked the strings with such percussive strength that, long before the introduction of the electric guitar, his sound had a vital, piercing tone. With the help of a microphone, he had no trouble being heard.

Reinhardt's love of music was transformed by the first jazz records to reach Paris. When he heard duets by guitarist Eddie Lang (Chapter 6) and violinist Joe Venuti, he recognized an immediate kinship with jazz improvisation and rhythm. At a time when most American guitarists played little more than "rhythm" (accompanying chords that supply the harmony and keep time), Reinhardt emerged as a soloist of stunning originality and a deeply personal romanticism.

Franco-American Relations

The turning point for European jazz came in 1934, the year Coleman Hawkins embarked on his five-year visit. A couple of years earlier, a few French fans, including critics Hugues Panassié and Charles Delaunay, had formed the Hot Club de France, an influential organization for enthusiasts and musicians. Then in 1934, Panassié published *Le jazz hot*, the first serious critical book on American jazz in any language—and the first to suggest the preeminent role of African Americans. That same year, he and Delaunay prepared to launch a magazine, *Jazz Hot* (still in existence today), and a band to represent the club's musical point of view: Quintette du Hot Club de France.

The Quintette, which arose out of informal jam sessions, included two powerful and like-minded soloists: Reinhardt and violinist Stephane Grappelli, a largely self-taught musician who had played both piano and accordion, accompanying silent movies from the age of fourteen before gravitating toward dance bands and jazz. Inspired by Eddie Lang and Joe Venuti, Reinhardt and Grappelli developed a hard-swinging and playful interaction. The setting in which they worked, however, was like no other in jazz. Instead of a piano and drums, the Quintette's rhythm section included two rhythm guitars (Roger Chaput and Joseph Reinhardt) and bass (Louis Vola).

Recordings by the Quintette drew avid praise in Europe, and were soon eagerly sought in the United States. If Bix Beiderbecke had shown that whites could master jazz with individuality, the Quintette du Hot Club demonstrated that Europeans could do the same. It confirmed the idea that jazz, though American in origin, was a musical art of universal potential. Grappelli was considered on a par with Venuti and the preeminent African American violinist of the Swing Era, Stuff Smith. Django was in a class by himself: after Lang's premature death in 1933, jazz guitar had receded in prominence, but Django brought it back with a vengeance.

Given Reinhardt's immediate acceptance by Americans (after the war, Ellington would sponsor his only visit to the United States), Delaunay began recording him with visiting musicians: Hawkins, Benny Carter, violinist Eddie South, trumpeter Bill Coleman, clarinetist Barney Bigard, and others. Hawkins was the most prominent of the guest soloists, but Carter was perhaps the most significant: in addition to playing superb alto saxophone and trumpet, he wrote arrangements that epitomized international jazz.

■ KING CARTER (1907–2003)

Press agents and pundits may have called Benny Goodman the King of Swing, but musicians privately reserved the royal epithet for a hero of the Swing Era who received little popular acclaim: the modest, soft-spoken jack-of-all-musical-trades Benny Carter. Born in New York City, Carter learned piano from his mother, but was largely self-taught as

> **Quintette du Hot Club de France**

Twenty World Jazz Musicians

By the late twentieth century, the world outside the United States had produced thousands of accomplished jazz musicians, some of them achieving international renown. Although most are outside the scope of this book, they have all enhanced jazz as a developing, international art. A small sampling follows (some are discussed in later chapters).

Danish violinist Svend Asmussen (b. 1916)
Dutch saxophonist Willem Breuker (b. 1944)
Cuban saxophonist Paquito D'Rivera (b. 1948)
Norwegian saxophonist Jan Garbarek (b. 1947)
French violinist Stephane Grappelli (1908–1997)
Swedish saxophonist Lars Gullin (1928–1976)
English vocalist Cleo Laine (b. 1927)
Brazilian percussionist Airto Moreira (b. 1941)
English saxophonist Evan Parker (b. 1944)
Danish bassist Niels-Henning Orsted Pedersen (1946–2005)
Cuban percussionist Chano Pozo (1915–1948)
Italian trumpeter Enrico Rava (b. 1939)
Cuban pianist Gonzalo Rubalcaba (b. 1963)
Norwegian guitarist Terje Rypdal (b. 1947)
Argentine bandoneon player Dino Saluzzi (b. 1935)
Brazilian guitarist Bola Sete (1923–1987)
French pianist Martial Solal (b. 1927)
English trumpeter Kenny Wheeler (b. 1930)
Austrian pianist Joe Zawinul (b. 1932)
Hungarian guitarist Attila Zoller (1927–1998)

Benny Carter—multi-instrumentalist, composer, arranger, and orchestra leader—was known among musicians as the King because he did everything with originality and panache. New York, 1941.

an instrumentalist, composer, and arranger. He began touring professionally at seventeen, and soon attracted attention with his playing and writing for Fletcher Henderson, Horace Henderson, Charlie Johnson, and McKinney's Cotton Pickers, which he took over in 1931. In addition to alto saxophone and trumpet, Carter tried his hand at clarinet (playing a renowned solo on his 1930 "Dee Blues"), tenor saxophone, soprano saxophone, trombone, and piano. He even sang once, imitating Bing Crosby. He formed his own orchestra in 1932.

The Complete Musician

Carter's importance to jazz has four components: instrumentalist, composer-arranger, bandleader, and social activist. Along with Johnny Hodges, Carter established the alto saxophone as a major jazz instrument, paralleling Hawkins's impact on tenor. He played with an unruffled, melodic flair, underscored by compositional logic. His improvisations flowed with timeless elegance—indeed, his style changed little between the 1930s and 1990s. He also developed a personal approach on trumpet, which he played less frequently; an excellent example is his recording of "More Than You Know."

As a composer, Carter emerged in the 1930s as one of the most accomplished tunesmiths in jazz; a few of his melodies became popular standards, including "When Lights Are Low" and "Blues in My Heart." His writing for big bands was acclaimed for its melodic ingenuity and streamlined rhythms. He was the first important jazz arranger to cut away the complex ornamentation of most dance bands, setting a standard for swing that would soon be echoed in the writing of Fletcher Henderson, Count Basie, and others.

The most imitated trademark in Carter's orchestrations was his writing for the reed section, which could swing with the impulsiveness of an improvised solo: the highlight of many of his works is a chorus by unified saxophones (*soli*). Carter's early recordings ("Lonesome Nights," "Symphony of Riffs") shimmer with timeless originality, and his most acclaimed album, *Further Definitions*, appeared in 1961 on a label (Impulse) associated with jazz's avant-garde. A favorite of singers, he wrote arrangements for Ella Fitzgerald, Ray Charles, Sarah Vaughan, and Peggy Lee, among others.

As a bandleader, Carter enjoyed little commercial success; at a time when most bands courted dancers, he concentrated on musical refinement. Even the ballad singers that he featured in the hope of getting a hit were framed in unusually understated settings. Carter was so much admired by fellow musicians, however, that he had his pick of players. Musicians who worked in his bands in the 1930s and 1940s include Ben Webster, Chu Berry, pianist Teddy Wilson, Dizzy Gillespie, trombonists Vic Dickenson and J. J. Johnson, drummer Max Roach, and Miles Davis.

As an activist, Carter steadfastly fought racism by opening doors closed to African Americans. In 1937, two years after arriving in Europe, he organized, at a Dutch resort, the first integrated and international orchestra in jazz history. Determined to create similar opportunities at home, he worked his way into the Hollywood studio system, one of the last bastions of segregation in the entertainment world. There, his temperament (mild-mannered but very tough), business savvy, and uncommon versatility allowed him to crack the

PHOTO BY CHARLES PETERSON, COURTESY OF DON PETERSON

"color bar." As a result, he enjoyed a rare level of financial security in jazz, living in Beverly Hills and driving a Rolls Royce. He worked on dramatic and musical films, from *Thousands Cheer* (1942) to *Buck and the Preacher* (1972), and more than two dozen television programs. In 1978, Carter was inducted into the Black Filmmakers Hall of Fame. It was at that point that he revived his career as a soloist, achieving his greatest success as a touring jazz musician in his seventies and eighties.

"I'm Coming, Virginia"

All of Carter's traits are apparent in his 1938 treatment of the 1926 standard "I'm Coming, Virginia," by black songwriters Will Marion Cook (the man who brought Sidney Bechet to Europe in 1919) and Donald Heywood. Carter leads an integrated and pan-national ensemble (it was recorded in Paris) in an arrangement that offers his own exceptional alto saxophone solo, a chorus by Django Reinhardt, and a signature climax featuring a four-part voicing of the saxophones.

LISTENING GUIDE

i'm coming, virginia

2.12

BENNY CARTER AND HIS ORCHESTRA
Benny Carter, Fletcher Allen, alto saxophones; Bertie King, Alix Combelle, tenor saxophones; Yorke de Souza, piano; Django Reinhardt, guitar; Len Harrison, bass; Robert Montmarché, drums

- Label: Swing (F)20; *Django: With His American Friends* (DRG 8493)
- Date: 1938
- Style: big-band swing
- Form: 24-bar popular song (**A A′ B**)

What to listen for:
- Reinhardt's acoustic guitar solo (chorus 3)
- Carter's supple arrangements for saxophone *soli* (choruses 1 and 5)

INTRODUCTION
0:00 The piano plays a four-bar introduction, lightly accompanied by the drums.

CHORUS 1
0:05 **A** The four saxophones enter with a *soli* in **block-chord** harmony. This arrangement by Carter is based on the original tune, but varies it through new rhythmic patterns reminiscent of speech.
0:16 **A′**
0:28 **B**

INTERLUDE
0:39 The saxophones continue their block-chord texture, accompanied only by a faint pulse on the bass drum.

CHORUS 2
0:44 **A** The Belgian tenor saxophonist Combelle takes a solo. Behind him, Reinhardt on guitar plays a heavy eight-beats-to-the bar pattern.
0:55 **A′**

| 0:58 | | Reinhardt relaxes into a more normal texture, playing chords on the **backbeat**. |
| 1:06 | **B** | |

CHORUS 3

1:18	**A**	Reinhardt enters with a dissonant harmonic **arpeggio** on guitar. Underneath him, the piano plays a stiff accompaniment.
1:22		Reinhardt plays a **blue note**, which tails off at the end of a phrase.
1:29	**A'**	
1:40	**B**	

CHORUS 4

1:51	**A**	Carter takes a solo. The other saxophones support him with simple chords in the background.
2:02	**A'**	
2:14	**B**	

INTERLUDE

| 2:22 | | The tenor saxophones interrupt with a **syncopated** phrase. The full band then plays a series of chords that modulate to a new key. |

CHORUS 5

2:28	**A**	The saxophone section reenters, this time with a much freer and rhythmically varied *soli*. It begins with a new riff in bare **octaves**, followed by a tumultuous plunge in block-chord harmonies.
2:37		Reinhardt interjects a brief phrase in octaves.
2:39	**A'**	
2:41		For dramatic relief, Carter reduces the sound of the ensemble to an octave.
2:50	**B**	
2:56		A familiar chord progression leads to the final cadence.

SINGERS

Singers have a peculiar relationship to jazz. Instrumentalists model themselves on the flexibility and expressiveness of the voice, while singers aim for the rhythmic freedom of instrumentalists. But there is a crucial difference: singers for the most part concentrate on melody, leaving the abstractions of ad-lib variations to instrumentalists. They occupy a middle ground between jazz and commercial entertainment, with a far greater chance of acceptance by the mainstream. Louis Armstrong reached more people singing than playing trumpet.

Most successful American pop singers who came along in the 1930s and 1940s were influenced by jazz. Few of them were true jazz singers, but the best were accepted as tasteful, creative interpreters of the same pop songs that fueled instrumental jazz. At they same time, they were resented for achieving a level of financial security not available to jazz instrumentalists—especially if they were hired as much for their looks as their voices. Singers were expected to charm audiences and give the musicians a breather. By the late 1940s, however, big-band jazz struggled to support itself, while the big-band singers were reborn as recording and television stars.

In the early days of the dance bands, instrumentalists who could carry a tune "doubled" as vocalists. But if an audience could hear lyrics, it was more likely to enjoy and remember the melody. So singers were added. That's how hits were made: people left theaters and ballrooms humming melodies and seeking them out in sheet music and on records. When Paul Whiteman recruited the first full-time singers in a dance band—Bing Crosby in 1926 and Mildred Bailey in 1929—he introduced a new and frequently rivalrous relationship between instrumentalists and singers.

Songbirds

By the time Mildred Bailey entered the Whiteman band, Bing Crosby was on his way toward becoming the most listened-to singer in history (see Chapter 5). He created a template for the jazz-influenced pop singer who garners ever-greater popularity by singing every kind of song, usually with diminished or nonexistent jazz content, and then translates that success into movie and broadcast stardom. Bailey created a different template and a demand for singers who could provide a feminine touch in the otherwise masculine world of the big bands.

FRANK DRIGGS COLLECTION

Bing Crosby and Mildred Bailey were neighbors in Washington State, though they first met in Los Angeles, where Mildred worked in a speakeasy and helped Crosby get auditions in vaudeville. Paul Whiteman hired them as the first full-time male and female vocalists to tour with a big band. Here they rehearse for a radio show, c. 1949.

Many women singers, however talented, doubled as eye candy and were obliged to pose flirtatiously for *Down Beat* and *Metronome*, the leading journals of swing music. They were routinely referred to with bird synonyms: a female band singer was a thrush, a canary, a sparrow, a chick or chickadee. Such images were far removed from those associated with 1920s blues divas like Bessie Smith and Ma Rainey, who were depicted as tough and independent. Bailey, with her light timbre and gentle embellishments, represented a stylistic extension of the more adaptable Ethel Waters, who roamed the blues and Tin Pan Alley with imperious self-assurance.

Those who followed Waters and Bailey, white or black, were confronted with songs that helped to define women as weaker vessels. Where blues singers used double entendres to celebrate sex, these younger performers tended to either pine for their men or offer cheerful fantasies of innocent romance. Great vocal artists emerged, even so, and the Swing Era produced two particularly ingenious singers who incarnated contrary views of life. Billie Holiday and Ella Fitzgerald, each in her way, exemplify a degree of cultural resilience beyond the scope of all but a few instrumentalists.

■ BILLIE HOLIDAY (1915–1959)

The life of Billie Holiday is shrouded in myths. Born in Philadelphia and raised (as Eleanora Fagan) in Baltimore, she was the illegitimate daughter of a teenage guitarist, Clarence Holiday, who declined to acknowledge his paternity until she became famous. Her young mother moved to New York soon after Billie's birth, leaving her in the care of abusive relatives. At ten, Holiday was remanded to a school for delinquent girls. In 1929, she joined her mother in New York, where she worked at menial labor and was arrested for prostitution. She began singing a year later, and by 1933 was ensconced at a Harlem club, where John Hammond heard her and invited her to record with Benny Goodman's band. A year later, she wowed the notoriously demanding audience at the Apollo Theater.

Billie Holiday recorded Lewis Allen's "Strange Fruit," a vivid description of a lynching and the first widely noted song about racism in American popular music, for the small Commodore label after Columbia Records refused. The band included Jimmy McGlin, guitar; John Williams, bass; and Eddie Dougherty, drums. New York, April 1939.

PHOTO BY CHARLES PETERSON, COURTESY OF DON PETERSON

Now a professional musician, Holiday renamed herself by combining the names of her father and the silent screen star Billie Dove—though she was also apparently nicknamed Bill in childhood. In 1935, Hammond built a series of recording sessions around her, directed by pianist Teddy Wilson and involving top musicians of the day, including Artie Shaw, Goodman, Roy Eldridge, Johnny Hodges, and several members of the Basie band, most significantly Lester Young, with whom she shared one of the most musically fertile partnerships in jazz.

Holiday briefly worked with big bands—first Basie and then Shaw, until racial injunctions forced Shaw to let her go. Mostly she sang in nightclubs, including, in 1939, New York's Café Society, the first major interracial night spot in the country. Her records, which were made with the growing jukebox market in mind, sold well, and her recording of "Strange Fruit" (1939), the vivid depiction of a Southern lynching, enhanced her standing with the New York intelligentsia. Her growing fame included a fling in Hollywood: she was cast as a singing maid in the film *New Orleans*, but walked off the set before it was finished.

Holiday suffered a long, public downfall that was caused by her dependency on narcotics and a thug who married her, encouraged her addiction, and betrayed her to the police to save himself. After a sensationalized drawn-out trial in 1947, she was jailed for eight months and deprived of her cabaret card—the permit (abolished in 1960) necessary for working in New York nightclubs. In the 1950s, Holiday continued to command a loyal following, recording with larger ensembles and strings, though her voice weakened. She began to focus on ballads, developing a more mannered, expressive style. As her voice declined, she experienced a few musical reprieves, including a triumphant 1957 appearance on a television broadcast, *The Sound of Jazz*, in which she was supported by an all-star band that included Young, Hawkins, Webster, and Eldridge. At the time she died, at forty-four, her voice was little more than a whisper.

Lady's Style

Often cited as jazz's greatest vocalist, Holiday initially drew inspiration from Ethel Waters, Bessie Smith, and Louis Armstrong. The Armstrong influence proved decisive: from him, she learned to swing, paraphrase and embellish a melody, and impart a blues feeling to everything she sang. When Hammond introduced her to Teddy Wilson, the pianist expressed disappointment. He preferred Ella Fitzgerald and thought Holiday was a gimmick—a woman who sang like Armstrong. But he quickly changed his mind and helped her to mature into the riveting artist whose voice expressed so much of the human condition.

Holiday does not fit the cliché of the jazz singer: scat-singing held no interest for her, and she rarely sang blues. Her range was limited to about an octave and a half, and her voice had a thin, edgy timbre. None of this mattered, because Holiday had a gift for altering a melody in such a way as to make it extremely personal. Even those of her signature numbers that were insufferably trite she managed to imbue with profound import. After her death, Frank Sinatra, born in the same year as Holiday, called her "unquestionably the most important influence on American popular singing in the last twenty years."

Jazz musicians adored her phrasing, which is at once guileless and clever and always rhythmically assured. They considered her one of them—a jazz artist of the first rank. She revised melodies to suit her voice and interpreted frivolous lyrics in a way that made them seem vital. Her musical romance with Young is unequaled, suggesting an intimate solidarity in performances like "A Sailboat in the Moonlight," which begins as singer-and-accompaniment and becomes a collaboration between two comparable voices riding out the night.

"A Sailboat in the Moonlight"

"A Sailboat in the Moonlight" is Holiday alchemy. The song, written by Carmen Lombardo, was a No. 1 hit for Guy Lombardo and His Royal Canadians (a band that specialized in sugary music with no jazz content). Its sentimental cadences emphasize a thoroughly banal lyric. Yet Holiday, abetted by Young and Count Basie's rhythm section as led by a good Teddy Wilson imitator (Jimmy Sherman), is rhythmically inspired and genuinely touching. How does she do it? The transformation begins immediately as she replaces the song's corny ascending melody with a repeated pitch, each of three notes ("a-sail-boat") articulated for rhythmic effect—not unlike the way Young begins many of his solos. From then on, she alters this note and that, stretches one at the expense of another, never obscuring the appealing qualities of the song (which has the saving grace of pretty harmonies). She makes the fantasy of sailing away with her lover to a remote rendezvous a dream worth cherishing.

LISTENING GUIDE

 a sailboat in the moonlight

BILLIE HOLIDAY

Billie Holiday, vocal; Buck Clayton, trumpet; Edmond Hall, clarinet; Lester Young, tenor saxophone; James Sherman, piano; Freddy Green, guitar; Walter Page, bass; Jo Jones, drums

- Label: Vocalion/OKeh 3605; *The Best of Billie Holiday* (Legacy 886972136127)
- Date: 1937
- Style: swing
- Form: 32-bar popular song (**A A B A**)

> **What to listen for:**
> - Holiday's melodic paraphrasing and rhythmic variations
> - Young's expressive countermelodies and responses to Holiday

INTRODUCTION

0:00   Clayton on trumpet plays a matched set of phrases, each ending on a **half cadence** (on the dominant). Jones accompanies on the high-hat cymbal.

CHORUS 1

0:08 **A**   *"A sailboat in the moonlight and you.*
Wouldn't that be heaven, a heaven just for two?"
As Holiday sings the song, she paraphrases the melody and swings hard against the beat. Young on tenor saxophone plays both underneath the solo (**countermelody**) and in answer to it (**call and response**). In the background, the clarinet plays sustained notes. The bass (Page) plays a simple accompaniment of two beats to the bar.

0:21   Over the **turnaround**, Young responds to Holiday by raising his volume and playing a phrase that lags noticeably behind the beat.

0:24 **A**   *"A soft breeze on a June night and you.*
What a perfect setting for letting dreams come true!"
Holiday continues to add rhythmic variations, while Young improvises a new line.

0:36   Young's response to the vocal line is bluesy.

0:40 **B**   *"A chance to sail away to Sweetheart Bay beneath the stars that shine,*
A chance to drift, for you to lift your tender lips to mine!"
The bridge provides contrast by moving to unexpected new harmonies.

0:52   The harmony moves to a half cadence.

0:57 **A**   *"The things, dear, that I long for are few:*
Just give me a sailboat in the moonlight and you!"
Holiday falls farther behind the beat.

1:03   She emphasizes the tune's title by singing the last phrase with a sharper timbre.

CHORUS 2

1:12 **A**   Sherman plays a light, spare piano solo. Behind him, Jones switches to a dry, **staccato** accompaniment on the cymbals. Page on bass occasionally fills in the texture by adding extra notes.

1:28 **A**

1:44 **B**   Clayton (trumpet) enters. Jones returns to a splashier high-hat sound, responding to the trumpet's phrases with sharp snare-drum accents.

1:53   In the background, someone shouts "Yeah!"

2:00 **A**   Young plays an eight-bar solo in a smooth, relaxed style.

2:09   The last phrase of the solo wraps things up by descending through a bluesy phrase to the **tonic**.

CHORUS 3 (abbreviated)

2:16   **B**   *"A chance to sail away to Sweetheart Bay beneath the stars that shine.*
A chance to drift, for you to lift your tender lips to mine!"
Holiday returns, her notes falling unpredictably within the measure. Young retreats to accompaniment, joining Hall (clarinet), who plays sustained notes deep in the background.

2:24   Holiday suddenly sings firmly on the beat, with the rhythm section instead of against it, helping to intensify the sense of groove.

2:32   **A**   *"The things, dear, that I long for are few:*
Just give me a sailboat in the moonlight and you!"
As if responding to Holiday, Page switches to a steady **walking bass** (four beats to the bar).

2:38   Holiday marks her last phrase by repeatedly hitting her highest pitch.

CODA

2:44   At the end of the vocal, the accompanying instruments (piano, tenor saxophone, and clarinet) combine in a brief polyphonic clamor.

▪ ELLA FITZGERALD (1917–1996)

If Billie Holiday is a singer associated with emotional pain—a wounded sparrow, in songbird parlance—Ella Fitzgerald is the irrepressible spirit of musical joy. Like Holiday, she rarely sang the blues, but where Billie had an unmistakable feeling for them, Ella saw blues as just another song form, useful for up-tempo scat improvisations. Her vocal equipment was also the opposite of Holiday's: she had four octaves at her disposal, and was not averse to adding falsetto (higher than her normal range) cries and low growls. In her peak years, her timbre had a luscious, ripe quality. She was an accomplished scat-singer, one of very few who could improvise on chords as imaginatively as the best instrumentalists. Benny Carter once orchestrated her solo on "Oh! Lady Be Good" as evidence of her compositional prowess.

Fitzgerald was born in Virginia and raised in Yonkers, New York, where she sang in church and taught herself to dance. When her mother died, she was sent to live with an aunt in Harlem, and treated as an orphan. By 1934, she had dropped out of school and was living off her wits on the streets. That November, she entered the Apollo Theater's amateur night as a dancer, but at the last minute chose to sing. Fitzgerald, who lacked Holiday's great physical beauty, was hooted when she walked onstage—a big, clunky girl, awkward in manner and badly dressed—until she broke into song. Her enchantingly girlish voice and dynamic rhythm triumphed, and she won the competition.

Because of her looks, however, bandleaders refused to hire her until Carter recommended her to Chick Webb, who was instantly hooked. He became her legal guardian, bought her clothes, and restructured his band to feature

Ella Fitzgerald, the voice of exuberant joy and vivacious swing, made an effortless transition from swing to bop to mainstream pop, maintaining top echelon stardom until her death. She is pictured here at the peak of the Swing Era with drummer Bill Beason at the Savoy Ballroom, 1940.

a voice he predicted would be heard for decades. From the summer of 1935, she was present on most of his recording sessions, and quickly attracted a following. Her 1938 recording of "A-Tisket, a-Tasket," based on an old nursery rhyme she set to a catchy melody during a hospital stay, made her famous. Within months she was billed as the "First Lady of Swing"—in later years the "First Lady of Song."

After Webb's death, Fitzgerald recorded dozens of ballads, swingers (up-tempo songs that swing), and novelties, effortlessly making the transition to bebop (her "Air Mail Special" is a bop version of a swing classic). Impressario Norman Granz recruited her for his Jazz at the Philharmonic concert tours (he also signed Holiday; see Chapter 11), and became her personal manager, building a new record label, Verve, around her. Fitzgerald's innovative songbook albums, each devoted to one songwriter, garnered tremendous acclaim in the 1950s and 1960s. She was regarded by many as the gold standard for both jazz and pop singing.

 "Blue Skies"

"Blue Skies," a pop standard frequently adapted by jazz musicians, was recorded for the album *Ella Fitzgerald Sings the Irving Berlin Songbook*. But her rendition is so adventurous (more Ella than Berlin), it was initially dropped from that album and included on another, *Get Happy!*—an emblematic Fitzgerald title (a typical Holiday title, by contrast, is *Songs for Distingué Lovers*). She begins with a scat intro, employing cantorial phrases (suggesting Jewish liturgical music). She sings the lyric at a medium clip, accompanied by Harry "Sweets" Edison's trumpet obbligato, mildly embellishing the melody, yet making every phrase swing. Then she takes off on a three-chorus scat improvisation, singing variations with the imagination of an instrumentalist. Note that she quotes from Wagner's "Wedding March" in chorus 2, and a few bars of Gershwin's *Rhapsody in Blue* in the last chorus before reprising the lyric for the final bridge.

LISTENING GUIDE

2.13

blue skies

ELLA FITZGERALD
Ella Fitzgerald, vocal, with Paul Weston Orchestra: John Best, Pete Candoli, Harry Edison, Don Fagerquist, Manny Klein, trumpets; Ed Kusby, Dick Noel, William Schaefer, trombones; Juan Tizol, valve trombone; Gene Cipriano, Chuck Gentry, Leonard Hartman, Matty Matlock, Ted Nash, Babe Russin, Fred Stulce, woodwinds; Paul Smith, piano; Barney Kessel, guitar; Joe Mondragon, bass; Alvin Stoller, drums

- Label: *Ella Fitzgerald Sings the Irving Berlin Songbook* (Verve 830-2); *Gold* (Verve 602517414549)
- Date: 1958
- Style: big-band swing
- Form: 32-bar popular song (**A A B A**)

What to listen for:
- Fitzgerald's imaginative scat-singing, with instrumental-like motives and riffs
- her varied rhythm and unusual vocal timbres
- unexpected quotations

INTRODUCTION

0:00   Over sustained orchestra chords, Fitzgerald begins to **scat-sing**, using open, resonant nonsense syllables ("da," "la") instead of words. The vocal line lazily moves through **arpeggios**: notes drawn from the underlying chords.

0:17   As the accompanying instruments come to rest on a dominant chord, the vocal line falls to its lowest note.

CHORUS 1

0:22   **A**   *"Blue skies smiling at me, nothing but blue skies do I see."*
Fitzgerald sings the melody to "Blue Skies" with its original text. In each **A** section, the melody gradually falls from the **minor** into the **major mode** (at "nothing but *blue* skies"). Behind her, the rhythm section plays a steady, even pulse, with **countermelodies** from muted trumpet (Edison) and piano.

0:34   **A**   *"Bluebirds singing a song, nothing but bluebirds all day long."*
Fitzgerald adds slight decorative touches to individual notes, and alters the melody at phrase's end (0:43).

0:46   **B**   *"Never saw the sun shining so bright, never saw things going so right.*
Noticing the days hurrying by, when you're in love, my, how they fly."
As the melody moves into the major mode and a higher register, the saxophones counter with a restrained lower accompanying line.

0:58   **A**   *"Blue days, all of them gone, nothing but blue skies from now on."*

1:08   The saxophones begin playing a riff.

CHORUS 2

1:11   **A**   Picking up on the rhythm and melody of the saxophone riff, Fitzgerald begins scatting.

1:17   For a few measures, she sings slightly behind the beat, adding rhythmic tension.

1:23   **A**   Using variable intonation (**blue note**), she gradually pulls the first note upward.

1:29   Using her head voice (higher register), she sings a series of relaxed **triplets**.

1:32   Unexpectedly, she quotes the beginning of Wagner's "Wedding March."

1:35   **B**   As the saxophones play gruff chords, Fitzgerald hints at singing in **double-time**.

1:42   She sings a phrase, then repeats it at a higher pitch level as the song returns to its original minor key.

1:47   **A**   Starting on a dramatic high note, she launches into a loose, bluesy phrase.

1:53   She sings a three-note motive; repeating it, she turns it into a **polyrhythmic** motive.

CHORUS 3

1:59   **A**   As the accompaniment intensifies, Fitzgerald digs into the beat, turning her line into a riff figure and using more percussive syllables ("bop," "dee-yowwww").

2:05   Searching for more consonants, she begins a new phrase with a misplaced (but arresting) "ssssssss" sound.

2:11   **A**   Fitzgerald marks the arrival at the next **A** section with a startling **dissonance**. She repeats it several more times to make it clear to the casual listener that it's not a mistake.

2:23   **B**   Picking up on a phrase she's just sung, she bounces back and forth between two notes in the major scale.

2:29   A lengthy phrase finally ends on the downbeat of the next **A** section.

2:35   **A**   More complicated rhythmic figures suddenly precede an extended passage in her upper register.

CHORUS 4

2:47   **A**   As the background orchestra reaches the peak of its intensity, Fitzgerald retreats to a simple riff figure.

2:54		She quotes a famous theme from Gershwin's *Rhapsody in Blue*.
3:00	**A**	She begins each phrase by leaning on the tonic, sometimes decorating it unexpectedly with triplets.
3:06		As the harmony moves to the major mode, her lines strongly evoke the blues.
3:12	**B**	*"I never saw the sun shining so bright, never saw things going so right. Noticing the days hurrying by, when you're in love, my how they fly."* The band retreats to a simpler texture. Fitzgerald returns to the song's lyrics and, at times, its original melody.
3:24	**A**	*"Blue days, all of them gone, nothing but blue skies from now on."* The last lines are distorted into soaring arpeggios.
CODA		
3:34		As Fitzgerald hits her high note, the band plays two sharp dominant chords, then drops out to let her add a bit more scat-singing.
3:37		The band ends with a caterwauling of chords, piano phrases, and drumming.

THE REST OF THE BAND

As swing soloists developed their virtuoso techniques, advancing harmonic and rhythmic ideas, the rhythm section had to make even more radical changes in order to keep up. Very quickly, thanks to brilliantly accomplished innovators on each instrument, the profiles of pianists, bassists, guitarists, and drummers were raised exponentially. No less than wind players like Coleman Hawkins and Roy Eldridge, these members of the rhythm section developed technical skills undreamed of by jazz's early musicians. As we will see in the next chapter, by the end of the Swing Era, every instrument of the ensemble could be featured, at least potentially, as a soloist. With rhythm players showing greater and greater flare in their individual roles as accompanists, the very nature and function of the rhythm section began to change.

┤ ADDITIONAL LISTENING ├	
Fletcher Henderson	"Queer Notions" (1933); *Blue Rhythm, 1931–1933* (Naxos 8.120672)
Coleman Hawkins	"Picasso" (1948); *Ultimate Coleman Hawkins* (Verve)
Bud Freeman	"The Eel" (1939); *Swingin' with the Eel* (Original Mono Recordings, 1929–1939)
Chu Berry and Roy Eldridge	"Body and Soul" (1938); *Roy Eldridge: Heckler's Hop* (Hep 1030)
Lester Young	"D. B. Blues" (1945); *Complete Aladdin Recordings of Lester Young* (Blue Note 32787)
Benny Carter	"When Lights Are Low" (1936); *When Lights Are Low* (ASV/Living Era 743625027624)
Django Reinhardt	"Nuages" (1942); *Django Reinhardt in Brussels* (Verve 513 947-2)

Benny Goodman	"Solo Flight" (1941); *The Genius of the Electric Guitar* (Sony Jazz 4K65564)
Teddy Wilson	"Blues in C Sharp Minor" (1936); *Teddy Wilson, vol. 2: Blues in C Sharp Minor, Original 1935–1937 Recordings* (Naxos 8.120665)
Duke Ellington	"Jack the Bear" (1940); *Never No Lament: The Blanton-Webster Band* (Bluebird 50857)
Count Basie	"Clap Hands, Here Comes Charlie" (1939); *The Lester Young / Count Basie Sessions, 1936–1940* (Mosaic 4-239)
Billie Holiday	"Strange Fruit" (1939); *Billie Holiday Complete Commodore Recordings* (GRP 401)
Ella Fitzgerald	"Air Mail Special" (1952); *1951–1952 Decca Recordings* (Jazz Factory)

FATS WALLER
christopher columbus

ART TATUM
over the rainbow

CHARLIE CHRISTIAN
swing to bop (topsy)

RHYTHM
IN TRANSITION

RHYTHM IS OUR BUSINESS

In May 1935, the No. 1 record in the country was Jimmie Lunceford's "Rhythm Is Our Business." Released a few months before Benny Goodman triggered the national craze known as swing, the song offered a foretaste of the coming deluge. "Rhythm is our business / Rhythm is what we sell," Lunceford's singer declared: "Rhythm is our business / Business sure is swell." If rhythm defined the swing bands, its foundation lay in the rhythm section: piano, guitar, bass, and drums.

In big bands, these musicians fused into a unified rhythmic front: supplying the beat and marking the harmonies. Each of the leading bands presented a distinct, well-designed rhythmic attack that complemented its particular style. The rhythm sections of Ellington, Basie, and Lunceford, for example, sounded nothing alike. Just as the soloists were champing at the bit of big-band constraints, rhythm players were developing techniques and ideas that demanded more attention than they usually received. In the 1930s, rhythm instruments made dramatic advances toward the foreground of jazz. In the process, they helped set the stage for bebop.

Jo Jones, the Count Basie drummer who was said to play like the wind, changed the feeling of swing with his brisk attack on the high-hat cymbal. New York, 1950.

wwnorton.com/studyspace

PIANO

Although swing bands, especially those led by pianists (Ellington, Basie, Earl Hines, Teddy Wilson), allowed piano solos, pianist-bandleaders limited themselves to introductions, solo choruses, and an occasional mini-concerto. Long before jazz, however, the piano had enjoyed a history of self-sufficiency. In Chapters 5 and 8, we saw how pianists achieved prominence with stride and boogie-woogie. These keyboard styles prospered and peaked in the 1930s.

Fats Waller, a master of comic poses and satirical interpretations of Tin Pan Alley songs, popularized stride piano and composed such classic jazz themes as "Ain't Misbehavin'" and the all-time jam-session favorite "Honeysuckle Rose." He's pictured here on a 1939 magazine cover.

■ FATS WALLER (1904–1943)

Thomas "Fats" Waller achieved, during a brief but incredibly prolific career, a matchless standing in jazz and pop, straddling the dividing line with his humor and instrumental technique. A radiant pianist, canny vocalist, musical satirist, and important songwriter, he made more than 500 records (most within a span of eight years), and succeeded as a composer on Broadway and as an entertainer in movies.

Waller was born in New York City, the son of a Baptist lay preacher. His mother taught him piano and organ, instilling in him a lasting love for Johann Sebastian Bach. She died when Fats was in his mid-teens, at which time he came under the spell of James P. Johnson. He began playing professionally at fifteen, on call to accompany silent movies. Three years later (1922), he recorded two pieces for solo piano, both stylistically indebted to Johnson. Like other stride pianists, Waller found additional work at rent parties, and also participated in cutting contests (competitive jam sessions in which participants vied for the audience's approval), winning admirers with his infallible keyboard touch and outgoing, ebullient personality. If he lacked Johnson's imaginative bass lines and breakneck speed, he was a more expressive interpreter of blues and ballads, exhibiting greater subtlety and a fluent rhythmic feeling that perfectly meshed with swing.

By the late 1920s, Waller had become a prominent figure in jazz and theater, thanks chiefly to the widely performed songs he wrote for theatrical revues. He was known as someone who could write the score for a show over a weekend and still have time to consume copious quantities of food and alcohol. Louis Armstrong established several of his songs as standards—including "Ain't Misbehavin'," "(What Did I Do to Be So) Black and Blue," and "Honeysuckle Rose." (After Ellington, Waller remains jazz's most successful pop songwriter.) Yet as he approached his thirtieth birthday, Waller was unknown to the general public.

Fats Goes Pop

In 1934, RCA-Victor signed up Fats Waller and His Rhythm, a six-piece band. The first tune he recorded, "A Porter's Love Song to a Chambermaid," written for him by James P. Johnson and Andy Razaf, introduced a new

Fats—a larger-than-life comic personality and irresistible vocalist who could kid a song and make it swing at the same time. The second song he recorded at that same session, "I Wish I Were Twins," became a best-seller. During the next five years, Waller was rarely absent from the pop charts.

Adapting the guise of a Harlem dandy—in a derby, vest, and tailored pin-stripes—Waller burlesqued the worst of Tin Pan Alley, creating satirical gems with painfully sentimental material like "The Curse of an Aching Heart." At the same time, he could be touchingly sincere with good material, like "I'm Gonna Sit Right Down and Write Myself a Letter." He possessed a mildly strident voice of surprising suppleness, using different registers for different effects: middle octave for straightforward singing, low notes for rude asides, high ones for feminine mockery. Humor enabled Waller to sweep up the musical debris of the day, inflecting it with his own spirit. Still, his immense success put him in a bind. RCA wanted nothing but hits, limiting his freedom to record more serious work, and jazz lovers failed to appreciate the artistry of his clowning. Significantly, at the time of his death (from pneumonia, at thirty-nine), Waller the recording artist had not recorded some of the finest songs by Waller the composer.

🎧 "Christopher Columbus"

"Christopher Columbus" represents Waller in a typically uproarious mood, very funny and very musical. The melody, by Chu Berry, who adapted the chords to "I Got Rhythm" for the bridge, generated several hits in 1936, though Waller's version (subtitled "A Rhythm Cocktail") was not among them. Fletcher Henderson, Benny Goodman, Andy Kirk, and Teddy Wilson all scored with it, but the tune didn't become a jazz hallmark until 1938, when Goodman interpolated it as the secondary theme in his version of "Sing, Sing, Sing." Andy Razaf, Waller's favorite lyricist, wrote the harebrained words, which Waller mocks, drawing on each of his vocal registers.

This performance shows Waller integrating stride piano into small-group swing, emphasizing rhythmic power—especially the cross-rhythms in his dashing solo chorus. His band remained fairly stable during the RCA years, with two prominent supporting roles taken by saxophonist and clarinetist Gene Sedric and trumpet player Herman Autrey. Accomplished musicians, Sedric and Autrey were nonetheless second-string players who reflect the dominating influences of the period: Sedric shows the inspiration of Hawkins and Chu Berry, while Autrey blends the sound and temperament of Armstrong and Roy Eldridge. The rhythm section has its hands full keeping up with Waller.

2.14

 # christopher columbus (a rhythm cocktail)

FATS WALLER AND HIS RHYTHM

Herman Autrey, trumpet; Gene Sedric, tenor saxophone; Fats Waller, piano and vocal; Albert Casey, guitar; Charles Turner, bass; Arnold Boling, drums

- Label: Victor 25295; *If You Got to Ask, You Ain't Got It! Fats Waller and His Rhythm* (Bluebird/Legacy 81124)
- Date: 1936
- Style: small-group swing
- Form: 32-bar popular song (**A A B A**)

> **What to listen for:**
> - Waller's stride piano, and cross-rhythms in chorus 4
> - his humorous changes in vocal timbre
> - background riffs played behind solos

INTRODUCTION

0:00   Waller plays the simple opening riff in **octaves**.

0:04   When the riff is repeated, it quickly subsides into a **stride** accompaniment.

CHORUS 1 (extended)

0:07 **A**   As the rest of the rhythm section enters in the first two sections of a 32-bar form, Waller begins to sing.
"*Mister Christopher Columbus sailed the sea without a compass.*
When his men began a rumpus,
[spoken gruffly] *Up spoke Christopher Columbus, yes!*"
He changes the timbre of his voice for comic effect.

0:22 **A**   "*There's land somewhere, until we get there,*
We will not go wrong if we sing, swing a song.
Since the world is round-o, we'll be safe and sound-o.
Till our goal is found-o, we'll just keep rhythm bound-o."
The band continues with another 16-bar **A A** section. Columbus is parodied in a high-pitched sing-song that gradually falls to Waller's normal speaking voice.

0:36 **B**   (sung) "*Since the crew was makin' merry—*
[spoken] *Mary got up and went home!*
There came a yell for Isabel, and they brought the rum and Isabel."
This section, which serves as the bridge to the broader 32-bar **A A B A** form, borrows its chord progression from "I Got Rhythm."

0:43 **A**   "*No more mutiny, no! What a time at sea!*
With diplomacy, Christory made history! Yes!"
A return to the **A** section.

CHORUS 2 (abbreviated)

0:50 **A**   (sung) "*Mister Christopher Columbus! Uh-huh!*
He used rhythm as a compass! Yes, yes! Music ended all the rumpus! Yes!
Wise old Christopher Columbus! [spoken] *Latch on, Christy! Yeah!*"
Waller reduces the melody line to a simple riff. Each line of text is answered by a short exclamation, as if Waller were in **call and response** with himself.

CHORUS 3

1:04 **A**   Sedric takes a tenor saxophone solo, spurred on by Waller's enthusiastic replies ("yes, yes!").

1:11 **A**

1:18 **B**   Waller signals the bridge by playing a two-note background line.

1:25 **A**

CHORUS 4

1:33 **A**   Waller plays the opening melody in exuberant stride style, emphasizing the offbeats.

1:40	**A**	
1:47	**B**	Over the bridge, he plays a complicated **cross-rhythmic** pattern.
1:52		He signals the end of the bridge with a descending octave pattern.
1:54	**A**	
2:00		At the end of the chorus, Waller interjects an excited "Yes!"

CHORUS 5

2:01	**A**	Autrey (trumpet) enters with an excited single-note pattern. Behind him, Sedric (tenor saxophone) plays a bluesy riff.
2:08	**A**	
2:15	**B**	During the bridge, the riff temporarily disappears (it will reappear during the last **A** section).
2:22	**A**	

CODA

2:30		(spoken) *"Well, look-a there! Christy's grabbed the Santa Maria, And he's going back! Yeah! Ahhhh, look-a there!"* The band moves suddenly to a quieter volume, with Waller playing the opening riff. In response, Autrey plays his own trumpet riff while Waller improvises some concluding remarks.
2:43		*"Uh-huh. . . . In the year 1492, Columbus sailed the ocean bluuuuue!* [quickly] *What'd I say?"* The band drops out entirely, leaving Waller the last word.

■ ART TATUM (1909–1956)

The peculiar nature of Art Tatum's genius is epitomized by the fact that twenty-first century listeners respond to his records much as 1930s listeners did—with gawking amazement. Whatever we may think of his music, there is no getting around its spectacular dexterity. The fact that Tatum was legally blind magnifies his legend. The son of amateur musicians, Tatum was born in Toledo, Ohio, with cataracts on both eyes. Minor gains made through operations were undone when he was mugged as a teenager and lost all sight in his left eye, retaining a sliver of light in the right.

Tatum began picking out melodies at three, attended the Cousino School for the Blind and the Toledo School of Music (where he studied violin and guitar as well as piano), led his own bands at seventeen, and signed a two-year radio contract before he was twenty. His reputation spread quickly. While passing though Ohio, Duke Ellington sought him out and encouraged him to head for New York where the competition would raise his sights and sharpen his wits. After singer Adelaide Hall hired Tatum in 1932, the New York stride pianists instantly acknowledged his superiority, a capitulation made easier by his friendly, unassuming demeanor. A couple of years later, George Gershwin threw a party at his home to introduce him to the classical elite.

Virtuosity

The word "virtuoso" is used to identify an artist of masterly technique and skill. Most accomplished artists in any field have achieved a measure of virtuosity; still, when it comes to Tatum, there is a temptation to call him a virtuoso and then retire the word. No other jazz player is so closely associated

Banjoist Elmer Snowden, the original leader of what became the Duke Ellington band, stands beside two incomparable pianists in a Greenwich Village nightclub, 1942: Art Tatum (right), who claimed Fats Waller as his primary influence, and Waller (center), who introduced Tatum to a nightclub audience by saying, "I play piano, but God is in the house tonight!"

with dazzling, superhuman nimbleness. That's because his style is fundamentally inseparable from his technique.

Tatum was championed by some of the great classical pianists of his time, including Sergei Rachmaninoff and Vladimir Horowitz. Jazz pianists universally regarded him as peerless. Waller, whom Tatum often named as his inspiration (you can hear the influence in Tatum's use of stride), once interrupted a number when Tatum entered a club where he was performing, and announced, "Ladies and gentlemen, I play piano, but God is in the house tonight!" Pianist Hank Jones has said that when he first heard Tatum's records, he felt certain they were "tricks" achieved through overdubbing.

Tatum was indefatigable. He worked in top nightclubs and then dropped by dives and after-hours joints, where he would play till dawn. If a particular piano was out of tune or worse, Tatum would play a two-handed run to test the keyboard and then avoid the bad or missing keys for the rest of the night. But though he was a frequent guest on radio broadcasts, he was never embraced by the mainstream. He appeared in few concert halls and recorded mostly for independent labels. Did his very brilliance put people off? Virtuosity is often regarded as a pitfall; an artist is expected to use it as the means to an end, not as the end itself. Tatum used his skill to create a thoroughly original approach to piano music, one that offers pleasure as much from his flashing runs and change-ups as his underlying harmonic and rhythmic ingenuity: means *and* ends.

Alone Together

Tatum was primarily a solo pianist. His style, complete in itself, depended on his freedom to change harmonies and rhythms at will. As an accompanist, he created backgrounds that were sometimes overly busy, threatening to obscure the soloist. There were exceptions (his album with Ben Webster, recorded shortly before Tatum succumbed to kidney failure, is a classic of mutual empathy), and, unexpectedly, he found his greatest popular success leading a trio with guitar (Lloyd "Tiny" Grimes) and bass (Slam Stewart). Audiences enjoyed watching the three instrumentalists challenge each other with oddball quotations from songs.

Alone, however, Tatum, was a fount of surprises. He developed set routines on many of his favorite songs, but no matter how often he played them, he was able to astound the listener with harmonic substitutions of unbelievable complexity. His ability to interject and superimpose additional harmonies influenced established musicians, like Coleman Hawkins, and helped inspire the bebop movement.

🎧 "Over the Rainbow"

Tatum's 1939 "Over the Rainbow"—the first of his five surviving versions, recorded over a sixteen-year span—was made when the song was new to the public. It was written by Harold Arlen and E. Y. Harburg for *The Wizard of*

Oz, a movie that debuted only days before Tatum made this recording. The fact that he brings so much feeling and control to a song new to his repertory is impressive; that he understands the mechanics of the song well enough to rewire its harmonies and deconstruct its melody is astounding.

This was one of many performances made by Tatum and other musicians for a company called Standard Transcriptions, which produced recordings exclusively for radio stations. Transcriptions, as the discs were called, could not be sold in stores. Broadcasters preferred creating their own music libraries to paying licensing fees to air commercial recordings. Eventually, the networks cut a deal with the labels, and transcription discs disappeared.

In some ways, however, transcriptions were superior to records: fidelity was enhanced because the discs were larger (sixteen inches instead of the usual ten), and the artists had more latitude in terms of length. This performance is a minute longer than a record would have allowed. Even so, Tatum has to hurry to squeeze in his ending.

LISTENING GUIDE

🎧 over the rainbow

2.15

ART TATUM, PIANO
- Label: Black Lion (E)BLP30194; *Art Tatum: The Standard Sessions, 1935–1943 Broadcast Transcriptions* (CD-919(2))
- Date: 1939
- Style: stride piano
- Form: 32-bar popular song (**A A B A**)

What to listen for:
- melodic paraphrase: clear statements or reminders of the melody throughout, with complicated harmonic substitutions
- dazzling virtuosic runs

INTRODUCTION

| 0:00 | | Tatum begins with an intensely dissonant **dominant chord**, rolled up from the bottom. It's answered by a pair of **octaves** in the right hand. |

CHORUS 1

0:07	**A**	Tatum plays the melody harmonized by chords, without the stride accompaniment. He plays **rubato**, adjusting the tempo for expressive purposes (sometimes accelerating slightly, at other times slowing down dramatically).
0:12		The first of many descending runs into the bass register.
0:14		Throughout the performance, Tatum plays the melody with faithful accuracy, but alters the chord progression with **harmonic substitutions**.
0:19		He decorates the end of the first **A** section with new chords and a dramatic upward-sweeping run.
0:23	**A**	For the second **A** section, he repeats the melody, in more or less the same sequence he had used earlier.
0:36	**B**	Tatum plays the bridge simply, accompanied only by sparse chords in the left hand.
0:40		Where the original tune is harmonically static, he adds a new series of chords.
0:52		He marks the end of the bridge with several runs.
0:57	**A**	Return of the original melody, now beginning in the bass register.
1:01		Another intensely dissonant chord.
1:08		He begins to move into a steady tempo.

CHORUS 2

1:17	**A**	In a moderate, relaxed tempo, Tatum uses a **stride** accompaniment in his left hand.
1:31		At the cadence, he throws in melodic lines that suggest a bluesy feeling.
1:36	**A**	
1:38		He moves from the original melody into a complicated, dissonant 16th-note line, featuring harmonic substitutions.
1:44		The intensity of this passage is "erased" by a descending fast run.
1:55	**B**	Once again, Tatum plays the melody to the bridge accompanied by simple left-hand chords.
2:01		As the phrase ends, the harmonies suddenly move into unexpected chromatic territory.
2:13		As Tatum nears the end of the bridge, his melodic line becomes increasingly fast and dissonant; it resolves directly on the downbeat of the new **A** section.
2:15	**A**	
2:20		As he settles into his groove, the harmonies take on more of a bluesy tinge.

CHORUS 3

2:36	**A**	
2:51		Over the last two measures of the **A** section, Tatum's improvisation drifts out of the main key and accelerates as it heads for a resolution on the downbeat of the next section.
2:56	**A**	
3:02		Over a few simple chords, he plays a blindingly fast passage.
3:11		Another bluesy cadence figure.
3:16	**B**	The bridge, which had been a point of relaxation, suddenly becomes more intense: over steady eighth-note chords in the left hand, the harmonization departs radically from the original.
3:26		Finally, Tatum resolves to the tonic harmony.
3:31		Suddenly, as if under extreme time pressure, he speeds up the performance and races through the rest of the tune in record time.
3:33	**A**	

GUITAR

In the 1930s, as we have seen, the guitar replaced the banjo in jazz bands (except those that played in the traditional New Orleans vein), chiefly emphasizing rhythm and harmony. Rhythm guitarists strummed a steady four-to-the-bar *chunk-chunk-chunk-chunk*, reinforcing the roles of the drummer and bassist. The guitar had lost the prominence it had earned as a solo instrument in the 1920s, when Eddie Lang and Lonnie Johnson appeared on records with Beiderbecke, Joe Venuti, Armstrong, and Ellington. Lang (who was white) and Johnson (who was black) had even recorded together, with Lang using a pseudonym (Blind Willie Dunn) to disguise the integrated nature of the session. Lang also recorded duets with Carl Kress, a pioneer of rhythm guitar. The short-term fate of the guitar may be measured by the fate of those three men: Lang died in 1933 (at thirty, of a botched tonsillectomy, like Benny Moten); Kress left jazz for mainstream studio work and to run a nightclub; and Johnson left jazz to reinvent himself as a blues (and, briefly, rhythm and blues) star.

Even rhythm guitar lost ground. While Freddie Green (who never recorded a single solo in a career of half a century) became a mainstay of the Count Basie band, adding immeasurably to the unique sound and style of the Basie rhythm section, other guitarists found their services no longer in demand. Many bandleaders, including Ellington, saw the instrument as an unnecessary accoutrement.

Plugging In

The problem with the acoustic guitar was volume. Whether the band was large or small, the guitar lacked the dynamic presence of other instruments. Various attempts were made to amplify it, using resonators, external microphones, and pick-ups (magnets coiled with wire that transmit an electrical impulse from the strings to an amplifier). Meanwhile, recordings by Django Reinhardt showed that the guitar was a jazz instrument of barely explored potential.

In the early 1930s, the Gibson Company began building prototypes for an electric guitar, achieving a breakthrough in 1936. The new instrument was taken up a few musicians, notably Floyd Smith of Andy Kirk's band, Eddie Durham of Count Basie's Kansas City Six, and Western swing musicians like Bob Dunn and Leon McAuliffe, who combined the traditions of Hawaiian steel guitar and jazz with the new technology to create a signature sound in country music: electric steel guitar. In the late 1940s, Gibson introduced the solid body electric guitar, and within a decade it was the representative instrument of rock and roll, urban blues, and country music.

Those early technological advances meant little, however, until one remarkable musician demonstrated the artistry possible on electric guitar. Charlie Christian showed that it was more than a loud acoustic guitar: it was a separate instrument with a flexible timbre and personality of its own.

Charlie Christian, seen here in 1940, was the first prominent electric guitarist. He was initially met with skepticism, until he used amplification to liberate the guitar from the rhythm section and establish it as a powerful solo instrument.

FRANK DRIGGS COLLECTION

■ CHARLIE CHRISTIAN (1916–1942)

In a career of tragic brevity (only twenty-three months in the public spotlight), Christian transformed the guitar and provided a powerful momentum to the younger musicians who would soon introduce bebop. In his hands, the guitar acquired the same rhythmic suppleness and dynamic confidence associated with the saxophone and trumpet. His warm, radiant sound had a suitably electrifying effect.

Charlie Christian was born in Texas and grew up in a poor section of Oklahoma City, where, according to his neighbor, novelist Ralph Ellison, he was a wonder in grade school, playing guitars made from cigar boxes and taking up trumpet, piano, and bass. His father and brothers were musicians as well, and Charlie began touring with Southwestern bands in his teens, soaking up the swing and blues echoing from Kansas City and Western swing bands. In 1938, Christian hooked up an electric pick-up to his acoustic guitar, and word of his prodigious gifts spread. Mary Lou Williams raved about him to John Hammond, who in 1939 arranged for him to audition for Benny Goodman. At first reluctant to hire a guitarist, Goodman changed his mind when he heard Christian's limber phrases soaring over the rhythm section.

Goodman signed Christian to his sextet, which made weekly radio broadcasts, and featured him on records with the big band. Extremely laconic, Christian usually let his music speak for him, yet three months after he signed with Goodman, he lent his name to a Chicago newspaper article (presumably ghostwritten) whose headline read "Guitarmen, Wake Up and Pluck! Wire for Sound; Let 'Em Hear You Play." The article argued that a guitarist is "more than just a robot plunking on a gadget to keep the rhythm going," and that "electrical amplification has given guitarists a new lease on life."

Christian made his case on record after record. Seemingly overnight, a flood of guitarists plugged in, determined to capture the spare clarity of Christian's solos—every phrase enunciated, logical and decisive. Recording with some of the finest musicians of the era, Christian always stood out with his ricocheting riffs, inspired melodies, and bluesy feeling. One of his most successful acolytes, Barney Kessel, later compared his importance to that of Thomas Edison. That may seem like an exaggeration, yet by the time Christian succumbed to tuberculosis at twenty-five, few would have argued the point. He had given the guitar a permanent new lease on life.

⊚ "Swing to Bop" ("Topsy")

This performance, one of Christian's best, exists by accident. In 1941, an engineer named Jerry Newman took his wire recorder (a predecessor to tape recorders) to Harlem after-hours clubs to document jam sessions. The sessions at Minton's Playhouse (discussed in Chapter 11) proved especially illuminating, because the rhythm section there included two men who later figured as key bebop innovators, drummer Kenny Clarke and pianist Thelonious Monk. Among the soloists who dropped by to jam were adventurous swing stars like Christian, Roy Eldridge, saxophonist Don Byas, and fledgling modernist Dizzy Gillespie.

When, years later, Newman's wire recordings were released commercially, they were greeted as a revelation, capturing the first steps in what proved to be the transformation from swing to bebop. Newman in fact released this track as "Swing to Bop," a title that couldn't have existed in 1941, because the word "bop" had not yet been coined. The tune is actually "Topsy," a swing hit by Eddie Durham and Edgar Battle, though the melody isn't played: Newman began recording this number as Christian was completing his first chorus. (This excerpt consists only of his six-chorus solo.) "Topsy" is the only swing tune that returned to the charts two decades later. When jazz drummer Cozy Cole recorded it in 1958, at the height of Elvismania, it unaccountably became the No. 1 rhythm and blues and No. 3 pop hit in the country.

Christian is inspired by the song's harmonies. Notice how consistently he varies his riffs and rhythmic accents, building on motives and playing with a relaxed lucidity—notice, too, how the harmonies of the bridge *always* liberate his melodic imagination.

LISTENING GUIDE

 ## swing to bop (topsy)

CHARLIE CHRISTIAN

Charlie Christian, electric guitar; Kenny Clarke, drums; unknown piano, bass

- Label: *Live Sessions at Minton's* (Everest FS-219); *Live Sessions at Minton's Playhouse: New York, May 1941* (Jazz Anthology 550012)
- Date: 1941
- Style: small-group swing
- Form: 32-bar popular song (**A A' B A**)

<table>
<tr><td colspan="2">What to listen for:</td></tr>
</table>

What to listen for:

- wide open jam session
- Christian's innovative polyrhythmic phrases
- bluesy riffs in the **A** sections, long harmonic lines in the bridge
- Clarke interacting with Christian

CHORUS 1

0:00	**A**	The recording fades in during the middle of Christian's six-chorus solo on electric guitar. He's just completing the first **A** section of the tune.
0:03	**A'**	For the **A'** section, the harmony changes to IV for four bars. In the background, the pianist loudly plays a **stride** accompaniment.
0:12	**B**	As the piano retreats to **comping**, the **walking bass** gradually takes over as the rhythmic foundation.
0:21	**A**	Christian's tone hardens. He begins playing a simple three-note figure, shifting it in different rhythmic positions in the measure.

CHORUS 2

0:29	**A**	The three-note motive now becomes the beginning of a longer, more involved phrase.
0:32		Christian throws in a **triplet**.
0:38	**A'**	
0:47	**B**	As he enters the more complex chord changes of the bridge, Christian uses harmonic improvisation in long, flowing lines. Clarke occasionally interrupts with bass drum accents.
0:56	**A**	The harmony returns to the tonic, and Christian turns the three-note motive into short repeated riffs.
1:02		Christian's riffs speed up; Clarke adds **counterrhythms**.

CHORUS 3

1:05	**A**	The next chorus begins with a new riff, loosely based on the three-note motive.
1:13	**A'**	
1:19		A final bluesy phrase rounds out the **A'** section. It's followed by silence.
1:22	**B**	Christian begins the bridge on a high note. The drums strongly accent the backbeat.
1:31	**A**	Christian's line becomes detached, falling firmly on the offbeat.

CHORUS 4

1:40	**A**	Christian repeats a simple riff.
1:46		When he extends it with a syncopated beginning, Clarke coincides with accents on the snare drum.
1:48	**A'**	The line suddenly rises to match the harmony.
1:57	**B**	A sudden return to straight eighth-note patterns, arpeggiating the underlying chords.
2:06	**A**	
2:11		The line ends with a single note, decorated with **tremolos** and repeated in a cross-rhythmic pattern.

CHORUS 5

2:15	**A**	The fifth chorus begins with a riff that uses the tremolo pattern to create a new polyrhythm (three beats against four).
2:17		In the distant background, another instrument can be heard tuning up.
2:23	**A'**	The line concentrates on a single note, played rhythmically on the beat and building intensity through repetition.
2:30		The first two **A** sections finish with a sharp, direct, and bluesy phrase.
2:32	**B**	Christian begins two beats early with a driving, descending **chromatic** pattern.
2:35		The pattern gets "turned around"—shifting slightly to an eighth note earlier, creating cross-rhythmic intensity.
2:41	**A**	The line again falls strongly on the offbeat.
2:49		Christian and Clarke coincide on strong offbeat accents.

CHORUS 6

2:50	**A**	Christian plays a new riff, starting with the flat fifth degree.
2:58	**A'**	He plays a pattern with strong rhythmic contrast, prompting Clarke to match it with drum accents.
3:04		Christian plays a phrase that accents the weakest notes in the measure (one-*and*-two-and, three-and-four-*and*).
3:07	**B**	Once again, he launches himself into the tune's chord pattern.
3:16	**A**	After the climactic final phrase, Christian retreats, allowing another instrument (trumpet) to continue the jam session.

BASS

Of all the instruments in the jazz ensemble, the bass was the slowest in reaching maturity. One reason is that since the bass traditionally served to bind the rhythm section, firming the tempo and outlining the harmonic progression, bassists had little incentive to expand their technical abilities. But as with rhythm guitar, the function was of more significance to the musicians who relied on its steady support than to listeners, who hardly noticed the bass unless it was featured in a solo. Until the late 1930s, the average bass solo was a predictable four-to-the-bar walk. Technique was so lacking that bad intonation was commonplace even in some top bands.

Some Prominent Bassists

Walter Page

There were a few exceptions. Walter Page codified the walking bass. Born in Missouri, he developed his style in the middle 1920s, while leading the Blue Devils in Oklahoma. An important figure in Kansas City, he worked for Benny Moten's orchestra before joining with Count Basie, who built his rhythm section on the metronomic reliability of Page's walking bass: pizzicato (or plucked) notes in stable, stepwise patterns (close together), usually four evenly stated pitches per measure. This style, ideal for Basie, was a dead end for others. Few bassists in the 1930s expanded on its potential.

Milt Hinton

Most prominent among those who did was Milt Hinton, a much-loved musician whose robust swing and excellent intonation reflected his genial personality. Hinton possessed an instinctive harmonic erudition that enabled him to make the leap from swing to bop. He expanded the bass walk by using more advanced harmonies and syncopating his rhythmic support with inventive, melodic figures. Initially known for his long stay with Cab Calloway and a shorter one with Louis Armstrong, he became the most in-demand, frequently recorded bassist of his generation, appearing on hundreds of jazz, pop, and rock and roll sessions, shifting effortlessly from Bing Crosby and Billie Holiday to Aretha Franklin and Bobby Darin—just to mention a few singers. At jam sessions with Dizzy Gillespie and other young modernists, he showed he could master the latest chord changes. As a soloist, he remained committed to swing. Hinton also won respect as an important jazz photographer.

Israel Crosby

Another remarkable bassist was the prodigy Israel Crosby, who became famous in the 1950s and 1960s for his virtuoso turns with the Ahmad Jamal Trio. He began recording at sixteen, with pianists Jess Stacey, Albert Ammons, and Teddy Wilson (Crosby created a powerful **ostinato**—a repeated melodic phrase, with the same pitches—for Wilson's "Blues in C Sharp Minor") and drummer Gene Krupa. He also spent three years with Fletcher Henderson's orchestra (1936–39). In each situation, he was encouraged to play solos that demonstrated a melodic and rhythmic confidence rare in those years.

John Kirby/Slam Stewart

By contrast, the best-known bassist of the Swing Era, John Kirby, was famous not because of his playing, which was conventional and flawed, but because he led the most popular small band of its day (1937–42), an unusually minimalist sextet that prefigured the cool style of the 1950s. The band featured Kirby's wife, the gifted vocalist Maxine Sullivan, and performed jazz adaptations of classical themes. Slam Stewart also won fame in this period, as part of the duo Slim and Slam, with singer-guitarist-humorist Slim Gaillard, and later as a member of the Art Tatum Trio. A gifted musician with rock-steady time and perfect pitch, Stewart was known for his ability to simultaneously scat-sing and improvise bass lines, which he often played with the bow.

Oddly enough, the man who did the most to advance the cause of the bass didn't play it. Duke Ellington was partial to the lower end of the musical spectrum; he often assigned the lead saxophone part to the baritone rather than the alto. In the 1920s, he wrote arrangements that required the elaborate participation of his Louisiana-born bassist Wellman Braud, whose large sound and solid beat had been heard in New Orleans as early as 1910. With Ellington, Braud helped to develop the walking bass and popularized the **arco** (or bowed) technique, heard in tandem with the wind instruments.

Count Basie's All American Rhythm Section brought a sizzling excitement to the Swing Era. Guitarist Freddie Green, drummer Jo Jones, bassist Walter Page, and Basie recording for Decca in New York, 1938.

FRANK DRIGGS COLLECTION

FRANK DRIGGS COLLECTION

Jimmy Blanton (c. 1940), a discovery of Duke Ellington, who wrote the first bass concertos for him, revolutionized the instrument and its role in the rhythm section, replacing the walking 4/4 approach with melodic, harmonic, rhythmic, and tonal nuances.

As Ellington's music grew beyond the skills of Braud, he added a second bassist (Billy Taylor) to play with him.

Ellington's greatest contribution to jazz bass, however, came with his discovery of Jimmy Blanton, the man who revolutionized the instrument. Blanton became such a central figure in the edition of the Ellington band that also introduced Ben Webster (in the early 1940s) that the band was later referred to by fans as "the Blanton-Webster band."

■ JIMMY BLANTON (1918–1942)

Blanton's brief life and career parallels that of Charlie Christian (they even succumbed to the same illness), and his transformation of jazz bass was every bit as complete as Christian's remaking of the guitar. In little more than two years—the same period in which Christian emerged (1939–41)—Blanton changed the way the bass was played and, by extension, the nature of the rhythm section. He expanded the walking bass into a fully involved musicianship that, while continuing to provide the harmonies and keep the tempo, added melodic, harmonic, and rhythmic nuances.

Jimmy Blanton started out on violin and switched to bass while attending Tennessee State College. He began working professionally on summer riverboat excursions (led by Fate Marable, who helped launch Louis Armstrong), and soon dropped out of college to work with a band in St. Louis. In 1939, Ellington heard him and invited him to join the band, then began writing pieces that made the most of Blanton's unparalleled authority. The bassist's attributes included a Tatumesque grounding in harmony that allowed him to add substitute chords, a distinctly attractive and supple timbre, and an authoritative rhythmic pulse.

Blanton recorded the first bass solos that departed from the walking-bass style in favor of a freely melodic conception. In his hands, the bass, no longer a cumbersome instrument, could maneuver with speed and flexibility. Blanton's work buoyed Ellington's music with a metrical panache in such works as "Jack the Bear," "Ko-Ko," and "Concerto for Cootie." Ellington also recorded piano-bass duets with him, though by then Blanton was already suffering from the effects of tuberculosis, which took his life at twenty-three.

DRUMS

Unlike the bass, the drums quickly reached a high plateau of accomplishment in the Swing Era. Because drums played a loud, dominant, visibly important role in the jazz band, they focused the attention of the audience. As a result, they became a selling point and drummers became showmen: they tossed their sticks in the air and surrounded themselves with exotic accoutrements, designing and even illuminating the heads of their bass drums. They often soloed with more physical exertion than was strictly necessary.

At the same time, a genuine musical virtuosity emerged, as drummers competed to create distinct and imaginative ways to keep time, shape arrangements, and inspire soloists. The nature of drumming would change radically after the Swing Era, promoting a different kind of virtuosity, but it already reached a kind of perfection in the 1930s, equal to that of the best pianists and wind players.

JAZZ GRAPHICS
Art and Commerce

The most significant visual documentation of jazz is achieved through photography, as exemplified in the images used throughout this book, and film. Photographs and movies allow us to see the great figures of jazz history in their prime and in settings particular to their eras. Yet jazz is also documented in the related but significantly different field of graphic design. All art is subject to marketing ploys. Just as book designers want you to judge a book by its cover, those who devise album jackets, concert posters, movie ads, and magazines hope to catch your attention with pictorial design.

Good graphic design provides us not only with the pleasure of aesthetically striking and informative images, but also historical insight into the way corporations sought to entice customers. In this section, we focus on the marketing of written and recorded jazz during the past century, beginning with sheet music, which was the most important outlet for new songs well into the 1920s. Unlike the plain covers on classical music scores, the sheet music for popular songs often had flamboyant and even witty covers that illustrated the themes or lyrics of the songs. We then look at the four types of recordings that dominated the market until the advent of the MP3 and other digital systems: 78-rpm records, LPs, 45s, and CDs.

"It's Nobody's Business but My Own," a satire of womanizing black preachers, was written by a white team (Skidmore and Walker) for the legendary comedian Bert Williams, a black man who had to perform in blackface makeup. He introduced it in the Ziegfeld Follies and recorded it in 1919. The stereotype drawings underscore the fact that it's a Negro dialect song.

"Big Indian Chief," a "two-step" ragtime number by the black songwriting team of Bob Cole and J. Rosamund Johnson, advertises its origin in a college production and implies (note the staff running across the top of the page) that it has a lyric; in fact, the sheet music is a piano instrumental of a song that was interpolated into an all-white 1904 musical, *An English Daisy*, after it was imported from London to Broadway.

All materials are from the Gary Giddins Collection.

Alberta Hunter and Lovie Austin were well-known performers and songwriters in 1923, when they wrote "Chirpin' the Blues" (not a chirpy number: "It takes a worried woman to chirp this weary song"). Hunter recorded it that year, and Bessie Smith never recorded it at all; yet, as the more promising and charismatic star, she is glowingly featured on the sheet music cover.

"Louis Armstrong's 125 Jazz Breaks for Cornet" is one of two portfolios that Armstrong created exclusively for the Chicago-based Melrose Publishing Company. He recorded the breaks and solos, which Melrose transcribed as sheet music—before destroying the discs! This volume came out in 1927, when relatively few people beyond jazz musicians and a small coterie of fans had heard of Louis Armstrong.

Eddie Green, a white song and dance man, wrote "A Good Man Is Hard to Find" in 1918, for the pioneering black music publishing company operated by W. C. Handy and Harry Pace. Its title became a catchphrase in American culture, and the song a jazz standard in the "red hot mama" mode, as popularized by Sophie Tucker and Bessie Smith. The sheet music, however, emphasizes the debonair vaudevillian Jack Norworth and depicts a high-born lady sharing the "Matrimonial News" with a parrot, as ships arrive on the horizon.

AIN'T MISBEHAVIN'

Lyric by
ANDY RAZAF
Music by
THOMAS WALLER
HARRY BROOKS

Harry James

Columbia Record 36887

MILLS MUSIC
1819 BROADWAY   NEW YORK 19, N.Y.

During the Swing Era, nothing sold sheet music better than endorsements from the most popular bandleaders, so when Mills Music reissued a piano arrangement of Fats Waller's 1929 classic "Ain't Misbehavin'" in 1945, it used a photo of Harry James, promoting his recent recording (lower left-hand corner), even though his version was only a minor commercial hit.

George Russell's *Lydian Chromatic Concept of Tonal Organization* is his argument on behalf of modes or scales as a way of systematizing harmony. Although his theory led directly to Miles Davis's *Kind of Blue*, his text of some 100 pages, as published in 1959, complete with graphs and paper slide rule, was too arcane for all but dedicated musicologists. The design, reminiscent of the Dutch painter Piet Mondrian, indicates modernism.

'ROUND MIDNIGHT

In Eb, (bb to ab)

WORDS BY
BERNIE HANIGHEN

MUSIC BY
COOTIE WILLIAMS
and THELONIUS MONK

PRICE 75 CENTS
IN U.S.A.

mph   ADVANCED MUSIC CORPORATION
NEW YORK
Printed in U.S.A.

the
LYDIAN CHROMATIC CONCEPT
of
TONAL
ORGANIZATION

BY
GEORGE RUSSELL

F#

CONCEPT PUBLISHING CO.
NEW YORK, N.Y.

The plain white sheet music cover for Thelonious Monk's " 'Round Midnight" indicates a musical seriousness and economical decision, as the song initially had marginal status as a pop hit. Note that the composer is listed third, after the lyricist and the bandleader who introduced the 1944 song, which Monk himself did not record until 1947.

Three projects involving Louis Armstrong show how graphic design figures in the promotion of jazz publications and concerts. *Swing That Music* (1939), the first (heavily ghostwritten) book issued under his name, forgoes a photograph in favor of reverberant musical notes and the names of many musicians, who are represented in the book merely by transcriptions of the way they might play the title song. The introduction by nasal pop singer Rudy Vallee, by no means a jazz performer, perceptively argues that Armstrong is the preeminent influence on contemporary vocalists. A 1947 issue of *Jazz Record*, aimed at collectors, uses a 1920s photo of Armstrong to underscore its concern with jazz's early years. The 1953 "Jazz Concert Programme" was sold during the historic tour undertaken by Armstrong and Benny Goodman, until illness forced Goodman to quit. Such programs invariably included publicity photographs of the participating musicians, with short biographies. Fans could purchase them and, between sets, ask musicians to sign their respective pages. Even at the height of its popularity, jazz stars were generally accessible to the fans.

Most early 78-rpm recordings were ten inches in diameter and were sold in plain wrapping paper sleeves with holes to reveal the labels. The short-lived Emerson Phonograph Company offered an arty sleeve design with jester and dancer (reflecting a late nineteenth-century graphic style) and a label logo involving the Statue of Liberty. "7 Inch Double Disc" refers to the diameter (the same as postwar 45s) and the fact that there is a different tune on each side—many 78s were recorded on one side only. "Honey Boy" is a 1916 raggy dance version of a minstrel song, played by a marching band.

Paramount Records was a leader in "Race Records," which targeted the African American market. The company is remembered for its extraordinary catalog advertisements, which were generally free of minstrel stereotypes and focused on the story content of the lyrics. The handout for "Keep a Knocking and You Can't Get In," a 1928 disc by the obscure vocalist and kazoo player James "Boodle It" Wiggins, boasts of the label's "electric method" of recording.

Ma Rainey had only been recording for three months when, in early 1924, Paramount put her picture on the 78 label and gave her the uncommon possessive credit: " 'Ma' Rainey's Dream Blues." This was testament to her great popularity as a performer, which the company hoped would extend to her records.

Paramount's ad for a 1922 recording by Alberta Hunter bills her as "The Idol of Dreamland" (a Chicago club) and "the most popular colored artist that ever appeared on the theatrical stage." Hunter, despite her work as a composer and performer of blues, had a versatile, mostly pop-oriented repertory, but in the 1920s every black woman singer was pigeonholed as a blues singer. After working as a nurse for two decades, Hunter enjoyed her greatest success in an astonishing New York comeback, in 1977, at the age of eighty-two. She continued to perform until her death in 1984.

Few record companies survived the Depression—even the formerly prosperous Columbia Records went into receivership. That began to change in the late 1930s, as the popularity of performers like Bing Crosby, Louis Armstrong, and the swing bands generated record sales. By 1940, there were three major American labels: Victor had been sustained by the RCA radio network; Decca began operating in 1934, with British financing; and Columbia was bought and relaunched by the CBS network. Audiences now clamored for older records that had long ago disappeared from shops. The labels responded with a new concept: *albums*—usually four discs in plain sleeves bound with a pictorial cover.

The Duke was the fifth in a series of albums collecting Ellington's Columbia recordings from the 1920s and 1930s. Note that the photograph emphasizes Ellington's supreme elegance and his association with the piano, as indicated by a thin black line—and that the name *Ellington* appears nowhere. Victor tested the market for Fats Waller by offering a compilation of "Favorites," commissioning a buoyant and colorful painting to attract customers. Boyd Raeburn, a bandleader, saxophonist, and arranger, played music that combined the headiest elements of bebop and classical music (especially Stravinsky)— something a record buyer might guess from the fantastic drawing on his 1946 *Innovations*, released by the small Jewel label: faces and instruments melt together along with an angel, a goatee, and dark glasses. Like crazy, man.

The entertainment industry was completely revolutionized in the postwar years with the introduction of magnetic tape and television. In the recording business, the big innovation was microgroove, which Columbia and RCA-Victor innovated simultaneously, but along different lines. In the end, the industry accepted RCA's seven-inch, donut-hole 45-rpm disc as a vehicle for single tracks, replacing the 78, and for Extended Play (EP) 45s (two songs per side). Columbia's twelve-inch Long Playing (LP) disc would serve as an extension of the album format, which was particularly suitable for classical music and jazz.

Inevitably, the 45 became the dedicated format for pop songs, but jazz labels often issued 45s of selected tracks from albums, in the hope of securing radio play that would generate interest in those albums. They also issued entire albums as 45 boxed sets. In Europe, the 45 remained a popular jazz format well into the 1960s. The 1958 release of "Topsy - Part 1" and "Topsy - Part 2," by the veteran swing drummer Cozy Cole, sold more than a million copies; Cole recorded another version in 1964, for Coral, that didn't do nearly as well, but served the purpose of keeping his name alive. "The Genius of Art Tatum" is an EP, No. 23 in a series of 27, containing the 69 piano solos Tatum recorded in December 1953; they were later released as ten LPs or four CDs—today, Tatum's complete works would fit on an iPod along with a few thousand other tracks. Note the painting by David Stone Martin, one of the most prolific and ubiquitous jazz artists of the 1950s. "John Coltrane" is another EP, containing two longish tracks, made specifically for the European market.

LPs also came in two formats. The ten-inch disc was briefly popular in the 1950s. It was less expensive than the twelve-inch and contained less music—typically, four tracks per side instead of six. "Bobby Hackett Trumpet Solos," released in 1950, gives equal emphasis to the musician, the songs and their composers, and the fact (posted on the upper right and lower left of the cover) that Long Play Microgroove Records were "unbreakable," an advantage over the brittle 78. From the first, the LP was used to package classic recordings. Billie Holiday's *Lady Day*, a compilation of her 1930s sides, introduced her early work to a new generation, and reminded older fans of how she had once sounded. The design is highly dramatic, with its oddly shadowed photograph blocked by large white letters and only the dancing red and blue letters for contrast.

The twelve-inch LP dominated the adult-listening market for nearly thirty-five years, ultimately giving way to CDs in the middle 1980s. Record collectors cherished them in a way that surpassed their feelings for 78s and was never equaled by the CD. One reason, some have speculated, is that cardboard is more "human" than plastic. Another reason is that tremendous care was expended on the cover graphics and liner notes, making the LP a more complete experience. The twelve-inch cover was more challenging and rewarding to visual artists than the five-inch CD booklet. Most important, the 35-to-50-minute playing time held the listener's attention, while the 75 minutes of music often crammed onto a CD exhausted the listener's patience, especially as the individual tracks also grew in length.

All the major labels offered extensive reissue programs to exploit their catalogs and provide an inexpensive means of producing product to keep national distributors interested in the labels' output. *Don Redman: Master of the Big Band* comes from one of the best of the 1960s reissue series, RCA-Vintage, which creatively assembled tracks of classic and relatively obscure jazz, pop, blues, and folk. Customers who came to trust the consistent good taste of a series like Vintage might purchase LPs by people they had never heard of, inevitably expanding their own knowledge of prewar American music.

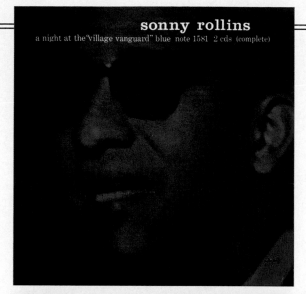

sonny rollins
a night at the "village vanguard" blue note 1581 2 cds (complete)

BLUE TRAIN **john coltrane** blue note 53428

Chico Hamilton's *Drumfusion*, a 1962 Columbia album, takes an aggressive approach by labeling the music "Dynamic" and serving up a dynamic cover, with its largely silhouetted Hamilton, uppercase lettering, and black trim. Also boldly noted is the stereo option, at a time when you could pay slightly less for a monaural version. The cover includes the names of the selections rather than the musicians, though this album helped to launch the career of tenor saxophonist Charles Lloyd. Blue Note usually took the opposite approach, promoting the names of the sidemen, but for two singularly important 1957 releases, John Coltrane's *Blue Train* and Sonny Rollins's *A Night at the Village Vanguard*, it focused on the leaders in close-up studies. No catalog of album covers is more celebrated than that of Blue Note, designed by Reid Miles and featuring the black and white photography (here color tinted) of the label's co-owner, Francis Wolff. These two covers are CD reissues—Blue Note music without Blue Note graphics is unthinkable.

One of the most unusual and arresting of album covers, for *Undercurrent,* by Bill Evans and Jim Hall (United Artists, 1962), has no design and no information—just a dreamlike black and white photograph by Toni Frissell of a woman who seems to be floating underwater. If you turn it upside down, you can see that it really shows a woman in a nightgown diving into a lake.

By the 1960s, jazz covers had become an art in their own right. Classical music albums usually settled for reproductions of famous paintings or posed portraits of the artists, and pop albums tended toward straightforward or romantic depictions of the performers. One especially influential cover was Dave Brubeck's *Time Out*. In 1959, a Columbia Records producer thought Brubeck's album so unmarketable that he refused to release it until the pianist mounted a protest. Why? All the selections were originals based on odd time signatures, and Neil Fujita's painting (which Brubeck insisted on) was thought too perplexing for the average consumer. *Time Out* remains one of the best-selling jazz albums of all time.

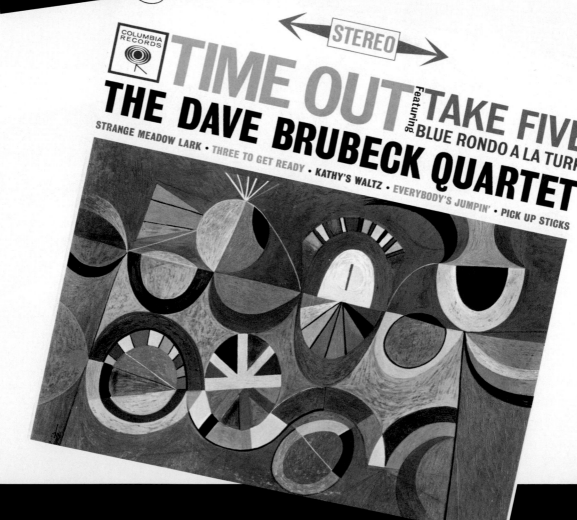

OUT THERE/ERIC DOLPHY

PRESTIGE/NEW JAZZ 8252

LOVE FOR SALE — CECIL TAYLOR

UA HI-FIDELITY

MILES

The release of Miles Davis's third LP arranged by Gil Evans, *Sketches of Spain*, was an event in 1960, a fusion of jazz and flamenco, its searing emotionalism conveyed by the classic simplicity of the uncredited cover—three layers of color in a manner reminiscent of the paintings of Mark Rothko, with a small full-figure silhouette of the trumpet player confronting a bull charging his first name; no last name necessary. The cover of Verve's 1963 landmark album *Getz / Gilberto* was widely imitated for its use of an abstract painting by the Puerto Rican–born artist Olga Albizu, confirming the idea that bossa nova was indeed a new style. The surreal illustration for Eric Dolphy's 1960 Prestige album *Out There* (signed by Prophet) telegraphs the idea that this music is not merely modern, but far out. On the other hand, United Artists came up with one of the most laughably deceptive covers in presenting the avant-garde Cecil Taylor's 1959 *Love for Sale* as a conventional interpretation of Cole Porter.

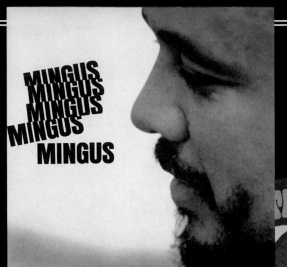

"The New Wave of Jazz is on Impulse!"—so proclaimed a major new label of 1960s jazz, known for its gatefold covers with orange spines (they stood out on record shelves) and a name with a built-in exclamation point. For a 1963 Charles Mingus album, it combined a close-up profile from a Joe Alper photograph with a kinetic typeface, repeating his name five times: *Mingus Mingus Mingus Mingus Mingus*. What more did you need to know? By the middle of the decade, rock covers brought a new style to graphic design, venturing into psychedelic whirls and colors. One of the first jazz covers to go that route was *Albert Ayler in Greenwich Village*, a 1966 Impulse! title, which, in its way, was as deceptive as Cecil Taylor's *Love for Sale*.

Miles Davis rejected Summer of Love graphics in favor of a startling new style for his breakout fusion album, *Bitches Brew*. The stunning cover art by Mati Klarwein and the startlingly crude title (by the standards of Columbia Records and of 1969) told listeners they were entering a brave new world before they put the platter on the turntable. No previous jazz album looked remotely like this. A couple of years later, a more naturalistic approach was back in favor. For Archie Shepp's 1972 *Attica Blues*, Impulse! countered the album's political theme (the riots at Attica prison) with a pensive study of the artist at work.

A decade after that, LPs were fighting a losing battle to CDs, even though the first digital discs had inferior sound; people bought records they already owned in the shiny new format, just as collectors of 78s had repurchased their favorites on microgroove. Usually the labels miniaturized the original LP cover art. But on occasion, they would contract a new one. When Chiaroscuro released Mary Lou Williams's 1971 *Nitelife* as a 1998 CD, the producer Hank O'Neal added a second disc of performances and commissioned a colorful painting by Richard Merkin, which made the music seem more urgent and contemporary.

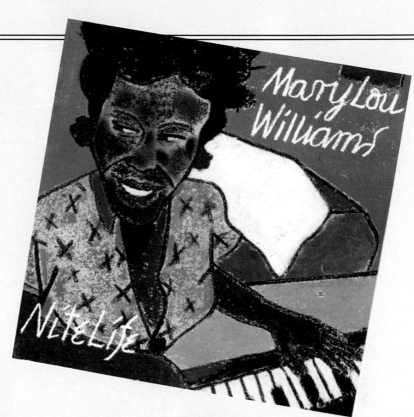

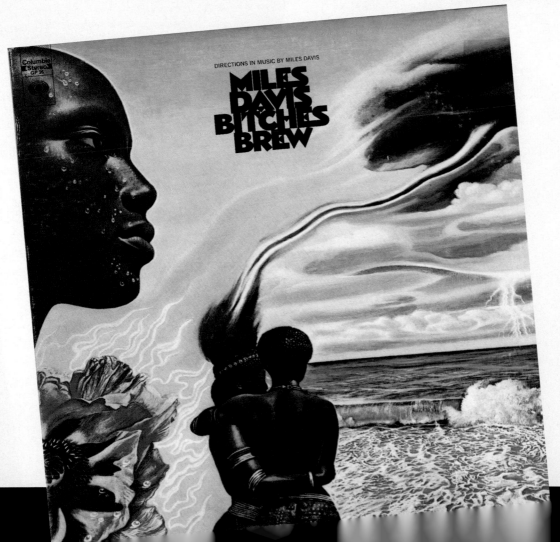

The diminutive size of CDs changed the nature of graphic design. More creative effort was expended on fancy boxed sets and oddly designed packages than on the typical single-disc album. Cover art was dominated by photographs rather than paintings or ornamental typeface. Of course, there are many exceptions, and graphic artists continue to find effective ways of communicating something about the artist or the music. For Danilo Perez's 2000 *Motherland*, Verve posed the pianist against an expansion bridge to evoke the connection he establishes between jazz and the music of his native Panama and other South American countries. You wouldn't know it from the cover, but Diana Krall's 2001 *The Look of Love* presents the singer-pianist, usually heard leading a trio, with a large orchestra; instead, Verve focuses entirely on her, especially her legs. The consumer can have no doubt that Jason Moran's 2002 *Modernistic* will live up to its title: Blue Note's design by P. R. Brown returns to basic black and white, but in a fashionably modern way, combining an alert eyeball and computer-like font to excite the buyer's curiosity.

■ CHICK (1909–1939) and GENE (1909–1973)

William Henry Webb, nicknamed Chick for his small size, was the first great swing drummer and the first to lead his own orchestra, a fiercely competitive outfit that ruled New York's Savoy Ballroom in the early 1930s. He didn't look the part of a powerful drummer and commanding bandleader: mangled by spinal tuberculosis, Webb was a dwarfed hunchback who lived most of his short life in pain. Drums of reduced size were built to accommodate him. Even so, his drumming had a titanic power, and even by contemporary standards his short solos and rattling breaks impart a jolt: each stroke has the articulation of a gunshot. He spurred his soloists with flashing cymbals or emphatic **shuffle rhythms** (slow, powerfully syncopated rhythms derived from boogie-woogie). Those who learned from him include most of the major Swing Era drummers, among them Gene Krupa, Sid Catlett, Jo Jones, Dave Tough, Buddy Rich, and Cozy Cole. Krupa said of Webb, "When he really let go, you had a feeling that the entire atmosphere in the place was being charged. When he felt like it, he could down any of us."

Born in Baltimore, Webb began teaching himself drums at three and bought his first set of traps at eleven. He came to New York in 1924, where two years later Duke Ellington arranged an engagement for him that led to his forming a stable band. He struggled until 1931, when he was booked into the Savoy. When Louis Armstrong came to New York that year, Webb's band was selected to accompany him. Soon Webb was recording with Armstrong and as the leader of his own band, introducing work by Benny Carter and Edgar Sampson that would become indispensable to the Swing Era. Some of these pieces were successfully adapted by Benny Goodman (including "Don't Be That Way," "Stomping at the Savoy," and "Blue Lou," all by Sampson). Webb, a generous nurturer of talent, became nationally known when he discovered Ella Fitzgerald, whose vocal on "A-Tisket, a-Tasket" made it one of the best-selling records of the decade.

Webb's rim shots and explosive breaks gave his music a unique kick. In 1937, he enjoyed the satisfaction of engaging in a "battle of the bands" at the Savoy with Goodman and trouncing him. The victory was particularly sweet because Goodman's drummer was the nationally publicized Krupa, who at the end faced Webb and bowed down in respect. But Webb didn't have long to savor his success; he died at thirty, of tuberculosis and pleurisy.

Gene Krupa, one of the white Chicagoans who congregated around Bix Beiderbecke, was the first drummer to achieve the status of a matinee idol. During four years with Goodman's band (1934–38), he created a sensation with his histrionic solos, characterized by facial contortions, broad arm movements, and hair falling over his brow. A solid musician, Krupa wasn't one of the Swing Era's best drummers, but he knew how to stir a crowd. His trademark was a dramatic figure played on the tom-toms ("Sing, Sing, Sing"). In 1938, given his growing fan base, Krupa was encouraged to leave Goodman to start his own band, which proved adventurous and tasteful, and made social history by hiring Roy Eldridge. In 1943, Krupa's career was

Chick Webb (c. 1939), a dwarfed hunchback whose drums were scaled to order, advanced big-band jazz and drumming as the indefatigable King of the Savoy Ballroom, finding commercial success as he launched the career of Ella Fitzgerald.

DUNCAN SCHIEDT COLLECTION

derailed by a trumped-up arrest for possession of marijuana. He won the case on appeal, but by then the Swing Era was in remission.

■ PAPA JO (1911–1985) and BIG SID (1910–1951)

No less mesmerizing and more musically accomplished was Jo Jones, born in Chicago and raised in Alabama, where he toured in tent shows as a tap dancer; gradually he transferred his fastidious dancing skills to the drums. As we saw in Chapter 8, Jones made his mark with Count Basie (1934–48, notwithstanding a few short sabbaticals), creating the fleet four-four drive that made Basie's rhythm section a Swing Era touchstone. It was said that "he played like the wind." His great innovation was to transfer rhythmic emphasis from the snare and bass drums to the high-hat cymbal: this created a tremendous fluidity, replacing *thump-thump-thump* with a sibilant *ching-a-ching-ching*. Jones created some of the most exciting moments of the Swing Era, announcing pieces on the high-hat, as in "Clap Hands, Here Comes Charlie," or spurring the soloists with razor-sharp stick work (note his accompaniment to Lester Young and Buck Clayton on "One O'Clock Jump"). In later years, he was reverently known as Papa Jo; on some nights, he would walk through the clubs he worked and drum on every surface.

Sidney Catlett was a masterly, flashy musician who played intricate cross-rhythms with a delicacy and precision that made them seem elemental. Born in Indiana, he played with several bands in Chicago before moving to New York, where he worked with Benny Carter, Don Redman, Fletcher Henderson, Louis Armstrong, and Benny Goodman, among others. The remarkable thing about Big Sid (he stood well over six feet), besides his infallible technique, was his willingness to play every kind of jazz with grace and commitment. He was as comfortable with Jelly Roll Morton and Sidney Bechet as with Charlie Parker and Dizzy Gillespie. He was one of the first drummers to work out a coherent, logical approach to solos. He created dynamics and contrasts with an array of cymbals, rim shots, bass drum rumbles, and unexpected rests—a good example is Louis Armstrong's "Steak Face." Catlett died of a heart attack backstage at a concert, at forty-one.

More Drummers

Many drummers distinguished themselves during the Swing Era. Dave Tough, a leader of Chicago's Austin High Gang, is considered the first white drummer to master African American percussion. The swing bands he worked with include those of Goodman (where he replaced Krupa), Tommy Dorsey, and Woody Herman, with whom he tailored discrete accompaniments for each soloist. Jimmy Crawford was a crucial member of the Jimmie Lunceford band (1927–43), perfecting a relaxed two-beat feeling while framing the ensemble's every phrase with scrupulous precision. Crawford later became a favorite of singers, including Billie Holiday, Frank Sinatra, and Ella Fitzgerald. Buddy Rich was regarded by other drummers as the instrument's foremost virtuoso for his unrivaled adroitness and speed. His show business career began in vaudeville before his second birthday; within a few years, he was touring theaters as "Traps, the Drum Wonder." After working with several important bands in the 1930s, Rich made his name with Tommy Dorsey's orchestra (1939–42). He later played with Benny Carter and Basie before forming his own successful bands, large and small.

THE BEST OF ALL POSSIBLE WORLDS

For Swing Era audiences, the music of the big bands seemed like a preview of paradise. It defined and unified American culture as no other style of music ever had or would—even the 1960s era of the Beatles, which evoked the optimism and broad reach of swing, exposed a "generation gap." Swing was innovated by men and women in their thirties, and if their initial audiences were young, their music almost immediately suspended all gaps. Swing was bigger than jazz. Country music performers like Bob Wills organized Western swing bands; comic personalities like Kay Kyser fronted novelty swing bands. Some liked it hot, others sweet; some liked it highbrow, others lowdown.

No matter how it was played, swing was an improbably luxurious music, chiefly the work of big bands averaging fifteen musicians plus singers, crisscrossing the country to play in ballrooms, up close to their fans, several sets each evening. Of course, it couldn't last. The irony of swing is that it flourished during the Depression, when luxury was in short supply except in popular culture; this was also the era of cinematic spectaculars like *Gone with the Wind* and *The Wizard of Oz*, of Fred Astaire/Ginger Rogers musicals and Cary Grant/Irene Dunne comedies, when actors played characters who wore tuxedos and gowns and hobnobbed with the very rich in laughably glamorous settings.

That fantasy crashed in the aftermath of the war, when the recovering economy was offset by the abruptly disclosed barbarism of the death camps, a new fear of nuclear devastation, and the reentry into civilian life of thousands of troops, attempting to pick up where they had left off. The music that dominated the next decade of American life emanated directly from swing bands—not from its stars, but rather from its mavericks, musicians considered tangential to or insignificant in the world of swing. They would lay the groundwork for rhythm and blues, salsa, star vocalists, and a way of playing jazz that was more intellectual and demanding than its predecessors. Ironically, the press tagged it with a silly, onomatopoetic name that stuck: bebop.

┤ ADDITIONAL LISTENING ├

Fats Waller	"Honeysuckle Rose" (1951); *Louis Armstrong: The California Concerts* (Decca Jazz 613)
	"I'm Gonna Sit Right Down and Write Myself a Letter" (1935); *A Handful of Keys, 1922-1935* (Jazz Legends 723724560123)
Art Tatum and Ben Webster	*The Tatum Group Masterpieces*, vol. 8 (1956) (Pablo PACD-2405-431-2)
Louis Armstrong and Sid Catlett	"Steak Face" (1947); *Satchmo at Symphony Hall* (GRP 011105066129)
Chick Webb	"Don't Be That Way" (1934); *Stompin' at the Savoy* (ASV/Living Era)
	"A-Tisket, a-Tasket" (1938); *Definitive Ella Fitzgerald* (Verve 731454908726)
Gene Krupa	"Let Me Off Uptown" (1941); *Anita O'Day's Finest Hour* (Verve)
Roy Eldridge	"Rockin' Chair" (1946); *Roy Eldridge, After You've Gone: The Original Decca Recordings* (GRP 011105060523)

PART III SUMMARY

SWING BANDS AFTER 1930

Swing, a buoyant, exuberant (mostly big-band) music that inspired teenage dancers to acrobatic feats, unified American culture as no other style ever had. The same tune might be played on the radio or a jukebox, on a movie soundtrack, or by a big band (hot or sweet) or small band. With its well-defined melodies, big-band swing was simple and accessible, and continued to balance composition against spontaneous improvisation.

Texture

- homophonic

Rhythm

- clearly articulated four beats to the bar

Instrumentation

- sections of trumpets, trombones, saxophones
- rhythm section: string bass, acoustic guitar, piano, drums

Form and repertory

- 32-bar popular song (**A A B A, A B A C**), 12-bar blues
- current pop songs

Special techniques

- call-and-response riffs
- improvised solos over simple backgrounds

Big bands

- Benny Goodman
- Fletcher Henderson
- Artie Shaw
- Jimmie Lunceford
- Cab Calloway
- Glenn Miller
- Gene Krupa

COUNT BASIE AND DUKE ELLINGTON

In the 1920s, thousands of local dance bands known as territory bands covered the country. In the same period, a new piano style called boogie-woogie developed in the Southwest and spread rapidly, securing a home in Kansas City and Chicago: a 12-bar blues, with a strong left-hand rhythmic ostinato that divided each measure into eight.

The most famous Kansas City pianist and bandleader was Count Basie, whose music making conveyed above all simplicity. Kansas City swing followed the same style as the big bands above, except that it placed more emphasis on head arrangements and soloists and featured a lighter rhythm section.

In the years before 1935, Duke Ellington was the dominant black name in dance bands. In a career spanning half a century, Ellington established a legacy through recordings that proves him to be, arguably, America's greatest composer.

Boogie-woogie pianists

- Pete Johnson
- Meade Lux Lewis

Territory bandleaders and musicians

- Benny Moten
- Walter Page
- Andy Kirk
- Mary Lou Williams

Count Basie Orchestra, 1930s–1940s

- Lester Young, tenor saxophone
- Herschel Evans, tenor saxophone
- Buck Clayton, trumpet
- Harry "Sweets" Edison, trumpet
- Eddie Durham, trombone
- Jo Jones, drums
- Freddie Green, guitar
- Walter Page, bass
- Jimmy Rushing, vocal

Duke Ellington Orchestra, 1940–

- Ben Webster, tenor saxophone
- Juan Tizol, trombone
- Lawrence Brown, trombone

- Rex Stewart, trumpet
- Billy Strayhorn, arranger/composer
- Sonny Greer, drums
- Jimmy Blanton, bass

- Johnny Hodges, alto saxophone
- Harry Carney, baritone saxophone
- Barney Bigard, clarinet
- Ivie Anderson, vocal

SWING ERA SOLOISTS

Soloists in big bands and smaller groups developed distinct personal syles that listeners could readily identify. Their popularity increased throughout the 1930s, portending a new respect for jazz musicians. At the same time, rhythm-section musicians developed technical skills and harmonic and rhythmic ideas that demanded attention.

Alto saxophone
- Benny Carter

Tenor saxophone
- Coleman Hawkins
- Ben Webster
- Lester Young
- Chu Berry

Trumpet
- Roy Eldridge
- Bunny Berigan

Guitar
- Django Reinhardt
- Charlie Christian (electric)

Vocalists
- Billie Holiday
- Ella Fitzgerald
- Mildred Bailey
- Ethel Waters

Piano
- Fats Waller
- Art Tatum

Bass
- Milt Hinton
- Jimmy Blanton
- Walter Page
- Israel Crosby
- John Kirby
- Slam Stewart

Drums
- Chick Webb
- Sid Catlett
- Gene Krupa
- Jo Jones
- Dave Tough
- Buddy Rich
- Jimmy Crawford

MODERN JAZZ

The war transformed the economy, speeded the pace of life, and spurred the demand for civil rights. Segregated black troops that had fought to liberate foreign lands from tyranny were more determined to liberate themselves from a second-class citizenship. Many young musicians, black and white, found a bond and a social message in the jazz represented by the incendiary brilliance of Charlie Parker and Dizzy Gillespie. Their music, which became known as bebop, emerged from the swing bands and found its own setting in small bands. In an era of rockets and atom bombs, bebop favored art over entertainment, unleashing supersonic tempos and volatile rhythms that frightened many listeners accustomed to the steady, stamping beat of swing.

Bebop became the standard language of jazz improvisation, yet it accommodated various musical styles, or schools. The West Coast fostered a cool way of playing, while the East Coast came up with a more visceral brew called hard

1940
- Charlie Parker joins Jay McShann's orchestra in Kansas City.

1941
- Parker begins playing in Minton's Playhouse jam sessions.

1944
- Dizzy Gillespie's band plays on New York's 52nd Street, known as Swing Street.
- Norman Granz establishes Jazz at the Philharmonic and produces *Jammin' the Blues*, featuring Lester Young.
- *Going My Way,* starring Jazz Age crooner Bing Crosby, is top-grossing movie of the year.

1945
- Charlie Parker records "Ko-Ko."
- Parker and Gillespie take their band to Los Angeles.
- United Nations founded.

1946
- Jackie Robinson becomes first African American in major league baseball.

- "Hollywood 10" blacklisted by House Un-American Activities Committee.

1947
- Louis Armstrong forms his All Stars band.
- Woody Herman forms his Second Herd, known as the Four Brothers band.
- Tennessee Williams's *A Streetcar Named Desire* (with Marlon Brando) opens on Broadway.

1948
- The last important clubs on New York's 52nd Street close.
- Dizzy Gillespie performs at Nice Jazz Festival in France.
- Billie Holiday breaks records at Carnegie Hall concerts.
- Microgrooves—LP 33⅓ rpm and 45 rpm—introduced.
- Apartheid imposed in South Africa.
- State of Israel founded.
- *The Texaco Star Theater*, starring Milton Berle, debuts on television.

Coleman Hawkins (left) led a prophetic session in 1944 at the Spotlight Club in New York, with one of his disciples, tenor saxophonist Don Byas (third from left), and an unknown pianist he championed named Thelonious Monk.

It happened here: In 1968, civil rights activists were blocked by National Guardsmen brandishing bayonets on Beale Street in Memphis. The demonstrators were also flanked by tanks.

Oscar Pettiford, shown at a recording session in the early 1950s, brought heightened virtuosity to jazz bass and introduced the cello as his second instrument.

bop. The revival of church, classical, and Latin influences led to soul jazz, Third Stream, and salsa. Miles Davis, one of the most influential and restless bop musicians, contributed innovations to all of these schools. His use of modes and free styles of improvisation also helped to ignite the avant-garde, which created a jazz rift more disputatious than the swing/bop schism.

Like jazz before and after, bop reflected the times. The relief and triumph that attended the Allied victory led almost instantly to disillusionment and paranoia, as the fear of nuclear devastation, Communist infiltration, and demands for racial equality generated social discord. Television responded with a homogenized view of American life, emphasizing middle-class satisfactions. Jazz no longer served as an optimistic booster. If it now alienated much of the audience that rallied around swing, it attracted a younger audience that admired its irreverence and subtlety. It was championed by beatniks, hedonists, students, and intellectuals.

1949

- "Rhythm and blues" displaces the label "race records."
- The club Birdland, named after Charlie Parker, opens in New York.
- Paris Jazz Festival brings Parker, Miles Davis, and other young musicians to Europe.
- West German Federal Republic and East German Democratic Republic established.
- Mao Tse-Tung establishes People's Republic of China.
- First flight of a passenger jet aircraft.
- George Orwell's *1984* published.
- Carol Reed directs Graham Greene's film script for *The Third Man*.
- Arthur Miller's *Death of a Salesman* opens on Broadway.

1949–50

- Miles Davis leads "birth of the cool" sessions.

1950–53

- Korean War

1951

- Dave Brubeck organizes quartet with Paul Desmond.
- J. D. Salinger's *Catcher in the Rye* published.

1952

- John Lewis forms Modern Jazz Quartet (in New York).
- Gerry Mulligan organizes "piano-less" quartet (in California).
- First pocket-sized transitor radios sold.
- Edward R. Murrow's *See It Now* comes to TV, helping to bring down Senator Joseph McCarthy.
- Ralph Ellison's *The Invisible Man* published.

1953

- Art Blakey and Horace Silver form the Jazz Messengers.
- George Russell publishes *Lydian Chromatic Concept*.

1954

- Miles Davis records "Walkin'."
- Clifford Brown and Max Roach form quintet.
- Supreme Court, in *Brown v. Board of Education of Topeka*, finds segregation in public schools unconstitutional.

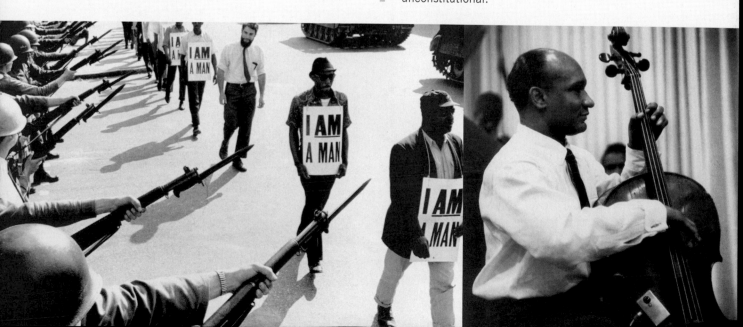

- Vietnam, at war since 1946, is partitioned into North and South Vietnam.

1955
- Miles Davis records *Round About Midnight* (with first quintet).
- Charlie Parker dies.
- Bus boycott begins in Montgomery, Alabama.
- Vladimir Nabokov's *Lolita* published.

1955–56
- Sonny Rollins records *Worktime* and *Saxophone Colossus*.

1956
- Art Blakey and His Jazz Messengers formed.
- George Russell records *Jazz Workshop*.
- Charles Mingus records *Pithecanthropus Erectus*.
- Louis Armstrong visits Africa, filmed by CBS.
- Dizzy Gillespie tours Middle East for the State Department.
- Clifford Brown dies in car crash.

- Riots prevent first black student from enrolling at University of Alabama.
- Rebellion in Hungary crushed by USSR.
- Lerner and Loewe's *My Fair Lady* opens on Broadway.

1957
- Gunther Schuller introduces term "Third Stream."
- Thelonious Monk spends six months at New York's Five Spot.
- Miles Davis and Gil Evans record *Miles Ahead*.
- Arkansas's Governor Faubus calls out National Guard to prevent school integration; Louis Armstrong cancels tour of Soviet Union in protest.
- Jack Kerouac's *On the Road* published.
- USSR launches first Sputnik satellite.

1958
- Davis and Evans record *Porgy and Bess*.
- First stereo records produced.

1959
- Dave Brubeck records *Time Out* (including "Take Five").

Bebop at New York's Royal Roost with drummer Max Roach, trumpet player Miles Davis, and trombonist Kai Winding, 1948.

Dizzy Gillespie once called Charlie Parker "the other half of my heartbeat." They posed playfully for the camera at the peak of bop, in 1949.

Gerry Mulligan, one of the architects of cool jazz, began as a big-band arranger, but became a major star playing baritone saxophone and leading a "piano-less" quartet. Half a century later, he remains the only baritone player to achieve mainstream recognition.

John Lewis, second from right, examines one of the scores he wrote for an RCA big-band recording by Dizzy Gillespie (left). New York, 1947.

Clarinetist Woody Herman, seen at a 1948 recording session, led a series of influential big bands from the 1930s until his death in 1987, making the transitions from blues to swing to bop to fusion.

Gil Evans, seen here in 1958, brought the art of arranging other people's music to the level of original composition; he's best known for the concertos he wrote for Miles Davis.

- Davis records *Kind of Blue*.
- John Coltrane records *Giant Steps*.
- Hawaii and Alaska become 49th and 50th U.S. states.
- Fidel Castro takes power in Cuba.

1960
- Davis and Evans record *Sketches of Spain*.
- Coltrane records "My Favorite Things."
- Charles Mingus and Eric Dolphy record *Original Fables of Faubus*.
- Harper Lee's *To Kill a Mockingbird* published.

1961
- Berlin Wall completed.
- U.S. sends "military advisers" to Vietnam.
- Joseph Heller's *Catch-22* published.

1961–62
- Bay of Pigs invasion provokes Cuban missile crisis.

1962
- First black student enters University of Mississippi.

- John Glenn becomes first American in space.

1963
- Count Basie tours Japan.
- President John F. Kennedy assassinated.

1964
- John Coltrane records *A Love Supreme*.
- Civil Rights Act passed.

1965
- Coltrane records *Ascension*.
- Miles Davis records *E.S.P.* (with new quintet).
- Malcolm X assassinated.
- Martin Luther King Jr. leads march in Selma, Alabama.

1967
- Wes Montgomery emerges as mainstream recording star.
- Six-Day War in Middle East.
- Thurgood Marshall becomes first African American Supreme Court justice.

BEBOP

In the mid-1940s, jazz stood at a crossroads. As swing, jazz had risen from its New Orleans origins to become an extroverted popular music, inseparable from mainstream American culture. With the arrival of **bebop,** jazz turned a sharp corner. It was suddenly an isolated music, appearing in tiny cramped nightclubs rather than brightly lit dance halls. Its music—small combo tunes with bizarre names such as "Salt Peanuts" and "Ornithology"—was complex, dense, and difficult to grasp. It traded in a mass audience for a tiny group of jazz fans who spoke of musicians known by terse, elliptical names: Bird (Charlie Parker), Diz (Dizzy Gillespie), Klook (Kenny Clarke), and Monk (Thelonious Monk). Like swing, bebop was still a music that prized virtuosity; if anything, its standards were even higher. But most people saw it as an outsider's music, steeped in drug abuse and tainted with an atmosphere of racial hostility.

For historians, one option has been to see bebop as a revolution, emphatically breaking with the past. In a 1949 interview, the great alto saxophonist Charlie Parker insisted that bebop was a new music, something "entirely separate and apart" from the jazz that had preceded it. This view requires us to think about the cultural forces that pushed

While **Kenny Clarke** devised his new techniques as a swing drummer in the 1930s, he came alive in after-hours jam sessions. As a member of the house band at Minton's Playhouse, he was central to the birth of modern jazz.

wwnorton.com/studyspace

musicians—mostly black—out of their conventional career paths into an unknown, risk-filled style. Historians today, however, tend to treat bebop as an evolution from swing, placing it firmly in the center of the jazz tradition. Indeed, it has been strongly argued that bebop is the first jazz style to cement its status as an art music.

We will begin with this evolutionary view, linking bebop back to the Swing Era—in particular to the backstage phenomenon known as the jam session.

BEBOP AND JAM SESSIONS

The swing musician's day began in the evening, as people drifted toward theaters and ballrooms for their after-work entertainment. By the time these audiences went home to bed, musicians in large cities, especially Manhattan, were gearing up for more work. "The average musician hated to go home in those days," remembered Sonny Greer, Duke Ellington's drummer. "He was always seeking some place where someone was playing something he ought to hear."

The jam session offered relaxation at the end of a hard day. Free of the constraints of the bandstand, musicians could come and go as they pleased. A version of "I Got Rhythm" could stretch out for half an hour. But jam sessions were also an extension of the workplace As the name suggests, "cutting contests"—duels pitting trombones, drums, or saxophones against each other—offered serious competition; if you lost, that was yet another stage in your jazz education. "Everybody would get up there and take [their] shots," one musician remembered. "Some of them we could handle and some of them we couldn't. But every time you do that you're sharpening your knife, see."

Bebop was the music of small clubs like Bop City in San Francisco. Crowded into this room one night in 1951 were Dizzy Gillespie (right, at the piano) and fellow trumpet players Kenny Dorham (standing to his left) and Miles Davis (head bowed, to his right); singer Betty Bennett; saxophonist Jimmy Heath (facing camera directly below her) and his brother, bassist Percy Heath (kneeling, to his right); vibraharpist Milt Jackson (kneeling, bottom left, facing left); and drummer Roy Porter (far left in back row, smoking cigarette).

To keep people from wandering in who didn't belong, jam sessions offered a series of musical obstacles. The simplest way to make an inexperienced interloper feel unwelcome was to count off a tune at a ridiculously fast tempo or play it in an unfamiliar key. Sometimes tunes would modulate up a half step with every chorus, challenging everyone's ability to transpose. Favorite tunes like "I Got Rhythm" would be recast with bristlingly difficult harmonic substitutions. Those who could take the heat were welcome; those who couldn't went home to practice.

In this way, the musicians who would become the bebop generation had their musical skills continually tested. The more ambitious of them embraced this atmosphere, experimenting with bizarre chords, improvising at unbelievable speeds, and generally making their peers and even their mentors feel slightly uncomfortable. When Ben Webster first heard Charlie Parker play, he asked, "Man, is that cat crazy?" and reportedly grabbed the horn away, exclaiming, "That horn ain't s'posed to sound that fast."

Dropping Bombs at Minton's

Charlie Parker and other bebop notables could be heard regularly at Minton's Playhouse, on 118th Street in Harlem, which hosted some of the most celebrated jam sessions in Manhattan. Many of the innovations that took place there reflected its professional clientele's liking for musical challenge.

Consider, for example, how drumming styles changed with bebop. As Kenny Clarke once explained it, his breakthrough in technique came when he was drumming for a swing band led by Teddy Hill in the late 1930s. During an exceptionally fast arrangement of "Old Man River," he found it nearly impossible to keep time in the usual fashion by striking his bass drum for each beat. Suddenly it occurred to him to shift the pulse to the ride cymbal. This innovation gave him two new weapons: a shimmering ride cymbal sound that became the lighter, more flexible foundation for all of modern jazz, and the powerful bass drum, now available to fill in the holes in the band's arrangements with its thunderous booms.

Kenny Clarke

Clarke's style was not popular with musicians who had become used to the heavy swing beat. "He breaks up the time too much," one musician complained. Reluctantly, Hill let Clarke go in 1940. But in an ironic twist, when Hill's own band collapsed shortly thereafter, his next employer was the owner of Minton's, looking for someone to hire for his new Playhouse. Realizing that the drum techniques that had irritated and bewildered musicians on the bandstand might delight them in a jam session, Hill brought Clarke into the Minton's Playhouse rhythm section, where he soon earned the nickname "Klook" for his combined snare drum and bass drum hits, known as "klook-mop." Because all this took place during the early years of World War II, Clarke's unexpected bass drum explosions were known as **dropping bombs.** Young, hip musicians soon fell in love with Clarke's simmering polyrhythms. Drummers like Max Roach and Art Blakey found in Clarke's playing the techniques they needed for a more modern style.

Over this new accompaniment, the rhythms played by soloists (inspired by Lester Young's fluid, discontinuous style) were disorienting and unpredictable. Listeners were startled by the spurts of fast notes, ending abruptly with a two-note gesture that inspired the scat syllables "be-bop" or "re-bop." Older musicians were not amused. While jamming at Minton's, Fats Waller

Minton's Playhouse opened for business in 1940. By 1947, it was famous enough as the birthplace of bebop that this photograph was staged for posterity. From the left: pianist/composer Thelonious Monk, trumpet players Howard McGhee and Roy Eldridge, and bandleader/manager Teddy Hill.

supposedly yelled out, "Stop that crazy boppin' and a-stoppin' and play that jive like the rest of us guys!"

Inspired by Count Basie, pianists dropped stride technique in favor of **comping,** a rhythmically unpredictable skein of accompanying chords that complemented the drummer's strokes and added yet another layer to the rhythmic mix. The acoustic guitar's insistent chording (*chunk chunk chunk*) once thickened the sound of a swing rhythm section, but for bebop the ride cymbal and walking-bass line were enough. Guitarists either abandoned bebop or, like Charlie Christian (Chapter 10), switched to electric amplification, which made them akin to pianists: they could take a more active, syncopated role in the rhythm section or step into the limelight as soloist.

The bassists' role didn't change—they remained timekeepers at the bottom of the texture—yet thanks to the jam session, a new generation of bass players raised the level of virtuosity. We have already met Jimmy Blanton (Chapter 10), who undergirded the Duke Ellington band during his brief lifetime. He was matched by Oscar Pettiford, a young black musician with Choctaw and Cherokee ancestry who handled the bass with rhythmic assurance and athletic swiftness. In jam sessions, even the bassists were prodded into taking a solo—a role that Pettiford embraced with glee. On a 1943 recording of "The Man I Love" with Coleman Hawkins, Pettiford plays a wonderfully melodic solo, his rhythmic gasps of breath between each phrase captured on the microphone with startling fidelity.

"Nobody Plays Those Changes"

Bebop was famous—even reviled—for its complex, dissonant harmonies. To be sure, these sounds had been part of the jazz vocabulary for some time. Art Tatum turned popular songs into harmonic minefields through the complexity of his chord substitutions, leaving other musicians—including a nineteen-year-old Charlie Parker, who worked as a dishwasher in a restaurant that featured Tatum—to shake their heads in wonder. Arrangers listened closely to Duke Ellington's instrumentation, trying to decipher how he voiced his astringent chords. Improvisers took their cue from Coleman Hawkins, who showed in "Body and Soul" how to use dense chromatic harmonies in popular song.

The challenge for the bebop generation came in translating these dissonant harmonies into a vocabulary all musicians could share. Soloists and members of the rhythm section had to learn to coordinate. This could be done deliberately, as when Dizzy Gillespie planned with bassist Milt Hinton on the roof of the Cotton Club how to play substitute harmonies in that evening's jam sessions. At other times it was the shock of discovery. When Charlie Parker first heard pianist Tadd Dameron's unusual chord voicings, he was so thrilled he kissed the pianist on the cheek. "That's what I've been hearing all my life," he said, "but nobody plays those changes."

The new harmonies fastened onto dissonances like the **tritone**—a chromatic interval known during the Middle Ages as the "devil in music" and during the bebop era as the **flatted fifth.** The tritone could be found in the complex chords that pianists like Dameron used, as well as the spiky solos musicians like Gillespie devised from them. Other extended notes (sixths, flat ninths) were added to the palette, making the job of harmonic improvisation that much more difficult. Keeping track of such nuances of harmony was a demanding task, turning a physical, emotional music into the realm of the intellectual. "With bop, you had to *know*," trumpet player Howard McGhee stated firmly. "Not feel; you had to *know* what you were doing."

◀)) **tritone/flatted fifth** the interval of three whole steps

On the Road

At the same time, nonmusical forces—racial and economic—were driving musicians out of swing into the unknown future, and it is these forces that form the basis for the revolutionary view of bebop. During the Swing Era, black bands were prevented by racial prejudice from two kinds of jobs. The first was a prime-time radio show with a commercial sponsor (such as "The Camel Cavalcade," sponsored by Camel cigarettes), through which the top white bands profited. The second was a lengthy engagement at a major hotel ballroom or dance hall in New York City. These jobs offered free late-night broadcasts, invaluable for publicity, as well as a chance for the band to rest from the rigors of travel. For several months of the year, musicians could unpack their bags, rehearse new tunes, and live with their families.

The top black bands, then, were forced onto the road. A few, like Ellington's and Calloway's, could afford the comforts of a private railroad car, but the rest toured the country in rattletrap buses. Continuous travel was enough to exhaust even the hardiest musician, and inevitably took bands through the heart of the Jim Crow South. As highly visible African American celebrities headquartered in New York, jazz musicians aroused the ire of white Southerners, from the man on the street to uniformed police. Musicians from the Deep South understood this, but their Northern colleagues had to learn the hard way how to stay out of trouble. They had to eat at "colored" restaurants, sit in the filthy Jim Crow car of a railroad, and avoid eye contact with white women—or risk violence. Few musicians were actually harmed, but the specter of public lynching (still active in some states) made it clear how far things could go.

Under these circumstances, musicians became bitter—especially the younger ones, who were impatient with the lack of change in racial mores. The most talented quit swing bands, sometimes out of exhaustion, sometimes disgust. Increasingly, they turned toward the jam sessions, hoping to find some way to carry on their music outside the system. Bebop absorbed this energy: it was subversive, "uppity," daring, and hell-bent on social change. "There was a message to our music," announced Kenny Clarke. "Whatever you go into, go into it *intelligently. . . .* The idea was to wake up, look around you, there's something to do."

By the early 1940s, a new approach to jazz, based on progressive chromatic harmonies and supported by an interactive rhythm section, was already in place. The final piece in the puzzle was a new kind of virtuoso soloist, taking Swing Era standards of excellence to unforeseen levels.

■ CHARLIE PARKER (1920–1955)

The most gifted alto saxophonist in jazz history, Charlie Parker earned his nickname "Bird" early in his jazz apprenticeship. Parker, who grew up in Kansas City, was touring as a teenager with a local territory band led by pianist Jay McShann. One day, the car in which he was traveling ran over a chicken. Parker yelled at the driver to stop. To everyone's surprise, he rushed to the dying bird and carried it back to the car. When the band arrived that night in a boarding house in a black neighborhood, he proudly presented the freshly killed chicken as the main ingredient for his meal. His bandmates gleefully called him "Yardbird"—slang for chicken. Over time, this nickname became shortened to "Bird," a term that bristled with overlapping meanings: melodious beauty, elusiveness, and the quickness of flight.

Parker didn't seem at first to have any special gift for music. He played baritone horn in his high school marching band, pecking out notes in the accompaniment. Eventually, he picked up the alto saxophone, teaching himself to play simple tunes like Fats Waller's "Honeysuckle Rose" by ear. When he tried to sit in on Kansas City jam sessions, though, he met only humiliation. One night, after he botched up "Body and Soul," the drummer Jo Jones "gonged" him out by throwing his high-hat cymbal on the floor. "Bird couldn't play much in those days," recalled one musician, "and he was mad about it, too."

Such experiences spurred him into a furious regimen of practicing. During one summer in the Ozarks, he learned how to play fluently in every key. He took as his model Lester Young, memorizing his recently recorded solo on "Oh! Lady Be Good" (Chapter 9). By the time he returned to Kansas City, his rhythm had become supercharged: one musician conveyed the impression of his performing by playing a Lester Young record twice as fast.

Now an expert soloist, Parker quickly earned a position in the Jay McShann Orchestra, one of the top territory bands. At the same time, he experimented with alcohol and pills; a serious car accident led him to morphine, which in turn led him to heroin—a substance that would haunt him throughout his life.

Parker's playing struck people at the time as both bluesy and modern. For his solo on "Hootie Blues" (1941), he upgraded the twelve-bar blues with new chromatic chord progressions and enlivened it with rapid flurries of notes. He also showed that he could be a model citizen in a swing band, blending beautifully in the saxophone section and devising endlessly varied riffs behind soloists during head arrangements.

Because of his heroin addiction, Parker didn't stay long with McShann—or with any other band. He

Throughout his brief career, alto saxophonist Charlie Parker appeared with a long list of trumpet players. In the late 1940s, his bandstand partner was young Miles Davis (right), barely out of his teens.

could rise from a drug-induced stupor to play a magnificent solo, but bandleaders found it too taxing to keep him. Instead, Parker settled into a precarious existence in New York, where drugs were readily available and where jam sessions offered a place to play. There he found a network of musicians similarly attuned to what he once called the "real advanced New York style" of modern jazz. Among them was Dizzy Gillespie.

This combo, which debuted at the Onyx Club on 52nd Street in late 1943, was probably the first bebop band. From left to right: Max Roach, drums; Budd Johnson, tenor saxophone; Oscar Pettiford, bass; George Wallington, piano; and Dizzy Gillespie, trumpet.

■ DIZZY GILLESPIE (1917–1993)

The intellectual force behind bebop was the trumpet player John Birks "Dizzy" Gillespie. His playing was astounding: brilliant solo lines that crackle in the upper register, accelerating to speeds not thought possible, matching Charlie Parker note for note. Yet it was his razor-sharp wit and steady hand that marked his fifty-year career. If Parker was bebop's inspiration, the Pied Piper of modern jazz, Gillespie pulled the style into shape like a master craftsman.

Like Parker, Gillespie came to New York from the provinces. He grew up in Cheraw, South Carolina, where his father labored as a bricklayer. Gillespie taught himself trumpet so unconventionally that his neck muscles protruded, frog-like, when he played. (Doctors have now dubbed this condition "Gillespie pouches.") He earned a scholarship to the Laurinburg Institute, across the border in North Carolina, where he studied both trumpet and piano. After hearing on the radio the music he wanted to play, he headed north—first to Philadelphia, joining local territory bands, and later to New York. By the time he was eighteen, his brash soloing style and excellent sight-reading had made him a valuable addition to Swing Era trumpet sections.

By 1939, Gillespie had reached the top of the heap. For the next several years, he was employed by the Cab Calloway Orchestra, perhaps the most lucrative black band in existence. He thrived in this atmosphere. Recordings reveal him as not only a top-flight soloist but also an arranger and composer: his tune "Pickin' the Cabbage," recorded by Calloway in 1940, combines a harmonic bite with a Latin groove. Still, Gillespie couldn't help feeling a certain dissatisfaction with the status quo: "I worked hard while I played with Cab, and practiced constantly. I could seldom get much encouragement from the guys in Cab's band. Mostly they talked about real estate or something, never talked about music. That atmosphere kept me acting wiggy and getting into a lot of mischief."

With Calloway

Gillespie had earned the nickname "Dizzy" back in Philadelphia for his fiery temperament and wicked sense of humor. He brought this unpredictable behavior onto the bandstand with the Calloway band, devising practical jokes and irritating the bandleader with his wild experimental solos. One night in 1941, a spitball flew directly into Calloway's spotlight. Gillespie was, in fact, innocent of this crime (a fellow musician had thrown it), but Calloway assumed he was the culprit. After a brief backstage confrontation erupted into violence, Gillespie was fired. But this only spurred him into action. For the next several years, he became a freelance artist, earning a living through whatever means possible. This included the small-combo, jam-session performances that led to bebop.

Gillespie became the nerve center for the new music. In Miles Davis's words, he was bebop's "head and hands," the "one who kept it all together." His apartment on 7th Avenue in Harlem was a gathering place for young bebop musicians eager to share information. Gillespie was quick to grasp the music's novelties and was generous enough to spread them as far as possible. In jam sessions, he showed pianists how to play the appropriate chords, and sat on the drum stool to demonstrate to drummers the more flexible, interactive style.

Thanks to his piano skills, Gillespie was fully aware of the harmonic possibilities of bebop. He not only learned to solo brilliantly over complex chord progressions, but also adapted dissonant chords into his compositions. Among them was "Salt Peanuts," a bracingly fast reworking of "I Got Rhythm": its strange title was sung on a riff based on a bebop drum lick (the quick alternation of snare drum and bass drum). "Salt Peanuts" introduced a humorous side to the new music, with verbal inanity covering the avant-garde complexity. "A Night in Tunisia" offered a more exotic groove. Completed in 1942, as the Allied troops invaded North Africa, "Tunisia" adapted modern chord changes to a Latin bass line, deepening Gillespie's fascination with Caribbean music.

Charlie Parker and Dizzy Gillespie posed together in 1951 at Birdland, the Broadway club named in Parker's honor. To their left is bassist Tommy Potter, while looking on from the right is the young saxophonist John Coltrane.

On 52nd Street

Gillespie and Parker first crossed paths in the early 1940s. Parker reveled in Gillespie's brilliant sound and his deep knowledge of harmony. Gillespie focused on the fluidity of Parker's phrases: "Charlie Parker brought the rhythm," he said. "The *way* he played those notes." The two worked side by side in 1942, when Earl Hines hired them for his big band (with Parker switching to tenor saxophone). None of Hines's recordings features them, but a private recording in a hotel room captures their skills offstage. Two years later, they again joined forces when Hines's vocalist, Billy Eckstine, started his own band. With Gillespie serving as music director, Eckstine's was the first big band to embrace bebop, astonishing those who heard it (including the teenaged Miles Davis in St. Louis).

Tunes like "Salt Peanuts" and "A Night in Tunisia," with their complex interludes, elaborate breaks, and sudden shifts of texture, seem naturally adaptable to the big-band (swing) environment. Yet the new style never found its way to a mass audience. Granted, the music was complex—perhaps too much so for commercial music. By the end of 1944, both Gillespie and Parker had quit the Eckstine band. Each turned instead to the jam-session-style small group as the best way to present their music to the public.

By the time Gillespie brought a quintet to 52nd Street, the emergent **Bebop arrives** style was known as "bebop," or "rebop," referring through scat syllables to the new rhythmic style. (An early Gillespie tune was titled "Be-bop," another "Bu-Dee-Daht.") It was a tightened-up version of what had been heard at Minton's, with one new wrinkle: at the beginning of a tune, where one might expect to hear a familiar harmonized melody, the horns played a bare, sinuous theme in disjointed rhythms, confusing those not already familiar with the Harlem jam sessions and offering no clue of what was to come. In this way, the jam-session style, already shielded from the public, became a way of transmuting the musicians' blues and standards into a new repertory. The white swing drummer Dave Tough, who heard the 1944 band, remembered its uncanny impact: "As we walked in, see, these cats snatched up their horns and blew crazy stuff. One would stop all of a sudden and another would start for no reason at all. We never could tell when a solo was supposed to begin or end. Then they all quit at once and walked off the stand. It scared us."

BIRD ON RECORDS

The first bebop recordings date from 1945—a chaotic period just before the end of the war that saw the emergence of small, independent record labels. Companies like Savoy, Apollo, and Dial saw jazz as a low-cost way of entering the business: no arrangements, no vocalists, just let the musicians do their thing. In the United States, while the melody of a tune is under copyright, its chord progression is not, leaving room for jazz musicians to create "original" tunes by superimposing a new melody over the changes of a copyrighted popular song. Tunes like "I Got Rhythm" were recast under unusual names like "Anthropology" and "Shaw 'Nuff," relieving the record company of the irritating obligation to pay royalties.

The intricacies of bebop can be sampled in three different recordings by Charlie Parker, each emphasizing a different aspect of his style.

🎧 "Ko-Ko"

"Cherokee," written by British bandleader Ray Noble in 1938 and turned into a popular hit the following year by Charlie Barnet, was an alleged tribute to Native Americans, with lyrics to match ("Sweet Indian maiden/Since I first met you/I can't forget you/Cherokee sweetheart"). Musicians liked it for its sixty-four-bar form, exactly twice the size of a standard thirty-two-bar **A A B A** form. Soloists shied away from the bridge, though, which jumped precipitously to a distant key and wound its way back home through continuous modulation. When Count Basie recorded this tune in 1939 (on two sides of a 78-rpm disc), the bridge appeared only during the head. The rest of the time, soloists and the arrangement retreated to the simpler harmonies of the **A** section.

Parker practiced this tune assiduously as a teenager in Kansas City, reveling in its difficult harmonic progression. It soon became his favorite showpiece. To accommodate him, the Jay McShann band concocted a loose head arrangement. When the band finally made it to New York, they played at the Savoy Ballroom, one of the few major venues that regularly broadcast black bands. To celebrate his New York debut, Parker let loose with a solo on "Cherokee" that seemed never to end, with the band spontaneously supplying riffs behind him. Like many others who heard that broadcast, the trumpet player Howard McGhee was struck dumb with amazement: "I had never heard anything like that in my *life*," he remembered. "Here's a guy who's playing everything that he wants to play . . . and *playing* it, you know. I never heard nobody play a horn like that—that *complete*."

Savoy Records

"Cherokee" was transformed into "Ko-Ko" in 1945, when Parker and Gillespie brought their 52nd Street band to the studio of Savoy Records. Originally a radio parts store in Newark, New Jersey, Savoy expanded into recording through the relentless miserliness of its owner, Herman Lubinsky. Like other small record company owners, Lubinsky would not tolerate a copyrighted melody. Thus it's not surprising that on the first take, after Parker and Gillespie follow a complex and abstract introduction with the melody to "Cherokee," someone interrupts them with "Hold it!" This was probably Parker, who may have calculated that a full chorus of the melody would cut into his solo time. In any case, a subsequent take left the "Cherokee" melody out altogether. The new name, "Ko-Ko," may have unconsciously been borrowed from the 1940 Duke Ellington recording by the same name. "Naming-day at Savoy," one critic has said, "must have been an exhilarating, if random experience."

The recording session was comically misassembled. Bud Powell was supposed to be the pianist, but in his absence Argonne Thornton (later known as Sadik Hakim) was hastily recruited. Gillespie substituted on piano for some tunes, but took over for the elaborate composed passages on "Ko-Ko" on trumpet. (The young Miles Davis, recently added to the band, doesn't play on this track, though he does on others recorded at the same session.) Gillespie sounds like the pianist on the released (master) take; but who, then, is playing piano on the rejected first take, when Gillespie is clearly on trumpet?

Somehow, out of this chaos came an unquestionable jazz masterpiece. Parker's two white-hot choruses, preceded by the boldly abstract introduction and immediately followed by a lightning-fast Max Roach drum solo, was a music so startlingly different that it demanded the new name, bebop.

ko-ko

CHARLIE PARKER'S RE-BOPPERS

Charlie Parker, alto saxophone; Dizzy Gillespie, trumpet; Curley Russell, bass; Argonne "Dense" Thornton, piano; Max Roach, drums

- Label: Take 1 (fragment)—Savoy MG-12079; master take—Savoy 597; *Savoy and Dial Master Takes* (Savoy 17149)
- Date: 1945
- Style: bebop
- Form: 64-bar popular song (**A A B A**; each section lasts 16 bars)

> **What to listen for:**
> - extremely fast tempo
> - Parker and Gillespie playing precomposed melody in octaves in the disorienting introduction and coda
> - Parker's constantly shifting accents, disruptive two-note "be-bop" rhythm
> - Roach's dropping bombs

TAKE 1 (fragment)

INTRODUCTION

0:00	In an elusive introduction, Gillespie and Parker play a single composed line in bare **octaves.** There is no harmonic accompaniment, the only rhythmic backdrop is the snare drum, played lightly by Roach with brushes.
0:05	The phrase ends suddenly with an octave drop, reinforced by sharp accents on the drums.
0:06	Gillespie plays a trumpet solo that implies a harmonic background through skillful improvisation. Many of the notes are **ghosted**—played so quietly that they are suggested rather than stated.
0:12	Parker enters, overlapping slightly with the trumpet. His improvised line is fluid, with a brief interruption by silence at 0:13. The drums add **cross-rhythms.**
0:18	A loud "thump" on the bass drum pulls the two instruments back together. The composed line is now harmonized.
0:21	Gillespie plays a high note, followed immediately by a note an octave lower from Parker. Roach responds with a "thump."
0:22	The two instruments play briefly without any accompaniment. During the brief silence, Roach exchanges his brushes for drum sticks.

CHORUS 1

0:24	**A**	The two horns begin playing the melody to "Cherokee," with Parker adding a harmonized line. The piano comps in the background.
0:29		As the melody nears the end of a phrase, Parker improvises a rapid bebop-style **countermelody.**
0:33		Someone—probably Parker, who has stopped playing—shouts, "Hey, hey! Hold it!" and whistles and claps his hands loudly. The tape suddenly ends.

MASTER TAKE

INTRODUCTION

0:00	The opening is identical to the previous take: the two horns enter with a precomposed melody in octaves.
0:06	Gillespie's solo is nearly identical to the previous take, suggesting that he had carefully prepared his line.
0:12	Parker's solo is strikingly different, underscoring the unpredictability of his improvisations.

CHORUS 1 (abbreviated)

0:25	**A**	Parker begins improvising in a steady stream to the chord progression to "Cherokee." Roach marks time through a shadowy halo on the ride cymbal. The bass is walking, and the piano comps.
0:27		Parker's line ends with a sudden dissonant pair of notes—a rhythm that was undoubtedly one source for the term "be-bop."
0:28		On the downbeat, Roach plays an unexpected accent on his bass drum—the first of many examples of **dropping bombs.**
0:35		Parker's improvisation is a continuous string of fast notes. The rhythms are disorienting, not simply because the tempo is extraordinarily fast, but because the accents are constantly shifting: sometimes on the beat, sometimes off.
0:37	**A**	Parker's line continues through this **A** section, in a phrase that recalls the opening of the solo. The drummer's improvisation is more intense and interactive.
0:44		After the first few notes of this phrase, an entire string of notes is ghosted until Parker suddenly returns to playing in full volume.
0:50	**B**	The bridge to "Cherokee" begins with a sudden shift away from the home key to more distant harmonies. Parker marks it by a relatively simple melodic phrase that ends with piercing, bluesy notes.
0:57		As the bridge begins to **modulate** back to the original key, Parker plays a long, involved phrase that continues through the beginning of the next **A** section.
1:03	**A**	
1:05		Two sharp drum accents signal the start of another Parker phrase.
1:13		Parker prepares for his next chorus by resting on a single note, echoed by the piano and accents from the bass drum.

CHORUS 2

1:16	**A**	Parker suddenly demonstrates his encyclopedic knowledge of jazz's history by quoting the famous piccolo obbligato from the New Orleans march "High Society."
1:29	**A**	
1:41	**B**	The piano marks the harmonic progression through simple chords. Parker disorients the listener with a series of phrases, alternately accenting the strong and weak beats of the measure.
1:48		As the harmony continues to move toward the tonic, Parker accelerates into particularly fast passages.
1:54	**A**	A line that started toward the end of the bridge continues through the beginning of this **A** section, ending on the disruptive two-note "be-bop" rhythm.
2:01		Parker's improvised line is interrupted by a squeak from his notoriously unreliable reed.
2:04		The two-chorus solo ends with a bluesy gesture.

CHORUS 3 (abbreviated)

2:07	**A**	Roach begins his chorus-long solo with a simple alternating of the bass and snare drums, followed by a lengthy passage on the snare drum.
2:10		He repeats the opening pattern.
2:12		The snare drum pattern continues, occasionally punctuated by accents from the bass drum.
2:18	**A**	Roach doesn't articulate the beginning of the second **A** section.
2:21		He plays a pattern of accents on the downbeat of each measure.
2:23		The drum accents turn into a cross-rhythm.
2:28		With a sudden two-note figure (*ch-bop!*), Roach ends his solo.

CODA

2:30		In a repetition of the introduction, Gillespie and Parker play the opening passage.
2:36		Gillespie improvises harmonically, while Roach quietly plays the backbeat behind him.
2:42		Parker fluently improvises on a harmonic progression that circles wildly through many key centers.
2:52		The back-and-forth octave exchange, which had previously served to introduce the first chorus, now returns as the piece's sudden and inconclusive end.

🎧 "Embraceable You"

Parker had an extraordinary musical memory. Through brief snippets quoted in his solos (such as the piccolo line from "High Society" in "Ko-Ko"), we can get a sense of how much music he processed and stored. He also loved classical composers, especially Stravinsky, whose early modernist pieces (*Petrushka, The Firebird*) deeply impressed the young saxophonist. And of course he knew hundreds of popular songs.

"Embraceable You" was recorded in 1948. Although the song is openly credited to George Gershwin, Parker avoids the well-known melody. At the beginning, where we expect to hear the tune, he substitutes a different pop song in its place: the 1939 "A Table in the Corner," recently recorded by swing bandleader Artie Shaw, fit into the harmonic progression of "Embraceable You" like a hand in a glove.

The remainder is a dazzling rhythmic swirl. Parker plays with a softness and earnestness that beautifully captures the song's romantic essence. Yet he barely touches the melody, floating instead on rapid, constantly shifting phrases. As is typical for a bebop recording, Parker's solo comes first, leaving Miles Davis the unenviable job of following in his wake. Davis may well have felt like trumpet player Howard McGhee, who also followed Parker on numerous recordings in the 1940s. "I used to hate to go to work," McGhee remembered, "knowing he would put a heavy whipping on me. And yet I couldn't wait to get there, because I knew what I was going to hear when I got there. And damn, he didn't never let me down."

LISTENING GUIDE

2.19

🎧 embraceable you

CHARLIE PARKER

Charlie Parker, alto saxophone; Miles Davis, trumpet; Duke Jordan, piano; Tommy Potter, bass; Max Roach, drums

- Label: Dial 1024; *Yardbird Suite: The Ultimate Collection* (Rhino/WEA 72260)
- Date: 1947
- Style: bebop
- Form: 32-bar popular song (**A B A C**)

What to listen for:
- extremely slow tempo
- Parker's improvisation within a romantic ballad
- his use of sequences, merely hinting at the song's melody
- early Davis solo

INTRODUCTION

0:00		The piano builds an introduction around a questioning four-note motive.

CHORUS 1

0:13	**A**	Parker quotes the melody to "A Table in a Corner." The accompaniment is simple: a slow **walking-bass** line, quiet piano chords, and the drums played almost inaudibly with brushes.
0:27		Having taken his quotation as far as it will go over the chord progression to "Embraceable You," Parker moves to bebop-style improvisation.
0:31		Over the next two measures, he plays a phrase that lags slightly behind the beat.
0:41	**B**	The high accented notes in his line derive from the melody to "Embraceable You" ("*Just* one look at *you* brings out the *gyp*-sy in me").

0:51		As Parker focuses his line onto one note, his tone becomes rougher and more intimate.
0:54		His rhythmic feeling begins to fall into **double time**.
1:00		Shifting suddenly to a more **staccato** articulation, Parker plays a line that's rhythmically unpredictable.
1:07		The next double-time lick is one of Parker's favorites.
1:10	**A**	
1:17		Parker plays a lick, then transposes by **sequence**, starting on a different pitch.
1:26		An impassioned entry results in a blown note.
1:29		The next phrase begins on a high note.
1:33		Parker plays another motive in sequence, moving it higher and higher.
1:38		Over a dominant chord, he raises the tension level by playing bebop dissonances.
1:40	**C**	After a silence, Parker continues in double time.
1:50		He begins his last phrase with a different rhythmic groove and more staccato articulation. His line emphasizes high notes on the downbeat, falling from there.

CHORUS 2 (abbreviated)

2:09	**B**	Davis begins quietly playing a lyrical line on muted trumpet. His line is restrained and simple, lacking Parker's dramatic rhythmic changes.
2:38		To signal the return to the **A** section, Roach adds a discreet roll with his brushes.
2:40	**A**	As Davis continues his solo, Parker plays hushed **countermelodies** behind him.
3:03		Roach suggests a double-time groove, but Davis declines to follow.
3:10	**C**	
3:19		Davis's improvisation, which is primarily **stepwise** (moving to adjacent notes), is interrupted by an octave lick; he repeats the lick a few seconds later.
3:26		The two horns together play the conclusion of "Embraceable You."

CODA

| 3:34 | | Underneath the horns' held-out note, the bass continues to walk while Roach plays a final roll. |

"Now's the Time"

Parker, who grew up with the blues in Kansas City, once described bebop as the collision of New York progressive intensity with the Midwestern blues. While working-class black audiences might have been alienated by bebop's intellectual complexity, he knew they would respond to what he called "red beans and rice music."

There were many kinds of blues in the 1940s. As African Americans adjusted to the demands of the industrial North, the blues changed, too. In addition to the swing bands, there were the harsh reinventions of Mississippi blues in Muddy Waters's electrified sound and the guitar virtuosity of T-Bone Walker. Parker added to the mix by melding the blues's vocal nuances to more chromatic harmonies and introducing a daringly fluid sense of rhythm. Parker showed how the blues could become modern, and many blues musicians showed they understood this by adopting his harmonies and rhythms. For their part, modern jazz musicians knew that every serious soloist must know how to play the blues.

"Now's the Time," an early Parker composition, is one of his simplest: it's built on a single riff, repeated and varied throughout the blues's twelve bars.

It was first recorded on the same session as "Ko-Ko" in 1945. Four years later, Savoy's proprietors conveniently ignored Parker's ownership of the melody, selling it as "The Huckle-Buck" for rhythm and blues saxophonist Paul Williams. "The one was jazz, the other was rock and roll, and we were hungry," explained go-between producer Teddy Reig. "And Lubinsky owned everything anyway." Linked in the public mind with a slow, erotic dance, "The Huckle-Buck" became a huge hit. It was soon covered by musicians ranging from Lucky Millinder to Frank Sinatra to Louis Armstrong. Even rock and roll singer Chubby Checker had a top-ten hit with it in 1961. Parker earned nothing from this, much as Ellington had felt robbed when his riff-laden "The Happy-Go-Lucky Local" was turned into the pop standard "Night Train."

This recording of "Now's the Time" comes toward the end of Parker's short life. By this point, Parker was recording for a major label (Norman Granz's Verve), and the sound is infinitely better. Nuances in the rhythm section, dimly audible in 1940s recordings, now take sonic precedence. In addition to Parker's masterful five-chorus solo, listen closely to Max Roach's drumming, which interacts brilliantly with Parker throughout.

LISTENING GUIDE

 now's the time

1.5

CHARLIE PARKER QUARTET
Charlie Parker, alto saxophone; Al Haig, piano; Percy Heath, bass; Max Roach, drums

- Label: Clef EPC208; *Bird's Best Bop* (Verve 731452745224)
- Date: 1953
- Style: bebop
- Form: 12-bar blues

What to listen for:
- explosive five-chorus Parker solo, at times imitating speech
- interaction between Parker and Roach
- solos by Roach and Heath

INTRODUCTION

0:00   Haig (piano) plays a four-bar introduction, accompanied by Roach's high-hat cymbal.

CHORUS 1 (HEAD)

0:05   Parker plays the opening riff. Roach answers in **call and response**.

0:10   As the harmony moves to IV, Parker ends his riff with a syncopated accent, doubled by the drums.

CHORUS 2 (HEAD)

0:20   In repeating the previous twelve bars, Parker leaves slight room for improvisation (notice the ad lib interpolation at 0:22).

CHORUS 3

0:35   Parker begins his five-chorus solo.

0:40   Over the "bluesiest" part of the progression (where the harmony moves to IV), Parker plays slightly behind the beat.

0:46   He plays a rapid **lick** (identical to the one at 1:08 in "Embraceable You").

CHORUS 4

0:49   Beginning of chorus.

0:53   Parker adds to his bluesy sound with a brief stuttering figure.

CHORUS 5

1:03   As he warms up, his rhythm imitates the looser, conversational quality of speech.

CHORUS 6

1:18   He takes a simple phrase and turns it into a complex **polyrhythm**.

CHORUS 7

1:32   Beginning of chorus.

1:44   Parker's last line signals the end of his solo, but still leaves us hanging.

CHORUS 8

1:46   After a brief pause, Haig begins his piano solo.

CHORUS 9

2:00   Haig's chorus begins with simple phrases, moves to fast, complicated phrases, and then returns to the style of the opening.

CHORUS 10

2:14   Heath (bass) takes a solo, accompanied by a tightly muffled cymbal and brief piano chords.

CHORUS 11

2:28   Roach takes a solo, alternating between the snare drum and bass drum.

CHORUS 12 (HEAD)

2:42   A repetition of the opening, but with more intense response from the rhythm section.

CODA

2:54   With a slight *ritard* (slowing down), Parker brings the piece to its end.

Bird's Last Flight

The collaboration between Charlie Parker and Dizzy Gillespie lasted only a few years. It foundered in 1945, when they took their band to Los Angeles in hopes of publicizing their new style of jazz on the West Coast. With its first exposure to bebop, California proved indifferent, even hostile. Disappointed, Gillespie took the band back home. Parker, still in thrall to drugs, cashed in his airplane ticket for money. For another year he remained in Southern California, sinking deeper into heroin addiction in a place where suppliers were few and far between. He not only titled a blues after a drug dealer ("Moose the Mooche"), but actually signed away his royalties for the record to him, hoping to keep his supplies intact. When heroin ran out, Parker switched to drinking heavily and using barbiturates.

The end of his California stay was unpleasant and highly public. In July 1947, Parker jumped at the chance to make a recording for Dial. The result is agonizingly captured on commercial recordings that he unsuccessfully tried to keep off the market. On "Lover Man," as he drifts in and out of the microphone's range, jagged fragments of bebop-style technique intermingle with a harrowing performance of the melody. Parker lasted only a few tunes before collapsing. Later that night, he strolled through his hotel lobby wearing only his socks, and was arrested after accidentally setting fire to his bed. Convinced he was a schizophrenic, the local police chained him to a cot and committed him to a state hospital. There he would remain for another six months.

For a brief time, Parker was free of his drug addiction. Feeling relaxed and physically fit, he returned to New York. But there was no escape from heroin. "They can get it out of your blood," he once said, "but they can't get it out of your mind." For the remainder of his life, his artistic genius was steadily undercut by physical and professional decline. Miles Davis, who played with him for several years, finally left in disgust in 1949, fed up with his "childish, stupid" behavior. "All we wanted to do was to play great music, and Bird was acting like a fool, some kind of . . . clown."

Parker's last years played out on two different levels simultaneously. In his more ambitious mode, he found a trace of commercial success through impresario Norman Granz, who consistently supported him and helped him gain a contract with Mercury Records. Granz found new venues for Parker's expertise, including recordings with strings, in which his alto saxophone was treated in much the same way that vocal stars were cushioned by the "classy" sound of orchestral instruments. One of these, the 1949 "Just Friends," was his most successful record. He also continued to perform straight-ahead bebop tunes and made some of his finest recordings (including "Now's the Time").

With strings

But his drug addiction made him increasingly unreliable and eventually wore him out physically. He was thirty-four at the time of his death in 1955, but the coroner estimated the age of his enervated body as fifty-three. His passing received little or purely sensationalist notice in the press, but all the musicians knew. In some ways, it marked the end of the bebop period.

The Elder Statesman

Dizzy Gillespie offered a different model. Unlike Parker, he disdained hard drugs. His career demonstrated how bebop could be the musical and professional foundation for working jazz musicians.

On returning from California in 1946, Gillespie sensed that the larger public was ready for his music in a more conventional framework. He formed a big band, once again adapting his bebop arrangements to the full resources of a swing dance orchestra. But leading a dance band was not comfortable for him: when he was not playing his trumpet, he had trouble knowing how to act. Eventually, he borrowed from an unexpected source: his former employer, Cab Calloway.

Gillespie become comfortable with a stage persona appropriate for his time: like Louis Armstrong, he balanced his artistry against his wit and penchant for genial silliness. Gillespie brought his bebop-flavored big-band entertainment to cheering crowds for the rest of his life. Audiences not ready for bebop could still enjoy his mordant sense of humor, his hip-twisting dancing, and his elaborate scat-singing translations of bebop riffs on tunes like "Oop-Bop-Sh'Bam" and "Ool-Ya-Koo." Through all this, the bebop lines shone through, the trumpet section performing brilliant lines that sounded as close to Gillespie's as possible.

As bebop declined in popularity through the 1950s, Gillespie remained clean-living, gregarious,

One night in 1953, an accident on stage pushed the bell of Dizzy Gillespie's trumpet upward. Realizing that this new design compensated for a lifetime habit of looking down while playing, Gillespie asked a trumpet manufacturer to make all of his horns that way.

© CHUCK STEWART

and generous to a fault. While some of his colleagues converted to the more militant forms of black Islam, Gillespie became devoted to Baha'i, a gentle religion committed to ideals of unity and peace. For years he managed to keep his big band active and nurtured the careers of such musicians as John Lewis, Ray Brown, Milt Jackson, John Coltrane, James Moody, Yusef Lateef, Jimmy Heath, Lee Morgan, Kenny Barron, and his protégé, trumpet player Jon Faddis. In the 1950s, when the State Department began to realize that jazz could be used as a weapon of propaganda overseas, Gillespie took his band on official tours, carefully balancing his patriotism against his insistence on speaking openly about the state of American race relations.

Over time, Gillespie's eccentricities melted into the stuff of celebrity. His goatee, his beret, his specially raised trumpet (designed to compensate for a lifetime habit of playing with the bell pointed down), and especially his cheek muscles made him instantly recognizable. In later years, as his chops gradually declined, Gillespie played less and joked more. Yet his musical inquisitiveness still led him to new discoveries, such as ethnic traditions he discovered overseas and the avant-garde traditions of the 1960s (in the 1980s, he employed avant-garde saxophonist Sam Rivers). As jazz continued to build a sense of tradition, Gillespie remained a central figure until his death in 1993. He was the elder statesman of bebop.

THE BEBOP GENERATION

Parker and Gillespie were only the most visible part of the bebop generation. In the 1940s, hundreds of young musicians, mostly but not exclusively black, were swept up into the new jazz, pulled by a modernist sensitivity to previously unseen social and musical realities. Like Amiri Baraka (see box), they felt in bebop a new aesthetics and derived from it a renewed sense of purpose.

The path was not easy. Some musicians, watching Charlie Parker, concluded that his musical achievements were somehow associated with drugs and became hooked on heroin. Theodore Navarro, one of Gillespie's most brilliant followers on trumpet, made just a few dozen recordings before succumbing to addiction. Nicknamed "Fats" or "Fat Girl" because of his stocky weight, he died emaciated from tuberculosis—just "skin and bones," as Miles Davis remembered him. Others, like Red Rodney, who for nearly a year played trumpet alongside Parker, found their careers interrupted by incarceration for drug use before finally kicking heroin once and for all.

Nevertheless, the technical achievements of this generation were remarkable. Who would have imagined, on first hearing Parker play in the early 1940s, that anyone could equal him in speed and fury? Yet hard on his heels came the alto saxophonist Edward "Sonny" Stitt, whose style so

Voices

In his autobiography, poet and critic Amiri Baraka (aka LeRoi Jones) reflects on his first exposure to bebop recordings in the mid-1940s.

I listened to bebop after school, over and over. At first it was strange and the strangeness itself was strangely alluring. Bebop! I listened and listened. And began learning the names of musicians and times and places and events. Bird, Diz, Max, Klook, Monk, Miles, Getz, and eventually secondary jive like *Downbeat*, *Metronome*, [jazz critics Leonard] Feather [and Barry] Ulanov, began to be part of my world and words. . . .

And I wasn't even sure what the music was. Bebop! A new language a new tongue and vision for a generally more advanced group in our generation. Bebop was a staging area for a new sensibility growing to maturity. And the beboppers themselves were blowing the sound to attract the growing, the developing, the about-to-see. . . .

My father had asked me one day, "Why do you want to be a bopper?" Who knows what I said. I couldn't have explained it then. Bebop suggested *another* mode of being. Another way of living. Another way of perceiving reality—connected to the one I'd had—blue/black and brown but also pushing past that to something else. Strangeness. Weirdness. The unknown!

closely resembled Parker's that for a time he switched to tenor, hoping to avoid the unflattering comparison ("Don't call me Bird!" he once begged a journalist). As for the tenor saxophone, Parker's influence was filtered through Coleman Hawkins's harmonic mastery and Lester Young's cool idiom, resulting in the syntheses pioneered by Lucky Thompson, Don Byas, and Illinois Jacquet. The trombonist J. J. Johnson kept pace with his peers by jettisoning his instrument's limited rips and smears for a cool, angular, and unbelievably swift sound. Bebop spread to the baritone saxophone (Serge Chaloff, Gerry Mulligan, Leo Parker), to the vibraphone (Milt Jackson), and to virtually any instrument playing jazz.

The unstable but brilliant Bud Powell transferred bebop's electric pace to the piano keyboard. He's seen performing at Birdland in 1949.

■ BUD POWELL (1924–1966)

Bud Powell, the finest pianist of the bebop generation, came by his talent naturally. His father was a New York stride pianist, his older brother played trumpet and hired young Bud for his first gigs, and his younger brother Richie became a bop pianist. Powell was drilled in classical music technique, but he also became fascinated by jazz. As a teenager, he frequented Minton's Playhouse, where Thelonious Monk spotted his talents: "I was the only one who dug him," Monk once said. "Nobody understood what he was playing." Monk may have initially intuited that the brilliant pianist was best suited to interpret his own challenging compositions. In return, Powell showed a stubborn loyalty to Monk's music, featuring Monk's knotty "Off Minor" on his first recording session in 1947.

Powell's career initially shot upward. He dropped out of high school at nineteen to join the swing band of Cootie Williams, then on leave from Duke Ellington. (To assuage Powell's parents, Williams served as his legal guardian.) Powell fit in beautifully with the music's elite, as broadcast recordings show. But while he was touring with the band in Philadelphia, he was brutally beaten by the police, leaving him with crippling headaches.

It was the beginning of a long nightmare. For a full third of his adult life, Powell was subjected to psychiatric supervision typical for black people of the day that now seems hostile and punitive. He was incarcerated and medicated, and underwent electroshock treatments so severe that they affected his memory. Alto saxophonist Jackie McLean remembered conversations about the day's events that ended in befuddlement. "He had to stop and think and ask me, 'Who?' and 'Tell me about it. . . . or 'What did I do?'" Combine this confusion with a weakness for alcohol so profound that a single drink might leave him slumped against a wall, and it's hard to believe that he was able to function at all, let alone forge a career as a jazz pianist.

Piano Style

Powell did more than that. His ingenious piano technique became the foundation for all bebop pianists to follow. While his left hand played a neutral backdrop of chords, his right hand would explode into a brilliant improvisatory cascade, rivaling (and even surpassing) Parker and Gillespie in rhythmic imagination. Watching Powell play was almost frighteningly intense. The jazz critic Ira Gitler, who observed him at close quarters, described him as "one with the music itself": "Right leg digging into the floor at an odd angle, pants leg up to almost the top of the shin, shoulders hunched, upper lip tight against the teeth, mouth emitting an accompanying guttural song to what the steel fingers were playing, vein in temple throbbing violently as perspiration popped out all over his scalp and ran down his face and neck."

Sometimes Powell used what pianists call block chords: combining his two hands to play a melody supported by rich chords, like a big-band *soli*. On other occasions, he played stride piano, borrowing from the overshadowing presence of Art Tatum: his version of "Over the Rainbow," for example, is stride scattered with Tatum-like runs. But most recordings featured him accompanied by bass and drums. Indeed, he did far more than any other pianist of his time in pioneering this now-standard piano trio format (piano, bass, drums), replacing the rhythm guitar favored by Art Tatum with the rhythmic power of drummers like Roy Haynes, Art Blakey, and Max Roach.

🎧 "Tempus Fugue-It"

Early 1949 was a good time for Bud Powell. He had just emerged from Creedmore Sanitorium, where he had been incarcerated for several months, and felt ready to make a record for Clef, one of the labels owned by the young Norman Granz (see below). It was a brief window, as he soon returned to Creedmore for more treatment. It's hard to imagine musical creativity taking place under these conditions, but Powell seems in full form, ready to display not only his pianistic fancy but also his talent as a composer.

On these recordings, accompanied by Ray Brown and Max Roach, he turned out a number of masterpieces. A dazzlingly fast and imaginatively reharmonized "Cherokee" revisited territory already claimed by Charlie Parker, while the relaxed and gentle "Celia" was dedicated to its namesake, his newborn daughter. The darkly colored "Tempus Fugue-It" suggests Powell's familiarity with Baroque music (a fugue is a challenging form of polyphonic composition) as well as the Latin proverb *tempus fugit* (time flies). The form is simple: thirty-two-bar **A A B A,** with the **A** section barely moving from the tonic. Harmonic variety is pushed to the bridge, which moves rapidly form chord to chord.

"Tempus Fugue-It" shows Powell pushing his technique to the limit. There are undoubtedly a few miscalculations that later recordings, armed with tape and digital technology, would have edited out. What we have instead is a document that captures the intensity Powell brought to his improvisation at the piano.

Un Poco Loco

Powell was also an important composer, drawing on his knowledge of Baroque counterpoint as well as his command of modern jazz harmony. In light of his mental instability, it's telling that some of his best-known tunes, like "Hallucinations" and "Un Poco Loco," have painfully self-reflective titles. "Un Poco Loco" is a blisteringly fast Latin tune, pitting Powell's frenetic energy against Max Roach's hypnotic polyrhythmic accompaniment.

By the end of the 1950s, Powell had moved to France, where adoring crowds watched him gradually disintegrate. There were times when he

2.20

 **tempus fugue-it**

BUD POWELL

Bud Powell, piano; Ray Brown, bass; Max Roach, drums

- Label: Clef 11045; *The Complete Bud Powell on Verve* (Verve 731452166920)
- Date: 1949
- Style: bebop
- Form: 32-bar popular song (**A A B A**)

> **What to listen for:**
> - Powell's translation of bebop soloing to piano
> - his complex chords, changes, and polyrhythmic ostinatos
> - his simple octaves at the end of chorus 2
> - harmonic variety in the bridge section

INTRODUCTION

0:00		Powell jumps in unaccompanied, playing a line in **octaves**. Its last few notes are accented by the drums.
0:04		He juxtaposes a dissonant note in the right hand with syncopated chords in the left.

CHORUS 1 (HEAD)

0:07	**A**	The opening melody is a sinuous bebop line with stops and starts. Each empty beat is filled in by a subtle brush hit on the drums.
0:14	**A**	
0:20	**B**	The melody is nearly overshadowed by a powerful bass line played in octaves by the left hand.
0:25		Dissonant chords are decorated with fast **grace notes** (ornamental, quickly played notes).
0:27	**A**	

INTERLUDE

0:34		Disjointed chords enter in unexpected rhythms, doubled by the bass and drums.
0:37		During a two-measure **break**, Powell begins his solo.

CHORUS 2

0:39	**A**	Powell plays a fast, elaborate melody in the right hand. When the melody pauses, we can hear his left hand alternating neutral, open harmonies with a sharp dissonance (the **flatted fifth**) deep in the bass.
0:45	**A**	He fills the next eight bars with a continuous phrase.
0:51	**B**	As the harmonies change, he improvises a line that matches the notes of each chord.
0:58	**A**	The drums interact with the line, adding sharp accents with the brushes.
1:01		Powell ends the chorus with simple octaves. (We'll see the same technique in Monk's "Thelonious" in Chapter 13.) The left hand maintains tension by lingering on the dissonant interval.

CHORUS 3

1:04	**A**	Powell plays a short fragment over and over that clashes **polyrhythmically** with the meter.
1:10	**A**	The same polyrhythmic effect is created by a new melodic fragment.
1:17	**B**	Over the rapidly moving harmony, Powell begins a line that disappears a few measures later, as if his concentration were temporarily thrown off.
1:20		After a few beats, he begins a new line that continues well into the next **A** section.
1:23	**A**	

CHORUS 4

1:29	A	Powell repeats the fragment from the previous chorus, with less precision.
1:35	A	In an apparent miscalculation, he begins playing the chords to the bridge. After a bar or two, he realizes his mistake and seamlessly corrects himself.
1:41	B	Now he plays the correct chords with exactitude.
1:45		For a few beats, he's suddenly disrupted from the groove, playing a few notes out of rhythm.
1:47	A	Within a few seconds, he returns to his brilliantly quick improvised line.

CHORUS 5 (HEAD)

1:53	A	Powell plays the head an octave higher, matching pitch to the heat of performance.
1:59	A	
2:06	B	
2:12	A	

CODA

2:18	As a signal for the ending, Powell repeats the last phrase.
2:19	He holds out the last chord, a dissonantly voiced tonic, with a **tremolo**.

returned to his youthful self, performing at the peak of his ability. On other occasions he would play haltingly or stop, staring blankly at the wall with what Miles Davis once described as a "secret, faraway smile." Within a few years, he died of tuberculosis. Like Charlie Parker, he was a musician whose legacy lay as much in what he could have done as in what he actually did.

JAZZ IN LOS ANGELES: CENTRAL AVENUE

Bebop was born in Harlem and nurtured on New York's 52nd Street, but it also resonated, three thousand miles away, on the West Coast. Although geographically remote, Southern California had rivaled New York as the center of the national entertainment industry since the birth of film. And jazz had been a part of California life ever since vaudeville brought the music west early in the century. Restless New Orleans musicians used California as a convenient second home, easily reachable by railroad lines running direct from the Crescent City. It was in Los Angeles that the first recording by a black jazz band (led by trombonist Kid Ory) was made in 1922, a year earlier than King Oliver's band in Chicago.

The jazz scene in Los Angeles spread along Central Avenue, which ran southward from downtown toward the black suburb of Watts. Los Angeles absorbed thousands of black workers through the Great Migration, but treated them with Southern disdain: musicians who worked there referred to it as "Mississippi with palm trees." Central Avenue was the core of a narrow, all-black neighborhood, thirty blocks long and only a few blocks wide. ("Housing covenants" in other neighborhoods prevented white residents from selling their property to people from other races.) The avenue was crowded and lively, and became even more so during World War II. With its extensive shipbuilding industry, California took a disproportionate share of defense contracts, pulling unemployed workers to the West Coast. During the war, Los Angeles's black population more than doubled, from 64,000 in 1940 to about 175,000 in 1945.

Central Avenue was a Mecca for entertainment, offering its share of blues, comedy, dance, and early rhythm and blues. In 1945, that scene began to include modern jazz, with Coleman Hawkins's quintet, bop groups led by trumpet player Howard McGhee, and Dizzy Gillespie and Charlie Parker's quintet. Musicians adopted the new language as quickly as possible. Soon there was a bevy of young California bebop practitioners, led by the young tenor saxophonist Dexter Gordon.

■ DEXTER GORDON (1923–1990)

Gordon was a product of the black middle class. His father, a jazz-loving doctor, counted Lionel Hampton and Duke Ellington among his celebrity patients and took his young son to hear the big swing bands that came regularly to the West Coast. At the integrated Jefferson High School, Dexter studied clarinet with Sam Browne, the school's first black teacher, who demanded excellence from all his students. He soon switched from clarinet to saxophone, with Browne keeping him after school to work on his scales. In the evenings, Gordon studied with swing veteran Lloyd Reese, who drilled local students (including Eric Dolphy and Charles Mingus) in the intricacies of complex chromatic harmony and ran a rehearsal band.

Like many aspiring tenor players, Gordon initially saw Coleman Hawkins as the model for harmonic improvisation. "Hawk was the master of the horn," he later said, "a musician who did everything possible with it, the right way." But his creative inspiration was Lester Young, whom he first heard when the Basie band came to Los Angeles in 1939. Gordon became fascinated by Young's "bittersweet approach" to melody and rhythm. "When Pres appeared, we all started listening to him alone. Pres had an entirely new sound, one we seemed to be waiting for."

Few saxophonists seemed more elegant than Dexter Gordon, who made looking cool a top priority for the bebop generation. "It ain't got nothing to do with money," he once told the young Miles Davis, "it's got something to do with hipness." New York, 1948.

Dexter Rides Again

The next phase of Gordon's education began when he joined the Lionel Hampton band at age seventeen. In the saxophone section, he sat next to Illinois Jacquet, a hard-blowing tenor saxophonist whose exuberant improvisation on Hampton's hit "Flying Home" foreshadowed the rhythm and blues revolution. From Jacquet, Gordon learned how to construct an extroverted solo. Other bands (Fletcher Henderson, Louis Armstrong) added invaluable professional experience. In New York, he was introduced to bebop, and studied music theory with Dizzy Gillespie. His first encounter with Charlie Parker's penetrating brilliance left him speechless. Under Parker's influence, he drifted into the bebop orbit, adding a new level of rhythmic intensity to his music—as well as an addiction to heroin that would haunt him for much of his life.

Of the new bebop saxophonists, Gordon was the most flamboyant. On the street, he cut a fine figure, dressing in the latest style with wide-shouldered suits accentuating his lanky frame and topped by a wide-brimmed hat that made him seem "about seven feet tall." He was so good-looking that some thought he should be an actor, an ambition that was in fact fulfilled: in 1960, he played a musician in the West Coast production of Jack Gelber's New York hit *The Connection,* and twenty years later earned an Oscar nomination for his lead role in the movie *'Round Midnight.*

But it was his musical style that turned people's heads. Gordon combined the looseness of Lester Young, playing slightly behind the beat, with Parker's rhythmic intricacies. He was also quirky and humorous, with a charming habit of quoting popular songs, suggesting that just beneath the language of bebop lay a world made up of beautiful Tin Pan Alley melodies. Before performing a ballad, he would often quote the tune's lyrics, as if inviting his listeners to take part in the deeper world of the song.

Wardell Gray ▶

Gordon's style of improvising was forged in the jam sessions he attended. He could be ruthless and efficient, using his quick-witted command of phrases to leave his competitors helpless. One of his partners was Wardell Gray, a fellow saxophonist from Oklahoma City who sparred with Gordon at Jack's Basket on Central Avenue, a fried-chicken joint where musicians gathered for late-night jam sessions. "There'd be a lot of cats on the stand," Gordon remembered, "but by the end of the session, it would wind up with Wardell and myself." A memento of these occasions was "The Chase" (1947), a frenzied tenor saxophone battle spread out over two sides of a 78-rpm recording for Dial. Featuring Gordon and Gray trading eight-, four-, and finally two-bar segments, it was one of the longest jazz improvisations on record.

🎧 "Long Tall Dexter"

In January 1946, Gordon brought a youthful all-star group into Savoy Records' studio. The rhythm section included pianist Bud Powell (twenty-one), drummer Max Roach (twenty-two), and veteran bassist Curley Russell (at twenty-eight the oldest musician present). The trumpet player was Leonard Hawkins, a high-school friend of Roach's from Brooklyn who was making his recording debut. But the focus was on Gordon, as the recordings from that day made clear: "Dexter Rides Again," "Dexter Digs In," and a blues that took a nickname inspired by Gordon's six-foot-five-inch frame, "Long Tall Dexter." The tune is built on a simple riff that, like the riff in Parker's "Now's the Time," strategically introduces an unexpected bit of dissonance (0:13).

Gordon's five-chorus solo on "Long Tall Dexter," beginning in a dramatic way with chorus 3, is a perfectly paced masterpiece, a condensation of what he might use to win out in a jam session. After he and Hawkins play a **send-off riff** (a composed segment that takes up the first four bars of a chorus), Gordon enters on an unexpected note, held for a long time before dissolving into a dissonance. The remainder of this chorus is simple and restrained, setting up what is to come. In chorus 4, he expands the range of his solo, sending his line into a number of sharp dissonances (e.g., at 0:51).

But it's with chorus 5 that Gordon begins ratcheting up the intensity. Restricting himself to a single note, he punches out riffs with rhythms so unpredictable that Powell and Roach are virtually pulled into the conversation. From here the riffs keep piling on, until at the beginning of chorus 7 we reach a climax of virtuosic display. At 1:20, Gordon drops to a honking low note—

the sort of gesture that would soon be a staple of nearly all rhythm and blues saxophonists. And in the solo's last few measures (1:39), Gordon cools down the temperature with false fingerings, a delicate and inventive way of inserting a bluesy gesture at the end.

🎧 long tall dexter

2.21

DEXTER GORDON QUINTET

Dexter Gordon, tenor saxophone; Leonard Hawkins, trumpet; Bud Powell, piano; Curley Russell, bass; Max Roach, drums

- Label: Dial 603; *Dexter Digs In* (Savoy Jazz 17546)
- Date: 1946
- Style: bebop
- Form: 12-bar blues

What to listen for:

- simple 12-bar blues riff, spiced with dissonance
- send-off riff in chorus 3
- Gordon's masterful five-chorus solo (choruses 3–7)

INTRODUCTION

0:00   Over a shimmer of cymbals, Roach creates a complex **polyrhythm** on the drums, alternating strokes on the snare and bass drum.

CHORUS 1 (HEAD)

0:04   Gordon (tenor saxophone) and Hawkins (trumpet) play the simple riff-based melody in **octaves**. Underneath, Powell comps with dense, dissonant chords on piano.

0:07   Hawkins adds a slight but noticeable rhythmic decoration to the head.

0:08   Roach punctuates the end of the phrase with a sharp snare drum accent.

0:09   As the harmony changes from I to IV, the riff figure adjusts by flatting one of the notes.

0:13   The horns play a simple ascending scale. When the harmony changes to V, they move it up a half step, creating an intense dissonance.

CHORUS 2 (HEAD)

0:18   As is typical for bebop blues, the head is repeated.

0:31   Gordon lets his last note tail off.

CHORUS 3

0:32   The two horns play a **send-off riff**—a composed four-bar melody designed to lead directly to the next soloist. This riff is built on a **harmonic substitution,** beginning with a remote harmony that modulates quickly back home to the tonic.

0:34   At its conclusion, the send-off riff becomes stridently dissonant, featuring **flatted fifths** against the prevailing harmony.

0:37   As the harmony shifts to IV, Gordon enters with a long-held note that finally descends to yet another dissonance, the chord's flatted fifth.

0:45   Roach punctuates the chorus's end with a few loud **fills**.

CHORUS 4

0:46   Gordon plays even strings of notes that climb into his highest register.

0:51   He plays a prominently dissonant note over the IV chord.

CHORUS 5

1:00   Gordon plays punchy, short riffs in continually changing rhythms. The drummer and pianist respond by filling in the spaces.

1:09   After reaching its melodic peak, the phrase winds down.

CHORUS 6

1:15   Gordon starts a new riff, maintaining a simple rhythm (long, short-short) while shifting the pitch in sequence.

1:20   Over the IV chord, he drops down to a sonorous low note. When he repeats the figure, the note moves up a half step to a sharp dissonance.

1:25   As the chorus ends, he plays a rhythmically intricate riff.

CHORUS 7

1:29   Gordon compresses the riff into a long, complex phrase that finally ends in a repeated note.

1:39   Using **false fingering,** he creates a note with a hollow timbre. Because it's slightly less than a half step higher and falls on the third degree of the scale, it has a distinctly bluesy tone.

CHORUS 8

1:43   Slightly off-microphone, Hawkins enters with the send-off riff. Gordon enters after a moment's hesitation.

1:48   Hawkins's solo begins with a simple two-note phrase. Immediately afterward, the drums stop playing for a several beats, creating an unexpected sense of space.

1:52   Hawkins plays the rest of his solo with a broad, open tone, **ghosted** notes, and occasional rapid bebop-style decorations.

1:57   Roach responds with rapid fills.

CHORUS 9

1:58   As Hawkins digs into a short riff, his timbre becomes coarser.

2:03   For a brief moment, he makes an apparent mistake: he hits a note that contradicts the IV harmony underneath.

CHORUS 10

2:12   Powell enters in octaves, emphasizing the first note with a "crushed" grace note. In the background, you can hear his rough singing.

2:16   He accompanies his intricate right-hand melodies with simple lines and two-note "shells" of chords in the left.

CHORUS 11

2:27   Powell suggests a faster, double-time feeling.

CHORUS 12

2:41   Instead of reprising the head, the two horns play a different (if equally simple) riff-based tune.

2:46   As the harmony shifts, the riff's top-most note is flatted.

CODA

2:54   A final new melodic phrase closes out the piece.

2:56   At the piece's end, Roach continues playing.

2:58   Powell has the last word with a dissonant lick that ends a **tritone** away from the tonic.

Homecoming

For Gordon, the 1950s were a mess. His playing time was continually interrupted by jail sentences for heroin use, culminating with a stint in California's notorious Folsom Prison. But in the next decade, he firmly reestablished his reputation as one of the finest saxophonists of his generation, recording masterful albums for Blue Note, including *Go!* (1962) and *Our Man in Paris* (1963). As the latter title suggests, he spent much of his time in Europe, where black musicians could take refuge from racial prejudice. For years he lived in an apartment in Copenhagen, where he mastered Danish, played locally, and toured the Continent. "Since I've been over here," he told an interviewer, "I've felt that I could breathe, and just be more or less a human being, without being white or black."

When he returned home to New York and opened at the Village Vanguard in 1976, he received the welcome he deserved. In his last years, Gordon occupied a role he was never to relinquish—the elder statesman of acoustic jazz. Shrewd promotion by Columbia helped his last albums succeed, and film acting made him for the first time widely visible. Until his death in 1990, Gordon remained a living example of what depth of experience could bring to jazz.

AFTERMATH: BEBOP AND POP

For a brief time in the late 1940s, bebop was aggressively marketed as popular music. As the swing bands began to fade, the music industry turned nervously to the new jazz style, offering it to the marketplace as both edgy modern music and comic novelty. Its public face was Dizzy Gillespie, whose peculiarities of dress (goatee, horn-rimmed glasses, and beret) gave cartoonists a convenient shorthand for jazz modernism. Jazz slang was parodied (endless repetitions of "cool," "daddy-o") and ultimately became beatnik clichés in the 1950s. Gillespie contributed to the confusion when he appeared in *Life* magazine in 1948, exchanging a "bebop handshake" with Benny Carter, their high fives supposedly representing the flatted fifth. "There was no such thing in real life," Gillespie later explained. "It was just a bunch of horseplay that we went through so they could pretend we were something weird. . . . We were helping to make bebop seem like just another fad, which it wasn't."

Bandleaders like Woody Herman and Benny Goodman enjoyed a number of hits with bebop-flavored arrangements, but their popularity quickly faded. Audiences became aware of bebop's dark underside through the highly publicized arrests of heroin addicts. The media began to treat the style as a vaguely degenerate idea whose time had passed. Leonard Feather published a landmark overview of the music's origins, *Inside Be-Bop*, in 1949; when it was later reprinted, he dropped the arcane word in favor of the more neutral title *Inside Jazz*.

Still, at the same time that bebop failed as popular music, it gained strength among musicians. As professionals, they saw it less as a fashion than a musical system to be mastered. Indeed, to become a jazz musician meant learning to play like Charlie Parker and Dizzy Gillespie. Nor has much changed today. More than sixty years later, young jazz novices still learn to improvise by studiously practicing transcriptions of Parker solos. Bebop has become the foundation for modern jazz and a symbol of professional identity for its musicians.

The challenge to bebop in the 1940s, if it couldn't be marketed as popular music, was finding a niche. How could anyone get large audiences to appreciate this music? The solution lay in offering the public bebop as it was: as a jam session (or cutting contest), but one that turned into a rowdy, aggressive public spectacle, held in large auditoriums across the country. Nobody was more central to this transformation than Norman Granz.

Norman Granz's tough, determined personality made him an ideal impresario for jazz; it combined with his idealism to make him a champion for civil rights. He's seen here in the 1950s.

JAZZ AT THE PHILHARMONIC

Granz (1918–2001), the son of Ukrainian immigrants, grew up in Los Angeles, where he supported himself in college by working part-time as a film editor. He was also a record collector, and became familiar with jazz in local clubs. Like John Hammond's, Granz's approach to jazz was both musical and political. He found the musicians endlessly fascinating and was repelled by the racial discrimination that determined their lives. His first concerts, held toward the end of the war (1944), were aggressively interracial, designed both to promote jazz and to attack long-held habits of segregation.

One of his earliest venues was Los Angeles's center of classical music life, the venerable Philharmonic Hall. By featuring his favorite freelance musicians there, both white and black, in jam-session-style groups, Granz attracted a large, jazz-loving audience. Such subversive behavior was not long tolerated. In 1946, his concerts at the Philharmonic were banned, allegedly because of the management's fear of violence from rowdy audiences. (Granz himself insisted the managers were horrified by the sight of mixed-race couples in the crowd.) By this time, Granz was ready to take his concerts on the road. As a kind of revenge, he named his touring show Jazz at the Philharmonic.

Jazz at the Philharmonic (JATP) did not distinguish between styles. At its core were a handful of stars from the Swing Era: Coleman Hawkins, Roy Eldridge, Buck Clayton, and Lester Young were eager for lucrative employment in the waning days of the big bands. But Granz also admired the innovations of bebop and included both Dizzy Gillespie and Charlie Parker in his early concerts, as well as soloists whose frenetic posturing evoked the nascent world of rhythm and blues. The result was a "nervous jazz," heavy on improvisation, that according to jazz critic Whitney Balliett hovered "somewhere between small-band swing and bebop."

Granz made the jam session format accessible to the casual fan by underscoring its competitive nature: honking saxophonists jostled for the microphone, trumpets screeched their highest notes. "I like my musicians to be friends offstage," he once said. "But when they're on stage, I want blood." Critics hated it, complaining of vulgarity and crassness. Audiences responded with gusto, even in staid concert auditoriums. The atmosphere at a JATP concert was as different from a classical music performance as one could imagine. Young people matched the visceral enthusiasm of what they saw onstage with ear-splitting whistles and cheers. The "heated teenage faces," Balliett noted, resembled the jitterbuggers who danced in the aisles at Benny Goodman's theater gigs in the 1930s but were "more warlike": "They rarely move from their seats, yet they manage to give off through a series of screams (the word 'go' repeated like the successive slams of the cars on a fast freight), blood-stopping whistles, and stamping feet a mass intensity that would have made Benny Goodman pale."

Granz profited handsomely from this madness, becoming in effect the first man to make a million from jazz and a major figure in postwar music. (He also recorded his concerts; see Chapter 12.) Well before the civil rights movement, he insisted that his band of black and white musicians perform before equally integrated audiences; if promoters balked, he was ready to withdraw the entire show. He took a special interest in the careers of Ella Fitzgerald and pianist Oscar Peterson, making both international stars and encouraging Fitzgerald to bridge the worlds of jazz and pop.

As twenty-first-century jazz listeners, we may thank Norman Granz for his long-term fight to have jazz performed in concert halls. Granted, the nature of jazz concerts has changed: even in the 1950s, the juvenile hysteria JATP thrived on was already being passed on to rock and roll performances. These days, a concert hall is but one option available for jazz musicians, and audience behavior is undoubtedly much closer there to a classical concert than Granz may have liked. Yet everyone can benefit from a smokeless, comfortable, and acoustically perfect place to hear jazz, to say nothing of the social prestige that rubs off on the music from such surroundings.

A SHORT-LIVED ERA

The bebop "era" didn't last long. Some might date it to 1955, the year of Charlie Parker's death, but in truth the excitement over bebop had long since passed. Not that musicians didn't acknowledge the debt they owed to Parker and Gillespie: if anything, they remained obsessed with mastering the new musical language. But the 1950s were dominated by new trends, based in bebop but shifting in new directions. The next chapter examines two such movements, drawing on different aesthetics and situated in the racial politics of the moment: cool jazz and hard bop.

ADDITIONAL LISTENING	
Jay McShann	"Hootie Blues" (1941); *Hootie Blues* (Stony Plain 1315)
Cab Calloway	"Pickin' the Cabbage" (1940); *New York, 1939–1940*, vol. D (JSP 2006)
Dizzy Gillespie and Charlie Parker	"Sweet Georgia Brown" (1943); *The Complete Birth of the Bebop* (Stash STCD 535)
Charlie Parker	"Parker's Mood" (1948), "Lover Man" (1946); *The Complete Savoy and Dial Master Takes* (Savoy Jazz 17149)
	"Just Friends" (1949); *Charlie Parker with Strings: The Master Takes* (Verve 2354)
Dizzy Gillespie	"Salt Peanuts" (1945); *Groovin' High* (Naxos 8.120582)
	"A Night in Tunisia," "52nd Street Theme" (1946); *Night in Tunisia: The Very Best of Dizzy Gillespie* (Bluebird/Legacy 828768486627)
Dexter Gordon	"Love for Sale" (1962); *Go* (Blue Note CD 98794)
Dexter Gordon and Wardell Gray	"The Chase" (1947); *Dexter Gordon: The Complete Dial Sessions* (Stash B000006N18)
Bud Powell	"Hallucinations" (1951); *The Definitive Bud Powell* (Blue Note 40042)
	"Un Poco Loco" (1951); *The Amazing Bud Powell*, vol. 1 (Blue Note 32136)
Woody Herman	"Caldonia" (1945); *Woody Herman, Blowin' Up a Storm: The Columbia Years, 1945-1947* (Legacy)

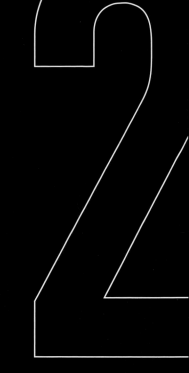

MILES DAVIS
moon dreams

MODERN JAZZ QUARTET
all the things you are

HORACE SILVER
the preacher

CLIFFORD BROWN
a night in tunisia

SONNY ROLLINS
autumn nocturne

WES MONTGOMERY
twisted blues

THE 1950s:
COOL JAZZ AND HARD BOP

NEW SCHOOLS

The emergence of bebop in the 1940s created a kind of Rubicon that many fans, critics, and musicians could not cross. They had come to jazz in the years of swing, when it functioned as dance music with an unembarrassed emphasis on entertainment, and they dismissed bebop as a fad; when it failed to fade, they lost interest in jazz. Far from fading, bop became so much the language of jazz that even young musicians who played in swing or traditional styles adapted elements of the new harmonies, rhythms, and melodies.

As we have seen, the leading bop figures were no less eager to please their audiences than their predecessors: Dizzy Gillespie was a master showman, and Charlie Parker introduced strings in an attempt to popularize his music. Still, the very intricacy of bebop made it a more introverted, intellectual listening experience. The music had evolved, and no single musician could be depicted as a defining figure for its entire canvas. Jazz now had a convoluted history: from New Orleans traditionalism to the styles developed in Northern and Midwestern cities to swing to bop. In the 1950s, additional styles grew out of bebop—cool jazz, hard bop, funk, avant-garde, and others—leading music historians to speak of jazz in terms of schools, as if it had splintered off into discrete realms.

Dave Brubeck pioneered unusual time signatures and became emblematic of jazz as a hip, sophisticated, modern music for the age of affluence. Los Angeles, 1953.

wwnorton.com/studyspace

It's important to remember, however, that although bebop caused a schism, it wasn't the first to do so. Conservative music lovers always prefer what they know. Hidebound critics in the 1920s attacked Armstrong and Ellington for sacrificing "authenticity"—Armstrong because he interpreted popular songs, Ellington because he orchestrated his music. Those critics shunned swing, just as some swing critics, in turn, shunned bebop; French critic Hugues Panassié wrote that Parker and Gillespie "gave up jazz in favor of bop." Later, some of the most ardent proponents of bebop would similarly shun the avant-garde.

The word "jazz" achieved its present-day historical meaning only in the aftermath of bop, when the multiplicity of schools necessitated a unifying term. During the Swing Era, "swing" was used to distinguish the popular dance music of the day from the New Orleans style of jazz. Now, with so many new schools competing for attention, "jazz" became an essential umbrella-term to cover them all.

Interpretations of History

Jazz was recognized as art music from almost the beginning; recall conductor Ernest Ansermet's remarks in 1919 about Sidney Bechet (see Chapter 4). After bop, as the association between jazz and dance diminished, the jazz world grew increasingly self-conscious of its status. Musicians sought respect as serious artists. They performed in major concert halls, collaborated with symphony orchestras and chamber groups, created ballets and theatrical scores. They expanded the parameters of improvisation and found new ways to combine it with composition. As jazz won acceptance as art music, it ceded its role as dance and entertainment music to new styles in pop, which peaked with the worldwide embrace of rock and roll. This development has been interpreted in various ways, reflecting either acceptance or resistance.

Modernists accept bebop and its successors as the natural outcome of a musical evolution that progresses from simplicity to complexity; in this narrative, jazz, like painting, literature, and classical music, is subject to inevitable change. Those who advocate *fusion* see the severance of jazz from pop music as a tactical error; in this narrative, jazz ought to take its cue from the public rather than from its most audacious artists. In the *ethnic* interpretation, jazz should look only to the African American elements that give the music its power, and shun experimentation and borrowings from other cultures, like Motown and hip-hop.

Finally, the *cyclical* view sees bebop as part of a normal cycle of innovation and elaboration. In the 1920s, for example, jazz was established as innovative new music, and the 1930s made those innovations more accessible (the Swing Era); this cycle is repeated in the 1940s (bebop) and 1950s (cool jazz, hard bop, funk); and again in the 1960s (avant-garde) and 1970s (assimilation). In jazz's post-cyclical history, all its styles compete for attention with its now classical past.

COOL JAZZ

The omnipresence of the word "cool" in present-day American speech derives in large measure from its association with the lingo of modern jazz. By the early 1950s, "cool" was used to describe a particular school of jazz born out of bebop that had a light, laid-back, reticent quality. As **cool jazz** grew in popularity, it was usually associated with white musicians who relocated from the East Coast to California, where the (largely segregated) film studios offered them financial security with musical "day jobs." Their style of music thus also became known as **West Coast jazz**.

There is much racial irony here, because the notion of coolness has deep roots in African American culture. Ralph Ellison recalled: "One countered racial provocation by cloaking one's feelings in that psychologically inadequate equivalent of a plaster cast—or bulletproof vest—known as 'cool.' . . . Coolness helped to keep our values warm, and racial hostility stoked our fires of inspiration."

Cool has a long pedigree in jazz as the antithesis of hot, which emphasized aggressive rhythms and improvisations, heavy timbre and vibrato, evocative blues scales, and overt expressiveness. As we have seen, musicians like Bix Beiderbecke and Lester Young dissented from the hot approach with music that was relatively unflappable—played with limited vibrato, restrained timbre, stable dynamics, melodic calm, and sophisticated harmonies that tempered the blues idiom. During the Swing Era, coolness was exemplified by such musicians as pianist Teddy Wilson, vibraphonist Red Norvo, bassist John Kirby (who adapted classical melodies for his small ensemble), arranger Eddie Sauter, and saxophonist-trumpeter-arranger Benny Carter.

At the height of bebop, Charlie Parker advanced the cool style with such compositions as "Yardbird Suite" and "Cool Blues," while his young disciple Miles Davis created a blues, "Sippin' at Bells," with so many intricate chord changes that the feeling of blues is deliberately obscured. An even more radical link between bop and the distinctive style that would soon be known as cool jazz is heard in the music of two stylistically dissimilar pianist-composers.

▮ LENNIE TRISTANO (1919–1978) and TADD DAMERON (1917–1965)

Lennie Tristano was a radical bopper, determined to carve out his own musical niche. He admired Charlie Parker, but his approach to jazz reflected his schooling in the European classics. Blind since childhood, Tristano began to play piano professionally at twelve, and studied at the American Conservatory in Chicago. He soon enticed a circle of bright young musicians who functioned as collaborators and even disciples. These included guitarist Billy Bauer and an ingenious fifteen-year-old alto saxophonist, Lee Konitz. In 1946, Tristano moved to New York, where he played with Parker and Gillespie and built a small but fervent following with his own groups, which included Bauer, Konitz, and Warne Marsh, a tenor saxophonist from Los Angeles stationed in New York for military service.

Tristano adapted the chord changes of popular songs, superimposing convoluted, spacey melodies (he telegraphed his intentions with such titles as "Supersonic" and "On a Planet"). These pieces sounded experimental and emotionally aloof, and showed off an extravagant virtuosity. One of his most memorable recordings is the justly titled "Wow," with whirling, meticulous, dual-saxophone phrasing. As a pianist, he created lengthy, winding phrases that employ counterpoint and two or more simultaneous meters.

By 1949, Tristano was conducting "free" sessions, which were entirely improvised. A few years later, he took a contrary approach, seeking increased

Pianist Lennie Tristano initiated a cult following to play his complex music, but he could also sit in with this unusual confluence of traditional, swing, and bebop musicians at New York's Birdland, in 1949: (left to right) Max Kaminsky, trumpet; Lester Young, tenor saxophone; Oran "Hot Lips" Page, trumpet; Charlie Parker, alto saxophone; Tristano.

control by replacing his drummer with taped percussion tracks. (This practice, though never accepted in jazz, prefigured the electronic dance mixes of the 1980s.) Tristano's music drew only a cult following, and by the early 1950s he was devoting most of his time to teaching. Yet his influence proved lasting, especially through the music of Konitz, the one alto saxophonist of the bop era with a sound and attack utterly unlike that of Charlie Parker.

Unlike Tristano, Tadd Dameron had limited keyboard technique and rarely improvised solos; he played what musicians call "arranger's piano," consisting of crafty accompanying chords. He was one of the few important bop composer-arranger-bandleaders who initially made his mark in swing. Born in Cleveland, he studied pre-med at Oberlin College before dropping out to compose full time for various entertainers and orchestras, mainly the Kansas City orchestra Harlan Leonard and His Rockets, for which he wrote such signature pieces as "Dameron Stomp" and "Rock and Ride." During that time, he became friendly with the young and unknown Parker.

While Tristano's classical training predisposed him to a difficult, intellectualized version of bop, Dameron's swing background inclined him to a gentler approach, defined by lyrical melodies and breezy rhythms, sometimes with a Latin feeling. Dameron wrote the most successful bop ballad, "If You Could See Me Now," and the fast instrumental anthem "Hot House," which combines intricate harmonies with a cool melody. His other pieces include the jazz standards "Good Bait" and "Our Delight." In 1948, Dameron was hired to organize a small band at the Royal Roost, a Broadway restaurant that had previously offered swing bands. There he put together an outstanding ensemble with trumpeter Fats Navarro and two tenor saxophonists, Wardell Gray (see Chapter 11) and Allen Eager, who represented divergent approaches to

Lester Young—respectively, earthy and ethereal. Dameron's spare melodies and plush voicings with this band and others ("Lady Bird," "Jahbero") prefigured the cool-school breakthrough of the following year.

MILES DAVIS AND THE BIRTH OF THE COOL

Every artistic movement sows the seeds of its undoing, as experimentalism always leads to more experimentalism. In 1945, Miles Davis played trumpet on Charlie Parker's first recording session, at age nineteen. It was apparent then that while he lacked the technical brilliance of Dizzy Gillespie (who consequently had to replace him on the explosive "Ko-Ko"), he offered a more lyrical approach to improvisation (as, for example, in his solo on "Embraceable You"), with an emphasis on personal timbre, longer tones, and suggestive silences.

Four years later, in 1949, Davis (whose life and career we will explore in greater detail in Chapter 14) emerged as the leader of a group of brilliant musicians who idolized Parker and Gillespie yet sought to explore ideas that would slow down the feverish pace of bebop in favor of supple melodies and plush harmonies. Above all, they aimed for a more balanced relationship between composition and improvisation. Instead of a performance that began with a written theme, followed by improvised choruses and a reprise of the theme, they challenged themselves to write music where the composer's hand was always apparent—where the improviser interrelated with the ensemble.

These precepts had already been explored by the big bands, especially in the work of Duke Ellington. But the young modernists, liberated from the jazz past by bop, also looked to classical music for chamber-like sonorities that favored the introspective middle range over rousing high notes. Temperamentally inclined toward emotional reserve, they filled out the instrumental palette with tuba and French horn, and preferred insinuating rhythms to the thumping beats that spurred dancers. After two years with Parker's band, Davis in particular had grown disenchanted with steeplechase harmonies and hurtling melodies. In his autobiography, he explained:

> Diz and Bird played a lot of real fast notes and chord changes because that's the way they heard everything; that's the way their voices were: fast, up in the upper register. Their concept of music was *more* rather than *less*. I personally wanted to cut the notes down, because I've always felt that most musicians play way too much for too long. . . . I didn't hear music like that. I heard it in the middle and lower registers. . . . We had to do something suited for what we did best, for our own voices.

Gil's Pad

In 1949, Davis at twenty-three was one of the youngest participants in the "cool" group and one of the least accomplished as a composer-arranger. He had made an immediate splash in jazz circles as Parker's trumpet player, but had yet to establish himself as a prominent stylist or bandleader. As an energetic and determined organizer, however, he assumed the pivotal role in a circle of second-generation bop musicians. He encouraged frequent discussions, organized rehearsals, promoted new compositions, and landed a record contract for which he settled on a nine-piece ensemble called the Miles Davis

Nonet. The ensemble's size suggested a middle road between a big band and a small combo, and its unusual brass-heavy instrumentation underscored links to classical chamber music. Several members of the nonet would become leading jazz figures for decades to come.

Gil Evans, at thirty-seven the oldest and most experienced member, did not play an instrument (in later years, he taught himself to play "arranger's piano") but was known as an ingenious orchestrator whose dramatic adaptations turned familiar melodies into virtually new compositions. Born in Canada in 1912 and self-taught, Evans led bands in California as early as 1933, but he achieved his signature style in his postwar work for the adventurous Claude Thornhill, who relished Evans's elaborately textured harmonies (prominently using two French horns, tuba, flute, and bass clarinet in addition to the usual jazz band instruments), including lengthy whole-note chords that seem to hang in the air like cloudbanks. Given a free hand with Thornhill's orchestra, Evans adapted jazz, pop, and classical themes—from Charlie Parker's "Donna Lee" to Modest Mussorgsky's "The Troubadour." (We will look at more of his music in Chapter 13.)

whole note in 4/4, note lasting four beats

Evans lived in a cellar apartment on New York's West 55th Street, conveniently located beneath a laundry and within blocks of the 52nd Street jazz clubs and rehearsal studios. Originally a storage room, Gil's pad (as it was known) became a meeting place for musicians who dropped by for conversation, a drink, or a nap. As Evans left the door unlocked, his place attracted a broad coterie of instrumentalists, composers, and singers eager to explore the wide-open terrain of modern jazz.

Among the regulars were two saxophonists who worked with him in the Thornhill band as well as Davis's nonet: Lee Konitz and Gerry Mulligan. Evans featured Konitz's fluid, unusually light alto saxophone on several Thornhill pieces. The lanky, multitalented Mulligan was then known primarily as a daring young arranger; within a few years, he would win lasting fame as the most popular baritone saxophonist in jazz history. Mulligan did most of the writing for the nonet.

John Lewis was another key nonet participant, a distinctive piano stylist who worked with Parker and Gillespie and would soon create the Modern Jazz Quartet and write many durable jazz classics. When Davis lined up a two-week engagement for his nonet at the Royal Roost (the only live engagement it ever played), he insisted that a sign be posted at the club entrance: "Arrangements by Gerry Mulligan, Gil Evans, and John Lewis." Never before had jazz arrangers received such prominent credit.

Coalition

The Miles Davis Nonet created a new coalition that was interracial, pan-generational, and culturally diverse. Of the key musicians, Davis, Lewis, drummers Kenny Clarke and Max Roach, and trombonist J. J. Johnson were black, while Evans, Mulligan, Konitz, and trombonist Kai Winding were white. Most of these musicians had apprenticed with swing bands; a few rode the first wave of bop (Davis, Lewis, and Roach had all worked with Charlie Parker); several had trained in classical music. The "birth of the cool" band (as the nonet later became known) was a collaborative experiment on every level. The improvisations were woven into an ensemble texture that favored the middle range, whether the instruments were high (trumpet, alto saxophone,

French horn) or low (trombone, tuba, baritone saxophone), as well as medium dynamics, economical phrasing, and plenty of rests.

As influential as it proved to be, the Davis Nonet initially garnered little interest from public or press. At three sessions in 1949 and 1950, involving more than twenty musicians and composers, it recorded twelve numbers; eight were issued on four records—one every four months or so. These sporadic releases failed to build long-term interest in the band. Not until 1954, when this handful of pieces was collected on an album called *Birth of the Cool*, were they acknowledged as innovative achievements and the genesis for the new cool jazz school that had, in the intervening years, become a national sensation.

🎧 "Moon Dreams"

"Moon Dreams," one of two arrangements written by Gil Evans for the nonet, is a radical example of the group's ambitions. The melody, composed by pianist Chummy MacGregor of the Glenn Miller band, is a conventional 1940s romantic ballad, though the forty-bar form indicates structural complexity. Johnny Mercer wrote lyrics in the hope of creating a pop hit for Miller, but although Miller recorded a vocal version with his Army Air Force Band, the song won favor with neither the public nor musicians. Evans's affection for it seemed peculiar.

Unlike every other piece we have examined thus far, "Moon Dreams" has no sustained improvised solo; instead, there are brief interludes by alto saxophone, baritone saxophone, and trumpet, which serve as transitional episodes in an orchestration that constantly calls attention to its subtly shifting harmonies, instrumental voices, and contrapuntal phrases. The most surprising element is the two-part structure: Evans orchestrates the forty-bar chorus only once, bringing it to a close with all instruments landing on F-sharp at 2:07. The rest of the performance is a new composition, built with minute and often dissonant instrumental details, suggesting an ominous breaking down of a pop melody as each instrument struggles to hold its place amid the chromatic chords.

contrapuntal describes composition using polyphonic texture (more than one melodic line)

LISTENING GUIDE

🎧 moon dreams

2.22

MILES DAVIS NONET
Miles Davis, trumpet; J. J. Johnson, trombone; Lee Konitz, alto saxophone; Gerry Mulligan, baritone saxophone; Gunther Schuller, French horn; Bill Barber, tuba; John Lewis, piano; Al McKibbon, bass; Max Roach, drums

- Label: Capitol T762; *The Story of America's Music* (Columbia/Legacy 074646143223)
- Date: 1950
- Style: cool jazz
- Form: 40-bar popular song (**A B A′ C C′**)

What to listen for:

- unusual, dark instrumentation (including French horn and tuba), subtly shifting harmonies
- Evans's imaginative arrangement, seamlessly moving from block chords to polyphony
- a lengthy, harmonically unstable coda

CHORUS 1

0:00	**A**	The band begins a slow ballad. Davis (trumpet) has the melody, the other horns play intricate harmonies in **block-chord** texture underneath. The sound is dominated by the lower instruments: tuba, baritone saxophone, French horn.
0:08		As the melody note is held, the horns swell in volume.
0:25	**B**	Konitz (alto saxophone) takes the lead, while the horns underneath create their own rhythmically independent line.
0:36		A return to block-chord texture, with the bass adding a line beneath.
0:51	**A′**	The band returns to the melody and harmony of the opening.
0:55		Schuller (French horn) leads from the middle of the texture.
1:12		Barber (tuba) plays a surprisingly fast and intricate **countermelody.**
1:17	**C**	Konitz retakes the lead.
1:24		His solo blends in with a faster, bebop-flavored line. The bass begins to ascend, step by step.
1:30		As the trumpet sustains a long held note, the background horns continue the faster rhythmic feeling.
1:43	**C′**	Mulligan (baritone saxophone) takes the melody.
1:57		Davis returns for the block-chord conclusion of the melody.
2:03		He hits the final note. Abandoning their tonic harmony, the other parts begin climbing up to reach that note.

CODA

2:07		Finally, all voices coincide on a single pitch (with the alto getting there last).
2:10		Konitz on alto is left holding the note; behind him, Roach accompanies quietly on cymbal.
2:13		The high note is suddenly accompanied by a new chord. As each line moves **chromatically,** the harmony becomes dissonant and unstable, held together by the unchanging alto note. Any sense of meter evaporates.
2:26		Konitz plays a quick ornament, continuing to hold the note.
2:34		As the harmonies continue to shift, the alto note finally fades out.
2:37		Konitz plays a fragment from the original melody, sounding plaintive in this unsettled harmonic atmosphere.
2:39		On horn, Schuller plays a new motive: a stuttering single note, ending with an upward turn.
2:48		Various horns trade back and forth fragments that resemble either Konitz's melodic fragment or Schuller's stuttering motive.
3:03		The tuba and baritone begin a descending scale.
3:07		The final chord is almost there, needing only the melody to fall into place.
3:11		As the chord resolves, the light cymbal pulse finally stops. The band sustains its chord, in a key different from the beginning one.

GROWTH OF THE COOL

As individual members of Miles Davis's circle carried each other's ideas over to their own bands, the influence of the nonet exceeded popular awareness of its recordings. A turning point came in 1952 with two events, one on each coast: in New York, John Lewis assembled what would become known as the Modern Jazz Quartet; in Los Angeles, Gerry Mulligan organized what would become known as his "piano-less" quartet.

■ GERRY MULLIGAN (1927–1996) and West Coast Jazz

If one group more than any other symbolized West Coast jazz, it was the Gerry Mulligan Quartet of 1952. Born in New York, Mulligan began writing big-band arrangements as a teenager for Philadelphia radio bands. Soon he was touring with bands, writing and playing saxophones and clarinet. In 1948, as a member of the Claude Thornhill band, he became a confidante of Gil Evans, who brought him into the "birth of the cool" circle, for which he did most of the writing—seven arrangements. Shortly afterward, in 1951, Mulligan hitchhiked to Los Angeles, seeking a job with Stan Kenton, the self-anointed king of progressive jazz.

Stan Kenton

Kenton and his hugely popular orchestra were often belittled for pomposity: he gave his pieces titles like "Artistry in Rhythm" and "Concerto to End All Concertos." Still, his canny ability to combine big band jazz, pop vocals, and experimental modernism (his 1951 recording of Bob Graettinger's "City of Glass" was an avant-garde assault on conventional jazz) made him a force to be reckoned with. In the 1940s and 1950s, Kenton hired dozens of important musicians and arrangers, many of whom looked to European classicism as a model of excellence and complexity. Almost all of them were white, encouraging simplistic characterizations of West Coast jazz as a white, intellectual, even pretentious kind of jazz.

Kenton was not especially responsive to Mulligan, and declined to hire him as a player—a decision he probably regretted once Mulligan's popularity on baritone saxophone soared. He did, however, record a few Mulligan compositions ("Young Blood," "Limelight," "Walking Shoes") that combined polyphony and simultaneous meters in ways that built on the achievements of the nonet. These arrangements influenced a generation of jazz composers, especially those living in California.

Gerry Mulligan, the only baritone saxophonist to become a major jazz star, was also an influential composer and arranger. In this photo taken in the 1950s, he's backed by his longtime bassist Bill Crow.

Piano-less

Mulligan returned briefly to New York to lead and record his own ten-piece band, but in 1952 he returned to Los Angeles and accepted a Mondays-only job at a small restaurant called the Haig, distinguished by its white picket fence and location: across the street from the Hollywood nightclub the Cocoanut Grove. There he formed a quartet consisting of baritone saxophone, trumpet, bass, and drums. According to legend, the Haig's bandstand was too small to accommodate a grand piano. In any case, the absence of a piano or chordal instrument was widely noted. An article in *Time* magazine drew attention to the "piano-less" group and its balmy music, which was thought to personify the laid-back temperament of Southern California. As crowds descended on the Haig, the quartet recorded a version of the Rodgers and Hart ballad "My Funny Valentine" that sold unusually well. The breezily swinging lyricism of cool jazz had found its star.

Without a piano to fill out the harmony, Mulligan and his young Oklahoma-born trumpet player, Chet Baker, expanded the contours of their

Chet Baker

music with contrapuntal interplay. Sometimes they achieved genuine two-part polyphony; at other times, one simply supported the other by playing whole notes to signify the song's chord sequence. Baker, an intuitive improviser, played almost exclusively in the middle register in a style that superficially resembled that of Miles Davis, but with lighter timbre and less dramatic force; he also won admirers as a soft-voiced ballad singer. The quartet's

Chico Hamilton

drummer, Chico Hamilton, known for the quiet rolling rhythms he created with mallets, later became an important bandleader in his own right. As an African American, Hamilton automatically symbolized postwar integration in jazz and the society at large.

The Gerry Mulligan Quartet lasted little more than a year before each man went his own way, yet its popularity was so lasting that the three key figures were taken up by Hollywood during the next several years: Mulligan and Hamilton appeared in movies, while actors playing jazz musicians mimicked Baker's baby-face looks and surly attitude. In later years, Mulligan divided his time between small groups and big bands, writing several jazz standards ("Rocker," "Line for Lyons," "Festive Minor") and winning polls as best baritone saxophonist for twenty years. A capable pianist, he came to dislike piano-less groups and refused to lead them except for occasional reunions with Baker. Baker's career was blighted by drug addiction, though he maintained a loyal following. Hamilton led bands for six decades, introducing such influential musicians as guitarist Jim Hall, bassist Ron Carter, and saxophonists Eric Dolphy, Charles Lloyd, and Arthur Blythe, among many others.

■ BOP, BLUES, AND BACH: JOHN LEWIS (1920–2001) and the MODERN JAZZ QUARTET

The Modern Jazz Quartet (MJQ) emerged, in some ways, as a reverse image of the Gerry Mulligan Quartet. It was an African American East Coast band that lasted more than forty years with only one change in personnel. As such, it was called the longest running chamber group in or out of jazz. Created by pianist John Lewis, who had written two of the nonet pieces, it was a genuine cooperative, with each member assigned specific extra-musical duties such as travel arrangements, finances, and public relations. Lewis was in charge of the music; his arrangements reflected a lifelong fascination with polyphony and counterpoint, and the conviction that J. S. Bach and blues were compatible.

Lewis was raised in Albuquerque, where he attended the University of New Mexico and saw the Duke Ellington band—a formative experience. While stationed in France as a soldier during World War II, he performed with drummer Kenny Clarke, who helped him to join Dizzy Gillespie's big band in 1946. In the next few years, Lewis resumed his studies at the Manhattan School of Music while working with Gillespie and participating in recording sessions with Charlie Parker and other modernists. He immediately

Pianist and composer John Lewis created the Modern Jazz Quartet, the most durable small band in jazz history (1952–97), with vibes virtuoso Milt Jackson (behind him).

FRANK DRIGGS COLLECTION

demonstrated a unique piano style: spare, light, melodic yet rhythmically firm and inflected with the blues. Gillespie encouraged him to compose for the band and to work up separate pieces that featured only the rhythm section, which consisted of Lewis, Clarke, vibraphonist Milt Jackson, and bassist Ray Brown—the nucleus of the MJQ.

By 1952, Lewis believed he had found the right musicians and the right concept. Milt Jackson, a native of Detroit, was the first major vibraphone player in a decade, since Lionel Hampton and Red Norvo in the 1930s. The vibes perfectly complemented the chimes-like sound Lewis coaxed from the piano, as well as offering a dramatic contrast: Jackson played with teeming energy, less subtle than Lewis and drenched in soulful blues figures he had learned in the church. Clarke, the most established member of the group, played with rambunctious, interactive enthusiasm yet also created a debonair, tasteful, distinctive brand of timekeeping with brushes or sticks. The least experienced member was bassist Percy Heath, a replacement for Ray Brown, who had left to tour with his wife, singer Ella Fitzgerald. Heath, the eldest brother in a celebrated family of Philadelphia musicians, had been playing bass for only a few years, having first taken it up after his discharge from the air force in 1946.

Milt Jackson

Percy Heath

Lewis was determined to undo popular misconceptions about jazz, not only in the manner of his music but in its presentation. He had ideas about the way the quartet should dress (in identical tuxedos or suits, in the tradition of the swing bands), enter and exit the stage, and introduce pieces. Every performance was to be regarded as a concert, whether they were actually playing a concert hall or a jazz club. This attitude puzzled many. As Percy Heath recalled:

> We had a hard time getting people to quiet down and listen. At that time in nightclubs, people were talking about hanging out. In order to break that down, instead of trying to play over the conversation, we'd use reverse psychology and play softer. Suddenly, they knew we were up there and realized the conversation was louder than the music. Of course, if it got too loud, we'd come off—just stop playing and walk off. It didn't take long for them to realize they were wasting their time, because we weren't going to entertain them in that sense. We didn't have funny acts, we didn't have any costumes. We were conservatively dressed, we played conservative music, and if you didn't listen you didn't get it. We were four instruments going along horizontally, contrapuntally. There was no back-up and soloist, the concept was changing.

Only after the MJQ was lauded in Europe did the American critics get on board. By the late 1950s, the MJQ ranked as one of the world's most successful jazz ensembles. In appearance and manner, it seemed genteel and cerebral. But its music was, in fact, profoundly rhythmic and emotionally intense—in other words, cool on the surface, hot at the core.

◉ "All the Things You Are"

At its first recording session, in December 1952, the MJQ recorded four pieces: two pop standards and two Lewis compositions, each of them arranged by Lewis to employ aspects of Baroque counterpoint (à la Bach) in a jazz setting. "All the Things You Are" is an important song in jazz history. Written for an unsuccessful 1939 Broadway musical by Jerome Kern and Oscar Hammerstein II, it was salvaged by Tommy Dorsey, whose recording of it topped the charts in early 1940. A few years later, it emerged as a personal favorite of the boppers. They admired the harmonic progression, which stimulates improvisation, and the poetic lyrics. Indeed, Charlie Parker, who recorded it many times, called the song "YATAG," an acronym for his favorite phrase in the lyric: "You are the angel glow."

At the beginning, Lewis's arrangement isolates each individual layer in the ensemble. The rapidly running bass line and the sporadic drumming fit strangely against the unison theme played by vibes and piano. Gradually, this framework is displaced by a more conventional, bebop-oriented one; but at no point do we feel that we are hearing a lone soloist accompanied by a rhythm section. The quartet always sounds like a quartet, with the primary melodic voice shifting between vibes and piano. Note the careful integration of the closing bass solo. Although rhythm and texture are always in play, the performance flows with seeming effortlessness.

LISTENING GUIDE

2.23

🎧 all the things you are

MODERN JAZZ QUARTET

Milt Jackson, vibraphone; John Lewis, piano; Percy Heath, bass; Kenny Clarke, drums

- Label: Prestige LP7059; *The Complete Modern Jazz Quartet Prestige and Pablo Recordings* (Prestige 4PRCD-4438-2)
- Date: 1952
- Style: cool jazz
- Form: 36-bar popular song (**A A′ B A″**; **A″** has 12 bars)

What to listen for:
- tightly integrated quartet playing
- contrapuntal piano parts
- composed elements within an otherwise improvised tune
- cool timbres

INTRODUCTION

0:00		In a moody introduction, Heath plays a double-time walking-bass line on a **Dorian scale**. On drums, Clarke enters with his own **ostinato** pattern: three quick accents, followed by a bass drum stroke and a mallet stroke on a cymbal.
0:08		Jackson (vibraphone) and Lewis (piano) play the melody in bare **octaves**. The bass ostinato undercuts the harmonies implied by the melody.
0:26		The melody line suddenly drops to a **dissonant** note, where it hangs unresolved.

CHORUS 1

0:29	**A**	With a sudden dramatic change in the rhythm section, the head begins. Jackson and Lewis play a varied version of the melody, harmonized by the piano's **block chords**.
0:38		The phrase ends with a rapid Latin figure. The **break** that follows is filled by the drummer.
0:41	**A′**	Jackson improvises over the pianist's simple line.
0:53	**B**	Lewis takes over for a delicate eight-measure solo.
1:04	**A″**	Jackson and Lewis return to a composed part of the arrangement, with chromatic harmonies and unexpected rhythms.
1:16		At the chorus's end, the melody collapses into a single unharmonized line.

INTERLUDE

1:22		A series of syncopated chords sets up Jackson's solo, which opens with a two-bar break.

CHORUS 2

1:27	**A**	Jackson plays a bebop-style solo, with dissonant passages and varied rhythms. Clarke plays a neutral accompaniment.
1:39	**A'**	In the background, Lewis comps quietly on the **offbeat**.
1:50	**B**	
1:57		Jackson reaches his highest point.
2:02	**A"**	Lewis's comping is often reduced to a single contrapuntal line.
2:12		As Jackson nears the end of his solo, his phrases become more bluesy.

CHORUS 3 (abbreviated)

2:19	**B**	Switching suddenly to the bridge, Lewis improvises briefly in the high register.
2:31	**A**	Heath takes a short solo, beginning with a phrase that recalls his opening ostinato. Behind him, Jackson and Lewis play a line that quietly lingers on dissonant notes.

CODA

2:48	Jackson and Lewis return to a composed part that reprises the final eight bars of chorus 1.
2:57	Without transition, we return to the introduction. Jackson and Lewis play one phrase, then stop.
3:09	Clarke ends with a cymbal explosion, followed by chords from Jackson and Lewis.

John Lewis, Gunther Schuller, and the Third Stream

Lewis, like Ellington, benefited from the loyalties of his musicians. The MJQ survived forty-two years with only one personnel change: drummer Kenny Clarke left the group in late 1954, unwilling to commit to a long-term endeavor that placed as much emphasis on composition as on improvisation. He was replaced by Connie Kay, a model of precision and nuance, who stayed until his death. (Kay also exerted an influence on early rock and roll as the leading session drummer for Atlantic Records.) During those forty years, Lewis merged the MJQ with symphony orchestras, chamber groups, big bands, singers, and individual guest soloists.

He wrote many benchmark works, including "Django," "England's Carol," "Afternoon in Paris," "Two Degrees East, Three Degrees West," "Little David's Fugue," the film scores *Odds Against Tomorrow* and *No Sun in Venice*, the ballet *The Comedy*, and the suite *A Day in Dubrovnik*. Lewis also functioned as an educator and jazz activist, directing the Lenox (Massachusetts) School of Jazz between 1957 and 1960 and the Monterey (California) Jazz Festival between 1958 and 1982. And as an early proponent of performing jazz classics with the respect given classical repertory, he co-founded and conducted Orchestra U.S.A. (1962) and the American Jazz Orchestra (1986–92).

The most controversial of Lewis's alliances gave birth to a short-lived idiom that composer, conductor, and musicologist Gunther Schuller called Third Stream. Schuller played French horn in the Miles Davis Nonet (1949–50) and worked with Lewis at the Lenox School and in Orchestra U.S.A. In a 1957 lecture, he suggested that a musical Third Stream would emerge, synthesizing elements in "Western art music" (classical) with "ethnic or vernacular" music (jazz). Collaborating with Lewis on the 1960 album *Jazz Abstractions*, Schuller introduced his own Third Stream example, "Variants on a

The "Four Brothers" sound—three tenor saxophones and a baritone saxophone—was named after a piece created for Woody Herman's 1947 orchestra. At a 1957 reunion recording session, the brothers were (left to right) Herbie Steward, Al Cohn, Zoot Sims, and Serge Chaloff.

Red Norvo

Lester Young's influence

Theme of Thelonious Monk." For several years, composers from both worlds self-consciously contributed to the Third Stream. Their music was not cool per se, but it had been stimulated by an environment nurtured by cool's architects. Although classical techniques would continue to figure in jazz as sources of creative stimulation (isolated examples of classical-jazz fusions may be found in prewar jazz as well), the movement soon faded and the term "Third Stream" fell into disuse.

Heating Up the Cool

For some important musicians, Third Stream acted as a buffer between cool jazz and counter-movements, including hard bop and avant-garde. Their experiments in blending jazz and classical music served as an apprenticeship for careers that assumed genuine significance in the late 1950s, when their music emphasized jazz roots and emotional complexity. In 1953, for example, the composer-bassist Charles Mingus (see Chapter 13) joined the Jazz Composers' Workshop, which consisted chiefly of white composers adapting their classical training to modern jazz. There he created several Third Stream works before developing a mature style that was more aggressive, jazz-rooted, and blues-driven.

Earlier, in 1950–51, Mingus played bass with the Red Norvo Trio. Norvo had started on xylophone in the 1920s, creating a stir in 1933 with his "Dance of the Octopus," a whimsical piece combining xylophone and bass clarinet; Schuller cited it as a precursor of the Third Stream. Norvo then led an audacious Swing Era orchestra, featuring vocalist Mildred Bailey (his wife). By the early 1950s, he had recorded with Charlie Parker and formed a trio made up of vibraphone, guitar (the influential Tal Farlow), and bass (Mingus). Its texture was light, but its swing and improvisational zest were hot. The pianist George Shearing developed a similar cool-bop sound with a quintet that included vibraphone and Latin percussion, yet stayed light on its feet and achieved enormous popularity.

Lightness was a significant aspect of cool jazz. Lester Young's influence on a generation of tenor saxophonists produced two approaches that tended to break down along racial lines. Black tenors (like Dexter Gordon, Wardell Gray, Illinois Jacquet, and Gene Ammons) modified Young's legato (smooth) phrasing into a more forthright attack, emphasizing the expressive robustness of his style. White tenors (like Stan Getz, Zoot Sims, Al Cohn, and Allen Eager) focused instead on Young's airy lyricism. As Dexter Gordon said, "We used to jam together—Zoot, Al Cohn, Allen Eager. Zoot and I worked in a club in Hollywood. He was playing Lester and I was playing Lester, but there was always a difference."

The most accomplished "white Lesters" worked together in the Woody Herman Orchestra (along with Gene Ammons). After Herman recorded Jimmy Giuffre's "Four Brothers," a fast bop piece that featured the reed section, the title phrase was used to define that reed section and any tenor who worked in what Stan Getz—the most widely admired of the "brothers" (see Chapter 16)—called "the Lestorian mode." These saxophonists perfected timbres that avoided vibrato while aiming for a high, delicate sound. Gerry Mulligan made the baritone saxophone sound almost like a tenor; Giuffre made the tenor saxophone sound almost like an alto; and Paul Desmond made the alto saxophone sound almost like a flute.

■ CHANGING TIME: DAVE BRUBECK (b. 1920)

Paul Desmond made his name with the Dave Brubeck Quartet, the most popular jazz group of the 1950s. Brubeck grew up in Concord, California, in a musical family; his first instructor was his mother, a classical pianist. He later studied with composer Darius Milhaud, whose 1923 ballet *La Creation du monde* was one of the first symphonies to employ blues harmonies. In the late 1940s, Brubeck organized an octet along lines similar to those of Davis's nonet, but with reversed priorities: more classical than jazz, it produced a ponderous, academic music, lacking rhythmic power. Then in 1951, Brubeck hooked up with Desmond and organized his first quartet (piano, alto saxophone, bass, drums). Success was almost immediate. He was pictured on the cover of *Time* in 1954, a rare acknowledgment for a jazz musician, and won acclaim with younger listeners by playing and recording on college campuses.

Paul Desmond

The Brubeck Quartet blew both hot and cool, in the contrast between Desmond's ethereal saxophone and Brubeck's heavy-handed piano. Both musicians excelled at unusual chord substitutions, but where Desmond improvised appealing melodies, Brubeck built his solos in a pattern that began with single-note phrases and climaxed with repetitive blocks of chords, generating either excitement or tedium, depending on the listener's taste. Brubeck's primary trademark was an innovative use of irregular meters such as 5/4 and 9/4. After decades of jazz played almost exclusively in 4/4 (even waltzes were rare), his approach to time was exotic, charming, and frequently catchy.

Brubeck's 1959 album *Time Out* became a national sensation, especially his "Blue Rondo à la Turk" (in 9/4) and Desmond's "Take Five" (in 5/4), which was released as a hit single. These meters were so unusual that musicians often mastered them by mentally subdividing the beats. A composition in 5/4 might be counted as 2 plus 3 or the reverse: "Blue Rondo à la Turk" breaks down to 1-2, 1-2, 1-2, 1-2-3. By the end of the twentieth century, unusual time signatures, some borrowed from Eastern music, were no longer uncommon.

HARD BOP

The counterstatement to cool jazz was essentially a revival of bop but with a harder edge. By the middle 1950s, the umbrella term **hard bop** was adopted by critics to describe a populous East Coast school of jazz that placed itself in direct opposition to the more arid precincts of cool.

Ironically, Miles Davis helped pilot the turn from cool to hard. Put off by underfed, overintellectualized music that claimed to be derived from his nonet, he switched directions in 1954, with recordings ("Walkin'," "Blue and Boogie") that restored jazz's earthy directness. Even his subsequent collaborations with Gil Evans emphasized powerful emotions and vigorous rhythms. As Davis moved forward according to his own lights (as did Mulligan, the Modern Jazz Quartet, Brubeck, Mingus, and other major stylists of the

1950s), hard bop came to embody a general attitude (tough, urban, straight-forward) and a new mainstream in jazz—one that made a point of resisting overt experimentation.

Born largely of musicians who came to New York from the nation's inner cities, especially Detroit and Philadelphia, hard bop was said to reflect the intensity and hustling tempo of city life. To these musicians, the cool school represented a more tranquil, stress-free environment. This idea paints a su-perficial gloss on the relationship between art and geography; obviously, West Coast musicians were as stressed as anyone else. Still, it seems fair to suggest that the West Coast school's expression of life's irritations was relatively in-troverted while the East Coast's was relatively extroverted.

One instantly apparent difference concerned timbre. If cool jazz aimed for a light timbre, hard bop preferred a sound that was heavy, dark, impassioned. The tenor replaced the alto as the saxophone of choice, and drummers worked in an assertive style that drove the soloists. Some hard bop bands winnowed bop's harmonic complexity in favor of elemental chords reminiscent of the sanctified church or rhythm and blues. They created a subset of hard bop called **soul jazz**. A subset of soul jazz in turn popularized an instrument that had previously been little used in jazz (like the cool school's French horn): the electric organ, a mainstay of church music (see Chapter 16). In effect, the soul musicians were attempting to reconnect modern jazz to popular music.

Ultimately, the contrast between cool and hard bop, though unmistakable, was not radical enough to suggest a schism like the one that divided swing and bop. For the most part, cool and hard bop represented the natural devel-opment of bop in a changing world.

Microgroove and Live Recordings

In 1948, Columbia Records patented a recording process called microgroove, or long-playing records (LPs): twelve-inch platters that turned at 33⅓ revo-lutions per minute and accommodated about twenty minutes of music per side with excellent fidelity. They were manufactured from a flexible plastic (or vinyl) that was promoted as unbreakable. By contrast, the three-minute 78-rpm platter that had dominated the industry for half a century was extremely brittle and easily shattered. As Columbia announced its breakthrough, its longtime competitor RCA-Victor introduced a similar system, also using microgrooves and improved vinyl, but smaller and with less playing time, a speed of 45 rpm, and a large donut-hole in its center.

The industry quickly accepted both technologies, reserving the LP for serious or extended works and the 45 for pop songs no longer than those heard on 78s. The LP had an immediate impact on jazz, particularly the new generation of hard bop musicians. Like every kind of recorded music, bebop had accommodated itself to the 78's time limit. While musicians could play longer pieces with extensive soloing in concert or at jam sessions, most per-formances were kept short to please audiences who expected to hear music familiar from records.

JATP and Long Solos

In 1944, when impresario Norman Granz organized his Jazz at the Philhar-monic (JATP; see Chapter 11), he began releasing recordings of its concerts.

Live recording, virtually unheard-of at the time, was done on disc-recorders with one microphone (tape had not yet been introduced), so audio control was narrow and sound-mixing impossible.

JATP events included a lot of rivalrous jamming that simulated a *crescendo* of yelps, screeches, and other climactic effects, wildly cheered by the audience and lasting a good ten or fifteen minutes. In order to release these numbers, Granz created new labels (Clef, Norgran) and divided the performances into sections, on several three-minute 78-rpm records—not unlike symphonies and operas.

When the LP arrived soon thereafter (it conveniently followed by a year the introduction of audio tape), it influenced the way music was played. Duke Ellington was one of the first to take advantage of the liberty it afforded him, composing extended works specifically for the new medium. At the same time, record producers encouraged musicians to play marathon solos to test the reaction of the fans. An early instance of this was a session by Zoot Sims, a "Four Brothers" saxophonist known for his smooth timbre, volatile swing, and fertile imagination. Backed by drummer Art Blakey, Sims was about to finish "East of the Sun" when the producer waved him on for an interpretation that ultimately ran eleven minutes.

Partly because of the LP, hard bop bands were especially inclined toward longer solos. Shunning counterpoint and complicated ensemble arrangements, they relied on the yeoman display of extended improvisations. The average performance consisted of a theme, solos by some or all the band members, and a reprise of the theme. The length of the improvisations threatened to alienate audiences accustomed to more succinct solos. At first the major labels, like Columbia and RCA, were disinclined to pursue hard bop. But new independent labels were delighted to take up the slack, among them Blue Note, Prestige, Contemporary, and Riverside. They realized that a large segment of the audience was eager for a style of jazz that was at once expansive and closer to its roots.

One way to maintain the interest of a mainstream audience is to fortify the beat with a pronounced rhythmic groove. A powerful accent on the second and fourth beats of each measure (backbeat) stimulates a physical response in the listener. In the 1950s, jazz fans congregated in nightclubs (not dance halls), where physical reactions like foot-tapping, finger-snapping, and head-wagging amounted to a kind of dancing while seated. The independent record companies liked the longer tracks for another reason: the fewer tunes on an album, the less they had to pay in songwriter royalties.

■ MESSENGERS: ART BLAKEY (1919–1990) and HORACE SILVER (b. 1928)

Drummer Art Blakey was the central figurehead of hard bop. Raised amid the Pittsburgh steel mills, Blakey was a tough, muscular leader who insisted that his sidemen put aside everything in their private lives when they mounted a bandstand and give their all to the music, as he did. He began on piano, switched to drums, and made his way to New York in 1942 to work with Mary Lou Williams. Two years later, Dizzy Gillespie recruited him for the Billy Eckstine band, positioning him to become one of the most influential percussionists of the bop era.

© CHUCK STEWART

Drummer Art Blakey pushed his Jazz Messengers to the pinnacle of hard bop for more than three decades, graduating dozens of major musicians, from Clifford Brown to Wynton Marsalis.

Blakey had an earthier approach than Kenny Clarke and Max Roach, and was their equal in finding precisely the right rhythmic figures or colorations to complement and inspire a soloist. He became famous for his **press-roll**: an intense rumbling on the snare drum, usually at a turnaround, which had the effect of boosting a soloist into the air for a few seconds and then setting him down in the next chorus, as the swinging pulse continued. Blakey's attentiveness made him an ideal drummer for Thelonious Monk, with whom he had a long association—even though Monk's own music was quirky and intricate while Blakey's was brash and straightforward.

In 1953, Blakey and pianist-composer Horace Silver formed a quintet (trumpet, tenor saxophone, piano, bass, and drums) called the Jazz Messengers. They made a few live recordings (including *A Night in Birdland*, with trumpet player Clifford Brown), and within two years had codified hard bop as quintet music that combined bebop complexity (in the harmonic improvisations) with blunt simplicity (in bluesy or gospel-inspired themes and backbeat rhythms). In 1956, after Silver left to organize his own quintet, Blakey formally assumed leadership, and the band became Art Blakey and His Jazz Messengers.

Blakey's musicians

The number of important musicians who either began or matured in Blakey's groups is remarkable. Among many others, it includes trumpet players Kenny Dorham, Lee Morgan, Freddie Hubbard, Woody Shaw, and Wynton Marsalis; saxophonists Hank Mobley, Jackie McLean, Benny Golson, Wayne Shorter, and Branford Marsalis; and pianists Cedar Walton, John Hicks, Keith Jarrett, Joanne Brackeen, and Mulgrew Miller. Blakey telegraphed the consistent attitude of his music in classic album titles: *Moanin'*, *Drum Suite*, *The Freedom Rider*, *The Big Beat*, *Indestructible*, *Hard Bop*, *Straight Ahead*.

In the three years he worked with Blakey, Horace Silver composed several of the tunes that incarnated the hard bop aesthetic. Born and raised in Connecticut, Silver soaked up a far-ranging assortment of musical influences. He learned Cape Verdean folk music from his father, an immigrant of Portuguese ancestry (Cape Verde is an island off the west coast of Africa, settled by the Portuguese), and studied tenor saxophone with a church organist. He listened to blues singers, boogie-woogie pianists, swing (he idolized Jimmie Lunceford), and especially bebop. At twenty-one, Silver was discovered in Hartford by Stan Getz, who took him on tour and into recording studios. During the next few years, he worked with major musicians, including Coleman Hawkins, Lester Young, and Charlie Parker; he appeared with Miles Davis on the 1954 sessions that helped turn the tide from cool to hard.

Beyond his ability to filter bop through gospel, rhythm and blues, and folk song structures, Silver brought to his music an uncanny ability to create catchy melodies that often sounded familiar and new at the same time. One of his earliest pieces, "Opus de Funk" (1953), a play on Stan Getz's "Opus de

Bop" (1946), popularized a word for Silver's brand of soulful jazz: funky. Partly derived from nineteenth-century slang for spoiled tobacco, *funky* also has a long history in African American usage to describe any kind of foul odor. (Jelly Roll Morton uses it in his version of "I Thought I Heard Buddy Bolden Say.") Thanks to Silver, the term was reborn to signify basic back-to-roots musical values. Many of his tunes became jazz standards; several attracted lyricists and vocalists. Significantly, a few were covered by pop or soul artists, including "Doodlin'," "Señor Blues," "Peace," and "Song for My Father."

🎧 "The Preacher"

One of Silver's best-known and most recorded tunes, "The Preacher" instigated what Silver later described as his only argument with the founders of Blue Note Records, Alfred Lion and Francis Wolf. They implored him not to record the song because it sounded too much like Dixieland. They were wrong but prophetic: over the next several years, "The Preacher" emerged as one of the few postwar jazz tunes to enter Dixieland repertory. Silver considered withdrawing it, but Blakey pulled him aside and encouraged him to hold his ground. It was at the "Preacher" session that the Jazz Messengers was born.

With its sixteen-bar structure, undemanding harmonies, and memorable melody, "The Preacher" suggests a distant past when American folk melodies, church music, and blues seemed to share the same terrain. Note the melodic similarities to "I've Been Working on the Railroad" or "Show Me the Way to Go Home," along with the blues-like chord structure (little harmonic movement in the first half of each eight-bar section, and a climactic use of the dominant chord in the second half). The lighthearted melody is echoed throughout the improvisations and emphasized by the piano chords. In allowing the slightly muddled playing of the background riffs to stand (instead of calling for another take), Silver adds to the churchlike mood established by such deliberate techniques as tremolos, false fingerings (alternate ways of playing a given note), two-beat and backbeat rhythms, and bluesy phrases.

© CHUCK STEWART

Horace Silver, seen here in the 1950s, established funk as the quintessence of soulful, rhythmically propulsive jazz, and wrote tunes like "The Preacher" and "Song for My Father," which were played by bands that ranged from Dixieland to rock.

2.24

🎧 the preacher

HORACE SILVER QUINTET
Kenny Dorham, trumpet; Hank Mobley, tenor saxophone; Horace Silver, piano; Doug Watkins, bass; Art Blakey, drums

- Label: Blue Note BLP5062; *Horace Silver and the Jazz Messengers* (UPC 724386447821)
- Date: 1955
- Style: hard bop
- Form: 16-bar popular song (**A A′**)

What to listen for:

- gospel-influenced groove, with gospel-like tune at beginning and end
- harsh, blues-oriented harmonies
- interplay between Silver's piano and horns
- Blakey's hard-swinging drums (press-roll)
- happy, upbeat mood

CHORUS 1 (HEAD)

| 0:00 | | A drum beat kicks off an introductory **break**, Mobley (tenor saxophone) and Dorham (trumpet) entering on the upbeat. |

0:01 **A** The two horns play in close harmony, as if mimicking the sound of gospel singing. The bass plays two firm beats to the bar, answered by the piano's bluesy background riff.

0:11 The first eight-bar section ends on a **half cadence.**

0:12 **A'**

0:15 The second eight-bar phrase moves in a new harmonic direction, heading for a **full cadence.**

CHORUS 2 (HEAD)

0:23 **A**

0:34 **A'**

0:43 As Blakey plays a fill (**press-roll**) on drums, Dorham (trumpet) begins to improvise.

CHORUS 3

0:45 **A** Dorham's opening lingers over a long held note before descending with a bluesy phrase. The bass begins to walk.

0:55 **A'** Dorham's improvisation begins to resemble straightforward bebop, with long strings of eighth notes.

CHORUS 4

1:06 **A** The next chorus rises to the top of the trumpet's register before falling into a more comfortable range.

1:17 **A'**

CHORUS 5

1:27 **A** Mobley (tenor saxophone) enters with a sharp, bluesy dissonance.

1:38 **A'** Holding out a note, he decorates it with short flutters.

1:43 During a bluesy lick, the melodic line rises as if aiming for a particular note, but never quite reaching it.

CHORUS 6

1:48 **A** As with Dorham, Mobley's rhythm moves closer to a bebop string of eighth notes.

1:59 **A'**

2:04 To vary his timbre, Mobley uses **false fingerings.**

CHORUS 7

2:09 **A** Silver (piano) enters with a simple riff, stressing the **flatted third** of the blues scale. Blakey reduces his drumming to a simple accompaniment, making it easier to hear the improvised bass line.

2:20 **A'** He hits a chord and plays it **tremolo** (with a small shake).

CHORUS 8

2:30 **A** Silver's second chorus begins with a descending riff. The notes are straightforward, but the rhythm is subtle and complicated.

2:40 **A'** He continues playing the same descending riff.

2:43 As the harmonies begin to change, Silver introduces a new motive.

CHORUS 9

2:50 **A** Dorham and Mobley play a riff in octaves. Against this pattern, Silver improvises phrases in **call and response.**

3:01 **A'**

3:04 Dorham and Mobley play different notes, as if they disagreed about where the riff should go. The saxophone drops out for a measure, yielding to the trumpet.

CHORUS 10

3:11	**A**	The horn players continue playing their riff. Behind it, Silver plays chords in tremolo.
3:21	**A'**	
3:25		Mobley follows Dorham's example, playing the figure clumsily, as if still learning it.
3:31		With the bass still walking, the two horns return to the opening melody.

CHORUS 11 (HEAD)

| 3:32 | **A** | The opening tune returns with a cymbal crash. The rhythm section reestablishes its initial two-beat gospel groove. |
| 3:42 | **A'** | |

CHORUS 12 (HEAD)

| 3:53 | **A** | |
| 4:03 | **A'** | |

CODA

| 4:13 | | A short drum figure leads to the final chord—a sustained bluesy dissonance on the piano, punctuated by a resounding cymbal. |

THREE SOLOISTS

By the 1960s, few observers could doubt that the unofficial rivalry between cool and hot had been decided in favor of hot. The stars of cool jazz retained their popularity, but most—including tenor saxophonists Stan Getz, Zoot Sims, and Al Cohn—had begun to play in an unmistakably harder style, reflecting the East Coast movement's impact. Moreover, the whole direction of jazz had developed an increasingly aggressive and brazen attitude, which would culminate in the raucous howls of the avant-garde.

By that point, the tenor saxophone had long since supplanted the trumpet as the most vital instrument in jazz. Many musicians who defined 1960s jazz by exploring the middle ground between bebop and radical avant-gardism had learned their trade playing hard bop—for example, saxophonists John Coltrane in Miles Davis's band, Wayne Shorter in Art Blakey's band, and Joe Henderson in Horace Silver's band. Coltrane (see Chapters 14 and 15) ultimately repudiated the structures and harmonies of bop in favor of avant-garde jazz, while others remained faithful to bop, adapting it to the freer environment of the 1950s and 1960s. Three major soloists who found their own paths amid the competing jazz schools were Clifford Brown, Sonny Rollins, and Wes Montgomery.

■ CLIFFORD BROWN (1930–1956)

The career of Clifford Brown lasted barely four years, but in that time he became one of the most admired and beloved musicians of his day. His death in an automobile accident at age twenty-five was mourned as a catastrophe for jazz. Born in Wilmington, Delaware, the son of an amateur musician, he took up trumpet at thirteen and attracted attention for his remarkable facility while studying at Maryland State College. After playing in Philadelphia and touring with a rhythm and blues band, word quickly spread that "he had it all"—gorgeous tone, virtuoso technique, infallible time, and a bottomless well of creative ideas.

Nor was his importance exclusively musical. At a time when the jazz ranks were devastated by heroin addiction, Brown embodied an entirely different attitude. Here was an immensely likable young man whose musical ability rivaled that of Charlie Parker, but who had none of Parker's bad habits. He didn't smoke or drink, let alone take drugs, and his example inspired other musicians to change the way they lived.

Brown received much encouragement from Dizzy Gillespie and especially Fats Navarro, with whom he shared a particular stylistic bond: each man was noted for his unusually rich timbre. When Navarro died of narcotics abuse, Brown was acknowledged as his heir—especially after he stepped into Navarro's shoes for a 1953 Tadd Dameron recording session. Weeks later, Brown joined Lionel Hampton's big band, which brought him to Europe. Upon returning, he participated in several recordings, as leader and sideman, but it was an Art Blakey engagement at Birdland in early 1954 that made him the talk of the jazz elite; two albums recorded at Birdland helped to clinch his growing reputation.

In the summer of 1954, Max Roach brought Brown to Los Angeles to make a concert recording. That event resulted in the formation of the **Brown-Roach Quintet** ▸ Clifford Brown–Max Roach Quintet, with which Brown was associated for the remainder of his short life. Often cited as the last great bebop ensemble, the quintet influenced the emerging hard bop bands with its exciting vitality and canny arrangements, including a few unlikely pieces ("Delilah," from the score of the film *Samson and Delilah*) and originals by Brown ("Joy Spring" became a jazz standard). Brown conquered Los Angeles as easily as he had New York, recording with the new quintet as well as with Zoot Sims and singer Dinah Washington. The latter association generated other requests from singers; on returning to New York, he made notable albums with Sarah Vaughan and Helen Merrill, as well as the most successful jazz album with strings since Charlie Parker's. In November 1955, the Brown-Roach quintet's talented tenor saxophonist, Harold Land, left and was replaced by Sonny Rollins, creating an even more potent ensemble.

Brown's work as a trumpet player penetrated every aspect of jazz on both coasts but especially in the East, where a succession of hard bop trumpeters modeled themselves after him, determined to replicate his plush timbre and infectious enthusiasm. He offered an alternate approach to that of the more introverted Miles Davis, and remained for decades a paradigm for upcoming trumpet players, including all those who succeeded him in Art Blakey's Jazz Messengers.

© CHUCK STEWART

Clifford Brown (trumpet) and Sonny Rollins (tenor saxophone) brought a new inventiveness and spirit to jazz and their instruments, teaming briefly in the classic band co-led by Brown and drummer Max Roach in 1956.

"A Night in Tunisia"

Clifford Brown's "A Night in Tunisia" is a posthumous recording (like Charlie Christian's "Swing to Bop," discussed in Chapter 10), one of many that have turned up since the introduction of portable recording devices. A few weeks before he died, in 1956, Brown sat in with the local band at a small jazz club in Philadelphia. Three numbers were taped, though the tape didn't surface until the early 1970s, when it was released to tremendous acclaim by Columbia Records. His five-chorus solo on this Gillespie classic is an inspired romp that, because of its length and the relaxed ambience, allows us a glimpse into the way Brown thinks in the heat of action, using various gambits, pivotal notes, and motives; and altering speed, range, and meter as he produces a stream of stimulating musical ideas.

This performance is also interesting for showing a great musician accompanied by a journeyman group working hard to keep up (the drummer, who owned the jazz club, is especially alert) and not always succeeding, while an eager audience adds percussion-like fills with its shouts and hollers. Brown's solo achieved theatrical renown in 1999, when it was heard in Warren Leight's play *Side Man*: one character plays the recently discovered tape for a couple of friends, who marvel and gasp in response.

LISTENING GUIDE

3.1

a night in tunisia (excerpt)

CLIFFORD BROWN

Clifford Brown, trumpet; Mel "Ziggy" Vines, Billy Root, tenor saxophones; Sam Dockery, piano; Ace Tesone, bass; Ellis Tollin, drums

- Label: Columbia KC32284; *The Beginning and the End* (Columbia/Legacy 66491)
- Date: 1956
- Style: hard bop
- Form: 32-bar popular song (**A A B A**), with an interlude

What to listen for:

- Brown's exploration of range and rhythm
- his use of motives to control portions of his extended improvised solo
- support by drums
- live audience interaction

INTRODUCTION

| 0:00 | | The rhythm section plays a **vamp**: an open-ended, two-measure figure in a Latin groove, with an asymmetric, syncopated bass line. Conversation can be heard in the background. |
| 0:12 | | A saxophone enters, playing a background riff. |

CHORUS 1 (HEAD)

0:17	**A**	Brown enters, playing the tune on the trumpet over the two-chord progression of the vamp. Every time he reaches for the high note, it falls slightly behind the beat.
0:25		As the phrase reaches a cadence, Brown's line is doubled by the other horns.
0:28	**A**	Brown repeats the **A** section, adding a melodic variation at 0:32.
0:37		The drummer marks the end of the eight-bar section with a drum **fill**.
0:39	**B**	For the bridge, the accompanying horns drop out, leaving Brown alone on the melody. The rhythm section leaves the Latin groove behind for a straight bebop-style four-four, with walking bass.
0:49	**A**	The band returns to the Latin groove of the opening.

INTERLUDE (16 bars)

0:59		The band plays a complicated interlude, designed to connect the head with the solos. The horns play a short riff with a constant rhythm; the melody changes slightly with each chord. Not everyone in the band knows this passage: the bass drops out entirely, while the pianist does his best to approximate the chords.
1:15		The interlude ends with a four-measure **break**. Brown plays a string of clean, even eighth notes that reach a peak at 1:17.

CHORUS 2

1:20	**A**	Brown's descending line connects smoothly with his solo, drawing applause from the crowd. The piano enters on the downbeat, the drums following a beat later.
1:31	**A**	Brown's playing remains relaxed and relatively simple.
1:37		A sudden burst of faster notes serves as a harbinger of rhythmic complexity to come.
1:42	**B**	At the bridge, Brown plays a descending line that interrupts the smooth rhythmic flow with unexpected **polyrhythmic** accents.
1:52	**A**	

CHORUS 3

2:03	**A**	The new chorus begins with a four-note motive, played in a simple descending pattern.
2:08		The next phrase is a mirror image of the first: another four-bar pattern, this time ascending.
2:12		The phrase ends with a bar left in the **A** section—enough space for an excited fan to yell, "Hey, Brownie!"
2:13	**A**	Brown plays a fanfare-like statement on a high-pitched note—A, the fifth degree of the home key of D minor.
2:24	**B**	Playing in the upper register of his trumpet, he starts a line that will continue throughout the bridge.
2:32		The lengthy phrase is finally rounded off with a quick two-note figure, prompting cries of "Oh, yeah!" from the excited crowd.
2:34	**A**	Brown now plays with the two-note figure, placing it in different parts of the measure; the drummer responds by playing unexpected bass drum accents (**dropping bombs**).

CHORUS 4

2:45	**A**	Brown returns to a high A, playing a series of **triplets** that encourage the drummer to follow his rhythm.
2:51		Aiming for a climax, he hits and holds a sharply **dissonant** note.
2:55	**A**	Again returning to a high A, Brown plays a sharp, detached **cross-rhythm** that is instantly reinforced by syncopated bass-drum accents.
3:02		Having played for several measures at the top of his horn, he starts a phrase too difficult to finish; he subsequently descends to a more comfortable register.
3:06	**B**	
3:14		Brown suddenly breaks into a quick, upward run.
3:17	**A**	Seizing on the run as a compositional idea, he folds it into a series of repeated phrases, each ascending higher than the last.
3:21		In response, he plays a rapid descending sequence based on a four-note motive.

CHORUS 5

3:27	**A**	Once again, Brown begins by blasting out a high A, but quickly shifts to a series of triplets. The accent for the triplet falls on the normally unaccented last note of each group.
3:38	**A**	Brown plays a pair of phrases, each beginning with insistent triplets.

3:48	**B**	The bridge begins with a fast barrage of notes.
3:51		In the midst of this fast passage, Brown turns a simple five-note scale into a complex polyrhythm.
3:57		The drummer marks the end of the bridge with an intense fill.
3:58	**A**	Brown's fast solo passage begins to disintegrate into shorter fragments.
CHORUS 6		
4:09	**A**	Brown begins again on a high A, playing a line strikingly similar to the line heard at 2:13.
4:15		Playing at the very top of his register, he squeaks out a line that is slightly out of tune until it descends into normal range.
4:19	**A**	For the last time, he begins on a high A before quickly descending.
4:22		He finds a new pattern and turns it into an ascending sequence.
4:30	**B**	
4:40	**A**	During his last melodic pattern, Brown plays dissonant intervals within a rhythm drawn from the "Night in Tunisia" theme.
4:51		His solo ends. As the excerpt fades out, a tenor saxophone solo begins.

■ SONNY ROLLINS (b. 1930)

One of the most influential and admired tenor saxophonists in jazz history, Sonny Rollins initially played a role in jazz similar to that of Clifford Brown. In the 1950s, countless young saxophonists and some older ones tried to assimilate his creative energy, brawny timbre, and rhythmic authority. He projected a measure of individuality and power—not unlike Louis Armstrong or Rollins's idol, Coleman Hawkins—that could not be contained in a conventional band.

Unlike Brown, however, Rollins enjoyed a long, vigorous career, performing for sixty years, snatching a few rest periods along the way to refuel but always challenging himself to change, even to the point of taking on different musical identities. At times, when he seemed to have reached an artistic peak, he would turn a sharp corner, altering his sound, repertory, and instrumentation. Unpredictability and playfulness rank high among his abiding (and controversial) attributes. Rollins represents continuity with the jazz past (through his use of pop tunes and swinging rhythms), while pointing the way to a promising future.

Born and raised in Harlem, Rollins studied piano and alto saxophone before taking up the tenor at sixteen. Two years later, Thelonious Monk invited him to participate in a program of rehearsals that went on for months, boosting his confidence and ambition. One of Monk's guiding principles, thoroughly adopted by Rollins, was that improvisation should elaborate the melodic as well as the harmonic content of a song. Why play a tune if you're going to discard it after the theme chorus (head)?

At nineteen, Rollins recorded as a sideman with Bud Powell and J. J. Johnson, among others, combining the gruff heaviness of Hawkins's sound with

Sonny Rollins, one of the most influential saxophonists and tune writers of the 1950s, focused on the lower register and never ceased pushing himself to greater heights. He's shown here in 1965.

© CHUCK STEWART

the quicksilver facility of Charlie Parker. Recording with Miles Davis a few years later, he revealed an unusual capacity for writing jazz pieces that other musicians jumped at the chance to perform ("Airegin," "Oleo"); with the Clifford Brown–Max Roach Quintet, he introduced the first widely noted bebop waltz, "Valse Hot."

In 1955, Rollins achieved an impressive stylistic breakthrough with the quartet album *Worktime*, following it a year later with *Saxophone Colossus*, one of the most lauded albums of the era. Rollins's music reflects a love of sentimental popular tunes that he heard on radio and in movies. He often astonishes audiences by dredging up and rigorously renovating such unlikely material as "There's No Business Like Show Business," "Toot Toot Tootsie," "Sweet Leilani," "I'm an Old Cowhand," "To a Wild Rose," and "Autumn Nocturne." In 1959, depleted by a decade of work and puzzled by the new stylistic currents, Rollins put his career on hold for more than two years, which he devoted to intense practicing. It was the first of three sabbaticals, each a restorative that inclined him toward further experimentation.

Expanding Bop

Rollins's music possesses great wit and concentration, evident in the frequent musical allusions within his solos. Although he has remained faithful to the precepts of bop, he has taken its harmonic complexity, vigorous swing, and melodic invention into diverse areas. These include calypso ("St. Thomas" was the first of many highly rhythmic jazz calypsos), avant-garde (he pioneered the saxophone-bass-drums trio to maximize his improvisational freedom), and rock (he has recorded with the Rolling Stones and written pieces that show rapprochement with post-1960s pop music).

In addition to humor, Rollins's solos are characterized by the following.

TIMBRE Rollins's sound is something of a paradox in that it frequently changes, yet it is always recognizably his. In the early 1950s, his tone was harsh and splintered, almost grating at times. In what many consider his greatest period, 1955–59, he produced an enormously attractive timbre: commanding, virile, and smooth as oak. In later years, he continued to experiment, eventually producing a sound remarkable in its sumptuous expressiveness.

MOTIVES Rollins broke with bebop's tendency to value new melodies, improvised on a song's harmonies, at the expense of the song itself. Instead of discarding the melody after the theme chorus, he reprises key phrases during the course of an improvisation as touchstones, reminding the listener that he is elaborating on a particular song and not just its harmonic underpinnings.

CADENZAS The cadenza, an unaccompanied episode played by an instrumentalist at the beginning or end of a performance (as in a classical concerto), is nothing new to jazz. Louis Armstrong, for example, ignited the 1920s with his cadenza on "West End Blues" (see Chapter 2). But no one has done as much with cadenzas as Rollins, who makes them an integral part of live and recorded performances. His sometimes go on longer than the ensemble sections, and almost always generate audience excitement.

EBULLIENCE The emotional meaning of a musical performance is entirely subjective: what thrills one listener may bore another. Still, Armstrong introduced a feeling of elation that has since remained a part of the jazz experience, whether achieved through high notes, big-band riffs, virtuosic runs, or other means. Rollins, perhaps more than any other soloist of his generation, often aims for transcendence. Sometimes he achieves it through obstinacy in prolonging a solo or revving up the rhythm until he reaches a satisfying climax.

This last aspect of Rollins's music works in concert, particularly in the outdoor and stadium settings he has favored since the 1980s, where audiences are primed to follow him in search of ecstatic release. It doesn't work in studio recordings, where expansive repetition quickly palls. As a result, Rollins split his music into two modes: the concert mode, which often aims for a spiritual intensity, and the studio mode, which is pre-planned and relatively understated. The two modes come together in his best live recordings.

🔊 "Autumn Nocturne"

Rollins's traits are all on display in his 1978 concert performance of "Autumn Nocturne," a fairly obscure 1940s song by little-remembered songwriters Kim Gannon and Joseph Myrow. Rollins recalled the tune from a staid 1941 record by Claude Thornhill's band, which features little improvisation. What Rollins does with it is far from staid. For the first two-thirds of the performance, he improvises a cadenza that hints at the melody with allusive fragments; these are instantly overrun as he ranges through several keys, shaping and distorting his timbre, and priming the audience for a dynamic transition into the ensemble chorus.

Rollins plays only one chorus of the tune, but note how he uses it to extend the emotional intensity established in the cadenza. He continues to toy with timbre, using astounding virtuoso passagework and dissonances to depart from the melody without really leaving it. At no point during the chorus are we in doubt that he is playing "Autumn Nocturne," yet the notes he actually plays consistently skirt the song's cloying melody. The response of the audience says a lot about the complexity of the experience Rollins offers, one involving suspense and laughter, tension and release, irreverence and romance.

🔊 autumn nocturne

3.2

SONNY ROLLINS

Sonny Rollins, tenor saxophone; Mark Soskin, piano; Aurell Ray, electric guitar; Jerome Harris, electric bass; Tony Williams, drums

- Label: Milestone M55055; *Don't Stop the Carnival* (Milestone M550552)
- Date: 1978
- Style: hard bop
- Form: 32-bar popular song (**A A B A**), with lengthy solo introduction

What to listen for:
- Rolllins's long, tension-filled solo, ranging from simple melodies (and quotes from various songs) to dissonant passagework
- his way of hinting at "Autumn Nocturne"
- his leading the band in after four minutes, followed by their impassioned performance

INTRODUCTION

0:00	Rollins begins improvising at top speed, ending with a descending run. In the abrupt silence that follows, we can hear murmurs of audience conversation.
0:07	Still warming up, Rollins plays fragments, some short, others lengthy.
0:18	He plays the opening melody of "Autumn Nocturne" in its home key of B-flat major.
0:27	The melody begins to lose rhythmic momentum in softer, disjointed passagework, finally running down to a loud, squawky note.
0:29	Rollins begins a new phrase with a bold, upward statement, then shifts it to a new key. As he reaches for upper notes, his tone is deliberately thin and strained.
0:39	A new phrase **modulates** to a different key.
0:48	A descending **chromatic scale** lands on a new note, suggesting yet another modulation.
0:52	Rollins rapidly repeats a short melodic pattern.
0:59	In the spirit of the original melody, Rollins plays in an earnest, romantic style.
1:09	Suddenly returning to B-flat major, he once again plays the opening melody to "Autumn Nocturne."
1:21	Rollins plays with a **triad** (three-note chord), moving it up and down experimentally. Sensing that the introduction is now going into overdrive, the audience begins to applaud and cheer.
1:28	The harmony becomes more "**outside**," with a descending melodic sequence built on the interval of a fourth.
1:41	Rollins moves into uncertain harmonic territory before returning to B-flat.
1:58	He suddenly shifts to a simple riff, played with greater volume and timbre intensity. He repeats the riff until the audience shouts its approval.
2:08	He fastens onto a two-note motive, moving rapidly between keys.
2:22	He quotes a phrase from "Today" by Randy Sparks ("I'll be a dandy and I'll be a rover").
2:29	Rollins holds a note and distorts it before moving to much faster material.
2:49	Settling in a major key, he plays more bluesy material.
2:59	A much faster passage moves through unsettled harmonies.
3:05	Rollins plays with a motive, dropping the last note a half step with each repetition.
3:25	He again holds and distorts a note.
3:31	Settling into F major, he ironically quotes "Home Sweet Home."
3:39	After playing a single note, he awkwardly answers it with a verbal squawk. He repeats the gesture, drawing yet more cheers from the crowd.
3:41	Once again, Rollins moves into a bluesy mode.
3:58	He begins to move down the chromatic scale. The notes become increasingly detached and accelerate in speed.
4:05	As the timbre of the notes becomes more distorted, the line reaches bottom and turns back upward.
4:11	Rollins settles into a slow, deliberate tempo, which becomes a cue for the band to enter.

CHORUS 1

4:18	**A**	As the audience roars its approval, Rollins plays the melody of "Autumn Nocturne" with fiercely distorted timbre. By sounding the beat clearly, the rhythm section makes it easier to hear the subtleties of Rollins's rhythmic gestures.
4:36		Off to the side, the electric guitar adds chords.
4:40		As the harmonic progression reaches the turnaround, Rollins launches into an extremely fast, **dissonant**, and heavily distorted passage.

4:46	**A**	Rollins returns to playing the melody.
4:54		He focuses his line on a single note, decorating it with **neighbor notes** (adjacent notes).
5:07		The last phrase becomes lost in an ecstatic, dissonant passage.
5:13	**B**	The bridge begins in a new key, with Rollins returning to the melody.
5:17		For several measures, the bass suggests a double-time rhythmic feeling.
5:27		The tune modulates to a new key. Rollins's improvisation becomes more earnest and impassioned.
5:35		As the tune begins to modulate back to the original key, Rollins plays another impossibly fast and distorted passage.
5:40		Williams signals the return with a drum roll.
5:42	**A**	
5:45		Rollins's melody descends instead of rising.
5:50		His line soars upward, reaching a brief climax.
5:54		As the tune nears its last few bars, Williams begins playing the cymbals more intently.
5:59		He plays a strong polyrhythm, augmenting it in the next measure by adding bass drum strokes.
6:07		A three-note rhythm ends the tune. All the musicians play their instruments simultaneously.
6:19		Seeming to have a few more notes in mind, Rollins tries to squeeze them out.
6:21		Finally, over a long saxophone **tremolo**, the tune ends to applause.

■ WES MONTGOMERY (1923–1968)

The arrival of Charlie Christian in the late 1930s opened the floodgates to electric guitarists who played in a linear style, adapting the single-note phrasing of horn players. Several combined linear solos with chords, voicing them in ways unique to the six-string configuration of the guitar. Those who achieved prominence in the 1950s include Barney Kessel, Tal Farlow, Johnny Smith, Billy Bauer, Jim Hall, and Kenny Burrell—each took Christian's example and developed a distinctive style of his own. None, however, had the impact of Wes Montgomery, who radically altered the instrument's sound with his innovative approach to chordal harmonies.

Born in Indianapolis, Montgomery was the second of three jazz musician brothers. His older brother, Monk, gave him a four-string guitar when he was twelve, but he showed little interest in it until he heard Christian's recordings several years later. Montgomery was twenty and married when he bought an electric guitar and amplifier, and began spending hours at night after work teaching himself how to play. When his wife complained that the amplifier was too loud, he dispensed with the pick and used his thumb, achieving unparalleled mastery with this technique as well as a remarkably mellow tone.

Montgomery elaborated on that dulcet sound by playing in octaves. From octaves, he moved on to full and intricate chords, manipulating them with the same speed and dexterity of his single-note improvisations, continuing to pluck and strum with his thumb. Soon he developed a signature approach

octave two notes with the same letter name, an eighth apart

Wes Montgomery set a new standard for jazz guitar and innovated a new style of soloing, combining single-note phrases, octaves, and rhythmic chords, and became a 1960s pop star in the bargain.

to soloing: after a theme statement, he would play choruses of single-note phrases, followed by choruses of more rhythmically intense octaves, climaxing with riff-laden chords. In 1948, he was hired by Lionel Hampton's big band and went on tour.

Bored with travel and one-night stands, Montgomery returned to Indianapolis and formed a group with his brothers, Monk on bass and Buddy on piano and vibes. Montgomery was thirty-four and virtually unknown when alto saxophonist Cannonball Adderley (see Chapter 13) heard him and alerted his record label to this major undiscovered talent. From the moment he arrived in New York, the critical reception was highly favorable; guitarists gawked at his impossibly fast thumb, and he came to be regarded as a musician's musician.

Then in the early 1960s, the guitar moved to the center of America's musical consciousness, and Montgomery's alluring octaves were seen as having great commercial potential. As he switched affiliations from a jazz label to a pop label in 1967, he emerged as a mainstream recording star, performing with large studio ensembles in easy-listening arrangements of pop songs that featured his octaves and minimized improvisation. Those records failed to reflect the stimulating jazz he continued to play in live performance, but firmly established him as one of the best-selling musicians of his time.

"Twisted Blues"

Montgomery's harmonic and rhythmic ingenuity led him to compose pieces that admiring musicians described as "tricky." "Twisted Blues" is a good example; as the title implies, it seems to start out as a blues, but goes off in a different direction, ending up as a thirty-two-bar structure built on a *near* sixteen-bar blues played twice. Montgomery initially recorded it with a small group in 1961, and made it an almost nightly part of his sets. By the time he rerecorded it in 1965, with a big band deftly arranged by Oliver Nelson, the piece was practically second nature to him. Although this version was made just as he was beginning to make the transition to a pop artist, it is far more effective than the original.

The tempo is taken way up, yet Montgomery plays with ease, phrasing on and against the beat, combining bebop harmonies with blues cadences, alternating chromatic riffs and melodic sequences. Toward the close of the third chorus, he introduces a rhythmic series of two-note chords (1:39). In the choruses that follow, he turns on the heat with his trademark octaves and chords. Note his interaction with the orchestra, which paces and inspires him, and the attentive playing by Grady Tate, Montgomery's preferred drummer.

3.3

 **twisted blues**

WES MONTGOMERY

Ernie Royal, Joe Newman, Donald Byrd, trumpets;
Wayne Andre, Jimmy Cleveland, Quentin Jackson,
Danny Moore, trombones; Tony Studd, bass trom-
bone; Phil Woods, Jerry Dodgion, alto saxophones;
Romeo Penque, Bob Ashton, tenor saxophones;
Danny Bank, baritone saxophone; Herbie Hancock
or Roger Kellaway, piano; Wes Montgomery, electric
guitar; George Duvivier, bass; Grady Tate, drums;
Candido Camero, congas; Oliver Nelson, conductor
and arranger

- Label: Verve MGV8642; *Goin' out of My Head*
  (Verve 000940202)
- Date: 1965
- Style: hard bop
- Form: 32-bar popular song (**A A'**)

> **What to listen for:**
> - Montgomery's use of sequences, motives,
>   cross-rhythms, bluesy chords
> - his gradual build from single notes to chords
>   and octaves
> - interaction between guitar and arranged big-
>   band accompaniment

INTRODUCTION

0:00		The full band enters with loud chords on the **offbeat**, played in the upper range of the trumpet's register.
0:02		Beneath the shrieking trumpets, the saxophones hold a **dissonant** chord.
0:04		The instrumentation now quiets down, with the trombones in the lead.

CHORUS 1 (HEAD)

0:08	**A**	Montgomery, introduced by two loud trumpet chords, plays a bluesy melody. The harmony behind it is *not* the tonic, but a IV chord—which we would normally find in the fifth bar of a blues.
0:11		The saxophone section responds to the guitar's melody with short, crisp chords, **doubled** by the guitar.
0:13		The first phrase is repeated.
0:17		Montgomery plays a short motive, leading the band to play a long chain of descending **chromatic** chords.
0:25	**A'**	Montgomery repeats his bluesy opening melody, answered by a corresponding melody in the saxophones.
0:38		The full band plays the descending chromatic chords, with trumpets shrieking in their extreme highest register.

CHORUS 2

0:42	**A**	Montgomery begins improvising in a bebop style over the rhythm section.
0:54		Over the gradually descending chromatic chords, he takes a melodic idea and repeats it (a **sequence**), starting each time on a different pitch to match the movement of the chords.
0:59	**A'**	
1:03		Montgomery plays a short three-note motive, drifting it up and down to match the harmony. The drums react to its **polyrhythm.**

CHORUS 3

1:16	**A**	Montgomery trims his line to simple, short phrases.
1:19		He hits a bluesy chord, followed by a bluesy phrase.
1:29		As the chords descend chromatically, Montgomery plays another motive in sequence.

1:32	**A'**	
1:39		Playing on two strings at once, Montgomery creates another polyrhythmic riff.
1:43		The change in harmony suddenly jolts him away from the blues lick into a more complex line.

CHORUS 4

1:48	**A**	Moving from single-note lines to chords and octaves, Montgomery plays short, choppy phrases, creating a **call and response** with a two-note riff in the upper register.
1:59		Playing in octaves, he creates another sequence—this time with a distinctive syncopated rhythm.
2:04	**A'**	Montgomery ends this part of his solo with a simple arranged riff, its opening rhythm doubled by the drums and piano.

CHORUS 5

2:20	**A**	For the next two choruses, the band enters with riffs (here, trombones) that accompany Montgomery for eight bars, leaving him free to improvise over the more complex chord changes of the next eight bars.
2:29		The trombones exit while Montgomery continues to play with a two-note motive that stretches into the upper register before tumbling back down.
2:37	**A'**	The saxophones enter with a new riff, and Montgomery continues to improvise over it.

CHORUS 6

2:53	**A**	The trombones play a two-note riff, which Montgomery uses as the backdrop for an extended **cross-rhythm**.
3:06		His syncopation finally collapses into a simple rhythmic line that falls directly on the beat.
3:10	**A'**	With the return of the two-note riff, Montgomery moves back to a syncopated pattern.
3:15		The trumpets join the trombones on the riff.
3:18		Montgomery fastens onto a two-note motive, played to a steady rhythm.

INTERLUDE

3:26		The drums play an eight-bar solo.

CHORUS 7

3:34	**A**	Two loud chords in the trumpets signal a return to the head.
3:50	**A'**	

CODA

4:05		The saxophones play a series of descending chords that land on the tonic.
4:06		The trumpets play a final sharp dissonance, holding the chord for a long time until the drums cut them off.

A Parable

Sadly, Montgomery did not have long to enjoy his skyrocketing success. The 1965 album that included "Twisted Blues" (*Goin' out of My Head*) received a Grammy Award, and his more commercial debut on the pop label A&M, *A Day in the Life*, was cited as the best-selling jazz album of 1967. From that point on, his record producers demanded he hew to the proven formula: familiar tunes played with octaves, backed by a large, easy-listening ensemble, with little improvisation to confuse the target audience. In 1968, he died suddenly of a heart attack, at forty-three.

Montgomery's career was interpreted by many as a jazz parable, with the moral being: for every album an artist does for the company, he ought to insist on doing one for himself. In concert, Montgomery continued to perform brilliantly, rarely playing the pop tunes that made him famous and never touring with large ensembles. Yet none of that work was formally documented after 1965. Indeed, the impact of his popular success was so pervasive that after his death, Verve released tracks by his quartet with an overdubbed string ensemble to simulate the pop recordings. Decades later, those tracks were released as Montgomery performed them, to much acclaim. By then, virtually every jazz guitarist had studied and many had mastered his innovative octaves and harmonies.

ADDITIONAL LISTENING

Lennie Tristano	"Subconscious-Lee" (1949); Lee Konitz, *Subconscious-Lee* (Prestige/OJC 186)
	"Wow" (1949); Tristano and Warne Marsh, *Intuition* (Capitol Jazz CDP 7243 8 52771 2 2)
	"Requiem" (1955); *Lennie Tristano / The New Tristano* (Rhino 71595)
Tadd Dameron	"Lady Bird" (1948); *Complete Blue Note and Capitol Recordings of Fats Navarro and Tadd Dameron* (Blue Note 33373)
Claude Thornhill	"Donna Lee" (1947); *Claude Thornhill and His Orchestra, 1947* (Hindsight)
Miles Davis	"Boplicity" (1949); *Birth of the Cool* (Capitol Jazz RVG Edition 30117)
Stan Kenton	"City of Glass" (1951); *City of Glass* (Capitol Jazz 7243 832084 2 5)
Gerry Mulligan	"My Funny Valentine" (1953); *Gerry Mulligan: Jazz Profile* (Capitol 54905)
	"Festive Minor" (1959); *What Is There to Say?* (Sony 52978)
Modern Jazz Quartet	"Django" (1954); *Django* (Prestige PRCD-7057-2)
John Lewis and the Modern Jazz Quartet	"England's Carol (God Rest Ye Merry Gentlemen)" (1960); *Modern Jazz Quartet and Orchestra* (Collectables Jazz Classics 6184)
Dave Brubeck	"Blue Rondo à la Turk," "Take Five" (1959); *Time Out* (Legacy 65122)
Art Blakey	"Moanin'" (1958); *Moanin'* (Blue Note 95324)
Horace Silver	"Songs for My Father" (1964), "Señor Blues" (1956); *Greatest Hits* (Collectables 1064)
	Silver City (Milestone)
Max Roach / Clifford Brown Quintet	"Joy Spring," "Delilah" (1954); *Clifford Brown & Max Roach* (Verve 731454330626)
Sonny Rollins	"St. Thomas," "Blue Seven" (1956); *Saxophone Colossus* (Prestige PRCD-8105-2)
Wes Montgomery	"Four on Six," "Airegin" (1960); *The Incredible Jazz Guitar of Wes Montgomery* (Riverside RCD-30790)

JAZZ COMPOSITION IN THE 1950s

DEFINITIONS: NEW AND OLD

Composition is not easily defined in music driven by improvisation. Before the advent of recordings, composers may have improvised in concert, but they committed formal composition to a written musical score. From the twentieth century on, records often supplanted or eliminated the need for scores. Coleman Hawkins's "Body and Soul" has been transcribed and published as a score, but the truest representation of the work is his recording, which alone documents such essential components as his timbre and rhythmic pulse.

Simply by calling it Coleman Hawkins's "Body and Soul," we contest the traditional attribution of composition, since the performance is based on a published melody written by Johnny Green. Indeed, international copyright laws fail to acknowledge the improviser's contribution: all "mechanical" (or composer) royalties that accrue from sales of Hawkins's record are divided between the song's composer, lyricist, and publisher. Hawkins does not participate in the profits, although Green's chord progression (which Hawkins does adhere to) is not copyrightable, while virtually every melodic phrase

Thelonious Monk, a powerful force at the jam sessions that fed the birth of modern jazz, works on a score at Minton's Playhouse in Harlem, 1948.

wwnorton.com/studyspace

Ridiculed as a charlatan for his unorthodox style, Thelonious Monk proved his bona fides to skeptics by recording an album of Duke Ellington tunes, backed by his partner from Minton's, drummer Kenny Clarke, in 1955.

PHOTO BY CAROLE RIEFF © CAROLE RIEFF ARCHIVE

Hawkins plays after the first two bars is his own invention. This financial iniquity is one reason jazz musicians of the bop era wrote their own (copyrighted) melodies based on standard harmonic progressions.

At what point does improvisation end and composition begin? If Hawkins had written his "Body and Soul" variations at a desk and published them as "Variations on a Theme by Johnny Green," no one would question his function as a composer or his right to reap financial reward. Yet as a jazz musician, Hawkins was trained to do something classical composers don't do: compose durable music spontaneously. His solo on "Body and Soul" became so renowned that it was subsequently transcribed and arranged for ensembles to perform. But that is one of several exceptions that prove the rule, which may be stated as follows: A composition is a musical work that may be played by any number of musicians and bands while remaining basically unchanged; an improvisation, though it may prove as durable and adaptable as a composition, exists first and foremost as a particular performance.

Back to the Future

In the postbop era of the 1950s, the nature of jazz composition changed. We have already seen (in Chapter 12) the influence of classical music on bop and postbop musicians, and the attempt to forge a Third Stream. Yet the major currents in 1950s composition derived less from classical borrowings than from reinvestigations of the jazz past: the most influential composers combined modern jazz with such traditional techniques as polyphony, stride piano, short breaks, and cadenzas, as well as standard jazz and pop themes. In this period, jazz began to produce full-time composers who did not necessarily work as instrumentalists.

The four composers we examine here represent four approaches to expanding the jazz canvas. Thelonious Monk worked almost exclusively with blues and song forms, rarely composing themes longer than thirty-two bars. Charles Mingus also worked with conventional forms, adding effects from gospel, ragtime, bop, classical music, and other sources, and expanding those forms into longer works. Gil Evans, as we've seen, focused on the work of other composers, radically altering it into imaginative new pieces. George Russell introduced modalism into jazz, which spurred fresh ways of approaching harmony and the connection between improvisation and composition.

■ THELONIOUS MONK (1917–1982)

After Duke Ellington, Thelonious Monk is the most widely performed of all jazz composers. This is remarkable when you consider the differences in their output: Ellington wrote between 1,500 and 2,000 pieces, while Monk wrote around 70. Ellington composed, in addition to orchestral, chamber, symphonic, and vocal works, dozens of popular songs, including major hits. Monk composed no hits and only one song ("'Round Midnight") that achieved a marginal mainstream acceptance. Yet every jazz player knows at least a few Monk pieces: they have been adapted for swing band, Dixieland, cool jazz, hard bop, avant-garde, and classical music settings. With the addition of lyrics, they have found increasing favor with singers. Although in his early years Monk was regarded as an eccentric, difficult, and not very talented pianist, his music is widely loved today, even among people who have no interest in or feeling for jazz. Grade school teachers have found that very young children respond enthusiastically to his melodies.

Years of Struggle

Born in North Carolina, Monk was four when his family moved to New York. In grade school, he began listening to his older sister's piano lessons and teaching himself. As a teenager, he added a middle name, Sphere—Thelonious Sphere Monk—and quit high school to tour with an evangelist, accompanying her on organ. He heard the leading stride pianist–composers, including Duke Ellington, James P. Johnson, and Mary Lou Williams, and began writing distinctive tunes that were melodically angular and harmonically dissonant. In 1939, he briefly studied music, and a year or so later was recruited by drummer Kenny Clarke to play in the house band at Minton's Playhouse.

Monk's involvement in after-hours jam sessions and cutting contests at Minton's, where he accompanied Charlie Christian, Dizzy Gillespie, and other advanced musicians, placed him at the center of bebop's development. Musicians, including the dazzling pianist Bud Powell, whom Monk mentored, admired his quirky rhythmic attack and progressive harmonies. Several of his compositions were enthusiastically taken up by swing and bop musicians, including "Epistrophy" (written by Monk and Clarke), "Hackensack" (introduced by Coleman Hawkins as "Rifftide"), and "52nd Street Theme," a bebop anthem that Monk himself never recorded.

The most important of Monk's early compositions was the ballad "'Round Midnight," which trumpet player Cootie Williams recorded in a big-band version in 1944, with Powell on piano. Williams made it his theme song, and after lyrics were added (by Bernie Hanighen), singers began to perform it. Dizzy Gillespie recorded an important version in 1946, adding an introductory passage that became part of the song, and Monk recorded the first of his many versions in 1947. By 1956, when Miles Davis made Monk's ballad the centerpiece of his album *'Round About Midnight*, it was fast becoming one of the most frequently performed songs in all of jazz. Monk's other ballads, each a distinctively poignant work, include "Ruby, My Dear," "Coming on the Hudson," "Reflections," "Ask Me Now," and "Crepuscule with Nellie."

"'Round Midnight"

In 1944, Hawkins hired Monk for the quartet he was leading, taking him on tour and recording with him. As word of Monk's unusual music spread, he found an important admirer in Alfred Lion, whose record company, Blue Note, signed him in 1947 and documented much of his most important work over the next five years. Monk was sometimes regarded as a figure apart from the bop movement, and his percussive piano style was mocked by many critics and fans.

In the years since Monk's death, medical observers have speculated that he may have had a neurobiological disorder called Asperger's syndrome, a non-debilitating form of autism, first described in 1944 and frequently associated with genius: others thought to have been similarly afflicted include Sir Isaac Newton, Albert Einstein, Ludwig Wittgenstein, Glenn Gould, and Stanley

Kubrick. Among the symptoms are a heightened ability to recognize and analyze patterns, exceptional talent in a particular area, undeveloped social and verbal skills, physical awkwardness, and compulsive behavior. It can also lead to mood disorders and depression. Monk was known for his long silences (in speech and in music), onstage dancing (he would twitchingly whirl in a circle as other musicians soloed), peculiar hats and sunglasses, and obsessive concentration on a few compositions.

Monk was further isolated in 1951, when he was imprisoned for two months on a trumped-up narcotics charge; by all reports he was innocent, but he riled authorities by refusing to testify against others. As a result, he lost his cabaret card, which functioned as a license (subsequently found to be unconstitutional) to perform in New York venues where liquor was sold. He spent the next six years composing and recording and occasionally performing in concert halls or in other cities.

Recognition

In 1955, Monk signed with a small new label, Riverside, and reluctantly agreed to begin his contract by recording well-known themes by Ellington and other popular songwriters. The idea was to disarm skeptical listeners by demonstrating that he could play in a conventional jazz setting, before focusing on original music. The plan worked. Monk's third Riverside album, *Brilliant Corners*, which featured Sonny Rollins and Max Roach, was hailed as a major jazz event in 1956, though the title piece proved so difficult to play that the final version had to be spliced together from three takes. Listeners around the world had no trouble humming the tune's irresistible, ominous, march-like cadences.

With Coltrane ▶ In 1957, Monk's cabaret card was restored, and he began a historic six-month residency at the Five Spot, leading a quartet that included tenor saxophonist John Coltrane. For contractual reasons (Coltrane was signed to another label, Prestige), little of this music was recorded, but it attracted the attention of dozens of New York artists: jazz and classical musicians, painters, actors, and poets. Monk was adapted as a hero of the beats, a generation of self-defined outlaw writers. His work with Coltrane had a lasting influence on both men: both thereafter spent most of their careers leading quartets that built on Monk's precepts. (A remarkable record of their collaboration was made at a Carnegie Hall concert for a Voice of America overseas broadcast; it remained unknown until the tape was discovered in the Library of Congress in 2005 and released on Blue Note.)

Monk's fame steadily grew. In 1962, he was signed by Columbia Records, the country's premiere record label, and two years later *Time* ran a cover story about him that cinched his standing as one of jazz's most admired musicians. Monk's quartet, with his longtime saxophonist Charlie Rouse, toured the world, finally reaping the rewards of his refusal to compromise. As he once witheringly remarked, "I say play your own way. Don't play what the public wants—you play what you want and let the public pick up on what you are doing—even if it does take them 15, 20 years."

Having achieved acceptance, Monk began to withdraw personally and professionally. His composing slowed to a standstill, though he seemed to open up emotionally with his joyous devotion to solo piano, perfecting a style that combined modern harmonies with stride rhythms, often inspired by old, forgotten, and unlikely tunes. Monk made his last records in 1971, and appeared in concert only a few times after that. By the middle 1970s, he had slipped into seclusion; soon he stopped speaking to anyone but his wife and a few friends. He spent his last years in the home of his longtime patron, the Baroness Pannonica de Konigswarter, and died of a stroke in 1982. In 2006, he received a belated Pulitzer Prize for music.

Style

Monk's compositions are abstractions of the song forms that had always predominated in jazz and popular music: **A A B A** tunes and blues. In some instances, he altered standard harmonic progressions with whole-tone and chromatic scales, so that "Just You, Just Me" became "Evidence," "Blue Skies" became "In Walked Bud," and "Sweet Georgia Brown" became "Bright Mississippi." Each new composition had its own unmistakable integrity. His quirky dissonances—including minor ninths, flatted fifths (or tritones), and minor seconds (or semitones)—had been widely regarded as mistakes until he popularized them. Monk played minor seconds, for example (two adjacent notes on the piano), simultaneously, as though his finger had accidentally hit the space between the two keys, making them both ring and forcing the listener to accept that jarring sound as a routine part of his musical language. Nellie Monk, his wife, described an incident in their home life that suggests a parallel with the way Monk altered the way we hear jazz: "I used to have a phobia about pictures or anything on a wall hanging just a little bit crooked. Thelonious cured me. He nailed a clock to the wall at a very slight angle, just enough to make me furious. We argued about it for two hours, but he wouldn't let me change it. Finally, I got used to it. Now anything can hang at any angle, and it doesn't bother me at all."

This doesn't mean that Monk advocated a kind of free jazz in which any note was acceptable, or that he didn't make mistakes. In "Thelonious" (below), which is chock-a-block with dissonances, there is a revealing moment (at

FRANK DRIGGS COLLECTION

Monk occasionally stood and danced in jerky, circular movements while another member of his band soloed. Here he responds to his longtime tenor saxophonist Charlie Rouse, 1960s.

1:52) where he concludes an arpeggio by landing on the wrong note. He then plays the right one, and combines them so as to resolve the error, making it a viable part of the performance. (Musicians call this a "save.") A fastidious composer-improviser, Monk paid scrupulous attention to details and demanded the same level of attention from his musicians.

Monk believed that a meaningful improvisation should flow from and develop the composed theme. Unsurprisingly, his compositions sound like his improvisations, and his improvisations often sound like his compositions—even when he didn't write the theme. For example, classical pianists have transcribed his solo interpretations of pop songs like "I Should Care" or "April in Paris," performing them as if they were Monk originals. His music has altered our perception of harmony, space, swing, and melody, all while remaining tied to the traditions from which it sprang.

"Thelonious"

A product of Monk's first session as a leader, "Thelonious" is considered his first masterpiece, a work that shuns the usual theme-and-variations format of bop and shows off his compositional ingenuity and fierce independence. In 1947, a *Billboard* reviewer called it a "controversial jazz disking worked out on a one note riff." But that repeated note, a B-flat (sometimes doubled as a B-flat octave), is a deceptively simple front for the descending chromatic chords that shadow this thirty-six-bar variant on the **A A B A** song. The **A** sections are eight bars, the bridge is ten, and the last **A** section includes a two-bar coda.

This pattern demands heightened attention from musicians, who, as a matter of habit, tend to think in terms of four eight-bar sections. As John Coltrane observed, "I always had to be alert with Monk, because if you didn't keep aware all the time of what was going on, you'd suddenly feel as if you'd stepped into an empty elevator shaft." In "Thelonious," the three wind instruments are used to voice the chords, and the only soloists are piano and, briefly, drums. The result is a kind of piano concerto, incorporating various elements of jazz history from stride to bop.

LISTENING GUIDE

3.4

thelonious

THELONIOUS MONK
Idrees Sulieman, trumpet; Danny Quebec West, alto saxophone; Billy Smith, tenor saxophone; Thelonious Monk, piano; Gene Ramey, bass; Art Blakey, drums

- Label: BLP 1510; *Genius of Modern Music*, vol. 1 (RVG 781510)
- Date: 1947
- Style: bebop, Monk-style
- Form: 36-bar popular song (**A A B A**; the bridge and the last **A** section are 10 rather than 8 bars long)

What to listen for:
- insistent repeated note, over chromatic chords
- unusual number of measures in **B** and last **A**
- Monk's unusual improvising, including stride piano in chorus 3

INTRODUCTION

0:00   Unaccompanied, Monk plays the main theme of the piece: a syncopated figure on the first note of the scale (the tonic). Pianistically, it is simple, built comfortably around an **octave**.

0:02   As Monk continues, he is joined by Blakey on cymbals. The theme ends on a **blue third**, which Monk holds out.

0:04   Blakey plays a brief solo, alternating snare drum with bass drum. In the background, we can hear Monk's voice counting off time.

CHORUS 1 (HEAD)

0:08   **A**   The entire band plays the theme: Monk's insistent, repetitive octave, supported by descending **chromatic** chords in the horns. The bass line for the **A** section remains consistent throughout the performance.

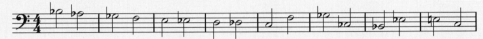

0:18   **A**

0:27   **B**   The bridge begins with a *cadence figure*, deriving its rhythm from the **A** section and promising a conclusion to its chromatic harmonies. But the harmony is *not* resolved: instead, the melody blends into a slower line that floats above ambiguous harmonies.

0:31   When the melody reaches the tonic, it is supported not by conventional harmony but by the **whole-tone scale**, which distorts our sense of tonality.

0:32   The melody slowly descends by half step.

0:37   As the melody reaches a half cadence, Monk connects the bridge to the concluding **A** section with a whole-tone scale.

0:38   **A**

0:47   The chorus ends with the cadence figure heard at the opening of the bridge, this time resolving to the tonic in the second bar.

CHORUS 2

0:49   **A**   Monk begins his solo with simple melodic fragments, all derived from his opening octave.

0:58   **A**   Suddenly, responding to the harmonies implied by the chromatic bass line, he shifts to a bebop-style improvised line.

1:07   **B**   Monk begins the bridge by paraphrasing its melody.

1:12   With a few dissonant notes and unexpected silences, he complicates his connection to the underlying harmony.

1:17   He finally returns to the tonic octave—a full bar early.

1:19   **A**   Monk plays a syncopated pattern with the tonic octave in the highest register of the piano, accompanied by only the bass and drums.

1:28   At the end of the chorus, he returns to the middle of the piano to play the cadence figure.

CHORUS 3

1:30   **A**   Sounding uncannily like a ragtime piano player, Monk begins playing in **stride** style, firmly doubling the bass line.

1:39   **A**   With his left hand shifting restlessly between chromatic chords, his right hand remains firmly rooted in the tonic.

1:48   **B**   Monk starts the bridge by once again paraphrasing its melody.

1:52   He "misses" a note by a half step, corrects it, and returns to a literal statement of the melody.

2:00   **A**

2:02   A new three-note motive borrows its rhythm from the bebop standard "Salt Peanuts."

2:09		Monk plays the cadence figure, connecting it seamlessly to the beginning of the next chorus.
CHORUS 4		
2:11	**A**	Once again, the chorus begins with an unaccompanied statement of the main theme.
2:16		Fastening onto a short chromatic **triplet**, Monk pulls it down the length of the piano.
2:20	**A**	He plays a long, involved melodic line based on the chromatic harmony.
2:29	**B**	The bridge begins in the upper octave; Monk plays it delicately.
2:41	**A**	The band returns with a full statement of the theme.
CODA		
2:50		The band plays the cadence figure, stopping on the next-to-last chord. While the horns hold out the unresolved harmony, Monk plays a lengthy descending whole-tone scale.
2:56		He ends his improvisation with a striking high note.
2:58		A three-note stroke from the drummer closes the performance.

Monk's 71

These are the seventy-one compositions officially attributed to Thelonious Monk (some were written in collaboration with other musicians or had lyrics subsequently added). The dates denote the earliest recorded versions by Monk; where a decade is given, Monk never recorded the tune. He may also have worked on other, disputed pieces.

1940s: "52nd Street Theme" (aka "The Theme"), "Harlem Is Awful Messy"

1946: "Introspection"

1947: "Humph," "In Walked Bud," "Off Minor," "'Round Midnight," "Ruby, My Dear," "Thelonious," "Well, You Needn't," "Who Knows?"

1948: "Epistrophy," " Evidence," "I Mean You," "Misterioso"

1950s: "Two Timer" (aka "Five Will Get You Ten")

1951: "Ask Me Now," "Criss Cross," "Eronel," "Four in One," "Straight, No Chaser"

1952: "Bemsha Swing," "Bye-Ya," "Hornin' In," "Let's Cool One," "Little Rootie Tootie," "Monk's Dream," "Monk's Mood," "Reflections," "Sixteen," "Skippy," "Trinkle Tinkle"

1953: "Friday the 13th," "Let's Call This," "Think of One"

1954: "Blue Monk," "Hackensack," "Locomotive," "Nutty," "We See," "Work"

1955: "Brake's Sake," "Gallop's Gallop," "Shuffle Boil"

1956: "Ba-lue Bolivar Ba-lues-are," "Brilliant Corners," "Pannonica"

1957: "Crepuscule with Nellie," "Functional," "Light Blue," "Rhythm-a-ning"

1958: "Blues Five Spot," "Coming on the Hudson"

1959: "Bluehawk," "Jackie-ing," "Played Twice," "Round Lights"

1960: "San Francisco Holiday"

1961: "Bright Mississippi"

1963: "Oska T"

1964: "Monk's Point," "North of the Sunset," "Stuffy Turkey," "Teo"

1966: "Green Chimneys"

1967: "Boo Boo's Birthday," "Ugly Beauty"

1968: "Raise Four"

1971: "Blue Sphere," "Something in Blue"

1972: "A Merrier Christmas"

"Rhythm-a-ning"

One of Monk's best-known pieces, "Rhythm-a-ning" has a long history, which testifies to his gift for collating bits of music and renewing them in his own way. The **A A B A** tune is based on the chord changes of "I Got Rhythm," but the primary eight-bar melody draws on two big-band recordings of the 1930s: Duke Ellington's "Ducky Wucky" (1932) for two measures, and Mary Lou Williams's "Walkin' and Swingin'," written for the Andy Kirk band (1936; see Chapter 8), for four. Williams's lick was later picked up by Charlie Christian and other musicians, but only Monk turned it into a post-bop classic, in part by connecting it seamlessly to the Ellington figure and adding a bridge of modern harmonies.

Although he wrote the piece much earlier, Monk did not record "Rhythm-a-ning" until 1957, at which point it became a regular part of his repertory. Our version dates from five years later, the period when he first signed with Columbia Records. Tenor saxophonist Charlie Rouse was Monk's most consistent partner; he joined the quartet in 1959 and stayed for eleven years. His soft, sandy sound suggests an uncanny affinity with Monk's piano, and his quick-witted responses provide countless moments of give and take with Monk's comping.

This performance is taken at a medium up-tempo, flowing smoothly through the introduction, theme, two choruses by Rouse, two choruses by Monk, theme, and coda. But close listening discloses how much each musician relies on Monk's cues and the demands of the piece. The drummer states the rhythm but also responds to rhythmic ideas introduced on piano. Rouse improvises variations on the theme, but also echoes melodic suggestions played by Monk. The bassist enables the others with his rock-solid harmonic and rhythmic foundation.

3.5

rhythm-a-ning

THELONIOUS MONK

Charlie Rouse, tenor saxophone; Thelonious Monk, piano; John Ore, bass; Frankie Dunlop, drums

- Label: Columbia CL2038; *Criss-Cross* (Legacy 074646353721)
- Date: 1962
- Style: bebop, Monk-style
- Form: 32-bar popular song (**A A B A**)

What to listen for:

- Monk's comping and Rouse's responses
- Monk's dissonant minor seconds (half steps) and right-hand ostinato
- drum's offbeat accents

INTRODUCTION

0:00	Monk plays the opening riff on solo piano.
0:02	At various points, he plays several adjacent keys (minor seconds) simultaneously— sometimes deliberately (as in the underlying harmony), but other times apparently from "sloppy" technique.
0:05	The second part of the tune is a repeated three-note riff, its last note falling in unexpected places and given extra weight by Monk, who doubles it in his left hand.
0:08	Dunlop on drums adds a response.

CHORUS 1 (HEAD)

0:09   **A**   With a cymbal crash, the entire band enters. Rouse (tenor saxophone) and Ore (bass) join the piano on the melody, with the drums reinforcing its syncopations.

0:14   Underneath the three-note riff, the bass begins to walk.

0:19   **A**

0:28   **B**   Over the chord progression to "I Got Rhythm," Monk continues the rhythm of the three-note riff, accenting the last note of each phrase.

0:36   A rising scale ends with a startling, splatted dissonance.

0:37   **A**

CHORUS 2

0:47   **A**   The first solo, by Rouse, is introduced by Monk's **comping**. Monk plays a dissonant chord that lands squarely on the opening beat of the chorus, then falls silent. Rouse paraphrases the theme's melody, accompanied by a crisp **backbeat** in the drums.

0:51   Monk plays the same chord, again falling on the **downbeat**. This pattern (a chord on the downbeat, followed by four measures of silence) continues throughout the **A** sections of this chorus.

0:56   **A**   Rouse moves away from the melody toward bebop-style lines. The drums similarly drift from the backbeat into more interactive rhythms.

1:05   **B**

1:10   Monk's chords become more frequent, falling every other beat.

1:15   **A**   Monk returns to his spare comping.

CHORUS 3

1:24   **A**   Monk signals a new chorus, still Rouse's, by placidly repeating a single chord.

1:29   For the next twelve measures, Monk stops playing altogether.

1:33   **A**   Rouse plays a phrase derived from the theme, then clashes with the bass line by repeating it a half step higher.

1:39   As Rouse returns to the tonic through a long descending line, the drums play complex patterns, accenting different **offbeats** in the measure.

1:43   **B**   Monk begins a new pattern of accompaniment, and Rouse improvises in response.

1:52   **A**   Monk returns to his favorite chord.

1:54   Rouse improvises another line that pulls a half step away from the tonic.

CHORUS 4

2:01   **A**   Monk begins his solo by borrowing a common harmonic pattern from bebop. He shifts to a distant chord and returns by a series of substitute chords to the tonic four bars later. (Since the bass immediately responds to Monk's chords, we can assume that this substitution was planned.)

2:10   **A**   Monk repeats his harmonic substitution, improvising a more dissonant line.

2:19   **B**   On the bridge, Monk plays dissonant **whole-tone** fragments in his right hand against loud single notes in his left hand. The drums disorient us by playing consistently on the offbeat.

2:29   **A**   Monk returns to the theme, occasionally altered by dissonant half-step splats and left-hand notes.

2:34   The last phrase reaches for a dissonant high note—the tritone, or **flatted fifth**.

CHORUS 5

2:38   **A**   Playing entirely in the upper register of the piano, Monk builds a line that consistently accents the dissonant flatted fifth.

2:47   **A**   Monk turns the flatted-fifth pattern into an **ostinato** in the right hand. The only accompaniment is the drum's accents and an occasional open fifth in the left hand.

2:53   The flatted-fifth pattern descends precipitously into the bass.

2:56	B	Infusing his harmonies with the whole-tone scale, Monk transforms the "I Got Rhythm" progression into a series of unsettling sounds.
3:05	A	Monk turns the opening theme into a descending scale that interacts with the improvised drum part.
3:09		To close out his solo, Monk turns the tonic chord into a peculiar ostinato.

CHORUS 6 (HEAD)

3:14	A	The band returns to repeat the head.
3:21		Monk responds to the theme with a dissonant **chord cluster** (with closely spaced notes), emphasizing the flatted fifth.
3:23	A	
3:27		Monk accents the end of the three-note riff with loud bass notes.
3:31	B	The bridge begins an octave lower than in the beginning.
3:40	A	

CODA

| 3:48 | | Over the last sustained piano chord, Monk repeats a jarringly dissonant minor ninth. |
| 3:50 | | Dunlop plays a short drum **fill**, but Monk's dissonance holds out just slightly longer. |

■ CHARLES MINGUS (1922–1979)

Charles Mingus was a bigger-than-life figure who made an indelible mark in many areas of jazz. As a bassist, he was among the most accomplished virtuosos of his time. As a composer, he expanded the variety and scope of American music, assimilating influences as far ranging as the sanctified church, New Orleans polyphony, swing, bop, Romantic classical music, and modern classical music. As a spokesman, he made jazz relevant to the civil rights era. As a memoirist, he brought new insights into the tribulations of African American artists trying to surmount the constrictions of prejudice.

Mingus was extremely sensitive to Negro stereotypes, which he exploited to poke fun at racist attitudes. He bristled at being called Charlie, which he thought disrespectful, and resented critical semantics that used the word "jazz" as a means of ghettoizing his art. About "Meditations on Integration" (1964), he wrote: "You'll say that it sounds almost classical. It *is* classical. You see, black faces aren't expected to play classical. But they do. We, too, went to school. We, too, studied music." He was also sensitive about his light skin, claiming a racially mixed background, including Chinese (he posed as a Chinese mandarin for the cover of his album *Mingus Dynasty*). A few days after the debut of "Meditations on Integration," he was the subject of a television portrait made in Toronto. Asked to describe himself, he said:

> I am Charles Mingus, a famed jazz musician but not famed enough to make a living in society, that is, in America, my home. I cannot even support my family, honestly that is, from the fame that I gain to the right of being a Negro musician. I am a human being born in Indian Territory, conquered by white skins, or invisible skins, transparent skins, people who killed and robbed to inherit the earth for themselves and for their children. Charles Mingus is a musician, a mongrel musician who plays beautiful, who plays ugly, who plays lovely, who plays masculine, who plays feminine, who plays music, who plays all sounds, loud, soft, unheard sounds, sounds, sounds, sounds, solid sounds, sounds, sounds. A musician just loves to play with sound.

Charles Mingus wrote grand tone poems, suites, jazz standards, parodies, and threnodies while leading his cutting-edge Jazz Workshop and maintaining his stature as one of the greatest bass players of all time. From the 1960s.

Slap That Bass

Born in Nogales, Arizona, Mingus was only three months old when his family moved to Watts, an area of Los Angeles with a large population of blacks and Mexican Americans. The family belonged to the African Methodist Episcopal Church, where Charles heard the gospel music that had a lasting influence on him. He played piano, trombone, and cello before taking up the bass in high school, studying with the excellent jazz bassist Red Callender and with Callender's teacher, Herman Rheinschagen, formerly of the New York Philharmonic. In later years, Mingus recalled being advised to switch from cello to bass because as a black man he could not succeed in classical music and would find work only if he learned to "slap that bass, Charlie!"

Mingus soon began playing dances and parties, and composing elaborate works that reflected his classical training, most notably "Half-Mast Inhibition" (a characteristically telling Mingus title), completed in his teens and reflecting his admiration for composer Richard Strauss. He worked in diverse ensembles, including a Dixieland band with Kid Ory, Louis Armstrong's big band, and studio sessions with singer Dinah Washington. In the late 1940s, he organized recording sessions for fly-by-night Los Angeles labels that were poorly distributed and little heard. The range of these recordings is remarkable: rhythm and blues, big-band swing, pop crooning, classicism, and original works that, slightly revised, helped define the style of his mature music.

At the same time, he toured with Lionel Hampton, who debuted Mingus's first important recorded work, "Mingus Fingers." Not until 1950, however, when he came to New York with the Red Norvo Trio, did he receive national attention. Mingus's virtuosity made him a mainstay of the city's best musicians, resulting in important engagements with Charlie Parker, Bud Powell, Stan Getz, Miles Davis, and the Duke Ellington Orchestra, among others.

In 1952, Mingus and drummer Max Roach organized their own record label, Debut, which lasted five years and documented Mingus's flirtation with cool jazz. Its most celebrated recording was of the Canadian Massey Hall concert of 1953, a bebop pinnacle featuring Parker, Gillespie, Powell, Mingus, and Roach. A year later, Mingus took a job with Art Tatum, whose harmonic ingenuity dazzled him as much as it had Charlie Parker a decade earlier.

Jazz Workshop

In 1953, as mentioned in Chapter 12, Mingus began contributing music to the Jazz Composers' Workshop, a pioneering cooperative launched by a handful of adventurous musicians. Except for Mingus, the participants were white and their music is little remembered, though one member, Teo Macero, would have a lasting impact as a Columbia Records producer who supervised recordings by Mingus, Monk, and Miles Davis. The music that emerged from this workshop tended to fuse cool jazz and classical techniques, prefiguring the Third Stream, which Mingus quickly recognized as an inadequate forum for the emotions he wished to express.

In 1956, Mingus signed with Atlantic Records and created his break-through album, *Pithecanthropus Erectus*, which demonstrated how explosive yet lyrical his music could be. The following year, he was invited to contribute a work to Brandeis University's Festival of the Arts ("Reflections"), a benchmark event for the Third Stream movement. He also completed his more significant second Atlantic album, *The Clown*, which introduced two musicians who remained longtime members of his circle, trombonist Jimmy Knepper and drummer Dannie Richmond, and placed Mingus in the forefront of advanced jazz thinkers. This album, played by a quintet he called the Charles Mingus Jazz Workshop, combined rousing passions with an almost nostalgic serenity, and demonstrated to anyone in doubt that Mingus might be the finest bass player alive, in or out of jazz. It also proved that he could produce a compelling work with little more than a fragment of composed music. The lead-off selection, "Haitian Fight Song," opens with a thunderous bass cadenza—"bass slapping" taken to a new and stirring level. The written material consists of two riffs amounting to eight bars, plus a twelve-bar blues format for the solos.

Mingus became increasingly notorious for outspoken comments on and off the bandstand. One piece, "Gunslinging Bird" (also known as "If Charlie Parker Was a Gunslinger, There'd Be a Whole Lot of Dead Copycats"), expressed his loathing for musicians who played clichés or failed to find original, personal ways of measuring up to his music. During public performances, he would occasionally stop a piece to berate a musician and then begin again.

Mingus's comments turned political after 1957, when President Eisenhower reluctantly sent federal troops to force Arkansas governor Orville Faubus to integrate Little Rock's Central High School. In 1959, Mingus recorded "Fables of Faubus," a piece that satirizes Governor Faubus with its melodically whimsical theme. Columbia Records, however, refused to let him sing his lyric, which he recorded for a smaller label (Candid) the following year, proclaiming Faubus "ridiculous" and "a fool." As the civil rights era heated up, other jazz musicians followed Mingus's example of speaking out through their music. Mingus inevitably heaped equal scorn on the "jazz industry," which deprived musicians of control over their own work.

Pithecanthropus Erectus/The Clown

Tradition and Discipline

For all his insistence on originality, Mingus remained respectful of jazz traditions. He never tired of citing as his core inspirations Ellington, Tatum, Parker, and the church, though his music took in far more than that. During the bop years, modernism had been embraced as a kind of religion by younger musicians, who belittled earlier styles of jazz. Mingus was the first composer of his generation to pay indelible tributes to great figures of the past, including Lester Young, the subject of his famous threnody (perhaps the best known of his tunes) "Goodbye Pork Pie Hat," and Jelly Roll Morton, in the affectionate parody "Jelly Roll."

We can see Mingus's versatility by comparing the fastidiously arranged "Far Wells Mill Valley," written for a friend on the West Coast and thus in the style of cool jazz (the instrumentation includes flute and vibes), with the raucous and self-descriptive "Wednesday Night Prayer Meeting." As the Jazz Workshop developed, Mingus retreated from writing out his ideas in favor of a more flexible form of collaboration with his musicians. This policy worked

© CHUCK STEWART

Mingus frequently rewrote pieces, revising scores within minutes of performing and recording them. From the 1970s.

for shorter pieces, but caused problems as Mingus continued to write exceedingly long orchestral works that required an organizational discipline he often lacked. In a famous 1962 debacle, for example, he held a concert at New York's Town Hall for which he was so unprepared that the musicians were seen correcting their scores as the curtains parted. Mingus began hiring arrangers and copyists to help organize his pieces; however many hands were involved, though, the end product always sounded like unadulterated Mingus. At the same time, he began revealing more of his personal life, encouraging documentary filmmakers to follow him around, writing unusually candid liner notes (in 1971, he published his memoir, *Beneath the Underdog*), inviting his psychiatrist to publicly analyze his music, and speaking at length on the bandstand.

Mingus's most successful and ambitious longer works include *The Black Saint and the Sinner Lady*, *Let My Children Hear Music*, *The Shoes of the Fisherman's Wife Are Some Jive Ass Slippers*, *Cumbia and Jazz Fusion*, and *Epitaph*—the work he presented in part at the 1962 Town Hall concert, completed posthumously by Gunther Schuller. Mingus's large body of work (some 300 compositions) spans cool jazz and hard bop, and combines experimental complexity with visceral pleasure. Some of his music, with its heady, polyphonic textures, gloomy dissonances, and intimations of outright terror, is as difficult for musicians to master as it is for listeners to understand. Mingus died in 1979, at fifty-six, from the effects of amyotrophic lateral sclerosis (Lou Gehrig's disease), having composed and conducted his final works from a wheelchair.

"Boogie Stop Shuffle"

Mingus generates express-train momentum with "Boogie Stop Shuffle," a twelve-bar blues that builds vibrantly on the eight-to-the-bar rhythms of boogie-woogie. Although he has only seven instruments at his disposal, he employs multiple textures and variations on the theme. The soloists express themselves freely, yet the main impression is of a tightly organized work in which the improvisations serve to elaborate on the composer's vision. The theme alone requires the first five choruses, with its ostinato, staccato chords, unison moaning, three-note riff, and bop variation punctuated first by cymbals (fourth chorus) and then by piano (fifth chorus). The expeditious tempo means that each of the eighteen choruses is played in about eleven seconds.

ostinato repeated melody

All the musicians heard here were important figures in the Jazz Workshop, especially Dannie Richmond, formerly a rhythm and blues tenor saxophonist who switched to drums under Mingus's tutelage and became his second in command. Pianist Horace Parlan developed a powerful left-hand style to compensate for the fact that his right hand was partly paralyzed by polio. The key soloist here, Booker Ervin, was one of the most instantly recognizable tenor saxophonists of his era, known for his huge sound and relentless energy.

This is the original recording of "Boogie Stop Shuffle" as edited (cut) by Mingus for the Columbia album *Mingus Ah Um*. After his death, Columbia reissued the album with the cuts restored. In some cases, such restorations are welcome. In this instance, we feel that Mingus knew what he was doing: increasing the excitement of the performance by cutting what he deemed to be inessential passages. Incidentally, fans of the Spider-Man movies may experience déjà vu: Spidey's theme song is suspiciously similar to "Boogie Stop Shuffle."

LISTENING GUIDE

3.6

🎧 boogie stop shuffle (edited version)

CHARLES MINGUS

Willie Dennis, trombone; John Handy, alto saxophone; Shafi Hadi, Booker Ervin, tenor saxophones; Horace Parlan, piano; Charles Mingus, bass; Dannie Richmond, drums

- Label: Columbia CL1370; *Mingus Ah-Um* (Sony/BMG Jazz 88697127572)
- Date: 1959
- Style: experimental hard bop
- Form: 12-bar blues

What to listen for:
- ostinato in 12-bar blues
- shifts between boogie-woogie and bebop grooves
- solos by Ervin, Parlan, and Richmond

CHORUS 1

0:00 The piece opens with an **ostinato riff** played by the tenor saxophones, piano, and bass, in a rhythm reminiscent of a **boogie-woogie** left hand.

0:04 As the harmony changes to IV in the 12-bar blues progression, the riff moves in sequence, starting four steps higher.

0:06 When the harmony falls back to I, the motive returns to its original pitch.

0:08 As the harmony falls from V to IV to I, the band plays a new, continuous phrase.

CHORUS 2

0:11 Parlan (piano) and Mingus (bass) continue the ostinato. Above it, the horns (three saxophones and trombone) mark the end of the ostinato's phrases with sharp, dissonant chords. These chords are extended, containing major triads that clash with the prevailing minor tonality.

0:19 By controlling their volume and bending pitches, the saxophones manage to match their sound to that of the trombone with a plunger mute.

CHORUS 3

0:22 The phrase played by the horns spills over into the next chorus. Each line now begins with a crisp, three-note riff on the same chords.

CHORUS 4

0:34 Suddenly the horns switch to a bebop-style line, played in unison. The bass ostinato continues underneath.

0:43 At the end of the last phrase, the line suddenly expands into a complex dissonant chord.

CHORUS 5

0:45 As the horns repeat the same line, the groove changes to a more standard bebop feeling: Mingus switches to a more conventional **walking-bass** line, while Parlan begins to **comp**.

CHORUS 6

0:55 A barely audible shift marks the spot where Mingus edited out the first two choruses of Ervin's tenor saxophone solo. What was originally his third chorus begins with a dramatic series of upward rips, supported by **block-chord** riffs by the saxophones and trombone.

CHORUS 7

1:07   Ervin uses **false fingering** while the background horns continue their riffs.

1:14   For a split second, he hits a high note before returning to a more comfortable register to round off his solo.

CHORUS 8

1:18   The horns and the bass return to the riff. Above them, Parlan oscillates between three piano chords.

CHORUS 9

1:29   In the upper register, Parlan plays a short, bluesy phrase, its endless repetitions forming a **cross-rhythm** against the background riff.

CHORUS 10

1:40   The groove switches once again, with the bass moving to a walking pattern. Parlan begins to improvise.

1:48   Toward the end of the chorus, Parlan lands on a harsh, bluesy dissonance.

CHORUS 11

1:52   Parlan continues on the same chord, effectively blurring the boundary between the two choruses.

CHORUS 12

2:03   Another bit of editing eliminates five choruses from the original. The ostinato returns in the bass, accompanied by a slow, mournful **countermelody** by the alto saxophone. Richmond on drums, preparing for a solo, plays more aggressively.

CHORUS 13

2:14   Richmond takes a solo. The first phrase fits neatly over the first four bars of blues form.

CHORUS 14

2:25   His second chorus begins with a short three-stroke motive.

2:28   Richmond plays a phrase that alternates between the snare drum and the tom-toms.

CHORUS 15

2:35   The ostinato bass line returns, supported by the horn chords from chorus 2.

CHORUS 16

2:47   A repeat of chorus 3.

CHORUS 17

2:58   A repeat of chorus 4.

CHORUS 18

3:09   A repeat of chorus 5.

CODA

3:18   As the horns sustain their last chord, the rhythm comes to a halt. The sound of the chord pulsates as individual horns change their volume.

3:21   The alto saxophone adds an anguished squeal.

3:24   The other horns join in, creating polyphonic chaos.

3:28   Inspired by the moment, Richmond begins an impromptu free-rhythm drum solo.

3:36   With a final cymbal crash, the tune comes to an end.

■ GIL EVANS (1912–1988)

The name Gil Evans, as Gerry Mulligan noticed, is an anagram of Svengali, and although no one could be less like the malevolent musical hypnotist of nineteenth-century fiction than the easygoing, often selfless Evans, he did have the power to make musicians and singers rise above themselves. Evans occupies a singular place in jazz: he composed several memorable pieces ("La Nevada," "Flute Song," "Proclamation," and "General Assembly" among them), but he was primarily an arranger, one who in Gunther Schuller's words "elevated arranging virtually to the art of composition."

As we've seen (in Chapter 12), Evans was a Canadian-born dance band arranger who came to New York to write for Claude Thornhill, and became one of the prime movers of cool jazz. In those years (1940s), he did not play an instrument or lead his own ensemble. With the decline of the big bands, he struggled as a work-for-hire orchestrator—although greatly admired by other musicians, he was considered too daring for the kinds of assignments that kept other arrangers busy. Evans took on random assignments, writing for Charlie Parker, Gerry Mulligan, swing trumpeter Billy Butterfield, and vocalist Helen Merrill, as well as a few anomalous projects, notably the first album by ballad singer Johnny Mathis.

Evans was forty-five when he achieved national recognition. Reuniting with Miles Davis for the groundbreaking 1957 album *Miles Ahead*, he crafted a series of trumpet concertos that emphasized the power and expressiveness of Davis's playing. He also wrote transitional interludes between selections, replacing the usual silences between tracks—a technique that remained unexplored until the Beatles did the same thing a decade later in *Sgt. Pepper's Lonely Hearts Club Band*.

Miles Ahead led to further collaborations with Davis (see Chapter 14) and invitations to write for others. More important, it established Evans as a recording artist in his own right, piloting his own albums with hand-picked ensembles. His choice of material ranged widely, as it had during his Thornhill years—from operetta (Kurt Weill's "Bilbao Song") to folk-blues (Lead Belly's "Ella Speed") to mainstream pop (Irving Berlin's "Remember")—but the majority of tunes were drawn directly from jazz.

Evans's reinventions of classic jazz pieces stimulated a revival of interest in jazz history. Like Monk and Mingus, Evans did not subscribe to the idea that modernism had trumped everything that preceded it. As for his transformations of contemporary music, John Lewis spoke for many when he said that Evans's version of "Django" taught him things about his own composition he had not previously realized.

Arranger Gil Evans (foreground) and trumpet player Miles Davis enjoyed one of the most fruitful partnerships in jazz. Here they record a radical rethinking of Gershwin's opera *Porgy and Bess*, New York, 1958.

© VERNON L. SMITH SR.

Cannonball Concertos

Evans is best known for his use of the concerto form: ensemble music designed to feature a single soloist. In addition to Miles Davis, he built works around soprano saxophonist Steve Lacy, mellophonist Don Elliott (a

The Composer's Arranger

So what exactly is an arranger? Simply put, an arranger takes an existing musical work and adapts it for a specific instrument or group of instruments. Depending on how many liberties are taken, the adaptation may result in a simple transference of the song or a radical transformation. During the big-band era, arrangers were hired to grind out "stock" arrangements of popular tunes. These stocks had little or no personality; their purpose was to allow a band to play the tune, nothing more.

Creative arrangers like Jelly Roll Morton, Bill Challis, Duke Ellington, Benny Carter, Don Redman, and Sy Oliver, however, made their arrangements as inventive and individual as improvised solos. The primary difference between, say, the music of Glenn Miller and Jimmie Lunceford is not the quality of the soloists or the selection of tunes, but the arranging style. Well-known pop tunes were covered by half a dozen or more big bands; fans bought the versions arranged in the style they found most pleasing.

In jazz, there are essentially two kinds of arrangements: written and head. A head arrangement (Count Basie's "One O'Clock Jump," for example) may be created through verbal instruction or trial and error as musicians work on a particular piece (see Chapter 8). A written arrangement involves a notated score that tells each musician precisely what to play at any given moment, except in those places set aside for improvisations or vocals. Gil Evans ultimately combined both methods, though his early work was mostly written. His music was characterized by a generous use of counterpoint, sonorous slow-moving chords, and a sound palette that combined very low instruments (like the tuba) with very high ones (like the flute). For Evans, a melody was a skeleton to be dressed from the ground up in his own harmonies, countermelodies, timbres, and rhythms. The same might be said of most good arrangers, but few performed this task with Evans's imagination or matched his ability to phrase passages so that they simulated the spontaneous excitement of a good improvisation.

mellophone is similar to a French horn), trumpeter Johnny Coles, and guitarist Kenny Burrell, among others. In 1958, Evans adapted classic jazz themes for an album, *New Bottle, Old Wine*, featuring alto saxophonist Cannonball Adderley. The instrumentation is typical Evans, favoring nine brasses (trumpets, trombones, bass trombone, French horn, and tuba). Other than Adderley, he uses only two woodwind players, and assigns them atypical jazz instruments: flute, piccolo, and bass clarinet.

Cannonball Adderley

Julian "Cannonball" Adderley (1928–1975), a former schoolteacher from Tampa, Florida, achieved instant recognition when he moved to New York in 1955, shortly after Charlie Parker's death: he was quickly acclaimed as "the new Bird." In 1958, he joined the Miles Davis Sextet, but within a year (after appearing on Davis's *Kind of Blue*), he would form his own quintet with his brother, trumpet player Nat Adderley, and enjoy a series of hit records that placed him at the forefront of the soul-jazz wing of hard bop—leaping high onto the pop charts in 1966 with "Mercy, Mercy, Mercy." Adderley combined bebop proficiency with funky backbeats, and his versatility perfectly suited Evans.

"King Porter Stomp"

Other than W. C. Handy's "St. Louis Blues," Jelly Roll Morton's 1923 piano piece "King Porter Stomp" was the oldest work on *New Bottle, Old Wine*. (In fact, it may have been older than Handy's tune, if we can believe Morton's claim that he composed it as a teenager.) In 1958, the title would still have been familiar to jazz fans because of Fletcher Henderson's arrangement, which became a Swing Era anthem after Benny Goodman's 1935 version hit the charts. But while Henderson's arrangement employed only one strain of Morton's piece, Evans returned to the 1923 original and adapted all four strains, including Morton's tricky up-beat syncopations in the **A** strain, which did not readily fit in with the Swing Era. Evans makes it swing harder than ever even as he transforms Morton's piece with dissonant harmonies and slashing bop-influenced phrases. The interaction between Adderley's improvisations and the written ensemble passages recalls the give-and-take perfected by Ellington in pieces like "In a Mellotone." Whether the ensemble's role is to initiate or respond in its exchanges with Adderley, it engenders the soaring illusion of unstoppable energy.

Alto saxophonist Cannonball Adderley, a former school-teacher from Tampa, Florida, who became an overnight sensation after sitting in at New York's Club Bohemia, recording in 1956.

LISTENING GUIDE

3.7

🔊 king porter stomp

GIL EVANS

John Coles, Louis Mucci, Ernie Royal, trumpets; Joe Bennett, Frank Rehak, Tom Mitchell, trombones; Julius Watkins, French horn; Harvey Philips, tuba; Cannonball Adderley, alto saxophone; Jerry Sanfino, reeds; Gil Evans, piano; Chuck Wayne, guitar; Paul Chambers, bass; Art Blakey, drums

- Label: World Pacific WP1246; *The Complete Pacific Jazz Recordings* (Blue Note 583002)
- Date: 1958
- Style: modernist big band
- Form: march/ragtime

What to listen for:

- Adderley's improvisation and the ensemble's response
- Evans's bold rhythms and inventive horn *soli*
- arpeggiated theme in strain **B**, Morton's theme in strain **D**

INTRODUCTION

0:00   Blakey (drums) plays a vigorous roll on the tom-toms, keeping the **backbeat** on the high-hat cymbal.

0:06   By pressing on the heads, he produces a subtle descent in pitch.

0:07   The horns enter unaccompanied on sustained chords. Over this background, Adderley (on alto saxophone) improvises.

STRAIN A

0:15   Adderley begins to solo over the rhythm section, while the low brass (trombones, tuba, horn) play short chords on the fourth beat of each measure.

0:26   All the horns join in on an extended *soli*, each horn occupying its own melody part, ending in a **tritone**-colored cadence.

STRAIN A

0:30   Adderley's solo continues, accompanied by lower brass chords.

0:35   The solo is interrupted by a line played by the trumpet and trombones.

0:39   Adderley reenters, accompanied only by the bass and drums.

STRAIN B

0:45   The new strain, starting in the minor mode, is marked by an **arpeggiated** theme scored
        delicately for guitar, piano, and clarinet.

0:49   The theme is answered by a sassy melody for the trumpets.

0:53   The arpeggiated theme is played again, this time in a higher register.

0:56   Once again, it's answered by the band.

STRAIN B

1:01   The arpeggiated theme is heard again, this time scored for trombone, alto saxophone,
        and clarinet. Underneath it, the lower brass reinforce the bass line.

1:05   The theme is followed by quiet **trills** from the reeds over a descending bass line.

1:09   The theme makes one more appearance.

1:12   The band responds with loud brass *soli*.

1:15   During a **break**, Adderley begins a solo.

TRANSITION

1:17   The composed line, **modulating** from the key of the first two strains to the key of the
        trio, is bolstered by rich *soli* scoring.

STRAIN C

1:21   In a new key, Adderley plays over just the drums and the bass.

1:29   He accidentally makes a distorted honking sound on a low note. Emboldened, he re-
        turns to this sound again and again—essentially turning a mistake into a motive.

STRAIN C

1:37   Under Adderley's solo, a low-pitched line for the trombones and the tuba descends,
        then ascends, through the **chromatic scale**. The guitar begins playing the chords to the
        tune very softly.

STRAIN D

1:53   The band now plays the piece's main theme, recognizably the same as it was originally
        written by Jelly Roll Morton.

1:57   As it continues, the theme is paraphrased—its harmonies and melodies changed.

2:01   Halfway through, when the melody is repeated, the rhythms are distorted.

2:08   During a one-bar break, the brass instruments (with Adderley on top) play a *soli*.

STRAIN D

2:09   Borrowing again from Jelly Roll Morton, the brass instruments play a riff made up of
        restrained and delicate chords, most of them falling securely on the beat.

STRAIN D

2:25   The brass chords turn into a background for an Adderley solo.

STRAIN D

2:42   The band plays a *soli* with familiar Swing Era rhythms, but its harmonies are unusually
        dissonant.

2:50   Adderley improvises a response.

STRAIN D

2:58 The *soli* becomes rhythmically sparse and its harmonies increasingly dissonant.

3:03 The band suddenly switches to a riff taken straight from the 1930s arrangement by Fletcher Henderson.

CODA

3:10 The coda—once again borrowed from Henderson—begins with a short riff fragment played over and over, creating a **cross-rhythm** against the underlying meter.

3:13 The drums stop: the horns ascend with a richly voiced *soli* to the final tonic chord.

Taking Charge

The first appearance of strain **B** on "King Porter Stomp" (0.46) represents a rare, early instance where Evans's piano comes to the fore. By the 1960s, however, he had decided to forsake freelance work in favor of leading his own orchestra. Seated at the piano (often electric), he used chords to pump up the energy level of the ensemble and its soloists. Evans's orchestra never achieved commercial success, but it was so admired by musicians—especially players who worked for him, sometimes turning down far more lucrative engagements to do so—that he managed to sustain it for more than twenty years. During much of that time, his band held down Monday night spots at New York jazz clubs, and toured Europe and Japan, where it was warmly received.

By 1970, Evans had begun to jettison the music that had made him famous, and, like Miles Davis, with whom he maintained a close friendship, added percussion instruments to his rhythm section and embraced a free-spirited fusion of jazz and rock. His 1969 album *Gil Evans*, though little noted at the time, was a major statement in that direction, preceding Davis's heralded *Bitches Brew*. A planned collaboration with Jimi Hendrix was halted by Hendrix's death; instead, Evans recorded orchestral versions of the rock guitarist's music—"Up from the Skies" is a superior example.

Evans also began devoting much of his performance energy to head arrangements. In 1961, he recorded a gripping version of his piece "La Nevada," actually shaping it (even handing out a last-minute riff scribbled on a matchbook) while the recording was in progress. By the 1970s and 1980s, having created an orchestra as steadfast as Ellington's, he routinely extended and revised pieces on the bandstand with physical gestures, piano chords, and vocal commands. Until his death in 1988, Evans continued to lead his band while also writing film scores (*Absolute Beginners*), mentoring young composers (Maria Schneider), and working with rock stars (Sting). His band continued into the 1990s under the direction of his son, Miles Evans, and thereafter in occasional reunions.

■ GEORGE RUSSELL (b. 1923)

Among the major jazz figures in the bop and postbop eras, George Russell is unique on two counts. First, he worked exclusively as a composer-bandleader, not as an instrumentalist; second, he devoted much of his life to formulating an intricate musical theory, published in 1953 and revised in 2001 as *George Russell's Lydian Chromatic Concept of Tonal Organization, Volume One: The Art and Science of Tonal Gravity.* (The planned second volume has not yet appeared.) As a result of his thesis and challenging music, Russell is generally perceived as an archetypal jazz intellectual—too difficult for the general public.

This is hardly fair. While some of his music was considered ahead of its time and presents challenges even today, a great deal of it is richly entertaining in a peculiarly pop-oriented way: his 1957 masterpiece "All About Rosie," for example, is based on a universal playground tune and charms audiences on those rare occasions when it is performed. His 1959 suite *New York, N.Y.,* which combines three original pieces with three adaptations of popular songs that celebrate Manhattan, was recorded with a rhyming rhythmic narration by singer Jon Hendricks that prefigures rap. Almost all of Russell's music since the 1970s incorporates funk and even disco rhythms.

Paradoxically, the *Lydian Chromatic Concept* is so dense that few people have actually read it, and fewer still can understand it, yet its influence is everywhere. Russell is the de facto father of modal jazz, the harmonic approach that produced such classics as Miles Davis's *Kind of Blue,* John Coltrane's *Giant Steps,* and Herbie Hancock's *Maiden Voyage,* as well as countless offshoots and imitations.

Theory and Practice

Russell, born of out of wedlock to a racially mixed couple, was adopted and raised by a black family in Cincinnati. In high school, he took up drums and received a scholarship from Wilberforce University to play in the college band. He left after two years and volunteered for the draft in 1941, only to learn at the recruitment center that he had tuberculosis. He was placed in a TB ward, but released prematurely. In 1944, Benny Carter hired him, and then fired him in favor of Max Roach. Russell described the experience of hearing the extraordinary Roach as marking the end of his ambition to play drums; he decided he would rather be a composer. A year later, he was stricken full-force by a tubercular attack, and spent fifteen months in a hospital. During this long recuperation, he began to formulate his Lydian concept.

Russell's theory was inspired in part by a conversation with Miles Davis, who wanted Russell to help him understand how chords relate to each other. Russell began to analyze chords in terms of related scales, which ultimately led him to the conclusion that using fewer chords, and focusing on their underlying scales or modes, would incline the improviser to think more melodically. Ultimately, it would even lead to the undoing of song and blues form. This was the basis for **modalism** as an

George Russell (seen here in the 1950s), the only major figure in jazz who did not play an instrument or sing, argued for the use of modes or scales as a substitute for chord changes with his Lydian Chromatic Concept and, more significantly, his challenging compositions.

© CHUCK STEWART

improvisational method. As Davis realized: "It's not like when you base stuff on chords, and you know at the end of 32 bars that the chords have run out and there's nothing to do but repeat what you've done with variations. I was moving away from that and into more melodic ways of doing things. And in the modal way I saw all kind of possibilities." The "modal way" would come to dominate jazz in the 1960s, particularly in the realm of jazz-rock fusion.

Russell believed that in every culture, the human ear detects the "greatest unity and finality" in the C Lydian scale: on a piano, the white keys from C to C but with an F-sharp—a tritone at the very center of the scale—instead of F. In building his theory, Russell set out to show how other scales relate to the C Lydian and to each other. He rejected the idea of major and minor keys and the harmonic rules contingent on them; instead, he advocated super-imposing different scales, so as to eliminate a tonal center. Charlie Parker showed that any note could be resolved (made to fit harmonically) within a chord. Russell believed that any chord could be re-solved within a scale.

Lydian concept

All this sounds complicated, and it is. Yet the net effect for other musicians was quite simple. Instead of improvising against a scrim of two or more chords in each measure, they could replace all the chords in, say, an eight-bar passage with one scale. The harmonic progression would no longer guide the direction of the piece. Instead, as Davis realized, "The challenge here, when you work in the modal way, is to see how inventive you can be melodically."

Pianist and composer Bill Evans (seen here in 1958) brought a romantic lyricism to jazz, etched in original chord voicings that influenced countless musicians.

Russell's ideas—which were communicated more in conversation or through musical examples (*Kind of Blue* popularized modality) than through his complicated text—liberated musicians from be-bop's harmonic grids. But although Russell felt vindicated by Davis's success, his own music was ignored, and he rankled at the new clichés that became ubiquitous in the 1960s and 1970s:

> I thought that *Kind of Blue* was beautiful music, of course. But I also thought that a lot of modal jazz that came out of it was a little simplistic. Too many jazzmen played simple modal tunes like "So What" and played long, long solos based on just a couple of modes. It could get very monotonous listening to that. . . . That kind of thing was only a part of what I intended with the theory. It should have opened up all kinds of new possibilities to musicians, not produced monotony.

Some of the best examples of what Russell intended may be found in his own work, beginning with "Cubana Be/Cubana Bop," a two-part arrangement he wrote for Dizzy Gillespie in 1947 that fused jazz and Afro-Cuban music and introduced modal orchestral writing. Russell's immersion in classical music, involving close study of Stravinsky, Stefan Wolpe, and others, produced a work for clarinetist Buddy DeFranco called "A Bird in Igor's Yard" (1949). Not until 1956 did he record under his own name: the result, *Jazz Workshop*, by the George Russell Smalltet, is among his finest achievements.

"Concerto for Billy the Kid"

Russell was held in great esteem by the most advanced jazz musicians of the 1950s, and he surrounded himself with many of them, including John Coltrane and Max Roach. But he also had a good ear for raw talent. His most influential discovery was the pianist Bill Evans, whom he eventually introduced to Davis (see Chapter 14). Evans had appeared on a few record sessions yet was virtually unknown when Russell recruited him for *Jazz Workshop*. To showcase his immense talent, Russell conceived "Concerto for Billy the Kid." Evans's rigorous solo, coming to a head in his whirling stop-time cadenza, is far removed from the more meditative approach that later became his signature, but it remains one of his most compelling performances.

Working with only six musicians in this piece, Russell creates tremendous harmonic density. His clashing scales give the performance a dramatically modernistic edge, though he also uses a standard chord progression (from the 1942 Raye-DePaul standard "I'll Remember April," an enduring favorite among jazz musicians) for the Evans sequence. In creating a capacious harmonic landscape that obliterates the usual tonal centers, Russell makes his sextet sound like a much larger ensemble. For all the dissonances, rhythmic change-ups, and fragmented melodies, the piece swings with a pure-jazz élan. The inventiveness of the composer and his soloists never wavers. After more than half a century, "Concerto for Billy the Kid" sounds not only fresh but avant-garde, in the truest sense of the term. It would sound modern if it were written and recorded today.

3.8

concerto for billy the kid

GEORGE RUSSELL

Art Farmer, trumpet; Hal McKusick, alto saxophone; Bill Evans, piano; Barry Galbraith, electric guitar; Milt Hinton, bass; Paul Motian, drums

- Label: Victor LPM1372; *The Complete Bluebird Recordings* (Lone Hill Jazz LHJ10177)
- Date: 1956
- Style: modernist small-group composition
- Form: original, including 32-bar **A A'** and 48-bar **A B A**

What to listen for:

- Latin rhythms at beginning and elsewhere
- Evans's stop-time cadenza in right hand and rhythmically tricky improvisation
- Evans's and drummer's sharp accents on dissonant chords

INTRODUCTION

0:00   The drums begin by playing a Latin groove: a syncopated rhythm on the cymbals alternates with the bass drum on the main beats and the snare drum on the backbeat.

0:05   Above the groove, two horns (muted trumpet and alto saxophone) play two independent lines in dissonant **counterpoint**. The rhythms are disjointed and unpredictable.

0:09   The horns become stuck on a dissonant interval—the **major second**, or whole step. They move this interval up and down.

0:11		Hinton enters on bass, doubled by piano, repeating two notes a half step apart. (This bass line will remain in place for most of the introduction.)
0:15		The horns play a descending riff that ends, once again, on a major second. This riff repeats at unpredictable intervals.
0:18		The texture is thickened by a new line, played by the electric guitar.
0:24		The horns switch to a new key and begin a new **ostinato** that clashes, poly-rhythmically, with the meter. Evans (piano) and Galbraith (guitar) improvise **countermelodies**.
0:34		The horns begin a new ostinato in **call and response** with the guitar.
0:44		The ostinato changes slightly, fitting more securely into the measure. Evans adds complicated responses.
0:58		Farmer (trumpet) removes his mute. The ostinato becomes a more engaging Latin riff, forming a four-bar pattern. Underneath it, Hinton plays a syncopated bass line.
1:11		In a dramatic cadence, the harmony finally reaches the tonic.
1:13		The drums improvise during a short two-bar **break**.

CHORUS 1 (32 bars, A A')

1:15	**A**	The rhythm section sets up a new Latin groove, with an unexpected syncopation on one beat. Evans plays a peculiar twisting line in **octaves** on piano, moving dissonantly through the chord structure.
1:22		Over one chord, the piano line is more strikingly dissonant.
1:28	**A'**	As the chord progression begins over again, Evans's melody continues to dance above the harmonies.

CHORUS 2

| 1:42 | **A** | The horns repeat Evans's line note for note. Underneath, Evans plays a *montuno*—a syncopated chordal pattern typically found in Latin accompaniments, locking into the asymmetrical bass line. |
| 1:56 | **A'** | |

TRANSITION

| 2:11 | | The walking-bass line rises and falls **chromatically,** while melodic themes are tossed between the instruments. |
| 2:21 | | The band returns to the Latin groove and the melodic ideas previously heard in the introduction. |

CHORUS 3 (48-bar A B A, each section 16 bars)

2:28	**A**	This new chord progression—based on "I'll Remember April"—begins with an extended passage of **stop-time**. Evans improvises for four bars in a single melodic line.
2:31		The band signals the next chord with a single sharp gesture while Evans continues to improvise.
2:35		The band enters every two bars, with Hinton filling in on bass.
2:42	**B**	The band's chords are irregular, often syncopated.
2:56	**A**	Evans's improvisations are so rhythmically slippery that the band misplays its next stop-time entrance.
3:08		A **walking bass** reestablishes a more conventional groove.

CHORUS 4

3:09	**A**	Evans plays a full chorus solo, featuring his right hand only.
3:23	**B**	He distorts the meter by relentlessly repeating a polyrhythmic **triplet** figure.
3:37	**A**	He switches to a series of bluesy gestures.

INTERRUPTION

3:50   The chorus is interrupted when the bass (doubled by piano) suddenly establishes a new triple meter. Against this, the horns play a dissonant line, harmonized in fourths (**quartal chords**).

CHORUS 5

3:55 **A**   We return to the piano solo, a full five bars into this chorus.

3:58   Evans joins with the drummer in playing sharp accents (or "kicks") on harshly dissonant chords.

4:05 **B**   Farmer takes a trumpet solo.

4:12   Underneath, McCusick (alto saxophone) adds a background line, harmonizing with the guitar's chords.

4:19 **A**   McCusick plays a melody previously heard in the introduction (at 0:34).

4:26   The trumpet suddenly joins the saxophone in quartal harmonies, fitting obliquely over the harmonic progression.

CODA

4:31   As the bass drops out, the instruments revisit ideas from the beginning of the introduction.

4:36   The guitar begins a final upward flurry.

4:39   Evans plays the final gesture on piano.

Unbowed

The *Jazz Workshop* album received glowing reviews. Critic Leonard Feather wrote of Russell, "Such men must be guarded with care and watched with great expectations." As a result, and despite poor sales, it provoked enough interest to enable Russell to sign with other labels and to tour with a small group. He initiated an especially productive collaboration with the saxophonist Eric Dolphy, who played an important role in the burgeoning avant-garde of the 1960s. One of Russell's earlier compositions, "Ezz-thetic," an ingenious variation on the Cole Porter song "Love for Sale," became something of a jazz standard, recorded by such musicians as Miles Davis and Lee Konitz.

After the critical success of "All About Rosie" and *New York, N.Y,* Russell was determined to maintain a band, but he found it increasingly difficult to find work in the United States. In 1963, he moved to Scandinavia, accepting a teaching post at the University of Sweden, touring with his sextet (which included many of the most admired young improvisers in Europe), and writing longer and more challenging pieces, including *Othello Ballet Suite* (1967) and *Electronic Sonata for Souls Loved by Nature* (1969), a major work that fused jazz, rock, and prerecorded tapes.

In 1969, Russell returned to the United States to teach at the New England Conservatory, where he spent more than twenty-five years. He reunited with Bill Evans to record his album-length concerto *Living Time,* and adapted that name for his orchestra, which made occasional appearances in New York and Europe. His later works include *Vertical Form 6* (1977), and *The African Game* (1983). *The London Concert* (1989) documents the bravura spirit, rhythmic ebullience, and uncanny beauty Russell could produce onstage; the album includes his arrangement of Davis's "So What," built not on the theme but rather on Davis's 1959 improvisation. Russell remained a controversial figure: the Jazz at Lincoln Center program in New York notoriously refused to book him on the grounds that his orchestra included electric bass.

ADDITIONAL LISTENING	
Thelonious Monk	"Round Midnight" (1947), "I Should Care" (1948); *The Complete Blue Note Recordings* (Blue Note 30363)
	"Brilliant Corners" (1956); *Brilliant Corners* (Riverside RCD-30501)
Charles Mingus	"Goodbye Pork Pie Hat," "Fables of Faubus" (1959); *Mingus Ah Um* (Columbia/Legacy Jazz 065512)
	"Haitian Fight Song" (1955); *The Charles Mingus Quintet Plus Max Roach* (Original Jazz Classics OJC CD440-2)
	Pithecanthropus Erectus (1956) (Atlantic/WEA 8809)
Miles Davis and Gil Evans	*Miles Ahead* (1957) (Legacy 65121)
	Porgy and Bess (1958) (Legacy 65141)
Gil Evans	"La Nevada" (1960); *Out of the Cool* (Impulse! 011105018623)
	"Up from the Skies" (1974); *The Gil Evans Orchestra Plays the Music of Jimi Hendrix* (Bluebird/RCA 663872)
Dizzy Gillespie (George Russell)	"Cubana Be / Cubana Bop" (1947); *The Complete RCA Victor Recordings, 1937-1949: Cubana Bop* (RCA 66528)
George Russell	"Ezz-thetic" (1961); *Ezz-thetics* (Riverside RCD-30188)
	"All About Rosie" (1957); *The Birth of the Third Stream* (Columbia/Legacy CK64929)
	New York, N.Y. (1958) (GRP/Impulse IMPD-278)

THE MODALITY OF MILES DAVIS AND JOHN COLTRANE

◼ THE SORCERER: MILES DAVIS (1926–1991)

We have encountered Miles Davis in earlier chapters, and will again in later ones. No one looms larger in the postwar era, in part because no one had a greater capacity for change. Davis was no chameleon, adapting himself to the latest trends. His innovations, signaling what he called "new directions," changed the ground rules of jazz at least five times in the years of his greatest impact, 1949–69.

- In 1949–50, Davis's "birth of the cool" sessions (see Chapter 12) helped to focus the attentions of a young generation of musicians looking beyond bebop, and launched the cool jazz movement.

- In 1954, his recording of "Walkin'" acted as an antidote to cool jazz's increasing delicacy and reliance on classical music, and provided an impetus for the development of hard bop.

- From 1957 to 1960, Davis's three major collaborations with Gil Evans enlarged the scope of jazz composition, big-band music, and recording projects, projecting a deep, meditative mood that was new in jazz.

At twenty-three, **Miles Davis** had served a rigorous apprenticeship with Charlie Parker and was now (1949) about to launch the cool jazz movement with his nonet.

wwnorton.com/studyspace

■ In 1959, *Kind of Blue*, the culmination of Davis's experiments with modal improvisation, transformed jazz performance, replacing bebop's harmonic complexity with a style that favored melody and nuance.

■ In 1969, *Bitches Brew* initiated an era of jazz-rock fusion (see Chapter 17), shifting the emphasis from melody to rhythm.

Davis's work throughout this twenty-year period involved a continuous rethinking of the four primary elements that define jazz and most other kinds of music: harmony, melody, rhythm, and instrumentation. Through all these changes, his approach to the trumpet remained relatively consistent and ardently personal. In the 1950s especially, his power as a performer had the effect of resolving musical opposites while leading jazz to a future beyond bop.

Yet Davis's importance goes beyond his musical questing. His personality —often belligerent, always independent, and given to periods of reclusiveness —mesmerized musicians and the public. He became an inescapable symbol of his time, and a magnet for artists in and out of music. Handsome, well-groomed, charismatic, Davis emerged as the archetypal modern jazz musician (distant, unflappable, romantic) and the civil-rights-era black man (self-reliant, outspoken, peerless). Imitated for his personal and musical attributes, including his dress and outspokenness, Davis generated a host of epithets: he was the man who walked on eggshells, the Prince of Darkness, the Sorcerer. Even though his record sales dropped almost to a standstill in the 1960s, and critics lambasted him for pandering to pop fashions, by the next decade he still retained an aura of mystery and respect. The poet and critic Amiri Baraka described Davis as "My ultimate culture hero: artist, cool man, bad dude, hipster, clear as daylight and funky as revelation."

Childhood and Early Start

Miles Dewey Davis III was born in Alton, Illinois, to a wealthy black family that moved to East St. Louis when he was a year old. His grandfather was an Arkansas landowner and his father a prominent dental surgeon and pillar of their St. Louis community. Davis's comfortable background instilled in him unshakable self-confidence, spurred by his father's education and prosperity and his equally strong-willed mother's fashion-conscious beauty.

Davis studied trumpet in school and received private lessons from a member of the St. Louis Symphony. He listened avidly to trumpet players, including the local phenomenon Clark Terry, who befriended Davis and would soon be widely respected for his work with Count Basie and Duke Ellington. When Billy Eckstine's orchestra visited St. Louis in 1944, Davis sat in with the band alongside its dynamic soloists, Dizzy Gillespie (who advised him to learn piano and harmony) and Charlie Parker. Later that year, Davis's father sent him to New York to study at the Juilliard School. He attended classes for a year and took piano lessons, before dropping out to pursue his real goal: to learn from and play with Parker.

From Bop to Cool

In 1945, Parker hired the nineteen-year-old Miles for his quintet and first recording date. Davis soloed on "Now's the Time" and "Billie's Bounce," but lacked sufficient technique to play on the pièce de résistance, "Ko-Ko," for which Dizzy Gillespie took his place (see Chapter 11). Although Davis worked with Parker's band on and off for the next three years, until December 1948, the "Ko-Ko" session characterized his dilemma during that period. He was attempting to forge a trumpet style in the shadow of Gillespie's (and Parker's) blazing virtuosity.

In addition to Parker, Davis toured with the big bands of Benny Carter and Gillespie, among others, and his relatively introverted style and improving technique earned him admirers. Some listeners, however, thought of him as a second-drawer bebop trumpet player who could not match the feats of fiery virtuosity of Gillespie or Fats Navarro. With Parker's quintet, Davis had to solo after the leader every night and in almost every piece, and the contrast did not favor him.

Davis's approach was different. He preferred the middle register to the more exciting high register, and focused on timbre and melody, playing fewer and longer notes. For a short time, he attempted to compensate for his perceived limitations as a trumpet player by writing excessively intricate tunes—such as "Sippin' at Bells," a blues with so many chord changes that the blues feeling is nullified. Parker played on Davis's first session as a leader and commented, sarcastically, that some of those harmonic changes were too complicated for a "country boy" like him.

In 1949, having left Parker, Davis began to experiment with the young musicians and composers who would form the "birth of the cool" nonet. That same year, he visited Paris to play the first Festival International de Jazz, an important presentation of old and young musicians, which gave him a more positive perspective on the respect that jazz and his own music enjoyed in Europe. He was now increasingly recognized for the emotional and rhythmic restraint of his solos. At twenty-three, he projected a lonely resilience that attracted many imitators. The sound of Miles Davis became unmistakable, though it would achieve far greater distinction in the next few years.

Miles Davis had no regular band when he assembled an "All-Stars" group for a 1953 Blue Note record session: (left to right) brothers Jimmy Heath (tenor saxophone) and Percy Heath (bass), with Davis at the piano and pianist Gil Coggins behind him.

PHOTO BY FRANCIS WOLFF/© MOSAIC IMAGES LLC

Drugs, "Walkin'," and the Harmon Mute

If his acceptance in Europe buoyed Davis's spirits, it also added to his bitterness and disillusionment about the realities of race in America. He had resisted the lure of narcotics during his years with Parker, but now in his midtwenties descended into heroin addiction, which took him into circles foreign to his privileged upbringing, forcing him to occasionally steal and pimp to feed his habit. Heroin hooked him for four years, during which time he completed *Birth of the Cool*, recorded as an accompanist to Sarah Vaughan, reunited with Parker, and freelanced as a leader of record dates that, despite the contributions of excellent musicians, often proved to be merely adequate.

A turning point came in 1954, when, after suffering withdrawal from heroin and recuperating at his father's farm, he returned to jazz with renewed energy and ambition. He now faced the double challenge of reestablishing himself as a serious force in jazz and as a reliable professional, no longer in

With Percy Heath on bass and "birth of the cool" colleague Gerry Mulligan on baritone saxophone, Davis (center) gave a triumphant drugs-free performance at the Newport Jazz Festival, Rhode Island, in 1955.

thrall to drugs. Under contract to Prestige Records, he presided over five remarkable 1954 sessions with many of the best musicians of the day (Thelonious Monk, Sonny Rollins, J. J. Johnson, Milt Jackson, Lucky Thompson), and an exemplary rhythm section—the first of several in his career—consisting of pianist Horace Silver, bassist Percy Heath, and drummer Kenny Clarke.

These performances revealed Davis to be a toughened, street-wise musician, thoroughly in charge of his timbre, and playing with steely resolve. His evenly phrased solos, combined with his dark good looks and quietly pugnacious stance, introduced a new kind of black masculinity in American entertainment, at once tender and invincible. He gave an excellent example of his coiled power in "Walkin'," an extended and mesmerizing performance that helped spur the hard bop school. Combining a twelve-bar blues with an eight-bar preamble, "Walkin'" has the dramatic grandeur of a march; while all the solos are accomplished, Davis's has the spellbinding logic of a fable, with meaningful silences and none of the high-note or speed-demon pyrotechnics associated with bebop trumpet.

Two months after recording "Walkin'," at a session with Sonny Rollins, he debuted three Rollins compositions that became enduring jazz standards ("Airegin," "Oleo," "Doxy") and a muting device, little known in jazz, that would become emblematic of Davis's style. The **Harmon mute**, introduced in the 1860s, was ignored during the 1920s jazz vogue for mutes generated by King Oliver and the Ellington brass men. Unlike other metal mutes, it is held in place by a cork ring, forcing the musician's entire air column into the mute to produce a thin, vulnerable humming sound. The Harmon mute augmented the brooding intensity of Davis's music.

Star Time

In the summer of 1955, Davis made a brief but much-acclaimed appearance at the Newport (Rhode Island) Jazz Festival, creating a stir with his version of Monk's " 'Round Midnight." It was the first time most critics and fans had ever seen a Harmon mute. On the basis of this performance, Davis's successful comeback was sealed. He was soon signed to a contract with Columbia Records—a major career leap from the independent jazz labels, like Prestige. Davis, however, still owed Prestige three years under his existing contract, which he fulfilled by recording five albums of music at two marathon sessions. The proliferation of Davis albums in the late 1950s from both labels boosted his celebrity.

On the cover of his first Columbia album, 'Round About Midnight (1955), Davis was photographed through a red lens, wearing dark glasses, embracing his trumpet, unsmiling—an iconic image. That album also introduced Davis's first great quintet, one of the most admired small bands of the era, with **First quintet** tenor saxophonist John Coltrane (see below), pianist Red Garland, bassist

Paul Chambers, and drummer Philly Joe Jones. Miles's old friend Gil Evans crafted the arrangement of "'Round Midnight," adding a tempo change and making the quintet sound fuller than on other selections.

Three aspects of this quintet were particularly noticeable. (1) The contrast between Davis's sparing, poignant solos and Coltrane's more demonstrative virtuosity reversed a similar disparity between Parker and Davis, this time favoring Davis. (2) The rhythm section boasted an assertive independence, thanks to Jones's insistent attack and Chambers's authoritative pulse and harmonic skill. (3) The diverse repertory combined original pieces with pop songs dating back to the 1920s or borrowed from Broadway shows.

Garland, a living thesaurus of pop music, suggested many of the tunes that Davis recharged with his interpretations. In this regard, Davis was also influenced by Frank Sinatra (see Chapter 16), who was revitalizing his own career at the same time, often with long-forgotten songs that were considered too dated or "corny" for modern jazz. By turning into jazz vehicles such unlikely titles as "Bye Bye Blackbird" (from 1926), "The Surrey with the Fringe on Top" (from the 1943 show *Oklahoma!*), and "If I Were a Bell" (from the 1950 show *Guys and Dolls*), Davis opened up jazz repertory.

Gil Evans and a Night at the Movies

After the success of *'Round About Midnight*, Davis's producer—mindful that Prestige would soon be issuing annual albums by the quintet—wanted to do something entirely different for his second Columbia release, in 1957. They

Arranger Gil Evans and Davis take a break during the momentous Columbia Records sessions that produced *Porgy and Bess*, 1958.

Miles Ahead

decided on an orchestral album arranged by Gil Evans. After several discussions, Davis and Evans settled on a nineteen-piece ensemble, extending the sonorities of the nonet's French horns and tuba to include flutes, piccolos, and harp. Davis would be the only soloist. The result, *Miles Ahead*, was a hit with the critics and public and a benchmark in recording history. Evans composed links between the selections, something never done before, to create the illusion of a suite without breaks. New post-production techniques (splicing and overdubbing) compensated for inadequate rehearsal and recording time, and allowed Davis to perfect his solos.

Ascenseur pour l'echafaud

Meanwhile, Davis had disbanded his quintet. At a loss for what to do next, he agreed to a tour of Europe, where he would perform with local musicians. Upon arriving, he learned that several engagements had been canceled, but he was offered something more intriguing: the chance to compose a film score for a French police thriller starring Jeanne Moreau and directed by Louis Malle. Gambling on Davis's ingenuity, Malle asked him to improvise the score at one late-night session, creating music cues while he watched the picture, *Ascenseur pour l'echafaud* (*Elevator to the Gallows*). To devise themes for the film, Davis improvised on scales instead of chords, simplifying the music harmonically and maximizing emotional content with slow, drawn-out phrases—often based on nothing more than a D minor scale. It was Davis's "eureka moment," and he returned home eager to elaborate on this way of improvising. (The success of *Ascenseur* inspired a brief vogue for movies with scores by or featuring jazz stars.)

His first problem was to create a new band. One musician he wanted to work with was alto saxophonist Cannonball Adderley (see Chapter 13), whom he recruited in 1958 after agreeing to appear as a sideman on an Adderley album. Davis had fired Coltrane because of his dependency on stimulants, but Coltrane had by now experienced what he later described as a rebirth—personal and (after working a year with Thelonious Monk) musical. Davis's new band—a sextet made up of trumpet, two saxophones, and his old rhythm section (Garland, Chambers, and Jones)—recorded *Milestones* (1958), his most mature work to date, exploring devices he had used in the film.

Porgy and Bess/ Sketches of Spain

Three weeks later, Davis returned to the studio for an ambitious project with Gil Evans, a reconceived version of George Gershwin's 1935 opera *Porgy and Bess*. Unlike the aggressively free-spirited music he made with his sextet, Davis's work with Evans on *Porgy* and other records possessed a sensuous luster that appealed to people who lacked the patience for long jazz improvisations. Surprisingly, these records, which redefined concerto form in jazz and exemplified Davis's soul-baring anxiety, doubled as make-out albums. This was particularly true of the third Davis-Evans epic, the 1960 *Sketches of Spain*: a fusion of jazz with Spanish classical and folk music (notably, the second movement of Joaquin Rodrigo's guitar concerto *Concierto de Aranjuez*), where the orchestrations frame Davis's chilling laments—the jazz musician as confessional poet.

Modal Jazz

In the year between *Porgy and Bess* and *Sketches of Spain*, Davis regrouped his sextet to record his most celebrated album, *Kind of Blue*. This album represented the fruition of the modal approach he had been perfecting since his film experience in Paris, and would alter the playing habits of countless musicians. Here, in contrast to the strenuous orchestral projects with Evans, Davis kept the compositional demands simple. At the same time, determined to stimulate his musicians, he did not show them the scores until they arrived at the recording sessions. His goal was to banish the clichés embedded in modern jazz.

By 1959, jazz had been fixated for fifteen years on chromatic harmony and the technical challenge of improvising smoothly and efficiently within it. The liberating innovations of Charlie Parker now loomed as an unavoidable and end-

Kind of Blue, the 1959 best-selling jazz recording of the LP era, popularized modality and changed the nature of improvisation: (left to right) John Coltrane, tenor saxophone; Cannonball Adderley, alto saxophone; Miles Davis; Bill Evans, piano.

lessly imitated model. His followers often made chord progressions more concentrated and difficult; soloing became a task rather like running hurdles, clearing a new obstacle every few yards. Davis had, in "Sippin' at Bells," tried to prove himself precisely in that manner. But **modal jazz** sent him in the opposite direction: fewer chords and less concentrated harmonies—or rather, scales (modes) that override harmonies, clearing away the hurdles. Modal improvisation was not new to jazz. It is an essentially basic idea, found in early jazz both in the use of the blues scale and in melodic paraphrase. In the 1950s, though, modalism emerged as a specific technique in reaction to the busyness of bop harmony. It offered a solution to the problem of revitalizing the relationship between improvised melodies and the harmonic foundations on which those melodies are based.

Davis, of course, was not alone in trying to move jazz beyond the dominion of chord changes. Charles Mingus, who publicly excoriated musicians for "copying Bird," wrote pieces with minimal harmonics to provoke fresh approaches. Dave Brubeck sought to inspire musicians with novel meters. George Russell, as we've seen, replaced chords with scales, creating his Lydian concept as a theoretical justification for modal jazz. As we will see in Chapter 15, a new jazz school—the avant-garde—arose at the same time (around 1960) to challenge all of jazz's ground rules.

Kind of Blue

The dark flowing introspection of *Kind of Blue*, which became one of the best-selling jazz albums of all time, underscored Davis's strengths and not his weaknesses. The modal arrangements and modified tempos suited his predilection for the middle range, his measured lyricism, his reserved disposition. It also provided an ideal middle ground between his laid-back ("walking on eggshells") style and the exuberance of the saxophonists, especially Coltrane, who even in the absence of multiple chord changes filled every scale and space with an almost garrulous intensity.

In order to realize this project, Davis made a couple of changes in the rhythm section. He hired drummer Jimmy Cobb, a musician steeped in hard bop, as a replacement for Philly Joe Jones. Cobb had been a member of

Adderley's group before both of them joined with Davis, and had also worked with singers Dinah Washington and Sarah Vaughan. He combined Jones's forcefulness with moderation, suggesting the restraint of Kenny Clarke.

On one track only, "Freddie Freeloader," a relatively conventional twelve-bar blues, Davis used his group's recently hired pianist, Jamaican-born Wynton Kelly, a veteran of hard bop known for his infectious blues playing; Kelly would remain with Davis's band through 1962. For the remaining four selections, Davis recruited Bill Evans, who had been his pianist through most of 1958. Evans's return to the fold for the two days it took to record *Kind of Blue* proved to be a crucial component in the album's success.

■ BILL EVANS (1929–1980)

One of the most influential musicians of his generation, Bill Evans was on the verge of achieving recognition when George Russell introduced him to Davis. Evans had attracted attention with his youthful virtuosity, but his percussive, linear cadenza on Russell's "Concerto for Billy the Kid" (see Chapter 13), however impressive, did not typify his approach to the piano. He was perfecting an improvisational style no less introverted and meditative than Davis's. Like Davis, too, he possessed an instantly identifiable sound on his instrument.

Born in Plainfield, New Jersey, Evans began classical piano and violin studies at six, and worked in dance bands as a teenager. Despite occasional jazz gigs, he did not seriously devote himself to jazz until after he graduated from Southeastern Louisiana College and served a stint in the army. Returning to New York, he freelanced with several groups. After wowing critics with his work for Russell, he was invited to record with his own trio in 1956. His debut album, earnestly titled (by his producer) *New Jazz Conceptions*, introduced "Waltz for Debby," a classic jazz ballad that marked him as a composer of promise. A perfectionist, Evans did not feel his "conceptions" were fully formed, and refused to record for the next two years except as a sideman.

During that interim, in addition to Miles Davis, he recorded with Mingus, Adderley, Gunther Schuller, Chet Baker, and others, finally returning to the studio under his own steam in 1958 with an album called *Everybody Digs Bill Evans*, festooned with admiring quotations from other musicians. A highlight of this session was his spontaneous "Peace Piece," improvised freely over a simple alternation of tonic and dominant chords.

Breakthrough Trio

In 1959, Evans made a significant leap, first with his work on *Kind of Blue*, and later that year with his third album, *Portrait in Jazz*. Drawing on his classical background and modal jazz, he developed an original approach to voicing harmonies. By thinking of chords as loosely connected to their roots (see box), he found ingenious ways to modulate

Bill Evans (center) created an ideal trio with bassist Scott LaFaro (left) and drummer Paul Motian, pictured here in 1961 at the Village Vanguard, where they made their most memorable recordings.

© STEVE SCHAPIRO

from one chord to another, adding harmonic extensions and substitute chords to alter standard progressions. His melodic and harmonic resourcefulness was especially apparent in his adaptations of standards, some of them unusual for jazz (like the sentimental ballad "My Foolish Heart" and the theme from the Disney movie *Alice in Wonderland*).

Portrait in Jazz also premiered a new approach to the piano trio, in which each member was a fully active participant. In the usual bebop piano trio as perfected by Bud Powell, the pianist was almost always the central figure, with the bassist and drummer serving as accompanists. Powell liked interacting with a vigorous drummer, but his bassists usually marked the harmonies and followed his lead. Evans favored the bassist, who was free to respond with strong melodic ideas of his own.

He found ideal allies in drumer Paul Motian and bassist Scott LaFaro, who was admired for his superb intonation, timbre, and melodic ideas. LaFaro's early death in a car accident shortly after the group reached its peak (*The Complete Village Vanguard Recordings, 1961*) derailed Evans for a while, but he rebounded with a series of interdependent trios. He continued to compose challenging, introspective tunes, among them, "Peri's Scope," "Turn Out the Stars," "Very Early," and "Remembering the Rain."

Evans's best-known piece (and one of Davis's most moving recordings), "Blue in Green," written for *Kind of Blue*, is a ten-measure circular sequence of chords that, as Evans configured them, has no obvious beginning or ending. Its hypnotic quality continues to challenge instrumentalists and singers. Elsewhere, Evans's **quartal harmonies** (built on fourths rather than thirds) help to define the modal achievement of *Kind of Blue*. On "Flamenco Sketches," the soloists are required to improvise on a sequence of scales, usually modulating every four or eight bars, though the soloist can extend his use of a scale if he desires. Evans's chords support the scales without linking them to a specific harmonic progression. Yet the piece that popularized modal jazz is the album's opening selection, "So What."

Voicing Chords

"Voicing" refers to the way notes or instruments are combined. We have already encountered instrumental voicings with big bands. Chord voicings similarly refer to the choices a musician makes in constructing harmony. Bill Evans was especially good at voicing chords in ways that made them sound fresh and open-ended: for example, instead of letting a definite C chord (C-E-G, with the root C at the bottom) advance to a definite F chord (F-A-C), his C chord might have the E or G on the bottom, and the F chord the A or C at the bottom, so that we hear the progression in a new way. If you drop the root notes altogether and add the interval of a ninth to each chord—D for the C chord and G for the F chord—you've come a long way from the original harmonies while staying within the original chord changes, and the possibilities for voicing seem limitless. Evans had a genius for realizing those possibilities.

🎧 "So What"

"So What" presents modal jazz in the context of a thirty-two-bar **A A B A** tune, which makes it easy to hear the only harmonic change. The **A** sections are based on the D Dorian mode, which on a piano keyboard is represented by the white keys from D to D; the bridge, a half step higher, shifts to the E-flat Dorian mode (the same scale, with the same intervals, starting on E-flat). In practice, this means that musicians improvise mostly on a D minor triad. A transcription of Davis's lyrical solo shows that a great deal of it employs just the triad's three notes (D-F-A), yet he found the experience melodically liberating; his variations are lucid, moving, and memorable.

The opening episode by the rhythm section is a remarkable prelude, thought to be sketched by Gil Evans. Paul Chambers's bass prompts a three-note piano phrase, leading to a bass-like figure played in tandem by bass and piano, followed by the pianist's enigmatic Spanish-style chords and the bassist's introduction of a swing beat and the theme. Davis's beautifully executed solo has been much studied: the singer Eddie Jefferson put lyrics to it, and George Russell orchestrated it for his big band. Note Evans's surprisingly dissonant piano clusters toward the end. Davis continued to play the piece for years, at ever-faster tempos. By the early 1960s, modal jazz was everywhere, as young musicians rose to the test of improvising in the absence of chord changes.

LISTENING GUIDE

1.7

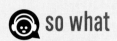 **so what**

MILES DAVIS

Miles Davis, trumpet; John Coltrane, tenor saxophone; Cannonball Adderley, alto saxophone; Bill Evans, piano; Paul Chambers, bass; Jimmy Cobb, drums

- Label: *Kind of Blue,* Columbia CL1355; *Kind of Blue* (Columbia/Legacy CL5173303)
- Date: 1959
- Style: modal jazz
- Form: 32-bar popular song (**A A B A**)

What to listen for:

- two-note riff ("So what!") in response to bass: first in piano, then horns
- bridge a half step higher than **A** sections
- modal improvisation
- contrast in styles between soloists

INTRODUCTION

0:00		Chambers quietly plays a rising bass line, evoking a two-note response from Evans on the piano: this prefigures, in slow tempo, the main head. The chords drift ambivalently, fitting no particular key area.
0:13		In a slightly faster tempo, Chambers and Evans combine on a precomposed melody.
0:20		The bass drops a step. Evans drifts elusively between chords.
0:30		After a pause, Chambers rumbles incoherently in the bass's lowest register.

CHORUS 1 (HEAD)

0:34	**A**	Suddenly striking up a steady tempo, Chambers plays a repetitive riff, answered by Evans with the famous two-note "So What" chord in **quartal** harmony (voiced in fourths). Cobb quietly supports on drums.
0:49	**A**	The response is now voiced by the three wind instruments. Cobb ratchets up the intensity by adding a **backbeat** on the high-hat cymbal.
1:03	**B**	In a subtle change, Chambers moves a half step higher. The horns play the riff in the new key.
1:17	**A**	All the instruments drop back to the original key.
1:30		Over drum **fills**, Davis begins his two-chorus solo.

CHORUS 2

1:31	**A**	Davis plays a few short phrases, answered by Evans with the riff.
1:37		Davis continues with a longer phrase. As it reaches its melodic peak, he pulls slightly behind the beat.
1:45	**A**	He plays short, concise phrases, leaving ample space for the rhythm section.
1:59	**B**	Evans moves a densely voiced **chord cluster** (with closely spaced notes) up a half step to signal the bridge. Davis plays over the harmonic cluster.
2:07		Evans returns to the "So What" motive.
2:14	**A**	The shift downward is signaled by a sharp drum accent.

CHORUS 3

2:28	**A**	Davis plays a hauntingly lyrical, sustained passage over a rhythmically active but harmonically static bass **ostinato**.
2:42	**A**	Chambers returns to a **walking bass**.
2:56	**B**	With a surprising dissonance, Davis signals modulation one beat early.
3:10	**A**	A drum crash leads the return back to the original key. Davis reprises his lyrical passage.
3:19		Davis's last phrase has a bluesy tinge.

CHORUS 4

3:24	**A**	While Cobb plays strong accents at the end of Davis's solo, Coltrane begins his two-chorus tenor saxophone solo with the same restrained mood.
3:38	**A**	Suddenly he switches to a more intense style of improvising, with flurries of fast notes. Evans responds with a peculiar **comping** pattern: holding a few notes, releasing others.
3:52	**B**	Cobb plays interactively on the snare drum, prodding Coltrane to greater intensity.
4:02		As Coltrane reaches the upper limits of his phrase, his timbre coarsens.
4:06	**A**	He plays a phrase in his lower register, repeating and extending it.
4:18		Cobb adds a Latin polyrhythm.

CHORUS 5

4:20	**A**	As in chorus 3, Chambers moves to a bass ostinato. Coltrane's line aims toward a melodic peak.
4:33	**A**	The bass returns to a walking-bass pattern.
4:41		Coltrane plays a motive, then repeats it in **sequence** (starting on a different pitch).
4:47	**B**	His improvisation lingers around a single note.
5:01	**A**	His last phrase begins in his highest register.

CHORUS 6

5:15	**A**	The rhythm section quiets down to allow Adderley (alto saxophone) to enter, mimicking Coltrane's extensive **double-time** lines.
5:29	**A**	For a moment Adderley digs into the groove, but soon returns to his double-time improvisation.
5:41		He suddenly moves up a half step, clashing against the background. Evans responds with the appropriate chord several seconds later.
5:42	**B**	
5:56	**A**	Adderley returns to the tonic by repeating, on varied tones, a two-note motive.

CHORUS 7

6:10	**A**	Adderley plays a pair of phrases in the same rhythm.
6:17		In the midst of his double-time improvisation, he inserts a trill.
6:24	**A**	He begins a simple rhythmic phrase with blues inflections, but once again moves back to faster passages.
6:38	**B**	A high-pitched phrase elicits a delayed chord from Evans.
6:50		Adderley's return comes a beat early, adding a touch of dissonance to the drummer's roll.
6:51	**A**	
7:00		His last phrase is distinctly bluesy.

CHORUS 8

7:05	**A**	The horns enter with the "So What" riff, shifting their role from the response to the call. Evans plays dense, dissonant chords.
7:19	**A**	Evans plays slow, single-note lines, recalling Davis's lyrical phrases.
7:33	**B**	On the bridge, he returns to short, dissonant chord clusters.
7:47	**A**	Back in the home key, he plays thinner chords: two notes a mere step apart.

CHORUS 9

8:02	**A**	Evans shifts the "So What" riff back to its original position. The bass continues to walk.
8:16	**A**	Chambers plays the call, with the horns joining Evans in responding with the "So What" chords.
8:30	**B**	
8:44	**A**	

CODA

8:58	Evans continues to respond to the bass, while the other instruments drop out. The music fades to silence.

■ JOHN COLTRANE (1926–1967)

No one united—and motivated—a larger circle of major jazz figures than Miles Davis; the musicians who passed through his bands would extend his influence beyond his own music, creating their own waves and ripples. Within this world, however, John Coltrane holds an exclusive place. His musical and personal impact eventually equaled—and, some would argue, surpassed—that of Davis. Coltrane became the most intrepid explorer of modal jazz and a cultural-ethical leader of the avant-garde jazz of the 1960s. His career was short-lived, barely a dozen years, and his later music alienated most of his early admirers, producing a windstorm of controversy that has not yet settled even now.

Although he was the same age as Davis (younger by four months), Coltrane made no significant recordings until 1955 (as a member of Davis's quintet), a decade after Davis had recorded with Charlie Parker. He made dozens of records during the next few years—many under his own name, establishing himself as Sonny Rollins's rival as the era's leading tenor saxophonist—and finally organized his own working band in 1959, the year of *Kind of Blue*. Despite the immense success of that album, it led to a falling off for Davis, as he cast about to perfect his next ensemble. Consequently, Coltrane's meteoric rise, at the age of thirty-five, had the effect of filling a leadership role vacated by Davis.

Davis continued to perform with creative authority in the early 1960s, but Coltrane seemed to personify the future of jazz. When, in late 1964, Davis presented his second great quintet (see below), Coltrane released *A Love Supreme*, the first small-band work since *Kind of Blue* to receive near-unanimous acclaim from critics and fans. Still, it soon became apparent that Coltrane and Davis were dissatisfied with the music they were creating, as they headed down very different paths, each in its way a departure from the central orthodoxies of jazz. For Davis, this meant examining rock, a fusion that he fully embraced a couple of years after Coltrane's death (see Chapter 17). For Coltrane, it meant embracing the expressionistic chaos of the avant-garde. Both roads were paved with modality.

The Long Apprenticeship

Born in Hamlet, North Carolina, John William Coltrane grew up in a racist, hardscrabble community, where his family's precarious situation was devastated by the death of his father when John was twelve. The loss distracted him from his studies while strengthening his growing obsession with music. At fifteen, he switched from clarinet to alto saxophone; when he wasn't practicing, he took odd jobs, like shining shoes, to help support his family. After graduating from high school, he moved to Philadelphia, where his musical training began in earnest.

Coltrane enrolled at the Ornstein School of Music and took an intensive course in theory at Granoff Studios, where he developed a fascination with scales, tenaciously playing them for hours at a time. He occasionally worked with local bands, usually in the rhythm and blues style popular in black communities. After service in the navy, he joined a big band led by a friend, saxophonist Jimmy Heath, the younger brother of Dizzy Gillespie's bassist, Percy Heath.

Together, Coltrane and Heath listened to classical music and bebop and worked at exploring the higher reaches of the saxophone, extending its range upward. In 1949, Gillespie brought both men to New York. Soon, Coltrane switched to tenor saxophone, working in various bands, some well known (Earl Bostic, Johnny Hodges), others buried in music's lower depths—he was known to "walk the bar," honking for tips in cheap dives. In this period, he discovered Nicolas Slonimsky's *Thesaurus of Scales and Melodic Patterns* (1947), a manual that codified his obsession with scales. Where Coleman Hawkins had emphasized every chord in a harmonic sequence, Coltrane experimented with a rapid-fire attack in an attempt to play every note in every chord, unleashing what critic Ira Gitler called "sheets of sound."

By the time Miles Davis hired him in 1955, Coltrane's attack was distinctive if not fully formed, but his career was hobbled by his self-destructive need for narcotics and drink. Within six months of his joining Davis, Coltrane was invited by Sonny Rollins to record with him ("Tenor Madness"), a prescient tribute when you consider that Coltrane's first important session with Davis had yet to be released. But critics were ambivalent: Coltrane was attacked for his harsh tone and lengthy solos. When Davis asked him why he played so long, Coltrane said, "It took that long to get it all in."

John Coltrane forged an expressionistic way of improvising that helped to instigate the avant-garde movement and led a classic quartet in the 1960s.

Awakening

Coltrane's dependency on drugs forced Davis to fire him twice. After the second time, in 1957, Coltrane turned his life around. Claiming to have undergone a profound religious experience (the subject of *A Love Supreme*), he renounced all stimulants, devoting himself entirely to music. He spent most of the year working with Thelonious Monk, an education in itself (documented on the album *Thelonious Monk Quartet with John Coltrane at Carnegie Hall*, first issued in 2005), exhibiting a glowing timbre and emotional urgency. His freelance work showed his talent as a composer ("Blue Trane," "Moment's Notice") and his facility with supersonic tempos and slow romantic ballads. In 1959, Coltrane signed with Atlantic Records, assuming a leadership role with unmistakable confidence—though it would take him a couple of years to recruit his ideal band.

© CHUCK STEWART

Early in 1959, Coltrane recorded *Kind of Blue* and albums with Adderley and Milt Jackson (of the Modern Jazz Quartet). In May, he recorded his own landmark album, *Giant Steps*, backed by leading bebop pianist Tommy Flanagan; Davis's bassist, Paul Chambers; and hard bop drummer Art Taylor. Coltrane composed all the selections, of which three became jazz standards— "Giant Steps," "Naima," and "Mr. P. C." (a tribute to Chambers). *Giant Steps* signifies an extension of *Kind of Blue*, with its investigation of scales and chords. Coltrane's subsequent work deepened his interest in the liberating implications of modal jazz. The melodic arc of his measured and poignant ballad "Naima," for example, is based on two scales. "Impressions" is a direct spin-off of "So What" (Coltrane even called it that the first time he played it), employing the **A A B A** format with a release built on a phrase from Maurice Ravel's "Pavane pour une infante défunte."

As Coltrane explored the relationships between chords and scales, "stacking" chords on top of a scale to see how many note combinations and phrase permutations he could develop, he also composed more complicated harmonic sequences. "Giant Steps" has been called his farewell to bebop, because the chord structure is so busy and difficult to play, especially at the roaring tempo he demanded. One of Coltrane's most influential pieces (it has become a test pattern for music students attempting to master fast-moving harmonies), it may be seen as a rejoinder to the scalar concepts of *Kind of Blue*.

🎧 "Giant Steps"

"Giant Steps" is a sixteen-bar composition in which almost every note of the melody is signaled by a new chord. Indeed, playing the chord changes is practically the same thing as playing the melody. The harmony extends the chord progression between equally distant tonal centers (the giant steps of the title). One goal of this harmonic sequence was to stimulate fresh ideas. Coltrane, taking a page from Miles Davis, decided not to show the piece to the musicians until the day of the recording session.

The piece's difficulty is especially evident in the piano solo. The chords alone would not have presented a problem for a pianist as harmonically sophisticated as Tommy Flanagan. The tune consists mostly of half notes, which in this instance means a chord change every two beats—no big deal if the tempo is leisurely or medium-fast. But the point of "Giant Steps" lay partly in playing it extremely fast, to trigger a sheets-of-sound jolt. Even for Coltrane, who had been working on these changes for years, the challenge was thorny, and his solo contains many repeated patterns. For Flanagan, the situation was virtually impossible. His solo begins with uncharacteristically jumpy phrases before retreating into a sequence of chords. (Flanagan later mastered the piece for his superb 1982 Coltrane tribute album, also called *Giant Steps*.) Coltrane's solo aims for a quite different effect from bebop; unlike most of the improvisations we've heard, including Coltrane's on "So What," the import of his eleven-chorus solo on "Giant Steps" resides less in details than in the aggregate attack—the overall whooshing energy.

3.9

 **giant steps**

JOHN COLTRANE

John Coltrane, tenor saxophone; Tommy Flanagan, piano; Paul Chambers, bass; Art Taylor, drums

- Label: *Giant Steps,* Atlantic LP311; *Giant Steps* (Atlantic/WEA 1311-2)
- Date: 1959
- Style: hard bop
- Form: 32-bar popular song

What to listen for:
- overall energy of Coltrane's 11-chorus solo
- repeated patterns in his solo
- continuous modulation

CHORUS 1 (HEAD)

0:00   Coltrane begins with a rhythmically simple melody disguising the dauntingly difficult chord progression voiced by Flanagan on piano. The tune changes keys 10 times in 13 seconds.

CHORUS 2 (HEAD)

0:13   Beginning of chorus.

0:26   The last two chords serve as the beginning of Coltrane's 11-chorus solo.

CHORUS 3

0:27   Coltrane launches into his solo with a pattern he'll return to again and again. The drummer changes from the open cymbal to a more tightly restrained sound.

CHORUS 4

0:40   Coltrane's intensity increases on a high, held-out note—a melodic peak that he reaches again two seconds later, over a different chord.

CHORUS 5

0:53   Coltrane repeats the opening of chorus 3 before shifting into a new direction.

0:59   A return to the melodic peak of chorus 4, again repeated over two different chords.

CHORUS 6

1:06   Coltrane takes a short break before continuing his solo.

1:11   Another short break may reflect a momentary lapse of attention at such fast speed.

1:18   At the end of the chorus, he reaches a new high note (a half step higher than before).

CHORUS 7

1:20   Coltrane's solo remains in the upper register, reaching the highest note at 1:22 and 1:24.

1:29   The end of the chorus settles into a familiar pattern, with one high note being replaced by the next.

CHORUS 8

1:33   Beginning of chorus.

1:40   Coltrane erupts into a rapid ascending E-flat major scale.

1:43   He seems to return to his high-note pattern. But instead of completing it, he dips back down to return to the customary opening for the next chorus.

CHORUS 9

1:46   Beginning of chorus.

CHORUS 10

2:00   His phrasing is choppier and more discontinuous.

CHORUS 11

2:13   The standard opening is interrupted by faster rhythmic gestures.

2:19   As Coltrane looks for ways to intensify his improvisation, the melodic line features **ghosted** notes and half-formed pitches.

CHORUS 12

2:26   Coltrane interrupts his usual chorus opening with a high-note flurry, continually circling his line back toward its melodic goals.

CHORUS 13

2:39   Coltrane's last chorus is built primarily around ever-higher notes, with a throaty timbre.

2:49   He finally tires and brings his line down.

2:52   A series of hard knocks on the side of the drum head signals the end of the solo, which spills over slightly into the next chorus.

CHORUS 14

2:53   Beginning of chorus.

2:55   Announced by a big cymbal crash, Flanagan (piano) starts his solo.

2:57   Early on, it becomes obvious that he can't remember all the chords; when he reaches an unfamiliar spot, his line stops.

CHORUS 15

3:05   Flanagan begins with a major scale that quickly becomes out of sync with the changing chords.

CHORUS 16

3:18   He halts his line to reestablish himself with the correct chord.

3:22   The gaps between lines become uncomfortably long.

CHORUS 17

3:31   Flanagan stops trying to create a single-note line, and simply plays chords.

CHORUS 18

3:44   Coltrane returns to solo, taking up his improvisation where he left off.

3:51   Long-held notes add expression to his line.

CHORUS 19

3:57   Coltrane's final chorus begins with a short break before plunging in for another continuous string of notes.

CHORUS 20 (HEAD)

4:10   He returns to the simple melody of the head.

CHORUS 21 (HEAD)

4:23   Beginning of chorus.

CODA

4:35   As the band holds out the final chord, Coltrane plays a skittering run that descends into his lower register. His last note is drowned out by a snare-drum roll.

"My Favorite Things"

Surprisingly, Coltrane followed *Giant Steps* in 1960 with a hit record—perhaps the most improbable jazz hit since Coleman Hawkins's "Body and Soul," twenty years earlier. His adaptation of "My Favorite Things," a cheerful waltz from Rodgers and Hammerstein's current Broadway hit *The Sound of Music*, was a rarity in every way: with its fifteen-minute running time, it was a particularly unlikely candidate for frequent radio play. Yet it *was* broadcast, making Coltrane a major jazz star while popularizing the use of modes in a more dramatic yet no less accessible manner than "So What."

Coltrane's arrangement transformed the piece by accenting the waltz meter with an insistently percussive vamp, and reducing the song's chords to two scales, one major and one minor. This gave the familiar theme an incantatory quality, underscored by deliberately repetitive improvisations and a surf-like rhythm. He accentuated the Eastern feeling by performing the piece on soprano saxophone, which has a higher range than the tenor and a keening timbre that suggests music from the Third World. The soprano had rarely been used in jazz since the days of Sidney Bechet; after "My Favorite Things," it was everywhere.

"My Favorite Things" was also the first recording to document the defining Coltrane quartet, with pianist McCoy Tyner and drummer Elvin Jones. (The quartet reached peak strength a year later with the addition of bassist Jimmy Garrison.) Tyner begins the piece with one of the best-known introductory passages in jazz. Like the 5/4 vamp of Dave Brubeck's "Take Five," it alerts audiences to what's coming—a combination of modal harmony and polyrhythm—in two measures. Throughout the performance, Tyner's ambiguous, persistent quartal chords create a constantly shifting background. If his harmonies recall Bill Evans, however, his touch is entirely different: weighty, forceful, and tense.

quartal chords chords based on the interval of a fourth (rather than third)

"My Favorite Things" suggested a procedure for interpreting all kinds of songs. Coltrane applied its style, for example, to the sixteenth-century English folksong "Greensleeves," Sigmund Romberg's "Softly, as in a Morning Sunrise," the pop standard "Body and Soul," the currently popular "Chim-Chim-Cheree" from the movie *Mary Poppins*, and other pieces.

The Quartet

McCoy Tyner, born in Philadelphia, attended the Granoff Studios and met Coltrane while still in his teens. Initially modeling himself after Bud Powell, Richie Powell (Bud's younger brother), Art Tatum, and Thelonious Monk, he went on to create a highly individual style. Coltrane worked with first-rate bop pianists, including Flanagan and Wynton Kelly, but not until Tyner did he find a true soul mate, with a heavy, harmonically advanced attack, a partiality for vamps, a gift for economy, and a rhythmic strength inseparable from his dramatic purpose. Coltrane said of him:

> He gets a very personal sound from his instrument and because of the clusters he uses and the way he voices them, his sound is brighter than what would normally be expected from most of the chord patterns he plays. In addition, McCoy has an exceptionally well-developed sense of form both as a soloist and an accompanist. Invariably in our group, he will take a tune and build his own structure for it.

© DUNCAN SCHIEDT

The quintessential John Coltrane Quartet: (left to right) McCoy Tyner, piano; Coltrane; Jimmy Garrison, bass; Elvin Jones, drums. In concert in Indianapolis, 1962.

Tyner's intensity was matched by that of drummer Elvin Jones, the youngest of three gifted brothers (the others were pianist Hank Jones and trumpet player–composer–orchestra leader Thad Jones) who grew up in Pontiac, Michigan. In the 1950s, he worked with key musicians in New York, including Davis, Mingus, Rollins, and J. J. Johnson, without earning recognition as an innovator in his own right. Then with Coltrane, Jones seemed to burst loose of all restraints, taking the dynamic style of Philly Joe Jones (no relation) to a new level. He quickly became known as a drummer's drummer, a master of polyrhythms.

Jones used two related approaches to polyrhythms: playing two rhythms simultaneously himself (for example, a three-beat rhythm and a four-beat rhythm) and playing a different rhythm from the rest of the band (for example, a three-beat waltz rhythm in contrast to the quartet's four-beat rhythm). His superimpositions of waltz meters gave Coltrane's band a rhythmic freedom—propulsive yet, in its way, as open-ended as the modal harmonies. He and Coltrane developed a mutual volatility that led them to long improvisational duels; at the height of some of these bombardments, Tyner would desist from playing altogether.

The cumulative fervor of these performances was liberating and spiritual, especially after Coltrane discovered bassist Jimmy Garrison. Raised in Philadelphia, Garrison came to New York as a protégé of Philly Joe Jones and landed a job with the free-jazz quartet of Ornette Coleman. One evening Coltrane sat in with Coleman's band and was so impressed by Garrison that he hired him for his own band. Elvin Jones called Garrison "the turning point" for the quartet: "His aggressiveness, his attitude toward the instrument gave us all a lift."

"Chasin' the Trane"

In 1961, Coltrane signed a lucrative contract with the fledgling label Impulse, which began to advertise itself as "The New Wave in Jazz." Recording live at the Village Vanguard, he performed a ferocious sixteen-minute blues, "Chasin' the Trane," so antithetical to "My Favorite Things" that it split his audience in two. Critics who once championed him went on the attack. *Down Beat* magazine accused him of playing "musical nonsense" and "anti-jazz." Others found the performance invigorating and defended him as the new hope of jazz. The oratory almost drowned out the music—was he a misdirected zealot or the hero of a new black consciousness?

"Chasin' the Trane" couldn't fail to cause a furor. Occupying one whole side of an LP, it is as relentless as it is long and played at tremendous velocity. Coltrane wails some eighty choruses, using **multiphonics** (chords played on an instrument designed to play only one note at a time), split tones (cracked notes played that way on purpose), cries, and squeals. He asked Tyner not to play on it, so that the primary drama is between Coltrane and Jones. Though the piece is a twelve-bar blues, there are instances when Coltrane seems determined to knock down the bar lines and play with complete freedom; Jones and Garrison forcefully pull him back to the blues structure by signaling the end of each chorus—a significant feat of concentration given the electrifying energy of the performance.

Here was jazz as an existential squawk, a taunting rush of unbridled release. In a sense, "Chasin' the Trane" logically expands on Coltrane's earlier work: it combines the vigorous attack of "Giant Steps" with the harmonic simplicity of the modal pieces. But it requires a new way of listening; without melodic phrases, toe-tapping rhythms, or anything remotely suggesting relaxation, the listener either enters the experience of musical exultation or is left in the cold. "Chasin' the Trane" doesn't really end, it stops; it doesn't really begin, it starts. The performance is all middle.

A Love Supreme

For the next six years, until his death, Coltrane's audience would be constantly "chasin' the Trane," as he took ever larger steps beyond the rudiments of conventional jazz, challenging the validity of everything he had mastered—ultimately alienating even Tyner and Jones. But first, he made another unexpected detour. In 1962 and 1963, he participated in a series of romantic recordings in which improvisation takes a back seat to individualized statements of pure melody. He recorded albums with Duke Ellington and vocalist Johnny Hartman, and one called *Ballads*—eight songs associated with pop crooners he had grown up with (Bing Crosby, Frank Sinatra, Dick Haymes, Nat King Cole). *Ballads* is a disarming showcase for his quartet at its most settled.

Then Coltrane created his most personal work. In December 1964, he recorded the autobiographical four-part suite and canticle *A Love Supreme*, to almost universally enthusiastic reviews. His influence was at this point pervasive.

In the gatefold cover of his masterpiece *A Love Supreme* (1964), John Coltrane published an open letter describing his triumph over drugs, and a hymn that he interpreted in the work's final movement.

An expanding coterie of musicians looked to him as a leader (he used his clout at Impulse to get several of them recording contracts), and a generation of listeners trusted him to map the no-man's-land of the new music.

A Love Supreme solemnizes Coltrane's 1957 devotional conversion, and his liberation from addiction, in four movements: "Acknowledgement," "Pursuance," "Resolution," and "Psalm." Though the arc of the piece moves from harmonic stability to chromatic freedom, *A Love Supreme* represented a type of avant-garde jazz that the public found approachable and satisfying; his old and new admirers closed ranks behind it. In retrospect, the album was a lull before the storm.

"Acknowledgement"

Coltrane's liner notes for *A Love Supreme* describe his religious experience and include a psalm that inspired the fourth movement, which is improvised entirely from the psalm's syllabic content. Unlike the usual canticle, this one is "sung" on the tenor saxophone. The first movement, "Acknowledgement," like the whole work, is a culmination of Coltrane's music thus far, involving scales, pedal points, multiphonics, free improvisation, and shifting rhythms. Toward the end of the movement, a vocal chant signals a harmonic change from one key to another.

Coltrane's sound demands attention instantly, with its heraldic phrases based on the pentatonic scale. It has the feeling of an invocation. Many listeners think the four-note vocal figure is the movement's theme, but in fact it is one of four; the others are motives that spur his improvisation. If the movement opens and closes with incantations, the central section suggests a kind of spiritual wrestling as Coltrane works his way through nagging motives to triumphant tonic chords, shadowed by the alert rhythm section.

Some critics were repelled by the religious aspect of his music, arguing that Coltrane abandoned musical coherence for an aesthetics of faith. This view (which may seem to find support in the 1971 founding of the still-active Church of Saint John Coltrane, in San Francisco) is no more helpful in understanding his music than it is in analyzing Bach's *B Minor Mass.* "Acknowledgement," including its freest passages, is in fact strictly ordered by musical logic.

---

acknowledgement

3.10

JOHN COLTRANE QUARTET
John Coltrane, tenor saxophone, voice; McCoy Tyner, piano; Jimmy Garrison, bass; Elvin Jones, drums
- Label: *A Love Supreme,* Impulse! A(S)77; *A Love Supreme* (Impulse! 314 589 945-2)
- Date: 1964
- Style: late Coltrane
- Form: open-ended

What to listen for:
- open-ended improvisation over an ostinato
- use of motives (A–D)
- intense climaxes
- "A love supreme" motive at 6:06

INTRODUCTION

0:00   The sound of a gong, combined with a piano chord, opens the piece. The music unfolds in free rhythm. Coltrane plays with a few notes from a **pentatonic scale** in the key of E, while the pianist scatters clusters up and down the keyboard.

0:03   The drums enter with a quiet shimmering in the cymbals.

0:15   The saxophone gently fades out.

0:20   The pianist settles on one chord, playing it with a fast **tremolo**.

0:29   As the bass and drums drop out, the drummer continues tapping on the cymbals.

IMPROVISATION

0:32   Garrison (bass) begins a four-note syncopated **ostinato**, which we'll call motive A.

0:40   Jones plays a Latin-style groove, with bass drum and tom-tom accents coinciding with accents in the ostinato.

0:48   Tyner (piano) enters, playing **quartal** harmonies.

1:00   The drums switch to a more intense, double-time feeling.

1:04   Coltrane enters with a three-note motive, repeated **sequentially** on a higher pitch: motive B.

He plays this motive three times, each time with more variation. The bass moves away from the ostinato, improvising within the pentatonic scale.

1:11   Tyner's chords begin to drift, pulling the harmony toward a more dissonant and **chromatic** sound.

1:16   Coltrane plays an ascending pentatonic scale: motive C.

1:21   He returns to motive B.

1:32   Reaching a climax, he ascends to a cadence figure, played with a roughened tone: motive D.

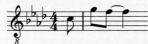

1:35   Coltrane descends with fast passagework, drawn from the pentatonic scale.

2:00   He begins playing with motive C.

2:11   He moves motive C in sequence, shifting the music out of the pentatonic scale. Tyner adjusts his harmonies accordingly. The drums become still more polyrhythmic.

2:31   Coltrane reaches an anguished high note; he descends in pentatonic spirals.

2:44   Again he returns to motive C, quickly sending it into other keys.

2:51   As the dissonance intensifies, the bass drifts away from the home key.

3:06   Coltrane **modulates** through all possible keys.

3:15   The band finds its way back to the home key.

3:26   For a moment, the intensity and volume begin to fade.

3:37   Coltrane begins again with motive C.

3:47   He begins modulating to new keys.

3:52   He finally reaches motive D, playing it repeatedly with an increasingly torturous sound.

4:13   Coltrane's improvisation renews itself with motive C. His modulations ascend in a chromatic swirl. On bass, Garrison follows him into the topmost register.

4:22	Coltrane reaches the tonic and falls downward through the pentatonic scale.
4:33	The improvisation gradually subsides.
4:55	He plays motive A, moving it restlessly through all possible keys. The bass and piano follow.
5:50	Finally all instruments come to rest on the tonic. As the mood dies down, Coltrane repeats motive A endlessly.
5:54	Garrison plays a close variant of motive A.
6:05	The saxophone disappears; in its place, Coltrane's overdubbed voice sings "a love supreme." Its incessant repetition induces a trance-like sense of calm.
6:36	Suddenly the voices sink down a whole step, settling into a new key (which will be the key of the next movement).

CODA

6:44	The voices disappear, leaving Garrison playing his variant of motive A. The piano and drums occasionally add tension, but the bass is at the center.
7:09	The piano drops out.
7:23	The drums drop out. Garrison continues the motive's rhythms, but begins improvising its melody.
7:40	Garrison ends by quietly strumming two notes at once.

Ascension

Within a year of *A Love Supreme*, Coltrane disbanded his quartet for an even more expressionistic group. He replaced Elvin Jones with Rashied Ali, another Philadelphian, but one tutored almost exclusively in the avant-garde; on occasion, Coltrane would use two or three drummers. His wife, Alice, a former student of Bud Powell with relatively workmanlike technique, replaced Tyner; after Coltrane's death, she would earn her own following as a composer of religious-themed music with internationalist echoes, elaborating on her husband's interest in the music of Africa, India, and the Middle East.

Jimmy Garrison continued to play with the group, which became a quintet with the addition of tenor saxophonist Pharoah Sanders. Born in Little Rock, Arkansas, Sanders was regarded as one of the most intractable members of the avant-garde. His shrieking, guttural explosions of sound, often within a modal framework, were thought to pick up where Coltrane left off, taking jazz into a realm where the only rule was the inspiration of the moment.

After Coltrane's death in 1967, Sanders's music grew increasingly restrained, backpedaling from modes to chords and melodic statements with minimal improvisation. Although the free music Coltrane embraced in his last years was undeniably a product of its time, notably the tragedies of the civil rights effort and the slaughter in Vietnam, it exerted lasting influence on musicians who adapted free improvisation along with ghosted notes, broken notes, squawks, and growls as part of the musician's arsenal.

ghosted notes notes played so softly they're barely audible

Coltrane's most extreme work is the 1965 album *Ascension*, a vexatious piece that takes the heady effusiveness of "Giant Steps" and "Chasin' the Trane" to the limit of musical reason. The piece, improvised by ten musicians, is based on a minor triad and a couple of ground chords for the ensemble passages; the format consists of free solos that alternate with free ensemble blowouts. Yet even *Ascension* offers a serendipitous logic. (Decades later, it was transcribed and performed as a "composed" piece.) Coltrane always claimed not to understand the fuss. "The main thing a musician would like to do," he said, "is to give a picture to the listener of the many wonderful things he knows of and senses in the universe."

MILES DAVIS'S SECOND QUINTET

After the back-to-back triumphs of *Kind of Blue* and *Sketches of Spain*, Miles Davis endured a slump of uncertainty. Coltrane, Adderley, and Evans had left to pursue their own careers, and Davis despised the avant-garde. He continued to release effective records, including a reunion with Coltrane that produced a minor hit in "Some Day My Prince Will Come." But his music was caught in a bind, much of it devoted to faster and harder versions of his usual repertory, including "Walkin'" and "So What."

Then in 1963, once again, he produced magic. He turned to younger musicians who would surely have had important careers on their own; under Davis's tutelage, they merged into a historic ensemble, greater than its very considerable parts. The rhythm section consisted of three prodigiously skillful musicians who valued diversity over an allegiance to one style of music: pianist Herbie Hancock, bassist Ron Carter, and seventeen-year-old drummer Tony Williams. Davis auditioned many saxophonists before temporarily settling on George Coleman, who played with facility and intelligence but lacked the drive and curiosity of the younger players.

After trying various musicians, Miles Davis introduced his second great quintet, with much younger players: (left to right) Herbie Hancock, piano; Tony Williams, drums; Ron Carter, bass; Davis; Wayne Shorter, tenor saxophone. Berlin, 1964.

In late 1964, Wayne Shorter, who had made his name as a saxophonist and composer with Art Blakey's Jazz Messengers, joined the band, a decision that changed his life and Davis's, and made this second great quintet a worthy follow-up to the 1955 group with Coltrane. This time, however, Davis took as much from his sidemen as he gave, drawing on their compositions (especially Shorter's) and sensibilities. These musicians were keenly interested in the avant-garde, and Davis adjusted his music to their new approach.

With the help of his young recruits, Davis struggled to make a separate peace in a confusing era. Jazz was beset on one side by avant-garde experimentalism that estranged much of the audience, and on the other by rock, which had matured from a teenage marketing ploy to the dominant pop music. Davis would eventually inch his way to a fusion of jazz and rock, but first he adapted modal jazz to include elements of the avant-garde in a **postbop** style far more extreme than cool or soul jazz. This approach, which attracted a number of musicians caught between bop conventions and the excitement born of the avant-garde (see Chapter 15), involved harmonic ambiguity, original compositions with new harmonic frameworks (rather than those built on standard songs), and a radical loosening of the rhythm section. Some of the tunes written by Davis's sidemen actually encouraged free improvisation; in these pieces, chord progressions were absent, and time and meter could evaporate and coalesce in the course of a performance.

Most first-rate rhythm sections work like the fingers in a fist. Coltrane's quartet, for example, achieved a fiercely unified front, devoted to supporting the leader. Davis's group was no less unified, but its parts interacted with more freedom, often rivaling the soloists. So much was going on between Hancock's unruffled block chords, Carter's slippery bass lines, and Williams's rhythmic brushfires that they all appeared to be soloing all the time. Davis gave them leave, enjoying the excitement they created, but he imposed a discipline that left space for the lyrical drama of his trumpet. Free of chord changes, unapologetic about fluffs, and stimulated by his band's ceaseless energy, Davis became a more expansive trumpet player. He began to forage in the upper register at precipitous tempos, ideas spilling from his horn with spiraling confidence despite infrequent technical failings. He cut back on his signature ballads, and began to jettison standard tunes and his old classics. Between 1965 and 1968, he found his own way to be avant-garde.

"E.S.P."

The 1965 album *E.S.P.* was a critical event, but not a popular success; it represented the first studio recording by the new quintet, and the seven new compositions, all by members of the group, challenged listeners who expected to hear the tender, meditative Davis who incarnated jazz romanticism. This music is audacious, fast, and free. The title of the album (and first selection) emphasized the idea that extra-sensory perception is required to play this music. Shorter composed "E.S.P." as a thirty-two-bar tune, but its harmonic structure is far more complicated than that of "So What."

The melody is based on intervals of fourths (recalling the indefinite quartal harmonies of "So What" and "Acknowledgement"), and married to a mixture of scales and chords in a way that offers direction to the improvisers without making many demands. The main part of the piece (**A**) hovers around an F major scale, while the **A'** sections close with specific harmonic cadences that are handled easily and quickly—especially at this expeditious tempo. The soloists (Shorter for two choruses, Davis for six, Hancock for two) take wing over the rhythm, bending notes in and out of pitch, soaring beyond the usual rhythmic demarcations that denote swing. Note, too, the equally free and multifaceted work of the rhythm section: the bass playing is startlingly autonomous, and the drummer's use of cymbals has its own narrative logic.

The public reception accorded *E.S.P.* and succeeding albums by Davis's quintet (*Miles Smiles, Sorcerer, Nefertiti*) suggested the tremendous changes that had taken place in the cultural landscape in the few years since *Kind of Blue* and *Sketches of Spain*. They were received favorably and sometimes enthusiastically by musicians, critics, and young fans, but achieved nothing of the broader cachet enjoyed by his earlier work: there was nothing easy or soothing about these records. By 1965, rock and roll could no longer be dismissed by jazz artists as music for kids, and Davis was feeling the heat. His response will be discussed in Chapter 17.

LISTENING GUIDE

3.11

 e.s.p.

MILES DAVIS QUINTET
Miles Davis, trumpet; Wayne Shorter, tenor saxophone; Herbie Hancock, piano; Ron Carter, bass; Tony Williams, drums

- Label: *E.S.P.,* Columbia CL2350; *The Complete Columbia Studio Recordings of the Miles Davis Quintet, January 1965 to June 1968* (Columbia/Legacy 827969092521)
- Date: 1965
- Style: postbop
- Form: 32-bar popular song (**A A′**)

What to listen for:
- rhythmic freedom and bent notes of soloists: Shorter, Davis, Hancock
- **Davis's shrill high notes and short phrases**
- **imaginative playing of rhythm section**

CHORUS 1 (HEAD)

0:00	**A**	The tenor saxophone and trumpet enter with the tune, which initially alternates between three notes. Because the notes harmonize equally well with two different chords, it's hard to determine the piece's key. Underneath, Carter (bass) plays two beats per bar, while Williams rattles busily on the cymbals.
0:07		The melody descends from a high note, while the bass rises chromatically. For several measures, the piano is silent.
0:13		The phrase ends with a dissonant bass note.
0:14	**A′**	The **A** section is repeated with a higher-pitched bass line.
0:21		The bass harmonizes underneath in **tritones** by playing two strings at once (**double stops**).
0:27		The tune ends in a major key that may be the tonic, but the sense of closure lasts less than a second.

CHORUS 2

0:28	**A**	Shorter (tenor saxophone) begins a two-chorus solo with an upward-rising line that ends in a bent note. Carter (bass) begins to walk.

0:35		Shorter plays pitches that are out of time and slightly flat before blending them back in to a continuous line.
0:42	**A'**	He improvises an even stream of notes.
0:49		He plays a descending three-note motive twice before continuing his line.

CHORUS 3

0:55	**A**	Shorter leaves spaces for Hancock (piano) to enter with chords.
1:02		With a sudden ascent, Shorter returns to the tune's melody. He ends a flurry of notes with a dismissive honk.
1:09	**A'**	Shorter plays with a motive that, in its alternation of two pitches, recalls the theme.
1:15		His melody is **chromatic**, matching the tension of Hancock's dissonant chords.

CHORUS 4

1:22	**A**	Davis begins his six-chorus solo. He concentrates on a few mid-register notes.
1:29		As the harmonies become more tense, Davis rises to a dissonant note.
1:34		His notes begin to crack.
1:36	**A'**	
1:41		Davis suddenly rises into the upper register. He plays a few shrill notes before tumbling, somewhat untidily, back down.

CHORUS 5

| 1:49 | **A** | As Williams (drums) and Hancock play more aggressively, Davis's solo becomes more disjointed, breaking into short fragments. |
| 2:02 | **A'** | Davis begins a new phrase with a repeated-note fanfare, followed by a series of short phrases. |

CHORUS 6

2:15	**A**	The trumpet hits an accent that coincides spontaneously with a drum accent.
2:29	**A'**	Carter takes his walking-bass line into the upper register.
2:35		As the bass drops back down, Davis rises step by step.
2:40		Davis again makes a sudden swoop upward.

CHORUS 7

| 2:42 | **A** | Davis screeches out a descending four-note line in his upper range. Williams's drumming hits a new level of intensity with powerful drum strokes. |
| 2:55 | **A'** | The band retreats to a lower volume. Davis plays a continuous line of notes in his middle register. |

CHORUS 8

3:08	**A**	Davis's new motive has a bluesy tinge.
3:21	**A'**	
3:31		Davis abruptly drops out; the space is filled by Hancock's **comping**.

CHORUS 9

| 3:34 | **A** | Davis plays a motive that rocks back and forth a half step, interrupting it with several swoops up to his highest register. |
| 3:47 | **A'** | He returns to a variant of the bluesy motive from chorus 8. |

CHORUS 10

4:00	**A**	Hancock starts his solo, imitating the rhythm of Davis's last motive.
4:06		Hancock introduces his own substitution in the harmonic progression.
4:13	**A'**	Playing a single-note line, he sounds like a saxophonist or trumpet player.

CHORUS 11

4:27 **A** Hancock plays a riff, then modifies it subtly to fit the chord progression.

4:40 **A'** His improvised line interacts with his left-hand chords.

CHORUS 12 (HEAD)

4:53 **A** As Davis and Shorter reenter with the tune's melody, Carter on bass returns to a slower pattern.

5:00 Carter plays tritone double stops, Williams adding a few cymbal colors.

5:07 **A'** Williams reestablishes his drum pulse, but fades in and out for the rest of the tune.

CODA

5:20 When the tune ends, Carter is on an unexpected note. He resolves it downward to the opening chord.

MILES DAVIS CHRONOLOGY		
1926	Born May 26 in Alton, Illinois.	
1944	Enrolls at Juilliard School, New York.	
1945–48	Performs with Charlie Parker.	
1948–50	Befriends Gil Evans, forms the Miles Davis Nonet ("birth of the cool" band).	
c. 1950	Becomes addicted to heroin.	
1954	Kicks drug habit.	"Walkin'" (Prestige)
1955	Forms first quintet, with John Coltrane, Red Garland, Paul Chambers, Philly Joe Jones.	'Round Midnight (Columbia)
1957–60	Writes score for French film; records with Evans.	Miles Ahead (1957), Porgy and Bess (1958), Sketches of Spain (1960)
1958	Adds Cannonball Adderley, expands to sextet.	Milestones
1959	Explores modal improvisation.	Kind of Blue (with Bill Evans)
1963	Forms second quintet, with Wayne Shorter, Herbie Hancock, Ron Carter, Tony Williams.	
1965–67	Records postbop albums.	E.S.P., Miles Smiles, Nefertiti

MILES DAVIS CHRONOLOGY		
1968–70	Moves into fusion (see Chapter 17).	*Filles de Kilimanjaro, In a Silent Way, Bitches Brew* (best-seller)
1975–80	Withdraws from music.	
1981	Returns to performing.	
1985	Signs with Warner Bros.	
1986		*Tutu*
1991	Dies September 28 in Santa Monica, California.	

ADDITIONAL LISTENING

Charlie Parker	"Donna Lee" (1947); *The Complete Savoy and Dial Master Takes* (Savoy Jazz 17149)
Miles Davis	*Kind of Blue* (1959) (Columbia/Legacy CK 64935)
	"Round Midnight" (1956); *X2 (Sketches of Spain / Round About Midnight)* (Legacy 886972965826)
	"Milestones" (1958); *Milestones* (Sony Legacy 85203)
	"Orbits," "Footprints" (1966); *Miles Smiles* (Columbia/Legacy 5099706568223)
	"Walkin'" (1954); *Walkin'* (Prestige PRCD-30008-2)
	"Someday My Prince Will Come" (1961); *Someday My Prince Will Come* (Columbia/Legacy 074646591925)
	"My Funny Valentine" (1964); *My Funny Valentine: Miles Davis in Concert* (Columbia/Legacy 827969359327)
Miles Davis and Gil Evans	*Sketches of Spain* (1959) (Legacy 074646514221)
Bill Evans	"Blue in Green" (1959); *Portrait in Jazz* (Riverside RCD-30678)
	"Peace Piece" (1958); *Everybody Digs Bill Evans* (Riverside RCD-30182)
	"My Foolish Heart" (1961); *Live at the Village Vanguard* (Fantasy FCD-60-017)
John Coltrane	"Naima" (1959); *Giant Steps* (Rhino/Atlantic R2 75203)
	"Chasin' the Trane" (1961); *The Complete 1961 Village Vanguard Recordings* (Impulse! 0111050-232-21)
	"My Favorite Things" (1960); *My Favorite Things* (Atlantic 1361-2)
	"Alabama" (1963); *Coltrane Live at Birdland* (Impulse! 011105019828)
	A Love Supreme: Deluxe Edition (1964) (Impulse! 731458994527)

PART IV SUMMARY

BEBOP

With the arrival of bebop in the mid-1940s, jazz turned a sharp corner. Emerging from Swing Era jam sessions, bebop was at the same time a rejection of the era's racial prejudice and resulting commercial restrictions. Bebop, with its fast tempos and complex harmonies, failed as popular music, but today, over sixty years later, young jazz musicians still learn to improvise by studying Charlie Parker and Dizzy Gillespie.

Texture

- homophonic, with occasional monophonic breaks

Rhythm

- unpredictable, extremely fast tempos

Typical instrumentation

- solo: saxophone (alto or tenor), trumpet
- rhythm section: piano, bass, drums
- other possibilities: trombone, vibraphone, electric guitar

Form

- original melodies written over standard forms (12-bar blues, 32-bar popular song)

Special techniques

- heads (unison lines at beginning and end)
- trading fours (between soloists, between soloists and drummer)
- comping (piano, guitar)
- interactive drums ("dropping bombs")

Bebop pioneers

- Kenny Clarke (drums)
- Dizzy Gillespie (trumpet)
- Charlie Parker (alto saxophone)
- Thelonious Monk (piano)

Bebop generation

- Art Blakey (drums)
- Wardell Gray (tenor saxophone)
- Dexter Gordon (tenor saxophone)
- Milt Jackson (vibraphone)
- Theodore "Fats" Navarro (trumpet)
- Bud Powell (piano)
- Max Roach (drums)
- J. J. Johnson (trombone)
- Miles Davis (trumpet)
- Red Rodney (trumpet)

COOL JAZZ

Cool (or West Coast) jazz grew out of bebop in the early 1950s. The style is characterized by a light, laid-back, reticent quality.

Texture

- basically homophonic, tending toward polyphonic lines

Rhythm

- unusual meters (five, seven)

Typical instrumentation

- solo: experimental (possible additions: flute, tuba, French horn, oboe)
- rhythm section: piano, bass, drums

Form

- 12-bar blues, 32-bar popular song, classically influenced compositions (fugue, atonal music)

Special techniques

- restrained timbre, vibrato
- limited range
- quiet rhythm section

Cool jazz pioneers

- Lennie Tristano (piano)
- Tadd Dameron (piano)

COOL JAZZ (continued)

Important cool bands/musicians
- Miles Davis Nonet ("birth of the cool")
- Lee Konitz (alto saxophone)
- Gil Evans (piano/arranger)
- Gerry Mulligan Quartet: Mulligan (baritone saxophone), Chet Baker (trumpet), Chico Hamilton (drums)
- Modern Jazz Quartet: John Lewis (piano), Milt Jackson (vibraphone), Percy Heath (bass)
- Dave Brubeck (piano), with Paul Desmond (alto saxophone)
- "white Lesters": Stan Getz, Zoot Sims, Al Cohn, Allen Eager

HARD BOP

Hard bop, centered on the East Coast, was a counterstatement to cool jazz: it was essentially a revival of bop but with a harder edge.

Texture
- homophonic, with occasional monophonic breaks

Rhythm
- assertive

Typical instrumentation
- solo: trumpet, saxophone, piano, bass, drums
- rhythm section: piano, bass, drums
- other possibilities: organ trio (Hammond B3 organ, guitar, drums)

Form: 12-bar blues, 32-bar popular song

Special techniques
- bop with a rough edge, resisting experimentation
- heavy, dark timbres
- African American aesthetic

Important hard bop bands/musicians
- Jazz Messengers: Art Blakey (drums), Horace Silver (piano)
- Clifford Brown (trumpet), Max Roach (drums)
- Sonny Rollins (tenor saxophone)
- Wes Montgomery (electric guitar)
- Miles Davis Quintet
- "black Lesters": Dexter Gordon, Wardell Gray, Illinois Jacquet, Gene Ammons

JAZZ COMPOSERS

Pianist Thelonious Monk, after Duke Ellington the most widely performed of jazz composers, worked almost exclusively with 12-bar blues and 32-bar **A A B A** tunes. He sometimes altered standard harmonic progressions with whole-tone and chromatic scales, and added quirky dissonances (such as minor seconds and tritones). Monk believed that a meaningful improvisation should flow and develop the composed theme.

Bassist Charles Mingus, among the most accomplished virtuosos of his time, composed in styles as far ranging as the sanctified church, New Orleans polyphony, swing, hard bop, and classical music. He was the first composer of his generation to pay tributes to great musicians of the past, such as Lester Young and Jelly Roll Morton.

Gil Evans "elevated arranging virtually to the art of composition," in the words of Gunther Schuller. His imaginative arrangements were characterized by the use of counterpoint, slow-moving chords, and very low instruments (tuba) combined with very high ones (flute). He's best known for his use of concerto form, featuring a single soloist.

George Russell, who worked exclusively as a composer-bandleader, devoted much of his life to formulating an intricate musical theory known as the Lydian chromatic concept. His ideas were the basis for modalism, which liberated jazz from bebop's harmonic grids and encouraged improvisers to think more melodically.

MILES DAVIS AND JOHN COLTRANE

Miles Davis was the archetypal modern jazz musician, a magnet for artists in and out of music. His unmistakable trumpet style was characterized by emotional and rhythmic restraint, while his continuous rethinking of harmony, melody, rhythm, and instrumentation led to works that changed the ground rules of jazz at least five times.

- 1949–50: "birth of the cool" sessions launched the cool jazz movement.
- 1954: "Walkin'" provided the impetus for hard bop.
- 1957–60: collaborations with Gil Evans enlarged the scope of jazz composition and projected a new meditative mood.
- 1959: *Kind of Blue*, featuring modal improvisation, transformed jazz performance in its favoring of melody and nuance.
- 1969: *Bitches Brew* initiated an era of jazz-rock fusion.

The pianist on *Kind of Blue* was Bill Evans, one of the most influential musicians of his generation, who in 1959 premiered a new approach to the piano trio (favoring the bass), with Scott LaFaro (bass) and Paul Motian (drums).

Davis's musical and personal impact was equaled (or surpassed) by that of tenor saxophonist John Coltrane, who became the most intrepid explorer of modal jazz. While Davis in later years leaned toward rock, Coltrane embraced the expressionistic chaos of the avant-garde. His "sheets of sound" harmonic improvisation can be heard in *Giant Steps;* modal improvisation in "My Favorite Things," "Chasin' the Trane," and *A Love Supreme*, with his quartet—McCoy Tyner (piano), Jimmy Garrison (bass), and Elvin Jones (drums); and free improvisation in *Ascension*.

PART V

THE AVANT-GARDE, FUSION, HISTORICISM, AND NOW

By the 1960s, jazz had accrued a convoluted history in little more than half a century. There had been so many jazz schools that Duke Ellington spoke for most listeners and musicians when he said, "I don't know how such great extremes as now exist can be contained under the one heading." The most extreme developments were still to come: the avant-garde and fusion. The former seemed to blow all the rules out of the water, advancing improvisation that was free from predetermined harmonies and rhythms. Fusion took a more popular approach, combining improvisation with rock's rhythms and instrumentation. Sometimes, as in the music of Miles Davis and Ornette Coleman, the avant-garde and fusion coalesced.

In a precarious era, defined by an apparently endless occupation in Vietnam and racist atrocities and political assassinations at home, jazz could hardly com-

1939
- *Jazzmen* published: first book to look back at early jazz.

1940
- The U.S. Good Neighbor Policy begins to have cultural ramifications as Walt Disney and others explore songs from South and Central America.

1940s
- "Jump" music popularized by Louis Jordan.

1942
- Bunk Johnson makes recordings.
- Sarah Vaughan wins talent competition at Apollo Theater.

1947
- Dizzy Gillespie records "Manteca" (with Chano Pozo).
- University of North Texas, Denton, offers first degree in jazz studies.

1948
- Machito records "Tanga."

1951
- *I Love Lucy* (with Lucille Ball and Desi Arnaz) debuts on TV, inadvertently spurring interest in Latin music.

1952
- Samuel Beckett's *Waiting for Godot* published.

1954
- Ray Charles's "I Got a Woman" is No. 1 R & B hit.
- George Wein establishes Newport Jazz Festival.
- Elvis Presley makes first records for Sun, in Memphis.
- *The Glenn Miller Story* (with Jimmy Stewart) released.

1955
- Hammond B3 organ introduced.

1956
- Cecil Taylor plays at Five Spot, records *Jazz Advance*.

As John Coltrane forged ever farther into the avant-garde, he recruited his wife Alice Coltrane as pianist, 1966.

Louis Jordan, playing alto saxophone at center stage, was the entertainer and musician who practically invented rhythm and blues. Here, he leads his Tympany Five (Josh Jackson, tenor saxophone; Bill Davis, piano; Jordan; Jesse Simprins, bass; Aaron Izenhall, trumpet; Eddie Byrd, drums) in a 1946 movie.

Composer and faculty member Gunther Schuller examines a score with guest "student" Ornette Coleman at the Lenox School of Jazz (Massachusetts), 1959.

pete in popularity with the accessible, verbal urgency of rock. Still, the avant-garde flourished artistically, expanding its base in Europe and ultimately demonstrating at least as much diversity as its predecessors. Coleman, its most radical yet lyrical proponent, eventually earned establishment plaudits that had been denied earlier jazz artists. His successors used every kind of music, from brass band marches to Javanese gamelan ensembles, to fashion new works and reinterpret old ones. A conservative movement also took hold, presenting big-band classics in repertory and advocating a return to generally accessible styles.

At the same time, jazz began to examine its own history in seminars and clinics, moving into the academy where orchestras were assembled as training grounds for young musicians. Although contrary theories of jazz history were advanced, by the twenty-first century most of the old battles had been settled and a universal modernism predominated, paying homage to the past while keeping its options open. The audience for jazz dwindled as the monopolized airwaves banished it, yet successful jazz festivals proliferated around the world and the overall level of virtuosity and commitment continued unabated.

- Frank Sinatra records *Songs for Swingin' Lovers*, with arranger Nelson Riddle.
- Duke Ellington makes comeback at Newport.

1957
- Lenox School of Jazz founded in Massachusetts.
- *The Sound of Jazz* broadcast on TV.

1958
- Bossa nova initiated in Rio de Janeiro.
- Ornette Coleman makes first recordings in Los Angeles.
- Mahalia Jackson brings gospel music, Chuck Berry brings rock to Newport Jazz Festival.

1959
- Coleman appears at the Five Spot, records "Lonely Woman."
- Ellington writes score to *Anatomy of a Murder.*

1960
- Coleman records *Free Jazz.*

1961
- Dizzy Gillespie, Charlie Byrd, and other musicians discover bossa nova in Brazil.

1963
- *Getz / Gilberto* is million-selling bossa nova record.

1964
- Albert Ayler records *Spiritual Unity.*
- Louis Armstrong has unexpected hit with "Hello, Dolly!"
- Beatles, Rolling Stones tour United States.

1965
- Association for the Advancement of Creative Musicians (AACM) founded.

1966
- Cecil Taylor records *Unit Structures.*
- Duke Ellington receives President's Medal of Honor.

1967
- Art Ensemble of Chicago (AEC) formed.
- First Montreux Jazz Festival in Switzerland.

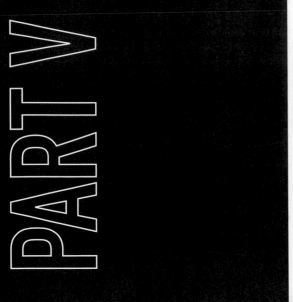

PART V

1968
- Martin Luther King Jr. and Robert F. Kennedy assassinated.
- USSR invades Czechoslovakia.

1969
- Anthony Braxton records *For Alto.*
- Miles Davis records *In a Silent Way, Bitches Brew.*
- Woodstock concert in Bethel, New York.
- Neil Armstrong becomes first man to walk on moon.
- Philip Roth's *Portnoy's Complaint* published.

1970
- Supreme Court, in *Roe v. Wade,* affirms abortion rights.
- U.S. invades Cambodia.

1971
- Louis Armstrong dies.

1972
- Mahavishnu Orchestra records *The Inner Mounting Flame.*

- Chick Corea forms Return to Forever.

1973
- George Roy Hill's *The Sting* (with Paul Newman and Robert Redford) revives interest in Scott Joplin and ragtime.
- Vietnam War ends.

1974
- Herbie Hancock records *Head Hunters.*
- Duke Ellington dies.
- President Richard M. Nixon resigns over Watergate scandal.

1974–86
- The Loft Era takes hold in downtown New York.

1975
- Keith Jarrett records *The Köln Concert.*

1976
- Weather Report records *Heavy Weather.*

He wore a wig and used an electronic pickup, but not even fusion could undermine the unmistakable timbre of Miles Davis, seen at a concert in London, 1989.

At a memorial service for John Coltrane, at St. Peter's Lutheran Church in New York, saxophonist Albert Ayler (in white suit) led his quartet in a dirge of astonishing intensity, July 21, 1967.

After you: Two of the great male vocalists to cross the divide between jazz and pop, Nat "King" Cole and Billy Eckstine, in New York, 1949.

Tenor saxophonist David Murray and composer-conductor Butch Morris helped to create a rapprochement between the avant-garde and older forms of jazz during the Loft Era of the 1970s and 1980s.

Berliners celebrate as East Germans (backs to camera) flood through the dismantled Berlin Wall into West Berlin at Potsdamer Platz, November 12, 1989.

Sonny Rollins played with undiminished power and endurance at a concert in New Orleans, 1995.

1978
- Pat Metheny Group formed.

1979
- Henry Threadgill's avant-garde group Air records music by Scott Joplin and Jelly Roll Morton.
- Charles Mingus dies.
- Revolution in Iran, Americans held hostage at U.S. embassy for over a year.

1981
- Sandra Day O'Connor becomes first female Supreme Court justice.

1982
- Thelonious Monk dies.

1987
- Jazz at Lincoln Center established.
- Soviet prime minister Mikhail Gorbachev institutes policies of *glasnost* and *perestroika*.

1989
- Berlin Wall falls.

1990–94
- Apartheid dismantled in South Africa.

1997
- Wynton Marsalis receives Pulitzer Prize for oratorio *Blood on the Fields*.

2001
- Terrorists attack World Trade Center and Pentagon.

2003
- U.S. invades Iraq.

2006
- Thelonious Monk receives posthumous Pulitzer Prize for his body of work.

2007
- Ornette Coleman receives Pulitzer Prize for recording, *Sound Grammar*.

2008
- Barack Obama is elected first African American president in U.S. history.

ORNETTE COLEMAN
lonely woman

CECIL TAYLOR
bulbs

CECIL TAYLOR
willisau concert, part 3

ALBERT AYLER
ghosts

DAVID MURRAY
el matador

THE AVANT-GARDE

Forward March

The word "avant-garde" originated in the French military to denote the advanced guard: troops sent ahead of the regular army to scout unknown territory. In English, the word was adapted to describe innovative composers, writers, painters, and other artists whose work was so pioneering that it was believed to be in the vanguard of contemporary thinking. **Avant-gardism** represented a movement to liberate artists from the restraints of tradition, and it often went hand-in-hand with progressive social thinking. Those who championed avant-garde art tended to applaud social change. Those who criticized it for rejecting prevailing standards couched their dismay in warnings against moral laxity or political anarchy.

In the end, however, all art, traditional or avant-garde, must stand on its merit, independent of historic influences. The art that outrages one generation often becomes the tradition and homework assignments of the next: the paintings of Paul Cézanne and Pablo Picasso, music of Gustav Mahler and Claude Debussy, and writings of Marcel Proust and James Joyce were all initially considered avant-garde. Two especially prominent twentieth-century avant-garde movements gathered steam in the decades following the world wars, and jazz was vital to both.

Sonny Rollins combined the harmonic progressions of bop with the freedom of the avant-garde and sustained an international following. He appeared with percussionist Victor See Yuen and trombonist Clifton Anderson at a stadium in Louisiana, 1995.

wwnorton.com/studyspace

THE FIRST AVANT-GARDE WAVE

The 1920s avant-garde, which included such sub-categories as surrealism, cubism, imagism, and twelve-tone music (introduced by Arnold Schoenberg in 1921), consciously sought to fracture artistic conventions. It was a response to the devastation of World War I, the expansion of women's rights, and startling advances in technology—radio, talking pictures, transcontinental flight—that seemed to shrink the world while expanding its potential. This avant-garde was provocative and sometimes rude, but generally hopeful.

Jazz was a new musical fashion, socially daring and emblematic of free-thinking young people. Although pilloried by some conservative tastemakers as low-born and vulgar, jazz was regarded by many members of the cultural elite as an inspirational resource and a powerful component of avant-garde modernism. Artists in diverse fields—painters Henri Matisse and Piet Mondrian, composers Igor Stravinsky and Kurt Weill, poets Hart Crane and Langston Hughes, photographer Man Ray, sculptor Alexander Calder, dancer Josephine Baker—found inspiration in jazz and its New World vitality.

Within jazz itself, as we have seen repeatedly, practically every new style was considered avant-garde. As early as the 1920s, traditionalists complained that Armstrong, Ellington, and swing music muddied the alleged purity of New Orleans jazz. Those complaints, however, were few and relatively calm compared with the outrage generated by bebop in the 1940s. Unlike purists who disparaged swing for commercializing jazz, the opponents of bop blamed it for sacrificing jazz's connection to mainstream popular culture. Instead of accommodating the dictates of the market place, bop proudly adapted the mantle of avant-gardism, self-consciously examining the relationship between jazz and society and between jazz and other kinds of music.

Even so, jazz remained largely accessible. Although it ceased to reign as America's dance music and aggressively challenged assumptions about melody, harmony, structure, meter, instrumentation, swing, and presentation, it continued to favor a strong, regular beat, standard harmonies, and hummable tunes. Bebop made jazz more intellectual while maintaining basic rules of musical coherence. The second avant-garde challenged those basic rules.

THE SECOND AVANT-GARDE WAVE

The avant-garde wave of the late 1950s and 1960s reflected conditions similar to those of the 1920s, only more so. The rebuilding of Europe and Asia after World War II was countered by new colonial wars, occupations, and the Cold War, in which America and the Soviet Union employed technology to threaten annihilation. The struggle for racial equality in the United States led to the Civil Rights Act of 1964, which outlawed discrimination on grounds of race, color, religion, sex, and national origin. Unsurprisingly, women now demanded professional, social, and sexual parity. Some of society's settled conventions, including the nuclear family (working dad, stay-at-home mom), unraveled.

The radical changes in racial and gender politics, as well as the threat of a push-button atomic war, created a very different avant-garde from the one that glorified modernism as a citadel of healthy change. Instead of expressing faith in a liberating future, the avant-garde of the Cold War bared uncertainty and anguish. It also celebrated the plebeian, the ordinary, the absurd. Instead of abstraction or surrealism, painters looked to comic strips, visual trickery, and commercial design. A characteristic literary work is Samuel Beckett's *Waiting for Godot* (published in 1952), an intricately symbolic play that recycled aspects of the most common form of popular entertainment, vaudeville. By the early 1960s, Beckett's themes—life is without meaning, the world is mad, mankind is abandoned ("to freedom condemned," as philosopher Jean-Paul Sartre put it)—permeated all the arts.

The most potent expressions of the avant-garde in the 1960s were apparent in the two art forms born in the twentieth century, movies and jazz. A powerful new direction in cinema emanated from France and Italy, often described as the New Wave. These films examined prevailing themes of confusion and desperation, and pioneered techniques in narrative style. Jazz in this period also developed new techniques to express its dramatic disavowal of tradition. The label *avant-garde* eventually attached itself permanently to this most controversial of jazz styles.

What's in a Name?

The jazz school that came to be called avant-garde was first known by other names, few of them neutral. One critic coined the term "anti-jazz" to attack its apparent rejection of mainstream jazz. Another widespread designation echoed the title of an album by Ornette Coleman, *Free Jazz,* released in 1961 with a cover reproduction of a Jackson Pollock painting, as if to underscore its challenging modernity. Some called it Black Music, arguing that its ferocity expressed the particular frustration of African Americans during the civil rights years. Others called it new music, the new thing, revolutionary music, and fire music. Ironically, the name that finally stuck had been indicated in the title of the first avant-garde album, Cecil Taylor's 1956 *Jazz Advance.*

As musicians in later decades enlarged the canvas of free jazz or new music, the inoffensive *avant-garde* emerged as an umbrella term to describe an inclusive, ongoing school of jazz that, despite many connections to mainstream jazz, evolved as a separate entity, a tradition in its own right. By definition, *avant-garde* is now something of a misnomer: music that is four or five decades old can hardly be representative of today's vanguard. Yet the word continues to apply because it defines an approach to jazz that remains outside the practices that govern the usual musical performance. It continues to question principles that the mainstream takes for granted.

Cover art was a strong selling point in the LP era, when Ornette Coleman used a Jackson Pollock painting to indicate the explosiveness of *Free Jazz*, released by Atlantic Records in 1961.

Breaking Points

As we saw in Chapters 11–14, postwar jazz innovators greatly enlarged the parameters of mainstream (or swing) jazz. The avant-garde stretched those parameters to the breaking point. Although the key figures of the avant-garde—most prominently Ornette Coleman, Cecil Taylor, and John Coltrane—approached music from very different angles, they collectively challenged the status quo. In refusing to be bound by rules of the past, they questioned and changed every facet of jazz's identity.

- Rhythm: The avant-garde dispensed with the steady dance beat, preferring an ambiguous pulse or several pulses at once.

- Harmony: The avant-garde did away with harmonic patterns based on chords or scales, creating a serendipitous harmony as the musicians instinctively felt their way through a performance.

- Melody: Depending on the soloist, melody could be lyrical or full of squeals and squawks; either way, melody no longer relied on harmonic patterns and resolutions.

- Structure: The avant-garde frequently rejected blues and songs, and encouraged *free* improvisation, in which the sheer energy or emotionalism of a performance dictated its overall shape.

- Instrumentation: The avant-garde favored the widest variety of instruments, from the hand drums and wood flutes of formerly colonized Third World countries to symphonic standbys like the cello and oboe.

- Presentation: Jazz was no longer entertainment. It could be witty, even funny, but it was a serious, challenging music, requiring the listener's full concentration—art for art's sake.

- Politics: Jazz became entrenched in the increasingly militant racial and antiwar struggles of the 1950s and 1960s; whether or not it referred to specific events, it adopted an assertive posture.

As the avant-garde developed beyond its initial stage, musicians embraced it as an arena in which anything could be tried. A spontaneous improvisation and a twelve-bar blues might follow one another in the same set, or in the same piece. The avant-garde refused to be pinned down to any one style or idiom.

Two pioneers, saxophonist Ornette Coleman and pianist Cecil Taylor, burst onto the scene with an originality that divided the jazz world, inciting international controversy. They were acclaimed as geniuses and derided as charlatans. At the height of the furor, the soft-spoken Coleman said, "Musicians tell me, if what I'm doing is right, they should never have gone to school." Many musicians and critics considered these two a threat. Duke Ellington once observed, "Bebop is like playing Scrabble with all the vowels removed." Coleman and Taylor removed the consonants as well.

■ ORNETTE COLEMAN (b. 1930)

Ornette Coleman is now almost universally revered as one of American music's most original figures. Several of his compositions are jazz standards, and his influence is beyond calculation. In 2007, he received the Pulitzer Prize—the first ever awarded for a recording (his album *Sound Grammar*). In 1959, though, he was the most disruptive figure in jazz. During a long engagement at New York's Five Spot that year, dozens of musicians came to hear his music. Some, including classical composers Leonard Bernstein and Gunther Schuller, declared him a genius. Others, including Miles Davis and Charles Mingus, were skeptical and derisive. Mingus expressed a prevailing confusion about Coleman's music when he said, "It's like not having anything to do with what's around you, and being right in your own world."

Coleman, who grew up in Fort Worth, Texas, began playing alto saxophone at fourteen and proceeded to work in rhythm and blues and carnival bands. In the late 1940s, he became enamored of the innovations of Charlie Parker and bebop. But his attempts to play in a style of his own were invariably greeted with hostility. The situation came to a head at a dance when he was attacked and his saxophone destroyed. He moved to New Orleans in 1949, where he met the gifted drummer Ed Blackwell, the first in a cadre of disciples who encouraged Coleman to persevere. Later that year, Coleman traveled with a rhythm and blues band to Los Angeles, where he took a job operating an elevator and taught himself theory. He remained unnoticed for five years, during which he wrote some of his benchmark tunes.

In 1956, Coleman and Blackwell formed the American Jazz Quintet, and Coleman also began rehearsing with other forward-thinking musicians, including three major interpreters of his music, with whom he formed his quartet: drummer Billy Higgins, bassist Charlie Haden, and Don Cherry, who played a compact cornet that looked more like a toy than a serious instrument (he called it a pocket trumpet). Two years later, Coleman was signed to record two albums for the Los Angeles–based label Contemporary. He was accompanied by Cherry, Higgins, and a few established bebop musicians suggested by the label.

Even without his own band, these albums proved Coleman to be a mature and inventive musician. The titles were deliberate provocations: *Something Else!!!!* and *Tomorrow Is the Question: The New Music of Ornette Coleman*. John Lewis of the Modern Jazz Quartet persuaded his label, Atlantic Records, to sign and record Coleman in Los Angeles and bring him to New York. Lewis also helped arrange for Coleman and Cherry to attend his Lenox School of Jazz in the Berkshires, and perform at the Five Spot in New York. The six Atlantic albums recorded between 1959 and 1961, all but one featuring his quartet (alto saxophone, trumpet, bass, drums), generated tremendous controversy, not least for album titles that continued to lay emphasis on the group's challenging attitude, which—without once mentioning the civil rights struggle—seemed to incarnate the authority of the New Negro: *The Shape of Jazz to Come, Change of the Century, This Is Our Music,* and *Free Jazz*.

Ornette Coleman generated controversy with just about everything he did in the late 1950s, not least playing a white plastic alto saxophone that underscored his raw timbre.

PHOTO BY CAROLE REIFF/© CAROLE REIFF ARCHIVE

Musical Style

Two aspects of Coleman's music were evident from the very beginning. First, his compositions possessed strong melodic, emotional character. Some suggested the solemnity of dirges, others were deeply bluesy, and many were as quirkily memorable and disarmingly simple as those of Thelonious Monk. Even his early detractors, put off by what they perceived to be a chaotic improvisational style, expressed admiration for such captivating melodies as "Turnaround," "Ramblin'," "Una Muy Bonita," "Congeniality," "Tears Inside," "R.P.D.D.," and "Lonely Woman."

Coleman found a perfect partner in Don Cherry, whose toy-like "pocket trumpet" blended with Coleman's plastic alto. At the Monterey Jazz Festival, 1960.

© ROY AVERY/CTS IMAGES.COM

Second, Coleman's sound on alto saxophone was jarring to many listeners, and this was the most alienating aspect of his music. His timbre had a rough-edged, elemental, vocal quality, a raw backwoods sound, as sharp and astringent as a field holler. That harshness was accentuated by his preferred instrument—a white plastic alto saxophone. The bop drummer Shelly Manne, who recorded with him, said that he sounded like a man crying or laughing through his horn. Coleman himself emphasized the value of "vocal" projection: "You can always reach into the human sound of a voice on your horn if you are actually hearing and trying to express the warmth of a human voice." He and his compositions sounded at once avant-garde and strangely primitive.

microtone an infinitesimal fraction of a half step

On a more technical level, Coleman was said to play the alto saxophone with **microtone** pitches, which challenged the familiarity of the **tempered**, or conventionally tuned, scale. The classical composer Hale Smith, who wrote for avant-garde jazz musicians, observed that Coleman's hearing was so acute that he played his in-between pitches in correct ratio to each other, so that if his E was slightly sharp, his F (and F-sharp, G, and so forth) was slightly sharp *to the same degree*. Coleman may have been at odds with the tempered scale, but he was in tune with himself.

Coleman has argued that there is no such thing as an absolute pitch, and that the playing of a pitch ought to reflect its context: an F, for example, ought not to sound the same in a piece expressing sadness and a piece expressing joy. He explained in his characteristically elliptical manner: "Jazz is the only music in which the same note can be played night after night but differently each time. It's the hidden things, the subconscious that lies in the body and lets you know: You feel this, you play this."

Coleman's approach to pitch was a decisive component in his overhauling of jazz, and his other innovations appeared to follow from it. He rejected preset harmony. On rare occasions when he played a standard song, he approached the piece solely through its melody, improvising on the song's melodic phrases rather than its chord changes. He offered an open-ended inspiration for musical creativity—both horizontally, in the linear development of solos, and vertically, in the serendipitous harmonies that followed.

This approach inclined him to dispense with the piano, which interfered with his music on two counts: it emphasized the tempered scale and promoted chords. The stark texture Coleman prefered (alto, trumpet, bass, drums) underscored the startling newness of his music. The listener hears a striking theme played by alto and trumpet, over a jolting rhythm that doesn't accent regular beats; the subsequent solos have no governing structure. Our ears are assaulted by the sharp pitch and the absence of a familiar frame of reference—there are no choruses, no harmonic resolutions, no steady meters.

That doesn't mean that rhythm and harmony are absent, only that they are improvised along with melody. Cherry developed a sound on the pocket trumpet that merged with Coleman's alto on the themes, sometimes harmonized in octaves. The chief source of harmony emanates from the bassist's response to the soloists. The drummer is free to spontaneously add to the musical whole; he produces plenty of rhythm, but not the toe-tapping, 4/4 meter kind. As Coleman explained, "Rhythm patterns should be more or less like natural breathing patterns."

"Lonely Woman"

Coleman wrote "Lonely Woman," his best-known and most frequently performed piece, in 1954, inspired by a painting he saw in a gallery. One reason it became popular is that most of his 1959 recording consists of statements of the melody, and Coleman's solo sounds almost like a transitional passage between melody statements, extending the feeling and character of the piece.

The unhurried, yearning melody comes as a surprise after the introduction, which suggests two rhythmic possibilities as Charlie Haden plays measured two-note chords (**double stops**) on the bass and Billy Higgins ignites a swift rhythm on the ride cymbal. The melody floats free of those specific cues, bluntly voiced by alto and trumpet. Throughout the piece, rhythm exerts a powerful presence. But try to count measures: there are no defining downbeats or upbeats. Still, the piece undoubtedly swings in a jazz sense—especially during Coleman's solo (for example, at 2:01–2:21), where he holds his rhythmic authority in reserve, suggesting swing without emphasizing it.

Although "Lonely Woman" has no underlying chord progression, the performance is harmonically interesting, from the octaves played by alto and trumpet to the two sections of the tune, each indicating a different harmonic sphere. Of particular interest is the creative bass playing by Haden, who implies major and minor key changes, augmenting the overall drama as he lags behind, doubles, or anticipates Coleman's phrases. Note that toward the end of the final chorus (4:02), Cherry hits a clinker. Coleman once said that it wasn't until he made mistakes that he knew he was on the right track. Whenever two or more musicians perform together, harmony is created, which means that in almost any context some notes will fit and others won't.

3.12

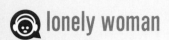 **lonely woman**

ORNETTE COLEMAN

Ornette Coleman, alto saxophone; Don Cherry, cornet; Charlie Haden, bass; Billy Higgins, drums

- Label: *The Shape of Jazz to Come,* Atlantic SD 1317; *The Shape of Jazz to Come* (Rhino UPC-075678133923)
- Date: 1959
- Style: avant-garde
- Form: loose **A A B A**

What to listen for:

- **A A B A** form without its usual rhythmic structure
- octave playing by Coleman and Cherry
- Coleman's simple, throaty timbre
- rhythm section freed from time-keeping

INTRODUCTION

| 0:00 | | The drummer (Higgins) begin quietly tapping out a short motive on cymbals. On bass, Haden joins in with a resonant **double stop** (playing two strings at the same time). |
| 0:07 | | Higgins switches to a rapid accompaniment. As if in a slower rhythmic space, Haden simultaneously holds down a **pedal tone** with one string while soloing with the other. |

CHORUS 1 (HEAD)

0:18	**A**	Coleman and Cherry enter, playing the melody in **octaves**. Like the bass line, the melody floats rhythmically above the drum accompaniment.
0:30		Coleman plays a short, plaintive reply. The bass falls to the dominant.
0:34		The two horns harmonize in parallel intervals.
0:36		On the upper string of the bass, Haden temporarily changes the harmony from **minor** to **major**. The mode changes back to minor when the horns reenter.
0:43	**A**	Coleman and Cherry repeat the melody.
0:55		As Coleman plays his plaintive reply, Haden doubles him on the bass.
1:03		On the last phrase, Coleman rises to a bluesy wail.
1:08	**B**	Over a new harmony, Coleman repeats a riff-like phrase. Behind him, Cherry and Haden creep upward **chromatically**, their background line accentuated by drum strokes.
1:16		Underneath Coleman's last phrase, the drum plays with richer timbres while the bass shifts to the dominant.
1:20	**A**	A drum stroke signals the return to the tonic harmony and the free-floating melody.

CHORUS 2

1:46	**A**	(indeterminate length) Coleman plays simple, bluesy phrases, unaffected by the rising chromatic line Haden suggests behind him.
2:01		As his emotional temperature begins to rise, Coleman's tone becomes rough and uneven.
2:08		He moves to a harder-swinging rhythmic feeling, evoking a cry of "whoo!" from one of the musicians.
2:21	**B**	The bridge is signaled by the return of the rising chromatic line in the trumpet, doubled erratically by the bass.
2:31		At the end of the bridge, the harmony and Coleman's line focus on the dominant.
2:33	**A**	With a dramatic return to the tonic, Coleman leads the group back to the **A** section. Haden, playing double stops, holds the bottom note in a pedal point while moving the upper voice up and down chromatically.
2:49		Rising in intensity, Coleman's line reaches its climax.

CHORUS 3

2:54	**A**	The two horns return to the melody in octaves.
3:17	**A**	
3:41	**B**	
3:47		Cherry hits high notes, followed by quick descending blurs.
3:53	**A**	
4:02		At one point, Cherry hits the wrong pitch.

CODA

4:19	The two horns combine to play bluesy wails.
4:25	Coleman holds out his last note; underneath, Cherry adds low, breathy comments.
4:32	The bass continues playing his double stops, rising chromatically until reaching the upper octave (at 4:42); he continues to play until the drums finally stop.

Free Jazz and Harmolodics

Coleman worked on two important projects at the close of 1960. On December 19 and 20, he participated in Gunther Schuller's Third Stream album *Jazz Abstractions*, as a featured soloist on "Abstraction" and "Variants on a Theme of Thelonious Monk." These twelve-tone compositions by Schuller (see Chapter 12) present Coleman's improvisations in the context of strict notation. He's backed by an ensemble of seven strings and a few other jazz musicians—notably, Eric Dolphy on bass clarinet.

On the 21st, Coleman returned to the same studio with what he called his Double Quartet, made up of his own group and some of the Schuller personnel, including Dolphy. This group recorded *Free Jazz*, an immensely influential work that offered, intentionally or not, a strong counterstatement to the concerto format represented by *Jazz Abstractions*. In *Free Jazz*, the entire ensemble was free to shape the thirty-seven-minute performance, although introductory sections were composed, and an order created for solos, duets, and broader collective improvisations. The composition comes to life in the give-and-take among the musicians, as they listen to each other and respond accordingly.

For all the fuss caused by *Free Jazz*, Coleman had by no means abandoned notation. Indeed, the rest of his career can be seen as an attempt to juggle the fastidious kind of composition represented by Schuller's work and the spontaneity of free improvisation. In working out a theory in which both approaches could coexist, Coleman coined a word, "harmolodic"—a contraction of harmony, movement, and melody, and a catch-phrase to characterize his take on ensemble music, written and improvised. One abiding aspect of harmolodic music is the idea that musicians may improvise register, even when their parts are notated. They may transpose written phrases to any key or octave while maintaining the music's melodic integrity.

In exploring the harmolodic landscape, Coleman composed music for string quartet, woodwind octet, symphony orchestra, rock bands, and other groups. He played trumpet and violin in addition to alto, deriving from them his own "unschooled" timbres. In 1972, he recorded his most elaborate piece, *Skies of America*, with the London Symphony Orchestra. Although the piece was conceived to combine symphony orchestra and his own ensemble, Coleman was forced by the record label to eliminate his band and appear instead as the only improvising soloist. In later concert performances, the piece emerged as intended; thanks to the harmolodic notion of free transposition and the free hand given Coleman's band, it can never be played the same way twice.

Prime Time

A few years after debuting *Skies of America*, Coleman put together an electric band, Prime Time, which also performed pieces that were mostly notated. This ensemble came as an unexpected addition to the fusion movement, which combined jazz and rock (see Chapter 17); several of the sidemen, including guitarist James Blood Ulmer, electric bassist Jamaaladeen Tacuma, and drummer Ronald Shannon Jackson, created offshoot bands that extended the idea of fusing different musical idioms. Significantly, Prime Time played some of the same themes created for *Skies of America* and Coleman's acoustic band. Through all these varied settings, Coleman never compromised his unmistakable sound.

■ CECIL TAYLOR (b. 1929)

While the leaders of bop served similar apprenticeships in big bands and developed styles that were sufficiently alike to allow them to perform and record together, the avant-garde's primary creators represent divergent backgrounds. Of the three main avant-garde leaders, only John Coltrane served his apprenticeship in jazz. Ornette Coleman's background, as we have seen, included rhythm and blues. Cecil Taylor's involved classical music. Significantly, they never performed in the same group, although Coltrane recorded once with Taylor and once with Coleman's sidemen.

Taylor was the first of the three to record as the leader of his own ensemble and the last to earn widespread recognition. He had his supporters, and his virtuoso keyboard attack was never much doubted; but detractors, weighing his music against the prevailing styles, questioned his ability to swing, play blues, and otherwise function in the conventional bop-derived jazz idiom.

Cecil Taylor attacked the piano as though it consisted of eighty-eight tuned drums, but could also be lyrical and romantically expansive. Despite his astonishing technique, he confounded the jazz audience for decades. New York, 1970s.

FRANK DRIGGS COLLECTION

Like Coleman's, his approach was so startling that even when he recorded standard songs, he made them all but unrecognizable.

His personal style also put listeners off. Like classical recitalists, Taylor never speaks onstage, though he often begins his concerts by reciting his poetry (not always audibly) as a kind of prelude to the music. More alienating is the length of his performances: concerts of three and more hours were, at least in his early years, not uncommon. Uniquely, he never performs the same work twice. Notoriously obsessive about practicing, he once had his ensemble rehearse for a year in order to perform one concert and make one recording—and the pieces were then retired.

Taylor has courted controversy throughout his career, arguing that since the musician prepares, the audience ought to prepare as well. This attitude has been criticized as arrogant, yet "preparation" is commonplace in attempting to understand other kinds of avant-garde art. Listeners with experience in modern classical music frequently find Taylor's music more accessible than jazz fans. This irks Taylor, who sees himself in the tradition of the jazz pianist-composers he admires, among them Duke Ellington, Bud Powell, Thelonious Monk, Lennie Tristano, Erroll Garner, and Horace Silver—each famous for his percussive style. Taylor takes that percussiveness to an unparalleled extreme. He is said to treat the piano as if it consisted of eighty-eight tuned drums.

Early Years

Cecil Taylor grew up on Long Island, New York, the son of educated African Americans whose own mothers were full-blooded Indian (Kiowa and Cherokee). His mother, a pianist, encouraged him to take up the instrument at five, the same year she took him to see Chick Webb's swing band at the Apollo Theater in Manhattan, an intoxicating event. A defining moment of his childhood was her death, when Taylor was fourteen. He developed an ulcer that year and grew increasingly introverted and devoted to music, studying percussion in addition to piano. In 1951, he enrolled at the New England Conservatory; there he grew resentful of the lack of respect accorded African and African American culture, which he recognized as a resource for much avant-garde music.

During summers and vacations, Taylor occasionally found work in jazz bands (including one led by Ellington's alto saxophonist Johnny Hodges), but those jobs were of short duration. One bandleader said he took pity on Taylor because he couldn't play the blues. Still, in 1956, shortly after graduating from the New England Conservatory, he convinced the Five Spot to hire his quartet—a six-week engagement that turned the neighborhood bar into a home for futuristic jazz—and recorded *Jazz Advance*.

Jazz Advance

Taylor's group included Steve Lacy, the first important soprano saxophonist in jazz since Sidney Bechet (Chapter 4), who until he hooked up with Taylor usually worked in Dixieland and swing bands; Lacy later became a prominent figure in the avant-garde. The rhythm section combined a classically trained bassist (Buell Neidlinger) with a self-taught drummer (Dennis Charles), whose inexperience pleased Taylor. Like Coleman, Taylor required malleable musicians who could follow him into new territory. For *Jazz Advance*, the band recorded intense versions of songs by Monk and Cole Porter, but the highlights were original compositions that suggested a free-form atonality and ferocious rhythmic attack.

On the basis of that album, Taylor's quartet was invited to play at the 1957 Newport Jazz Festival, where he received respectful if somewhat uncomprehending notices. Other record sessions and engagements followed, but the public remained indifferent, and Taylor took day jobs to support himself. As of 1960, he was regarded as one of several forward-thinking musicians who played mostly in Greenwich Village, exploring the spacier precincts of modern jazz and not yet the leader of a movement.

A turning point came the next year, as he began to work with more accomplished musicians who hastened his break with the last vestiges of tradition. These included tenor saxophonist Archie Shepp, who later recorded with Coltrane and made an important series of politically outspoken avant-garde recordings, and two musicians who played critical roles in Taylor's music: alto saxophonist Jimmy Lyons, who worked with him for twenty-five years, and drummer Sonny Murray, who worked with him for only a few years but profoundly influenced his approach to rhythm.

Unit Structures

Rather than writing conventional scores, Taylor preferred an arcane system of sketches, fragments, codes, and arrows. He did not, however, provide his musicians with these scores. Instead, he played episodes on the piano, which the musicians picked up by ear and developed by way of improvisation. As he explained it:

> The eyes are really not to be used to translate symbols that are at best an approximation of sounds. It's a division of energy and another example of Western craziness. When you ask a man to read something, you ask him to take part of the energy of making music and put it somewhere else. Notation can be used as a point of reference, but the notation does not indicate music, it indicates a direction.

Taylor coined the term *unit structures* (also the title of a celebrated 1966 album) as a means of describing his method. Rather than compose a single theme to spur improvised variations, he constructed his works out of modules, or units; the group worked through each unit in sequence. Because each unit was flexible (the band could work it through quickly or expansively), the rehearsal of a particular piece could run ten minutes or an hour.

Jimmy Lyons/Sonny Murray ▸ Jimmy Lyons, with his quick ear and particular affinity for Taylor's method, became a kind of translator, interpreting Taylor's figures on alto saxophone and showing the other musicians how to phrase and develop them. Lyons brought to Taylor's music a vivid tie to the bebop past, through his timbre and phrasing. Sonny Murray, on the other hand, helped to trigger Taylor's most radical departure from the past: a way of playing rhythm based not on a preset meter, but on the energy level of the performance. In Ornette Coleman's music, the usual 4/4 patterns disappear, yet the rhythm section still plays a supportive role, maintaining a pulse that suggests swing. Working with Murray, Taylor intensified the level of interaction with the drums, so that rhythm followed from the force of the band's energy. The center of that force could be the piano or the drummer or another soloist.

Andrew Cyrille ▸ Not surprisingly, Taylor performed duets with many drummers, from bebop innovator Max Roach to John Coltrane's mainstay, Elvin Jones, to major avant-garde drummers around the world. After he and Murray parted, Taylor developed his second closest association (after Lyons) with the drummer Andrew Cyrille, who had played and studied every kind of jazz drumming; he worked with Taylor from 1964 to 1975, and then formed his own Taylor-influenced ensemble. Cyrille explained Taylor's process:

> We had a magical dialogue. This kind of improvising is a matter of very close listening and trading of information. It's like a game. We put forth sounds, ideas, rhythms, and melodic fragments that turn into much longer statements, and we surprise each other with replies and continue to evolve within the dialogue. It can be endless. And when we decide to resolve what's happening, it's as though we've finished a conversation. We have grown, matured, to some degree even mellowed.

Taylor's rhythmic attack was an example of his fundamental differences with Coleman. Both musicians were emotional, but if Coleman wore his heart on his sleeve, Taylor was virtuosic and intellectual. Coleman avoided the piano, developed his theories outside the framework of the educated tradition, perfected a raw timbre descended from the roots of African American music, and eventually employed relatively conventional notation and a dance-beat fusion he called *Dancing in Your Head*. Taylor emphasized the piano's drum-like quality, studied modern classical theory and atonality, avoided any kind of conventional notation (even in his several big bands), and turned to dance in the tradition of ballet—he even collaborated on a project with the great dancer Mikhail Baryshnikov.

Taylor's particular kind of emotional commitment is evident in his method as a performer, which has been captured in several films. His hands work so quickly they become a blur, as he produces great cascades of sound. He pummels the keyboard with both hands, occasionally using the flat of his palm or his elbows. In the more meditative passages, he seems to pluck the keys, judging the particular sound of each one, producing delicate melodies that echo nineteenth-century Romanticism.

◉ "Bulbs"

In 1961, under the aegis of Gil Evans, Taylor assembled a quintet to record "Bulbs," a summation of everything he had achieved in the first stage of his career. From the first notes, we hear how figures introduced on the piano are quickly echoed by the other instruments. The blend of two saxophones is characteristic of Taylor, especially at 0:54, where they are voiced in thirds to suggest the driving edge of a big-band reed section.

Harmonically, the piece demonstrates a variety of approaches, from traditional triad harmonies to whole-tone and pentatonic scales to free passages. Taylor's melodic units are often subtle, yet by following their appearances and reappearances (note the nine motives or thematic riffs, A–I), we find that the overall work has an integral unity that may not be apparent at first. Taylor's piano solo introduces and develops particular figures, which he later reprises in accompanying the saxophonists. His percussive attack, **chord clusters** (dissonant chords with closely spaced notes), and melodic/rhythmic patterns animate the entire performance.

Lyons's solo is startling in its wit and historical finesse. Despite Taylor's accompanying dissonances, his initial phrase has the fluid feeling and warm timbre associated with Charlie Parker. His responsiveness to Taylor produces a whimsical moment at 3:12, when he quotes a phrase from Franz von Suppé's *Poet and Peasant* Overture—a fragment known to many for its use in Looney Tunes cartoons. In the last minute, motives seem to multiply in a burst of polyphony that suggests, however distantly, an avant-garde take on New Orleans traditionalism.

LISTENING GUIDE

 bulbs

CECIL TAYLOR ORCHESTRA
Jimmy Lyons, alto saxophone; Archie Shepp, tenor saxophone; Cecil Taylor, piano; Henry Grimes, bass; Sonny Murray, drums

- Label: *Into the Hot: The Gil Evans Orchestra,* Impulse! A(S)9, 12922; *Mixed* (GRP 270)
- Date: 1961
- Style: avant-garde
- Form: Taylor's unit structures

What to listen for:

- jazz improvisation without a set structure
- figures introduced in the piano echoed by other instruments
- Taylor's percussive piano playing, with dense chord clusters
- Lyons's solo, quoting von Suppé

HEAD

0:00   A short piano **arpeggio** by Taylor leads to a **chromatic** line played by the saxophones. Grimes bows a few dissonant notes on bass.

0:08   A two-note motive frames dense, dissonant piano chords, moving up and down the chromatic scale. We will label this motive A.

0:11   Taylor plays a chord with a distinct harmony, answered briefly by the saxophones.

0:15   After a slight pause, the band erupts into an arching phrase in the **whole-tone scale**. It's followed by dark chords over a rumbling oscillation in Taylor's left hand.

0:21   The whole-tone scale returns, only to be interrupted by a rising chromatic line that suggests a cadence (motive B).

0:27   Another whole-tone phrase is followed by more bass rumbling. Shepp briefly improvises on tenor saxophone.

0:42   Taylor plays a melodic fragment, then repeats it.

0:47   Shepp improvises over a dissonant chord.

0:54   The band is suddenly roused into a more rhythmic groove. Over a bass and piano **ostinato**, the saxophones harmonize in thirds.

1:05   Over a whole-tone riff, Taylor plays a Latin-based melody. When he repeats it, he shifts it upward.

1:19   In a faster tempo, the piano and saxophones play an intricate riff accompanied by a descending bass line.

1:26   The horns repeat the melody while Taylor improvises freely.

1:33   Chaos ensues, as each instrument goes in its own direction.

1:41   Taylor plays dissonant **chord clusters** up and down the keyboard.

PIANO SOLO (TAYLOR)

1:45   The texture thins out; the bass begins to walk.

1:51   Taylor plays a back-and-forth pattern (motive C).

1:57   He switches to shorter patterns. Each new pattern tends to be repeated before being discarded for a new one.

2:01   Taylor plays two-note clusters, followed by an octave riff (motive D) by Shepp. He follows it with several more patterns.

2:18   One passage begins with the rhythm for motive C before dissolving into chromatic chaos.

2:22   Shepp distantly echoes Taylor's ideas.

2:29   Taylor reintroduces motive A.

2:32   Behind Taylor, Shepp enters with a riff figure (motive E).

2:42   Shepp enters with another riff figure (motive F), followed by a return of motive A.

ALTO SAXOPHONE SOLO (LYONS)

2:51   Lyons improvises, accompanied by Taylor's aggressively dissonant piano chords.

3:00   In his comping, Taylor revisits motives A and C; these ideas penetrate Lyons's improvisation.

3:12   Lyons briefly quotes von Suppé's *Poet and Peasant* Overture.

3:19   As the harmony passes through the whole-tone scale, Shepp plays motive D.

3:25   After Taylor plays motive A, his comping becomes more dense and polyrhythmic, spurring Lyon to new levels of intensity.

3:37   Shepp reenters with motive E.

3:48   A return of motive A leads to a repetition of motive E.

3:59   A return to the whole-tone scale and motive D.

4:06   A final Shepp riff is based on motive B.

TENOR SAXOPHONE SOLO (SHEPP)

4:10   Shepp begins his solo. His tone is warm, rich, and somewhat indistinct in pitch.

4:16   Taylor again includes motives A and C in his accompaniment.

4:36   Shepp's improvisation hints at motive F.

4:42   Taylor foregrounds motive C.

4:49   In response to Taylor's new harmony, Shepp plays motive F.

4:59   Taylor's accompaniment becomes sharper and more percussive, creating a call and response with Shepp's saxophone.

5:21   A return to motive A.

5:39   Taylor reintroduces motive B; as Shepp and (eventually) Grimes join in, the tempo grinds to a halt.

HEAD (abridged)

5:45   The band returns to the sequence first heard at 0:16, beginning with the arching whole-tone phrase and concluding with motive B.

5:58   After a brief pause, the band returns to the opening chromatic melody.

CODA

6:06   Taylor plays a questioning piano melody (motive G), rising to an unresolved dissonance. It's imitated with near exactitude first by the unaccompanied alto saxophone, then by the tenor.

6:13   The alto and tenor play a riff (motive H) accompanied by occasional sharp piano chords.

6:19   Entirely unaccompanied, the two horns play a final, concluding riff (motive I).

6:21   The two saxophones and piano overlap motives G, H, and I in an intricate polyphonic texture.

6:28   As the polyphony reaches its climax, Murray adds a brief roll on drums.

6:34   The polyphonic texture dies down, and the instruments briefly regather on motive I.

6:37   As the bowed bass and tenor saxophone hold out a note, Taylor and Lyons trade short, percussive patterns.

Mature Taylor

Taylor recorded "Bulbs" at a time when his professional fortunes were at ebb tide. His records did not sell, and audiences were put off by the nonstop fury of his live appearances. In 1962, he left for Copenhagen, where he performed with the young saxophonist Albert Ayler (see below) and recorded his trio, with Lyons and Murray. These performances represented his most forceful incursion into rhythmic freedom to date. Back in America, Taylor found little work and made no records for four years. In 1966, he recorded two of his most admired ensemble albums, *Unit Structures* and *Conquistador!* These were followed by another long silence, as he embarked on several years of teaching at colleges in the Midwest.

In 1973, he returned to New York and released a self-produced album, *Spring of Two Blue J's*, a work (conceived half for solo piano and half for his quartet) that signaled a new maturity. The solo section in particular suggested an emotional coherence and generosity new to his music. Over the next several years, Taylor garnered awards, grants, critical renown, and a cult audience, especially in Europe; in 1988, a festival was devoted to him in Berlin, resulting in more than a dozen albums, including works for large orchestra. He now played the major jazz clubs and continued to perform internationally as a recitalist (for example, *Air Above Mountains*, *For Olim*, *Willisau Concert*), and as leader of bands of various sizes (*3 Phasis*, *Dark to Themselves*, *The Owner of the River Bank*), attracting a growing coterie of musicians and fans. He remains a symbol of the avant-garde innovator at his most unbowed and uncompromising.

🎧 *Willisau Concert,* "Part 3"

Taylor's piano recitals usually consist of a long work created for the event, followed by brief encores. His performance in Willisau, Switzerland, is one of his most impressive and lucid, showing off his theme-and-variations method as applied to the units that comprise the finished piece. The main piece consists of two movements totaling little more than an hour, and it's followed by three encores, averaging ninety seconds each. The first encore ("Part 3"), discussed here, is a capsule example of Taylor's vivacious keyboard style, exemplifying his virtuosity and organizational coherence.

Taylor begins with a five-note motive and in a very brief time explores several tonal centers while ranging over the entire breadth of the keyboard. His use of space and contrast underscores the drama, setting off a characteristically explosive passage (at 0:42) when the notes cascade down from the treble range at great speed. He employs dissonance, but contrasts those episodes with consonant harmonies. The details are carefully articulated. Playfulness governs the temperament of this etude-like piece, which, despite its brevity, feels complete and satisfying.

LISTENING GUIDE

3.14

🎧 willisau concert, part 3

CECIL TAYLOR, PIANO
- Label: *The Willisau Concert,* Intakt 072
- Date: 2000 (Willisau Jazz Festival, Switzerland)
- Style: avant-garde
- Form: Taylor's unit structures

> **What to listen for:**
> - the "Willisau chord" and consonant harmonies in the midst of dissonance
> - Taylor's playful ranging over the entire keyboard

0:00	Taylor begins with a simple motive: five notes, spread out over several octaves.
0:05	He repeats the motive, with variations; when he pauses momentarily, you can hear him humming.
0:13	With sudden rhythmic movements, Taylor repeats a chord that sounds like the dominant.
0:22	He begins quietly exploring a new chord (which we will call the "Willisau chord"), combining dissonant notes over a **minor triad**. This chord is occasionally interrupted by dense **chord clusters** and bass rumblings.
0:29	Taylor moves the chord down **chromatically**.
0:31	After a brief pause, he begins spreading the chord out over the keyboard. Once again, he moves downward chromatically.
0:37	The harmony changes to a new chord, somewhat closer to the dominant sound of 0:14.
0:40	The left hand rises with an emphatic **octave** run.
0:42	Suddenly the texture changes. Beginning in the uppermost register, Taylor uses both hands to alternate chords in a dizzyingly fast array of complex chromatic chords, descending across the entire keyboard.
0:46	Having reached the bottom of the keyboard, he starts once again at the top. A few seconds later, he does so again.
0:50	The dissonant chords are replaced by the dominant chord, split between notes in the right hand and loud, percussive octaves in the left.
0:54	Suddenly we return to the Willisau chord. As at 0:32, it's spread across the keyboard and descends chromatically.
1:02	The bass continues to drop, revealing a new chord that offers a point of contrast.
1:09	Taylor moves rapidly back and forth between loud chord clusters in the bass and in the upper register.
1:12	Returning to the Willisau chord, he once again moves down chromatically.
1:21	A sudden loud percussive outburst in the bass shuts the piece down.

THE NEW THING

Ornette Coleman and Cecil Taylor emerged as core figures in a much larger faction that divided the jazz world in half, generating strident brickbats on both sides. Many critics dismissed avant-garde jazz as political music, and indeed its musicians over the years did associate themselves with various causes, from civil rights and anti–Vietnam War to Black Power, Marxism, mysticism, and pacifism. Its proponents sometimes characterized the New Thing, as it was most often called in the middle-1960s, as "people's music," although it alienated far more people than it attracted.

The most charismatic figure of the era was John Coltrane, who, as we saw in Chapter 14, commanded respect at the outset for having proved himself a master of the bop idiom. Unintentionally, Coltrane became an unofficial referee between certified jazz masters, like himself, who embraced the avant-garde and provocateurs whose radical styles generated contempt. The contrast can be seen in the work of two dominant saxophonists, Eric Dolphy and Albert Ayler.

■ ERIC DOLPHY (1928–1964)

Eric Dolphy, a virtuoso alto saxophonist, flutist, and bass clarinetist, was born in Los Angeles, where he played in dance bands in the late 1940s and jammed with local and visiting musicians, including Charles Mingus. Dolphy attracted little attention until 1958, when he came to New York as a member of drummer Chico Hamilton's quintet, which also included a cellist. A year later, he began an on-and-off-again association with Mingus, lasting until shortly before Dolphy's death from heart failure and diabetes. In 1960, he appeared on Coleman's *Free Jazz*; in 1961, he toured Europe as a member of Coltrane's band, appearing on several of his albums, including *Africa/Brass* and *Live at the Village Vanguard*.

During his brief time in the sun, Dolphy made many records, often with another tragic figure of the period, trumpeter Booker Little, who died of uremia at twenty-three, including a series of discs taped during their engagement at the Five Spot. As noted earlier, Dolphy was also affiliated with the Third Stream. He performed works by classical composers (including the influential Edgard Varèse), and single-handedly made the bass clarinet a significant instrument in jazz.

Dolphy built his style on bebop, but stretched its harmonies and his own timbre into areas of extreme dissonance. Although he played flute with a centered pitch, he favored a vocalized and strident sound on alto saxophone and bass clarinet, which gave his robust, chromatic phrases an electrifying immediacy. Dolphy's liberal approach to intonation reflects the influence of Coleman, but his evident control of intonation also made it more palatable to skeptics like Mingus. As an interpreter of Mingus's music, Dolphy helped to maneuver Mingus closer to the avant-garde fold. His key albums include *Live! At the Five Spot*, *Out There* (accompanied by drums, bass, and cello), *Out to Lunch*, and *Last Date*.

© CHUCK STEWART

Eric Dolphy, seen here in the 1960s, popularized the bass clarinet while also playing alto saxophone and flute, bringing an energetic, conservatory level of virtuosity to the avant-garde.

■ ALBERT AYLER (1936–1970)

Albert Ayler exploded on the scene with a musical style so extreme that observers competed to find suitable metaphors. The poet Ted Joans likened Ayler's tenor saxophone sound to "screaming the word 'FUCK' in Saint Patrick's cathedral on a crowded Easter Sunday." Writer Amiri Baraka (aka LeRoi Jones) described his childlike melodies as "coonish churchified chuckle tunes," and critic Dan Morgenstern compared his group to "a Salvation Army band on LSD."

The subject of these tributes was born in Cleveland, where he studied alto saxophone for over a decade, beginning at age seven. In his teens, he worked with rhythm and blues bands, then joined the army, at which time he switched to tenor saxophone (he later added soprano as well). While stationed in France, Ayler experimented with the tenor's so-called hidden register—the highest pitches, verging on caterwauling tempests that few saxophonists knew how to control. Although he continued to perform in the bop idiom for a few years, he felt stifled by the harmonies and rhythms. Sitting in with Cecil Taylor in Copenhagen in 1962 helped to liberate his instincts.

Ayler soon returned to the United States with a trio (bass and drums), and in 1964 issued an album that, among other things, transformed a tiny label created to spread the international language of Esperanto, ESP-Disk, into a major source for avant-garde jazz. The album, *Spiritual Unity*, was both cheered and ridiculed. Ayler's huge sound evoked lusty hysteria. His room-filling timbre, ripe with opulent overtones, sounds as if he is playing two or three notes at a time (multiphonics). His rejection of musical gestures that might link him to conventional jazz offended some and influenced others, including Coltrane, who insisted that he learned as much from Ayler as Ayler did from him, an important endorsement.

In a span of barely eight years, 1962 to 1970, Ayler went through several stylistic changes, at one point focusing on composition almost to the exclusion of improvisation; one of his groups included a front line of saxophone, violin, and trumpet (his brother Donald), and played waltzes and other works that suggested classical music. In the end, he reluctantly tried to reach the rock audience with a flower-power brand of fusion. Its failure exacerbated an already present despondency, and he died, a suicide, at thirty-four.

Just as audiences had begun to accept the avant-garde of the early 1960s, along came tenor saxophonist Albert Ayler (seen here in 1968), who raised the bar, playing hair-raising improvisations on simple tunes.

"Ghosts"

"Ghosts" was Ayler's signature theme, recorded by him many times in different contexts. On his first important album, *Spiritual Unity*, two of the four selections are alternate versions of this piece. "Ghosts" combines three primary elements in Ayler's music: old-time religious fervor, marching, and simple, singable melodies. In his early versions of the piece, the theme statement is followed by a free improvisation. By the time Ayler performed this 1966 version, he was leading a five-piece ensemble that aimed for total group music.

There are no solos, although Ayler's powerful sound occasionally dominates the performance. Nor is the theme stated with unequivocal clarity. Rather, the musicians play around it, each contributing to the interpretation without really spelling it out. The result might be considered an example of musical *trompe l'oeil*—the art of illusion. After an authoritative opening, the instruments splinter away from the center. If we listen closely, noting the individual contributions, the performance seems incoherent, a jumble of scattered sounds that sporadically meet to convey the tune. But if we step back, listening at a distance, it's all perfectly logical. These musicians work together so closely that each one knows how to minimally fill out the canvas without overwhelming it.

The performance consists of three sections: an introduction, a collective interpretation of the theme, and a coda. Though "Ghosts" never swings in a traditional jazz sense, it never lacks for strong rhythms. In one passage (1:09–1:22), the performance suggests a kind of Scottish dance. Elsewhere, we hear the insistence of a march, accenting the first beat of each measure; the martial aspect is underscored by a bugle call in the coda. Most surprising is the nostalgic quality of the piece, especially as it concludes. The performance cuts against the grain of convention, but it leaves us with the conventional feelings generated by folk music—the vague recognition that we've heard this before.

LISTENING GUIDE

3.15

◉ ghosts

ALBERT AYLER QUINTET

Albert Ayler, tenor saxophone; Don Ayler, trumpet; Michel Samson, violin; William Foxwell, bass; Beaver Harris, drums

- Label: HatMUSICS 3500; *Lörrach, Paris, 1966* (hatOLOGY 573)
- Date: 1966
- Style: avant-garde
- Form: idiosyncratic

What to listen for:
- phrases of the tune: A, B, C, and D
- march rhythms coinciding with chaos
- ecstatic multiphonics

INTRODUCTION

0:00 Ayler begins with a simple **diatonic** phrase, fluffing the highest note. His phrase, slow and with much **rubato**, is echoed by the trumpet and supported by the bowed bass.

0:04 Over repeated **double stops** in the violin, Ayler plays intense, distorted sounds in his upper register.

0:09 Ayler stops; the violinist gradually slows to a halt.

0:13 Ayler plays simple melodies in a major key, loosely doubled by the trumpet.

0:27 The violinist plays chords that are deliberately out of tune.

0:33 All the instruments join in a loose **polyphonic** texture.

THE TUNE

0:41 Ayler and the trumpet suddenly shift to a brisk tempo, joined by the drum set. The melody they play is the opening phrase of "Ghosts" (A). Around it, the violinist and bassist add their own melodies and rhythms.

0:47 Ayler repeats the melody, occasionally adding **counterpoint**.

0:54 They begin a new phrase of the tune (B), setting a firm tempo that is not matched by any of the other instruments.

0:58 The trumpet continues the melody while Ayler harmonizes above it.

1:02 They repeat B.

1:09 On another repetition of B, Ayler again harmonizes above, the melodic content suggesting a Scottish dance.

1:22 The tune slows to a stop.

1:28 Ayler holds out a note, raising it through microtonal inflections before allowing it to sag down again.

1:33 Everything coalesces on a single note: the violinist saws back and forth on top of it.

1:38	Ayler returns to the mood of the introduction, adding rubato **pentatonic** phrases that are echoed by the other instruments.
1:49	He reinitiates the tempo, beginning a new melodic phrase (C) marked by a more chromatic opening. The bassist follows with a similar line, while the drummer plays on the cymbals.
1:57	As the trumpet moves to the next melody phrase (D), Ayler plays ecstatic squawks, alternating between his gruff middle register and the extreme upper reaches of his horn. His intensity is matched by the drummer's shift to the louder drums in his kit.
2:05	The trumpet returns to the beginning of the tune (A).
2:22	As Ayler and the trumpet harmonize loosely on the second melodic phrase (B), the drummer's strokes become still louder while the violinist rapidly plays scales.
2:30	The horns repeat B. The drums retreat, leaving the violin in the foreground.
2:35	The trumpet slows down the tempo, ending on a dramatically held-out note.
2:45	The violinist returns to playing double stops, accelerating in tempo.

CODA

2:50	Ayler reenters with his introductory phrases.
3:00	He ends with a phrase that sounds strikingly like a bugle call.
3:08	At the end, the trumpet continues to hold out his last note after all the other instruments have stopped; applause follows.

THREE PARADOXES

The avant-garde carried jazz to what musicians and other artists often refer to as the cutting edge—the last frontier of hip adventurousness. It ratcheted up the emotional expressiveness of music (unlike the classical avant-garde, which often preferred an extreme intellectualism, shorn of overt emotional content), but the audience reared in the swing and postswing eras found it loud, incoherent, and unappealing. Their children had an easier time with rock and roll.

Although the avant-garde eventually generated an international cult audience that supported the key figures, it was never going to be a commercially successful music. Cecil Taylor was nearly sixty years old when a MacArthur Foundation grant gave him his first taste of financial independence. Ornette Coleman (another MacArthur winner) supplemented his income with several nonmusical ventures. Others followed the classical avant-garde into the academy, where they found teaching positions and students eager to learn their music. The popular outlook for jazz looked bleak in the late 1960s, as rock achieved a level of sophistication and excitement—melodic, danceable, verbally relevant—that attracted people who a decade earlier might have been drawn to jazz.

Given the avant-garde's permanent outside status, it is worth contemplating three paradoxical aspects of its achievement: (1) for all the outrage it generated, the avant-garde engrossed and influenced many established musicians; (2) despite its insistence on the New Thing, the avant-garde turned out to be more inclusive than any previous jazz style; and (3) although it failed to find popular or commercial acclaim, the avant-garde proved as durable as mainstream jazz.

First Paradox: Older Musicians

Older musicians, who had already attained popular acceptance working in established idioms, found the lure of the cutting edge irresistible. Major jazz stars, including Sonny Rollins (Chapter 12), Charles Mingus (Chapter 13), Miles Davis, and John Coltrane (both Chapter 14), adjusted their performing styles to address techniques associated with the avant-garde. In every instance, they overcame their own initial skepticism to explore the new musical freedoms.

Consider Coltrane. In 1958, he and a few other hard bop musicians appeared as sidemen on Cecil Taylor's album *Hard Driving Jazz*. The other musicians were appalled at Taylor's procedures, but Coltrane was intrigued. In 1960, Coltrane co-led, with Ornette Coleman's trumpet player Don Cherry, an album issued as *The Avant-Garde*. The following year, he hired Eric Dolphy and recorded *Live at the Village Vanguard*, the breakthrough album that included the fifteen-minute blues rant "Chasin' the Trane." And in 1965, he assembled eleven avant-garde musicians for the ultimate free-jazz blowout, *Ascension*.

Similarly, Sonny Rollins teamed with Don Cherry and Coleman-drummer Billy Higgins in 1962 to record *Our Man in Jazz*, a surprisingly witty session combining extended improvisation with interactive group dynamics; the next year, he toured Europe with Cherry. Although Rollins ultimately returned to a bop-based music, his serious flirtation with the avant-garde left a lasting imprint—his timbre grew more expressive and his improvisational style more aggressive. His 1966 "East Broadway Run Down" is a classic example of his use of consecutive motives to shape his solos.

At the same time, lesser-known veteran musicians found that the avant-garde created an environment suitable to their music. Working in the outer precincts of jazz, they had been ignored or derided as weird and lacking in seriousness. The avant-garde gave them validity; it shone a light on artists who created their own world yet remained invisible. For some, like the pianist and composer Herbie Nichols, the avant-garde came too late to earn them proper recognition; after his death, Nichols was honored as a prophet—a 1990s band called the Herbie Nichols Project devoted itself to his sly and thorny compositions. Others, like the brilliantly idiosyncratic pianist and composer Andrew Hill, were revitalized by the avant-garde; after a decade of obscurity, Hill went on to create a powerful body of work (his album *Point of Departure* is a benchmark of 1960s jazz) that continues to grow in stature.

■ SUN RA (1914–1993)

The most peculiar of these invisible men was a pianist, composer, and bandleader who called himself Sun Ra. Born Herman Blount in Birmingham, Alabama, Sun Ra came to Chicago in the 1930s, touring with a college band and then leading his own group as Sonny Blount. During the war, he was imprisoned for two months after declaring himself a conscientious objector. In 1946, he worked with a rhythm and blues band before hiring on for a year as pianist for Fletcher Henderson—an important association that grounded him in the big-band tradition.

After studying black nationalism and Egyptian history, Blount created a cosmology involving the planet Saturn, renamed himself Sun Ra, and organized a band he called the Arkestra. His 1950s recordings are like no others in that era and were heard by only a few people, basically his followers in

Chicago. They combined familiar and experimental jazz textures with rhythm and blues (including doo-wop singing), unusual time signatures (7/4 was a favorite), and electric instruments (he was one of the first musicians to use electric piano and Moog synthesizer). Sun Ra and his acolytes, who included a broad mixture of accomplished and untried musicians, privately pressed and distributed their records, both albums and singles, some of them recorded in a garage.

In 1961, Sun Ra brought his followers to New York, and by the mid-1960s he had found regular work in jazz clubs and at festivals; his elaborate theatrical presentation included singers, dancers, stage props, and bizarre costumes. Despite the financial burden, he insisted on leading a big band, playing a repertory that acknowledged no boundaries between swing, avant-garde, pop (he played songs like "Hello, Dolly!"), classical music (he collaborated with composer John Cage), and fusion (see Chapters 16–17). Increasingly celebrated as a visionary maverick, Sun Ra continued to tour the world until his death. Highlights among his dozens of albums are *Jazz in Silhouette*, *The Heliocentric Worlds of Sun Ra*, *Atlantis*, and *When Angels Speak of Love*.

Pianist, composer, and bandleader Sun Ra (seen here in the 1970s) created a cosmology in which he came to Earth from Saturn, but his avant-garde Arkestra ran the gamut from doo-wop to "Hello, Dolly!"

Second Paradox: Openness to All Forms

Although critics routinely pilloried the avant-garde for rejecting settled jazz conventions, it ultimately proved to be the most inclusive form of jazz in history. The innovators of bop, for example, apprenticed in swing bands but played exclusively in their own modern styles as they became prominent; they never played Dixieland or attempted to create new versions of Jelly Roll Morton tunes. A later innovator, Miles Davis, constantly changed his perspective, but it was always focused on the future, never the past.

Yet the avant-garde, which seemed to incarnate the very definition of futurism, welcomed every kind of musical influence and allusion. It brought instruments previously ignored or underemployed in jazz (bass clarinet, cello, tuba, wood flutes, soprano and bass saxophone, exotic rhythm instruments, the African kalimba, and the Australian didgeridoo, among others) into the thick of things. The avant-garde was impatient with clichés, but not with historical styles and achievements. Like Sun Ra, it refused to be limited to any one idiom, including avant-garde jazz.

The full canvas of avant-garde interests did not became apparent until a second generation of avant-garde musicians, most of them schooled in the Midwest, made names for themselves in the 1970s. For the first time since the early days in New Orleans, these musicians came together as members of collectives (not unlike the New Orleans fraternal societies), which helped to arrange rehearsals, secure work, and encourage the creation of new music. One such organization, called BAG (Black Artists Group), arose in St. Louis. In Los Angeles, the composer and pianist Horace Tapscott organized the Underground Musicians' Association. Several New York musicians, including Cecil Taylor, Andrew Cyrille, and Archie Shepp, attempted to launch the Jazz and People's Movement. Each of these organizations eventually failed, but one that didn't was the influential AACM—the Association for the Advancement of Creative Musicians, which went on to produce concerts for more than four decades.

Muhal Richard Abrams (1985), pianist and composer, created the hugely influential cooperative AACM (Association for the Advancement of Creative Music) in Chicago, but found more acclaim in New York.

AEC members ▶

■ MUHAL RICHARD ABRAMS (b. 1930), AACM, and AEC

The AACM originated in Chicago as the brainchild of the pianist, composer, and bandleader Richard Abrams. A member of several of Chicago's bop-based ensembles going back to the late 1940s, Abrams founded the Experimental Band in 1961, as a way of allowing musicians to write new music and hear it performed. In 1965, he and other musicians from the Experimental Band launched the AACM, with Abrams as president, insisting that each member create original music. "We were not in the business of showcasing standards," Abrams explained. Noting that jazz musicians played new music in the early years, he argued that the AACM "was just hooking up with the real tradition. Besides, there was so much talent, so much originality, and we thought it should be encouraged."

Abrams, a reticent but charismatic and resolute man, also insisted on high personal standards of morality and behavior; his quiet integrity inspired younger musicians to adopt his values. The saxophonist Joseph Jarman recalled, "Until I had the first meeting with Richard Abrams, I was like all the rest of the 'hip' ghetto niggers; I was cool, I took dope, I smoked pot, etc. . . . In having the chance to work in the Experimental Band with Richard and the other musicians there, I found something with meaning/reason for doing."

Jarman became a charter member of the most important band to emerge from the AACM, the Art Ensemble of Chicago (AEC), along with saxophonist Roscoe Mitchell, trumpeter Lester Bowie, bassist Malachi Favors Maghostut, and drummer Famoudou Don Moye. The AEC popularized the use of "little instruments"—an array of bells, whistles, and drums that originated at AACM concerts as a way of incorporating African instruments. Hundreds of these little instruments, enough to cover the stage, generated a uniquely tintinnabulating suspense as the group focused on long meditative preludes of tinkling, shaking, and hand drumming before turning to the "big" instruments.

The AEC's theatricality also extended to startling facial makeup and Lester Bowie's white lab coat, which became his trademark—an indication of the wit that animated his music. Concerts unfolded in an unbroken stream-of-consciousness, climaxing with a hard-swinging number or blues. The AEC bannered its music with the motto "Great Black Music: From the Ancient to the Future," and invariably fused elements of free improvisation, notated compositions, and a variety of rhythms, from extreme rubato to modern dance beats.

Bowie took the mix further with other bands, including Brass Fantasy and New York Organ Ensemble, creating an unlimited American jukebox with a repertory that included pop songs, swing themes, early rock and roll and country music hits, and hip-hop. Ironically, the AACM dictum to write new music triggered a generous investigation of repertory outside the usual jazz curricula. The most prolific of AACM artists, Anthony Braxton (see Chapter 18), wrote hundreds of original pieces but also launched a series of *In the Tradition* projects that reinvestigated the compositions of Charlie Parker.

■ THE AACM IN NEW YORK: LEROY JENKINS (1932–2007) and HENRY THREADGILL (b. 1944)

Though AACM musicians began recording in 1966 (for an adventurous Chicago jazz and blues label, Delmark), they were largely ignored outside of Chicago for several years. The AEC began to attract attention in Paris during a 1969 tour, but the real breakthrough came in 1976, when Abrams, who adopted the name Muhal, and other AACM musicians moved to New York. Suddenly, Muhal Richard Abrams seemed to be everywhere, recording for several labels (representative albums include *Young at Heart / Wise in Time, The Hearinga Suite,* and *Blu Blu Blu*) and performing an immense variety of concerts, from solo piano to big band.

Two other important AACM bands that took hold in New York were the Revolutionary Ensemble and Air. Violinist Leroy Jenkins created the former with bassist Sirone (born Norris Jones) and percussionist Jerome Cooper. Jenkins developed a distinctive timbre and style, combining classical and jazz techniques, and encouraged collective rubato improvisations, as in *The People's Republic.* Sirone and Cooper developed solo bass and drum recitals, something unheard-of in jazz. After the Revolutionary Ensemble broke up in 1977, each member separately worked with Cecil Taylor.

Henry Threadgill led the trio Air, with bassist Fred Hopkins and drummer Steve McCall, in the late 1970s and early 1980s. Threadgill, an alto, tenor, and baritone saxophonist and flutist, also built what he called the hubcapphone—two tiers of hubcaps played with mallets. In addition to Threadgill's rhythmically knotty originals, including a couple of tangos, Air played interpretations of Scott Joplin rags and Jelly Roll Morton piano pieces (*Air Lore*).

Threadgill later inaugurated a series of bands notable for the unpredictability of his writing and unusual instrumentation. Among these were the Henry Threadgill Sextet (*Rag, Bush and All*), consisting of seven musicians (he counted the two percussionists as one component); Very Very Circus (*Spirit of Nuff...Nuff*), with trombone, French horn, two electric guitars, and two tubas; Make a Move (*Where's Your Cup?*), with guitar and accordion; and Zooid (*Up Popped the Two Lips*), with guitar, tuba, cello, and oud (a Middle Eastern type of lute).

Third Paradox: The Eternal Avant-Garde

By 1980, it was clear that the avant-garde, which had been accused of annihilating the jazz audience, had no less staying power than swing or bop. Indeed, it had created its own tradition, with different schools in Germany, Scandinavia, Russia, England, and just about every place else where improvising musicians congregated. It rescued American jazz from what many perceived to be popular compromises, but no longer circled its wagons around any particular approach. The idea of free jazz had come to mean not jazz without rules, but rather the freedom to play anything musicians can devise.

The musicians who gave jazz this freedom gathered in New York in the 1970s, in one of the largest migrations since the height of bebop. Among them were three prominent saxophonists from St. Louis's Black Artists Group: altos Julius Hemphill and Oliver Lake and baritone Hamiet Bluiett. They appeared in individual recitals, saxophone duets, and with groups of every size.

From California came tenor saxophonist and bass clarinetist David Murray (see below), alto saxophonist Arthur Blythe, flutist James Newton, bassist Mark Dresser, and composer-trumpeter Butch Morris. Morris pioneered a form of big-band music he called "conductioning": through a system of conducting gestures, he was able to improvise orchestral pieces by spontaneously cuing the soloists and ensemble sections.

The influx of musicians spurred the need for new performing venues. Some important concerts took place in private homes, recalling the old days of New York rent parties. And several full-time concert spaces were created in loft apartments in New York's largely abandoned warehouse district. As a result, the period became known as the Loft Era, and the variety of its music "loft jazz."

THE LOFT ERA (1974–86)

Loft jazz created tremendous excitement in New York's downtown area. New record labels, some of them owned by the musicians, documented the music, and a new audience heard it live in lofts, galleries, churches, and other spaces not usually associated with jazz. The Loft Era lasted for about twelve years; it ended as the established clubs and record labels began to accept these musicians as part of mainstream jazz culture.

Knitting Factory One landmark event was the opening in 1987 of the Knitting Factory, a large downtown venue that replaced the lofts and encouraged musicians to cut across discrete idioms and reach broader audiences. In 1994, the club moved to a larger space, three stories tall, where several performing spaces could operate at the same time. The musicians who became Knitting Factory regulars had an immediate impact not only on jazz but on the entire arts community. One, the saxophonist and composer John Zorn, combined a background in the classical avant-garde and Jewish klezmer music, while guitarist James Blood Ulmer's "harmolodic" bands meshed jazz with the sounds of Delta blues and country music.

A critical byword of the Loft Era was "eclecticism," used to signal an enlightened approach to all styles of music. These musicians fused jazz, pop, free improvisation, funk, sambas, Indian ragas, and anything else they found appealing. Drummer Beaver Harris, a baseball player in the Negro leagues before he turned to music, summed up the attitude with the name of his band, the 360 Degree Music Experience, and a recording, *From Ragtime to No Time*.

■ DAVID MURRAY (b. 1955)

If one musician came to represent the synthesis between the avant-garde and the jazz tradition it was saxophonist David Murray. Born in Oakland, California, Murray came from a musical family, but one that disdained jazz. The Murray Family Band—mother on piano and directing, father on guitar, and three sons on reeds and percussion—played four nights a week and all day Sunday at the Missionary Church of God in Christ. A teacher introduced him to jazz, but he was not allowed to play it at home until his mother died, when he was thirteen. He promptly joined a local soul band, playing alto saxophone. After falling under the spell of Sonny Rollins, he switched to tenor and proceeded to explore the entire history of the tenor, memorizing

The Five Spot

The jazz club that embodied the transitions from bebop to avant-garde to loft jazz started out as a family-operated bar on New York's downtown Bowery. The owners, Iggy and Joe Termini, cared little about jazz, but in the middle 1950s a musician who held jam sessions in his loft offered to hold the sessions in their bar if the Terminis would buy a piano. In 1956, the Five Spot played host to two important engagements. Alto saxophonist Phil Woods organized an all-star tribute to Charlie Parker and recorded it—the first of many *Live at the Five Spot* albums. Then an unknown pianist, Cecil Taylor, began a long residency that attracted a following of painters, writers, actors, and musicians.

The room was unprepossessing, small and dark, with a bar along one wall and the stage at the rear. Filled with smoke and the bohemian chatter of artists and other regulars, it achieved national renown in 1957 when it presented a long engagement by Thelonious Monk's quartet, featuring John Coltrane—the first of several extended Monk appearances through 1962, averaging six to eight months a year. In 1959, the Five Spot became the focal point for the jazz world when it presented Ornette Coleman in his New York debut. Coleman held the stage for three months, frequently returning over the next few years. Other important engagements featured saxophonist Eric Dolphy, who recorded a series of albums there, and Charles Mingus.

In 1962, the Five Spot moved a few blocks from its original address (5 Cooper Square) to Third Avenue and Seventh Street. While most jazz clubs booked bands by the week, the Five Spot encouraged long residencies. Charles Mingus used one such engagement in 1964 to audition saxophonists for his band (he decided on Clifford Jordan, but during the course of the gig other saxophone stars, including Coleman Hawkins and Sonny Rollins, sat in). By 1967, however, the neighborhood had changed: rock palaces like the Circus and the Fillmore opened nearby, and the Termini brothers could no longer afford to operate a jazz club. They darkened the stage and sold food from a street-side vestibule, closing altogether in 1972.

Miraculously, the brothers returned to jazz two years later, a block away at 2 St. Marks Place. In 1974, they enlisted a Chinese chef to prepare a very basic menu, stocked a bar without bothering to renew their liquor license, and tested the waters with French horn player David Amram and a comedian. Shortly thereafter, Art Blakey opened with his new band, and over the next two years the Five Spot was among the most reliable jazz clubs in the world: Taylor, Coleman, Mingus, Don Cherry, Jackie McLean, and many others appeared, each for a week-long gig. Squeezed between a sausage stand and a hotel for transients, the Five Spot remained bleak and unassuming, except for the music and the conglomeration of jazz posters and record albums hanging on the walls. The neighborhood had changed again: this time a new crop of jazz musicians took over the downtown lofts, priming a new audience. In addition to the old wing of the avant-garde, you could hear such newcomers as David Murray, James Blood Ulmer, and Air. Then in 1976, the State Liquor Authority finally caught up with Iggy and Joe, who quietly retired for good.

Outside the Five Spot Café in 1958, tenor saxophonist Lester Young, wearing his porkpie hat, is greeted by pianist Hank Jones. The club was better known for long engagements by modernists like Monk, Coleman, Taylor, and Mingus.

© JAN PERSOON/CTS IMAGES.COM

David Murray, tenor saxophonist, bass clarinetist, composer, and leader of large and small bands, arrived in New York at the height of the Loft Era at age twenty and was soon known internationally. Copenhagen, 1991.

solos by Coleman Hawkins, Lester Young, Ben Webster, and a particular favorite of his, Paul Gonsalves, a star of Duke Ellington's band in the 1950s and 1960s.

Murray came to New York in 1975 as a twenty-year-old college student to research a thesis on the tenor saxophone, but after getting a taste of performing (and receiving rapturous reviews), he dropped out of college and embarked on a remarkable career. He was initially hostile to the avant-garde, but eventually warmed to Archie Shepp and Albert Ayler. His best-known composition, "Flowers for Albert," is a requiem for Ayler. Murray's stylistic approach made it clear that he did not accept a barrier between the avant-garde and the jazz tradition.

By the late 1970s, Murray was well on his way to becoming one of the most frequently recorded musicians in jazz history, and the leader of several bands at once, including a large orchestra. He played with musicians of every generation, perfecting an ebullient improvisational style at ease with and without preset harmonies. His timbre was gruff but his intonation was essentially correct, except when he worked the "hidden" register, usually to climax his solos. As a composer he wrote several pieces with a blues or gospel mood ("Morning Song," "The Hill," "Blues for Savannah," "Shakhill's Warrior"), and recorded an album of spirituals, *Deep River*. He wrote complex pieces for his octet and big band, including orchestrations of improvisations by Gonsalves and Coltrane.

Murray co-founded the World Saxophone Quartet, the first successful jazz ensemble without a rhythm section, along with the three BAG saxophonists: Julius Hemphill, who wrote most of the group's repertory, Oliver Lake, and Hamiet Bluiett. After Hemphill's death, his place was taken by Arthur Blythe, whose ripe pear tones suggested an earlier approach to the saxophone. Murray also played in Clarinet Summit, focusing exclusively on bass clarinet, an instrument he did more to popularize than anyone since Eric Dolphy, and worked with musicians from other cultures, notably the Gwo-Ka Masters, a percussion ensemble from Guadeloupe.

"El Matador"

As a newcomer to jazz, Murray enhanced his credibility by collaborating with several established artists on various projects. One of these was a brilliant pianist, Don Pullen, who had worked in many areas of jazz and pop (including Charles Mingus's group and his own quartet, co-led with saxophonist George Adams); switching to organ, Pullen played a key role in Murray's acclaimed album *Shakhill's Warrior*. After Pullen's death in 1995, Murray recorded a tribute album to him, *The Long Goodbye*. On one track of this quartet session, "El Matador," written by Murray's frequent associate Butch Morris, he plays a duet with pianist D. D. Jackson—a Murray protégé and a Canadian of African American and Chinese parentage. Jackson's intense and flashy keyboard attack, combining conventional and avant-garde techniques, is not unlike Pullen's.

In "El Matador," Murray and Jackson explore Spanish scales and feelings dear to Pullen, as exemplified by his classic 1988 trio record "At the Café Centrale." Yet unlike Pullen's piece, which is raucously festive, "El Matador" is dark and ruminative, progressing from a solemnly heraldic theme (suggesting the matador entering the ring) to piercing climactic cries. It combines tender respect for the fallen hero—underscored by Murray's heavy use of vibrato in his opening phrases—with a candid expression of grief. During its two dramatic choruses, Murray is the lead voice, as Jackson creates a setting that sustains and, in a sense, fields the saxophonist's tonal variations. They converge in harmonic consonance, diverge in spiky dissonance, and exult together on attaining tonic chords.

LISTENING GUIDE

3.16

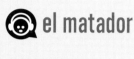 **el matador**

DAVID MURRAY

David Murray, tenor saxophone; D. D. Jackson, piano

- Label: *The Long Goodbye: A Tribute to Don Pullen* (DIW 930)
- Form: **A B A′ B′** (**A′ B′** are one step lower than **A B**)
- Date: 1996
- Style: loft jazz

What to listen for:

- use of the "Spanish" scale
- Murray's ecstatic, high-register climaxes
- subtle interaction in free rhythm between the musicians

CHORUS 1

0:00   **A**   With a slow and stately tone, Murray begins with a fanfare motive in the key of D. The opening melodic gesture establishes a "Spanish" scale: a major scale with two **flatted** notes, the second and seventh degrees.

The rhythm is free and unmetered. Underneath, Jackson plays a simple but rich chordal accompaniment on piano.

0:08   Jackson echoes Murray's last melodic fragment, letting it fall several octaves.

0:15   A new chord, outside the scale, begins a movement away from the tonic—a **modulation**. The chords begin to rise.

0:20   The harmonic movement reaches an upper chord, then begins to fall by step.

0:26   **B**   We arrive on a new tonic (G), having moved to it by a half-step **cadence** typical of the Spanish scale. As Murray repeats a simple figure,

the harmony shifts between the tonic and its surrounding chords, the flatted second and seventh degrees. The two musicians move back and forth at their own pace, with Murray often lagging behind.

0:49   The oscillations finally stop. Jackson allows the harmonies to subside.

0:54   **A′**   Murray repeats the opening section, this time in a new key (C).

1:05   Again, the chords begin to move from the tonic.

1:17   We begin another Spanish-scale cadence.

1:20	**B′**	We arrive, by half step, on F.
1:24		As the harmonies surround the tonic, Murray repeats the cadence melody.
1:49		Jackson plays the lower chord simply, using it to return to the opening tonic (D).

CHORUS 2

1:51	**A**	Murray now plays more expansively, letting his improvisation rise into the upper register; the Spanish scale takes on a more bluesy tone. Jackson uses the sustain pedal on the piano to blur his harmonies, creating a fuller sound.
2:05		While Murray plays loose, expansive melodic figures, Jackson pushes the modulation forward.
2:16		As the modulation nears its goal, the two musicians join forces, Murray harmonizing Jackson's melody in thirds.
2:23	**B**	We arrive on the new tonic (G). Murray lets loose with a long, rhythmically intricate run.
2:29		Over the oscillating chords, Murray hits a long, agonized high note. His descent is mildly dissonant against the harmony.
2:38		The volume of his playing increases.
2:44		As his lines reach higher and higher, Murray's tone begins to disintegrate.
2:50		He reaches a climax with an extraordinarily high note, barely supported by his breathing.
2:53		Jackson signals the new section by forcefully descending the bass line toward the new tonic.
2:55	**A′**	Murray celebrates the new key with a **major scale**.
3:03		Descending into his lower **register**, Murray's sound becomes harshly distorted.
3:05		His gestures take on an ecstatic rhythm, barely touching on actual pitches.
3:14		As Jackson moves forward with the modulation, his playing is similarly rough: octaves are played with crushed **grace notes**.
3:20	**B′**	As Jackson plays his chords with abandon, Murray responds with lines that sometimes support the harmonies, but more often clash with them. The timbre often is enriched with **multiphonics**.
3:42		Murray's playing becomes more detached; he rises steeply in register, reaching a high, wailing note.
3:51		Jackson momentarily lightens the sound of his piano playing to highlight the climax. Echoing the piece's opening fanfare, Murray moves to a high note, sustaining a tone several octaves above the saxophone's normal range.
3:55		As Jackson triumphantly plays his F major chord, Murray gradually descends in a disruptive flurry of notes.
4:02		The harmony changes once again.
4:05		Murray's line restarts in the lower register, finally reaching a note sustained through **false fingerings**.
4:12		After a brief pause, the chords descend back to the opening key, D. Murray fades out with a trill.
4:27		At the end, all you can hear is the faint sound of Murray's breath.

AVANT-GARDE VISIONS

By 2008, the avant-garde had continued to develop for half a century, influencing every kind of jazz with its approach to timbre, instrumentation, and repertory. Yet it struggled to survive even in the few American and European cities where it attracted a significant audience. In New York, avant-garde musicians continued to create their own venues and record labels. Among the key activists were saxophonist-composer John Zorn, who created a performance space (Tonic) and a label company (Tzadik, Hebrew for "righteous one"), and bassist William Parker, who worked with dozens of major cutting-edge musicians, including a decade with Cecil Taylor. In the 1970s, Parker and his wife, dancer and choreographer Patricia Nicholson-Parker, helped to start various multicultural arts organizations. In 1996, they introduced the ongoing Vision Festival, combining jazz, dance, and poetry.

Vision Festival eventually developed into a major nonprofit arts producer, presenting concerts year-round. It also promoted political activism, in trying to get the city of New York to support the study of what it calls *avantjazz*. In a mission statement, Vision Festival emphasized the international and multimedia aspects of art that "exhibits a disciplined disregard for traditional boundaries," and incarnates "the freedom to choose any tradition or vocabulary." Still, avant-garde jazz is all but unknown outside of a few cities, an educated taste for a small, eager audience.

ADDITIONAL LISTENING

Ornette Coleman	"Turnaround" (1959); *Tomorrow Is the Question!* (Original Jazz Classics OJCCD-342-2)
	Free Jazz (1960) (Atlantic 1364-2)
	"R.P.D.D." (1961); *Ornette* (Atlantic 73714)
Gunther Schuller	"Variants on a Theme of Thelonious Monk" (1960); *John Lewis: Golden Striker / Jazz Abstractions* (Collectables 6252)
Cecil Taylor	"Rick Kick Shaw" (1956); *Jazz Advance* (Blue Note 84462)
	"Enter, Evening" (1966); *Unit Structures* (CDP7-84237-2)
	"Spring of Two Blue-J's, Part I" (1973); *Jazz-View I* (CDD008)
	"3 Phasis" (1978); *3 Phasis* (New World 80303)
Eric Dolphy	"Out There" (1960); *Out There* (Prestige PRCD-8101-2)
	"Out to Lunch" (1964); *Out to Lunch* (Blue Note 98793)
Albert Ayler	"Bells" (1965); *Bells/Prophecy* (ESP-Disk 4006)
	"Our Prayer / Spirits Rejoice" (1966); *Live in Greenwich Village* (Impulse! 273)
Sonny Rollins	"The Bridge" (1962); *The Bridge* (RCA/Bluebird 828765247221)
Andrew Hill	"Point of Departure" (1964); *Point of Departure* (Blue Note 99007)
Sun Ra	"Space Is the Place" (1972); *Space Is the Place* (Impulse! IMPD-249)
	"Saturn" (1958); *Jazz in Silhouette* (Evidence ECD22012-2)
Muhal Richard Abrams	"Blues Forever" (1981); *Blues Forever* (Black Saint 0061-CD)
Art Ensemble of Chicago	"Nice Guys" (1978); *Nice Guys* (ECM 827876)
Air	"Weeping Willow Rag" (1979); (currently out of print)
David Murray	"Shakhill's Warrior" (1992); *Shakhill's Warrior* (DIW-850)
World Saxophone Quartet	"I Heard That" (1980); *Revue* (Black Saint BSR0056-CD)

JIMMY SMITH
the organ grinder's swing

FRANK SINATRA
the birth of the blues

SARAH VAUGHAN
baby, won't you please come home?

DIZZY GILLESPIE
manteca

MONGO SANTAMARIA
watermelon man

STAN GETZ/CHARLIE BYRD
samba dees days

FUSION I (TO 1960):
R & B, SINGERS, AND LATIN JAZZ

NEW IDIOMS

In the late 1960s, as jazz musicians began to employ the instrumentation, rhythms, and repertory of rock in an effort to reposition jazz in the sphere of popular music, the word "fusion" was coined to denote this new synthesis, also known as **jazz-rock**. Yet fusions of one sort or another have always played a role in jazz history. Jazz, after all, emerged as an American phenomenon through the melding of traditions from Africa, Europe, and Latin America, and from such sources as blues, ragtime, and Tin Pan Alley.

No musical form grows in a cultural vacuum. Europe's classical composers worked with popular airs and folk styles, and jazz has similarly borrowed from other forms. In the words of saxophonist Dexter Gordon, "Jazz is an octopus"—it will take whatever it needs or can use. In Chapter 12, we saw how the Third Stream attempted to merge the techniques of jazz and classical music. In this chapter and the next, we examine jazz's ongoing relationship to popular music, beginning in the 1940s. We will use the term **fusion** to describe all music situated on the boundary between jazz and pop. Some fusions are natural, while others are more deliberate, whether motivated by genuine creativity or meretricious pandering. The most successful fusions tend to create new idioms in their own right—among them, in this case, organ trios, jazz-pop vocals, and bossa nova.

Sarah Vaughan was called the Divine One in praise of her peerless voice and musicianship, which won over the boppers and the general public. At Birdland, 1949.

wwnorton.com/studyspace

Until now, our narrative has focused on jazz as a series of chronological creative leaps. Each generation of musicians expanded on styles and accomplishments of the preceding generation while reflecting their own times. We have seen jazz develop in a fairly straight line, from the relatively insular community of New Orleans to the international popularity of swing to the modernist reformation of bop to the art-for-art's sake credo of the avant-garde.

In looking at jazz from a "fusion" perspective, we find an alternative approach for examining its evolution. Instead of tracking influences as they exist within jazz proper (for example, the lineage from Louis Armstrong to Charlie Parker to Miles Davis to Ornette Coleman), this narrative tacks back and forth between jazz and parallel changes in popular culture. It focuses on the stylistic developments and fashions beyond the parameters of jazz, including new dance grooves and advances in musical technology, that have altered jazz itself.

Historical Background: Before World War II

In the early years of the twentieth century, New Orleans musicians played to please audiences and employers, tailoring their music to a specific situation: advertising wagons, street parades, funerals, and dancing in saloons or at pavilions, among others. As jazz moved around the country, finding opportunities in nightclubs and vaudeville shows, it continued to mind the needs of the audience, frequently incorporating comedy routines and double-entendre song lyrics.

In Chicago, New York, and elsewhere, jazz continued to encourage dancing, but a gap quickly widened between musicians who played jazz for the sake of playing jazz and those who organized ensembles to suit the prevailing tastes of the public. By the middle 1920s, the split was inescapable: jazz musicians groused as society band leaders inhibited their rhythms and reduced their improvisations to occasional breaks in otherwise gummy-sweet ballroom arrangements. Attempts to enliven those dance bands with jazz indicated an early fusion of jazz and pop music.

With the coming of the Swing Era in the middle 1930s, jazz was thoroughly integrated into the popular entertainment industry. Jazz bands played dance music, performing the latest pop songs, often with singers. The art vs. commerce chasm continued to divide hot swing bands from sweet ones, yet each borrowed elements from the other—sweet bands ventured cautiously into jazz, and hot bands promoted pop singers, ballads, and novelty songs. Huge audiences clamored for both kinds of music. The most enduring bands alternated "commercial" numbers with more creative ones that featured improvisation, advanced harmonies, and provocative rhythms. There was relative peace in the kingdom, until the bands began to fade in popularity.

Swing's Triple Pop Legacy

As the big bands began to lose steam, it became evident that bebop would not be their only successor. Three other, more listener-friendly schools of music were emerging from the Swing Era that would simultaneously dominate American popular music in the postwar era—until the arrival of rock and roll: (1) rhythm and blues, (2) mainstream pop vocals, and (3) Latin jazz.

In Chapters 11–13, we looked at bebop as the prevailing jazz to appear after swing, pioneered by musicians like Charlie Parker and Dizzy Gillespie, who apprenticed in swing bands. But as bebop fractured the connection between jazz and pop, it opened the door to other, more accessible interpretations of songs and dance rhythms. These, too, emerged from the heady days of the dance orchestras and were obvious candidates to take up the slack.

THE R & B CONNECTION

During the 1940s, an offshoot of swing called "jump" music was popularized by bandleader Louis Jordan and other former swing band musicians. This new kind of race music, which countered the experimental trends of modern jazz, eventually became known as rhythm and blues (R & B). Some R & B bands maintained a strong relationship with bebop, but the gap steadily widened. The jump style usually focused on blues played at a fast tempo and featured brash vocals backed with ensemble riffs. Lyrics might be risqué, satirical, serious, or socially relevant, but they were almost always marked by a humorous attitude. Several black bandleaders of the 1930s and 1940s—including Lionel Hampton, Cab Calloway, Lucky Millinder, and Buddy Johnson—made jump blues a part of their repertory, and produced some of R & B's leading lights. Millinder, for example, hired Dizzy Gillespie and Thelonious Monk, among other jazz innovators, but also featured future R & B stars like Sister Rosetta Tharpe, Wynonie Harris, and Bullmoose Jackson.

Singer, saxophonist, songwriter, and leader of the Tympany Five, Louis Jordan (seen here in the 1950s) liked to clown, but was a stern taskmaster who took his music very seriously.

Another jazz element (in addition to big-band swing) that proved essential to R & B was the eight-beats-to-the-bar rhythm of boogie-woogie, the heavy-beat style of piano playing that lent itself especially well to early blues shouters like Big Joe Turner (Chapter 8). Turner's recordings ultimately found success in jazz (in the 1930s), R & B (1940s), and rock (1950s), though his style remained essentially unchanged through the years. As his career illustrated, it was only a matter of time before the appeal of R & B reached the white mainstream. The breakthrough was largely engineered by Louis Jordan.

■ LOUIS JORDAN (1908–1975)

Louis Jordan was an alto saxophonist, singer, and songwriter as well as an influential bandleader. A phenomenon in American entertainment history, he recorded nearly sixty charted hits between 1942 and 1951; many of them reached the No. 1 and No. 2 positions on the R & B charts and crossed over to the predominantly white mainstream pop charts. Jordan was born in Arkansas, and began playing saxophone in his father's touring group, the Rabbit Foot Minstrels. He worked in other bands in the South and Midwest before arriving in New York in 1936, to join the Chick Webb Orchestra. During his two years with Webb, he achieved only marginal recognition as a musician and singer—but it was enough to encourage him to start his own group.

In 1938, Jordan organized the band that he eventually named Louis Jordan and His Tympani Five. The ensemble, which consisted of two saxophonists (including Jordan), one trumpet player, and a three-man rhythm section, played with such zest that it seemed to have the power of a big band. At the height of the Swing Era, Jordan demonstrated that a small group could achieve great commercial success. Widely imitated in the 1940s, he set the direction that the music industry followed after the war, as small bands took over in jazz and pop.

Jordan's music derived much of its appeal and humor from Southern black culture. He wrote comical pieces detailing sexual and marital mores that blacks related to and that whites could readily understand. His songs were political only in that they celebrated the good times in Negro communities, emphasizing personal peccadilloes rather than hardships. Jordan had absorbed the lessons of minstrelsy, but in a way that humanized blacks, depicting them as no better or worse than anyone else. His songs helped to create new archetypes of blackness, stemming from ethnic pride.

In the 1940s, Jordan's popularity was such that he recorded successful duets with Bing Crosby, Louis Armstrong, and Ella Fitzgerald, and appeared in several movies. His tunes blended elements of jazz, boogie-woogie, and Latin rhythms like the rumba, and he put them over with the kind of showmanship he had learned working on the minstrel and vaudeville circuits. Several of his hits have endured as all-time standards, including "Is You Is or Is You Ain't My Baby," "Caldonia," "Let the Good Times Roll," and "Saturday Night Fish Fry." Although his career slowed down in 1951 because of illness, his influence carried on in the music of Chuck Berry, Bill Haley, and Ray Charles.

R & B's Influence on Jazz

Rhythm and blues was not only a forerunner of rock; it was also a lateral influence on jazz. Several musicians of Jordan's generation managed to succeed on both sides of the R & B–jazz divide, as the need for a party music increased in direct proportion to the sophisticated challenges proffered by modern jazz. Consider these tangled examples:

Earl Bostic The alto saxophonist Earl Bostic studied harmony and theory before he took jobs playing and writing arrangements for big bands, including those of Don Redman, Cab Calloway, Louis Prima, Artie Shaw, and Lionel Hampton. He received little popular recognition until 1951, when he recorded a rhythm and blues version of a song made famous a decade earlier by Duke Ellington, "Flamingo"; the record established him as the No. 1 instrumentalist of the year. His small band became, in turn, a training ground for such future jazz luminaries as saxophonist John Coltrane and pianist Jaki Byard.

When Duke Ellington's celebrated alto saxophonist Johnny Hodges took a five-year sabbatical from the Ellington orchestra to lead his own small group, he had a hit straightaway, in 1951, with the R & B tune "Castle Rock"; it did so well that even singer Frank Sinatra (see below) recorded a version. Significantly, Hodges himself did not solo on his own recording. In a way, he was slumming to attract a mainstream audience. He had come of age in the 1920s: musicians who came up with Jordan in the 1940s recognized that the template for commercial success had changed. The younger audience now wanted brazen, brassy music with a strong backbeat. A musician like Hodges, known for the dynamic elegance of his playing, would have to meet that audience on its terms, not his.

Wild Bill Davis The most influential of Jordan's sidemen proved, unexpectedly, to be a keyboard player and arranger, Wild Bill Davis. Born in Missouri, Davis studied music at Tuskegee Institute and Wiley College, where he developed a piano style influenced by Fats Waller and Art Tatum. After freelancing with big bands in Chicago, he was hired by Jordan in 1945, and served as his pianist and chief arranger for four years. Upon leaving Jordan in 1949, he began to focus on the organ, an instrument he had played intermittently ever since hearing a recording of Fats Waller on the pipe organ in the 1930s. Davis's work on organ attracted the attention of musicians, but found relatively little pop success; he's best remembered for adapting his organ arrangement of the song "April in Paris" for the Count Basie Orchestra—No. 8 on the R & B charts in 1956.

Davis's replacement in Jordan's band, from 1949 to 1951, was the more experienced jazz pianist and arranger Bill Doggett, who had worked with several big bands; he had arranged Thelonious Monk's "'Round Midnight" for the Cootie Williams Orchestra. After hearing Davis play the Hammond electric organ, Doggett followed suit, and in 1956 scored the No. 1 record in the country with his rock and roll organ opus "Honky Tonk (Parts 1 & 2)." The success of that record reflected a period when rock and roll, as yet undefined, sought inspiration from R & B and technical know-how from jazz musicians. In later years, Doggett returned to the jazz-pop mainstream, writing arrangements for Ella Fitzgerald, Louis Armstrong, and the vocal group the Ink Spots.

Bill Doggett

■ RAY CHARLES (1930–2004)

One musician can be said to have single-handedly represented a fusion between swing, bop, R & B, gospel, and rock: the blind singer and pianist Ray Charles, whose influence was so pervasive that no one contested Frank Sinatra's nickname for him (adopted by his record label), "the Genius." Initially, though, Charles was a divisive figure among churchgoing blacks, who resented his pioneering use of gospel techniques to intensify his vocals and rhythms.

African American church music had always found a way into jazz (recall the call-and-response method used by big bands), and complaints had long been raised about mixing religious music with "the devil's music"—Louis Armstrong was criticized in 1938 for his recording of "When the Saints Go Marching In." Charles went much farther than anyone else, merging pop and gospel to an unparalleled degree. Observers said that he was singing no differently than a Baptist church singer, except that he sang "baby" instead of "Jesus." He additionally emphasized the church connection by playing the kind of basic, bluesy piano chords associated with gospel music, and hiring a backup choir of women singers, called the Raelettes.

Charles struggled as a musician for several years before he turned to his gospel roots. Born to an impoverished family in Georgia, he was raised in Greenville, Florida, by his mother, who took him to the Shiloh Baptist Church on Sundays. At seven, Charles was blinded by glaucoma, and at fourteen he was orphaned. He

Blind from early childhood, Ray Charles (1959) combined his love of jazz, R & B, pop, country music, and gospel into a heady brew and often recorded with his vocal group, called the Raelettes.

PHOTO BY CAROLE REIFF/© CAROLE REIFF ARCHIVE

left school and tried to earn a living in jazz and hillbilly bands. In 1948, he moved to Seattle, where he found acceptance in the black musical district and made his first records. Over the next several years, he led a trio in imitation of Nat "King" Cole (see below). By emulating Cole's cool, jazzy style, Charles placed a few hits on the R & B charts.

Meanwhile, on road tours, Charles perfected an original style that combined the blues, advanced bebop harmonies, and the testifying shouts and backbeat rhythms of gospel. In 1952, he signed with Atlantic Records; his recording of "I Got a Woman" reached the No. 1 slot on the 1954 R & B hit parade. In 1958, he brought a band to the Newport Jazz Festival, a septet modeled after the hard bop groups of Art Blakey and Horace Silver but with two saxophonists, two trumpeters, and backup singers. The diversity of his music, which ranged from bop themes by Max Roach and Milt Jackson to original gospel-inspired rock and roll tunes like "I Got a Woman" and "A Fool for You," astonished the audience and the other musicians.

During the next few years, Charles triumphed in every area of international show business. On his 1959 two-part hit "What I Say," a rock and roll landmark that firmly secured the white audience, Charles and the Raelettes used gospel-style call and response to mimic the sounds of lovemaking. That year, he signed with a better financed label, ABC-Paramount, insisting on the right to use big bands and string orchestras and to choose his own material. His hugely popular version of "Georgia on My Mind," a 1930 tune by Hoagy Carmichael arranged by swing band musician Ralph Burns, proved that he could sing anything—a point he drove home with albums of country and western songs, many of them adapted to the style of the old swing bands.

Soul Jazz

Ray Charles and other vocalists reached a larger audience than any jazz musician could. They flourished not as singers with big bands, as in the Swing Era, but instead as solo attractions leading their own groups, usually trios. For jazz musicians who wanted to reach this mainstream audience, the most successful avenue was a new school called **soul jazz**. An obvious offshoot of hard bop as perfected by Art Blakey, Horace Silver, and Cannonball Adderley (see Chapter 12), this style also employed a strong backbeat, an aggressive urban sound, and gospel-type chords, but it simplified the result—preferring basic harmonies, shorter solos, and clearly defined dance rhythms. Soul jazz paid particular attention to ethnic orientation, sometimes through slang or colloquial spelling, as in such titles as Horace Silver's "Doodlin'" and pianist Bobby Timmons's "Moanin'" (written for Art Blakey) and "Dis Here" (written for Cannonball Adderley). Other song titles celebrated the aspects of black life that had characterized Louis Jordan's music: soul food, churchgoing, and Saturday night parties.

In the 1960s, the exemplary modern jazz label Blue Note enjoyed a series of unlikely hits as successful hard bop records were assimilated into the mainstream: these included Herbie Hancock's "Watermelon Man" (adapted to a Latin style by bandleader Mongo Santamaria; see below), Lee Morgan's "The Sidewinder" (used for a series of razor ads), and Silver's "Song for My Father" (covered by soul singer James Brown). The leaders of soul jazz attempted to cut out the middle man: rather than make records that generated pop versions, they made three-minute singles suitable for pop radio. In 1965, pianist Ramsey Lewis topped the charts with a trite ditty called "The 'In' Crowd";

in 1967, Adderley did as well with an abbreviated version (in which his solo was cut) of "Mercy, Mercy, Mercy"; the uncut version appeared only on an album.

■ JIMMY SMITH (1925–2005)

The enormous popularity and influence of organist Jimmy Smith was a direct expression of the fusion between jazz and R & B. His was the kind of music that sustained a popular audience for jazz in black communities of the 1950s and 1960s. Like "the Genius" Ray Charles, Smith picked up his own nickname, "the Incredible Jimmy Smith"—and his imitators and rivals were everywhere. He launched a new kind of trio centered around the Hammond B3 organ, supported by drums and either guitar or tenor saxophone. The music was brash, bluesy, lean, and rocking, and it became ubiquitous in urban bars around the country, whether it was live or on jukeboxes.

Smith was born in Norristown, Pennsylvania, and studied piano with his parents, occasionally getting pointers from a young pianist in nearby Willow Grove, Bud Powell (a lasting influence on Smith and almost every other major postwar keyboard player; see Chapter 11). At nine, he won an amateur contest broadcast on Philadelphia radio, playing boogie-woogie. He began touring with his father, honing a song and dance act in nightclubs. Thus far, he had been schooled largely in blues and gospel music. After serving in the navy during World War II, he returned to Philadelphia to study theory, harmony, piano, and string bass.

Jimmy Smith made the Hammond B3 one of the most popular instruments of his time, sustaining a feeling for soul music amid the complexities of modern jazz. In this 1950s photo, drawbars can be seen at lower left.

For several years, Smith played piano with local R & B bands. In 1953, while traveling with one such group, he heard Wild Bill Davis play organ and was smitten. He later recalled hearing Davis as early as the 1930s, but in those early years the organ was mostly associated with the enormous pipe instruments in theaters and churches. Count Basie and Fats Waller occasionally recorded organ solos, but they were regarded as diversions, indicative of the influence of church or classical music (Waller was a lifelong devotee of Bach). During the war, however, organs were routinely used in military chapels, and returning servicemen like Smith were more receptive to it as a jazz instrument.

The Hammond B3

Smith's fascination with the organ coincided with an important technological advance. The inventor Laurens Hammond had introduced the first Hammond organ (model A) in 1935. His goal was to replicate the opulent sound of a pipe organ through purely electronic means, creating a relatively compact, portable alternative. Model A never caught on with the public or musicians: it was expensive, bulky, and complicated, involving two keyboards, foot pedals, and a system of drawbars (similar to stops) to control volume and timbre. In 1955, Hammond presented the model B3, an altogether tidier version that caught Smith's attention—so much so that he went into semi-seclusion for three months to study it. Wild Bill Davis warned him that it might take him a decade just to learn the bass pedals, but Smith wasn't discouraged:

> When finally I got enough money for a down payment on my own organ I put it in a warehouse and I took a big sheet of paper and drew a floor plan of the pedals. Anytime I wanted to gauge the spaces and where to drop my foot down on which pedal, I'd look at the chart. Sometimes I would stay there four hours or maybe all day long if I'd luck up on something and get some new ideas using different stops.

Smith's mastery of the foot pedals combined with his earlier study of the bass allowed him to play complete bass lines with his feet, setting a powerful precedent for subsequent jazz organists. He also realized that the B3's keyboard, called a "waterfall keyboard" for its light construction, rounded edge, and absence of an overhanging lip, encouraged rapid melody lines and glissandos played with the palm of the hand. Smith's tremendous technique enabled him to develop an attack that combined R & B rhythms, bebop virtuosity, and gospel, which was connected with organ music in the lives of many African Americans.

Smith introduced his trio in Atlantic City in September 1955. The following January, he scored a much touted New York debut at Harlem's Small's Paradise. Blue Note signed him and promptly released his album, *A New Star—A New Sound: Jimmy Smith at the Organ*. The timing could not have been better: 1956 was the year Bill Doggett released his single "Honky Tonk" (see above), establishing the organ as a trendy new sound. But Smith showed how much more could be done with the instrument. At first, jazz critics were predictably ambivalent. Smith typically played a torrent of notes with the right hand, supplementary chords or drones with the left, and bass walks with his feet, often sparking his solos with glissandos that varied in speed (some were sensuously slow-moving) and texture—a consequence of his peerless ability to combine keyboards, drawbars, and pedals.

Smith recorded prolifically, using album titles that echoed the same categories Louis Jordan had popularized: leisure time (*House Party*, 1957), church (*The Sermon*, 1958), and food (*Back at the Chicken Shack*, 1960). In 1962, he signed with a larger label, Verve, and achieved even greater success, often with big bands or in collaboration with guitarist Wes Montgomery. At a time when the avant-garde was splintering the "serious" jazz audience, Smith maintained a fervent popular following.

◉ "The Organ Grinder's Swing"

"The Organ Grinder's Swing" is the leadoff track of an album (*Organ Grinder Swing*) that captures Smith at his peak. At the time of its release, 1965, it was regarded as a welcome return to the trio format after several big-band albums. By then, most critics agreed that Smith was a musician to be reckoned with. The album included several unlikely tunes in addition to "The Organ Grinder's Swing," a 1936 Swing Era novelty recorded by, among others, Will Hudson (its composer), Chick Webb (vocal by Ella Fitzgerald), Benny Goodman, and, most memorably, Jimmie Lunceford. Smith's version is only a bit longer than two minutes, yet it demonstrates his rigorous personality, wit, and technical mastery.

The session teamed Smith with the versatile studio drummer and occasional ballad singer Grady Tate and reunited him with his frequent and perhaps finest partner, the Detroit-born guitarist Kenny Burrell, who performed with everyone from Ray Charles to John Coltrane. Smith and Burrell are superb blues players, yet their approaches are different and they seem to temper each other. Burrell, with his cool sound, economy, and harmonic subtlety, brings out the lyricism in Smith, while Smith's rowdier attack inspires Burrell to lay on the funk.

This performance opens with a gunshot blast from the drums and Smith's signature organ squawk, delaying the actual theme, which has a faded nursery school quality in melody and lyrics ("Who's that coming down the street? / Good old organ grinder Pete"). The trio ignores the lyrics, but Smith inserts a couple of amusing vocal breaks that consist of well-timed mumbles. When he goes into the main theme, note the bagpipe feeling suggested by the full timbre, a good example of Smith using the drawbars. At 1:48 and 1:56, he employs, albeit for only a few seconds, his trademark gambit of repeating a note or a tremolo. In concert, Smith would hold a chord while soloing over it for several choruses, until the audience begged for mercy.

Kenny Burrell

tremolo: rapid alternation between two or more notes

LISTENING GUIDE

🎧 the organ grinder's swing

JIMMY SMITH

Jimmy Smith, Hammond B3 organ; Kenny Burrell, electric guitar; Grady Tate, drums

- Label: *Organ Grinder Swing,* Verve V(6)8628; *Organ Grinder Swing* (Verve 731454383127)
- Date: 1965
- Style: soul jazz
- Form: 12-bar blues

What to listen for:

- rock-solid, steady groove
- complementary blue styles of Smith and Burrell
- Smith's electrifying soloing, with organ tremolos
- sudden surprise ending

CHORUS 1

0:00   A short blast from the drums leads directly into the opening chorus, marked (as each chorus is) by a loud, squawking organ chord. Smith plays rhythmically tricky riffs on the organ, connected by a simple rocking back and forth between two notes. He's supported by his own walking bass line and the guitar's steady, syncopated two-chord **comping**.

0:12   The organ holds out simple blues chords, falling from V (0:12) to IV (0:13), reinforced by the drums.

0:14   On the last beat of the measure, the harmony resolves to I. During the two-bar **break** that follows, Smith quietly mumbles an inaudible phrase.

INTERLUDE

0:18   Over a **pedal point**, Smith plays a portion of the well-known children's melody popularized in the 1932 song "The Organ Grinder." Behind him, the drum plays a syncopated pattern on the cymbals.

0:27   The band stops for a two-bar break while Smith continues playing.

0:30   The band reenters. As in the blues, the harmonic progression moves to IV, resolving to I at 0:33.

0:35   Once again the harmony moves to IV, in preparation for a half cadence on V.

0:40   A shorter one-bar break announces the entrance of the guitarist (Burrell), who begins with a high-pitched **blue note**.

CHORUS 2

0:41   Burrell keeps his solo simple, remaining largely in a **pentatonic** blues scale.

0:53   As the harmony changes, he shifts to a more dissonant scale.

0:55   A two-bar break leaves his line exposed; after a short pause, it ascends in **triplets**.

CHORUS 3

0:59   Burrell's second chorus begins with a high note, nearly obscured on the downbeat by Smith's chord.

1:13   During another two-bar break, Smith returns. His melodic line is frequently doubled by additional notes.

CHORUS 4

1:16   Beginning of chorus.

1:23   Smith builds a short rhythmic motive, placing it polyrhythmically against the background beat. Underneath, we can hear his voice in a wordless mumbling, which has both a comic and rhythmic effect.

1:31   He's more aggressive during this two-bar break, entering almost immediately with an active line.

CHORUS 5

1:34   Smith's second chorus begins with a phrase accented sharply on the backbeat.

1:38   For a time, he reduces his line to a **tremolo** between the tonic and a blue note.

1:42   Moving much faster now, he spills a short bluesy phrase against the beat.

1:48   The break during this chorus lasts for four bars, filled in (once again) by Smith's vocalized and rhythmic mutterings.

CHORUS 6

1:54   Beginning of chorus.

1:56   As before, another tremolo yields to an irregular fast bluesy phrase (2:00), finally resolving to a more beat-oriented polyrhythm (2:03).

2:07   As the harmony changes, Smith returns to his simple blues chords. When he resolves to the tonic, the tune simply stops.

SINGERS IN THE MAINSTREAM

The 1950s are often described as a golden age for singers of the classic American songbook. The claim is justified on several counts, and may be attributed to at least four factors.

1. The number of gifted vocalists was remarkable; most of them had apprenticed with big bands and were now aiming for solo careers. After the war, tens of thousands of servicemen returned home, their tastes in music conditioned by prewar (big band) styles and the singers who dominated V-Discs—recordings made expressly for the armed forces. Thus, these singers had a made-to-order audience, providing a link between the present and a fondly recalled past.

2. In addition to new songs constantly ground out for movies, theater, and record sessions, an astonishingly large repertory of songs written between the 1920s and 1950s had become part of the country's musical diet. Many key composers and lyricists were still alive and available to promote their catalogs; some (Irving Berlin, Richard Rodgers, Oscar Hammerstein, Duke Ellington, Hoagy Carmichael, Harold Arlen, and others) were as well known to the public as the performers.

3. The 45-rpm single, introduced in the late 1940s, furthered the careers of rising stars and often offered novelty songs and other "one-hit wonders." At the same time, the 33-rpm long-playing (LP) album attracted an older and more affluent audience, and proved to be an ideal forum for mature performers like Ella Fitzgerald and Frank Sinatra.

4. The rise of television in the 1950s helped sustain the careers of established performers, particularly singers. Variety shows, combining music and comedy, were broadcast nearly every day, in the afternoon as well as during prime time, and most were initially built around singers who had become famous during the war. Guest performers invariably included other vocalists (including African Americans, who were not permitted their own programs). The TV audience had limited patience for instrumental music, jazz or classical, but it never tired of singers.

Nat "King" Cole (1949) was considered one of the finest pianists in jazz as leader of an influential trio with guitar and bass—then he started to sing and became one of the most successful entertainers of all time.

Touched by Jazz / Touched by Pop

As singers moved to the center of the music industry, many maintained a connection to jazz or swing, as Bing Crosby had done in the 1920s and 1930s, because that was the music they had grown up with. They weren't necessarily jazz singers, but they were products of the Swing Era, and when their appeal to young listeners faltered in the years of rock and roll, they returned to their jazz roots.

To choose one of many examples, Rosemary Clooney was a best-selling recording artist between 1951 and 1954. Her biggest hit, a nonsense song about food, "Come On-a My House," was so popular it put her on the cover of *Time* magazine and led to a film and television career. She had recorded it under duress: it was a novelty number—sung in an Italian accent, accompanied by harpsichord—and she considered it beneath her. Its phenomenal success, however, allowed her to record LPs that were more meaningful to her, like a 1956 collaboration with Duke Ellington, *Blue Rose*. During the last thirty years of her career, she performed almost exclusively with jazz musicians, singing the classic American songbook. Clooney was essentially a popular artist who learned her trade touring with a big band.

Rosemary Clooney

In contrast, Nat King Cole was an accomplished jazz pianist who enjoyed an unexpected triumph as one of the most successful pop singers of all time. Born in Alabama, the son of a pastor, Cole sang and played in church, and began to record while still in his teens. In 1939, he formed the highly influential King Cole Trio, which popularized the combination of piano, guitar,

Nat King Cole

and bass. His singing on the novelty song "Straighten Up and Fly Right" helped him achieve a commercial breakthrough in 1943, yet during the next few years he was still known primarily as an excellent pianist who occasionally sang numbers with an R & B appeal similar to the recordings of Louis Jordan.

After the war, however, Cole began recording ballads like "Mona Lisa" and "Too Young," smash hits that outsold most of his white rivals'. Although he continued to record with jazz musicians on the piano, he was now a pop star, standing at a microphone and backed by a studio orchestra that combined big-band instrumentation with string sections. Cole's popularity was so great that in 1956 he became the first African American entertainer to be offered his own television show, sponsored by Revlon cosmetics. When Southern affiliates protested, though, Revlon withdrew its support, complaining that Negro women did not use cosmetics. Cole's much-quoted response was "Revlon is afraid of the dark."

Although Cole's success never waned (he recorded more than 115 charted singles between 1943 and 1964), his jazz abilities were increasingly obscured by such commercial projects as albums of country songs and Spanish songs. In the years following his death, as his early records were re-released, younger jazz fans were surprised to discover his immense talents as a jazz musician.

Frank Sinatra (1956) achieved widespread fame as a skinny, bow-tied ballad singer in the early 1940s, but after he remade himself as a jet-set swinger, he became a deeper artist and a stylistic icon of the era.

© HERMAN LEONARD PHOTOGRAPHY LLC/CTS IMAGES.COM

■ FRANK SINATRA (1915–1998)

No popular singer had a more fabled career than Frank Sinatra, universally admired by jazz artists—from classic prewar figures like Louis Armstrong, Duke Ellington, and Count Basie (all of whom he performed with) to such modernists as Miles Davis and John Coltrane, who acknowledged his influence and recorded several of the songs he introduced. Born in Hoboken, New Jersey, Sinatra started out as an imitator of his idol, Bing Crosby, but developed a deeply personal style as he listened to the way singers like Billie Holiday interpreted lyrics, turning them into statements of private anguish.

Sinatra believed that every song tells a story and that a singer's phrasing should emphasize the meaning of the lyric. As a young man, he practiced holding his breath under water to increase his lung power so that, like an instrumentalist, he could sing eight-bar phrases without pausing. He never developed the rhythmic confidence of a Crosby or a Holiday, but he won immediate recognition as a ballad singer who could delve deeper into the emotional core of a song than anyone else. From 1939 to 1942, Sinatra received international acclaim as the "boy singer" with the big bands of Harry James and Tommy Dorsey. His debut as a star in his own right was front page news, attracting screaming female fans who fainted in his presence (some were paid to do so); newspaper writers called them "swooners" and referred to Sinatra as "Swoonatra."

His more enduring nickname was "the Voice." In the early 1940s, Sinatra earned his own radio show and a film career in Hollywood. He often covered hits associated with Crosby, demonstrating particular affection for songs written in the 1920s. At the same time, he attracted prominent songwriters who were eager to write specifically for him. In those years, Sinatra rarely recorded anything at a fast tempo.

The Second Act

With the end of the war, Sinatra's career fell apart. Returning servicemen who resented his failure to serve ignored his recordings and broadcasts. They preferred Crosby, who had made a more vigorous contribution to the war effort, participating in entertainment tours in America and overseas; the years 1946 to 1949 turned out to be the most successful in Crosby's career. As Sinatra's career declined, excessive drinking and smoking marred his voice, gossip columnists pursued his rocky personal life (divorces, public brawls), and a newer crop of singers, like Clooney and Cole, won the hearts of younger listeners. Under contract to Columbia Records, he no longer had the clout to choose material, and was humbled into recording dreadful novelties—on "Mama Will Bark," for example, he barked like a dog (it didn't sell).

In perhaps the most celebrated comeback in American show business, Sinatra set about reinventing himself. He affected a new persona: the jet-set hipster-gambler-drinker-womanizer, sporting a fedora and holding a trench coat over his shoulder. He rebuilt his film career with powerful dramatic performances, winning an Academy Award for one of them (in *From Here to Eternity*). His most profound change, however, was musical. Although he remained a nonpareil ballad singer, Sinatra focused increasingly on up-tempo swing numbers, accompanied by studio orchestras arranged by some of the finest writers in popular music—most notably the orchestrator Nelson Riddle, known for his imaginative way of expanding the big-band sound with strings, harp, flutes, and other colorful instruments.

Sinatra did not improvise as freely as a jazz singer, but he embellished the melodic line to make it more interesting. His baritone became weightier, more virile. He continued to phrase in order to accentuate meaning, no matter the tempo. If he failed to swing in the easy legato manner associated with jazz, he did create his own kind of swing: a buoyant, foot-tapping, on-the-beat style that his detractors unfairly characterized as "a businessman's bounce." Ellington got to the root of Sinatra's art when he said, "Every song he sings is understandable and, most of all, believable, which is the ultimate in theater."

Working with Riddle (who also wrote albums for Cole, Clooney, and many other singers, as well as television and film scores), Sinatra was one of the first artists to conceive of the LP as a nontheatrical opera, where the selection of songs reflected a particular concept or theme (young love, loneliness, travel, dance). By 1956, Sinatra was king of the LP—he was also the anti–Elvis Presley, who was king of the 45 single. Sinatra's most successful years coincided with those of Presley, who more than anyone else turned rock and roll into a national spectacle. Presley ignited his audience no less than Sinatra had the swooners, who now found in Sinatra a powerful link to the bands they had known as teenagers. He remained a force in the entertainment industry for the rest of his life.

💀"The Birth of the Blues"

"The Birth of the Blues," recorded in 1952 with a studio orchestra consisting of big-band veterans, captures Frank Sinatra in transition: it was one of the first records to show the 1940s ballad crooner recreating himself as the 1950s swinger. The purity of his timbre is evident throughout, especially in half-time episodes (at 1:07 and 2:33), when he takes the time down to a near-rubato crawl. We also hear him toying with his voice, using an occasional groan or croakiness to underscore feeling. He sings several melodic embellishments, including a motive introduced at the outset as he accentuates the word "blues," bending it into a two-note phrase.

The song is typical of Sinatra's repertory of the period. Written for a Broadway revue in 1926 by the thriving team of Buddy DeSylva, Lou Brown, and Ray Henderson, it was revived by Bing Crosby for a 1941 movie, *Birth of the Blues*. Although it is not a blues, the lyric poetically evokes the beginnings of jazz. The tune features an imaginative verse that, unlike most verses, is as well-known as the thirty-two-bar **A A B A** chorus and is always performed as an essential part of the song. Sinatra makes the most of its dramatic quality, as he does the bridge (2:05)—reaching exciting high notes and ultimately retreating into his ballad mode, all without breaking a sweat.

The arrangement by Heinie Beau (who worked with Tommy Dorsey and other bandleaders in the Swing Era and went on to arrange for singers and television shows through the 1970s) adds an introduction and a coda to resolve the main melody. Note that he singles out two instruments to play obbligato responses to the vocal: alto saxophone (Fred Stulce) in the verse and trumpet (Zeke Zarchy) in the chorus, imitating "the wail of a downhearted frail." Notice, too, the *wah–wah* effects played by the brasses, a jazzy sound associated with King Oliver in the 1920s, and that the piece begins and ends with the drums. The arrangement's stylistic diversity suits Sinatra's always impressive command of the material.

LISTENING GUIDE

4.2

💀 the birth of the blues

FRANK SINATRA

Frank Sinatra, vocal; Alex Stordahl and His Orchestra, including Zeke Zarchy, trumpet; Frank Stulce, alto saxophone; Heinie Beau, arranger

- Label: Columbia 39882; *Frank Sinatra Sings His Favorite Hits* (Columbia/Legacy 65420)
- Date: 1952
- Style: jazz-pop fusion
- Form: 32-bar popular song (**A A B A**), with verse

What to listen for:
- Sinatra's use of rubato and timbre variation
- the horn obbligatos and *wah-wah* effects
- use of drums at beginning and end

INTRODUCTION

0:00	After an opening drum shot, the band enters with a *fortissimo* (very loud) *soli.* On the last note, the trumpets play **shakes** (quick trills between two notes, in imitation of a wide vibrato).
0:03	Sinatra answers on the same melody: *"These are the blues!"*
0:06	The band repeats the melody at a lower pitch.

0:10	Sinatra again responds, ending with a long, exaggerated downward slide: "*Nothing but blues!*"
0:13	The brass play a series of short riffs, each featuring the **blue** (lowered) **third**.

VERSE

0:19	Sinatra enters on a long-held note, singing slightly behind the beat: "*Oh, they say some people long ago . . .*" Behind him, a saxophone plays a bluesy countermelody.
0:29	"*. . . were searching for a different tune, one that they could croon as only they can.*" Sinatra sings over the walking bass and rhythm guitar. Underneath, the trombone occasionally hits the low dominant.
0:41	During a one-measure **break**, he starts a new section: "*They only had the rhythm, so . . .*"
0:48	"*they started swayin' to and fro.*"
0:54	"*They didn't know just what to use, this is how the blues really began.*"
1:03	The full band rounds off the verse with strong **staccato** chords.
1:07	The tempo is interrupted by a break, featuring Sinatra supported only by saxophone chords. The break uses **rubato:** each chord is held for an unusually long time. "*They heard the . . .*"

CHORUS

1:13	**A**	"*. . . breeze in the trees . . .*" Sinatra resumes the original tempo over a walking bass. The melody rises gradually by **sequence**.
1:19		"*. . . singin' weird melodies . . .*" On "*weird,*" he bends upward with a long-held note, supported by rich, resonant saxophone chords.
1:25		"*. . . and they made that the start of the blues!*" His melody is accompanied by descending **chromatic** chords in the saxophones.
1:37		The next line starts with a rubato break. Sinatra decorates his line with unexpected melismas. "*And from a . . .*"
1:40	**A**	"*. . . jail came the wail of a downhearted frail, and they played that as a part of the blues!*" Each of Sinatra's phrases is answered by a loud, wailing trumpet.
1:59		The full brass plays a series of descending chords to round out the two **A** sections.
2:05	**B**	"*From a whip-poor-will way up on a hill, they took a new note.*" At the start of the bridge, Sinatra's melodic line reaches its peak.
2:12		He cuts his line off brusquely, leaving room for the brass to answer with distorted timbre. The last note of the riff falls off.
2:17		"*Pushed it through a horn until it was worn into a blue note.*"
2:24		As the horns respond again, the drums play on the **backbeat**.
2:28		The tempo is interrupted again by a rubato break, with Sinatra exaggerating the downward slide on each note. "*And then they . . .*"
2:33	**A**	"*. . . nursed it, they rehearsed it, and then sent out that news, that the Southland gave birth to the blues.*" Sinatra begins his line quietly, only to build to a climax.

CODA

2:52	As Sinatra holds out his last note, the harmony moves away from the tonic, signaling the start of the coda.
2:58	"*They nursed it . . . then they rehearsed it . . .*" His statements rise chromatically, each answered by a brass choir.
3:04	"*And they sent out that news!*" As the music moves toward its final climax, Sinatra's voice becomes emphatic.
3:08	"*That the Southland . . .*" He sings an unaccompanied held note, finally supported by the drums.
3:14	"*. . . they gave birth to the blues!*" As he sings his last phrase, he hits his highest note.
3:18	The band plays a descending bluesy line before ending with a sustained chord, finally cut off with a drum stroke.

▪ SARAH VAUGHAN (1924–1990)

With Sarah Vaughan, we approach the jazz-pop fusion from the opposite vantage point. Sinatra was a pop performer steeped in the tradition of Tin Pan Alley and swing. Vaughan was a dedicated jazz singer who applied bop harmonies, rhythms, and improvisational ideas to popular music. The leading figures of bop attempted to make their music accessible (Charlie Parker recorded with strings, Dizzy Gillespie sang comical novelties), but they could never reach as far into the mainstream as Vaughan, who had one of the most admired and lustrous voices in twentieth-century music. Jazz musicians crowned her with two enduring nicknames, "Sassy" to denote her artistic temperament, and "the Divine One" to denote her art.

Vaughan was born in Newark, New Jersey, where she sang in the Mt. Zion Baptist Church, and learned piano from her mother, the church organist. At twelve, Sarah was good enough to sub for her mother at the organ. Shy and awkward at eighteen, she sang "Body and Soul" at the Apollo Theater's Amateur Night, winning the competition and an important job. In the audience that night was pianist Earl Hines, and though he was not impressed by her gawky demeanor, he was astonished by her voice. He gave her a spot in his orchestra, playing second piano to Hines and sharing vocals with the influential ballad singer (and, subsequently, leader of the first bebop orchestra) Billy Eckstine.

Word of Vaughan's gifts quickly spread, and in 1944 she recorded one of the first bop sessions (Parker and Gillespie were among her sidemen). Two years later, she headlined at New York's Café Society, developing a confident stage presence that eventually became world famous: sensuous, imperious, and yet humorously self-deprecating. One of her characteristic lines, uttered midway through a set as she wiped perspiration from her brow, was "I come up here every night looking like [the famously beautiful singer] Lena Horne, and go home looking like Sarah Vaughan." Inevitably, she was signed by a major record label (Columbia).

Taking Risks

As an established singer, Vaughan rarely played piano in public, but she continued to play in private, exploring substitute chord changes that ultimately informed her vocal improvisations. Her greatest asset, though, was her voice, a contralto with a range exceeding four octaves and excellent intonation, which allowed her to attempt far-reaching melodic and harmonic embellishments with the authority of an instrumentalist. She had a strong feeling for the blues (reflecting her gospel training) and, in marked contrast with Sinatra, an instinctive feeling for swing: no businessman's bounce for her. By the time she signed with Columbia, in 1949, Vaughan was admired for her stunning creativity at any tempo.

The record label, however, didn't want that kind of creativity, which it felt would alienate a mainstream audience that wanted to hear familiar songs in a familiar style. During her five years with Columbia, Vaughan was allowed to record only one outright jazz session (with sideman Miles Davis, who later compared her brilliance to that of Charlie Parker), but the presence of large string orchestras could not rein in her improvised embellishments. Nor could she fake interest in the kind of novelties that governed the pop charts in the early 1950s—the era of million-sellers like "The Doggie in the Window" and "Hot Diggity, Dog Diggity."

Vaughan was poised between two careers—that of an indomitable jazz creator and an exquisite pop star, a predicament that took on contractual formality when she signed with Mercury Records in 1954. The company acknowledged her dual appeal by having her alternate between jazz and pop record dates. In her first year with Mercury, for example, Vaughan achieved a major hit with "Make Yourself Comfortable," a forgotten ditty by the man who conceived "The Doggie in the Window," and also recorded an ageless jazz classic (called simply *Sarah Vaughan*) featuring trumpet player Clifford Brown. Significantly, she refused to sing inferior songs in concert, no matter how well they sold.

The 1950s were the years when Ella Fitzgerald expanded her audience with her songbook series, helping to establish the pantheon of American songwriters while sustaining her jazz following with astonishing flights of scat-singing. Some of Vaughan's best work similarly resulted from a fusion of jazz and pop, in theme albums like *Great Songs from Hit Shows*. Bad songs disengaged her, but sugary arrangements of good ones rarely fazed her; sometimes overwrought orchestrations, dripping with syrupy violins, inspired her to bolder melodic embellishments.

As long as she could work in both fields, everything was fine. But by the 1960s, a new generation of record executives was less than enchanted by her free-thinking spontaneity and rapier wit. Vaughan complained that producers handed her sheet music for new songs on the day they were to be recorded, depriving her of rehearsal time on the assumption that unfamiliarity with the material would tame her creative impulses.

By 1967, she had had enough of their attempts to market her as a middle-brow pop star. When her contract ended, she turned her back on the industry and refused to record for four years. This turned out to be the beginning of the most successful phase in her career. Like Sinatra, Vaughan reinvented herself, but not by changing her music. Instead, she modified her place in the business, working in major concert halls with a trio instead of nightclubs, although she occasionally performed with big bands, guest stars, and even symphonic orchestras. When she resumed recording, she did so on her own terms and continued to successfully combine concerts and recordings until her death in 1990.

"Baby, Won't You Please Come Home?"

This song is even older than "The Birth of the Blues." The earliest recorded version dates from 1922 (sung by Eva Taylor, the wife of Clarence Williams, its composer and publisher), and it may have been written as early as 1919. Hundreds of jazz and pop performers recorded it in the 1920s and 1930s and again in the 1950s. The swing bands and bop musicians largely ignored it, however, so it was an unusual choice for Sarah Vaughan in 1962.

The setting is also unusual. At a time when she usually recorded with large studio orchestras, this was one of two albums Vaughan made with just guitar (Barney Kessel, a disciple of Charlie Christian and himself a prominent guitarist) and bass (Joe Comfort, a big-band veteran who often worked with Sinatra and Riddle). The spare, elegant accompaniment gives the singer no place to hide; her every note adds prominently to the harmonic and rhythmic contours of the performance. Under these circumstances, most pop singers stick close to the melody. Vaughan, with infallible intonation, plays freely with the material.

The arrangement consists of an introduction, three choruses of the thirty-two-bar **A A′** tune, and a protracted coda. Each chorus is treated with a different rhythmic approach: a cool medium tempo is followed by a funkier backbeat treatment and then by double-time swing. Notice how frequently Vaughan alters her vocal quality, from the soulfully seductive timbre of her first notes to the speech-like cadence at the end. She constantly modulates her vibrato, especially at the ends of phrases to underscore the rhythm. For example, she amplifies the word "name" (0:30) and changes the emphasis on "part," cutting it short in the first chorus (0:39) and extending it with vibrato in the second (1:21); in the third chorus, she puts the emphasis instead on the preceding "heart" (1:55).

Unlike Sinatra, Vaughan doesn't build to climactic high notes. With her entire range at her disposal, she casually rises to high notes or dips down to low ones to define the melodic embellishment of the moment, taking particular liberties in the first half of the third chorus. Some of her phrases are short, playing against the support of the guitarist, and others are surprisingly long—even breathless, though she is never really short of breath. While Sinatra sings long phrases to underscore the meaning of the lyric, Vaughan uses them to extend the melodic idea of her improvisation. Although she is singing an old pop song in a way that would have been accessible to everyone, she leaves not the slightest doubt that she is a true jazz vocalist.

LISTENING GUIDE

4.3

🎧 baby, won't you please come home?

SARAH VAUGHAN

Sarah Vaughan, vocal; Barney Kessel, guitar; Joe Comfort, bass

- Label: Roulette R(S)52118 (*Sarah Plus 2*); Angel (UPC 094637133927)
- Date: 1962
- Style: jazz-pop fusion
- Form: 32-bar popular song (**A A′**)

What to listen for:
- different keys for each chorus, dramatic shifts in tempo and groove
- Vaughan's virtuosic, wide-ranging voice, with variation in timbre and vibrato
- superb ensemble

INTRODUCTION

0:00	To introduce the song, the guitar and bass play the last eight bars of the chorus. The guitar's chords are bluesy, bending notes expressively. The bass sets a slow, shuffle groove.
0:09	The harmony comes to rest in a **half cadence** (on the dominant).

CHORUS 1

0:10	**A**	*"Baby, won't you please come home? 'Cause your mama's all alone."* Vaughan sings the repeated notes in the melody pleadingly, each note bent slightly and dragged behind the beat.
0:14		Having started without **vibrato**, she relaxes and allows her voice to flourish at phrase's end.

0:21		*"I have tried in vain, never no more to call your name."*
0:31	**A'**	*"When you left, you broke my heart, because I never thought we'd part."* Displaying her voice control, Vaughan connects the new stanza (*"When you left"*) to the last in a long, continuous phrase.
0:39		At the end of the line, her voice drops off suddenly, suggesting a more speech-like sound.
0:42		*"Every hour in the day, you will hear me say, Baby, baby, won't you please come home?"* For the last two lines, Vaughan switches to a bluesier sound.
0:51		Kessel (guitar) plays a chord that signals a **modulation** to a higher key.

CHORUS 2

0:52	**A**	*"Baby, won't you please come home? 'Cause your mama's all alone."* Kessel digs into the pulse, planting each chord solidly into each beat. Comfort suddenly plays a straightforward **walking bass**. Vaughan matches this rhythmic groove precisely: she turns the melody into a series of steady repeated notes, adding tiny embellishments to reinforce each beat.
0:56		As the line continues, her timbre begins to thin out, as if her breath were about to expire. And yet by the phrase's end, she has plenty of breath to complete her line with grace and style.
1:03		*"I have tried in vain never no more to call your name."* Vaughan begins to differentiate her lines with skillful **syncopation**.
1:08		In a sudden rise to the upper octave, she shows off her higher register.
1:13	**A'**	*"When you left, you broke my heart, because I never thought we'd part."*
1:18		Vaughan shifts to her lower register, where her timbre becomes dark and sultry.
1:24		*"Every hour in the day, you will hear me say, Baby, won't you please come home?"* For the final couplet, she sings in **call and response** with the guitar.
1:33		Kessel signals another modulation.

CHORUS 3

1:34	**A**	*"Baby, won't you please come home? 'Cause your mama's all alone."* The groove switches to double-time: Kessel **comps** while Comfort plays a fast walking bass. Vaughan's voice swings hard against the beat.
1:43		*"I have tried (Lord knows I've tried) in vain never no more to call your name."* As she improvises, words appear in strange rhythmic positions.
1:47		Vaughan's line descends deep to a note implied by one of the underlying chords.
1:50		At the phrase's end, she lets her timbre broaden and her volume increase, leading seamlessly to the next couplet.
1:52	**A'**	*"When you left, you broke my heart, because I never thought we'd part."*
1:59		The tempo slows down dramatically to an approximation of the opening groove.
2:01		*"Every hour in the day, you will hear me say, Baby, won't you please come home?"* Vaughan's timbre becomes loud and brassy.

CODA

2:12		*"Baby, won't you please come home?"* For the conclusion, the band repeats the last four bars of the tune. Vaughan swoops up to her highest note.
2:17		*"Baby, won't you please . . ."* As they near the final cadence, the harmonies slow down.
2:22		*"Come on home? Come on home? Come on home?"* Vaughan sings the last words in different octaves, contrasting her lyrical high voice with a deep, resonant low one.
2:30		*"Come on home!"* Her last phrase collapses from song into speech.
2:31		A final guitar chord ends the song.

Meanwhile: Jazz on TV

As the gap widened between modern jazz and an increasingly uncomprehending public, jazz began to embody four very different cultural clichés—each far removed from the optimistic "Let's Dance" status that buoyed the music during the Swing Era. The use of jazz on television in the late 1950s tells the story.

In one cliché, jazz was associated with urban mavericks, especially beatniks, and treated with a comical disdain. Such depictions emphasized jive talk, eccentric haircuts and goatees, and aimless scat-singing. This formula had nothing to do with music and underscored the idea that jazz musicians and enthusiasts were cultural outsiders and probably not very bright.

The second cliché also fostered a negative image: the sound of jazz—particularly sultry high notes played on alto saxophone—served as cues in dozens of shows to introduce a woman of doubtful virtue or a bad part of town. Television's detective shows almost always featured jazz scores. The most famous was *Peter Gunn* (1958–61), with a theme by composer Henry Mancini that became a big hit. *M Squad* (1957–60) had music by Count Basie and Benny Carter, while Nelson Riddle scored *The Untouchables* (1959–63).

The third cliché was largely positive though no less tiresome, and possibly did more damage than the others. This one postulated that jazz was the exclusive property of the super-hip. If you didn't qualify, you were a "square" or "out to lunch." Jazz embodied the sleek, affluent, postwar adult world for sexy people with expensive hi-fi's; it was the antidote to rock and roll, regarded as kids' music. Cutting-edge comedians like Lenny Bruce revered jazz; stylish writers like Jack Kerouac and Norman Mailer pondered its meaning. This sort of jazz lover disappeared in the middle 1960s, as the Beatles, Bob Dylan, and others certified rock's adult bona fides.

The fourth role was the most positive and realistic: the actual presentation of jazz musicians on variety shows, late night gabfests, and arts programming like *Omnibus* (1953–57), which hired the classical conductor Leonard Bernstein to explain "What Is Jazz?" Several isolated "special" programs were devoted entirely to jazz, including the acclaimed 1957 *The Sound of Jazz*. The overall portrait of jazz was severely circumscribed by public taste and racial imperatives.: singers were favored, African Americans were limited to guest appearances, and true modernists were rarely welcome. Even so, more jazz was seen on television in the 1950s and 1960s than in the past thirty years of cable TV—it was too much a part of the cultural landscape to ignore.

LATIN JAZZ

The dance beats of the Caribbean, which are closely related to actual West African sources, have always exerted a powerful influence on jazz history, beginning with New Orleans. As Jelly Roll Morton counseled: "If you can't manage to put tinges of Spanish into your tunes, you will never be able to get the right seasoning, I call it, for jazz." Yet in the postwar era, the Latin "tinge," especially as developed in Cuba and Brazil, fused with jazz to create riveting new developments. The Cuban influence produced an exciting, wildly percussive dance movement (salsa), while the Brazilian influence introduced a laid-back, melodious counterstatement to rock (bossa nova).

Cuban music maintained a large following in the United States in the big-band era and after, spurring a fashionable a series of dances: the rumba in the 1930s, the mambo in the 1940s, and the cha-cha-cha in the 1950s. In those years, Cuba was a popular destination for vacationing Americans, who returned with a taste for those exotic, sexy dances. The most successful of the Cuban bands working in the United States offered little in the way of jazz, but they kept ballrooms hopping and were much admired for their rhythmic vitality and colorful showmanship, which often involved extravagant costumes and beautiful dancers and singers.

Latin Pop, Good Neighbors, and Copyright

The most famous of all the Latin bandleaders was Xavier Cugat, a Spanish-born violinist whose family moved to Cuba when he was a boy. He played with Havana's Grand Opera Company and the Berlin Symphony before traveling to Los Angeles, where he worked as a newspaper cartoonist specializing in celebrity caricatures. Cugat organized his first band in 1929, and quickly found success in nightclubs in Los Angeles and New York. His fame peaked in the 1940s thanks to hit records and frequent appearances on radio and in the movies—rather incredibly, Cugat appeared in more Hollywood musicals than any other bandleader.

▶ **Xavier Cugat**

Cugat's band did not play jazz, but it furthered a vogue for Latin music and bandleaders, of which there were soon a great many. (Desi Arnaz brought that image to television in *I Love Lucy*.) Their success was encouraged by the Good Neighbor Policy, initiated by the United States in the late 1930s to counter its own interventionist policies, combat Nazi propaganda, and promote good ties with countries throughout Latin America.

Another factor in the growing popularity of Latin music was the 1940 battle between the American Society of Composers, Authors, and Publishers (ASCAP: the songwriters' union founded in 1914 to license music and protect copyrights) and the recently formed Broadcast Music Incorporated (BMI). ASCAP composers didn't want their music played on radio for free, and radio broadcasters, who formed BMI, balked at paying high licensing fees. Both sides finally agreed to new rates, but before they did, ASCAP songs were taken off the air, creating a musical vacuum that South American songwriters, most notably the Brazilian composer Ary Barroso, whose songs included "Brazil" and "Bahia," helped to fill.

Walt Disney hired Barroso and others to provide music for his contributions to the Good Neighbor Policy, movies that combined animation with live action: *Saludos Amigos* and *The Three Caballeros*. These films introduced several South American songs that gained tremendous popularity in North America. Everyone from Bing Crosby to Charlie Parker recorded them. Hollywood also began promoting a new generation of Latin leading men in musicals and dramas that pretended to take place in Havana or Rio, but were actually filmed on the studio lots. The most prominent Latin import was the wildly effervescent Brazilian entertainer Carmen Miranda, known for performing her songs in outrageous costumes that involved huge fruit-salad hats. Her impact in spreading Latin music was far from frivolous. Miranda's pre-Hollywood recordings helped to trigger interest in **samba** (a traditional music with African roots) in her native country. In Hollywood, she insisted on being accompanied onscreen by her own band, and performed authentic sambas with wit and brio—her expressive arms and facial gestures emphasized the music's stirring rhythms.

▶ **Carmen Miranda**

■ MARIO BAUZÁ (1911–1993) and MACHITO (1908–1984)

A profound realignment of Cuban music and jazz began to take place during the war but was little noticed until the late 1940s. This brew had been fermenting for years, partly in protest against Cugat's showboating popularization of Latin music. The new Cuban-jazz fusion was known as Cubop or Afro-Cuban jazz, and its relatively little-known godfather was the trumpet player and arranger Mario Bauzá. Born in Havana, Bauzá came to New York

▶ **Cubop/Afro-Cuban jazz**

Machito (seated far right) pioneered Afro-Cuban jazz and attracted many stars to the Brazil Club in Los Angeles (1946), including radio singer Lina Romay (black jacket) and Bing Crosby (center); also shown are his singer Graciela (fifth from right) and trumpet player and composer Mario Bauzá (seated second from right).

FRANK DRIGGS COLLECTION

as a teenager and worked with important big bands, most notably that of Chick Webb. Like the R & B innovators who found little recognition playing in swing bands, Bauzá bided his time—until 1939, when he attempted to form an Afro-Cuban band with Frank Grillo, soon to be known as the bandleader, singer, and maracas player Machito.

Machito was also raised in Havana, where he began performing in the 1920s. He moved to the United States in 1937, and worked with several Latin ensembles before he and Bauzá launched their first band, which was forced to fold for want of steady engagements. Bauzá joined Cab Calloway's orchestra and Machito recorded with Xavier Cugat. A year later, 1940, everything changed: Machito formed the Afro-Cubans, a ten-piece band (two saxophonists, two trumpeters, pianist, bassist, four percussionists), and never looked back. Bauzá soon left Calloway to become Machito's music director, and hired innovative young arrangers to give the band a jazz sound.

During the next few years, the two men grew closer as Bauzá married Machito's sister Estela. Their progress was delayed as Machito served in the army, but on his return his ensemble created much interest among modern jazz musicians. The California-based bandleader Stan Kenton, known for his embrace of orchestral modernism, later recalled that when he went to see Cugat, a member of the band told him, "Man, if you think this is good, you should go and hear Machito—he's the real thing!" In 1946, Machito and Kenton shared a bill and Kenton recorded his tribute, "Machito."

Clave ▶ The foundation of Cuban music, and specifically of Cubop, is the **clave** (Spanish for "keystone"): a time-line pattern on which other rhythms may be stacked. A crucial difference between jazz and Latin rhythms is that jazz has a fairly symmetrical forward momentum (swing), charged by a strong backbeat. Clave is asymmetrical, creating tension within each measure by its fluid, constantly changing nature. It originated in West Africa and was adapted by Cuban musicians as the defining organizing rhythmic principle for their music.

The most widely played clave patterns are the **son clave** and the **rumba clave**. The son clave is a two-bar phrase that can be notated as

played as shown here or with the measures reversed. The rumba clave is similar but with one important change:

.

That subtle rhythmic shift allows rumba clave to fit compatibly with a more Africanized 6/8 meter.

In a Latin band, the rhythm section is larger than the jazz configuration of piano, bass, and drums; it consists of a team of percussionists who may out-number the members of the reed or brass sections, as with Machito's Afro-Cubans. In addition to trap drums, the instruments played by a typical Cubop

Jazz Goes to the Movies

Jazz has always been part of the mix in Hollywood movies, even in the silent era, when ragtime was played by theatrical pianists and organists. From the beginning, jazz justifiably represented the sound of urban life; with less justification, it also came to signal immorality, in the form of wayward flappers, dissolute roués, and other lost souls.

During the Swing Era, the association between jazz and moral laxity briefly disappeared, as big-band music was celebrated for its all-American vitality, wartime sentimentality, and promise of good times. No sooner did the war end than jazz lost its Hollywood smiley face and came to represent urban decay and despair. Consider the episode in Frank Capra's Christmas perennial, *It's a Wonderful Life* (1946), in which Jimmy Stewart is required to experience what his idyllic town would be like if he had never been born. The place has gone to hell, particularly the friendly neighborhood bar, which in his absence has been invaded by bullies, rummies, hookers, and . . . Negro jazz!

In the 1950s, jazz stood for the same negative qualities in the movies as it did on television: the humid saxophone glissando became ubiquitous in melodramas whenever the camera turned to a "bad" woman or wandered into the city's tenderloin.

Most of the jazzy film scores of the period were created by composers under contract to the Hollywood studios who were masters of their craft, especially as arrangers. Yet when they wrote jazz-influenced scores, they tended to settle for overstatement and hackneyed formulas. A few producers and directors rebelled and hired true jazz composers. A big push in this direction came from Europe (as we saw in Chapter 14), when the French director Louis Malle hired Miles Davis to improvise a score for his 1957 film *Ascenseur pour l'echafaud*.

The Hollywood director Robert Wise, who would go on to direct such blockbusters as *West Side Story* and *The Sound of Music*, initiated a breakthrough for jazz with two films, *I Want to Live* (1958) and *Odds Against*

Tomorrow (1959). Both pictures explored the sleaziest elements in society—a junkie-prostitute-murderess and a racist psychopath. But the music was exceptional: John Mandel, a swing band arranger in the 1940s, wrote the former, featuring a West Coast "cool" band that included baritone saxophonist Gerry Mulligan, who appeared in the film. *Odds Against Tomorrow* was scored by pianist John Lewis, creator of the Modern Jazz Quartet. One of the best and most significant scores was composed by Duke Ellington for Otto Preminger's *Anatomy of a Murder*, also in 1959. This assignment was considered unusual because the film is about a Midwestern country lawyer, not a city slicker. Ellington nevertheless was encouraged to write in his own style and without restraint. His much-admired score shows that jazz has an emotional resonance that can echo beyond the city's mean streets. Still, the average jazz-style film score can be depended on, even now, to illuminate the travails of drug addicts, prostitutes, and criminals.

Director Otto Preminger (left) signed Duke Ellington (right) and his aide de camp Billy Strayhorn to score *Anatomy of a Murder*. Ellington played a pianist named Pie Eye in the 1959 film.

percussion team are timbales, congas, bongos, maracas, claves (short wooden sticks), and guiros (see Chapter 1 for descriptions of these instruments).

The Dizzy Factor

Machito sparked a great deal of interest, but the real breakthrough for the Afro-Cuban jazz movement was triggered by Dizzy Gillespie (see Chapter 11). Once again, the seeds had been planted by Mario Bauzá. During the two years he spent with the Cab Calloway Orchestra, Bauzá persuaded Calloway to hire the young, untested Gillespie, whom he then privately instructed in the essentials of Cuban music, including clave. In 1946, backed by a contract with RCA-Victor, Gillespie organized a big band and started working toward a fusion of jazz and Cuban music. After Bauzá introduced him to Chano Pozo, the brilliantly flamboyant congas player who occasionally worked with Machito's band, Gillespie invited Pozo and bongo player Chiquitico (Diego Iborra) to appear with his band at Carnegie Hall, marking the first public presentation of a serious jazz-Latin fusion.

Chano Pozo, the Cuban-born conga player (seen here in 1948), encouraged Dizzy Gillespie to explore a Cuban-jazz fusion.

Gillespie had already displayed a penchant for Afro rhythms in "A Night in Tunisia," but he now delved deeply into the arena of Cuban music, a subject about which he knew virtually nothing—in consulting Bauzá, he initially called the congas "one of those tom-tom things." He was a fast learner, eventually becoming a fair congas player himself. But in Pozo, he had a master: a tough, wiry man who had been something of an underground legend in Havana. He had limited command of English, but Gillespie gave him a free reign to instill Latin polyrhythms in his band from 1947 until the end of 1948, when Pozo's life was cut short at age thirty-four by a bullet in a Harlem bar. In December 1947, the Gillespie band recorded their major works together, "Cubana Be" and "Cubana Bop," arranged by George Russell in an early example of modal jazz, and the instantly influential "Manteca." Recalling the response to "Manteca," Gillespie said, "It was similar to a nuclear weapon when it burst on the scene. They'd never heard a marriage of Cuban music and American music like that before."

"Manteca"

"Manteca" was originally Pozo's idea. The title, which literally means grease or lard in Spanish but which was also Cuban slang for marijuana, is loudly invoked by Pozo throughout the recording. We hear his conga drumming from the outset, interlocked with a Latin syncopated bass line strikingly different from the walking-bass line that characterized swing and bebop. Thereafter, the orchestra adds riff after riff, saturating the musical space with cross-rhythms.

Pozo apparently wanted nothing but this tumultuous Latin groove, stretched out over a single tonic chord (another example of modal jazz). "If I had let it go like he wanted it," remembered Gillespie later, "it would've been strictly Afro-Cuban, all the way." Gillespie's job was to link these exotic sounds to jazz. In the introduction, his rapid-fire bebop solo ricochets past the riffs like an express train. Later on, he complements the "Manteca" tune with a sixteen-bar bridge that suddenly shifts to the distant realms of chromatic harmony. The whole piece, it seems, is in constant tension, moving from one world to another, giving the musicians a background they feel comfortable with. One of Gillespie's soloists, "Big Nick" Nicholas, was a hard-swinging tenor saxophonist, so the arrangement drops him into an "I Got Rhythm" chord progression with a steady four-four bass. It is as fine an example of cultural fusion as we are likely to find in mid-century America.

LISTENING GUIDE

4.4

🎧 manteca

DIZZY GILLESPIE AND HIS ORCHESTRA

Dizzy Gillespie, Dave Burns, Elmon Wright, Benny Bailey, Lamar Wright Jr., trumpets; Bill Shepherd, Ted Kelly, trombones; Howard Johnson, John Brown, alto saxophones; Joe Gayles, George "Big Nick" Nicholas, tenor saxophones; Cecil Payne, baritone saxophone; John Lewis, piano; Al McKibbon, bass; Kenny Clarke, drums; Chano Pozo, congas and vocal

- Label: Victor 20-3023; *Dizzy Gillespie: The Complete RCA Victor Recordings* (Bluebird 7863)
- Date: 1947
- Style: big-band Latin jazz
- Form: 40-bar popular song (**A A B A**; the bridge lasts 16 bars) with interludes

What to listen for:

- Latin syncopated bass line and conga drumming, alternating with bebop groove and walking bass
- layered riffs supplied by orchestra
- brilliant Gillespie improvisations, with bebop dissonances
- "I Got Rhythm" chord progression (interlude 2)

INTRODUCTION

0:00	The piece opens with an interlocking duet between the Afro-Cuban drumming of Pozo and the bassist. Pozo's repeated pattern emphasizes a strong **backbeat** on beat 2 (the high-pitched drum), and two drum beats that fall *just before* beat 1. The syncopated bass line falls strongly off the beat.
0:05	The drum set fills in the texture, adding its own pattern but also playing a bass drum accent firmly on the beginning of each measure. Pozo begins chanting, *"Manteca! Manteca!"*
0:08	The baritone saxophone enters with yet another polyrhythmic riff, a two-note riff in **octaves**.
0:13	The baritone saxophone is doubled by tenor saxophones.
0:16	The brass instruments enter: the trombone section on its own riff, the trumpet section doubling the saxophones but adding a chord at the end.
0:19	Gillespie adds his own improvised layer in bebop style.
0:24	He suddenly accelerates to a faster passage.
0:30	The full band enters with a sudden explosion on a **triplet** rhythm (*da*-da-da, *da*-da-da, *da*-da-da, *da*-da-da, *daaah!*).
0:32	The final note is held and allowed to decay, each instrument falling away at its own rate. The texture once again reduces to the bass-conga duet (with the drums playing quietly behind them).

CHORUS 1 (HEAD)

0:38	**A**	The saxophones play a short riff, answered by the full band. Each line ends in a **shake**—a rapid tremolo that marks the end of the phrase. Behind them, the bass plays various asymmetric riffs.
0:44		The conga drum adds improvised accents.
0:46		At the end of the **A** section, the full band repeats its answer, its syncopations accented by the drum set.
0:49	**A**	
1:00	**B**	Playing a sustained chord, the saxophones **modulate** to a new key. The congas continue their rhythm, but the bassist has shifted to a walking-bass pattern.
1:12		Gillespie takes over the melody on trumpet, the saxophones harmonizing underneath him.
1:22	**A**	

INTERLUDE 1

1:33		We return to the bass-conga duet, with subtle changes in the bass line.
1:36		As Pozo shouts, "*Manteca!*" the trombones double the bass.
1:39		The saxophones play their octave riff.
1:42		Over a **cross-rhythm**, the full band enters with the high trumpets on top.

INTERLUDE 2 ("I GOT RHYTHM")

1:48	**A**	With a flourish, Nicholas enters on tenor saxophone, improvising against **block chords** played by the full band. The chord progression is the jam-session favorite, "I Got Rhythm," with a walking bass.
1:52		The background chords, voiced at the peak of the trumpet section's range, feature intense bebop dissonances.
1:54		Nicholas's line lands strongly on the **flatted fifth** (a melodic dissonance).
1:59	**A**	The band is now silent, leaving Nicholas to play with the rhythm section. He quotes the opening of "Blue Moon." The congas are still heard, but they subordinate their Latin rhythms to the prevailing bebop groove.
2:05		Again, Nicholas hits the flatted fifth.

CHORUS 2 (abbreviated)

2:10	**B**	The brass play a syncopated version of the melody, backed by a **countermelody** from the saxophones.
2:21		Entering on a stunning high note, Gillespie improvises over the second phrase.
2:31		As Gillespie reaches the end of the phrase, he throws in a series of bebop dissonances (including the flatted fifth).
2:32	**A**	The band returns to the opening riff.
2:38		Pozo bellows "*Manteca*!" over the entire band.

CODA

2:43		A conglomeration of riffs gradually declines in volume. Pozo continues to yell, changing his pitch and rhythm. The sound retreats to the bass and congas.
2:55		The bassist, now the focus of attention, plays variations on his line.
3:03		A few short drum strokes end the piece.

A New Movement / Salsa

The fascination with Cuban rhythms quickly spread. An especially important recording following on the heels of "Manteca" came about in 1948, when, as part of a recorded survey called *The Jazz Scene*, Machito was asked to contribute a selection. He chose a 1943 Bauzá composition (frequently cited as the first piece written in the Afro-Cuban idiom), "Tanga." At the center of this performance was a tenor saxophone solo by jazz star Flip Phillips (formerly of the Woody Herman band), but the context was an intricate clave developed by six percussionists. It was probably no coincidence that in Havana, *manteca* and *tanga* were both terms for marijuana: if "Manteca" approached the merger from a jazz angle, "Tanga" defined the same union from a Cuban purview. Still, as Chico O'Farrill, a principal Afro-Cuban composer hired by both Bauzá and Gillespie, noted, "I truly believe jazz ended up influencing Cuban music more than Cuban music influenced jazz."

"Tanga"

By 1950, the Latin influence was widespread. Charlie Parker recorded with Machito (they connected on "Tico Tico," one of the songs introduced by Disney's *Saludos Amigos*); Bud Powell drew on clave for his trio recording of "Un Poco Loco"; and Stan Kenton regularly used bongos, maracas, and other Latin devices. In the mid-1950s, Afro-Cuban jazz receded; like bop itself, Cubop polarized the mass audience. But Machito's career continued unabated, not least at vacation resorts in places like the Catskills, where he promoted the mambo and cha-cha-cha. He made two kinds of records: those that featured jazz solos and those that did not. Soon, the Cuban style became part of a broader appreciation of Latin American styles, which included the Brazilian bossa nova (see below), the tango (an Argentine dance), and mariachi (Mexican street music).

The Afro-Cuban tradition sparked yet another kind of fusion, between Cuba and other areas in the Caribbean, especially Puerto Rico, as blended together on New York's streets. Puerto Rican musicians named the new Afro-Caribbean result **salsa** (sauce). By the 1970s, salsa was a full-blown urban tradition, with several ballrooms accommodating its orchestras and the loyal dancers and fans who followed them.

In these bands, the jazz input was not an option but a given. Every salsa group employed accomplished jazz improvisers as well as singers and rhythm sections that built disarmingly danceable clave rhythms. Many key figures in the salsa movement were born in New York and had grown up with strong ties to the twin traditions of Machito and Gillespie—among them, Tito Puente, Ray Barretto, Eddie Palmieri, and Willie Bobo. Barretto, for example, was encouraged early on by Charlie Parker, played straight jazz as often as he did salsa, and was the first musician to play the conga in 4/4 jazz time, with no trace of clave.

At the same time, established jazz stars hired Latin rhythm sections to give their music a clave foundation. One of the most successful was a vibraphonist from St. Louis, Cal Tjader. Tjader initially made his name in the 1950s cool school working for pianist George Shearing, who used Latin rhythms on many of his albums. In 1955, Tjader went out on his own; two years later, he was able to hire two of the prized percussionists in Tito Puente's band, Willie Bobo and Mongo Santamaria. Tjader's group enjoyed much success during the next several years, culminating in 1964, when his landmark recording *Soul Sauce* sold 100,000 copies.

Cal Tjader

© CHUCK STEWART

Mongo Santamaria (seen here in the 1960s) played congas with several Latin jazz bands, but achieved stardom when he started his own group and adapted jazz and pop themes to clave rhythms.

■ MONGO SANTAMARIA (1922–2003)

In 1961, Mongo Santamaria left Tjader to start his own group. Within a year, he had a top-ten hit: "Watermelon Man," an Afro-Cuban treatment of a new piece by the young pianist with Miles Davis's quintet, Herbie Hancock (see Chapter 17). *Salsa* was not yet a household term and bossa nova had only begun to stir interest, yet his "single" helped pave the way for a flexible Latin-soul fusion that covered mainstream hits in addition to creating its own tunes.

Santamaria was born in Havana, where he studied violin, and turned to drums after hearing Chano Pozo. Arriving in the United States in 1950, he spent most of the next seven years working with Tito Puente. He didn't become known in the jazz world until he joined with Tjader, an association that led to his making freelance records as a leader. An innovator of *charanga*, a standard Cuban style featuring flute and violin, Santamaria added saxophones and trumpet to give the music more weight and thrust.

In the wake of "Watermelon Man," Santamaria became the archetypal crossover musician whose audience encompassed fans of salsa, jazz, soul, and middle-of-the-road pop. His first name became so well-known that Mel Brooks used it as a punch line in the movie *Blazing Saddles*. Although many of his records reflected commercial ambitions, Santamaria was a versatile musician. He occasionally collaborated with Dizzy Gillespie, and his composition "Afro-Blue" remains a jazz standard, best known in a version by John Coltrane.

🎧 "Watermelon Man"

Santamaria instantly saw the potential of "Watermelon Man," and worked up an arrangement for his band before most people had heard Hancock's original. The tune is a variation on the sixteen-bar blues form, moving from the tonic to the subdominant in the four-bar **A** sections and to the dominant in the eight-bar **B** section. The **A** sections include long rests, more than a measure each (for example, at 0:12 and 0:19), which Santamaria fills with vocal shouts and laughter. This use of space emphasizes the unchanging pulse of the rock-steady vamp.

Everything about the performance, including the sculpted ensemble phrasing of the theme, is subordinate to the repetitive force of that vamp. After the second chorus, there's a brief transition before the only solo, played by Santamaria's longtime trumpet player Marty Sheller. It's a pleasant solo, but was it improvised or composed? It hardly matters, though it is interesting to note that it became a standardized part of the arrangement: in Santamaria's 1965 version of the piece, arranged by Hancock, the trumpet solo is virtually identical. This is an example of a record in which jazz feeling is maintained (in the solo and in the blending of the ensemble instruments), but not jazz substance—essentially, it is dance music.

watermelon man

LISTENING GUIDE

MONGO SANTAMARIA

Mongo Santamaria, congas; Marty Sheller, trumpet; Pat Patrick, Bobby Capers, flutes and tenor saxophone; Rodgers Grant, piano; Victor Venegas, bass; Frank Hernandez, Kalil Madi, drums; Kako, Chihuahua Martinez, Joseph Gorgas, Latin percussion; Martinez and La Lupe, vocal effects

- Label: Battle 909; *Watermelon Man* (Concord, Milestone MCD-47075-2)
- Date: 1962
- Style: Afro-Cuban jazz
- Form: 16-bar blues: **A** (4) **A** (4) **B** (8)

> **What to listen for:**
> - rock-steady vamp: montuno
> - four extra bars in last blues phrase
> - Latin percussion (congas, guiro, woodblock)

0:00   The tune begins with a **montuno**: a one-to-two-bar syncopated vamp in the piano that is repeated ad infinitum. In this case, the piano chords come straight from the original Herbie Hancock version. There are also various percussion instruments: conga drums, guiro, and woodblock.

CHORUS 1 (HEAD)

0:07   **A**   The horns sneak in, building with a *crescendo* to the first note of the phrase.

0:11   At the end of the phrase, the concluding chords are played slightly behind the beat.

0:12   The male vocalist responds with a series of distorted shouts.

0:15   **A**   The melody is repeated, with the first note played higher to adjust to the change of harmony to IV.

0:19   The vocalist's response is a high-pitched laugh.

0:23   **B**   The horns play, in **block chords** that oscillate back and forth between the harmonies IV and V.

0:33   As the band takes a one-measure **break**, the horns play the opening melody one more time.

CHORUS 2 (HEAD)

0:39   **A**   The band plays the melody again; a male vocalist responds with a single prolonged shout.

0:47   **A**

0:51   After the second phrase, a woman responds, "That's right, baby, come on!" then laughs.

0:55   **B**

INTERLUDE

1:11   The band repeats the montuno one more time.

CHORUS 3

1:15   **A**   Marty Sheller begins a trumpet solo. His phrases are followed by a riff, played by the saxophones.

1:23   **A**   As the harmony changes to IV, the background riff is transposed upward. Sheller's lines are short and simple, with some colored by a bluesy tone.

1:31   **B**

1:41   The one-bar break is silent for a few beats before Sheller reenters on a syncopated riff with a tenor saxophone.

INTERLUDE

1:47   Another two-bar interlude featuring the montuno. Toward the end, a percussionist
         fills in space on a cowbell.

CHORUS 4

1:51   **A**

1:55   After the first and second phrases, the two vocalists harmonize a response:
         "Watermelon man!"

1:59   **A**

2:07   **B**

CODA

2:23   The tune fades out rapidly after the end of the chorus.

© CHUCK STEWART

Antonio Carlos Jobim, Brazil's greatest songwriter (seen here in the 1960s), wrote the melodies and often the lyrics that João Gilberto and other musicians interpreted to launch the bossa nova, a new approach to the samba.

Bossa Nova

The Brazilian dance known as the samba originated in the nineteenth century as an amalgam of African dances and march rhythms that laid particular emphasis on the second beat of the measure, or more specifically the eighth note leading from beat one to beat two. Although it was grounded on a version of clave, samba does not use clave as an organizing rhythmic principle: the overall feeling of the samba is more relaxed than that of Cuban music. The dance found acceptance in the United States in the 1930s and 1940s through hit songs like "Brazil" and "Tico Tico" and the Hollywood stardom of Carmen Miranda.

Then in 1958, the revered Brazilian singer and actress Elizete Cardoso released an album (*Canção do Amor Demais*) that created a stir in Rio de Janeiro and beyond. Recorded at the request of playwright, composer, and diplomat Vinícius de Moraes, it consisted of the songs he wrote with another young composer, Antônio Carlos Brasileiro de Almeida (Tom) Jobim, and it introduced Brazil to a new style of music soon known as **bossa nova** (new flair). On a couple of tracks, Cardoso was accompanied by the young guitarist João Gilberto.

The album was a culmination of several years' work that began when Vinícius hired Jobim to write music for his play *Orfeu da Conceição*, based on the legend of Orpheus and Eurydice. A year after the album's release, Vinícius helped to spur an international triumph when his Orpheus play was adapted by a French filmmaker, Marcel Camus, as *Orfeo Negro* (*Black Orpheus*), a classic film with an irresistible score by the guitarist-composer Luiz Bonfá plus a couple of new tunes by Jobim. Those songs were more in the traditional style of the boisterous samba than the "new flair," but they brought attention to the melodically infectious music of Brazil.

The key figures in the new movement were now assembled: Vinícius de Moraes, who had published his first samba in 1953; Tom Jobim, often cited as the finest composer of popular songs since the golden age of Gershwin, Berlin, and Porter; and João Gilberto, who was not only the key interpreter of bossa nova, but the man who created the style by which the Jobim–de Moraes songs would be known. Often concertizing alone, sometimes for ninety minutes or two hours at a stretch, Gilberto accompanied his spare, unemotional yet moving vocals with infallibly soft rhythmic guitar.

Although detractors insisted that they were merely reinterpreting the traditional samba, Jobim and company insisted that bossa nova represented a break with tradition no less meaningful than bop's break with swing. The public agreed. Bossa nova incarnated a young, innovative attitude with poetic, sometimes self-mocking lyrics and melodies that, though occasionally melancholy, were almost invariably as gentle as a summer's breeze. Rhythmically, bossa nova seemed to sway rather than swing. Harmonically, it delighted in intricate chord changes not unlike those of bop, favoring seventh and ninth chords and melodic dissonances. The title of one of Jobim's best-known songs, "Desafinado," is Portuguese for "out of tune"; its melody makes bold use of bop's signature interval, the flatted fifth, and its lyric uses the phrase that Gilberto initially coined to describe Gilberto's "new flair"—bossa nova.

seventh/ninth chord: chord featuring the interval of a seventh or ninth

■ CHARLIE BYRD (1925–1999) and STAN GETZ (1927–1991)

As of 1960, bossa nova was a phenomenon largely confined to Brazil. Two factors changed that. First, as far as the United States was concerned, the Cuban Revolution of 1959 put a damper on celebrating anything Cuban, from cigars to music. Brazil was now the logical place to turn to for South American rhythms. Second, touring jazz musicians discovered Jobim's songs and embraced them.

Not surprisingly, the first American to seriously study Jobim's music was Dizzy Gillespie, during a visit in 1961. He added such bossa nova benchmarks as "Desafinado" and "Chega de Saudade" to his repertory and recorded them shortly after returning. Then he made the commercially disastrous decision to postpone releasing his Brazilian album, *New Wave!*, which left the field open to other musicians, also visiting Brazil in 1961.

One of those musicians was guitarist Charlie Byrd, who toured South America for three months with his trio. Byrd, born in Virginia, was one of the few modern guitarists who concentrated on the acoustic rather than electric guitar—a reflection of his admiration for Django Reinhardt and studies with the classical guitarist Andres Segovia. By 1961, he was an established jazz player in the Washington, D.C., area. Meetings with Jobim and João Gilberto raised his sights, and made him realize that the "texture and volume" of bossa nova was more conducive than other kinds of Latin music to the guitar.

Stan Getz was a major jazz star known for his gorgeous timbre long before he discovered the bossa nova. Here he performs with bassist Ray Brown in Paris, 1960.

There was a noticeable difference from the Cuban approach, for example, from the Xavier Cugats and those kinds of things—a more delicate and light way of playing. Also appealing were the ingenious melodies of Jobim and Bonfá and those people. They emulated American popular songs to some extent, but they had a lot of innovation in their own tradition, and they were very inventive people themselves.

Byrd could not interest an American label in recording his interpretations of bossa nova until he recruited Stan Getz for the project. Getz, one of the most influential tenor saxophonists of the 1950s, along with Dexter Gordon, Sonny Rollins, and John Coltrane, was born in Philadelphia and demonstrated a prodigious talent while in high school. At seventeen, he became a member of Stan Kenton's band, and then worked with Benny Goodman and other prominent bandleaders. Woody Herman hired him in 1947, placing him in what quickly evolved into a distinctive bebop reed section known, after a record of that name, as the "Four Brothers."

Getz's brief solo on Herman's "Early Autumn" made him an overnight jazz star—his supple timbre had a cool, romantic, otherworldly quality that was instantly recognizable. His reputation soared in the 1950s until problems with narcotics forced him to decamp for Europe. In 1961, intent on reestablishing himself in the United States, he completed a pioneering album with composer Eddie Sauter (*Focus*), which fused jazz and classical techniques—and proved his artistry but not his commercial potential. When Getz, who worked with Machito during the Afro-Cuban jazz vogue, listened to the recordings Byrd brought back from Brazil, he was sold on bossa nova.

Jazz Samba

Joining with Byrd's trio (plus a second drummer), Getz recorded *Jazz Samba* early in 1962. Byrd wisely realized that Getz would dominate the album. A record plugger convinced Verve Records to issue a single of "Desafinado," edited down to two minutes from the nearly six-minute album version, highlighting Getz's solo. The single was the kind of hit that drives album sales: *Jazz Samba* reached the No. 1 spot on the pop music charts. Within a year, more than two dozen jazz and pop albums claiming to have something to do with bossa nova were released, including creative ventures by Gillespie, Sonny Rollins, Cal Tjader, and Sarah Vaughan. There had been nothing like it in American pop since Elvis Presley triggered rock and roll—and nothing like it in jazz since the Swing Era.

Getz / Gilberto

In 1963, Getz, aiming for greater authenticity, recorded with the Brazilians who created bossa nova and had begun performing in New York. The million-selling *Getz / Gilberto* comprised eight songs by Jobim (who played piano), including the track that became emblematic of the entire bossa nova fad, "The Girl from Ipanema." For these recording sessions, Getz asked Gilberto's wife Astrud, who was present, to translate some of the song lyrics. Although she had never sung professionally, Getz liked the wispy innocence of her thin voice and persuaded Gilberto to let her sing on this one track—which became a milestone in the globalization of the jazz–bossa nova fusion.

🎧 "Samba Dees Days"

As the punning title suggests, "Samba Dees Days" is not a Brazilian bossa nova. It was written by Charlie Byrd for the *Jazz Samba* session, in an attempt to meet what he considered the challenge of composing a samba tune. His piece catches the rhythmic excitement of Brazilian jazz but also the more wistful elements, as in the interval of a third at 0:03 and 0:05 and in subsequent **A** sections, and the bluesy feeling in the last half (0:26) of the sixteen-measure bridge. The first half of the bridge uses a familiar device in the songs of Tom Jobim, also commonplace in jazz: the repetition of one note. One of the Jobim songs included on *Jazz Samba*, in fact, is "Samba de una nota só" ("One-Note Samba"), which Byrd described as "the most recorded [song] of all" in Brazil.

The star of the performance is Stan Getz, whose effortless phrasing, combined with the understated playing of the two drummers, captures the music's easygoing polyrhythms. His playing has an irresistibly breezy confidence as he alternates long and short phrases, bounces along on the one-note idea of the bridge, and rises to a couple of high-note climaxes (1:54, 3:10) that were something of a Getz specialty—increasing not only his range but also the power of his timbre. His fluid attack is especially noteworthy as he navigates the turnarounds, the measures that end one chorus and lead to another; his manner of moving from one chorus to the next emphasizes the cumulative drama and overall coherence of the performance. Even his final chorus contributes to that unity by echoing aspects of Byrd's solo. In Getz's most penetrating playing, we have the convergence of a uniquely attractive timbre, tender but forceful; an immense gift for melodic invention; and the ability to lucidly communicate his ideas and emotions, which made him the ideal musician to establish Brazil's bossa nova as a major North American event.

LISTENING GUIDE

4.6

 ## samba dees days

STAN GETZ AND CHARLIE BYRD

Stan Getz, tenor saxophone; Charlie Byrd and Gene Byrd, acoustic guitars; Keeter Betts, bass; Buddy Deppenschmidt, Bill Reichenbach, percussion

- Label: *Jazz Samba,* Verve MGV8432; *Jazz Samba* (Verve 731452141323)
- Date: 1962
- Style: Latin jazz
- Form: 40-bar popular song (**A A′ B A′**)

What to listen for:
- easygoing polyrhythm in a relaxed Brazilian groove
- single syncopated note in bridge
- Getz's seamless improvising and high-note climaxes

INTRODUCTION

0:00		Getz plays a series of lazy unaccompanied **arpeggios**, which establish the key of the piece.

CHORUS 1 (HEAD)

0:02	**A**	Getz plays the melody—a series of short phrases, discreetly doubled in thirds by Byrd's guitar. Behind the melody, the accompaniment (including maracas) keeps a quiet Latin rhythm.
0:08		The first eight-bar section ends with a **half cadence** on the dominant chord.
0:10	**A′**	The next eight-bar phrase begins on the same chord, but ends (0:17) with a **full cadence** on the tonic.
0:18	**B**	The bridge (lasting 16 bars instead of 8) begins with Getz and Byrd playing a single **syncopated** note.
0:22		Getz and Byrd repeat the gesture, this time ending with a bluesy phrase.
0:26		As the harmonic progression changes, the melody slowly sinks back to the dominant (at 0:33).
0:35	**A′**	
0:41		The arrival on the tonic signals a two-bar **break**.

CHORUS 2

0:43	**A**	Getz begins with a simple, riff-like rhythmic figure.
0:47		Many of his phrases end early, leaving a great deal of open space.
0:51	**A′**	As he warms up, his melodic ideas begin to cohere into longer and longer phrases.
0:59	**B**	On the bridge, Getz opens up the repeated note to a full octave, complementing it with bluesy phrases.

| 1:07 | | As the harmonies change, his phrases become more active, moving rapidly in arpeggios. |
| 1:14 | **A'** | |

CHORUS 3

1:22	**A**	As Getz plays a long phrase, he accents the **backbeat** (coinciding with the background maracas).
1:30	**A'**	
1:38	**B**	Getz builds a longer, highly decorated phrase around the single note.
1:50		As the phrases increase in intensity, his volume rises.
1:54	**A'**	The last phrase begins with his highest note (a D-sharp).

CHORUS 4

2:02	**A**	Byrd begins his solo quietly, playing single-note lines on guitar. Behind him, the details of the Latin rhythmic background are more clearly audible.
2:10	**A'**	
2:18	**B**	At the beginning of the bridge, Byrd switches to a series of chords.
2:26		He plays a phrase polyrhythmically against the beat, adjusting the notes to match the underlying harmony.
2:33	**A'**	
2:37		To signal the end of his solo, Byrd plays a bluesy gesture.

CHORUS 5

2:41	**A**	Getz begins his second solo mimicking the rhythms and phrases of Byrd's improvised melody.
2:49	**A'**	As Getz suggests the melody of the head, he reduces the rhythm to even quarter notes.
2:57	**B**	Once again, Getz's bridge focuses on a single note, embedding it within an ornate, complex line.
3:02		His bluesy response is played with particular intensity.
3:05		He plays a series of ascending arpeggios, each culminating in a high note; the last of these high notes (at 3:11) is the **dominant**.
3:13	**A'**	He returns to the head.

CODA

3:19		Getz improvises unaccompanied for two bars. After a sharp drum stroke, Byrd follows with his own two-bar phrase.
3:23		Getz and Byrd exchange another two bars. Each of their lines remains largely within the blues scale.
3:27		Switching to the **major scale**, the two musicians play a composed-out line.
3:30		The piece concludes with two quick strokes.

Bossa Nova at Fifty

As the initial excitement over bossa nova waned, it continued to enjoy popularity as easy-listening lounge music, devoid of most of the features that had made it so captivating to jazz musicians. For example, the Brazilian pianist Sergio Mendes first made his mark with a deft fusion of Brazilian rhythms and hard bop jazz solos, underscored by his own Horace Silver–influenced keyboard style. But he didn't become an international celebrity until he leached out the jazz content, added cooing voices, and covered American Top Forty tunes.

Still, bossa nova never completely lost its bite, as became evident in 2008 when its fiftieth anniversary was celebrated in Brazil with festivals, concerts, panels, articles, and books. By now it had fused with rock and classical music. The samba received a forceful jolt in the music of young singers like Marisa Monte, who created a repertory that drew on bossa nova in the context of rock and soul music. Born in Rio de Janeiro and trained in opera, Monte became a leading figure in a style called MPB, for *Música Popular Brasileira* (Brazilian Popular Music).

At the same time, a more faithful development of bossa nova was maintained by Rosa Passos, a native of Bahia who began on piano but took up guitar after hearing João Gilberto. At eleven, she sang on local television, and soon developed into a premier interpreter of Jobim and other Brazilian songwriters while contributing to the repertory as a prolific lyricist. After disappearing from public view for several years to raise a family, Passos began a busy recording career in 1996, touring the world—sometimes in tandem with the classical cellist Yo-Yo Ma, who called her voice "the most beautiful in the world."

⊦ ADDITIONAL LISTENING ⊦	
Louis Jordan	"Is You Is or Is You Ain't My Baby" (1943); *Jumpin' and Jivin' at Jubliee* (Koch 00617742103526)
	"Caldonia" (1945); *Classics: 1943-1945* (Classics 886)
Earl Bostic	"Flamingo" (1951); *Flamingo* (ASV/Living Era 5635)
Ray Charles	"I Got a Woman" (1958); *Ray Charles Live* (Rhino Atlantic 81732)
	"Georgia on My Mind" (1960); *Definitive Ray Charles* (WEA International/Atlantic 81227355629)
Jimmy Smith	"The Sermon" (1958); *The Sermon* (Blue Note 24541)
Rosemary Clooney and Duke Ellington	"Grievin'" (1956); *Blue Rose* (Legacy 803188)
Nat King Cole	"Straighten Up and Fly Right" (1943); *King Cole Trio: That's What (1943-1947)* (Naxos)
	"Sweet Lorraine" (1940); *Hit That Jive, Jack: Nat King Cole Trio, The Earliest Recordings, 1940–41* (GRP 011105066228)
Frank Sinatra	"I've Got You Under My Skin" (1956); *The Capitol Years* (Capitol 94317)
Sarah Vaughan	"It's Crazy" (1954); *Sarah Vaughan with Clifford Brown* (Verve 731454330527)
	"My Funny Valentine" (1973); *Live in Japan* (Mobile Fidelity MFCD 2 844)
Machito	"Tanga" (1949); *The Original Mambo Kings: An Introduction to Afro-Cubop* (Verve 513876)
Charlie Parker and Machito	"Tico Tico" (1951); *Charlie Parker South of the Border: The Verve Latin-Jazz Sessions* (Verve 527779)
Stan Getz and João Gilberto	"Desafinado" (1962); *Getz / Gilberto* (Verve 731452141422)
Rosa Passos	"Por Causa de Você" (2007); *Entre Amigos / Among Friends* (Chesky JD 247)

17

FUSION II:
JAZZ, ROCK, AND BEYOND

By the 1950s, a revolution was occurring outside the gates of jazz and popular music. A new music, dubbed **rock and roll**, unsettled the music industry by attracting a sizable body of white teenagers to an odd but compelling fusion of the fluid rhythms of black race records and the insistent plaintive sound of white "hillbilly" music. It was led by Elvis Presley, a Memphis truck driver who added pelvic-twisting dances to his blues-country mixture; Chuck Berry, a St. Louis bluesman who mimicked white country music with his "Maybelline"; and Little Richard, a gospel singer from Georgia who dressed in outrageous drag costumes and whooped his way onto the mainstream pop charts.

In retrospect, it seems that jazz musicians should have been paying attention to this new music; but few were. Early rock and roll was seen as music for teenagers, created by amateurs and catering to untutored tastes. At best it was errant nonsense, at worst a juvenile plague—"the martial music of every side-burned delinquent on the face of the earth," as Frank Sinatra arrogantly characterized it. Jazz, by contrast, was firmly part of an adult sensibility that surely would triumph over such rubbish. When Presley joined the army in 1958, trading in his pompadour for a crisp army uniform, it seemed that youthful rebellion had indeed been contained.

Miles Davis, who devoted as much time to his painting as to his music, was a work of art himself. He's seen here in Malibu, California, in 1989, just two years before he died.

wwnorton.com/studyspace

475

All that changed in the 1960s, when popular music became overwhelmed by rock and jazz musicians found themselves struggling for survival in a new world not of their making. The result, as we have seen, was a new pop-jazz mixing known as fusion, which many assumed was simply the next phase of jazz, displacing all that came before. This has not happened. Instead, the term "fusion" has fallen from favor, replaced by market-driven terms like "smooth jazz" and "contemporary jazz."

Jazz-Rock Background

The changes that transformed a generation of jazz musicians can be traced back to the 1950s. The success of rock and roll meant a new source for popular song, which came from the Brill Building on Broadway in New York City. There Carole King, Neil Sedaka, Neil Diamond, and other young songwriters churned out hundreds of new tunes aimed directly at the youthful market-place. Few of these songs, with their puerile, adolescent lyrics (Sedaka's "Stupid Cupid," for example), appealed to jazz musicians, who were still attuned to the sophisticated harmonies and lyrics of Gershwin, Porter, and Rodgers. But they provided an alternative for a pop repertory separate from the adult world.

A different signal was sent by the breakthrough success of the Kingston Trio, which sold 6 million copies of "Tom Dooley" in 1958. Within a few years, a folk revival brought a new aesthetic: austere, simple, and moralistic. Veterans like Pete Seeger and fresh-faced singers like Bob Dylan and Joan Baez became the lodestars of politically active youth, who felt it better to make their own music with harmonicas and guitars than to sully themselves with inauthentic and old-fashioned "commercial" music.

British invasion ▶ In 1964, the rock revolution went into full swing with the British invasion—the stunning success in the American marketplace of English pop groups, led by the Beatles and the Rolling Stones. These groups did two things. First, they brought back into circulation pop styles from the 1950s that had struck the mainstream as obscure or extreme—those of early rock and rollers Chuck Berry and Little Richard, rockabilly pioneers Carl Perkins and Gene Vincent, and Chicago blues artists Bo Diddley and Muddy Waters. Indeed, the Rolling Stones, who derived their name from a Muddy Waters song, originally labeled themselves a blues band. By marketing this raucous music as "cool," the British artists turned pop aesthetics on its head. They also brought in a new "anti-establishment" attitude, identifying this rebellion with youth culture.

Second, the British invasion also brought its own music. The Beatles were gifted songwriters: to the surprise of their handlers, John Lennon and Paul McCartney (and to a lesser extent, George Harrison) created the bulk of their own material. In doing so, they effected a crucial shift in the music industry away from "mere" performers toward **singer-songwriters**. Recording artists were soon expected to create their own songs, infusing them through performance with an unmistakable aura of authenticity. When Bob Dylan went electric in 1965, bringing his heightened, expressive poetry into the rock sphere, it became clear that rock and roll—or **rock**, as it soon became known—needed no outside interpreters. This left jazz musicians out in the cold. Throughout the 1960s, they tried giving the new rock tunes their own interpretive spin, but the results (like the 1966 *Basie's Beatles Bag*) were meaningless—not because the performances were inept, but because the entire jazz-rock enterprise now seemed suspect.

To be sure, the music business did not change overnight. Pop song "standards" continued to be written by the likes of Burt Bacharach (his inventive "Alfie" and the unavoidable "Raindrops Keep Falling on My Head"). There were new musicals, supplying an endless stream of hit songs and profits for record companies: *My Fair Lady* (1956, filmed in 1964) sold 5 million albums, and *The Sound of Music* (1959, filmed in 1965) and *Camelot* (1960, filmed in 1967) each sold 2 million. Jazz musicians continued to mine them for new material: the 1964 season of musicals included jazz versions by Cannonball Adderley (of *Fiddler on the Roof*), Duke Ellington (of *Mary Poppins*), and Louis Armstrong (of "Hello, Dolly!"). As the decade went on, though, even this material dried up. Industry executives nervously watched as musical soundtrack albums—their bread and butter—declined steadily in sales. The end of an era was in sight.

Record sales overall, however, did the opposite of decline. Beginning in 1955—when rock and roll records first began to appear—sales increased by about 36 percent per year, reaching $600 million in 1959. In the 1960s, the growth was astronomical. Sales broke the $1 billion mark in 1966 and the $2 billion mark by 1972. Everyone in the industry knew that these staggering increases were due to rock. Record companies inevitably adjusted, filling their staffs with business-savvy rock enthusiasts. Rock became a sprawling business, swallowing up opera and musicals (*Jesus Christ Superstar, Tommy, Hair*), bluegrass and country music (the folk-rock movement), the avant-garde (Frank Zappa, Captain Beefheart), and race music (Motown, soul). It even collided with world music: after the Indian virtuoso Ravi Shankar took a place of honor at the 1969 Woodstock concert in Bethel, New York, rock fans began to expect their virtuoso musicians to improvise over long stretches of time.

THE CHALLENGE TO JAZZ

In the late 1960s, rock groups began to shift away from the tight pop format of 45-rpm singles in favor of album-oriented loose improvisation (signaled by the shift from AM to FM radio). Groups like Cream, which teamed guitarist Eric Clapton with bassist Jack Bruce and drummer Ginger Baker (all originally jazz or blues fans from England), featured a freewheeling, blues-drenched improvisation that some compared to electrified jazz. In San Francisco, Jerry Garcia's Grateful Dead similarly favored extended "jams" that embedded improvisation in a broad context, including bluegrass, gospel, country, and blues. And in the virtuoso electric guitarist Jimi Hendrix, rock had its most formidable improviser, capable of stunning audiences with the intensity of his solos.

Within the more traditional pop sphere, groups like Blood, Sweat and Tears experienced extraordinary popular success by trading electric guitars for saxophones and trumpets. Not even jazz repertory was sacrosanct: on the group's second album (1967), which sold an astonishing 3 million copies, you could hear an eclectic reworking of Billie Holiday's "God Bless the Child." Later albums featured

Record business

The rock musician who appealed most to jazz musicians was guitarist Jimi Hendrix, who fused the blues with the raw power of amplified sound. Had he not died accidentally in 1970—just days before he was to meet with Gil Evans about a recording session—he may well have played an active role in jazz-rock fusion.

bits of Thelonious Monk mixed with Prokofiev. With results like that, who needed jazz musicians?

Jazz musicians who wanted a taste of success now faced a number of obstacles, each of which presented its own challenges:

YOUTH Rock was the music of the teenager—a term that had been in existence only since the 1940s, but by the 1960s denoted the huge demographic slice of the American population known as the "baby boomer" generation. Teenagers were affluent, with access to what historian Eric Hosbawm describes as "an unprecedented share of middle-class parents' prosperity." And they were permanent: to be sure, thirteen-year-olds grew up, but new ones inevitably took their place. The rock musicians they preferred were similarly young. The phrase "Don't trust anyone over thirty" made it difficult for older jazz musicians, who had spent their lives mastering their idiom, to believe they could ever again be accepted by a younger audience.

ELECTRONICS Rock was built on the electric guitar and remained indebted to the sheer power of amplification. Thanks to the stacks of amplifiers that now lined every rock stage, an electric guitarist could drown out an entire big band by playing a single chord. Rock musicians used new technologies with unbridled enthusiasm: *wah-wah* pedals, phasers, feedback, new electric keyboards and synthesizers all produced an entirely new range of timbres for the upcoming generation. Jazz was familiar with this kind of experimentation—indeed, it had pioneered the electric guitar in the 1930s—but struggled to keep up with the rapid pace of change.

RECORDINGS Rock musicians depended far more on the studio than on live performance—initially, probably, to compensate for weak-voiced singers. But technology made the studio infinitely more flexible. New multitracking systems made it possible to create entire sonic landscapes on a recording. A handful of pioneering artists like Lennon and McCartney with the Beatles and the Beach Boys' Brian Wilson broke down the barriers keeping young musicians out of the engineer's booth, and made studio production part of their creative process. Jazz musicians had made some efforts to master editing, but remained trapped in the belief that recordings should transparently demonstrate what a band sounds like in person.

RHYTHM Rock and roll originally came from the same loose rhythm as jazz—as Chuck Berry's "Rock and Roll Music" had announced, "It's got a backbeat, you can't lose it." But by the 1960s, its groove had shifted away from swing toward a steady, pounding, even eighth-note 4/4. Jazz musicians who had grown up on the more flexible, uneven eighth notes of swing found it hard to adjust; many refused to do so for aesthetic reasons.

GROUPS Rock groups were *bands*, submerging individual musicians into a collective sound. The loose combos of jazz were much more openly focused on the contribution of each musician—not only the soloist, but also the rhythm section. It would take a revolution in thought for jazz to come up with a new collective aesthetic, replacing the solo with a group-oriented creative process. This happened in the avant-garde, and it also happened in fusion.

VIRTUOSITY By the time of bebop, virtually every respectable jazz musician was capable of instrumental feats far beyond the norm. Rock had little patience with that kind of technique. Through the "do-it-yourself" ethos of the folk or blues revival and the naive primitivism of the teenage garage band, rock shifted attention toward other qualities—the band, the song, the singer. Not until rock itself moved more toward virtuosity would jazz musicians find a place in its aesthetic.

Funk

Ultimately, the fusion that began in the late 1960s was designed to meet each of these obstacles. It was electronic music, created in a studio by younger musicians, often in groups; it fused a strong dance-beat rhythm with a modified cult of jazz virtuosity. The vocabulary that allowed jazz musicians to create this fusion came not from mainstream rock but from a different kind of music: the contemporary version of race music, better known as soul or **funk**.

Although soul music (as we have seen) dated back to the 1950s, when Ray Charles redefined blackness through music by dragging religious grooves into the secular marketplace, and soul-jazz instrumentalists like Horace Silver and Jimmy Smith emphasized backbeat rhythms, a new and more intense kind of funk was born in the 1960s. Specifically, it was the revolutionary new music created by James Brown when he entered the national spotlight in 1965 with crossover hits like "I Got You (I Feel Good)" and "Papa's Got a Brand New Bag." Brown felt it first in the recording studio: "I had discovered that my strength was not in the horns, it was in the rhythm. I was hearing everything, even the guitars, like they were drums. On playbacks, when I saw the speakers jumping, vibrating a certain way, I knew that was it." Soon he had spawned an entire section of black pop music, infusing it with an African polyrhythmic intensity.

James Brown

Funk used rhythmic contrast in fascinating new ways. Unlike rock, where the prevailing 4/4 rhythmic groove dominated the texture, each layer in a funk or soul tune was independent rhythmically, allowing endless possibilities for inventive bassists, guitarists, and drummers to offer fresh new support.

© CHUCK STEWART

Fusion was inspired by the electrifying James Brown, seen here dancing with his horn section in the 1960s. Jazz musicians adopted his tight, multilayered rhythm section, while his flexible, open-ended tunes were perfect for modal improvisation.

Jazz drummers interested in this music had to learn to switch from a swing feeling to a new funk groove—but the best of them understood that there was freedom as well as responsibility in this new way of playing. Bassists moved away from walking-bass lines to more asymmetric, syncopated lines. Soloists understood that their lines were only one part of the overall texture, contributing to but not dominating the groove.

Funk offered an opportunity for jazz musicians to continue to draw on their mastery of chromatic harmony. Unlike rock, which often reduced its chords to their most basic forms, funk was harmonically sophisticated, supporting denser, jazz-oriented harmonies and opening the door for chromatically based semi-atonal sounds. Moreover, it was also open to modal improvisation. In James Brown's hands, a funk tune was flexible and open-ended, typically featuring lengthy stretches on a single harmony. The band would move to a contrasting bridge only on a cue from the vocalist.

Funk was a new dance groove—one that, like rock, was based on the steady eighth note. Young people could easily relate to it—as could young musicians, eager to find a way to link jazz with the dance music of their generation. Moreover, this dance groove was not opposed to harmonic improvisation: one of the most surprising and stimulating things fusion musicians discovered is that a steady beat was enough to hold their audience even when they explored the most dissonant harmonic territory.

Breaking Down Barriers

By 1967, jazz was in a state of crisis. Coltrane had died, leaving the free jazz movement without its most charismatic leader. The music was losing its audience, as nightclubs began closing and concerts drying up. Critics had started to take the new rock artists seriously, lifting the Beatles to new heights (with the Rolling Stones as a scruffy alternative). Even *Down Beat*, the main jazz trade magazine, now started including ads for electric guitars and turning toward rock. Seeing the writing on the wall, young jazz musicians started forming groups, like the Free Spirits and the 13th-Floor Elevators, that had the look and feel of rock bands. Something needed to be done to bridge the gap between jazz and pop. "Everybody was dropping acid and the prevailing attitude was 'Let's do something different,'" recalled guitarist Larry Coryell. "We were saying, 'We love Wes, but we also love Bob Dylan. We love Coltrane but we also love the Beatles. We love Miles but we also love the Rolling Stones.'"

Charles Lloyd ▸ The first groups to begin to break down the barriers found opportunities in the California jam-band scene. One was led by Charles Lloyd, a Coltrane-influenced tenor saxophonist. Born in 1938, Lloyd moved from Memphis to Los Angeles to study composition at the University of Southern California, and became known as a skillful arranger. He formed his own group in 1965; under the shrewd management of George Avakian, who understood the youth-oriented scene, he landed a spot at the 1966 Monterey Jazz Festival, where his music was suddenly labeled as "psychedelic jazz"—a stance Lloyd was only too happy to play up ("I play love vibrations," he told the press).

The group did not sound strikingly different from other jazz at the time—although Lloyd undoubtedly drew attention with his young rhythm section, which marked the electrifying debut of pianist Keith Jarrett and drummer Jack DeJohnette (see below). Lloyd benefited from the loose cultural boundaries on the San Francisco scene, where jazz drifted into a melting pot with many kinds of music. On the radio, he remembered, "They would play my music alongside Jimi Hendrix or the Grateful Dead, or Ravi Shankar. . . . All the San Francisco groups loved our music." On one San Francisco gig in 1966, Elvin Jones and the Joe Henderson Quartet appeared on the same stage as Jimi Hendrix, Big Mama Thornton, and the Jefferson Airplane.

In 1968, Tony Williams, the brilliant drummer with the Miles Davis Quintet of the 1960s, formed a group called Emergency with the electric guitarist John McLaughlin (see below), whom he brought over from the U.K., and organist Larry Young. The band was an attempt to revive the spirit of Williams's organ trio roots in Boston in the late 1950s and early 1960s, but with an aggressive edge. They began to explore a new sound, an organ trio playing "electric music": caustic, loud, hard-driving, harmonically dissonant, with extended improvisation. The group lasted only a few years, producing a handful of exciting but uneven recordings that failed to capture the band's intensity in live performance. Still, they pointed the way toward a hard-edged style of group improvisation that would form the basis for fusion.

Tony Williams

THE DAVIS BREAKTHROUGH

The breakthrough toward fusion happened only when it had captured the attention of the biggest name in jazz—Miles Davis. By 1968, Davis, by contemporary standards an old man (already over forty), had become dissatisfied with the direction taken by his postbop quintet. A reviewer who came to his apartment was startled to notice that piled on his coffee table were albums by the Fifth Dimension, which had just had a hit with "Up, Up, and Away"; and Sly and the Family Stone, one of the most daringly inventive funk groups.

Some of the change could be attributed to his new young wife, Betty Mabry. Having studied fashion design and worked as a model for youth-oriented magazines like *Jet* and *Seventeen*, Mabry understood the new look and embodied it in person: with her startling Afro and miniskirts, one musician remembered her as "walking eye-candy." She was also a musician who wrote pop arrangements and had taken the plunge as a singer, and counted Jimi Hendrix and Sly Stone among her friends.

Davis had always been searching for new artistic impulses to rescue him from the tired routines of modern jazz. As his jazz style became increasingly complicated, he yearned for a release. He heard it in the blues of Chicago great Muddy Waters, which offered the sound of simplicity in "the $1.50 drums and the harmonicas and the two-chord blues. . . . I had to get back to that now because what we had been doing was just getting really abstracted."

Rock put that kind of simplicity back into the spotlight, and Davis was determined to borrow from it. He began changing the instrumentation of his group, pushing his

Miles's Musicians Through the Years

The number of people invited by Miles Davis to play with his band became legend: just to be associated with the "master" was enough to entrance most players, including (for example) Keith Jarrett, a pianist who hated electronic instruments, but who nevertheless played electric piano for Miles. Musicians who played with him during the turbulent period from 1968 through 1971:

Herbie Hancock	Chick Corea
Tony Williams	Keith Jarrett
Wayne Shorter	Benny Maupin
Joe Zawinul	John McLaughlin
Jack DeJohnette	Dave Holland
Billy Cobham	

A different group was added to the ever-changing Davis roster in the 1970s:

John Scofield	Airto Moreira
Sonny Fortune	Michael Henderson
Dave Liebman	Pete Cosey
Steve Grossman	Mike Stern
Kenny Garrett	Bob Berg
Al Foster	George Duke

rhythm section to play their electric equivalents. Ron Carter didn't like the electric bass, so Davis replaced him with a young British player, Dave Holland. He also switched from the acoustic piano to the new electronic keyboards now available. These sounds were in the air: Cannonball Adderley had already introduced the electric piano of Joe Zawinul (who had borrowed it in turn from Ray Charles). By putting a Fender electric piano in front of Herbie Hancock, Davis hoped for a new direction as well as a new sound. When Hancock failed to return on time from a honeymoon in Brazil, he hired the young Chick Corea as an able replacement on keyboard. He also brought in Gil Evans, whose own band was moving in the same direction, to help arrange the sounds.

The results of these experiments can be heard on the 1968 album *Filles de Kilimanjaro,* a peculiar blend of modal jazz and abstracted soul rhythm, featuring harmonies floating over ostinato bass lines. Tony Williams's drum parts don't sound like "rock," but they are clearly influenced by the new music, and form a firm foundation for the shifting bass ostinatos that underscore most of the pieces. Davis quickly realized that by maintaining a steady beat, Williams could hold together complicated textures, no matter how bizarre the harmonies involved. "Mademoiselle Mabry" (all the song titles were in French) is based in part on Jimi Hendrix's "The Wind Cried Mary." The album was labeled "Direction in music by Miles Davis"—making it clear that the "music" could no longer be contained by the genre "jazz," and that Davis was fully in charge.

In a Silent Way

More dramatic changes came with his next album, *In a Silent Way.* Among the new musicians in the band was John McLaughlin (see below), who added the crucial missing ingredient to the jazz-rock mix: the distorted sound of an electric guitar. On the title track, Davis drastically simplified a tune by Joe Zawinul; in place of Zawinul's carefully crafted harmonic progression, Davis asked McLaughlin to play a simple E major chord, the most basic sound on the guitar. The musicians thought it was a rehearsal, but Davis shrewdly kept the tapes running. Their spontaneous interactions over this static harmonic background became part of the texture of the recording.

Increasingly, Davis came to rely on studio post-production. This was not new to jazz—as we have seen (Chapter 13), Charles Mingus edited his music to eliminate irrelevant solos; but Davis took advantage of the new technologies firmly in place at Columbia Records. Whatever happened in the studio was now raw material for future editing. Davis's partner was producer Teo Macero, who served for him the same role that producer George Martin played with the Beatles. At day's end, Macero cut and spliced the session's recordings into unexpected new patterns: "I had *carte blanche* to work with the material," he later said. "Shhh/Peaceful" was stitched together from hours of performing, interwoven into new shapes and patterns. Musicians on these recordings were often surprised—and pleased—to hear how their loose interactions were combined and recombined. The overall effect sacrificed the purposeful intensity of earlier jazz for a deeper sense of groove. *In a Silent Way* consisted of two long tracks, each taking up a full side of the LP recording, exploring the new rock atmosphere in depth. It was a startling change, as Davis acknowledged in an interview: "This one will scare the shit out of them."

Bitches Brew

Davis's leadership was sparse and intermittent, leaving plenty of room for his musicians. "He'd go out and play, and you'd follow," said Chick Corea. "Whenever he'd stop playing, he never told the group what to do, so we all went and did whatever." Earlier in the 1960s, the rhythm section from his quintet had learned to take advantage of the chance to create new textures on the spot—they called it "controlled freedom." By the end of the decade, Davis had gathered large conglomerations of musicians: two drummers, two bassists, two percussionists, a bass clarinet, an electric guitar, and the three electric keyboards of Hancock, Corea, and Zawinul. The texture was dense but light: while the musicians "had egos," Zawinul remembered, their respect for each other meant that "nobody stepped on anybody's feet." The musicians were a full generation younger than Davis and often looked the part, sporting casual hippie clothing and long hair. Yet Davis insisted that his music drew less from conventional rock than from the new currents in African American music: "I don't play rock, I play *black*."

During this time, Miles remained under contract to Columbia Records, which kept the jazz star for its cultural capital (much as it retained a contract with the classical pianist Vladimir Horowitz) even as the label as a whole moved solidly toward rock. Davis's recordings sold steadily, but at a volume that was soon overwhelmed by newer rock acts like Blood, Sweat and Tears. Davis must have seen how much jazz's audience had been eroded, and yearned for freedom from the "jazz" label. "If you stop calling me a *jazz* man," he apparently told Columbia producer Clive Davis, and sell him alongside Chicago and Blood, Sweat and Tears, "I'll sell more." The answer was his next album, *Bitches Brew*.

To record *Bitches Brew* (1969–70), hours were spent in the studio. "It was loose and tight at the same time," said Davis. "Everybody was alert to different possibilities that were coming up in the music." Some of the tunes came from his then-current band's repertory, but others took shape only after the fact through ingenious editing. Because each song was long—the title track lasted twenty-seven minutes—*Bitches Brew* was a sprawling double album, decorated with an elaborate drawing by the Israeli artist Mati Klarwein. No one in their right mind would have considered it "commercial": it was too dissonant, too texturally dense, and radio-unfriendly (although "Spanish Key" was released, in highly abbreviated form, as a single). Nevertheless, *Bitches Brew* found a niche in the new album-oriented rock of the late 1960s, selling a half million copies during its first year. Davis never looked back. Neither did the music industry, which now loudly trumpeted the new category, marked in the record store as "fusion."

■ MAHAVISHNU

Bitches Brew may have been the revolutionary album that launched fusion, but it could not serve as a model for other musicians. Instead, fusion as a style—the intense, electric-guitar sound—became shaped around the new, disciplined sound of the Mahavishnu Orchestra.

Mahavishnu was created by John McLaughlin (b. 1942), an English guitarist from Yorkshire. Like many young guitarists of the period, he was initially caught by the music of blues musicians from America, such as Muddy Waters and Lead Belly. To this he added the dazzling guitar of flamenco, which showed him how bluesy gestures could be linked with blindingly fast

John McLaughlin

Through the teachings of his guru, Sri Chinmoy (whose portrait is prominent in this early 1970s photo), John McLaughlin became devoted to Indian music. He brought Indian tala (meters) into the music of the Mahavishnu Orchestra, and in 1975 formed Shakti, an acoustic group featuring tabla player Zakir Hussain and Ravi Shankar's nephew, the violinist L. Shankar.

passagework and constantly shifting cross-rhythms. Recordings by Django Reinhardt and the modern guitarist Tal Farlow inspired him toward becoming a jazz musician; but he retained an openness to music of all kinds—including the rock that had begun to affect all youth culture in the 1960s. He soon began performing with the Graham Bond Organization, which placed him alongside future Cream members Ginger Baker and Jack Bruce.

It took an invitation by drummer Tony Williams to incite McLaughlin to come to New York in 1969. After a year of playing with Williams and Miles Davis, he was ready to strike out on his own. McLaughlin, fascinated by religion from the East, became drawn to the teachings of Sri Chinmoy, an Indian "New Age" guru who also counted rock guitarist Carlos Santana among his disciples. As a result, he immersed himself in the classical music of India, which offered a bewildering variety of unusual meters, or *tala*, for improvisation. It was Chinmoy's suggestion that led McLaughlin to give his band the unusual name of Mahavishnu Orchestra. By 1970, fusion was hot, and Mahavishnu was immediately signed by Columbia Records to a sizable advance. The risk paid off: the band's first two albums, *The Inner Mounting Flame* (1972) and *Birds of Fire* (1973), sold 700,000 copies—enough to allow a so-called jazz band to compete in the same league with the more popular rock bands.

It's easy to see how the Mahavishnu Orchestra could have competed in the world of rock. It was loud, fast, intensely distorted music, more suited to concert dates with ZZ Top and Emerson, Lake and Palmer than to the confined quarters of a jazz club. McLaughlin was out in front, playing a bizarre-looking electric guitar with two different necks—one six-stringed, the other twelve-stringed. Through his lengthy solos, played at sledgehammer volume, McLaughlin raised the level of virtuosity associated with rock guitarists like Hendrix to a new level. Yet he was also part of a band. A typical Mahavishnu tune would feature McLaughlin playing seamlessly alongside the amplified violin of Jerry Goodman. The rest of the band included Jan Hammer, a rock keyboardist who had to be convinced that a "jazz" group wouldn't damage his reputation, and drummer Billy Cobham, a rhythmic powerhouse who, like McLaughlin, had just played with Miles Davis.

Although it seemed to some that the Mahavishnu was "like a car that could only function at 100 miles per hour," it was also inventive. Rhythmically, it relied on *talas* from Indian music, which sometimes moved in groupings reminiscent of Dave Brubeck—five, seven, or nine—but could also be considerably more complicated: "Birds of Fire" asks the musicians to improvise in a meter of eighteen, while "The Dance of Maya" somehow squeezes a hard-driving boogie-woogie into a meter of twenty. Harmonically, the band played chords that were far removed from popular song. Some were known as **slash chords**—simple triads sitting precariously on top of completely unrelated bass roots. (The term comes from fake-book notation: an E major triad over a C bass would be shown as E/C, pronounced "E slash C.") These chords were not atonal—the triads offered a point of stability—but they pushed the harmony far into the realm of dissonance. Many of Mahavishnu's compositions and improvisations were built on such unstable combinations.

■ CHICK COREA (b. 1941) and RETURN TO FOREVER

One musician who used the Mahavishnu Orchestra's hard-focused style as a way to enter the fusion field that would be both artistically satisfying and commercially successful was keyboardist Chick Corea, who spent much of the 1970s with a guitar-based version of his group Return to Forever.

Born in Boston, Corea learned his jazz by transcribing the harmonic voicings of Horace Silver and mastering Bud Powell's solos on the keyboard. His tastes were broad, including Latin music (his first recording session was with Mongo Santamaria), Miles Davis's fusion, and avant-garde jazz. In particular, the intellectual quality of free improvisation appealed to him. Shortly after leaving Davis in 1970, he joined saxophonist Anthony Braxton and bassist Dave Holland in Circle, an avant-garde group that recorded six albums that year. But just as suddenly, he found this kind of improvisation alienating. "It was like group therapy, just getting together and letting our hair down," he said later. "Everybody yelled and screamed. Then after a while nobody cared." Religion forced a change in his attitude. After seeking help in Scientology, he formed the first of his groups known as Return to Forever in 1972. This band dabbled in fusion, mixing the Brazilian influence of vocalist Flora Purim and her husband, the percussionist Airto Moreira, with Corea's electric piano.

Within a few years, though, Corea had heard Mahavishnu, which made him rethink his goals. "More than my experience with Miles," Corea recalled, "John's band led me to want to turn the volume up and write music that was more dramatic and made your hair move." Jan Hammer's use of the synthesizer as a fluid, singing solo voice inspired him to switch to playing an entire rack of synthesizers. To capture the sound of McLaughlin's lead, he hired guitarist Bill Connors, who was replaced a year later by Al DiMeola, a pyrotechnic soloist who once proclaimed that his goal was "to be the fastest guitarist in the world." During the mid-1970s, Return to Forever was a powerful vehicle for Corea's tautly disciplined compositions, using the volume and intensity of the Mahavishnu sound to overwhelm its audiences.

The mid-1970s version of Return to Forever matched Chick Corea's compositional genius with the volume and intensity of the Mahavishnu Orchestra. Left to right: Lenny White, drums; Corea; Al DiMeola, guitar; Stanley Clarke, bass.

■ WEATHER REPORT

The most artistically and commercially successful fusion group of the 1970s was Weather Report. Like the others, it too was a band with roots in the Miles Davis experience: one of its founders was Joe Zawinul, and the other, Wayne Shorter, had been Davis's saxophonist from 1964 to 1970. While other fusion bands came and went, Zawinul and Shorter's partnership lasted uninterrupted for a decade and a half, evolving from its loose, experimental playing in the early 1970s to a hard-driving, funk-oriented band that topped the charts while delighting critics.

Wayne Shorter

As we have seen (Chapter 15), Shorter was a leading voice in Miles Davis's 1960s quintet. He also led his own postbop groups that released no fewer than ten albums in those same years, each full of his inventive, harmonically original compositions. Shorter contributed new tunes to Weather Report's book and added his saxophone solos, although to many, the rich ensemble textures submerged his solo voice. (Drummer Jack DeJohnette summed up the attitude of a generation by entitling one tune "Where or Wayne.")

Joe Zawinul

The strong hand in the group was Zawinul, who came to the United States from his home country of Austria, where he survived the hardships of World War II in countryside music camps that sheltered its most talented youngsters. There he experimented with his first instrument, the accordion, by gluing felt onto the soundboard, creating a pungent nasal timbre that prefigured his later synthesizer style. By 1959, he had arrived in America, where he accompanied the vocalist Dinah Washington before joining Cannonball Adderley's band. For the next decade, Zawinul was the only white musician in his band—a decision that reflected a love for black Americans he had cultivated in Austria, listening to jazz and watching movies like the 1942 *Stormy Weather* (featuring Cab Calloway and Lena Horne) over and over. "To me," he later said, black Americans "are the easiest to understand, the closest to my environment."

© LEE TANNER

The dominant fusion band of the 1970s and 1980s was Weather Report, which arose from the imaginations of keyboardist Joe Zawinul (seen here in 1972, adjusting the volume on his Fender Rhodes electric piano) and soprano saxophonist Wayne Shorter.

Weather Report became a mecca for the new sounds of technology. Inspired by the sound of Ray Charles's group, Zawinul began to play the electric piano in the mid-1960s, using it to write and perform on Adderley's biggest hit, "Mercy, Mercy, Mercy." He soon became a master of the synthesizer, using it extensively beginning with Weather Report's third album, *Sweetnighter*. But he despised the preset sounds on his instruments, working deep into the equipment to create his own timbres, sometimes detuning the intervals to mimic non-Western instruments. Mastering the ARP 2600 even required him to play backward, using an inverted keyboard with the top notes starting on the left-hand side.

In the long run, the band started moving away from free-jazz improvisations and atmospheric textures toward straight-ahead African American popular grooves. "We were a black band," Zawinul explained. "In spite of me not being black, it was always a black band, more or less." The albums became funkier: *Black Market* (1975) opened with its title track, a percussive, riff-oriented tune that rolled along on its syncopated, pentatonic bass line. But the band did not find its center of gravity until it stumbled onto a new member.

Zawinul was standing outside the Gusman Theater in Miami when a young man walked up and introduced himself: "Excuse me, Mr. Zawinul, my name is John Francis Pastorius III, and I am the greatest bass player in the world."

This unabashed introduction proved to be well grounded. Jaco Pastorius was the first bassist who did not play acoustic. He was born the year the electric bass was invented and first marketed. For many years, it was used primarily in small dance bands, the poor relation to its delicate and expensive acoustic cousin. Musicians put up with its generally muddy sound only because they could easily increase the volume at will. But they soon found a way to make the instrument speak: James Jamerson, for example, used his electric bass to create the lively, dancing bass lines that energized dozens of Motown hits in the 1960s. It took a virtuoso of Pastorius's character to show that the same creative intensity could be applied to jazz.

Jaco Pastorius

Pastorius grew up in Fort Lauderdale, Florida, where he learned his craft by playing in local rhythm and blues bands. He loved his electric bass, creating his own version with the frets removed (the holes filled in by wood filler), flying over the soundboard with extraordinary quickness. By manipulating the controls on his amplifier, he developed a rich, singing sound on the instrument—"that ballad voice," Zawinul called it. His skills astonished the jazz community. On his first album, *Jaco Pastorius*, he sealed his claim on the jazz tradition by playing the bebop standard "Donna Lee" (a tune that even its composer, Miles Davis, found difficult) as a solo number.

In a career that lasted barely a decade, Jaco Pastorius brought the electric bass to the center of fusion. In a reflective mood, he could play warm melodies with a singing timbre, while on faster tunes he could unleash endless torrents of notes. Philadelphia, 1978.

Pastorius became "the warhead" with Weather Report, firmly grounding its rhythm section while playing fluid melodic lines one would normally expect from a guitarist. (In concert, he even played a feedback solo à la Hendrix.) "Jaco . . . brought the white kids in," Zawinul remembered. "He was all of a sudden a real white All-American folk hero." With this new foundation, Weather Report reached its peak with the best-selling 1976 recording *Heavy Weather*. This album featured a splendid Zawinul composition, "Birdland," a tribute to the New York club named after Charlie Parker. Although its overall texture is heavy-driving funk, it evokes a genial, big-band feeling in its refrain. Zawinul's skill as a composer is evident here: the piece is built on some of the simplest aspects of music—the G major scale and the G blues scale—but leaves us hanging for minutes at a time. Only with the climactic refrain do we feel we have arrived.

"Teen Town"

Named after a neighborhood in Miami, "Teen Town" displays Pastorius's creative efforts. On this recording, he plays two roles: the electric bass soloist and the substitute drummer. The tune features a peculiar chord progression, cycling through four major triads. The chords are simple but ambiguous: no one key can contain them all. Over this shifting background, Pastorius plays a melody line that snakes its way through different rhythmic shapes and unexpected accents. It sounds improvised but is composed, as we can

major triad: three-note chord, with bottom interval a major third (e.g., C-E-G, B♭-D-F)

tell when it begins to repeat. Still, there are moments when Pastorius the improviser trumps Pastorius the composer, adjusting his line to the heat of performance.

While Pastorius is clearly in front, the tune is also a dialogue—sometimes with Shorter, who plays brief solos that hint at his remarkable melodic invention, but more often with Zawinul on keyboards. By the end of the performance, the dialogue is wide open. In live performance, Weather Report would extend this last section, allowing room for Shorter and Zawinul to trade melodic and harmonic ideas with Pastorius, before the final lick closed the tune off.

4.7

🎧 teen town

WEATHER REPORT

Joe Zawinul, Fender Rhodes piano, melodica, Oberheim polyphonic synthesizer, ARP 2600; Wayne Shorter, soprano saxophone; Jaco Pastorius, electric bass, drums; Manolo Badrena, congas

- Label: *Heavy Weather,* Columbia CK 65108; *X2 (Heavy Weather/Black Market)* (Columbia/Legacy 886973301128)
- Date: 1976
- Style: fusion
- Form: eight-measure cycle

What to listen for:

- up-tempo 1970s dance groove
- peculiar harmonic progression in eight-bar cycle
- interchange between Pastorius and Shorter and between Pastorious and Zawinul

INTRODUCTION

0:00   A series of rapid-fire snare drum hits opens the tune.

0:01   Shorter on soprano saxophone and Zawinul on synthesizer play the melody harmonized in thirds (Zawinul on top, Shorter below). Behind them, the drummer begins a rapid, steady pattern, with high-hat cymbal accents on the backbeat and the snare falling on the third beat of the measure. Distantly in the background, the percussionist adds Latin rhythms.

0:03   The drummer punctuates the space in between melody phrases with loud bass drum accents.

CHORUS 1

0:08   An accented pair of high notes announces the first chorus. Pastorius begins a lightning-fast line on electric bass, accompanied by the synthesizer. The chords in the background are **major triads** from different keys: each new chord cancels out the previous one.

CHORUS 2

0:16   The chords begin to repeat, establishing an eight-bar cycle. Pastorius continues his line, changing the rhythm and pitches.

CHORUS 3

0:23   Pastorius's line bridges the boundary between one chorus and the next. Underneath, Shorter emerges from the background with long-held saxophone notes.

0:27   Pastorius's line rises in volume and pitch.

0:29   A short bluesy phrase is followed by bass drum accents.

CHORUS 4

0:31 On this chorus, Pastorius plays the pair of accented high notes, this time doubled by the drums.

0:34 His line becomes intensely **syncopated**. In its wake, the drummer answers with his own snare drum and bass drum accents.

0:38 Pastorius plays the repeated high notes again, linking them to a longer melody line.

CHORUS 5

0:39 Pastorius repeats the line from the first chorus note for note, making it clear that the solo is a composed piece, not an improvisation.

0:41 The first phrase is answered by short decorative passages by Shorter.
0:45 After the next phrase, the drummer lays a loud bass drum accent right on the downbeat.

CHORUS 6

0:46 Pastorius repeats the line from the second chorus.

0:49 The end of his line is doubled by sharp snare drum accents.

CHORUS 7

0:53 Pastorius's line disappears, replaced by the synthesizer. Unlike Pastorius's rapid-fire solo, it's slow, drawing attention to the increasingly dissonant synthesizer chords behind.

0:59 Pastorius reenters.

CHORUS 8

1:01 After playing only a single phrase, Pastorius drops out again. In the absence of melodic activity, the bass and snare drums add syncopated **fills**.

INTERLUDE (INTRODUCTION)

1:08 Zawinul and Shorter play the introductory melody again, this time with the synthesizer on a softer and more resonant timbre.

1:23 At the end of the second phrase, the harmony suddenly shifts into a new direction: the piece has **modulated** to a new key.

CHORUS 9

1:24 Doubled by synthesizer, the bass plays a mighty ascending line. Each phrase is answered by a loud "boom" from the drums.

CHORUS 10

1:31 Over the bass line, the synthesizer adds a slow line that rises **chromatically**.

CHORUS 11

1:39 The synthesizer line rises until it disappears into the upper range. The background chords, now played by an ethereal electric piano, become more extended and dissonant.

CHORUS 12

1:47 Shorter plays a few tentative notes on saxophone before retreating to silence. In his absence, the drummer fills in with syncopated accents.

CHORUS 13

1:54 The chord progression is doubled by a slow synthesizer line.

CHORUS 14

2:02 Pastorius begins improvising in the style of the opening chorus. His line is dissonant against the background chords.

CHORUS 15

2:09 Pastorius begins with the phrase that opened the fifth chorus, but sends it off into an unexpected direction.

2:13 Shorter sneaks in with a descending line.

2:16 Pastorius ends the chorus with a closing phrase: a rhythmically catchy lick using just two notes.

CHORUS 16

2:17 The texture thins out. It becomes easier to hear the conga drums improvising alongside the drumming.

2:23 Pastorius repeats the closing phrase from the end of the last chorus.

CHORUS 17

2:24 Shorter plays another short solo.

2:30 Pastorius repeats the closing phrase.

CODA

2:31 The harmony suddenly comes to a stop on a sustained chord. The drumming continues.

2:38 The drummer adds ferocious bass drum accents, culminating in a cymbal crash.

2:40 The sound of the drummer becomes distant, as if heard from far away.

2:42 The synthesizer enters with the opening of the introduction.

2:46 The harmony shifts in unexpected directions. The final chord is heard over the accented pair of high notes.

Pastorius's fall was as steep as his climb. Within a few years after joining Weather Report, he was deep into drugs, almost daring himself to perform his complicated solos in states of extreme intoxication. By 1982, he had left the group, and quickly fell into a state of mental illness. By the end he was homeless, living out on the streets. His end was violent: one night in 1987, he was badly beaten by a bouncer as he tried to break into a nightclub in his hometown of Fort Lauderdale. He never recovered from his injuries, dying a week later at age thirty-five, a shadow of himself.

◼ CHAMELEON: HERBIE HANCOCK (b. 1940)

One of the ironies of the 1970s is that two of its most popular jazz stars were pianists of extraordinary ability who managed, somehow, to sell their music based on its simplicity. During his years with Miles Davis, Herbie Hancock had already established himself as a postbop composer of subtlety and bristling complexity. Yet by the early 1970s, under the name Headhunters, he had created a mixture of funk and jazz that was little more than syncopated bass lines repeated and extended ad infinitum. He once observed: "We jazz listeners tend, 90% of the time, to like clever, complex treatments of simple ideas. That's what we respect. . . . But what I found out is that . . . there's a much more subtle kind of challenge in going towards the simple."

Keith Jarrett (see below) seemed even less likely to break through with the public—indeed, he despised rock, rejecting its electronic paraphernalia ("I can get toys in a toy shop," he sniffed) and preferring to play his unamplified acoustic piano in hushed silence. Yet his biggest album, *The Köln Concert*, enraptured listeners with extended repetitions of gospel grooves and simple ostinatos.

Hancock's most famous tune is "Chameleon," and it's hard to avoid applying this title to his ability to adapt to new surroundings in an instant. Hancock manages to keep several careers in motion simultaneously. He is a superb postbop pianist who is also a pop performer in 1970s funk, 1980s hip-hop, and contemporary duets with Sting, Christina Aguilera, and Josh Groban. In concert, he will appear simultaneously at a Steinway piano and a "keytar" (a portmanteau of keyboard and guitar), playing acoustic jazz as well as contemporary R & B tunes. Everyone respects him, but no one knows how to pin him down.

Early Years

Born in Chicago, Hancock grew up playing classical music well enough to win a concerto competition at age eleven, as well as rhythm and blues. He soon drifted into jazz, listening to Bill Evans and Oscar Peterson and learning how to play bluesy. By the time he had become a professional jazz musician, he had developed an extraordinary ear for harmony—how to voice it to suit his expressive needs, how to work it into every fabric of his compositions. In the 1960s, everyone in jazz knew his album *Maiden Voyage,* with its title track suspended on cool ambiguous harmonies and the innovative use of slash chords on "Dolphin Dance."

Yet Hancock had always had an ear for the pop world. Early in his career, he wrote "Watermelon Man," a disarmingly simple blues tune that evoked the vendors on his Chicago street in the summer. The word "watermelon" had its dangers: thanks to minstrel shows, it evoked decades of racist stereotypes in which that succulent fruit was the favorite of plantation "darkies." Using the title required courage. "I looked at myself in the mirror," Hancock remembered, saying, "'Now wait a minute, man. You are projecting something from the black experience, tell what the thing is. What are you ashamed of?'" In the hands of Mongo Santamaria (see Chapter 16), it became his first popular hit.

Once the rock revolution was underway, Hancock, who had studied electrical engineering in college, found a new fascination for the keyboards that Miles Davis shoved in his direction. Immediately after leaving Davis in 1970, he formed a highly experimental group, combining his complex postbop jazz impulses with textures created by an array of synthesizers (helped out by electronic wizard Patrick Gleeson). This was an exciting band for him, one in which everyone had adopted an African name: bass clarinetist Bennie Maupin was Mwile, trumpeter Eddie Henderson was Mganga, while Hancock reserved for himself the title Mwandishi—Swahili for "composer."

The group struggled, though, and Hancock began to feel he had made a mistake. He was by this time practicing Nichiren Shoshu Buddhism, a religion that required its devotees to chant an invocation. During his meditations, Hancock came to realize he had been a "jazz snob." The music he *really* admired was the new funk sound of James Brown, Sly and the Family Stone, and Tower of Power. "I decided that it was now time to try some funky stuff myself and get me some cats who could play that kind of music."

The harmonic sophistication of Herbie Hancock, seen here at a 1963 recording session, appealed directly to the jazz aficionado. Yet his best-selling songs fit squarely into pop territory.

PHOTO BY FRANCIS WOLFF/© MOSAIC IMAGES LLC

Headhunters

He recast his band as the Headhunters, finding new musicians with little jazz experience but with a knowledge of funk: the drummer Harvey Mason, who could improvise expertly within a funk groove; Paul Jackson, master of syncopated bass lines; and percussionist Bill Summers, who brought with him the traditional West African music he had studied at the University of California at Berkeley. The music they recorded on their 1974 album of the same name spoke a new language: simple, yet intensely polyrhythmic. The big hit, "Chameleon," was little more than a simple bass line locked into a steady clave rhythm that cycled back and forth between two chords. Over this foundation, Hancock added layer after layer, recreating the web of sounds that energized a James Brown recording, and using his electronic keyboards instead of rhythm guitars. Although the piece lasts over fifteen minutes, shifting to a new bass ostinato halfway through that provides space for Hancock to explore more subtle harmonizations, it was the simplicity of the piece that won him a mass audience.

Some people disliked *Head Hunters*, feeling that in trying to combine jazz and funk, Hancock was doing neither. "I don't even think this is well-done funk," Lester Bowie complained in a Blindfold Test in 1979. "They were basically jazz cats—they don't know nothing about funk, that's why they sound so funny. They ain't been on the road up and down doing that stuff. . . . It's beat-your-head-into-the-concrete type music." Hancock was hurt by this criticism, but not by the distinction between jazz and funk. "Some of the dance music I do," he once said, "is not done for art." When he balanced his inventive complexity with the duties of simplicity, the results could be devastating: albums like *Thrust* (1974) and *Man-Child* (1975) wove a jazz sensibility into modern funk grooves.

Not every album worked. Hancock's disco efforts in the late 1970s were particularly lame, marred by excessive repetition ("We thought it would be hypnotic rather than monotonous," he later explained) and his use of the Vocoder, an electronic device invented by Wendy Carlos and Walter Moog that allowed his spoken voice to be converted into a spooky, electronically modified keyboard sound. But in the early 1980s, while in Los Angeles, he was sent tapes by Bill Laswell and Michael Beinhorn, then working with the hip-hop group Material in Brooklyn, featuring the novel sound of scratching by turntablist Grand Mixer DXT. Intrigued by what he heard, Hancock added his own melody on top. The end result, released as "Rockit" (1983), became an underground success, complete with MTV video (with robots banging their heads in time with the music). These days, Hancock is a familiar presence in the pop world, as comfortable in the world of hip-hop as he is within the jazz tradition.

■ KEITH JARRETT (b. 1945)

Keith Jarrett is a difficult and highly idiosyncratic pianist. When he improvises, he grunts and yowls (which can be heard on most of his recordings). While his hands stay perfectly balanced on the keyboard, his body seems possessed. Gyrating and twisting, his contortions often push him off the bench into areas far below the keyboard. He is notoriously intolerant of distractions, such as flash photography or inattentive audiences, and has at times simply refused to play. Nevertheless, he has attracted a wide audience, because his keyboard playing is among the best in jazz today.

Jarrett was born in Allentown, Pennsylvania, and quickly became a musical prodigy with classical training. Along the way he learned to improvise, a skill that earned him a spot at the Berklee School in Boston. After a brief stint in Art Blakey's Messengers, he played in the Charles Lloyd Quartet (see p. 480), where his extravagant improvisations caught public attention. For a few years, he survived a stint with Miles Davis, a remarkable feat for someone who believes that fusion was a mistake. "The main reason I joined the band was that I didn't *like* the band," he explained. "I liked what Miles was playing very much and I hated the rest of the band playing together." He tolerated electric pianos only out of a desire to help Davis achieve his artistic goals, writing about the band's recordings at the Cellar Door, a Washington, D.C., club: "You don't usually see this kind of comet go by more than once or twice in a lifetime."

FRANK DRIGGS COLLECTION

Keith Jarrett, shown playing with bassist Cecil McBee, burst onto the jazz scene in the late 1960s with the Charles Lloyd Quartet. He's probably the most eclectic pianist active today, his irrepressible creativity surfacing in free jazz, acoustic fusion, and traditional jazz standards.

The Köln Concert

Jarrett's best-known music is restricted to the piano. His improvisations ranged widely, sometimes simple and meditative, other times flashing by blindingly fast, but always with a profound melodic quality. Performances went on for as long as Jarrett felt necessary: one series from Japan, *The Sun Bear Concerts*, stretched out to a full ten LPs. The most famous is *The Köln Concert* (1975), a double LP set that, having sold more than 4 million copies, ranks among the top-selling jazz albums of all time. According to Jarrett, everything about the concert was wrong: "It was the wrong piano; we had bad food in a hot restaurant; and I hadn't slept for two days. . . . But I knew something special was happening when I started playing."

The Köln Concert, recorded live in Cologne, Germany, brought his music to people who were not jazz fans but who were attracted by a different kind of fusion: one that brought jazz into a compelling, real-time mixture with gospel, folk music, and whatever else captured Jarrett's attention in the spur of the moment. "I was trying to get rid of all the way of playing that was normal," he explained, "and just leave a giant hole to jump into when I finally went there." The slew of New Age pianists he has inspired have spun simple imitation of his style into endless albums. For Jarrett, playing is a spiritual experience, one that has lasted over the decades, with recorded concerts in Tokyo, Milan's La Scala, and New York's Carnegie Hall.

American and Euopean Concerts

Jarrett's activity outside of solo piano is vast and diffuse, fueled less by a desire to please his audience than by inner inspiration. His albums range over classical music (some recorded on pipe organ and clavichord), avant-garde improvisations, and spiritual practices (for example, *Hymns*, dedicated to the Sufis). There is even a folk-rock album.

In the 1970s, Jarrett divided his time between two different quartets, one American and the other European. The American group pitted him firmly within avant-garde jazz: surrounded by bassist Charlie Haden, tenor saxophonist Dewey Redman (both had played with Ornette Coleman), and drummer Paul Motian, Jarrett was inspired to create a wide spectrum of pieces running from gospel to free jazz, often with him leaving the piano to pick up a soprano saxophone or bass recorder. His European group paired him with the Norwegian saxophonist Jan Garbarek (see below), and was filled out with other musicians from Scandinavia: drummer Jon Christensen and bassist Palle Danielsson. This group was equally far-ranging but less abrasive in approach. According to Manfred Eicher, who recorded the group for his ECM records, Scandinavian musicians "play a different blues. It's not of urban America . . . they know isolation and they know stillness and they know tranquility because that is all around them."

🎧 "Long as You Know You're Living Yours"

Jarrett's "different blues" can be heard on this recording, which took place not in the United States but in Oslo, Norway. The tune, with its intriguingly long title, is one of Jarrett's ebullient gospel pieces, a delightful romp in F major introduced by an open-ended vamp. The melody seems simple but is anything but. The harmonies shift unpredictably back and forth, and the rhythm of the tune is slippery, never pausing before launching off on another tangent. The tune has no form to speak of: it unfolds, phrase after phrase, over a sprawling thirty measures.

It is a surprise, then, when the tune suddenly shifts into unexpected territory. The bass moves up to a new note and becomes stuck on a pedal point. Jarrett's harmonies move away to dissonant chords but obsessively return again and again. Over the drummer's increasingly agitated accompaniment, Jan Garbarek on tenor saxophone plays a wonderful modal improvisation, starting low before inching his way upward to his highest register. We hold our breath, waiting to hear how it turns out—and the answer, once again, is deceptively simple: a return to the opening melody, now heard as the triumphant answer to all the turmoil of the interlude, safely relegated to the past.

LISTENING GUIDE

4.8

🎧 long as you know you're living yours

KEITH JARRETT

Keith Jarrett, piano; Jan Garbarek, tenor saxophone; Palle Danielsson, bass; Jon Christensen, drums

- Label: *Belonging*, ECM 1050 (829115)
- Date: 1974
- Style: acoustic jazz-pop fusion
- Form: free-form gospel

What to listen for:

- jazz-gospel groove
- vamp at beginning and at 4:26, sprinkled with dissonant chords
- surprising move in bass to pedal point on A at 2:45
- improvisation by Garbarek, into his highest register

VAMP

0:00   Jarrett plays a few chords on the upbeat to introduce the **vamp**—a short, repeated chord progression that precedes the main melody.

0:01   Jarrett's chords cycle back and forth between the **tonic** and the **subdominant**, creating a gospel flavor. The bassist plays a syncopated line, landing solidly on the tonic on virtually every downbeat. The drummer plays in straight eighth notes, accenting strongly on the main beat of each measure while adding syncopated fills in between.

0:16   Jarrett adds a chord that increases the tension by ratcheting up the level of dissonance.

0:33   After playing the tonic in the bass, Jarrett sounds as though he's abandoning the chordal vamp for the main melody. Yet a few notes later, he quickly retreats.

0:49   Again, he intensifies the sense of harmonic movement by adding an extra chord.

HEAD

0:59   Garbarek (saxophone) finally enters with the main melody, doubled by Jarrett's piano—a simple diatonic melody, with unpredictable **syncopations**.

1:05   The harmony moves to a new chord, suggesting a half cadence on the dominant; the tune doesn't pause, but continues in its syncopated way.

1:10   The harmony returns to the tonic.

1:17   A new phrase begins on the dominant chord.

1:28   New chords lead to a strong cadence, which comes a few seconds later.

1:32   A new phrase of the melody begins and remains on the tonic.

1:39   The melody becomes more wide-ranging, soaring to the upper tonic and spreading out rhythmically in **triplets**.

HEAD

1:52   The melody ends; but Jarrett immediately begins it again, prompting Garbarek to follow after just a few notes. The melody follows the same pattern as before.

INTERLUDE

2:45   The bass unexpectedly moves up from the tonic to a new note, A—the same note that Garbarek sustains on the saxophone. The bass will remain on this note for the next minute and a half.

2:47   Jarrett's first chords are sharply dissonant; in a few seconds, they resolve back to the main chord (A7). Throughout this passage, Jarrett moves back and forth between the stability of the main chord and his highly inventive dissonances.

2:53   Garbarek rises from the A by a half step, creating a sharply dissonant note that resolves a few seconds later.

2:59   By way of contrast, Garbarek descends to a lower-pitched melody, which will eventually resolve to a lower note.

3:13   Surprising us by jumping in ahead of the beat, Garbarek soars upward to a new high note (C-sharp); he gradually descends to a low point by 3:21.

3:21   The line soars upward to the same note before descending once again.

3:26   The drummer's improvisation becomes more unpredictable, his intense accents disturbing the previously steady 4/4 accompaniment.

3:39   Garbarek fastens onto a three-note rhythmic motive (short-short-long).

3:44   He rises to a new high note, rocking ecstatically back and forth on a polyrhythmic rhythm with distorted timbre.

3:50   Sounding a bit like Coltrane, Garbarek ascends yet higher, straining with distorted timbre.

3:56   Having reached a note several octaves above the place where he started, Garbarek pushes the limit of his playing abilities.

4:01   Somehow, he manages to move up *slightly* higher.

4:05   The climax is over: a steadier rhythm in the drums signals that the band will draw a close to this episode. Garbarek steadily descends.

4:12   As the snare drum marks time, Garbarek settles on a lower note. Jarrett plays the basic A7 clearly on the downbeat.

VAMP

4:26 The harmony suddenly relaxes to the tonic. The bass, now free from its pedal point, plays ecstatic **glissandos**.

4:32 For a brief moment, we can hear Jarrett's voice in the background.

4:41 The piano stops for a few measures; this makes it easier to hear the drummer accenting the main beats on the cymbals.

4:51 Jarrett adds a brief but intense dissonance to the vamp.

4:56 He begins hinting at the head, playing a few of its melodic ideas lightly and leaving lots of space to be filled in by the bass.

5:04 Yet another opportunity to hear Jarrett's voice in the texture.

HEAD

5:09 Jarrett and Garbarek return to the opening melody. For the next minute, the band joyfully plays through the head with renewed intensity.

6:02 The piece finally ends on the tonic, slowly decaying in volume.

■ PAT METHENY (b. 1954)

Fusion entered a new phase when it was passed on from veterans like Miles Davis to young musicians who were fluent in contemporary pop. These musicians no longer treated rock as an exotic seasoning; they had learned it as the music of their own generation, a basic language that would require jazz to fundamentally change its nature.

Such was the case with the guitarist Pat Metheny. Born in Lee's Summit, Missouri, near the very center of the continent, he was initially infatuated with Wes Montgomery. By listening to album after album, he learned the guitarist's basic tricks: how to play in octaves, how to use the thumb. But other sounds filtered in through the radio: Bob Dylan, the Beatles, the country music of Waylon Jennings, Brazilian bossa novas. His music would embrace it all, his guitar drawing jazz into an ongoing dialogue with the whole new landscape of pop music.

Metheny entered the jazz field professionally as a teenager. By 1975, he had played with vibraphonist Gary Burton (himself an early aficionado of fusion) and recorded his first album, *Bright Size Life*, with the young Jaco Pastorius on bass. His sound is already fully formed on this album: a warm tone from a hollow-bodied guitar, spread out through two amplifiers and a decay unit to a rich, singing voice. His lines are broad and melodic, and his compositions, often explicit in their geographical references ("Missouri Uncompromised," "Omaha Celebration"), betray a country openness. He soon found a composing partner in Lyle Mays, an introverted pianist whose intellectual musical ideas fused with Metheny's lyricism. The two formed the Pat Metheny Group in 1977, launching the long-haired guitarist as the fresh face of fusion jazz.

Pat Metheny Group

Jazz had long struggled to be heard against the dominant guitar sound of 1960s rock. Metheny was the first musician of his generation to reclaim the guitar as a solo jazz voice. His sound is immediately recognizable, even as his band has added new electronic voices, such as the guitar synthesizer. Melody dominates the ensemble: on some recordings, the guitar is amplified by a voice, giving it a warmer, richer sound. At times, the balance spills over into pop. Any given performance includes a full array of amplifiers and synthesizers; some of the background sound is generated by sequencers, spinning out loops created in advance. But the jazz element is what Metheny prizes most. He studied the tradition, familiarizing himself with music going back to Louis Armstrong, and can flesh out his compositions with spontaneously improvised melodic ideas.

In fact, Metheny is something of a jazz nerd. During his youthful radio-listening days, he also heard the music of Ornette Coleman, and some of that peculiar avant-garde sensibility is present in the guitarist's music. On the album *80/81*, he set himself against bassist Charlie Haden and saxophonist Dewey Redman, risking his fusion sound on the freefloating challenge of Ornette's tunes. In 1985, he recorded an album featuring Coleman himself (and his band Prime Time, which included Ornette's son Denardo on drums), titled *Song X*. Metheny is almost deferential to his elder, expressing the openness and optimism of Coleman's music by adding yet another layer to the "harmolodic" texture.

One of the first members of the rock generation to tackle fusion, Pat Metheny has been recording albums for over thirty years. His distinctive amplified hollow-body guitar has graced many pop-oriented projects, but he has also recorded with avant-garde giant Ornette Coleman. Philadelphia, 1979.

WORLD MUSIC

A different type of fusion pulls in music not only from outside the jazz tradition, but outside the United States. We might call it "crossover" or "world music."

Jan Garbarek (heard on "Long as You Know You're Living Yours") provides a good example. He was born a displaced person, the son of a Polish father who had been sent to Norway during World War II to build railroads for the Nazis. Growing up in Norway, he became infatuated with John Coltrane, especially his use of Third World music in his 1960s albums. The musicians who visited Norway brought startling juxtapositions of culture. The trumpeter Don Cherry, part black and part Native American, refused to act according to any stereotype: dressed in African garb, he recited Indian philosophy and insisted to his Norwegian audience that they take their folk heritage seriously. Later, George Russell moved to Oslo, bringing with him a wide-open theoretical approach capable of embracing Indonesian gamelan music, European classical music, and bebop. Garbarek became a jazz ethnomusicologist, learning to sing folk traditions and infusing his music with their essence. For over thirty years, he has recorded his distinctive blend of music, which he refuses to call jazz—much as he refuses to call *anything* after *Bitches Brew* by that name. It is simply Norwegian music. We could multiply his example by the hundreds to take in all the music that fuses jazz with overseas traditions.

■ PAUL WINTER CONSORT

There are other ways for jazz to be global. Paul Winter, for example, has taken on stewardship of the entire earth. He began as a straight-ahead saxophonist who served as cultural ambassador in Latin America and Brazil, where he became entranced by the folk traditions he heard. By 1967, his band had morphed into the Paul Winter Consort—a term he borrowed from

Elizabethan music for its evocation of diversity. Winter soon began to draw from unusual sources—the cry of the wolf, the singing of humpbacked whales—and even performed for the whales in the North Pacific. Ranging from high-pitched squeals to earth-rattling depths, whale songs became the basis for a new kind of fusion, marketed through Winter Consort recordings such as *Common Ground* in 1978. Later recordings have placed him in sacred space (his *Missa Gaia* is set in the Cathedral of St. John the Divine in New York City) and deep in the wilderness (several take place in the Grand Canyon).

■ OREGON

The theme for the Consort was "Icarus"—an arching folk-like melody situated within complex jazz harmony. The composer, Ralph Towner, joined several other musicians in the Winter Consort when they broke away to form their own group in 1970. For more than thirty years, this band, called Oregon, has pioneered the fusion of jazz with all kinds of world music.

Ralph Towner ▶

Each musician in Oregon has a primary instrument, but the fluid nature of the band allows experimenting with other instruments: Ralph Towner was originally a trumpet player and pianist who belatedly became intrigued by the acoustic guitar, which he picked up at age twenty-two. He is now a virtuoso on the six-string and twelve-string guitar, and some performances might find him wandering to the acoustic piano or picking up a French horn. Bassist Glen Moore also played violin and flute. Paul McCandless specialized in the oboe, a rare example of that double-reed instrument finding a place in jazz. Percussionist Colin Walcott (who never played the trap set) was the group's firmest link to world traditions: although he learned percussion in college, he became a devout fan of the music of India, studying the tabla (a pair of drums) with Alla Rakha and the sitar with Ravi Shankar.

Oregon is an exemplar of what could be called New Age jazz—quiet, thoughtful, serene. Yet its compositions are intricate enough, and skillfully wedded to the instruments at hand, that its music is both engaging and a challenge to listen to. And like the avant-garde Art Ensemble of Chicago, it features real-time interaction.

World music groups are numerous, and include many kinds of music—Indian (Shakti, featuring John McLaughlin with Zakir Hussein), jazz/bluegrass/old-time (Bela Fleck, David Grisman, the Turtle Island String Quartet with David Balakrishnan), and European (Pierre Dørge and his New Jungle Orchestra from Denmark).

SMOOTH JAZZ

When Bill Clinton was asked early in his presidency to name his favorite saxophonists, he replied: "Lester Young and Kenny G." The first name points back into the jazz tradition (and to the only saxophonist nicknamed "the President"). The second—undoubtedly far better known to his voters—points toward **smooth jazz**.

The term first appeared in the late 1980s, when the label "fusion" had run out of steam. But the idea behind it—an innocuous, listener-friendly blending of jazz with an upbeat, celebratory brand of R & B and funk—dates back to the 1960s and 1970s, when producer Creed Taylor helped Wes Montgomery break through with cover recordings of the Beatles. Taylor's record label, CTI, offered recordings by George Benson, Quincy Jones, and Nat Adderley with a distinctive gatefold cover and carefully monitored the content of the records, which stayed on the boundary between jazz and pop. The instrumentalists were cushioned by the orchestrations of Don Sebesky, a trombonist who worked behind the scenes as an arranger.

In the 1970s, this style found its mass audience. Among the albums released then was *Mister Magic*, recorded by the Philadelphia saxophonist Grover Washington Jr. in 1975; its sales were not eclipsed until his 1980 *Winelight*, featuring "Just the Two of Us." Guitarist George Benson, who had struggled for years to escape the shadow of Wes Montgomery, hit it big with *Breezin'*, featuring "This Masquerade," an electrifying remake of a Leon Russell tune with Benson singing along with his playing. Musicians like Donald Byrd, a competent hard bop trumpet player, abandoned acoustic jazz for fusion with the 1972 *Black Byrd*. Some groups even dropped the word "jazz" when it threatened to limit their appeal. Thus, the Jazz Crusaders became simply the Crusaders, exemplifying jazz-influenced dance music.

The audience for this music was affluent, well-educated—and increasingly black. After the civil rights revolution removed legal barriers in the workplace, black professionals finally felt comfortable with their success, and marked their affluence in their consumer tastes. More often than not, they embraced jazz as their music. Their tastes were conservative, shadowing closely rhythm and blues.

The Radio Effect

The new music was radio driven. While record companies prefer broad categories (corresponding to sections of a record store), radio searches for finer and finer divisions of taste. By the late 1980s, a new category had emerged, sometimes called "new adult contemporary," but soon adopting other labels: "jazz lite," "quiet storm," and "smooth jazz." The music was pioneered by stations like KTWV in Los Angeles, known as The Wave, and monitored by marketing companies like Broadcast Architecture. The target audience was the "money" demographic, ages twenty-five to fifty-four: adults who had "graduated" from rock to a less abrasive music, but were still shy of embracing jazz. Smooth jazz was the perfect soundtrack for their lifestyle. In 1987, *Billboard* finally amended its charts, placing jazz in the category "traditional jazz," while dubbing its pop-oriented cousin "contemporary jazz."

The king of smooth jazz was Kenny G, or Kenneth Gorelick. A saxophonist from Seattle, he made his mark with the Jeff Lorber band; but it was as a solo artist that he ascended from the ranks of mere jazz players into the stratosphere. He is currently ranked No. 25 of all performers by the Recording Industry Association of America—having sold 48 million recordings, including 12 million for *Breathless*, undoubtedly the highest total ever for anyone considered to be a jazz artist. His name has evoked howls from jazz musicians, especially when he dubbed his solos—what Pat Metheny colorfully called "his lame-ass, jive, pseudo bluesy, out-of-tune noodling"—over Louis Armstrong's vocal in a remake of "What a Wonderful World."

Kenny G

There are many things to dislike about smooth jazz—for example, its use of some of the worst aspects of pop recording. Jazz has always depended on real-time interaction, even in the studio. But pop recordings long ago dispensed with the concept of live performance. Tunes are constructed layer by layer, with each musician recorded separately, often wearing headphones, listening and performing with tracks created days or weeks before. The sound may be beautiful, even precise (thanks to digital sampling and synthesized drum tracks), but it comes at the cost of the interactive quality of jazz. We can't blame technology per se: many jazz pieces, including two highlighted in this chapter ("Teen Town" and "Tutu") have been recorded in this way.

The most important thing about smooth jazz is that it reaches a wide audience, including those who otherwise would never hear any kind of jazz. For most listeners, it's probably background music (for example, the Weather Channel uses smooth tracks as the underscore for its local forecasts).

JAM BANDS, ACID JAZZ, HIP-HOP

If smooth jazz is a commodity consumed through recordings and radio play, other types of fusion are inescapable from the sweat and noise of contemporary music. We can distinguish between roughly three: jam band jazz, acid jazz, and jazz/hip-hop.

© ALAN NAHIGIAN

John Medeski, flanked by Chris Wood on bass (left) and Billy Martin on drums (right), has brought the Hammond B3 organ sound into a twenty-first-century aesthetic by combining it with the most modern synthesizers and samplers. Cape Cod Music Festival, 1999.

Jam Band Jazz

The **jam band** concept has its roots in 1960s rock. It took its cue from the Grateful Dead, the psychedelic rock band that turned away from the commercial scene to celebrate the pleasures of communal improvisation. The Dead was not terribly concerned with recordings, although a surprising number of performances were taped by their dedicated followers, known as "Deadheads." The band became an international phenomenon, devoted to the freedom of the improvised moment.

In more recent years, the jam band phenomenon was carried on by Phish, an improvisational rock group led by guitarist Trey Anastasio. Phish began in the early 1980s as a pick-up band playing small gigs in its home state of Vermont; by the time it disbanded in 2004, it had become known worldwide. Phish reached a highly educated, dedicated audience, astronomically larger in size than anything jazz was able to muster (hundreds of thousands attended its concerts every year). Like the Grateful Dead, Phish could not be construed as a jazz band; but in its enthusiasm for open-ended improvisation, it opened the door to a much wider audience for new bands who might want to follow in their footsteps.

One such band was founded by Charlie Hunter, a guitarist from the San Francisco Bay area who plays an eight-stringed guitar. On the lower two strings, he plays bass lines, separately amplified for the proper sound; the rest of his hand is free for guitar licks, perfectly synchronized with the overall groove.

■ MEDESKI, MARTIN AND WOOD

Another group is Medeski, Martin and Wood—a band that Phish helped publicize by playing their tapes in between Phish's own sets. The group was started by John Medeski, a former classical pianist who became turned off by the music's social pretensions ("all these rich people in fur coats") at age fourteen. He studied at the New England Conservatory, where he met bassist Chris Wood. On one of their early gigs, they discovered the drummer Billy Martin, a New Yorker who brought "that more danceable element" to their music.

The group began as a piano trio in New York, but by the early 1990s they had set off on the road, touring in their own van (complete with camper) and booking their own gigs. Medeski, Martin and Wood found themselves on gigs with alternative rock bands like Los Lobos and the Dave Matthews Band, as well as putting on free gigs at the Knitting Factory in New York. Although Medeski was an acoustic pianist, he found electric instruments more suitable to the band's peripatetic life. He soon became an expert on the Hammond B3 organ, the Clavinet, the Wurlitzer electric piano, the Mellotron (another Wurlitzer instrument), the ARP String Ensemble, and the Yamaha synthesizer. Each instrument has its own amplifier and its own sound, adding a different texture to their music. "I can hit three notes on any of my keyboards, and each will sound different," says Medeski.

Medeski dislikes the term "jam band," finding it "demeaning"; but his group's music is very much part of that scene, better suited to coffeehouses and rock clubs than jazz nightclubs and building on the grooves of earlier fusion groups like the organ trios of Jimmy Smith. Inevitably, their audiences affect what they create—in part because each night's show is taped, digitized, and loaded onto the Internet for everyone to enjoy. Much of their music seems retro, aimed at a camp audience that enjoys hearing modern versions of older soul-jazz styles. But it is also thoroughly modern. Many of their recordings have been shaped by hip-hop professionals like DJ Logic and Scott Harding, both of whom help the band conceive of their music as a whole, not just as a collection of individual soloists.

John Scofield is a jazz guitarist and composer with a taste for funk and soul. A Miles Davis alumnus from the mid-1980s, he has recorded albums featuring mainstream jazz, drums and bass, and the music of soul genius Ray Charles. At the Blue Note, New York, 1999.

🎧 "Chank"

In 1998, Medeski, Martin and Wood received a phone call from an older musician who had become a fan. John Scofield was an electric guitarist who had played with Miles Davis in the early 1980s. Over the years, Scofield had earned a reputation as a skillful composer as well as performer within the neo-funk groove. His playing combined a searing, distorted blues sound with a deep knowledge of modern postbop scales. His command of chord progressions made him accepted within mainstream jazz, but he yearned for a change of groove. "I'm at a point now where I'm bebopped out," he complained.

John Scofield

Scofield arranged for Medeski, Martin and Wood to play on his next recording session, which produced the album *A Go Go*. Scofield was the composer for the date, providing tunes that were disarmingly simple, often little more than a few guitar licks set against a funk groove. But the rhythmic flow was designed for improvisation. "I'm not a huge fusion fan per se," Scofield said. "I like swing. But some grooves make you want to play, if you're a jazz musician."

"Chank" was written as a tribute to Jimmy "Chank" Nolen, a guitarist in James Brown's stellar rhythm section. Scofield's part was basically a rhythm line—not necessarily the role most jazz guitarists hanker for. But the line was essential in setting up the overall groove. Scofield remembers the bass line as reminiscent of James Brown's seminal "Cold Sweat" (1967): on the offbeat, except for the first beat of the measure. "[Saxophonist] Maceo Parker and [trombonist] Fred Wesley describe funk as 'about the one,' and on that tune, everything comes back to it. It was a whole way of breaking up the bass and drum rhythm."

The form is simple, derived again from James Brown's practice: an **A** section over a single chord, used for modal improvisation, followed by a bridge. The bridge is cued by each soloist, who can play as long as he wants: "On 'Chank,' you play four-bar phrases, not choruses." The group, which had played together only three times in rehearsal, mesh beautifully on this tune. The album as a whole jump-started Scofield's career, selling 100,000 copies—nowhere near as much as, say, Hancock's *Head Hunters*, but a quantum leap from his usual sales.

LISTENING GUIDE

🎧 chank

4.9

JOHN SCOFIELD

John Scofield, electric guitar; John Medeski, Hammond B3 organ; Chris Wood, electric bass; Billy Martin, drums

- Label: *A-Go-Go*, Polygram 539979
- Date: 1998
- Style: jam band fusion
- Form: **A A B A** (**A B** during the solos)

What to listen for:
- Scofield's intricate rhythms and electrified timbres
- each soloist's improvised A section, ending with his signal for the bridge
- composed coda, with descending melody

INTRODUCTION

0:00		Scofield (electric guitar) plays a dissonant chord in a syncopated rhythm.
0:02		After a brief pause, he follows with a brief **pentatonic** lick.
0:04		Scofield repeats the guitar chord, this time following with a rhythmically tricky passage.
0:08		Having established the pattern, Scofield plays it repeatedly.
0:15		On an upbeat, the drums enter, followed by the electric bass.
0:16		The drums and bass add their own rhythmic layers, sometimes reinforcing Scofield's syncopations, at other times creating new patterns. The bass begins squarely on the downbeat before shifting to the offbeat.

HEAD

0:32	**A**	Medeski (organ) plays a melody with strong, sustained **blue notes**, in a simple repetitive pattern that contrasts with the syncopated accompaniment.
0:38		The last note of the line dissolves in a bluesy **glissando**.
0:48		Having completed two complete phrases, the organ rests, giving the drums, bass, and guitar room to continue the groove for another eight bars.
0:57	**A**	The melody is repeated in a higher register.
1:05		Medeski begins the melody harmonized in thirds.
1:13	**B**	The bass note moves to IV. After a few beats, the guitar and organ play syncopated chords, followed by a riff.
1:21		The band reaches a **half cadence** (on the dominant chord).
1:22		A brief drum solo closes the bridge after only five bars.

| 1:24 | **A** | Medeski returns to the opening melody, again harmonized in thirds. |

SOLO 1

1:40	**A**	Medeski plays a few **staccato** chords.
1:42		Scofield enters for his guitar solo with a forceful electric sound. Some of his phrases are loud, others suddenly quiet.
1:49		As Scofield plays, Medeski **comps** quietly in the background.
1:56		Scofield's lick begins quietly on the downbeat with fast repeated notes.
2:08		Scofield plays a line with expressive, upward-bending blue notes.
2:16		He stitches together several short ideas into a long continuous phrase.
2:28		In the background, the organ holds out sustained notes.
2:44		Scofield returns to the repeated-note idea, interacting aggressively with Medeski's comping.
2:50		As Scofield ends his phrase with a short, distorted passage, the organ plays a brief riff.
2:53		Scofield echoes the riff, adding brief rhythmic decorations.
2:56		His guitar sound becomes more distorted.
3:00		With a change in the timbre of his guitar, Scofield repeats a simple four-note riff, playing it in **call and response** with a lower-pitched blues line.
3:06		At times, his lines become blurred in pitch and rhythm.
3:16		Scofield begins to suggest the tune's opening melody.
3:20		He follows this with a rapid repeated riff.
3:24		By referring once more to the opening melody, he signals the bridge.
3:32	**B**	

SOLO 2

3:43	**A**	Medeski begins his organ solo with a fiercely repeated riff, placed polyrhythmically against the bar.
3:47		In the background, Scofield plays a variant of the line he introduced at the beginning of the tune.
4:00		Medeski's next line is a string of fast notes, moving "outside" the main chord until it descends into the bass register.
4:07		His licks become shorter, interacting more with Scofield's syncopated accompaniment.
4:14		Medeski focuses on a single bluesy note.
4:24		He begins a simple four-note riff, then repeats it at different pitch levels, some dissonant against the prevailing harmony.
4:31		He starts a longer and faster melody that once again moves into dissonant territory.
4:46		To signal the bridge, Medeski plays the opening melody, which quickly disintegrates into polyrhythmic improvisation.
5:01	**B**	

HEAD (abbreviated)

| 5:12 | **A** | Medeski leads a version of the head that's reduced to two phrases. |

CODA

5:28		The band moves to a composed passage (lasting nine and a half measures). As the bass slowly ascends, the guitar and organ play a bizarre melody, harmonized in dissonant intervals that fall just short of octaves.
5:32		The melody is repeated, with the bass slightly higher and the intervals slightly more dissonant.
5:40		The melody moves in faster note values.

5:43	The passage comes to rest on a half cadence, followed by a brief drum solo.
5:47	The passage is repeated exactly.
6:06	As the passage is repeated one more time, the guitar begins playing a solo over harmonies played by the organ.
6:24	The bass shifts down **chromatically** to a new harmony; the organ lingers on a fragment of the melody, repeated polyrhythmically against the bass.
6:28	A strange synthesized sound fills up the melody space, gradually growing louder.
6:31	Suddenly the bass rises in pitch as it speeds up, as if the tape were being run faster.
6:40	The bass finally stops, ending the piece.

Acid Jazz

The term comes from England—specifically, the lively "rave" scene in dance clubs of the late 1980s and early 1990s. Late at night (so late that the events often took place in secret locations to avoid curfew regulations), DJs would play electronic music to crowds of dancers, enhanced by light shows and artificial fog. The music was known as "acid house," a repetitive, hypnotic music with a powerful bass line. One night, DJ Chris Bangs, tired of the usual selection, offered an alternative, woven together from soul jazz tracks in his record collection. He called it **acid jazz**, and the term quickly spread. Dancers heard the music as retro, a chic evocation of now-forgotten soul jazz from the 1960s, available only on LPs. For many young people, it was their pathway into the jazz tradition—albeit a notion of tradition quite different from the usual modernist narrative.

The acid jazz craze brought back to life styles that had been shunted to the fringes. During a time when giants like Coltrane, Mingus, and Ornette Coleman were roaming the earth, soul jazz rarely received critical attention. Some critics saw it as trivial and monotonous as well as relentlessly commercial—a "regression" that informed jazz minds should simply ignore. Yet the music didn't go anywhere. Bands continued to play soul jazz; and even when the movement itself faded in memory, their recordings still formed a large part of many record collections. As DJs hungry for new beats combed through piles of used vinyl looking for new material, they discovered these sounds and recycled them back into dance music. Acid jazz was thus created out of a pastiche of recordings.

Groove Collective

Many of the new groups associated with acid jazz have only a tenuous connection to jazz. Some, like the Brand New Heavies, simply sound like the 1970s soul bands revisited. Others lie more securely on the jazz-pop borderline. One such group is the Groove Collective, a collection of roughly a dozen instrumentalists that first performed at the Giant Step, a dance venue in Manhattan. Some aspects of the Groove Collective's music relate to the dance hall: they use a DJ, for example, to blend their sounds, and they often base their grooves on hip-hop dance music. But the band also features fine jazz soloists, including saxophonist Jay Rodriguez and trombonist Josh Roseman. The music has a bohemian feeling, but it is hardly out of touch with the modern scene. As one band member said, "Groove Collective has the energy of a rock band. We are not cool dudes with a beatnik feel and berets and dark glasses."

A tune like "Rentstrike," from their first album, provides a good example. The first minute seems historical: to judge from the faint recording quality and the sound of scratched vinyl, it sounds like classic bebop from the 1940s. But the music then fades abruptly into a contemporary dance groove: cycling endlessly between two chords, slightly out of tonal kilter. The bebop tune was, of course, "faked"—but it was worked into the main theme of the piece. In and around the ambiguous harmonies of the main theme, the jazz musicians find a way to take short solos that don't disturb the group aesthetic.

Jazz/Hip-Hop

The latest area to be affected by the jazz fusion impulse is African American **hip-hop**. Hip-hop arose from the streets of the Bronx in the 1970s, and by the 1980s had spread to the rest of the country and to the world. Few jazz musicians had any interaction with it (although as we have seen, Herbie Hancock's "Rockit" is a splendid early example of hip-hop's use of turntable scratching), and by the 1990s it had become a symbol of everything jazz was not: young, countercultural, and in touch with the reality of the streets in black communities.

Two things had to happen for jazz/hip-hop fusion to work. First, young hip-hop artists had to discover jazz. Musicians from bands like A Tribe Called Quest and Digable Planets began raiding their parents' cabinets, finding old Blue Note records and pulling cuts to use as samples on their recordings. The results were explosive in popularity. In 1994, Us3 transformed a Herbie Hancock song, "Cantaloupe Island," into a new mix entitled "Cantaloop (Flip Fantasia)," which rose into the top twenty. Blue Note enjoyed an unprecedented prosperity as it saw earlier recordings suddenly rise up the charts, thanks to their popularity on hip-hop records. So many artists were sampling Blue Note records that the company—figuring that if it couldn't beat them, it might as well join them—opened up its vaults to hip-hop DJ Madlib to plunder at will.

The second thing was that jazz musicians had to find a way to use hip-hop. The financial incentives were obvious: embracing hip-hop opened up a new, hip audience for their music. But at the same time, yielding up older swing grooves for new ones offered a new artistic challenge. Numerous recordings since the mid-1990s have put respectable, aging jazz soloists in the midst of hip-hop tracks. On *Stolen Moments*—a tribute album designed to fight AIDS, recorded in 1994—you can hear Lester Bowie mixed in with Digable Planets, Herbie Hancock with Me'Shell NdegéOcello, and Ron Carter with MC Solaar.

The nature of the fusion depended on who was in charge. Recordings controlled by hip-hop artists tend to keep jazz well in the background, reduced to short sampled loops or buried in the mix. Such was the case, for example, with *Jazzmatazz*, an album by Guru (aka Keith Elam), who honored Roy Ayers and Donald Byrd but kept them distinctly behind Guru's rapping. Jazz artists, for their part, are willing to absorb just enough hip-hip to make their own music more stylish. Branford Marsalis's fusion band, called Buckshot LeFonque (after one of Cannonball Adderley's pseudonyms), adds a rapper and a turntablist to an otherwise conventional electric jazz ensemble.

MILES TO GO

To close this chapter, we return to Miles Davis, whose flirtations with fusion did not end with *Bitches Brew*. In the 1970s, he turned forcefully toward contemporary black pop with an album called *On the Corner*. The cover art suggests an unfamiliar environment for the son of a wealthy dental surgeon— colorful but low-grade street life, including pimps and hustlers dressed in yellow platform shoes. Davis felt it was important to reach this audience, and did so through a dense interlocking of bass-heavy, rhythmic layers. Critics panned the album, finding it difficult and formless. These days, *On the Corner* and other albums from this period (*Big Fun, Get Up with It*) are seen as foreshadowing the ambient rhythms of techno music.

Davis went into seclusion in 1975, and for a time it seemed he would not come back at all. He was suffering from sickle-cell anemia, degeneration of his hips, bleeding ulcers, and walking pneumonia—all of which he treated by self-medicating through a new addiction to cocaine. Then in 1980, incredibly, he returned to the public light and began recording and touring again. Gradually, he found a style and a way of playing that suited his temperament. The albums kept improving, and audiences found his aura even more impressive.

It was not easy for older jazz fans to adjust to the new Miles Davis. Critic Martin Williams was shocked to see a man reaching sixty dressed "in what looked like a left-over Halloween fright-suit, emitting a scant handful of plaintive notes." Those who were accustomed to seeing Davis in the solo spotlight now had to watch him play a lick here, his trumpet on a portable microphone, shift to a keyboard to add a chord, and otherwise control the stage through his wandering presence. His repertory included new pop songs, such as Cyndi Lauper's "Time After Time" and Quincy Jones's "Human Nature," from Michael Jackson's *Thriller*, as well as a range of constantly shifting funk tunes. He still continued to attract superb young players, like the saxophonist Kenny Garrett. More than ever, playing with Miles was the ultimate credential.

⦿ "Tutu"

In 1985, irritated with the company's lackluster support for his albums, Davis decided to finally terminate his long-standing contract with Columbia Records. He signed instead with Warner Bros., which offered him an enormous advance—compensated in part by their appropriating half the copyrights to his compositions. Davis was fascinated by the new pop singer-songwriter Prince, finding his music extraordinary ("the new Duke Ellington of our time"), and wanted to feature him on his next album—along with electronic samples and overdubs.

Warner Bros. put him in touch with Marcus Miller, a bassist who was also a producer and arranger. "Wow," he said, "if Miles is willing to start using drum machines and stuff, let me show my take on that." For the opening track of the album, Miller devised what he felt would be an appropriate backdrop for Davis: a brooding, shuffling sound that was intended to evoke the Prince of Darkness, Davis's infamous nickname. The voicings in the tune were inspired by Herbie Hancock's playing—darting chromatic chords, suggesting harmonies while undermining them at the same time.

Davis was working with a band at this time, but none of his musicians appear on the recording. His role was simply to respond with his trumpet to the synthesizer textures and drum machine tracks (augmented by a few musicians, such as Miller and keyboardist Adam Holzmann) presented to him in the studio. The result may seem artificial and stilted. But it is also the same process by which Davis made some of his finest recordings with Gil Evans, like *Sketches of Spain* and *Porgy and Bess*: Davis as the star soloist, surrounded by gorgeous textures. There is little doubt that the trumpet sound on this recording is Davis: the Harmon mute, the plaintive wail, the elliptical phrasing are all unmistakable. "As soon as Miles walked into the studio and played his first three notes," Miller said, "it became his."

LISTENING GUIDE

4.10

🎧 tutu

MILES DAVIS

Miles Davis, trumpet; Marcus Miller, soprano saxophone, synthesizer, electric bass, drums; Paulinho DaCosta, percussion

- Label: *Tutu,* Warner Brothers 25490
- Date: 1986
- Style: jazz-pop fusion
- Form: chorus (**A A B**) with solo improvisation over a vamp (ostinato)

What to listen for:

- brooding sound of rhythm section's ostinato
- Davis's trademark sound (elliptical phrases, including extreme high notes) in a modern dance groove
- improvisation mixed with prerecorded music

INTRODUCTION

0:00		A short bass drum hit leads to a loud orchestral chord in the synthesizer. As the sound slowly decays, we hear a quiet pulse and a few strikes on the conga drum.
0:03		A second orchestral chord is followed by more aggressive drumming.
0:08		Davis enters with a muted trumpet, playing a descending line.

VAMP

0:13		The bass plays a simple, loping **ostinato**, doubled by the synthesizer. Its continually repeated asymmetric rhythm locks in with the driving percussive groove, featuring the ride cymbal. Above the ostinato, Davis plays simple lines, circling around a **blue note**.
0:21		As Davis reaches for a high note, his sound becomes distorted.
0:25		As if responding to Davis's rhythms, the ostinato temporarily adds a few notes.
0:30		The bass breaks briefly away from the ostinato to play a short lick.

HEAD

0:33	**A**	Davis plays the main melody, supported by the synthesizers and the bass line: an eight-bar phrase, voiced with modern **quartal** chords. The ostinato continues as accompaniment.
0:47		For a few bars, the melody is silent. Davis hits a long held note before completing his phrase with a flourish and then dissolving into the lower register.
0:54	**A**	
1:08	**B**	The melody (now doubled by the bass line) descends in a syncopated phrase. The harmony is ambiguous, drifting outside the main key.
1:13		A quiet ascending line in the synthesizer brings us back to the tonic, signaled by an orchestral chord.

SOLO

1:14		The ostinato is silent, opening up the texture. Davis interacts with Miller's improvisations on bass, with quiet synthesizer chords and massive orchestral hits.

HEAD

1:28	**A**	Davis leads the return to the main melody.
1:38		Over the melody's last held note, he improvises new patterns.
1:41	**A**	
1:51		Again, he adds brief improvised lines.
1:55	**B**	

SOLO

2:01		Again, the ostinato is silent. Miller plays another descending bass run, echoed by Davis, who squeezes a few notes into spaces left by the synthesizer.
2:09		Davis is quiet while the percussion takes over with a strong **backbeat**.
2:15		A delicate wash of synthesizer sound precedes Davis's reentrance with a repeated two-note motive.
2:26		His bluesy high note is undercut by a deep sagging sound in the bass.
2:29		Davis suddenly inserts a faster, more nervous phrase.
2:34		After he hits a high note, the whole background bends slightly in pitch.
2:36		As Davis enters on the downbeat, the bass ostinato begins again. Over a percussion background featuring the ride cymbal, Davis plays repeatedly with two notes, hitting them in unpredictable rhythmic patterns.
2:49		The overall rhythmic texture intensifies with bass licks and percussive hits.
3:00		A wash of synthesizer sound leads us back to the main melody.

HEAD

3:03	**A**	A return to the main melody, with more frequent improvised comments by Davis and Miller.
3:13		Davis's line suddenly ascends to a perilously high note.
3:16	**A**	He now begins to add to his version of the melody—sometimes doubling the synthesizer, but at other times departing from it with improvised comments.
3:30	**B**	

SOLO

3:37		Davis's playing becomes sparser. Interacting with the conga drum, he makes the most of a few intense notes.
3:44		He threads a piercing line through an increasingly dense intersection of sounds.
3:50		A loud synthesizer hit silences Davis's line, opening up the texture.
3:59		A faint background chord grows in volume, leading us once again back to the main melody.

HEAD

4:04	**A**	Davis plays against the main melody, nearly obliterating it with harsh high notes.
4:12		As the melody nears the end of its phrase, he plays a steady descending line over it.
4:18	**A**	Davis's improvisation focuses on a short bluesy phrase, repeated with ever varying rhythmic nuances.
4:31	**A**	Instead of moving to the bridge, the melody continues, punctuated by Davis's commentary.

SOLO (CODA)

4:45		Davis plays short phrases in call and response with the bass ostinato.
4:59		The track begins to fade out.

"Tutu" was recorded in a single take, with only a few trumpet clams edited out. On a whim, Davis decided to title the tune (as well as the entire album) after Desmond Tutu, the Anglican clergyman who was one of the heroes of the freedom movement in South Africa. Not all of the album wore well; but the title track stands as a tribute to Davis's genius. On the cover of the album, we can see stark photographs by Irving Penn, showing a blank closeup of Davis's face as well as a beautiful profile of his hands, frozen as if playing one of his favorite notes.

ADDITIONAL LISTENING

Tony Williams Lifetime	"Emergency!" (1969); *Emergency* (Verve 731453911727)
Charles Lloyd Quartet	"Forest Flower—Sunrise" (1966); *Forest Flower: Live in Monterey* (Rhino 71746)
Miles Davis	"Filles de Kilimanjaro" (1968); *Filles de Kilimanjaro* (Sony BMG Special Markets 723796)
	"Shhh/Peaceful" (1969); *In a Silent Way* (Columbia/Legacy 696998655669)
	"Spanish Key" (1969); *Bitches Brew* (Columbia/Legacy 074646577424)
Mahavishnu Orchestra	"Vital Transformation" (1971); *The Inner Mounting Flame* (Columbia/Legacy 65523)
Return to Forever (Chick Corea)	"Song of the Pharaoh Kings" (1974); *Where Have I Known You Before / No Mystery* (Beat Goes On 799)
Weather Report	"Birdland," "Black Market" (1976); *X2 (Heavy Weather / Black Market)* (Columbia/Legacy 886973301128)
Jaco Pastorius	"Donna Lee" (1975); *The Essential Jaco Pastorius* (Columbia/Legacy 886970128728)
Pat Metheny	"Have You Heard" (1989); *The Road to You: Recorded Live in Europe* (Nonesuch 79941-2)
Herbie Hancock	"Palm Grease" (1974); *Thrust* (Columbia/Legacy 074646498422)
	"Chameleon" (1973); *The Essential Herbie Hancock* (Columbia/Legacy 827969459324)
Keith Jarrett	"The Windup" (1974); *Belonging* (ECM 1050)
	"Death and the Flower" (1974); *Death and the Flower* (Impulse! / The Verve Vault 00076742904623)
George Benson	"This Masquerade" (1976); *Breezin'* (Warner Bros. 3111)
Oregon	"Aurora" (1973); *Vanguard Visionaries* (Vanguard 73150)
Groove Collective	"Rentstrike" (1993); *The Best of Groove Collective* (Shanachie 016351511027)
Charlie Hunter	"Mitch Better Have My Bunny" (2001); *Songs from the Analog Playground* (Blue Note 33550)
Medeski, Martin and Wood	"Beeah" (1993); *It's a Jungle in Here* (Gramavision 879495)

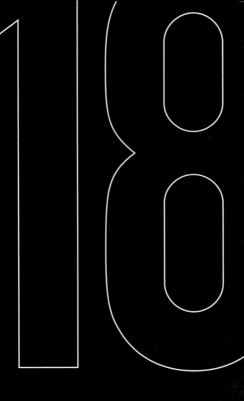

ANTHONY BRAXTON
piece three

WYNTON MARSALIS
processional

RONALD SHANNON JACKSON
now's the time

HISTORICISM:
JAZZ ON JAZZ

THE WEIGHT OF HISTORY

In 1925, shortly after joining Fletcher Henderson's big band in New York, Louis Armstrong showed Henderson's arranger, Don Redman, a handbook containing music that he and his mentor, King Oliver, had composed in Chicago. Armstrong encouraged Redman to select one for the purpose of orchestrating it. Redman decided on "Sugar Foot Stomp," which Oliver had recorded as "Dippermouth Blues," and wrote an arrangement in which Armstrong was asked to perform Oliver's famous cornet solo.

"Sugar Foot Stomp" helped put Henderson's band on the map: it was a startling example of a modern New York recording based on written and improvised material taken from a traditional New Orleans (by way of Chicago) jazz recording, and the piece quickly became a favorite among dancers and musicians. This was not the first nor last time Henderson looked to jazz history for inspiration. A year earlier, he had recorded "Copenhagen," a piece introduced only months before by the Wolverines (a white Chicago band featuring cornetist Bix Beiderbecke); Henderson's record served as a critique, showing that New York was paying attention to Chicago even as it moved in a new

John Lewis, who believed in jazz education, helped launch the Lenox School in the year that he brought the Modern Jazz Quartet to Paris, 1957.

HERMAN LEONARD PHOTOGRAPHY LLC/CTS IMAGES.COM

wwnorton.com/studyspace

direction. Then in 1926, Henderson recorded "King Porter Stomp," based on the third strain of a Jelly Roll Morton piece of the same name; a decade later, that arrangement would be embraced as an anthem of the Swing Era.

We have previously considered jazz as (first) an art-for-art's sake tradition whose masters move the music along with radical leaps of creativity; and (second) as a "fusion" tradition in which jazz evolves in response to contemporary pop culture. The Henderson examples offer us a foundation for a third way of interpreting jazz history: the "historicist" narrative, which begins with the precept that jazz creativity is inextricably bound with its past. This narrative is especially useful in considering today's jazz.

Historicism: A Definition

Historicism, which originated in the nineteenth century, is opposed to the notion that great men and women and their works arise independently of history; instead, it connects each new undertaking to those of the past. The German philosopher Friedrich Hegel called this exchange between past and present a "dialectic." For artists, the dialectic means grappling with, rejecting, and expanding time-honored accomplishments.

In the 1980s, critical theorists put forth a **New Historicism**, which says that a work of art must be viewed within the context of the place and time of its creation. Rejecting the **New Criticism**, which analyzes works of art as sufficient unto themselves, the New Historicists look beyond a work to the historical and social conditions that may help us interpret it. Despite their differences, these two schools of criticism were never really at war in jazz; on the contrary, they complemented each other. Perhaps the leading advocate **Martin Williams** of the New Criticism as applied to jazz was the writer and producer Martin Williams, who always focused on the particularity of a musical work. His approach, not unlike the Listening Guides in this book, analyzed a piece by breaking down its chorus structure and examining the components that went into making it a success or failure.

Williams paid relatively little attention to historical details that might have furnished a different kind of interpretation. In the 1970s, while working at the Smithsonian Institution in Washington, D.C., he created *The Smithsonian Collection of Classic Jazz*, an anthology of jazz recordings that revolutionized the teaching of jazz. Yet as an example of pitfalls inherent in the New Criticism, consider that Williams included Jelly Roll Morton's "Dead Man Blues" (Chapter 4) while excising its comic introduction. He considered it irrelevant, dated, and even embarrassing. A historicist, on the other hand, would find value in that bit of tomfoolery: it tells us something of Morton's times and of his background, intentions, and attitude.

Williams was by no means opposed to historical inquiry or interpretation. But neither did he subscribe to the historicist idea, popularized in the 1940s, that familiarity with the personalities and backgrounds of musicians was necessary to appreciate the quality of their music. From the 1950s until the 1970s, his art-centric approach predominated.

Historicism at Work

In the twenty-first century, we see countless examples of filmmakers, composers, choreographers, writers, painters, architects, and others attempt to energize the present by mining the past. We live in an age of homages and interpretations. In the 1950s and 1960s, jazz musicians strove to create new and original works of art; today, musicians are as likely to perform or pay tribute to those same works. The ways in which they apply historicist principles tend to fall into three categories:

1. The revival of entire idioms, such as traditional jazz or swing. This usually involves an immersion in jazz repertory—the faithful interpretation of classic or neglected works.

2. Original music that celebrates music of the past. This may range from momentous tributes to playful parodies of artists.

3. Modernist interpretations of jazz classics, as a way of using the past to spur the present.

These principles have found favor throughout much of jazz history.

RECLAIMING THE PAST: BUNK (1940s)

Although jazz has mined its past almost from the beginning, the first genuine movement to counter prevailing musical tastes in favor of an older, neglected jazz style did not take place until the late 1930s. The kick-off came with the publication of the 1939 book *Jazzmen*, edited and partly written by Frederick Ramsey Jr. and Charles Edward Smith. A serious if faultily researched work, *Jazzmen* argued that true jazz was an essentially New Orleans–derived, African American, blues-based music—hardly a controversial position. But in romanticizing jazz's traditional roots while ignoring modern swing stylists (Lester Young, Roy Eldridge, Billie Holiday, and Lionel Hampton are mentioned only in passing or not at all), it created a nostalgic longing for early jazz and raised questions of authenticity to banish those who didn't heed the party line. In the course of researching a section on New Orleans for *Jazzmen*, writer William Russell discovered a New Orleans trumpet player of uncertain years named Willie "Bunk" Johnson (1889–1949), and made him one of the book's heroes.

Johnson, who predated the actual year of his birth by a decade, claimed to have played with Buddy Bolden in 1895 (he would have been six at the time) and to have influenced Louis Armstrong—a boast that Armstrong gently debunked. In 1942, fitted with a new set of teeth, Johnson recorded for the first time in his career; he continued to record over the next five years, while touring the country from San Francisco to New York and spurring a major revival of traditional jazz. Bunk Johnson was exhibited as a musician of Arcadian purity: an uncompromised purveyor of the "real" jazz.

Though plagued by technical limitations, Johnson was at his best an intriguing musician. He had a rosy, glowing tone and an undeniable penchant for the blues. Still, he rarely measured up to the great established figures from New Orleans, like Sidney

Jazzmen

Bunk Johnson brought his New Orleans Jazz Band to New York and became the focal point for the New Orleans revival: (left to right) Big Jim Robinson, trombone; Johnson, trumpet; Baby Dodds, drums; Lawrence Marrero, banjo; George Lewis, clarinet; Alton Purnell, piano; Alcide "Slow Drag" Pavageau, bass. Decca Records, New York, 1945.

Bechet (with whom he recorded), and was as frequently ridiculed by young modernists as he was idolized by his fan base, which consisted chiefly of conservative white men. As a result, a schism developed that eventually divided jazz into two mutually scornful camps: the revivalists and the boppers.

To their credit, Johnson and his admirers forced a reconsideration of early jazz, which was so remote to most swing fans that King Oliver and Jelly Roll Morton died broke and forgotten. Bunk also introduced a clique of veteran New Orleans musicians, born at the turn of the century, who accompanied him on tour and in the studio; they interpreted a narrow traditionalist repertory with sincerity and emotional candor. The best known among them, **George Lewis** clarinetist George Lewis, later played an important role in reestablishing the French Quarter in New Orleans as a jazz tourist attraction. His plaintive sound sustained an international following long after the Bunk Johnson phenomenon ended, offering a refuge for those who stubbornly refused to tackle bop.

DEFINING THE PAST: MAINSTREAM (1950s)

The 1950s offered a nonstop parade of new jazz schools, brilliant improvisers, and innovative composers (as delineated in Chapters 12–14). Not surprisingly, this creative commotion also instigated a historical investigation of the older schools seemingly left in the dust. Diehard traditionalists had circled their wagons around Bunk Johnson during the Swing Era. In the postbop era, it was the swing generation that required critical resuscitation.

In 1958, the critic Stanley Dance coined the term **mainstream** to describe that giant swath of jazz situated between reactionary traditionalism and radical modernity—in short, all those musicians, from Louis Armstrong and Duke Ellington to Benny Goodman and Lester Young, who played in prebop styles. Dance, who despised bebop, sought to renew interest in musicians who were still relatively young (not yet fifty, for the most part) but were treated in the jazz press as dinosaurs. He succeeded, but in the 1960s, to his dismay, with the avant-garde at center stage, *mainstream* came to encompass bop musicians. Then in the 1970s, when fusion or jazz-rock dominated the spotlight, the mainstream was said to include just about everyone who played acoustic jazz. The important thing, however, is that *mainstream* came to represent the ongoing language of jazz creativity while holding it at a distance from the latest trends.

Dave Brubeck speaks to a class at the Lenox School in Lenox, Massachusetts, in 1959, while Gunther Schuller and John Lewis look on.

Jazz eventually began making inroads into academia and the arts establishment, but this was an exceedingly slow process. In the unsympathetic atmosphere that would deny Duke Ellington the Pulitzer Prize (see Chapter 8), jazz activists began to take matters into their own hands, setting up their own schools and exploring jazz history in books, magazines, and public discussions. Jazz had begun to look at itself as a historical phenomenon with distinct roots and a proud lineage.

At the same time, musicians were crossing stylistic divides. Unlike the 1940s, when jazz musicians were swing players, modernists, or traditionalists, musicians in the 1950s practiced a new rapprochement. Louis Armstrong and Dizzy Gillespie, who feuded in the early years of bop, played together on television. In the tradition of Ellington's musical portraits, modernists composed tributes to jazz pioneers. John Lewis helped launch the Modern Jazz Quartet with his cortege for Django Reinhardt. Charles Mingus created memorable portraits of Lester Young ("Goodbye Pork Pie Hat"), Jelly Roll Morton (the partly satiric "Jelly Roll"), and others.

Schools: The Lenox School of Jazz

Much of the historical and educational activity was stimulated in an area rarely singled out in jazz histories: Massachusetts, its eastern (Boston) and western (Lenox) borders. The first dedicated jazz curriculum was launched in 1957 as the Lenox School of Jazz, in the Berkshires near the classical music festival at Tanglewood. Never before had a faculty been convened for the exclusive purpose of teaching jazz; never before had an integrated but largely black faculty been recruited to teach whites anything. The Lenox School, under the direction of John Lewis (see Chapter 12), offered a star-studded roster of musicians and composers to a small, international selection of students who had submitted audition tapes through the mail.

Composer Bill Russo (arm raised) rehearses his Choir Ensemble with such notables as cellist-educator David Baker (third from left), Ornette Coleman (center, seated), and pianist Steve Kuhn (right, seated) at the Lenox School, 1959.

The Lenox School invented jazz pedagogy as it went along. The staff included Dizzy Gillespie, Oscar Peterson, Ray Brown, Jimmy Giuffre, George Russell, Max Roach, Gunther Schuller, J. J. Johnson, and Ornette Coleman (who, although registered as a student, also taught), along with several ensembles. In the first year, there were thirty-four instructors for forty-five students; as the number of students doubled, the staff also increased. For the educators, some of whom continued to teach at other institutions, the experience was a revelation; most of them had learned by doing—now they were at the frontier of discovering how to pass on their knowledge.

The goal at Lenox was to combine jazz history with jazz technique, and to rid jazz of semi-mystical notions of racial or "natural" talent. The courses ranged from writer Marshall Stearns's "The History of Jazz" to Schuller's "The Analytical History of Jazz"—from chronological history to musicological history. The school had grown out of public discussions of folk music and jazz that had taken place in the city of Lenox since 1950, under the aegis of a jazz club called the Music Inn. Each summer the Music Inn sponsored jazz workshops organized by Stearns, an English professor who later wrote an important jazz history and founded the Institute of Jazz Studies at Rutgers University. These discussions led directly to the creation of the Lenox School, which lasted four years, closing after the 1960 season. They also inspired Schuller's Third Stream movement (see Chapter 12).

By the time Lenox folded, jazz studies had begun to make headway in accredited schools. The most important of these were the Berklee School of Music in Boston and the University of North Texas in Denton. North Texas offered the first degree in jazz studies in 1947, and eventually accumulated one of the largest libraries of American music; its big-band workshop has served as the training ground for many gifted players. Berklee began to offer undergraduate degrees in jazz performance and composition in the middle 1960s, and continues to boast the best-known jazz department in American education. By 2000, countless musicians could claim an undergraduate background in jazz studies.

Festivals: Newport

George Wein

Perhaps Boston's most influential contribution to jazz history was the impresario George Wein, who founded the Newport Jazz Festival, across the state line in Rhode Island. Wein, a pianist and bandleader, was known in Boston as the proprietor of two jazz clubs, Storyville and Mahogany Hall, which specialized in Dixieland and swing, though Storyville broadened its menu to include modernists such as Charlie Parker and Stan Getz. In 1954, Wein answered the call of socialites Elaine and Louis Lorillard, who wanted him to program jazz concerts in one of the least likely, most insular settings imaginable: a tennis and croquet court in Newport, patronized by old money.

George Wein, a Boston-based pianist and club owner, changed the presentation of jazz forever when he produced the Newport Jazz Festival, featuring Count Basie in 1956.

The shutters of many mansions were closed in outrage, but Wein prevailed, and jazz was accepted as a symbol of postwar social enlightenment and good times. Within two years Hollywood appropriated the Newport Jazz Festival as the setting for the movie *High Society,* and in 1958 an independent production company visited Newport to shoot the much-imitated documentary *Jazz on a Summer's Day.* Wein became the most powerful impresario in jazz.

Taking a cue from the scholarly events at Music Inn and the Lenox School, Wein programmed panels and workshops along with the concerts, which presented every major jazz star from Armstrong and Ellington to Miles Davis and Thelonious Monk. He also regularly invited the participation of musicians not always accepted in the jazz world; his motive may have been commercial, but his choices reflected the historicist idea of placing jazz in the wider context of contemporary music. These artists included gospel singer Mahalia Jackson, Frank Sinatra, Ray Charles, and Chuck Berry.

Audience insurrections in the late 1960s caused a suspension of the festival in Newport, but Wein reestablished his operation in New York, where it grew far larger. Eventually he created jazz festivals in France, New Orleans, and elsewhere, and even returned to Newport. By the time he stepped down in 2006, jazz festivals had become annual events on the cultural calendars of countries on six continents.

AVANT-GARDE HISTORICISM (1970s)

Historicism practically disappeared during the avant-garde 1960s, when the emphasis in jazz was on pushing boundaries. But it made a major and apparently permanent comeback in the late 1970s, as the second wave of the avant-garde looked to the past in order to vary its music. We saw in Chapter 15, for example, how New York's loft scene favored a boundless eclecticism.

Significantly, the Loft Era coincided with a surge in jazz education, as influenced by Martin Williams's *Smithsonian Collection of Classic Jazz* and similar compilations designed to examine jazz from a historical perspective. Record companies were releasing comprehensive boxed sets encompassing entire careers, movements, record labels.

At the same time, great jazz artists whose careers had faltered during the height of rock (1967–74) returned to jazz, creating tremendous interest in musicians from all eras. Some players had disappeared into studio work (commercial recordings for films, television, commercials, and so forth), the academy, and pit bands (mostly on Broadway and in Las Vegas); others relocated to Europe or simply kept low profiles. Now they were greeted as "living legends." Suddenly, you could see long-absent musicians who had started out in the 1920s, like Benny Carter and Doc Cheatham, or in the bop era, like Dexter Gordon, Red Rodney, and James Moody. In this atmosphere, musicians frequently experimented with different styles, and the audiences seemed ready for almost anything.

■ ANTHONY BRAXTON (b. 1945)

Few musicians in this period proved more startling or prolific than Anthony Braxton, who initially made his mark on alto saxophone but eventually appeared in concerts and on records playing every instrument in the saxophone and clarinet family, plus flute and piano. Born in Chicago, Braxton began on clarinet at eleven; after three years in the army, he attended Roosevelt University as a philosophy major. At the same time, he joined the AACM, and in 1967 launched the Creative Construction Company, a trio with violinist Leroy Jenkins and trumpet player Leo Smith.

In 1969, Braxton released a two-disc album, *For Alto*, consisting entirely of unaccompanied alto saxophone solos. The sheer audacity of the venture generated a firestorm, with a by-then-familiar response: he was either a genius or a fraud. Some critics argued that the album was not jazz, but most had to concede that it demonstrated Braxton's thoroughgoing mastery of the alto saxophone. It also showed his knowledge of avant-garde classical music as well as cutting-edge jazz—he was interested equally in free improvisations and structural blueprints. Braxton kept his listeners guessing with the variety of his associations, including bands led by Chick Corea (Circle), Dave Holland, and Dave Brubeck, and duets with Max Roach. He issued dozens of recordings under his own name, with the instrumentation ranging from synthesizer to twin orchestras.

Braxton's historicism caused more controversy than accord. In 1974, for example, he formed a band, In the Tradition, to present jazz and pop standards (originally it confined itself to pieces by Charlie Parker), but the band performed in ways that undermined the feeling of the original works.

Anthony Braxton wrote music for every conceivable ensemble and played every conceivable saxophone, including the giant contrabass. At the Kitchen, New York, 1977.

© BOB PARENT/COURTESY OF DALE PARENT

His choice of instruments (like the huge contrabass saxophone), harmonies, and rhythms often seemed to counter the traditions he promised to explore. He was criticized for not swinging and for titling his pieces with drawings that resembled circuit diagrams. Ultimately, his music proved so varied and touched on so many idioms and styles (from brass band marches to atonal big-band swing), that the single word "jazz" could not contain it. Braxton eventually found a home in academia as a professor of music. In 1994, he created the Tri-Centric Foundation to present multimedia and interdisciplinary concerts in New York.

🎧 "Piece Three"

Braxton released one of his most widely noted albums, *Creative Orchestra Music*, in 1976. It was his first work with a large ensemble, and the selection of musicians emphasized the historicism that characterized the Loft Era; here were musicians associated with swing (Seldon Powell), bebop (Jon Faddis), fusion (Dave Holland), Euro modernism (Kenny Wheeler), and every kind of avant-garde music in and out of jazz. Each of the album's six selections illustrated a different type of composition, employing aspects of big-band jazz, parade music, and free improvisation. "Piece Three" remains unique in attempting to construct and deconstruct the sort of march that James Reese Europe's regimental band might have played during World War I.

The title simply means that it's the third selection on the album—it's also designated by one of Braxton's mathematic diagrams. As a composition, it represents the kind of wry, unexpected gambit he does best. From the very beginning, the music startles with its authenticity: whoever heard of a march on a jazz album? Yet for all the jubilance of the opening four strains, the last of which suggests the kind of music heard in an old German beer garden more than it does a military cadence, we soon realize that the composer has other things on his mind.

The *oom-pahs* are suddenly stuck in a repetitive rut, as though the melody had been wrung out. Dissonant chords signal the entrance of trumpeter Leo Smith, playing pitches of no use in a march. Yet the bass lines, harmonies, and rhythms are controlled and deliberate. No less surprising is the appealing ostinato for reeds and flute that sets up the droll, tailgate trombone playing by George Lewis, and the brief spot of parade drumming that introduces Braxton's quizzical clarinet solo. These touches of contrast and humor occur throughout the piece. Note the persistent echoing and harmonizing of the glockenspiel (metal bars played with two hammers). When the march is reconstructed for the finale (6:34), the harmonies are what, in an ordinary march, would seem nothing more than a cliché. Here they have the effect of an ironic wink, as the piece waddles off in the sunshine.

4.11

🕮 piece three

ANTHONY BRAXTON

Kenny Wheeler, Cecil Bridgewater, Leo Smith, trumpets; Jon Faddis, trumpet and piccolo trumpet; George Lewis, Garrett List, trombones; Jack Jeffers, bass trombone; Jonathan Dorn, tuba; Anthony Braxton, alto saxophone and clarinet; Seldon Powell, alto saxophone and flute; Ronald Bridgewater, tenor saxophone; Bruce Johnstone, baritone saxophone and bass clarinet; Roscoe Mitchell, bass saxophone; Dave Holland, bass; Karl Berger, glockenspiel; Warren Smith, Barry Altschul, snare drums; Frederick Rzewski, bass drum; Philip Wilson, marching cymbals

- Label: *Creative Orchestra Music 1976,* Arista 4080; *Creative Orchestra Music 1976* (Mosaic Box)
- Date: 1976
- Style: avant-garde historicist
- Form: idiosyncratic

What to listen for:
- march rhythm and cadences (in strains A–D)
- dissonance and unpredictable meters as march gets "stuck" (solo 1)
- ostinato in reeds and flute, trombone glissandos, glockenspiel (solo 2)
- solos by Smith, Lewis, Braxton
- grand return of march (strain E), with piccolo trumpet countermelody

INTRODUCTION

0:00 The piece begins with the band playing standard introductory material for a march: a thunderous line in octaves that snakes its way upward to a **half cadence** on the dominant chord.

STRAIN A

0:03 The trumpets play the melody, doubled by the glockenspiel, over a steady two-beat accompaniment in the tuba and percussion. The saxophones answer with riff figures. Underneath, the trombones play simple supporting lines.

STRAIN B

0:17 After a brief pause, the new strain begins. The instrumentation remains the same, while the harmony begins not on the tonic but on the dominant.

STRAIN C

0:31 The third strain begins on yet another chord. The tune in the trumpets continues as before, while the saxophone riffs become more elaborate.

STRAIN D

0:45 The melody shifts to the tuba, doubled by the bass drum, and falls on the downbeat. The upbeats are filled with chords played crisply by the brass. The harmony shifts back and forth between the tonic and the dominant.

SOLO 1

0:59 Suddenly, the bass line moves to a new, **dissonant** note. The harmony on the upbeat sounds as though it ought to resolve—but it doesn't.

1:03 The bass line and chords, which had been alternating in simple duple meter, suddenly switch to a new meter in groups of three. Adding to the confusion, we hear a caterwauling trumpet sound in the uppermost register.

1:06 The harmony remains stuck on the dissonance. The trumpet player, Smith, descends to a more normal register, but his choice of notes remains decidedly "outside."

1:11 The bass line and chords now change meter unpredictably: sometimes in groups of two, sometimes in three, four, or even five.

1:21 Smith's melodic line occasionally contains fragments of melody, but the overall impression is of a *sound*, hovering dissonantly above the constantly changing accompaniment.

1:33 As if to stabilize his line, Smith leans into a single sustained note. This, too, eventually disintegrates into higher unstable pitches.

1:50 The trumpet sounds as if it were mimicking human speech.

2:16 Struggling to read their parts, the accompaniment players occasionally miss some of Braxton's relentlessly changing meters.

SOLO 2

2:33 The solo and accompaniment suddenly come to a stop. In their place we hear a simple five-note line, played by the clarinets in octaves. They continue to repeat it as an **ostinato**.

2:41 A saxophone joins the ostinato.

2:48 A flute adds a part of its own, creating a thin harmony.

2:55 With a dramatic **glissando**, Lewis enters on trombone. He begins with simple, idiomatic trombone gestures, but soon adds stratospheric assaults on the upper register and extraordinarily quick passages.

3:03 In the background, another flute begins to improvise.

3:09 The glockenspiel and clarinet join the ostinato.

3:15 Using the trombone's slide, Lewis punctuates his solo with loud glissandos.

3:40 As Lewis finishes his solo, the snare drum interrupts the texture with a faster rhythmic figure that displaces the ostinato.

SOLO 3

3:43 A cymbal crash introduces the next section. While a percussionist keeps time on the side of his instrument, brass instruments play chords in a steady short-short-long rhythmic gesture. Braxton starts a disjointed solo on clarinet.

3:47 More and more instruments continue to join the chords, making them heavier and more dissonant. Each instrument adds its own note, and several begin to drop by half step.

3:59 The saxophones interrupt with a long, low-pitched dissonant chord.

4:08 As Braxton continues improvising, the glockenspiel adds notes above him.

4:13 The saxophones play another dissonant chord. After a brief pause, they play two more dissonant chords, one immediately following the other.

4:25 Faddis on piccolo trumpet adds notes that complicate the rhythm. Another dissonant chord follows.

4:37 After reaching a peak of intensity, the background chords quiet down.

4:40 A higher-pitched dissonant chord is followed by a new burst from the piccolo trumpet.

4:51 The dissonant chords begin to increase in number, each emphasized by the crash of a cymbal.

4:58 Yet another dissonant chord. As Braxton reaches the climax of his solo, his tone becomes shrill and distorted.

5:09 A loud cymbal announces three more dissonant chords, augmented by crazy decoration from the glockenspiel.

5:27 Three more dissonant chords, each with its own cymbal crash.

INTERLUDE

5:42 A few strokes of the snare drum dissipate the previous section.

5:44 The saxophones enter with a chromatic unison line.

5:46 As with the interlude to Sousa's "Stars and Stripes Forever," the entire band descends on a **chromatic scale**.

5:48 The gesture is repeated twice, each time at a higher pitch (a **sequence**).

5:54 The phrases become shorter, each ending with a half-step dissonance.

5:59 As the clarinet trills wildly, the band inexorably moves toward a big cadence.

STRAIN E

6:04   In a slower, grander tempo, the band triumphantly returns to the opening mood of the piece. The cymbal plays on every beat, while the piccolo trumpet improvises a **counter-melody** on top.

6:20   A descending line signals a repetition.

STRAIN E

6:22   As the band plays the strain one more time, the snare drums cement the groove with **press-rolls**.

6:34   To signal the end, Braxton adds a slight intensification to the harmonic progression.

6:40   One last blast ends the piece.

THE NEOCLASSICISTS (1980s)

The Loft Era musicians, as we have seen, borrowed from old styles as resources: they combined swing, funk, and free rhythms to create an independent music seasoned with humor, irony, nostalgia, sarcasm, and deep feelings. For them, the aging battle cry of "free jazz" meant the freedom to play whatever they liked—even ragtime, even a march.

In the manner of Hegel's dialectic, however, that thesis invariably triggered an antithesis in the early 1980s. The ensuing movement involved a more conservative approach toward historicism, which may be defined as **neoclassical**. This approach was predicated on fidelity to a specific canon of masterpieces. Instead of looking at marches or swing or bop as generic styles that could be interpreted and reinterpreted, it paid homage to particular musicians and works, infusing them with a contemporary luster—at best. Yet neoclassicists also argued that jazz must swing in a certain way, that harmonies and melodies had to conform to traditional practices, that jazz had clear-cut borders defined by its key artists.

This kind of traditionalism found acceptance in the early 1980s for several reasons, including the conservative temper of the time. Ronald Reagan had just been elected president, promising to implement (despite his own messy personal life) traditional American values, a harsh approach toward law and order, and a reversal of "great society" programs of the 1960s, including welfare and civil rights. He represented a backlash against the excesses associated with a period roiled by a tragically unnecessary war, political assassinations, and student revolt.

Reagan frequently referred to the allegedly golden age of his youth and often confused real life with movie plots. His popularity reflected both the pragmatic yearning for a steadying hand at the tiller of government and the purely sentimental longing for a paradise lost. These anti-intellectual and wishful feelings precipitated hostility toward the arts, especially those thought to appeal to an *elitist* (this was a prominent code word) audience. Arts funding was reduced, while books and other art works were censored or removed from public display. In this atmosphere, nostalgia for an orderly, swinging style of jazz was practically a given.

The American Jazz Orchestra revitalized jazz repertory in residence at Cooper Union's Great Hall: (first row) Danny Bank, Norris Turney, Loren Schoenberg; (second row) Benny Powell, Eddie Bert, Bob Milliken, John Eckhardt, bassist John Goldsby, pianist Dick Katz. Standing: director of the Great Hall Roberta Swann, artistic director Gary Giddins, music director John Lewis. New York, 1986.

Established players who had been alienated by the avant-garde and fusion began to explore jazz history by paying homage to deceased or neglected musicians. At first the trend seemed novel, but it grew into a tidal wave of tributes and interpretations. Joe Henderson recorded albums of music by Billy Strayhorn and Miles Davis; Kenny Barron and musicians associated with Thelonious Monk formed a quartet, Sphere, to play his music. Philly Joe Jones organized a big band to play music by Tadd Dameron. Steve Lacy focused on works by the overlooked pianist-composer Herbie Nichols. Keith Jarrett, who had almost exclusively played original music as a bandleader, now launched a standards trio to reinvestigate pop and jazz classics.

Repertory vs. Nostalgia

The most expansive tribute bands were orchestras created to examine big-band jazz, either by performing original arrangements or by commissioning new versions of classic works. The **jazz repertory** movement got its start in the middle 1970s, with the debuts of two groups. The New York Jazz Repertory Company, launched by George Wein, produced two seasons of concerts at Carnegie Hall by rotating music directors: Cecil Taylor led a large orchestra that included former students; George Russell conducted his own music; Paul Jeffrey conducted orchestral versions of music by Thelonious Monk with Monk playing piano; and so forth. And the National Jazz Ensemble, a solitary orchestra with stable personnel, directed by bassist Chuck Israels, played new versions of venerable jazz works.

By the middle 1980s, those organizations had long since disbanded, but the neoclassical movement whetted the appetite for more ambitious jazz repertory concerts. At first these were isolated events, involving large bands and small. Duke Ellington's music was frequently revived. Other presentations recreated famous events, like the 1938 Benny Goodman Carnegie Hall Concert and Paul Whiteman's 1924 *Rhapsody in Blue* concert.

In 1986, the American Jazz Orchestra debuted, conducted by John Lewis, whose association with jazz historicism dated back to the Lenox School. In addition to music by Ellington, Goodman, Count Basie, Jimmie Lunceford, Mary Lou Williams, Woody Herman, Dizzy Gillespie, and Gil Evans, the orchestra performed arrangements that had rarely if ever been heard. These included Ellington's *Black, Brown, and Beige*, conducted by Maurice Peress with a revised ending based on instructions Ellington dictated to Peress shortly before his death. Several composers from the various eras of jazz history—Benny Carter, Jimmy Heath, Muhal Richard Abrams, David Murray—were invited to write and conduct new works during the orchestra's seven years.

American Jazz Orchestra

Similar orchestras were created in San Diego, Washington, D.C. (under the aegis of the Smithsonian Institution), and elsewhere. From 1992 to 2002, Jon Faddis, a remarkable high-note trumpet virtuoso and former protégé of Dizzy Gillespie, led the Carnegie Hall Jazz Band, which premiered new versions of classic jazz works and often created unexpected transformations, such as an arrangement of John Coltrane's *A Love Supreme* for full orchestra. The band also recovered long neglected works, including Lalo Schifrin's suite *Gillespiana*.

The most durable of the new repertory orchestras debuted in 1987 at Lincoln Center, New York's leading cultural institution. The Lincoln Center Jazz Orchestra, under the direction of Wynton Marsalis (see below), achieved outstanding successes that led to the development of an independent jazz wing for the center, including a multiplex that housed concert halls, a night club, and educational facilities. Encouraged by the Jazz at Lincoln Center program, university and high school music departments began to introduce jazz repertory into student orchestras.

Jazz at Lincoln Center

Some performers took a more nostalgic attitude. Singer-pianists Harry Connick Jr. and Diana Krall demonstrated popular appeal by resurrecting performance styles of the 1940s and 1950s. Connick was the first of several male singers to invoke the manner of Frank Sinatra, though he also spiced his performances with piano playing that reflected Monk's percussive wit. Krall initially made her name with a trio that echoed the instrumentation (piano,

Harry Connick Jr./ Diana Krall

© ALAN NAHIGIAN

Wynton Marsalis (right), trumpet player, composer, and activist, helped to create the jazz wing at Lincoln Center, emphasizing jazz's swinging tradition and often performing with major figures from earlier eras, including trumpet player Clark Terry and saxophonist Jimmy Heath. New York, 1990.

guitar, bass) and songs of Nat King Cole. She later recorded ballads with lush studio orchestras in the manner of mainstream 1950s singers.

Less rewarding were a cluster of **retro-swing** orchestras, which played for dancers and triggered a revival of ballroom dancing. They were good for dancing but not for listening, as they usually performed in a generic style that lacked the individuality of the great swing bands. They appealed to a nostalgic desire for the world as it was, and soon faded away. Jazz nostalgia even found its way into such movies as Bertrand Tavernier's 'Round Midnight, in which tenor saxophonist Dexter Gordon created a character based on Bud Powell and Lester Young; Clint Eastwood's Bird, a fictionalized biography of Charlie Parker, with Parker's saxophone solos grafted to a modern rhythm section; and Robert Altman's Kansas City, in which 1930s musicians were viewed as a positive counterstatement to the city's appalling crime and corruption.

■ WYNTON MARSALIS (b. 1961)

Young neoclassical musicians in the 1980s found an unmistakable leader in Wynton Marsalis, an audacious trumpet virtuoso who loudly denied that avant-garde jazz and electric fusion had anything to do with jazz. Marsalis also sought to alter the personal styles of musicians. Ridiculing the dashikis (loose pullovers), occasional facial paint, and general informality that characterized the way musicians appeared onstage, he insisted on a suit-and-tie dress code that reinstated the elegance of Swing Era bands.

Marsalis was the ultimate Reagan-era jazz musician. He launched his recording career with simultaneous jazz and classical releases, winning Grammy Awards in both categories. Highly intelligent, impeccably groomed, and fiercely outspoken, he changed the discussion in jazz from one of progressive modernism—with its liberal borrowings from world, popular, and classical music—to the strict interpretation of mainstream jazz parameters. He insisted that jazz had to swing with a particular regularity.

Though lambasted as divisive by many musicians, Marsalis was quickly accepted by the popular culture, frequently appearing in televised concerts, in magazine articles, and as a key voice in Ken Burns's film Jazz. He was the first straight-ahead jazz musician to achieve that degree of renown in more than a decade. Yet Marsalis was as hard on himself as he was on anyone else. He was involved in every kind of jazz historicism. As the artistic director of Jazz at Lincoln Center, he conducted dozens of jazz repertory concerts, interpreting composers from Ellington and Armstrong to Mingus and Gil Evans. He recorded fanciful interpretations of Morton and Monk. He also created a massive body of original work that probes African American history, tradition, and music in such formats as jazz ensembles, chamber groups, and ballet.

From New Orleans to New York

Marsalis was born in New Orleans to a musical family. His father, Ellis, was a well-known pianist and educator who instilled in him a sense of dedication and discipline. His brothers are also musicians, most prominently saxophonist Branford, an equally skilled musician who often challenged his brother's precepts by working in diverse musical settings, including a tour with rock singer Sting. At fourteen, Wynton played Haydn's Trumpet Concerto with the New Orleans Philharmonic; his early taste in jazz ran to funk and fusion.

In 1980, while studying at Juilliard, Marsalis auditioned for Art Blakey and won a coveted position with Blakey's Jazz Messengers. After making a dynamic showing on Blakey's *Album of the Year*, he toured with a Herbie Hancock quartet and then organized his own quintet, with Branford. This group was modeled on one of the few sixties acoustic jazz groups to achieve mainstream acceptance—the 1963–68 Miles Davis Quintet. His deliberate turn to the musical past, along with his dark suits and sober demeanor, delighted many people. If he hadn't felt compelled to use his celebrity to attack less well-placed musicians, his success might have proved even more widespread.

Unfortunately, the mass media that accepted Marsalis as an engaging personality and musical spokesman was no longer responsive to jazz itself. It could absorb Marsalis as a celebrity, but could not roll the clock back to a time when musicians appeared on radio and television and when record releases by its most creative players were well-publicized events. Marsalis's exacting historicism underscored the fact that jazz now competed less with pop or classical music than with its own past. Young fans were challenged with a choice: do you buy a new tribute to Monk, or do you buy Monk? As jazz record sales plummeted, even Marsalis—despite his Grammys and a 1997 Pulitzer Prize for his oratorio *Blood on the Fields*—was dropped by his label, Columbia Records, which turned its corporate back on jazz altogether.

Marsalis seemed to understand this, and increasingly devoted his energies to touring, education, and relentless fund-raising to ensure the success of Jazz at Lincoln Center. His music became increasingly eclectic, combining references to earlier forms of jazz in a manner that could only be described as pastiche. For a while, his trumpet playing turned from the Miles Davis template to an earlier style that employed mutes and vocalized sounds, à la Ellington. At the same time, he developed greater clarity in his improvisations, making the most of long phrases and high-note gambits. He also loosened some of his strictures, though not about the avant-garde; he even recorded an album with Willie Nelson.

🎧 "Processional"

Marsalis's *In This House, On This Morning*, recorded during 1992 and 1993, represented his most ambitious work to date. Written for septet, it chronicles a Sunday in the life of a religious congregation, from devotional prayers through the sermons and hymns of the church service to the "Pot Blessed Dinner." It is structured in three movements, each of which is made up of smaller units. "Processional," from the first part, follows "Devotion" and "Call to Prayer" and precedes "Representative Offerings" and "The Lord's Prayer."

If we compare "Processional" with Anthony Braxton's "Piece Three," we see that it introduces a gospel theme that's as credible as Braxton's march. Braxton, however, bulldozes his march before reconstituting it, while Marsalis uses subtler touches to give his take on gospel music a modernist affect, mostly through odd structural changes that slightly distort our expectations. Those alterations have a historical accuracy in that Southern black rural music tended to be less precise and codified than city music. But Marsalis also owes a great deal to Igor Stravinsky, the Russian composer who began turning classical music on its head through unusual metrical shifts as early as 1913, with *The Rite of Spring*. (Marsalis recorded Stravinsky's *L'histoire du soldat* as

Fiddler's Tale in 1999.) In "Processional," phrases come up a bit short (2:14) or long (2:37) or peculiar (the "threes" at 3:49). Such oddities, thoroughly rehearsed, give the piece a spry whimsy.

Other references to the past are much in evidence. The **A** theme is in the style of folk songs and hymns like "Down by the Riverside" and "I've Been Working on the Railroad," and consequently recalls Horace Silver's similar piece, "The Preacher" (Chapter 12). The harmonies underlying the **C** theme suggest those of "Sweet Georgia Brown" (1:04). The use of the tambourine is as evocative of gospel traditions as Braxton's glockenspiel is of march tradition. An Ellington influence is apparent in the blending of bowed bass and horns (0:42), the superbly vocalized trombone playing by Wycliffe Gordon (throughout), and Marsalis's half-valve trumpet effects (2:53). Each of these details emphasizes the literalness of Marsalis's approach to the past.

half-valving: pressing trumpet valves only halfway down

LISTENING GUIDE

4.12

 processional

WYNTON MARSALIS SEPTET

Wynton Marsalis, trumpet; Wycliffe Gordon, trombone; Wessell Anderson, alto saxophone; Todd Williams, tenor saxophone; Eric Reed, piano; Reginald Veal, bass; Herlin Riley, drums

- Label: *In This House, On This Morning,* Columbia C2K-53220
- Date: 1993
- Style: historicist
- Form: **A A B A**, with contrasting **C** section and interludes

What to listen for:
- simple gospel playing (with tambourine on the backbeat) interrupted by modernist tricks
- vocalized trombone playing by Gordon
- unpredictable structure: phrases cut short or extended, horns "trading threes"
- Marsalis's half-valving

INTRODUCTION (TRANSITION)

0:00   The band moves out of the preceding movement, "Call to Prayer" (echoes of which can be heard in the first few seconds). A hoarse-sounding trombone leads with a descending **glissando** into this new movement.

A (16 bars)

0:03   The trombonist (Gordon) plays a pair of four-bar phrases. The groove solidly evokes the gospel church: the tambourine accents on the **backbeat**, while the bass bounces fluidly between a syncopated two-beat pattern and a **walking bass**. The piano plays simple, churchy chords.

0:13   The second eight-bar phrase echoes the first, moving to a more extended cadence, backed by a walking-bass pattern.

A

0:23   Behind the trombone, a choir of trumpet, alto saxophone, and tenor saxophone plays a riff in **block-chord** harmony.

0:33   As Gordon plays the second phrase, the horn choir moves its accompanying harmonies to a simpler rhythmic pattern.

INTERLUDE

0:42   The trombone's melody is interrupted by a simple four-note, descending **pentatonic** riff, played by the three horns and the bowed bass. After a short pause, Gordon begins to play.

0:44   He's cut short by a two-bar **break**, in which the bass bows a simple variation of the descending riff. Once again, Gordon restarts his line.

B (8 bars)

0:47   As the harmony moves to IV, the horns play a rhythmically intricate riff.

0:49   At the end of the first phrase, a bar is deliberately cut short (it lasts for only two beats instead of four).

0:54   The second phrase is interrupted by a return of the descending riff (harmonized). This time, the line is cut short after its third note.

A (abbreviated)

0:56   The opening melody returns; but by inserting a few strategic **rests**, Marsalis forces it into unexpected rhythmic shapes. The tambourine continues to play the backbeat, but its position within the meter is continually changing.

C (16 bars)

1:04   After a short break, the tenor and alto saxophones play simple quarter-note melodies. Each line is designed to fit within the new harmony, but they often clash with sharp dissonances. Riley (drums) enters, displacing the tambourine with a firm backbeat on the snare drum.

1:14   As the harmony shifts to more distant chords, the melody lines become more rhythmically independent. In response, Riley plays more complex polyrhythms.

A

1:24   With a plunger mute, Gordon returns us to the mood of the opening, playing in between the tambourine backbeats with an intensely distorted timbre.

1:28   After his first phrase, a band member responds with an appreciative grunt.

1:34   In the second eight-bar phrase, Gordon shows his command of the instrument, playing soulful yet rhythmically intricate lines.

A

1:44   As the horns return to their riff, Gordon improvises in response to their call.

INTERLUDE

2:04   In a two-bar break, the horns and bass play the four-note pentatonic riff.

B

2:06   Behind the trombone, the horns play increasingly complicated harmonies and rhythms.

2:14   Once again, the phrase is interrupted by the descending riff—this time only three notes (which means a bar and a *half*).

A

2:16   Gordon returns to the main melody.

2:25   The bass and the pianist's left hand set up a **counterrhythm**—three eighth notes against the prevailing quarter-note pulse. Against this, we can hear two lines: one played by the trombone and the trumpet, the other by the saxophones. Riley improvises his own accompaniment on the tambourine.

2:35   In a two-bar break, the bass enters with a plucked version of the descending riff.

B

2:37   Over the harmony of the bridge, the horns combine on a complex block-chord figure. The concluding drum figure adds an extra measure, making the phrase five bars long.

2:43   The second measure of the next phrase is slightly longer, pushing the downbeat arrival (at 2:46) one beat late.

C

2:48   The rhythmic groove suddenly shifts away from gospel toward a modern jazz sound. The bass plays a walking-bass line, while the piano voices the chords as postbop harmonies. Marsalis takes a solo.

2:53	Marsalis squeezes out several notes through **half-valving**.	

C

3:08	Anderson begins a four-bar solo on alto saxophone.
3:12	His improvisation is matched by four bars by Williams on tenor: the two are **trading fours**.
3:17	Anderson's and Williams's lines become increasingly complicated as they play off each other's ideas.

C

3:27	As the saxophones continue trading fours, the accompaniment by the drums and piano heats up in intensity.
3:41	Williams begins playing rapid passages in double-time.

C

3:46	Anderson mimics Williams's rapid passage before returning to a normal groove.
3:49	Williams's response comes in after only three bars: the soloists are now "trading threes."
4:00	The two horns enter on a set of composed lines, moving in steady quarter notes (reminiscent of 1:04).
4:03	In the background, Gordon begins a trombone **glissando**, starting softly but growing in intensity.

A

4:05	The glissando pulls us back into the gospel groove: the trombone is in the lead, the horns playing riffs behind.

CODA

4:12	In a two-bar break, the piano and bass interrupt with a rising line that modulates to an unfamiliar key a half step higher.
4:14	The main melody of the **A** section is repeated in the new key.
4:21	The band stops on a blue note, holding it out as if deliberately slowing the tempo to prepare for a final cadence. After a slight pause, though, the melody line continues as before.
4:24	An unexpected missing downbeat masks a sudden modulation to the original key. The missing beat forces the tambourine's backbeat to fall on the downbeat.
4:27	As it approaches the cadence, the band disorients us further by playing a melodic figure in three different rhythmic shapes.
4:31	Finally, the band lands on its final cadence.
4:35	As the piece is ready to move on to the next movement, the track cuts off.

ALTERNATIVE ROUTES TO HISTORY

Between Wynton Marsalis's historicist fidelity and Anthony Braxton's historicist revisionism, less extreme ways of dealing with the past won the hearts of most musicians. Some musicians simply devoted concerts and albums to works by a well-known composer, like Ellington or Monk. Others wandered so far afield from jazz traditions that they opened up what was, in effect, virgin territory—rock songs, country blues, classical themes, folk idioms.

Jazz in the twenty-first century may be characterized, to a degree, by the number and variety of these projects. They tend to be more conventional than the loft generation's radical interpretations, while ignoring strictures favored by the neoclassicists. A short list of examples does double duty as a guide to some of the most gifted and influential jazz musicians on the current scene:

- Clarinetist Don Byron (b. 1958) has interpreted the works of Mickey Katz, a Jewish musical satirist and composer of *klezmer* (Yiddish dance music); novelty composer Raymond Scott, whose pieces were often adapted for Looney Tune cartoons; and 1930s jazz bassist John Kirby, known for "swinging the classics."

- Guitarist Bill Frissell (b. 1951) plays concert sets that range over every kind of American music, moving in a kind of stream-of-consciousness from Monk to Aaron Copland to Bob Dylan to Charles Ives to traditional folk and country tunes.

- Singer Cassandra Wilson (b. 1955) has expanded the vocalist's repertory by reaching back to Delta blues singers like Son House and Robert Johnson and to recent pop performers like Joni Mitchell, Dylan, and the Monkees.

- Singer Dee Dee Bridgewater (b. 1950) has recorded albums of instrumental pieces by Horace Silver, outfitted with new lyrics, and French chanson; she expanded her reach as a singer-actress on and off Broadway.

- The Bad Plus Trio, consisting of pianist Ethan Iverson (b. 1973), bassist Reid Anderson (b. 1970), and drummer Dave King (b. 1970), plays a unique repertory that includes Nirvana, Blondie, Aphex Twin, Queen, Radiohead, and Ornette Coleman.

- Guitarist Marc Ribot (b. 1954) has adapted the melodies of avant-garde saxophonist Albert Ayler to solo guitar, collaborated with punk rock groups, and created the band Los Cubanos Postizos to explore Afro-Cuban compositions.

- Trumpet player Nicholas Payton (b. 1973) has performed tributes to Cannonball Adderley, Herbie Hancock, and 1930s Kansas City swing; recreated solos by Louis Armstrong and King Oliver; and recorded duets with ninety-year-old trumpeter Doc Cheatham.

- Pianist Uri Caine (b. 1956) combines classical, rock, electronica, and jazz techniques in predominantly jazz settings to interpret the music of Mahler, Bach, and Mozart; he created a musical montage to recreate the ethnic complexity of early Tin Pan Alley.

- Trumpet player Dave Douglas (b. 1963) has formed discrete bands to pay homage to Wayne Shorter, Mary Lou Williams, and Booker Little; he has also played klezmer music and introduced the band Tiny Bell Trio to interpret Baltic folk tunes.

- Italian alto saxophonist Francisco Cafiso (b. 1989), who began recording at fourteen, has recreated the entire body of Charlie Parker's recordings with strings, accompanied by the thirteen-piece chamber orchestra I Solisti di Perugia.

- Trumpet player Wallace Roney (b. 1960) has participated in Chick Corea's Bud Powell tribute band and Gerry Mulligan's recreation of the "birth of the cool" sessions, and performed in concert a faithful rendition of Miles Davis's *Kind of Blue* album.

These projects (the tip of the iceberg) show how historicist jazz links modern creativity to the "jazz tradition" and other kinds of music. They have liberated jazz from the orthodox repertory that governed jazz in the postbop era, which consisted of standards by pantheon songwriters, new tunes based

© JIMMY KATZ

Drummer Ronald Shannon Jackson (seen here in the 1990s) injected a vibrant backbeat in performances with avant-garde ensembles, but really let go when he organized his own free-fusion ensembles with jazz and rock musicians.

on the harmonies of those standards, and new works of various quality. The new historicism has more in common with the repertory of the Swing Era bands, which routinely adopted pop songs as well as an occasional classical theme and even a few ethnic styles, from Cuban to Yiddish.

■ RONALD SHANNON JACKSON (b. 1940) and JAMES CARTER (b. 1969)

Two unpredictable stylists of the new historicism, from different generations, found mutual inspiration in the conflation of modern and historical styles. Drummer Ronald Shannon Jackson and saxophonist James Carter are known for aggressive virtuoso skills and a willingness to look beyond the usual jazz parameters. That willingness has led them to explore the avant-garde and fusion as well as traditional jazz (both separately and together), although everything they play is anchored by an improvisational enthusiasm that kept them at the center of 1990s jazz.

Jackson was born in Fort Worth, Texas, where his mother played church piano and his father stocked jukeboxes and ran a record store. He was exposed early to bluesmen like Howlin' Wolf and B. B. King and jazz musicians like Charlie Parker and Erroll Garner, while hearing hillbilly and rhythm and blues on the radio and classical music in school. Jackson studied piano, then switched to drums, and began working professionally at fifteen. He enrolled at Lincoln University in Pennsylvania, but dropped out to pursue his career. Upon resuming his education at the University of Bridgeport (Connecticut), where he studied sociology and history, he received a scholarship from the New York College of Music in 1967.

Over the next three years, Jackson worked with many adventurous musicians, backing singer Betty Carter, playing timpani for Charles Mingus, and touring with Albert Ayler. But jazz was in the economic doldrums, and for five years Jackson played mostly weddings and bar mitzvahs. In 1975, he was having breakfast in a Greenwich Village restaurant when Ornette Coleman walked in and mentioned he was looking for a drummer for his band Prime Time (see Chapter 15). Jackson's subsequent recordings with Coleman, the fusion albums *Dancing in Your Head* and *Body Meta*, aroused much interest. He combined supple attentiveness with a heavily jubilant rhythmic feeling; in effect, he had brought funk to avant-garde jazz. This was reaffirmed in 1978, when he recorded with Cecil Taylor: on *3 Phasis*, Jackson, without warning, infused the climax of the piece with a backbeat rhythm that inspired Taylor and the whole ensemble.

Decoding Society   Soon Jackson was leading his own band, called the Decoding Society because it sought to find the common denominator that brought various musical forces into harmony:

> The thing I'm trying to do is organize the music, and you have to rehearse constantly, because we're talking about putting together all the musical ideas of the past 30 years. It's got to swing—swing is the egg in the meatloaf—but it can be

bop, reggae, rock, classical. It has to be a total experience for everyone involved, like going to a Buddhist meeting, where we deal in our energies, not in egos or who we are or what we do.

In 1994, the Decoding Society recorded an exemplary quartet album, *What Spirit Say*, featuring James Carter on tenor and soprano saxophones. At twenty-five, Carter already had a richly comprehensive resume. He was considered by some to be the representative musician for an era in which historicism simultaneously boosted involvement with the jazz past and knocked down borders for the jazz present.

Born in Detroit, Carter began on saxophone at eleven, and five years later toured Scandinavia with a student ensemble. While still in his teens, he worked with Wynton Marsalis and Lester Bowie, the two trumpet players who incarnated the divide in 1980s jazz, publicly feuding with each other after Marsalis declared that Bowie and the Art Ensemble of Chicago weren't jazz musicians. Even so, they apparently agreed on Carter's overwhelming musicianship, revealed in his mastery of saxophones from soprano to baritone. Carter later played in Marsalis's Lincoln Center Jazz Orchestra, but his inclinations ran to the open-endedness of Loft Era historicists; on moving to New York in 1990, he enlisted in two of Bowie's ensembles, including a fusion group centered on the Hammond B3 organ.

Carter recorded his first album, *JC on the Set*, in 1993, a dramatic debut that led to a series of quartet albums. He defied categorization, playing with harmonic sophistication on one number and in gritty funk mode on the next—equally comfortable with blues, ballads, and free improvisation. He soon became involved in a series of historicist projects, including Robert Altman's film *Kansas City*, in which he helped recreate the musical and social atmosphere of the 1930s.

James Carter (2001) brings tremendous vitality to his playing on tenor and baritone saxophone and avoids pigeon-holing by changing from swing and bop to soul and funk, all of it leavened with an avant-garde irreverence.

For his 1996 album *Conversin' with the Elders*, Carter recruited an unparalleled quartet of musicians from two widely divergent jazz eras: tenor saxophonist Buddy Tate and trumpeter Harry Edison from Count Basie's 1930s orchestra, and Bowie and baritone saxophonist Hamiet Bluiett from the Loft Era cooperatives. In 2000, Carter simultaneously released two albums: *Chasin' the Gypsy*, a thoughtful, scrupulously arranged interpretation of music by Django Reinhardt, and *Layin' in the Cut*, a set of improvisations with a fusion rhythm section. A few years later, he returned to the early fusion tradition that had intrigued Bowie: he formed a trio with organ, tenor saxophone, and drums.

"Now's the Time"

Thus far in this chapter, we've heard modernist resurrections of the march and gospel traditions. With Ronald Shannon Jackson's "Now's the Time," we return to the blues: a fusion version of a classic bebop blues by Charlie Parker (analyzed in Chapter 11). Parker's theme picked up fusion associations shortly after he recorded it in 1945, when it was adapted as a rhythm and blues hit, "The Hucklebuck."

Jackson's version is highly sophisticated (it's more harmonically dissonant, for example, than Parker's), and yet partakes of the partying sensibility associated with pop music.

The first chorus is striking: Jackson introduces a variation on the melody by playing a shalmei, considered the oldest of reed instruments and a predecessor of the double-reed oboe. The dissonant guitar chords add to a sense of strangeness, but as the blues changes kick in, we recognize familiar ground. The repetitiveness of the blues chords—through twelve choruses—gives the performance a quality of inevitability, but the constant contrariness of dissonant harmonies and contrapuntal melodies renders the piece as unmistakably contemporary.

Structurally, the performance is simplicity itself: theme, consecutive solos by James Carter's soprano saxophone and Jef Lee Johnson's guitar, return of theme, coda. But the primary interest stems from the collective effort by the quartet. We are always aware of each of the four musicians. The change-ups, syncopations, and other contributions by bass, drums, and guitar, particularly in support of the saxophone solo, have the effect of keeping the piece on edge and flush with small surprises. Compare this group activity with the Parker recording, where the rhythm section is relatively unified in support of his solo. Despite the dissonances and melodic eruptions, including Carter's high-note squawks, the integrity of the blues harmony is never threatened. We invariably know where we are.

LISTENING GUIDE

4.13

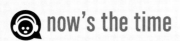 **now's the time**

RONALD SHANNON JACKSON

Ronald Shannon Jackson, drums and shalmei; James Carter, soprano saxophone; Jef Lee Johnson, electric guitar; Ngolle Pokossi, electric bass

- Label: *What Spirit Say,* DIW 895
- Date: 1994
- Style: avant-garde historicist
- Form: 12-bar blues

What to listen for:

- electric rhythm section, ethnic double-reed instrument (shalmei)
- Carter's distorted timbre and high solo on soprano saxophone
- bass pedal point in choruses 6, 9, 10
- Johnson's guitar responses to the saxophone

CHORUS 1 (INTRODUCTION)

0:00 Jackson plays a riff on the shalmei, answered by dissonant and strangely timed chords from Johnson on electric guitar.

0:07 The guitar arrives on IV. Jackson plays **syncopations** (sudden accents on the offbeat) that mirror the original melody to "Now's the Time."

0:18 By the time the harmony returns to I in the tenth bar, Pokossi enters on electric bass.

CHORUS 2 (HEAD)

0:21 Carter enters with the head to "Now's the Time" on soprano saxophone, the melody roughly doubling Jackson's ongoing shalmei riff. The guitar **comps** behind them.

0:29 The harmony arrives on IV.

0:32 The guitar begins improvising a complementary melody in the background.

0:38 Jackson drops out, leaving Carter alone on saxophone.

0:42 Carter begins the next chorus with an ascending riff.

CHORUS 3

0:43 Carter's riff ends with a blue note that coincides with a cymbal crash as Jackson reenters on the drums. The guitar breaks his chords into gentle **arpeggios**.

0:51 As the harmony turns to IV, the bass abandons his walking-bass line, playing simple, syncopated patterns.

0:58 Carter plays a riff, then lowers it a half step.

1:02 The chorus ends with a simple, melodic bluesy phrase.

CHORUS 4

1:05 Carter suddenly plays his ascending riff an octave higher.

1:09 As the bass plays ascending **octaves**, Jackson ratchets up the intensity of his drumming while Carter increases the speed of his line to fast bebop-style notes.

1:12 When the harmony arrives on IV, the bass continues playing simple syncopations. In the background, the guitar adds its own melody.

1:25 Carter begins the next chorus with an even higher riff.

CHORUS 5

1:26 Playing with intensely distorted timbre, Carter begins two octaves above where his solo began in chorus 3.

1:28 With an extra effort, he reaches yet another octave higher—well above what a soprano saxophonist would normally try to play.

1:33 Arriving on IV, the bass plays only the root of the chord.

1:37 Carter's improvised line begins to descend.

1:43 His last phrase sounds relaxed and bluesy.

CHORUS 6

1:47 The bass switches to a **pedal point**, freezing the harmony on the tonic for the next eight measures. Against this neutral backdrop, Carter toys with a two-note motive.

1:55 Carter accelerates to double-time.

2:00 As the bass begins walking again, Carter returns to his high register, tooting out a repeated note.

2:05 An extremely high-pitched squawk warns us that he's ready to make yet another assault on his high register.

CHORUS 7

2:07 For the next eight measures, Carter plays notes even he can't fully control. The first note he hits wavers uncertainly in pitch. The next note is higher still, but lasts for only a split second.

2:10 He begins once again on the lower pitch, getting it under better control before moving upward again. Having found the higher note, he holds it for several seconds.

2:13 For a second, he achieves his highest note: B, four octaves above middle C.

2:17 A disorienting squawk brings him down to his normal register.

CHORUS 8

2:27 On guitar, Johnson begins his solo with a simple two-note riff that he transposes and plays in a variety of rhythmic positions.

2:46 His last phrase ends on an unsettling dissonance.

CHORUS 9

2:48 Johnson starts with a three-note motive, heard against the background of another pedal point in the bass.

2:54 As the bass returns to walking over the IV chord, Johnson improvises a line that will run uninterrupted through the entire chorus—and beyond.

CHORUS 10

3:08 Johnson's line becomes simpler, coinciding with yet another pedal point in the bass.

3:16   As the harmony becomes more intense, Johnson plays a rapid series of chords. For the remainder of the chorus, his improvisation blurs unsteadily between melody and chords.

CHORUS 11 (HEAD)

3:27   Carter returns to play the head. In response, Johnson repeats the riff, distorting it into new shapes.

3:32   The horn and guitar now play the riff in harmony.

3:34   Over the IV chord, the harmony takes on a peculiar tone as Carter moves to other modes.

3:43   Carter plays an elaborate, repeating blue note, prompting Johnson to imitate him.

CHORUS 12 (HEAD)

3:47   Over a rapidly repeated bass note, the two instruments play the riff in harmony.

3:51   Carter takes his line "outside" into uncharted harmonic territory.

3:54   Over the IV chord, Carter inserts sudden high-pitched shrieks into his line.

CODA

4:08   The guitar and saxophone come to rest on a single note. Jackson keeps the tension going with a quiet roll on the snare drum.

4:10   Johnson plays a descending bluesy line.

4:12   Carter answers with an ascending line. His last few notes are underscored by cymbal crashes.

THE HISTORICIST PRESENT

When musicians get together and grouse about the current state of jazz, they almost invariably reserve a generous measure of derision for the incessant waves of historicist tributes and interpretations. In 2008, the Grammy Awards, which has always treated jazz as a poor relation, awarded its most coveted prize, album of the year (for 2007), to Herbie Hancock's *River: The Joni Letters*. It was the first time in forty-three years that that accolade had gone to a jazz recording—since the 1964 bossa nova classic *Getz / Gilberto* (Chapter 16).

No one contested the merit of Hancock's album, which consists of highly inventive adaptations of Joni Mitchell songs, performed by a quintet including no fewer than three Miles Davis alums (Hancock, saxophonist Wayne Shorter, and bassist Dave Holland). But neither could anyone imagine a jazz album even being nominated that did not offer either a fusion with pop or a tribute to the past—unlike *Getz / Gilberto*, which celebrated a new idiom in jazz and pop.

With *River*, Hancock brought off a jazz-pop fusion *and* a memorial to another era. How long jazz can continue gazing into a rear-view mirror while gliding forward is anyone's guess.

⊦ ADDITIONAL LISTENING ⊦	
Fletcher Henderson	"Sugar Foot Stomp" (1925); *Fletcher Henderson* (Columbia/Legacy 074646144725)
Charles Mingus	"My Jelly Soul Roll" (1959); *Blues and Roots* (Atlantic 1305-2)
Don Byron	"The Dreidel Song" (1992); *Don Byron Plays the Music of Mickey Katz* (Nonesuch 79313)
Bill Frisell	"Shenandoah" (1999); *Good Dog, Happy Man* (Nonesuch 79536)
Cassandra Wilson	"Dust My Broom" (2007); *Loverly* (Blue Note 5099950769926)
Marc Ribot	"St. James Infirmary" (2001); *Saints* (Atlantic 83461)
Nicholas Payton	"Wild Man Blues" (1995); *Gumbo Nouveau* (Verve 731453119925)
Uri Caine	"Symphony No. 2 (Resurrection) / Primal Light" (1996); *Urlicht/Primal Light* (Winter & Winter 4)
Francisco Cafiso	"Just Friends" (2008); *A Tribute to Charlie Parker* (Giotto Music)
Gerry Mulligan (with Wallace Roney)	"Godchild" (1992); *Re-birth of the Cool* (GRP 011105967921)
Anthony Braxton	"Donna Lee" (2002); *What's New in the Tradition* (Steeplechase 37003)
Wynton Marsalis	"Donna Lee" (2002); *Live at the House of Tribes* (Blue Note 7/132)
Ronald Shannon Jackson	"American Madman" (2000); *Earned Dreams* (KnitClassics 3034)
James Carter	"'Round Midnight" (1994); *The Real Quietstorm* (Atlantic Jazz 82742)
	"Nuages" (2000); *Chasin' the Gypsy* (Atlantic 83304-2)

JAZZ TODAY

AFTER HISTORY

In the 1990s, a new term became fashionable: *post-historical*. Intended to convey the essentially insupportable idea that history is somehow over, that the great political and cultural movements are behind us, it was applied to every aspect of modern life, including jazz. Many people found the concept appealing because it fostered two liberating illusions: first, that our generations are perched atop the historical mountain, looking down at the past, like gods; and second, that history's afterlife is a clean slate, upon which we are free to scrawl our own blueprints for the future. A cursory glance at post-post-historical history suggests that (as throughout human history) such arrogance leads to military debacles and moral chaos. No surprise there.

Even so, if we adapt the post-historical theory to jazz, we may find a helpful way of sorting through the three narratives we have already examined in order to define jazz in the twenty-first century. So let's pretend we are looking down from the mountain crest.

The art-for-art's-sake account, in which jazz is seen to have evolved in a vacuum of inspired innovations, from Buddy Bolden's slow blues to Ornette Coleman's free jazz, would seem to be at an impasse if not necessarily at an end (there's no way of knowing). After the avant-garde era, musicians freely mined the idioms of jazz's past, but the next movement, neoclassicism, represented a retrenchment—away from the avant-garde, not a continuation toward another frontier.

Jason Moran, a brilliant young pianist and composer, is a representative jazz musician for the early years of the twenty-first century, at home with classic jazz, hip-hop, and everything between.

© JIMMY KATZ

wwnorton.com/studyspace

The fusion narrative takes us beyond the avant-garde into diverse attempts to combine the practices of jazz with those of rock, soul, hip-hop, and other kinds of pop music, domestic and international. But that also now seems a dead end, as the farther pop departs from melody and harmony, the less it offers as source material for jazz. Some would argue that the pinnacle of jazz-rock fusion was created by Miles Davis nearly forty years ago. When a modern jazz group plays a song by, say, Radiohead, it's an isolated stunt, not a meeting of minds.

The historicist model is very much alive, as jazz musicians continue to mine the past. Yet it fails to describe the overall state of jazz in today's world. No matter how many instances of historicist jazz we compile, we are simply collating individual interpretations and homages, which can hardly define an era in which those instances account for a small percentage of overall jazz performances.

It would seem, then, that while each of these templates gives us a way of understanding jazz history, none provides us with a satisfactory label with which to describe contemporary jazz. Still, this is far from a period of chaos: a live-and-let-live conformity has taken over in the absence of warring factions. If jazz is in a post-historical phase, it's a relatively peaceful one—traditionalists and modernists have declared a truce. A different and broader narrative may give us a better sense of the present situation.

Jazz as Classical Music

Some commentators have described jazz as America's classical music, but what exactly does that mean? The dictionary definitions of "classical" have changed over the past hundred years, largely in response to the existence of jazz. In 1885, the American musicologist J. C. Fillmore offered a simple and influential definition of the word "classic" as applied to music: "having permanent interest and value." The 1933 *Oxford English Dictionary* upheld the inclusiveness of that general description: "of the first rank or authority; constituting a standard or model." The 1969 *American Heritage Dictionary* limited the definition: "any music in the educated European tradition, as distinguished from popular or folk music." In 1972, the *OED* added a new restriction: "opp. JAZZ," followed by supporting extracts, including this one from a 1947 magazine: "The lowbrow, of course, divides all music into 'classical' and 'jazz'."

The lowbrow needn't detain us. Let us raise our sights to encompass the original meaning— "having permanent interest and value": no one can deny that a survey of twentieth-century music shows that jazz has proved as lasting as the most admired "classical" works of the same period. Only the most rigorous standards of excellence, applied ecumenically, can give *classical* real meaning.

Throughout this book, we refer to *classical music* as the European tradition of composed music that produced the great symphonic, chamber, and operatic repertories. Here we let *classical* represent not one tradition as opposed

Cyrus Chestnut has the kind of pianistic skills that recall the dazzling Art Tatum, but he also draws heavily on Southern church music and even recorded a tribute to Elvis.

© JIMMY KATZ

to another, but rather the status to which all serious and lasting kinds of music (including rock) aspire. Bach, after all, was not considered classical in his day; time and semantics defined the tradition in which we place him.

Four Phases

In this formulation, jazz has undergone four phases of development. These phases are not stylistic schools, like swing and bop, but broader stages that mark its overall place in the cultural world.

1. The first phase (1890s–1920s) was the period of genesis. Every musical idiom begins in, and reflects the life of, a specific community where music is made for pleasure and to strengthen social bonds. In jazz, the primary breeding ground was the black South, especially New Orleans, where a mixture of musical and cultural influences combined to create a freewheeling, largely improvised, blues-based music that suited every social gathering, from dances to funerals. The strength and originality of this music allowed it to spread beyond geographical, racial, and cultural boundaries. Listeners of every background responded to its novel vitality.

2. In the second phase (1920s–1950s), jazz was transformed from a community-based phenomenon to an authentic art of unlimited potential. Spreading around the world, it revolutionized musical performance and conception, influencing both classical and popular artists. It became a universal art spurred by gifted individuals who could express singular artistic visions within its general yet constantly shifting parameters. Within twenty years, jazz found worldwide popular acceptance as a generation's dance music, and spurred intellectual interest with a subsequent modernism.

3. The third phase (1950s–1970s) was largely defined by the limits of modernism, which increased artistic possibilities while alienating the general public. Jazz became more of a listener's than a dancer's music. It continued to sustain a large following, but passed from center stage in favor of newer, more popular styles (rhythm and blues, rock and roll). These newer styles fulfilled the unchanging social needs of the overall community—music that suited dancing and singing and required little in the way of learning or imaginative concentration. In this period, jazz also moved from the ballroom to the classroom.

4. The fourth stage (1970s–), at which jazz presently finds itself, may be defined by its classical status on two counts.

   ■ Jazz has now moved so far from center stage that its survival is partially dependent on an infrastructure of academic study and institutional support, including public and private grants. Its absence from the commercial marketplace guarantees a limited international audience. In some areas of the United States, for example, people can live their entire lives without encountering jazz on television or the radio, in the movies or on jukeboxes. It is a specialty interest, like European classical music.

   ■ Jazz and its musicians are weighed down by the accomplishments of its past. Virtually every young jazz artist who comes along is defined to some degree by the presumed influences of his or her predecessors. These young musicians are also obliged to compete with the past in a way that did not exist in jazz before the 1990s. The commercial ramifications are familiar, because they replicate the struggle of European classical music

Pianist Gonzalo Rubalcaba began recording as a teenager in Cuba, but word of his superb technique and originality—combining aspects of jazz, Latin, and classical music—soon brought him international acclaim.

Pianist Brad Mehldau brought a powerfully meditative approach to pop standards, jazz classics, and original pieces in a series of five albums called *The Art of the Trio*.

during the past century, as listeners continued to support the performances of famous nineteenth-century masterworks while neglecting modern composers as either too difficult or simply too new.

On the other hand, the classical status is liberating for young jazz artists, who range freely between past and present, creating their own narratives as they attempt to forge new techniques, or to fuse jazz techniques with those of popular and classical music, or to elaborate on acknowledged jazz masterworks. What's more, the classical stage offers a more reasonable way of anchoring jazz in history than the post-historical analysis: it assumes an evolving growth within its new status, leaving open the possibility of new jazz styles and stars.

LINGUA FRANCA

If the present era is not dominated by a single jazz school, it does offer something akin to a universal *lingua franca*. This useful term derives from seventeenth-century Europe, when a hybrid language developed that promoted communication between different peoples who interacted in Mediterranean seaports. Whatever their stylistic preferences, today's jazz musicians can all speak the same language—a musical patois grounded in bebop, with respect for previous jazz schools and knowledge of later ones.

One reason for this is the prevalence of education. In the past, musicians learned by doing—they traveled in bands or memorized solos from recordings. They almost always leaned toward the style that was dominant at the time they came of age. In today's world, apprentice work is largely replaced by undergraduate studies. Musicians are less likely to pick up the latest chord changes by ear than to learn them in the classroom.

At a time when pop music squeezes every other kind of music into the slimmest margin of commercial significance, jazz students are motivated to master the music's lingua franca—the shared pool of styles and techniques—as a necessity of surviving as professional musicians. Yet neither education nor the marketplace has succeeded in making them assembly-line performers. Something at the heart of jazz, and every kind of art worth its name, rejects slavish imitation; it thrives only on acute individualism. If jazz in the twenty-first century no longer seems rife with the kind of adventurous innovators of earlier eras (and only time can tell if that's true), it has produced one of the best-equipped musical generations ever. The achievements of contemporary musicians continue to sustain jazz as a singular, exciting, and still surprising musical art.

For Example: Pianists

If we examine the state of jazz as reflected on only one instrument, we can survey the way individual visions and the lingua franca combine to create extraordinary musical diversity. Consider the list in the box below: fifty pianists who have influenced jazz in the years since 1990. They were by no means alone. Many established pianists defined this period with the renewed vitality of their work, from bop masters like Hank Jones and Tommy Flanagan to avant-garde pioneers like Cecil Taylor and Andrew Hill to 1980s neoclassicists (all born in the middle 1950s) like Geri Allen, Fred Hersch, Mulgrew Miller, and Uri Caine.

The list consists exclusively of pianists born no earlier than 1960, which means they were all raised in the "classical" era, long after the stylistic wars of the past were resolved. A paradox is immediately apparent: although almost any one of them could effectively sit in on a job if another one was called away, this group represents a comprehensive variety of musical approaches. They all know the common language, but are highly particular in the way they develop it.

Matthew Shipp spent much of his career as pianist with the David S. Ware Quartet, while recording a series of albums that stretched his talents as composer and improviser.

Bill Evans and Cecil Taylor (whom we first encountered, respectively, in Chapters 14 and 15) were born within a few months of each other in 1929. Yet we don't think of them as sharing much common ground, because their approaches are so very different. Of the musicians listed below, Brad Mehldau is a lyrical pianist in the Evans tradition and Matthew Shipp is a percussive one in the Taylor tradition, but their grounding in jazz history is such that they might easily cross into each other's realms (unlike Evans and Taylor).

Some of these musicians came to jazz in their late twenties or thirties after working in other fields, including European classical music, rhythm and blues, fusion, and smooth jazz. In making the leap to jazz, they bring with them applicable aspects of those other idioms, increasing the pool of shared knowledge. Note, too, the geographical diversity: Vijay Iyer, who grew up in New York State, traces his heritage to India and employs elements of Indian music (largely unexplored in jazz), especially in his collaborations with the alto saxophonist Rudresh Mahanthappa—who, though born in Italy and raised in Colorado, shares Iyer's heritage and his education in American universities. Jazz internationalism is a given in today's climate, fostered by constant travel to the numerous jazz festivals in Europe, Japan, Canada, South America, and elsewhere. The common language is exponentially enlarged through cultural exchange.

Diana Krall first became famous with a trio and repertory modeled on Nat King Cole, and similarly allowed her vocal talents to obscure her ability as a pianist.

Not all of these pianists are major figures, but all are accomplished ones. Most have recorded with major labels, including Blue Note, ECM, Verve, BMG, Columbia, Sunnyside, and Warner Bros. All have made recordings as leaders, though many are usually heard in sideman engagements. Some of the best-known pianists of recent years are not included here because they are primarily known as singers, though they could sustain careers as keyboard artists—among them Diana Krall (b. 1964 in British Columbia), Harry Connick Jr. (b. 1967 in New Orleans), and Norah Jones (b. 1979 in Brooklyn).

These pianists are proof (similar lists can be devised around other instruments) of life after history, or rather that jazz history is in the making. Indeed, we may well ask whether a comparable list of fifty pianists born in or after 1960 could be made from the rolls of classical or rock musicians.

■ JASON MORAN (b. 1975)

For a closer look at the life of the contemporary jazz musician, we could hardly ask for a more exemplary career than that of Jason Moran. In the years since he made his first album (*Soundtrack to Human Motion*, 1998), he has earned nearly unanimous acclaim, demonstrating with wit and imagination

Fifty Twenty-First-Century Jazz Pianists (with year and place of birth)

© JIMMY KATZ

Pianist Bill Charlap recorded a series of rigorously produced CDs, leading his own trio and revitalizing the American songbook, from George Gershwin to Leonard Bernstein.

Helio Alves (1966, São Paulo)
Frank Amsallem (1961, Algeria)
Django Bates (1960, England)
Jonathan Batiste (1986, New Orleans)
Stefano Bollani (1972, Italy)
Michael Cain (1966, Los Angeles)
Marc Cary (1967, New York)
Bill Charlap (1966, New York)
Cyrus Chestnut (1963, Maryland)
George Colligan (1969, Baltimore)
Xavier Davis (1971, Grand Rapids)
Eliane Elias (1960, São Paulo)
Orrin Evans (1975, Philadelphia)

Antonio Faraò (1965, Italy)
Amina Figarova (1966, Azerbaijan)
Anat Fort (1970, Israel)
Robert Glasper (1978, Houston)
Aaron Goldberg (1974, Boston)
Larry Goldings (1968, Boston)
Edsel Gomez (1962, Puerto Rico)
Benito Gonzalez (1975, Venezuela)
Darrell Grant (1962, Philadelphia)
Tord Gustavsen (1970, Norway)
Kevin Hays (1968, New York)
Ethan Iverson (1973, Menomonie, Wis.)
Vijay Iyer (1971, Rochester, N.Y.)
D. D. Jackson (1967, Ottowa)
Geoffrey Keezer (1970, Eau Claire, Wis.)
Rodney Kendrick (1960, Philadelphia)
Guillermo Klein (1970, Argentina)
John Medeski (1965, Louisville)
Brad Mehldau (1970, Jacksonville, Fl.)
Jason Moran (1975, Houston)
Leszek Możdżer (1971, Gdańsk)
Junko Onishi (1967, Japan)
Danilo Pérez (1966, Panama)
Jean-Michel Pilc (1960, France)
Mika Pohjola (1971, Finland)
Eric Reed (1970, Philadelphia)
Marcus Roberts (1963, Jacksonville)
Renee Rosnes (1962, Saskatchewan)
Gonzalo Rubalcaba (1963, Havana)
Stephen Scott (1969, New York)
Matthew Shipp (1960, Wilmington)
Travis Shook (1969, Oroville, Calif.)
Edward Simon (1969, Venezuela)
Craig Taborn (1970, Minneapolis)
Jacky Terrasson (1966, Berlin)
Anthony Wonsey (1971, Chicago)
Bojan Zulfikarpašić (1968, Belgrade)

the triumphs possible in jazz despite its relatively remote standing in America's cultural life. Born in Houston, he began playing classical piano at six and continued with it, reluctantly, for seven years. He now says he came to hate music, piano, and practicing, preferring to listen to the hip-hop records that flourished during his childhood.

Moran's attitude changed radically when he was thirteen; at a memorial service for one of his father's friends, he heard a Thelonious Monk record, "'Round Midnight," and found himself riveted by Monk's keyboard touch, rhythmic intensity, and melodic playfulness. As he learned more about Monk, he delved deeper into jazz and particularly jazz piano—Bud Powell, Horace Silver, McCoy Tyner, Herbie Hancock. Like any young jazz lover, he allowed each musician to lead him to other musicians: soon he was also soaking up older pianists like Art Tatum and Erroll Garner and more obscure or idiosyncratic modernists like Herbie Nichols, Randy Weston, Ahmad Jamal, and Cecil Taylor.

This wide-ranging process provided him with a musical platform broader than that of his predecessors. It could not fail to combine elements of the avant-garde (he searched out the cutting edge of musical possibilities), historicism (he roamed as freely through the past as he did the present), and fusion—his increasing love of jazz by no means diminished his enthusiasm for the pop music of his generation, specifically the beats of hip-hop.

© JIMMY KATZ

Moran was bored with piano lessons as a child, until he heard Thelonious Monk, whose flair for haberdashery he also inherited.

Mentors

After graduating from the jazz program at Houston's High School for the Performing and Visual Arts, Moran moved to New York, where in 1993 he enrolled at the Manhattan School of Music, chiefly to study with Jaki Byard (1922–1999). Over the next four years, he found "a role model for life" in Byard, the school's most distinguished jazz faculty member. Byard, a brilliant and stubbornly individual instrumentalist, was well-known for his longtime association with Charles Mingus and his own recordings, which revealed a style that combined the techniques of stride, swing, bop, and avant-garde—an approach so far ahead of its time that some critics dismissed him as a tongue-in-cheek eclectic.

Byard was an ideal mentor for Moran (and several other young pianists, including Fred Hersch and D. D. Jackson), breaking down the various techniques and instilling a respect for their separate virtues. Moran has referred to him as "a jazz leftist," for his stylistic inclusiveness. In the same period, Moran sought out two other pianists, who had also absorbed much of the instrument's varied history but were more firmly aligned with the 1960s and 1970s avant-garde: Andrew Hill and Muhal Richard Abrams (see Chapter 15). As he developed his own style, Moran added compositions by his three primary teachers into his repertoire—helping to keep alive a body of work that had been largely neglected.

In 1996, at twenty-one, Moran began appearing as a sideman with prominent musicians, including the saxophonists David Murray (see Chapter 15) and Steve Coleman, who had begun to exert much influence in the 1980s. Coleman created a pan-stylistic collective centered in Brooklyn called M-Base—an acronym for Macro-Basic Array of Structured Extemporizations. It was one of the first groups to combine aspects of avant-garde and mainstream jazz with hip-hop, electronic pop, and world music.

One of Coleman's most gifted associates was another alto and soprano saxophonist, Greg Osby, who used Moran on several projects, including the 1997 Blue Note album *Further Ado*, Moran's debut on record. The next year, Blue Note signed Moran to his own contract, launched with the album *Soundtrack to Human Motion* and participation (along with Osby) in the label's New Directions concert tour.

Osby has noted that Moran, though fascinated by avant-garde theories, hip-hop, and electronics, particularly *musique concrète* (the use of environmental and manufactured sounds from nonmusical sources), is essentially a traditionalist. "We're like the anti young lions," Osby observed, adding, "Jason is kind of an old soul."

Keeping It New

As Moran began to release a series of albums in 1998, one a year, it quickly emerged that he saw each one as a distinct project, with its own goals and parameters. He organized a durable trio, with bassist Tarus Mateen and drummer Nasheet Waits, that grew increasingly empathetic in the course of concert and club tours, but he planned his records to try something different every time. Even so, a few characteristics remained stable—the surprising breadth of his repertory, his love of electronic enhancements, and his humor.

Soundtrack to Human Motion includes works based on classical compositions by Maurice Ravel and Alban Berg as well as a free improvisation and the first in his series of "Gangsterism" pieces. The latter is a series of thoroughly camouflaged variations on a theme by Andrew Hill, "Erato," each one discretely designed—for example, Moran has described "Gangsterism on a Lunchtable" as an attempt to "do my John Cage interpretation of hip-hop," referring to the classical composer famous for using ambient noises in his music.

Moran's albums have included fresh yet faithful renditions of work by Byard and Ellington, movies themes (including *Godfather II* and *Yojimbo*), a collaboration with the veteran saxophonist and pianist Sam Rivers (b. 1923), an album-length exploration of blues forms, and such idiosyncratic original works as "Ringing My Phone," in which he finds notes on the keyboard that match up with the notes of his wife and mother-in-law speaking Turkish in a taped phone conversation. In every instance, the challenge is to mesh contemporary musical ideas with tradition to create music that is recognizable yet new. This challenge was underscored when he set out to honor his first influence.

In 2007, Moran was commissioned to compose an original piece in celebration of the ninetieth anniversary of Thelonious Monk's birth. He based the work (*IN MY MIND: Monk at Town Hall, 1959*) on a celebrated big-band concert. The piece calls for an eight-piece ensemble, video projections, and recorded excerpts from Monk's Town Hall rehearsals. Moran explained: "The hard part is actually trying to unlearn what learned me. I want to reconnect with Monk, not with people talking about his 'quirky rhythms' or 'off-centered humor.' I want to get past all that and say this was a real human being who shaped the world of jazz and the world of music, partially because of what he did at the instrument but mostly because of the way he thought."

 ## "You've Got to Be Modernistic"

Like Monk, Moran has developed a self-sufficient approach to the piano, recognizing that playing solo piano is very different from working with a trio. His 2002 album *Modernistic* is a benchmark achievement and a particularly strong example of his ability to combine classicism and maverick innovation. Whereas many pianists would be content simply to master James P. Johnson's 1930 "You've Got to Be Modernistic," Moran suggests its essential character while giving it a radical facelift, taking it through so many variations that by the end we feel as though we've been on a completely different trip from the one intended by Johnson.

James P. Johnson (1921), as we saw in Chapter 5, made the better part of his living as the composer of such Jazz Age anthems as "Charleston," but was also the greatest of stride pianists.

To understand Moran's interpretation, we need to consider Johnson's original recording (see Listening Guide in Chapter 5). "You've Got to Be Modernistic" is basically a ragtime work, made up of three sixteen-bar strains. Moran works with the original material, but adds his own variations (including new **C** and **D** strains) and frequently alters or stops the tempo. Johnson's modernism was apparent in his introduction and the first two strains (**A** and **B**), which are ornamented by augmented chords and the whole-tone scale. Although Moran is basically faithful to Johnson's primary theme, he adds incremental dissonances and extends its final melodic figure. Here and in the subsequent strains, Moran halts the flow in unexpected places, as if to look around and tweak this chord or twist that rhythm before returning to the grid.

Moran's reading suggests an asymmetrical impulsiveness that threatens the integrity of the piece, despite his frequent return to the stride underpinning. The effect is ironic in the sense that he holds the original work at a distance, partaking of it and then rejecting it, as he lingers on passages he wants to emphasize or alters the tempo and harmonies. He defamiliarizes the piece; passages that seem stable when Johnson plays them now seem unmoored, free to go in any direction the pianist wishes to take them, thanks to his strategically misplaced notes or wildly divergent harmonic progressions. Intermingled with his versions of Johnson's first theme are harmonic cycles that can be considered Moran's *own* strains, which, like much of his playing, are elusive and idiosyncratic.

LISTENING GUIDE

 you've got to be modernistic

JASON MORAN, PIANO

- Label: *Modernistic,* Blue Note 39838
- Date: 2001
- Style: historicist/modernist
- Form: march/ragtime with alterations

What to listen for:

- theme phrase, from James P. Johnson's **A** strain (see Chapter 5), recurring throughout
- descending chromatic chords in **B** strain, from Johnson
- harmonic cycles within the "**C**" and "**D**" strains
- disappearing and then returning triple meter in "**D**" strain

INTRODUCTION

0:00   After a held-out bass note, Moran plays a series of chords descending the **whole-tone scale**.

A STRAIN

0:06   Moran faithfully plays the first four bars of James P. Johnson's "You've Got to Be Modernistic." This section (we'll call it the *theme phrase*) is his main point of contact with the original.

0:09   On its first appearance in Johnson's composition, the theme phrase ended with the left hand playing a tonic chord with a mild dissonance (we'll call it the *tonic chord passage*). Moran lingers on this passage, repeating it and gradually building in volume.

0:14   Moran defamiliarizes the theme phrase by playing a deliberately inaccurate bass note.

0:18   On its second appearance in Johnson's composition, the theme phrase was followed by chords from the whole-tone scale. Moran extends this passage, pulling it temporarily outside the meter of the piece.

0:21   On its last repetition, Moran plays the theme phrase for six bars, leading through **whole-tone, or augmented, chords** (made up of major thirds) to a full cadence.

0:29   He lengthens the tonic chord passage by two bars.

A STRAIN

0:32   Moran plays the theme phrase.

0:37   The left hand suddenly drops to a remote key. Over this harmony, the right hand improvises a wild passage.

0:42   Moran repeats the theme phrase.

0:46   The left-hand chords drop once again. Moran pulls the harmony upward step by step while the right hand plays sharp dissonances.

0:51   Moran repeats the theme phrase; as before, he extends the whole-tone response.

0:57   The last repetition of the theme phrase is undistorted, coming to a full cadence.

B STRAIN

1:06   Moran plays the opening **B** strain: descending chromatic chords divided between the hands, culminating in a bluesy phrase.

1:11   The second time through, the left hand is overwhelmed by dissonant passagework in the right hand. Not until the phrase's end (at 1:15) does the original melody and tempo return.

1:15   For four bars, Moran adheres closely to Johnson's original.

1:20   The third repetition of the opening disintegrates into harsh dissonance and free rhythm.

1:23   Suddenly, Moran returns to the original tempo and meter. Landing on the **tonic**, he plays the note insistently.

INTERLUDE

1:30   Over a **pedal point**, Moran plays a series of descending **tritones**.

1:36   The phrase ends with a simple ragtime cadence, followed once again the tonic chord passage (repeated and extended).

1:40   He repeats the descending tritones.

1:47   Suddenly he inserts a passage that sounds as though it might **modulate** to a new key; but it resolves quietly back to the tonic.

1:54   He repeats the tonic chord passage to support bizarre right-hand improvising.

2:10   The harmony works its way back to the descending tritones, followed by a **turnaround**—a short concluding chord progression. We can now recognize an **eight-bar cycle:** six bars of pedal point with descending tritones, followed by two bars of turnaround.

"C" STRAIN

2:19   (cycle 1) As the left hand settles into a familiar routine, Moran begins improvising with his right hand.

2:29   (cycle 2)

2:38   (cycle 3) His left hand remains constant, but his right hand becomes increasingly wild, spreading dissonant flurries across the chord progression.

2:47   (cycle 4)

2:57   (cycle 5) He batters several notes at the top of the keyboard.

3:06   (cycle 6) The texture on the piano thickens as Moran adds complex passagework.

3:12   At the climax, we suddenly return to the simple ragtime cadence, now densely voiced at top volume. It is followed by a thunderous repetition of the tonic chord passage.

A STRAIN

3:17   Moran returns to the theme phrase.

3:21   The left-hand chords become loosened from their moorings, moving up or down a half step in a spastic rhythm.

3:34   He repeats the theme phrase, followed by the whole-tone chords.

3:41   He again repeats the theme phrase, this time reaching a full cadence.

"D" STRAIN

3:49   (cycle 1) The tonic chord drops down, then moves back up step-by-step in a **triple meter**. This establishes yet another cycle, six bars long.

3:54   (cycle 2) Moran adapts **stride** technique to this unusual meter: the bass line is played not on the downbeat, but in the middle of the measure (chord—bass—chord).

3:57   His right hand begins improvising within the cycle.

4:00   (cycle 3)

4:05   (cycle 4) His lines grow faster, occasionally disrupting the left-hand foundation.

4:10   (cycle 5) The right hand becomes thickened with chords, which interrupt and displace the left-hand chords.

4:15   (cycle 6) Gradually, the stride accompaniment and triple meter disappear into a complex, disjointed rhythmic flux. We still hear Moran moving slowly through the chords, however, and can recognize the end of each cycle by the return to the tonic.

4:25   (cycle 7)

4:34   (cycle 8)

4:42   (cycle 9) Finally, Moran settles back into a smooth stride accompaniment, once again in triple meter. The right hand improvises rich, mellifluous chords.

4:50   (cycle 10)

4:58   (cycle 11) The right hand begins to play behind the beat, distorting our sense of meter.

5:05   (cycle 12) The stride foundation dissolves into left-hand chords.

CODA

5:12   Before the cycle is complete, the theme phrase from strain **A** slips back in. The tempo slows down dramatically, and the piano texture is simplified.

5:16   As the phrase continues, the music becomes hushed, as if Moran were preparing for a big cadence.

5:22   He plays the upward-rising whole-tone chords quietly and slowly.

5:26   A sudden loud octave jolts us awake. Moran plays the final cadence with a certain bluesy bluntness.

5:30   He continues to fool us, however, dropping from the tonic to remote harmonies.

5:40   The piece ends on unresolved V7 chord.

"Planet Rock"

Moran's adaptation of Afrika Bambaataa's "Planet Rock," a perfect companion piece to "You've Got to Be Modernistic," was recorded for the same album. Bambaataa's 1982 single is generally regarded as one of the first and most influential rap tunes; its primary melody is deeply ingrained on Moran's generation. Moran brings to his interpretation the same mixture of fidelity and independence he brought to James P. Johnson's work, creating a powerful jazz performance that respects each component of the original: the rhythms, melodies, even the vocal timbres. Bambattaa began as a Bronx-based disc-jockey and came to be regarded as a hip-hop godfather when "Planet Rock" brought beat-box electro-funk to the dance floor.

"You've Got to Be Modernistic" reclaims a piece from the distant past, which suggests a historicist approach, while "Planet Rock," based on contemporary pop, suggests a fusion approach. Yet the overriding impression created by both pieces is of the undeniable originality of Moran, forging his own path with the materials that interest him. His inventiveness is inseparable from his sense of musical tradition and his openness to the music around him.

Moran employs techniques that parallel Bambaataa's use of scratched and otherwise manipulated vinyl discs, including prepared piano strings and reverse sounds created by running a tape backward. His attempt to recreate the pitches of Bambaataa's vocal line in verse 1 is an attempt to explore a technique that he continued to develop in his later work—as he duplicated speech patterns on the piano. Moran's use of reversed tapes and dubs is not itself new; Bill Evans recorded a dubbed album of solo piano, *Conversations with Myself*, in the 1960s. But where Evans used soundboard tricks to expand his harmonic and melodic options, Moran is largely concerned with rhythmic effects. He shows that hip-hop rhythms, which many consider anathema to jazz, are just another source for creative music-making, and that jazz, as ever, is ultimately whatever its most creative proponents make of it.

LISTENING GUIDE

planet rock

4.15

JASON MORAN

Jason Moran, piano and electronics

- Label: *Modernistic,* Blue Note 3983
- Date: 2001
- Style: historicist/fusion
- Form: verse-refrain, with a 16-bar chorus in the middle

What to listen for:

- backward chords, prepared piano strings
- bass-line vamp
- the different verse, refrain, and chorus melodies

INTRODUCTION

0:00   The piece opens with a peculiar sound—a taped piano chord played backward. It begins quietly before exploding into sound at the end.

0:02   With his left hand, Moran plays a series of **pentatonic** fragments. The sound of the piano is acoustically filtered, creating a distinctive timbre.

0:07   After three short phrases, Moran pauses.

0:09   He plays a more syncopated line, followed again by a pause and a repeat of the line.

0:16   He plays a single note in **octaves**, with a noticeable difference in timbre. By sticking foreign objects—erasers, clothespins, paper clips—into the strings, Moran has turned his keyboard into a "prepared piano."

VAMP

0:18   Moran plays the bass line from the Bambaataa recording of "Planet Rock"—a syncopated pattern alternating bass notes with a chord on the **backbeat**. This line, distinguished by its timbre, is recorded separately and heard throughout as a repeating track.

0:22   Every two bars, the bass line is punctuated by the sound of a left-hand chord combined with the electronically manipulated "backward" piano chord.

0:34   As the backward chord disappears, we approach the beginning of the song.

VERSE 1

0:38   As painstakingly as possible, Moran matches the pitches of the original rapped vocal line to Bambaataa's version ("*Just start to chase your dreams*"). Since the original line was spoken, not sung, the pitches create strong **dissonances** against the repeating bass line.

REFRAIN

0:54   When Moran reaches the simple refrain, he plays it with literal precision.

1:02   On its repetition, he emphasizes the refrain melody in octaves.

VERSE 2

1:10   Moran shifts to a different part of Bambaataa's version, again matching the pitches of the original rap ("*You're in a place where the nights are hot*") to notes on the piano. Once again, the notes clash against the bass line.

1:23   To mimic a place where several voices join together on the original recording ("*hump bump bump, get bump, now let's go, house*"), Moran brings out the line with octaves.

REFRAIN

1:26   Moran returns to the refrain.

INTERLUDE

1:42   Moran moves to a line chanted by the group as a whole ("*Go rock it, don't stop it!*").

1:54   To convey the sense of **call and response** between group and in-studio audience on Bambaataa's recording, he pits two full, rich chords in the middle register against the same chords an octave higher.

2:06   With three chords, Moran emphasizes the dominant in a half cadence.

CHORUS 1 (16 bars)

2:10   Moran plays a simple but wandering ascending melody, stretching over sixteen bars. Each note lasts two beats and is distorted at the end by a backward sound.

2:20   He begins to harmonize the melody.

2:28   As the line ascends into the upper register, another piano part (recorded as a different track with its own distinctive timbre) appears below.

2:38   The melody finally rests on a single note.

CHORUS 2

2:42   Moran repeats the ascending melody, clearly establishing the chorus structure. Two different layers of piano begin improvising almost immediately, adding dense, complicated chords as well as unpredictable new melodies.

3:10   The melody ends.

CHORUS 3

3:14   The timbre suddenly changes. The bass line shifts to a sinister low register (where the ringing on the backbeat chord is particularly noticeable). Moran plays the melody backward, then reverses its sound so that it appears with a distinctive timbre. All of this is used as background for more aggressive improvisation in another piano line.

3:23   In one measure, the bass line skips a backbeat.

3:42   Moran marks the end of the melody with loud chords and an insistently repeated note in the treble.

CHORUS 4

3:46 The sound of the melody returns to a normal timbre. This time, as it ascends, the melody is harmonized by a descending bass line (both parts are superimposed over the consistently repeating bass track). Above it, an improvised line plays increasingly dissonant patterns.

3:55 As the piece nears a climax, the improvised line switches to octaves.

4:14 The melody ends, clearly establishing the tonic, while improvisation around it continues to swirl.

INTERLUDE

4:18 Several different lines intersect, all rocking back and forth in a limited range and merging into a kind of rumble, augmented by a return of the backward sound.

4:27 A dissonant line begins to emerge from the mix.

4:34 Switching to octaves, the line plays with fragments from the refrain melody.

4:39 A particularly harsh chord seems to prompt the bass to drop out for a few beats.

4:43 He plays a line from the opening.

REFRAIN

4:46 Moran returns to the refrain melody.

4:50 The timbre suddenly returns to a fuller, richer sound, doubled and even tripled by octaves.

CODA

4:57 The melody stops; in its wake, numerous other voices emerge, chaotically echoing its motivic ideas.

5:05 As the improvisations continue, the bass line begins to slow down.

5:10 The bass line is doubled at the lower octave.

5:28 The performance disappears in a gradual fade-out.

JAZZ TOMORROW

No one has ever successfully predicted the future of jazz. It's unlikely that Buddy Bolden could have foreseen the worldwide acceptance of music he played to entertain dancers in the tenderloin district of *fin de siècle* New Orleans. Louis Armstrong helped to spur the Swing Era, but he could not have seen it arising from his Hot Five recordings of the 1920s—no more than swing musicians could have predicted bop or bop musicians the avant-garde. All we can say with assurance is that jazz is here to stay. It continues to represent a way of playing and thinking about music, attracting musicians like Jason Moran who continue to confound, delight, and amaze discriminating music lovers around the world.

ADDITIONAL LISTENING	
Jason Moran	"Gangsterism on a Lunchtable" (2002); *Modernistic* (Blue Note 39838)
	"Ringing My Phone" (2002); *The Bandwagon* (Blue Note 80917)
Bill Charlap	"Autumn in New York" (2003); *Live at the Village Vanguard* (Blue Note 724359704425)

Cyrus Chestnut	"Precious Lord" (2002); *You Are My Sunshine* (Warner Bros. 48445)
Anat Fort	"Rehaired" (2004); *A Long Story* (ECM 000850502)
Vijay Iyer	"Imagine" (2004); *Reimagining* (Savoy Jazz 17475)
D. D. Jackson	"Serenity Song" (2005); *Serenity Song* (Justin Time 222)
Brad Mehldau	"The Very Thought of You" (2006); *Brad Mehldau Trio Live* (Nonesuch 376252)
Danilo Pérez	*Panamonk* (1996) (Impulse! 1142994)
Eric Reed	"Evidence / Think of One" (2000); *E-Bop* (Savant 633842205120)
Marcus Roberts	"Someone to Watch Over Me" (1994); *Gershwin for Lovers* (Sony/BMG Masterworks CK66437)
Gonzalo Rubalcaba	"Los Bueyes" (2004); *Paseo* (Blue Note 81832)
Stephen Scott	"The Pit and the Pendulum" (1992); *Aminah's Dream* (Verve 73145179962)
Marc Cary	"New Blues" (1996); *Listen* (Arabesque AJ1025)

PART V SUMMARY

AVANT-GARDE JAZZ

Avant-garde jazz (1950s–1960s) was no longer entertainment but serious and challenging music, requiring the listener's full concentration; in a performance, anything could be tried. It also became increasingly entrenched in the racial and antiwar struggles of the time.

Texture
- varies widely, but tends toward polyphony (independent lines)

Rhythm
- free

Instrumentation
- varies widely, including instruments from all over the world

Form
- original compositions

Special techniques
- free improvisation, dispensing with harmonic background
- use of timbre as improvisational device
- ambiguous rhythmic pulse rather than steady dance beat

Pioneers of avant-garde jazz
- Ornette Coleman (alto saxophone)
  Quartet: Billy Higgins (drums), Charlie Haden (bass), Don Cherry (pocket trumpet)
- Cecil Taylor (piano)
  Jimmy Lyons (alto saxophone), Sonny Murray (drums), Steve Lacy (soprano saxophone), Archie Shepp (tenor saxophone), Andrew Cyrille (drums)
- Eric Dolphy (alto saxophone, clarinet, flute)
- Albert Ayler (tenor saxophone)
- Herbie Nichols (piano)
- Andrew Hill (piano)
- Sun Ra (piano)

Older musicians attracted to avant-garde jazz
- John Coltrane, Charles Mingus, Sonny Rollins

Avant-garde collectives

Underground Musicians' Association, Los Angeles

Association for the Advancement of Creative Musicians (AACM), Chicago
- Muhal Richard Abrams (piano)
- Anthony Braxton (saxophone)
- Leroy Jenkins (violin)
- Henry Threadgill (saxophone)
- Art Ensemble of Chicago: Joseph Jarman (saxophone), Roscoe Mitchell (saxophone), Lester Bowie (trumpet), Malachi Favors Maghostut (bass), Famoudou Don Moye (percussion)

Black Artists Group (BAG), St. Louis
- World Saxophone Quartet: David Murray, Julius Hemphill, Oliver Lake, Hamiet Bluiett, Arthur Blythe

Loft jazz (1970s)
- David Murray (tenor saxophone)
- Arthur Blythe (alto saxophone)
- Ed Blackwell (drums)
- James Newton (flute)
- Butch Morris (trumpet)
- John Zorn (saxophone)
- James Blood Ulmer (guitar)
- Beaver Harris (drums)

FUSION

Fusions of some kind have always played a role in jazz history. Symphonic jazz in the 1920s and the Third Stream in the late 1950s attempted to merge the techniques of jazz and classical music. And from the beginning, jazz has had an ongoing relationship to popular music. As jazz has responded to contemporary pop culture over the years, new schools of music have emerged, along with musicians at home in both worlds.

1940s – 1960

Rhythm and blues, or "jump music" (blues played at a fast tempo, boogie-woogie rhythm)
- Louis Jordan (alto saxophone)
- Earl Bostic (alto saxophone)
- Wild Bill Davis (organ)
- Bill Doggett (piano)

Soul jazz (gospel-type chords, basic harmonies, clearly defined dance rhythms)
- Ray Charles (piano, vocal)
- Jimmy Smith (organ)

Singers
- Rosemary Clooney
- Nat King Cole
- Frank Sinatra
- Sarah Vaughan

Latin jazz

Cubop/Afro-Cuban jazz/salsa (asymmetrical clave rhythm, large percussion section)
- Mario Bauzá (trumpet)
- Machito (bandleader)
- Dizzy Gillespie (trumpet)
- Chano Pozo (percussion)
- Cal Tjader (vibraphone)
- Mongo Santamaria (percussion)

Brazilian bossa nova (more relaxed and melodious)
- Luiz Bonfá (guitar)
- Vinícius de Moraes (composer)
- Tom Jobim (composer)
- João Gilberto (guitar)
- Stan Getz (tenor saxophone)
- Charlie Byrd (guitar)

FROM 1960

Jazz-rock fusion

Texture
- homophonic

Rhythm
- rock-based (even eighth notes)

Instruments
- electronically amplified bass, guitar, keyboards, synthesizers, "bottom- heavy" rhythm section

Form
- contemporary popular song (verse-chorus), original compositions

Special techniques
- high volume
- modern recording techniques (editing, sampling)

Early jazz-rock fusion bands
- Charles Lloyd Quartet
- Emergency (Tony Williams, drums)
- Miles Davis: *Filles de Kilimanjaro* (1968), *In a Silent Way* (1969), *Bitches Brew* (1970)

1970s jazz-rock fusion
- Mahavishnu Orchestra: John McLaughlin (guitar), Jan Hammer (keyboard), Billy Cobham (drums)
- Chick Corea (keyboard) and Return to Forever
- Weather Report: Wayne Shorter (saxophone), Joe Zawinul (keyboard), Jaco Pastorius (electric bass)
- Herbie Hancock (keyboard) and Headhunters
- Keith Jarrett (piano)
- Pat Metheny Group: Metheny (guitar), Lyle Mays (keyboards)

World music
- Jan Garbarek (saxophone), Paul Winter Consort, Oregon

Smooth jazz
- Grover Washington Jr. (saxophone), George Benson (guitar), Donald Byrd (trumpet), Kenny G (saxophone)

Jam-band jazz
- Charlie Hunter (guitar), Medeski, Martin and Wood

Acid jazz
- Groove Collective

Jazz/hip-hop
- Us3, Buckshot LeFonque (Branford Marsalis), Herbie Hancock, Miles Davis

HISTORICIST JAZZ

Throughout much of jazz history, musicians have faithfully reinterpreted classic or neglected works (from the jazz repertory), written original music that celebrates music of the past, and created modernist interpretations of jazz classics. By looking at ways musicians have followed these principles, we find a new way of interpreting jazz history: the historicist narrative.

Avant-garde historicist (1970s)
- Anthony Braxton (saxophone, clarinet, flute, piano)
- Arthur Blythe (alto saxophone)
- Henry Threadgill (saxophone) and Air

Neoclassicist (1980s)
- Wynton Marsalis (trumpet)

Repertory groups
- American Jazz Orchestra
- Carnegie Hall Jazz Band
- Lincoln Center Jazz Orchestra
- Mingus Big Band

Nostalgia
Harry Connick Jr., Diana Krall (singer-pianists)

Experimental historicist
- Don Byron (clarinet)
- Uri Caine (piano)
- Cassandra Wilson (singer)
- Dave Douglas (trumpet)
- Bill Frissell (guitar)
- Mark Ribot (guitar)
- Nicholas Payton (trumpet)
- Francisco Cafiso (alto saxophone)
- Ronald Shannon Jackson (drums)
- James Carter (saxophone)

Musicians by Instrument

Trumpet/Cornet

Nat Adderley (1931–2000)
Louis Armstrong (1901–1971)
Chet Baker (1929–1988)
Mario Bauzá (1911–1993)
Bix Beiderbecke (1903–1931)
Bunny Berigan (1908–1942)
Terence Blanchard (b. 1962)
Buddy Bolden (1877–1931)
Lester Bowie (1941–1999)
Clifford Brown (1930–1956)
Billy Butterfield (1917–1988)
Roy Campbell (b. 1952)
Don Cherry (1936–1995)
Buck Clayton (1911–1991)
Johnny Coles (1926–1996)
Ted Curson (b. 1935)
Olu Dara (b. 1941)
Miles Davis (1926–1991)
Kenny Dorham (1924–1972)
Harry "Sweets" Edison (1915–1999)
Roy Eldridge (1911–1989)
Jon Faddis (b. 1953)
Dizzy Gillespie (1917–1993)
Bobby Hackett (1915–1976)
Roy Hargrove (b. 1969)
Freddie Hubbard (b. 1938)
Harry James (1916–1983)
Bunk Johnson (1889–1949)
Sean Jones (b. 1978)
Freddie Keppard (1890–1933)
Ryan Kisor (b. 1973)
Nick LaRocca (1889–1961)
Booker Little (1938–1961)
Wynton Marsalis (b. 1961)
Howard McGhee (1918–1987)
Jimmy McPartland (1907–1991)
Bubber Miley (1903–1932)
Lee Morgan (1938–1972)
Ray Nance (1913–1976)
Fats Navarro (1923–1950)
King Oliver (1885–1938)
Oran "Hot Lips" Page (1908–1954)
Manuel Perez (1871–1946)
Marcus Printup (b. 1967)
Red Rodney (1927–1994)
Ernie Royal (1921–1983)
Charlie Shavers (1920–1971)
Woody Shaw (1944–1989)
Bobby Stark (1906–1945)
Rex Stewart (1907–1967)
Idrees Sulieman (1923–2002)
Clark Terry (b. 1920)
Charles Tolliver (b. 1942)
Cootie Williams (1910–1985)

Saxophone

George Adams (1940–1992)
Cannonball Adderley (1928–1975)
Gene Ammons (1925–1974)
Albert Ayler (1936–1970)
Gary Bartz (b. 1940)
Sidney Bechet (1897–1959)
Chu Berry (1908–1941)
Hamiet Bluiett (b. 1940)
Arthur Blythe (b. 1940)
Earl Bostic (1913–1965)
Anthony Braxton (b. 1945)
Pete Brown (1906–1963)
Don Byas (1912–1972)
Harry Carney (1910–1974)
Benny Carter (1907–2003)
James Carter (b. 1969)
Serge Chaloff (1923–1957)
Arnett Cobb (1918–1989)
Tony Coe (b. 1934)
Al Cohn (1925–1988)
George Coleman (b. 1935)
Ornette Coleman (b. 1930)
Steve Coleman (b. 1956)
John Coltrane (1926–1967)
Paul Desmond (1924–1977)
Eric Dolphy (1928–1964)
Jimmy Dorsey (1904–1957)
Allen Eager (1927–2003)
Booker Ervin (1930–1970)
Herschel Evans (1909–1939)
Bud Freeman (1906–1991)
Chico Freeman (b. 1949)
Von Freeman (b. 1922)
Jan Garbarek (b. 1947)
Stan Getz (1927–1991)
Benny Golson (b. 1929)
Dexter Gordon (1923–1990)
Wardell Gray (1921–1955)
Shafi Hadi (b. 1929)
John Handy (b. 1933)
Coleman Hawkins (1904–1969)
Tubby Hayes (1935–1973)
Jimmy Heath (b. 1926)
Julius Hemphill (1938–1995)
Joe Henderson (1937–2001)
Johnny Hodges (1906–1970)
Illinois Jacquet (1922–2004)
Joseph Jarman (b. 1937)
Budd Johnson (1910–1984)
Louis Jordan (1908–1975)
Rahsaan Roland Kirk (1936–1977)
Lee Konitz (b. 1927)
Steve Lacy (1934–2004)
Oliver Lake (b. 1944)
Harold Land (1928–2001)
Yusef Lateef (b. 1920)
Charles Lloyd (b. 1938)
Jimmy Lyons (1931–1986)
Rudresh Mahanthappa (b. 1978)
Branford Marsalis (b. 1960)
Warne Marsh (1927–1987)
Jackie McLean (1931–2006)
Roscoe Mitchell (b. 1940)
Hank Mobley (1930–1986)
James Moody (b.1925)
Gerry Mulligan (1927–1996)
David Murray (b. 1955)
Big Nick Nicholas (1922–1997)
Charlie Parker (1920–1955)
Evan Parker (b. 1944)
Leo Parker (1925–1962)
Chris Potter (b. 1971)
Dewey Redman (1931–2006)
Joshua Redman (b. 1969)
Sam Rivers (b. 1923)
Sonny Rollins (b. 1930)
Charlie Rouse (1924–1988)
Edgar Sampson (1907–1973)
Pharoah Sanders (b. 1940)
Gene Sedric (1907–1963)
Archie Shepp (b. 1937)
Wayne Shorter (b. 1933)
Zoot Sims (1925–1985)
Sonny Stitt (1924–1982)
Buddy Tate (1913–2001)
Joe Thomas (1909–1986)
Lucky Thompson (1924–2005)
Henry Threadgill (b. 1944)
Frank Trumbauer (1901–1956)
David S. Ware (b. 1949)

Ben Webster (1909–1973)
Paul Williams (1915–2002)
Phil Woods (b. 1931)
Lester Young (1909–1959)
John Zorn (b. 1953)

Clarinet

George Baquet (1883–1949)
Alvin Batiste (1932–2007)
Barney Bigard (1906–1980)
Peter Brötzmann (b. 1941)
Don Byron (b. 1958)
John Carter (1928–1991)
Kenny Davern (1935–2006)
Buddy DeFranco (b. 1923)
Johnny Dodds (1892–1940)
Paquito D'Rivera (b. 1948)
Irving Fazola (1912–1949)
Jimmy Giuffre (1921–2008)
Benny Goodman (1909–1986)
Edmond Hall (1901–1967)
Jimmy Hamilton (1917–1994)
Woody Herman (1913–1987)
George Lewis (1900–1968)
Jimmy Noone (1895–1944)
Alphonse Picou (1878–1961)
Perry Robinson (b. 1938)
Pee Wee Russell (1906–1969)
Louis Sclavis (b. 1953)
Tony Scott (1921–2007)
Artie Shaw (1910–2004)
Omer Simeon (1902–1959)
Wilbur Sweatman (1882–1961)
Frank Teschemacher (1906–1932)
Dr. Michael White (b. 1954)
Bob Wilber (b. 1928)
Lester Young (1909–1959)

Trombone

Ray Anderson (b. 1952)
Bob Brookmeyer (b. 1929)
Lawrence Brown (1907–1988)
George Brunis (1902–1974)
Jimmy Cleveland (1926–2008)
Willie Dennis (1926–1965)
Wilbur De Paris (1900–1973)
Vic Dickenson (1906–1984)
Tommy Dorsey (1905–1956)
Eddie Durham (1906–1987)
Honoré Dutrey (1894–1935)
Carl Fontana (1928–2003)
Curtis Fuller (b. 1934)
Tyree Glenn (1912–1974)

Wycliffe Gordon (b. 1967)
Al Gray (1925–2000)
Slide Hampton (b. 1932)
Bill Harris (1916–1973)
Jimmy Harrison (1900–1931)
Conrad Herwig (b. 1959)
J. C. Higginbotham (1906–1973)
Jack Jenney (1910–1945)
J. J. Johnson (1924–2001)
Jimmy Knepper (1927–2003)
George Lewis (b. 1952)
Melba Liston (1926–1999)
Albert Mangelsdorff (1928–2005)
Glenn Miller (1904–1944)
Miff Mole (1898–1961)
Benny Morton (1907–1985)
Joe "Tricky Sam" Nanton (1904–1946)
Kid Ory (1886–1973)
Big Jim Robinson (1892–1976)
Frank Rosolino (1926–1978)
Roswell Rudd (b. 1935)
Jack Teagarden (1905–1964)
Juan Tizol (1900–1984)
Steve Turre (b. 1948)
Bill Watrous (b. 1939)
Dicky Wells (1907–1985)
Kai Winding (1922–1983)
Trummy Young (1912–1984)

Piano/Keyboard

Muhal Richard Abrams (b. 1930)
Toshiko Akiyoshi (b. 1929)
Geri Allen (b. 1957)
Mose Allison (b. 1927)
Albert Ammons (1907–1949)
Lil Hardin Armstrong (1898–1971)
Lynne Arriale (b. 1957)
Kenny Barron (b. 1943)
Count Basie (1904–1984)
Jonathan Batiste (b. 1986)
Eubie Blake (1887–1983)
Ran Blake (b. 1935)
Paul Bley (b. 1932)
Stefano Bollani (b. 1972)
Joanne Brackeen (b. 1938)
Dave Brubeck (b. 1920)
Ray Bryant (b. 1931)
Jaki Byard (1922–1999)
George Cables (b. 1944)
Uri Caine (b. 1956)
Bill Charlap (b. 1966)
Ray Charles (1930–2004)
Sonny Clark (1931–1963)
Gerald Clayton (b. 1984)

Nat King Cole (1919–1965)
Harry Connick Jr. (b. 1967)
Chick Corea (b. 1941)
Eddie Costa (1930–1962)
Marilyn Crispell (b. 1947)
Albert Dailey (1939–1984)
Tadd Dameron (1917–1965)
Walter Davis Jr. (1932–1990)
Duke Ellington (1899–1974)
Bill Evans (1929–1980)
Victor Feldman (1934–1987)
Tommy Flanagan (1930–2001)
Red Garland (1923–1984)
Erroll Garner (1921–1977)
Vince Guaraldi (1928–1976)
Al Haig (1924–1982)
Herbie Hancock (b. 1940)
Barry Harris (b. 1929)
Hampton Hawes (1928–1977)
Fred Hersch (b. 1955)
John Hicks (1941–2006)
Andrew Hill (1931–2007)
Earl Hines (1903–1983)
Jutta Hipp (1925–2003)
Elmo Hope (1923–1967)
Ethan Iverson (b. 1973)
Vijay Iyer (b. 1971)
D. D. Jackson (b. 1967)
Ahmad Jamal (b. 1930)
Keith Jarrett (b. 1945)
James P. Johnson (1894–1955)
Pete Johnson (1904–1967)
Hank Jones (b. 1918)
Duke Jordan (1922–2006)
Wynton Kelly (1931–1971)
Kenny Kirkland (1955–1998)
Diana Krall (b. 1964)
Steve Kuhn (b. 1938)
Billy Kyle (1914–1966)
John Lewis (1920–2001)
Meade "Lux" Lewis (1905–1964)
Ramsey Lewis (b. 1935)
Harold Mabern (b. 1936)
Marian McPartland (b. 1918)
Jay McShann (1916–2006)
John Medeski (b. 1965)
Brad Mehldau (b. 1970)
Misha Mengelberg (b. 1935)
Mulgrew Miller (b. 1955)
Thelonious Monk (1917–1982)
Jason Moran (b. 1975)
Jelly Roll Morton (1890–1941)
Phineas Newborn Jr. (1931–1989)
Herbie Nichols (1919–1963)
Horace Parlan (b. 1931)

Danilo Perez (b. 1966)
Oscar Peterson (1925–2007)
Michel Petrucciani (1962–1999)
Enrico Pieranunzi (b. 1949)
Bud Powell (1924–1966)
Mel Powell (1923–1998)
Don Pullen (1941–1995)
Luckey Roberts (1887–1968)
Jimmy Rowles (1918–1996)
Gonzalo Rubalcaba (b. 1963)
Hilton Ruiz (1952–2006)
Matthew Shipp (b. 1960)
Horace Silver (b. 1928)
Pine Top Smith (1904–1929)
Willie "the Lion" Smith (1893–1973)
Martial Solal (b. 1927)
Billy Strayhorn (1915–1967)
Joe Sullivan (1906–1971)
Sun Ra (1914–1993)
Ralph Sutton (1922–2001)
Horace Tapscott (1934–1999)
Art Tatum (1909–1956)
Cecil Taylor (b. 1929)
Jacky Terrasson (b. 1966)
Bobby Timmons (1935–1974)
Lennie Tristano (1919–1978)
McCoy Tyner (b. 1938)
Mal Waldron (1925–2002)
Fats Waller (1904–1943)
Cedar Walton (b. 1934)
Randy Weston (b. 1926)
Gerald Wiggins (1922–2008)
Jessica Williams (b. 1948)
Mary Lou Williams (1910–1981)
Teddy Wilson (1912–1986)
Jimmy Yancey (1898–1951)
Joe Zawinul (1932–2007)

Organ

Count Basie (1904–1984)
Milt Buckner (1915–1977)
Wild Bill Davis (1918–1995)
Joey DeFrancesco (b. 1971)
Barbara Dennerlein (b. 1964)
Bill Doggett (1916–1996)
Richard Groove Holmes (1931–1991)
Jack McDuff (1926–2001)
Jimmy McGriff (1936–2008)
Don Patterson (1936–1988)
Shirley Scott (1934–2002)
Jimmy Smith (1925–2005)
Dr. Lonnie Smith (b. 1942)
Fats Waller (1904–1943)

Larry Young (1940–1978)
Joe Zawinul (1932–2007)

Bass

Jimmy Blanton (1918–1942)
Wellman Braud (1891–1966)
Ray Brown (1926–2002)
Steve Brown (1890–1965)
Red Callender (1916–1992)
Ron Carter (b. 1937)
Paul Chambers (1935–1969)
Curtis Counce (1926–1963)
Bob Cranshaw (b. 1932)
Israel Crosby (1919–1962)
Bill Crow (b. 1927)
Richard Davis (b. 1930)
Mark Dresser (b. 1952)
George Duvivier (1920–1985)
George "Pops" Foster (1892–1969)
Jimmy Garrison (1933–1976)
Henry Grimes (b. 1935)
Charlie Haden (b. 1937)
Bob Haggart (1914–1998)
Percy Heath (1923–2005)
Milt Hinton (1910–2000)
Dave Holland (b. 1946)
Chuck Israels (b. 1936)
David Izenzon (1932–1979)
Bill Johnson (1872–1972)
Sam Jones (1924–1981)
John Kirby (1908–1952)
Peter Kowald (1944–2002)
Scott LaFaro (1936–1961)
Malachi Favors Maghostut (1927–2004)
Cecil McBee (b. 1935)
Christian McBride (b. 1972)
Charles Mingus (1922–1979)
Red Mitchell (1927–1992)
Charnett Moffett (b. 1967)
George Mraz (b. 1944)
John Ore (b. 1933)
Walter Page (1900–1957)
William Parker (b. 1952)
Jaco Pastorius (1951–1987)
John Patitucci (b. 1959)
Gary Peacock (b. 1935)
Niels-Henning Ørsted Pedersen
    (1946–2005)
Oscar Pettiford (1922–1960)
Tommy Potter (1918–1988)
Gene Ramey (1913–1984)
Curly Russell (1917–1986)
Eddie Safranski (1918–1974)
Slam Stewart (1914–1987)

Steve Swallow (b. 1940)
Jamaaladeen Tacuma (b. 1956)
Miroslav Vitous (b. 1947)
Wilbur Ware (1923–1979)
Peter Washington (b. 1964)
Buster Williams (b. 1942)
Reggie Workman (b. 1937)

Drums/Percussion

Rashied Ali (b. 1935)
Paul Barbarin (1899–1969)
Joey Baron (b. 1955)
Ray Barretto (1929–2006)
Louis Bellson (b. 1924)
Han Bennink (b. 1942)
Ed Blackwell (1929–1992)
Brian Blade (b. 1970)
Art Blakey (1919–1990)
Candido Camero (b. 1921)
Terri Lynne Carrington (b. 1965)
Sid Catlett (1910–1951)
Joe Chambers (b. 1942)
Kenny Clarke (1914–1985)
Jimmy Cobb (b. 1929)
Cozy Cole (1909–1981)
Jimmy Crawford (1910–1980)
Andrew Cyrille (b. 1939)
Alan Dawson (1929–1996)
Jack DeJohnette (b. 1942)
Warren "Baby" Dodds (1898–1959)
Hamid Drake (b. 1955)
Frankie Dunlop (b. 1928)
Al Foster (b. 1944)
Milford Graves (b. 1941)
Sonny Greer (1895–1982)
Chico Hamilton (b. 1921)
Eric Harland (b. 1979)
Beaver Harris (1936–1991)
Roy Haynes (b. 1925)
Al "Tootie" Heath (b. 1935)
Billy Higgins (1936–2001)
Greg Hutchinson (b. 1970)
Susie Ibarra (b. 1970)
Ronald Shannon Jackson (b. 1940)
Elvin Jones (1927–2004)
Jo Jones (1911–1985)
Philly Joe Jones (1923–1985)
Connie Kay (1927–1994)
Gene Krupa (1909–1973)
Jack "Papa" Laine (1873–1966)
Mel Lewis (1929–1990)
Shelly Manne (1920–1984)
Charles Moffett (1929–1997)
Airto Moreira (b. 1941)

Joe Morello (b. 1928)
Paul Motian (b. 1931)
Sonny Murray (b. 1936)
Lewis Nash (b. 1958)
Tony Oxley (b. 1938)
Sonny Payne (1926–1979)
Chano Pozo (1915–1948)
Tito Puente (1923–2000)
Buddy Rich (1917–1987)
Dannie Richmond (1935–1988)
Ben Riley (b. 1933)
Herlin Riley (b. 1957)
Max Roach (1924–2007)
Mongo Santamaria (1922–2003)
Zutty Singleton (1898–1975)
Grady Tate (b. 1932)
Art Taylor (1929–1995)
Dave Tough (1907–1948)
Kenny Washington (b. 1958)
Jeff "Tain" Watts (b. 1960)
Chick Webb (1909–1939)
Tony Williams (1945–1997)

Guitar/Banjo

Howard Alden (b. 1958)
Danny Barker (1909–1994)
Billy Bauer (1915–2005)
George Benson (b. 1943)
Kenny Burrell (b. 1931)
Charlie Byrd (1925–1999)
Charlie Christian (1916–1942)
Joe Cohn (b. 1956)
Eddie Condon (1905–1973)
Larry Coryell (b. 1943)
Eddie Durham (1906–1987)
Herb Ellis (b. 1921)
Tal Farlow (1921–1998)
João Gilberto (b. 1931)
Freddie Green (1911–1987)
Grant Green (1935–1979)
Lonnie Johnson (1899–1970)
Robert Johnson (1911–1938)
Jim Hall (b. 1930)
Charlie Hunter (b. 1967)
Barney Kessel (1923–2004)
Carl Kress (1907–1965)
Biréli Lagrène (b. 1966)
Eddie Lang (1902–1933)
Russell Malone (b. 1963)
Pat Martino (b. 1944)
John McLaughlin (b. 1942)
Pat Metheny (b. 1954)
Wes Montgomery (1923–1968)
Joe Morris (b. 1955)

Mary Osborne (1921–1992)
Joe Pass (1929–1994)
Les Paul (b. 1915)
Bucky Pizzarelli (b. 1926)
Jimmy Raney (1927–1995)
Django Reinhardt (1910–1953)
Emily Remler (1957–1990)
Marc Ribot (b. 1954)
John Scofield (b. 1951)
Sonny Sharrock (1940–1994)
Johnny Smith (b. 1922)
Johnny St. Cyr (1890–1966)
Leni Stern (b. 1952)
Ralph Towner (b. 1940)
James "Blood" Ulmer (b. 1942)
George Van Eps (1913–1998)
T-Bone Walker (1910–1975)
Muddy Waters (1913–1983)
Chuck Wayne (1923–1997)

Vibraphone

Gary Burton (b. 1943)
Terry Gibbs (b. 1924)
Lionel Hampton (1908–2002)
Stefon Harris (b. 1973)
Jay Hoggard (b. 1954)
Bobby Hutcherson (b. 1941)
Milt Jackson (1923–1999)
Joe Locke (b. 1959)
Steve Nelson (b. 1955)
Red Norvo (1908–1999)
Terry Pollard (b. 1931)
Cal Tjader (1925–1982)

French horn

Vincent Chancey (b. 1950)
John Clark (b. 1944)
Tom Varner (b. 1957)
Julius Watkins (1921–1977)

Violin

Svend Asmussen (b. 1916)
Regina Carter (b. 1966)
Stephane Grappelli (1908–1997)
Leroy Jenkins (1932–2007)
Joe Kennedy Jr. (1923–2004)
Ray Nance (1913–1976)
Jean-Luc Ponty (b. 1942)
Jenny Scheinman (b. 1973)
Stuff Smith (1909–1967)
Eddie South (1904–1962)
Joe Venuti (1903–1978)

Singers

Karrin Allyson (b. 1963)
Ernestine Anderson (b. 1928)
Ivie Anderson (1905–1949)
Louis Armstrong (1901–1971)
Mildred Bailey (1907–1951)
Chet Baker (1929–1988)
Tony Bennett (b. 1926)
Connee Boswell (1907–1976)
Boswell Sisters
    Martha (1905–1958)
    Connee
    Helvetia "Vet" (1911–1988)
Dee Dee Bridgewater (b. 1950)
Cab Calloway (1907–1994)
Betty Carter (1929–1998)
Ray Charles (1930–2004)
June Christy (1925–1990)
Rosemary Clooney (1928–2002)
Freddie Cole (b. 1931)
Nat King Cole (1919–1965)
Bing Crosby (1903–1977)
Billy Eckstine (1914–1993)
Roy Eldridge (1911–1989)
Ella Fitzgerald (1917–1996)
Slim Gaillard (1916–1991)
Johnny Hartman (1923–1983)
Jon Hendricks (b. 1921)
Billie Holiday (1915–1959)
Shirley Horn (1934–2005)
Alberta Hunter (1895–1984)
Denise Jannah (b. 1956)
Eddie Jefferson (1918–1979)
Etta Jones (1928–2001)
Sheila Jordan (b. 1928)
Diana Krall (b. 1964)
Dave Lambert (1917–1966)
Lambert, Hendricks & Ross
    Dave Lambert
    Jon Hendricks
    Annie Ross
Peggy Lee (1920–2002)
Abbey Lincoln (b. 1930)
Carmen McRea (1920–1994)
Helen Merrill (b. 1930)
Mills Brothers
    John Jr. (1910–1936)
    Herbert (1912–1989)
    Harry (1913–1982)
    Donald (1915–1999)
Carmen Miranda (1909–1955)
Anita O'Day (1919–2006)
Jackie Paris (1926–2004)
John Pizzarelli (b. 1960)

King Pleasure (1922–1981)
Ma Rainey (1886–1939)
Dianne Reeves (b. 1956)
Annie Ross (b. 1930)
Jimmy Rushing (1903–1972)
Nina Simone (1933–2003)
Frank Sinatra (1915–1998)
Bessie Smith (1894–1937)
Mamie Smith (1883–1946)
Kay Starr (b. 1922)
Big Joe Turner (1911–1985)
Sarah Vaughan (1924–1990)
Dinah Washington (1924–1963)
Ethel Waters (1896–1977)
Lee Wiley (1908–1975)
Joe Williams (1918–1999)
Cassandra Wilson (b. 1955)
Nancy Wilson (b. 1937)

Composers/Arrangers

Muhal Richard Abrams (b. 1930)
Anthony Braxton (b. 1945)
Alan Broadbent (b. 1947)
Bob Brookmeyer (b. 1929)
Ralph Burns (1922–2001)
Benny Carter (1907–2003)
Bill Challis (1904–1994)
Al Cohn (1925–1988)

Ornette Coleman (b. 1930)
Steve Coleman (b. 1956)
Tadd Dameron (1917–1965)
Miles Davis (1926–1991)
Duke Ellington (1899–1974)
James Reese Europe (1881–1919)
Gil Evans (1912–1988)
Clare Fisher (b. 1928)
Frank Foster (b. 1928)
George Gershwin (1898–1937)
W. C. Handy (1873–1958)
Neal Hefti (1922–2008)
Fletcher Henderson (1897–1952)
Bill Holman (b. 1927)
Antonio Carlos "Tom" Jobim
   (1927–1994)
Quincy Jones (b. 1933)
Scott Joplin (1868–1917)
Louis Jordan (1908–1975)
Stan Kenton (1911–1979)
Michel Legrand (b. 1932)
John Lewis (1920–2001)
Abbey Lincoln (b. 1930)
Johnny Mandel (b. 1925)
Wynton Marsalis (b. 1961)
Gary McFarland (1933–1971)
Glenn Miller (1904–1944)
Thelonious Monk (1917–1982)

Butch Morris (b. 1947)
Jelly Roll Morton (1890–1941)
Gerry Mulligan (1927–1996)
Jimmy Mundy (1907–1983)
David Murray (b. 1955)
Oliver Nelson (1932–1975)
Chico OíFarrill (1921–2001)
Melvin "Sy" Oliver (1910–1988)
Hall Overton (1920–1972)
Don Redman (1900–1964)
Johnny Richards (1911–1968)
Nelson Riddle (1921–1985)
George Russell (b. 1923)
Luis Russell (1902–1963)
Eddie Sauter (1914–1981)
Maria Schneider (b. 1960)
Wayne Shorter (b. 1933)
Billy Strayhorn (1915–1967)
Cecil Taylor (b. 1929)
Henry Threadgill (b. 1944)
Charles Tolliver (b. 1942)
Fats Waller (1904–1943)
Ernie Wilkins (1922–1999)
Clarence Williams (1898–1965)
Mary Lou Williams (1910–1981)
Spencer Williams (1889–1965)
Gerald Wilson (b. 1918)
John Zorn (b. 1953)

Primer on Music Notation

Jazz is a largely improvised music, but much of it is also composed, from the *heads,* or themes that kick off the solos, to big-band orchestrations. Today, nearly all jazz musicians are fluent in the traditional forms of music notation. While we don't expect readers of this textbook to know how to read music, a few pointers about how it works may prove helpful.

There are two ways music notation is used in jazz. The first is *prescriptive,* and operates along the same principles as classical music: a composer writes music on a page for instrumentalists to translate into sound. Jazz notation sometimes lacks the kind of details that indicate dynamics, articulation, and even melodic notes (a jazz chart may consist exclusively of chord symbols). Rather than providing painstaking instructions, jazz composers rely on musicians to know how to interpret their symbols, as in the example below.

Charlie Parker, "Billie's Bounce"

The second approach is *descriptive,* which puts into notation a musical work that already exists, perhaps as a spontaneously created arrangement, like Count Basie's "One O'Clock Jump," or as an ad lib solo, like Coleman Hawkins's improvisation on "Body and Soul." This is known as **transcription.** It can be simple or elaborate, depending on what the transcriber wants to show, and will *always* be incomplete—nothing in writing can capture the totality of sound or the rhythmic nuance of swing as heard in a performance.

Both ways rely on the traditional forms of music notation. The basic guidelines that follow will allow you to make sense of written music, or perhaps even write or transcribe some of your own.

Pitch

Pitches, or notes, are written on five lines grouped together as a **staff** or in the spaces in between.

Each line or space represents a different note—A, B, C, D, E, F, or G. Pitches that lie outside the range of the staff can be added by drawing extra lines (called **ledger lines**) above or below the staff.

The precise range of pitches is defined by the **clef** written at the far left of the staff: the **treble clef** for the higher pitches, the **bass clef** for the lower. The treble clef, also called the G clef, curls around the second line from the bottom of the staff, marking the G above middle C. The bass clef, also called the F clef, has two dots that enclose the second line from the top of the staff, the F below middle C.

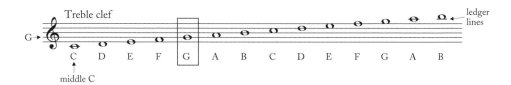

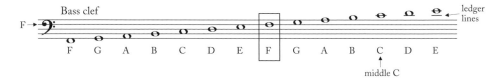

Simple mnemonics—for "line notes" and "space notes"—can help you remember where the notes fall on the staff.

The two clefs combined make the **grand staff,** with middle C (notated with a ledger line) lying precisely in the middle; it can be written in either the treble or bass staff.

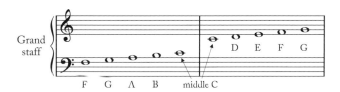

The keyboard below shows over three octaves of notes and how they are notated on the musical staff.

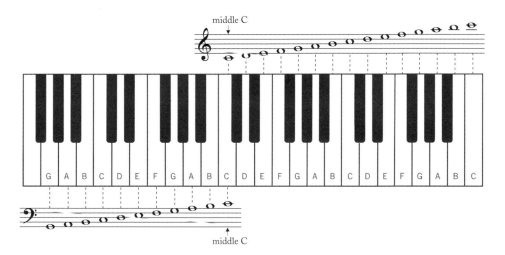

Major and Minor Scales

As we saw in Chapter 1, the piano white keys from C to C make up a **diatonic scale**—in this case a **major scale**—with C as the **tonic,** or home, pitch. Any major scale is constructed by a pattern of half (H) steps and whole (W) steps: W W H W W W H. (A half step is the shortest distance between any two notes, white or black, in either direction; a whole step is equal to two half steps.) The pattern is easy to see on a keyboard if you start from C.

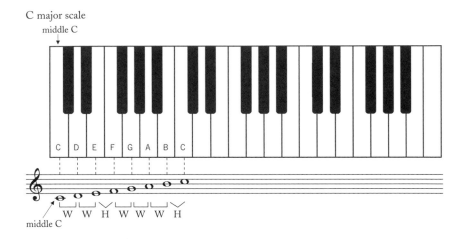

To preserve this pattern, all other scales will necessarily need some of the black keys—either **sharps** (♯), which raise a pitch by a half step, or **flats** (♭), which lower a pitch by a half step. A major scale starting on E, for example, requites four sharps (F♯, C♯, G♯, D♯).

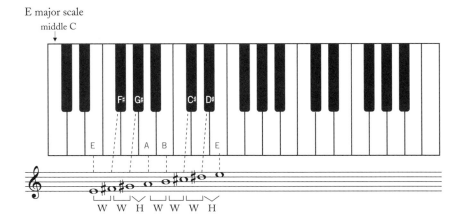

To convey music in E major, or any other key besides C, musicians use a **key signature,** to the right of the clef. The E major key signature automatically ensures that every F, C, G, and D will be raised a half step—unless a natural sign (♮) restores the note to its white key.

Key signatures range from blank (for C major) to up to seven sharps (for C♯ major) or six flats (for G♭ major). You can easily tell what key corresponds with a key signature through a simple bit of mnemonics: the tonic (starting pitch) of the major scale is either the next-to-last flat, or one half step higher than the last sharp.

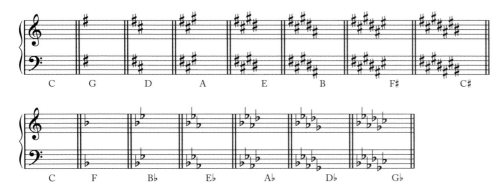

When building a major scale, how do you know when to use sharps and when to use flats? The main thing to remember, in addition to the whole- and half-step pattern, is that each scale contains all seven letter names. So starting on F, for example, the major scale is F, G, A, B♭, C, D, E, F. The fourth note has to be B♭, not A♯, because there's already an A.

F major scale

Each major scale has a **relative minor** scale: a minor scale that uses the same key signature. To find a major scale's relative minor, take the tonic (beginning) pitch of the major scale and count down one and a half steps. (Do this process in reverse to find a minor scale's relative major.) The relative minor of F major is thus D minor. The key signature for both scales is one flat, B♭.

The minor scale has its own pattern: W H W W H W W. Chapter 1 described the difference in sound between major and minor, resulting mostly from the interval between the first and third notes of the scale. This interval in a major scale is a **major third** (two whole steps) and in a minor scale is a **minor third** (a whole and half step).

You can't tell what key a piece is in *just* by looking at the key signature; one flat, for example, could indicate either F major or D minor. You need to also look at the beginning and especially the end of the piece, which will usually feature the tonic note and harmony.

Western musical notation assumes **fixed intonation**: there are no notes smaller than a half step. Yet we know that in playing **blue notes**, jazz musicians often make use of **microtones**. To show tiny variations in pitch requires the use of idiosyncratic notation: arrows, downward slurs, lines from one note to the next.

Rhythm

Staves are divided by vertical **bar lines** into **measures,** or **bars,** which allow musicians to keep regular beats and accents throughout the piece.

The longest-held note is normally the **whole note,** an oval that usually fills up a measure. From there, notes are divided in half: a whole note equals two **half notes,** a half note two **quarter notes,** a quarter note two **eighth notes,** an eighth note two **sixteenth notes,** and so on. Each division marks a smaller amount of time. At a moderate tempo, the beat will usually be assigned to the quarter note, with sixteenth notes moving by at blinding speed.

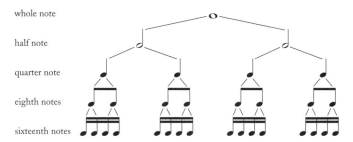

The parts of a note are shown below. Eighth and sixteenth notes are written with a flag attached to the stem or, when two or more are joined together, with beams. Each note value has a corresponding **rest,** indicating a silence that lasts as long as the equivalent note.

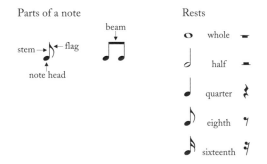

Beats usually divide into two, but when a note is (exceptionally) divided into threes, it's called a **triplet,** and special notation is required: the three notes grouped together are marked by a bracket with the number 3 attached.

Meter

Most jazz is in duple meter, which is indicated by the **meter signature** 4/4 (sometimes abbreviated as *C*) to the right of the key signature. The top number shows the number of beats to the measure (four), while the lower number designates which note gets one beat (the quarter note). Another form of duple meter (with two beats to the measure) is 2/4; triple meter, with three beats to the measure, is 3/4.

Vernon Duke, "I Can't Get Started"

Ludwig van Beethoven, Symphony No. 9, 4th movement

Richard Rodgers, "My Favorite Things"

When the beat is divided into three instead of two throughout a whole piece, however, a different meter signature is required. In a duple meter of four beats, with each beat divided into threes, a **dot** is added to the quarter note, which makes it equal to three eighth notes rather than two. (A dot attached to any note adds half that note's value; so a dotted half note would be equal to three quarter notes.) Such a measure is notated as 12/8; each measure contains the equivalent of twelve eighth notes, or four dotted quarter notes.

The first example below shows a measure of 4/4 and a measure of 12/8, with the beats written below; in 4/4 the quarter note divides in twos, and in 12/8 the dotted quarter divides in threes.

George David Weiss, "What a Wonderful World"

A **tie** mark, seen in the example above, is an arc that connects two identical notes and adds the duration of the second note to the first; the second is not played.

As we have seen, jazz musicians don't rigidly divide the beat up into twos or threes, but use an infinite variety of divisions, known as **swing eighth notes** (see Chapter 1). But these are written as "straight" eighth notes, which are easier to read and to transform into actual music. Musicians can then swing them as they please.

Western notation can't show the continuous cycles of African American music, but it does include a symbol for repetition, **repeat marks**: double bar lines with two dots at the beginning and end of a passage, instructing the performer to play that passage twice. We can also use this notation to show cycles that repeat indefinitely. (See also "Heart and Soul" example in Chapter 2.)

Count Basie, "Splanky"

An arc that connects *different* notes, seen in the example above, is known as a **slur.** A slur instructs the performer to play smoothly, or **legato.** Accent marks emphasize a given note. And notes underscored with small dots are meant to be played crisply, with little sustain; this is known as **staccato** playing.

Dizzy Gillespie, "Salt Peanuts"

staccato mark

Harmony

Harmony is created by combining several notes at once to make **chords.** The most common type of chord is the **triad,** three notes that are alternate scale degrees: for example, C-E-G, D-F-A, E-G-B, and so on.

Triads in C major

A chord can be built on any note, but be sure to check the key signature of the key you are in; if you're playing in F major, remember that every B is flatted.

Triads in F major

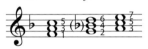

The chords built from notes in the C major scale are shown below. They are all either major chords (with a major third as the bottom interval) or minor chords (a minor third is the bottom interval)—except for the chord built on B, the "leading tone," which is a **diminished** chord. As the diagram shows, chords are identified with a Roman numeral that signifies the scale degree: I for the chord built on scale degree 1, V for the chord built on scale degree 5, and so on. Uppercase numerals indicate major chords, lowercase minor or diminished.

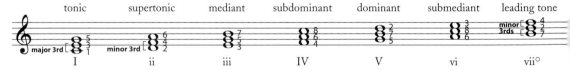

If you have access to a piano, play these chords to get a sense of major, minor, and diminished. Then try adding another third to a chord—for example, 1-3-5-7 or 5-7-2-4. These are **seventh chords,** reflecting the interval from the bottom note to the top. Continue to experiment, using your ear to add notes, and you will quickly find your way to the rich colors that are part of every jazz musician's harmonic palette.

This primer is a very basic starting point. Many of the elements discussed here can be heard in the Jazz Studio demonstrations on StudySpace. You can expand your understanding by investigating a music theory site on the Internet or taking a course in music fundamentals. The more you know about the mechanics of music, the greater appreciation you will have for the spontaneous creativity of jazz.

Glossary

I chord   chord built on the first degree of the scale; known as the *tonic*.

IV chord   chord built on the fourth degree of the scale; known as the *subdominant*.

V chord   chord built on the fifth degree of the scale; known as the *dominant*.

A A B A form   the most common 32-bar *popular song* form, referring to melody and harmonic progression (but not text). Each portion is eight bars long, with **B**, the *bridge*, serving as the point of contrast. **A** = statement, **A** = repetition, **B** = contrast, **A** = return.

A B A C form   the second most common 32-bar *popular song* form, referring to melody and harmonic progression (but not text). Each portion is eight bars long, with the **A** section returning in the song's middle. Can also be considered **A A′** form.

accelerando   a gradual speeding up of *tempo*.

acid jazz   a form of contemporary music created by DJs in the 1990s, relying heavily on samples taken from jazz recordings from the 1950s and 1960s.

alto saxophone   one of the most common saxophones used in jazz performance, smaller and higher-pitched than the tenor.

arpeggio   the notes of a chord played in quick succession rather than simultaneously.

arrangements   composed scores for big bands, with individual parts for each musician.

arco   a stringed instrument (such as the string bass) played with a bow.

art music   a form of music with high aesthetic standards and social prestige, created by professional artists for a well-educated public and insulated from the commercial world.

atonal   music with no key center.

augmented chord   an unstable chord made up of two major thirds; found in the whole-tone scale.

avant-garde jazz   a modernist style of jazz exploring new methods that radically oppose existing traditions; among the elements of jazz undermined by the avant-garde are rhythm, harmony, melody, structure, instrumentation, manner of presentation, and politics.

backbeat   a simple *polyrhythm* emphasizing beats 2 and 4 of a 4/4 measure (rather than 1 and 3).

ballad   (1) a slow, romantic *popular song;* (2) a long, early type of folk song that narrated a bit of local history.

bar   see *measure*.

baritone saxophone   the largest and deepest saxophone used in jazz performance.

bass   in the *rhythm section* of a jazz band, an instrument—*string bass, electric bass,* or *tuba*—that supports the harmony and plays a basic rhythmic foundation.

bass clarinet   a *wind instrument* pitched lower than a standard *clarinet*.

bass drum   the large drum front and center in a jazz *drum kit,* struck with a mallet propelled by a *foot pedal;* it produces a deep, heavy sound.

bebop   A style of modern jazz pioneered in the mid-1940s; it has become the basis for most contemporary jazz.

bell   the flared opening at the end of a brass instrument.

bent notes   see *blue notes*.

big bands   large jazz orchestras featuring sections of saxophones, trumpets, and trombones, prominent during the Swing Era (1930s).

block chords   a *homophonic texture* in which the chordal accompaniment moves in the same rhythm as the main melody.

blue notes   notes in which the pitch is bent expressively, using *variable intonation;* also known as blue notes.

blues   a musical/poetic form in African American culture, created c. 1900 and widely influential around the world.

blues form   a twelve-bar *cycle* used as a framework for improvisation by jazz musicians.

blues scale   the melodic resources for the *blues;* includes simple *pentatonic* and *diatonic* scales combined with *blue notes*.

blue third   the lowered third degree of the scale, featured in the *blues*.

bongos   in *Latin percussion,* an instrument with two drumheads, one larger than the other, compact enough to sit between the player's knees.

boogie-woogie   a blues piano style in which the left hand plays a rhythmic *ostinato* of eight beats to the bar.

bossa nova   "new flair"; Brazilian form of *samba* music.

bottleneck guitar   *guitar* played with a glass slide over the finger to create a *glissando* effect.

bow   a string instrument, such as a *string bass,* played by drawing a bow with horsehair across the strings; also known as *arco*.

brass instruments   *wind instruments,* some of which are indeed made of brass, that use a cuplike *mouthpiece* to create the sound.

break   a short two- or four-bar episode in which the band abruptly stops playing to let a single musician solo with a *monophonic* passage.

bridge (release)   the middle part (or **B** section) of 32-bar *A A B A form,* which connects, or "bridges," between the **A** sections; it typically ends with a *half cadence*.

broken octaves   a form of left-hand piano accompaniment that alternates the lower note of an octave with the higher one.

cadence stopping places that divide a *harmonic progression* into comprehensible *phrases*. See *half cadence, full cadence*.

cadenza a classical-music word for a monophonic solo passage that showcases the performer's virtuosity.

cakewalk ragtime dancing featuring *syncopated* rhythms.

call and response a pervasive principle of interaction or conversation in jazz: a statement by one musician or group of musicians is immediately answered by another musician or group.

changes jazz slang for a harmonic progression. See *rhythm changes*.

Charleston rhythm a dance rhythm from the 1920s, consisting of two emphatic beats followed by a rest.

chart a shorthand musical score that serves as the point of reference for a jazz performance, often specifying only the melody and the harmonic progression; also known as a lead sheet.

Chicago style style of jazz in the 1920s that imitated the New Orleans style, combining expansive solos with *polyphonic* theme statements.

chord a combination of notes performed simultaneously.

chord clusters *dissonant* chords with closely spaced notes.

chorus (1) a single statement of the harmonic and rhythmic jazz *cycle* defined by the musical form (e.g, 12-bar blues, 32-bar popular song); (2) the repeated portion of a *popular song*, often introduced by its *verse*.

chromatic harmony complex harmony based on the *chromatic scale*.

chromatic scale the scale containing twelve *half steps* within the *octave*, corresponding to all the keys (black and white) within an octave on the piano (e.g., from C to C).

clarinet a *wind instrument* consisting of a slim, cylindrical, ebony-colored wooden tube that produces a thin, piercing sound.

classic blues see *vaudeville blues*.

classical music *art music* from the European tradition.

clave a Latin *time-line pattern*.

clusters see *chord clusters*.

coda Italian for "tail": a concluding section to a musical performance.

collective improvisation method of improvisation found in New Orleans jazz in which several instruments in the *front line* improvise simultaneously in a dense, *polyphonic* texture.

comping a rhythmically unpredictable way of playing chords to accompany a soloist; typically one of the *variable layers* in the *rhythm section*.

congas in *Latin percussion*, two tall drums of equal height but different diameters, with the smaller one assigned the lead role.

consonant the quality of a harmony that's stable and doesn't need to *resolve* to another chord.

contrapuntal adjectival form of *counterpoint*.

cool jazz a style of modern jazz in the 1950s that used a "cool," relaxed approach to timbre and experimented with such basic elements as form, texture, instrumentation, and meter.

coon song an early form of *ragtime* popular song that yoked polyrhythmic accompaniments to grotesque racial stereotypes.

cornet a partially conical *brass instrument* used often in early jazz and eventually supplanted by the *trumpet*.

countermelody in *homophonic texture*, an accompanying melodic part with distinct, though subordinate, melodic interest; also known (especially in classical music) as obbligato.

counterpoint *polyphonic texture*, especially when composed.

counterrhythm see *cross-rhythm*.

country blues an early style of blues, first recorded in the 1920s, featuring itinerant male singers accompanying themselves on guitar.

crash cymbal a cymbal that produces a splashy, indeterminate pitch, not unlike a small gong, used for dramatic punctuations.

crescendo an increase in volume.

cross-rhythm a rhythmic layer that conflicts with the underlying meter.

cup mute an orchestral *mute* with an extension that more or less covers the *bell* of a *brass instrument*.

cycle a fixed unit of time, repeated indefinitely, that's used as the framework for improvisation in jazz.

cymbals broad-rimmed, slightly-convex circular plates that form part of the jazz *drum kit*. See also *crash cymbal, high-hat*, and *ride cymbal*.

decrescendo a decrease in volume.

degree individual notes in a scale (e.g., the first note of a scale is the first degree).

diatonic scale the seven-note scale most commonly used in Western music. See *major scale, minor scale, Dorian mode*.

diminished (or diminished-seventh) chord an unstable chord made up entirely of minor thirds.

discography the science of record classification.

dissonant the quality of an unstable harmony that *resolves* to another chord.

dominant a chord built on the fifth degree of the scale that demands resolution to the tonic chord.

Dorian mode a diatonic scale with an arrangement of half and whole steps (found on the piano white keys from D to D) that falls between major and minor.

double (1) to play more than one instrument; (2) to reinforce a melody with one or more different instruments.

double bass see *string bass*.

double stop on a bowed string instrument (violin, bass), two strings played at the same time.

double time a technique in which a jazz ensemble, especially the *rhythm section*, plays twice as fast without changing the length of the overall cycle.

downbeat the first beat of a *measure*, or bar.

dropping bombs a technique devised in *bebop* in which the bass drum plays strong accents.

drum kit (or drum set, trap set, traps) a one-man percussion section within the rhythm section of a jazz band, usually consisting of a *bass drum, snare drum, tom-toms*, and *cymbals*.

duple meter the most common form of *meter,* grouping beats into patterns of twos or fours; every *measure,* or bar, in duple meter has either two or four beats.

dynamics volume, or loudness.

electric bass a four-stringed guitar used in popular music, amplified through an electric speaker.

electric piano an electrically amplified keyboard, such as the Fender Rhodes, capable of producing piano sounds.

Ellingtonians musicians who played with Duke Ellington for years or even decades.

embouchure the shaping and positioning of the lips and other facial muscles when playing wind instruments.

extended chords *triads* to which additional pitches, or *extensions,* have been added.

extensions notes added to extend a chord beyond the triad (such as the sixth, seventh, ninth, or thirteenth).

fake book a collection of *charts* or lead sheets used by jazz musicians (so-called because jazz musicians improvise, or "fake," their way through a performance).

false fingerings on a reed instrument (especially the saxophone), playing the same note with different fingers, often producing unusual timbres or slight pitch differences.

field holler an unaccompanied, rhythmically loose vocal line sung by a field worker.

fill a short drum solo performed to fill in the spaces in an improvised performance.

fixed intonation a tuning system that fixes pitches at precise frequencies. See *variable intonation.*

flat a musical symbol (♭) that lowers a note by a half step.

flatted third the lowered third degree of the scale, typically found in the blues.

flatted fifth see *tritone.*

flatted scale degree note played a half step lower.

flugelhorn brass instrument with a fully conical bore, somewhat larger than a trumpet and producing a more mellow, rounded timbre.

folk music a form of music created by ordinary people for their own use, insulated from the commercial world and the world of social elites.

foot pedal the mechanism that propels the mallet to hit a *bass drum.*

form the preconceived structures that govern improvisation in jazz. These may include *cycles* of various kinds, popular song (like *A A B A*), or compositional forms such as *march/ragtime.*

forte a loud dynamic.

foundation layers continuous, unchanging patterns whose very repetition provides a framework for a musical piece.

free improvisation improvisation in an atonal context, where the focus shifts from harmony to other dimensions of music: timbre, melodic intervals, rhythm, and the interaction between musicians.

free rhythm music that flows through time without regularly occurring pulses.

frequency the vibrations per second of a musical note.

front the nominal star of a jazz band, but not really its leader or music director.

front line in *New Orleans jazz,* the melody instruments: trumpet (or cornet), trombone, and clarinet.

full cadence a musical stopping point on the *tonic* that marks the end of a phrase.

funk a type of groove with a highly sycopated bass line and multiple contrasting rhythmic layers, favored by jazz musicians after about 1970.

fusion the joining of two types of music, especially the mixing of jazz and rock in the 1970s.

ghosting playing notes so lightly that they are almost inaudible.

glissando sliding seamlessly from one note to another, as exemplified on the trombone; also known as smear.

grace note a short, decorative note sounded either immediately before or simultaneously with a longer melodic note.

groove a general term for the overall rhythmic framework of a performance. Grooves include *swing, funk, ballad,* and *Latin.*

guiro in *Latin percussion,* a scraped gourd with ridges.

guitar a plucked string instrument with waisted sides and a fretted fingerboard; the acoustic guitar was part of early jazz *rhythm sections,* while the electric guitar began to be used in the late 1930s and came to dominate jazz and popular music in the 1960s.

half cadence a musical stopping point on the *dominant.* Half cadences sound incomplete; they serve like a comma or a semicolon in punctuation, providing a stop but not signaling full closure.

half-valving depressing one or more of the valves of a brass instrument only halfway, producing an uncertain pitch with a nasal sound.

half step the smallest interval possible in Western music.

hard bop a *bebop* style of the 1950s that refused the experiments of *cool jazz* and linked its aesthetic with African American culture; included the more populist *soul jazz* and was played by great bebop artists of the day.

Harlem Renaissance an artistic movement of the 1920s that attempted to display African American abilities in painting, drama, literature, poetry, criticism, and music; jazz was usually not included by critics of the time, although in retrospect the music of Duke Ellington seems central.

harmonic improvisation a new melodic line created with notes drawn from the underlying *harmonic progression;* also known as running the changes.

harmonic progression a series of chords placed in a strict rhythmic sequence; also known as changes.

harmonic substitution the substitution of one chord, or a series of chords, for harmonies in a progression.

Harmon mute a hollow mute, originally with a short extension but usually played without it, leaving a hole in the center and creating a highly concentrated sound.

head a composed section of music that frames a small-combo performance, appearing at the beginning and again at the end.

head arrangement a flexible, unwritten arrangement created by a band.

high-hat two shoulder-level *cymbals* on an upright pole with a foot pedal at its base; the pedal brings the top cymbal crashing into the lower one with a distinct *thunk*.

hip-hop a form of contemporary music that arose in the 1970s, featuring rapping, turntable styling, and the dance and fashion of inner-city youth.

Historicism the theory that artistic works do not rise independently of history but must be understood in relation to the past.

homophony a *texture* featuring one melody supported by harmonic accompaniment.

horns jazz slang for *wind instruments*.

inside see *playing inside*.

interval the distance between two different pitches of a scale.

irregular meter a meter featuring beats of unequal size (some are divided into twos, others into threes). A meter of five, for example, features two beats—one divided into three notes, the other divided into two notes (as in Dave Brubeck's "Take Five"). Similar combinations of seven, nine, and eleven are possible.

jam session an informal gathering at which musicians create music for their own enjoyment.

Jazz Age the 1920s; the era in which jazz became a popular, prominent form of music.

jazz repertory a movement that arose in the mid-1970s to critically examine and perform jazz from earlier eras.

keeping time playing the *foundation layers* for a musical piece.

klezmer a Jewish dance music.

Latin music dance grooves from the Caribbean, Central America, or South America (such as rumba, samba, mambo, bossa nova, or merengue) that feature syncopated bass lines and lively polyrhythm.

Latin percussion a wide variety of instruments including congas, bongos, timbales, maracas, and guiro.

legato a smooth, unbroken connection between notes.

licks short melodic ideas that form a shared basic vocabulary for jazz improvisers.

mainstream term first coined for music during the 1950s that was neither modernist (bebop, cool jazz, hard bop) or historicist (New Orleans jazz); today, it refers to styles that are neither aggressively innovative nor backward-looking, but falling in the center of the tradition.

major scale or mode the most common scale in Western music, sung to the syllables *do, re, mi, fa, sol, la, ti do*. The pattern of whole and half steps is W W H W W W H.

major second a whole step, or an interval made up of two half steps.

major triad a triad featuring a major third between the two lower notes.

maracas in *Latin percussion*, a gourd filled with beans and shaken.

march form a musical form exemplified by composers like John Philip Sousa, consisting of a series of sixteen-bar *strains*, usually repeated once and not brought back; for example, A A B B C C D D; the third strain, or *trio*, *modulates* to a new key (usually *IV*) and is often twice as long.

march/ragtime form *march form* as adopted by ragtime composers like Scott Joplin.

measure (or bar) a rhythmic unit lasting from one downbeat to the next.

melismatic several notes sung to a single syllable.

melodic paraphrase a preexisting melody used as the basis for improvisation.

meter the organization of recurring pulses into patterns. See also *duple meter*, *irregular meter*, and *triple meter*.

microtones melodic intervals smaller than a half step.

minor scale or mode a diatonic scale similar to the *major scale*, but with a different pattern of half steps and whole steps (W H W W H W W); normally used in Western music to convey melancholy or sadness.

minor triad a triad featuring a minor third between the two lower notes.

modal improvisation the process of using a scale as the basis for improvisation.

modal jazz a style of jazz devised in the 1950s that relied heavily on *modal improvisation*.

modulate to move from one key (B-flat, G, D minor, etc.) to another.

monophony a *texture* featuring one melody with no accompaniment. See also *break*, *stop-time*.

montuno a syncopated *vamp* that serves as a rhythmic foundation in Latin music.

motive a short melodic or rhythmic idea.

mouthpiece on a brass instrument, a cuplike rest for the musician's lips, into which air is blown; on a reed instrument, the piece of hard plastic to which a reed is attached.

multiphonics complicated sounds created on a wind instrument (through intense blowing) that contain more than one pitch at the same time; used often in avant-garde jazz.

mutes physical devices inserted into the bell of brass instruments to distort the timbre of the sounds coming out. See *cup mute*, *Harmon mute*, *pixie mute*, *plunger mute*, and *straight mute*.

neighbor note a note one half or whole step away; neighbor notes leave and return to a note by step.

New Criticism criticism that emphasizes close examination of a work of art with little concern for the cultural or biographical circumstances under which it was created.

New Orleans jazz the earliest jazz style, developed early in the twentieth century and popularized after 1917 in New York and Chicago; native to New Orleans, it features *collective improvisation.*

ninth an interval a step larger than an octave, used to create *extended chords.*

obbligato see *countermelody.*

octave two notes with the same letter name; one pitch has a frequency precisely twice the other (in a ratio of 2 : 1).

offbeat a note that falls in between the basic beats of a measure.

organ in jazz, an electrically amplified keyboard with *pedals* that imitates the sound of a pipe organ; used in *soul jazz* in the 1950s and 1960s.

ostinato (Italian for "obstinate") a repeated melodic or rhythmic pattern.

ostinato riff a riff that's repeated indefinitely.

outside see *playing outside.*

pedals the bass notes on an *organ,* played on a keyboard with the feet.

pedal point a passage in which the bass note refuses to move, remaining stationary on a single note.

pedal tone the bass note that creates a *pedal point.*

pentatonic scale a scale of five notes; for example, C D E G A.

percussion in the *rhythm section* of a jazz band, the drums, cymbals, congas, and other instruments that are struck to provide the music's rhythmic foundation.

phrase a musical utterance that's analogous to a sentence in speech.

phrasing the manner of shaping phrases: some musicians play phrases that are short and terse, while others are garrulous and intense.

piano a stringed keyboard instrument on which a pressed key triggers a hammer to strike strings; a standard part of the *rhythm section.*

piano a soft dynamic.

pickup a small microphone attached to the bridge of a *string bass* or to an acoustic *guitar* to amplify its sound.

pitch the vibrations per second, or *frequency,* of a sound.

pixie mute a small mute inserted into the bell of a brass instrument; players like Cootie Williams and "Tricky Sam" Nanton modified its sound further with a *plunger mute.*

pizzicato the technique of playing a string instrument by plucking the strings with the fingers; usually the preferred method in jazz for playing the *string bass.*

playing inside improvising within the structure of a *tonal* harmonic progression

playing outside improvising outside the structure of a *tonal* harmonic progression.

plunger mute the bottom end of a sink plunger (minus the handle), used as a mute for a brass instrument.

polyphony *texture* in which two or more melodies of equal interest are played at the same time.

polyrhythm the simultaneous use of contrasting rhythms; also known as rhythmic contrast.

popular song a type of song created by professional songwriters, especially in the period from the 1920s to the 1960s; usually falls into one of the basic song forms, such as *A A B A* or *A B A C.*

press-roll an intense rumbling on the *snare drum.*

programmatic music that attempts to link itself to specific places, people, or events.

quartal chords (or harmonies) chords built using the interval of a fourth (rather than a third).

quarter tone a *microtone* that divides the half step into equal parts.

ragtime a style of popular music in the early twentieth century that conveyed African American polyrhythm in notated form; includes popular song and dance, although it's primarily known today through compositions written for the piano.

reed instruments *wind instruments* whose *mouthpieces* are inserted between the lips, with the player blowing a stream of air into a passageway between a thin, limber reed and the hard part of the mouthpiece.

refrain in *popular song* or *folk music,* a musical section that returns regularly.

register the range of an instrument or voice: upper register means its highest notes, lower register its lower notes.

resolve what an unstable (or *dissonant*) note or chord does when it moves to a stable (or *consonant*) note or chord.

rest a moment of silence, indicated by a sign in musical notation; for example, ⅃ indicates a quarter rest (a quarter note's duration of silence).

retro-swing a form of dance music popular toward the end of the twentieth century that appropriated dances from the Swing Era with musical accompaniment from 1940s rhythm and blues.

rhythm changes a harmonic progression based on the George Gershwin tune "I Got Rhythm."

rhythmic contrast see *polyrhythm.*

rhythmic layers in the repetitive cyclic structures of jazz, highly individualized parts that contrast with one another, even as they create a unified whole. See also *polyrhythm.*

rhythm section instruments that provide accompaniment for jazz soloing: harmony instruments (piano, guitar), bass instruments (string bass, tuba), and percussion (drum set).

ride cymbal a cymbal with a clear, focused timbre that's played more or less continuously.

ride pattern a steady pulsation played on the ride cymbal that forms one of the foundations for modern jazz.

riff a short, catchy, and repeated melodic phrase.

ring shout an African American religious dance, performed in a circle moving counterclockwise; often cited as the earliest and most pervasive form of African survival in the New World.

rip a strong *glissando* rising to the top of a note, especially on a trumpet.

ritard a gradual slowing down of *tempo*.

rock and roll a form of contemporary music, combining rhythm and blues with elements from popular song and country music and marketed at white teenagers; since the 1960s, when it became known simply as **rock,** it has been the dominant form in the music industry.

root the bottom note of a *triad*.

rubato (Italian for "stolen") an elastic approach to rhythm in which musicians speed up and slow down for expressive purposes; rubato makes musical time unpredictable and more flexible.

rumba clave a slight variation of the *clave* pattern, used in the rumba.

salsa a form of Latin popular music, founded in the 1970s.

samba a traditional Latino music with African roots.

saxophone invented by Adophe Sax in the 1840s, a family of single-reed *wind instruments* with the carrying power of a brass instrument. See *alto saxophone, tenor saxophone, soprano saxophone,* and *baritone saxophone*.

scale a collection of *pitches* within the *octave*, forming a certain pattern of whole and half steps, from which melodies are created.

scat-singing improvising by a vocalist, using nonsense syllables instead of words; popularized by Louis Armstrong.

secondary ragtime a pattern of *polyrhythm* in which a short motive of three pitches, implying a meter of three, is superimposed on a duple meter.

send-off riffs ensemble *riffs* played in the first few bars of a *chorus* by the entire band. They interrupt or immediately precede a solo, "sending" the soloist off on his way; the soloist then completes the rest of the chorus.

sequence a short melodic pattern repeated on different pitches. See also *transpose*.

seventh an *interval* one step smaller than an *octave*, often used as an *extension* for chords.

shake for *brass instruments*, a quick *trill* between notes that mimics a wide *vibrato*, often performed at the end of a musical passage.

sharp a music symbol (♯) that raises a note a half step.

shuffle rhythms slow, powerfully syncopated rhythms derived from *boogie-woogie*.

sideman any musician employed by a bandleader; often used to describe members of a swing band.

singer-songwriter in contemporary popular music, a perfomer who creates his or her own music; this contrasts with the practice in the music industry before the 1960s that set songwriters apart from performers.

single reed a *reed instrument*, such as the *clarinet* or *saxophone*, that uses only one reed; in jazz, double-reed instruments such as the oboe or bassoon are rarely used.

slash chords complex *extended chords* in which the root is a note not normally part of the *triad* (e.g., an A major chord with an F root, written as A/F and spoken as "A-slash-F").

slide an elongated trombone tube that adjusts the length of a column of air when the player slides it.

small combo the standard small group for jazz, combining a few *soloists* with a *rhythm section*.

smear see *glissando*.

smooth jazz a highly popular form of contemporary jazz, featuring inoffensive soloing and digitally processed rhythm tracks, favored on some radio stations.

snare drum smaller drum in a jazz *drum kit*, either standing on its own or attached to the *bass drum*, and emitting a penetrating, rattling sound.

soli a passage for a section of a jazz band (saxophones, trumpets, trombones) in block-chord texture.

soloist any instrument in the jazz ensemble whose improvisation is featured in a performance.

son clave the standard version of the *clave* pattern.

soprano saxophone the smallest and highest-pitched saxophone used in jazz performance.

soul jazz a popularized form of *hard bop* that employs a strong backbeat, an aggressive urban sound, and gospel-typechords.

spiritual African American religious song.

staccato a short, detached way of playing notes or chords.

standard a popular song that has become part of the permanent repertory for jazz musicians.

stepwise in melody, moving from one note in the scale to the next.

stock arrangements standard arrangements of popular songs made available by publishing companies for swing bands.

stop-time a technique in which a band plays a series of short chords a fixed distance apart (e.g., a measure), creating spaces for an instrument to fill with monophonic improvisation; often used in early jazz.

straight mute a standard orchestral mute that dampens the sound of a brass instrument without much distortion.

strain in *march form*, a 16- or 32-bar section.

stride piano a style of jazz piano relying on a left-hand accompaniment that alternates low bass notes with higher chords.

string bass the most common bass used in jazz, the same acoustic instrument found in symphony orchestras; also known as double bass.

subdominant the fourth degree of the scale, or the chord built on that scale degree.

swing (1) jazz from the period 1935–1945, usually known as the Swing Era; (2) a jazz-specific feeling created by rhythmic contrast within a particular rhythmic framework (usually involving a walking bass and a steady rhythm on the drummer's ride cymbal).

swing eighth notes a jazz soloist's flexible division of the beat into unequal parts.

symphonic jazz a form of jazz popular in the 1920s that attempted to elevate the music through symphonic arrangements.

syncopation an occasional rhythmic disruption, contradicting the basic meter.

synthesizer an electronically amplified keyboard that creates its own sounds through computer programming.

tailgate trombone (or smears) exaggerated *glissandos*.

tempo the speed of a piece of music.

tenor saxophone a common type of saxophone, larger and deeper than the alto.

territory bands in the 1920s and early 1930s, dance bands that serviced a "territory," defined by a day's drive from an urban center.

texture the relationship between melody and harmony: a melody supported by harmonic accompaniment (*homophony*), a melody by itself (*monophony*), or two or more melodies played at the same time, creating their own harmonies (*polyphony*).

third the basic interval for tonal harmony; in a major scale, it's formed by skipping over a scale degree (e.g., moving from *do* to *mi*).

thirty-two-bar popular song a standard song form, usually divided into shorter sections, such as A A B A (each section eight bars long) or A A′ (each section sixteen bars long).

timbales in *Latin percussion*, two drums mounted on a stand along with a cowbell, played with sticks by a standing musician.

timbre the quality of sound, as distinct from its pitch; also known as tone color.

timbre variation the use of a wide range of *timbres* for expressive purposes.

time-line pattern a repeated, asymmetric pattern that serves as a basic foundation layer in African (and, to a lesser extent, African American) music.

tom-toms cylindrical drums with no snare used in a *drum kit*, typically tuned to different pitches.

tonal music music characterized by an overall tonal center (the *tonic*) that serves as the center of gravity: all other harmonies are more or less dissonant in relation to this tonal center.

tonic the first degree of the scale, or the chord built on the first scale degree.

tonic triad the chord built on the first scale degree.

trading fours in a jam session, "trading" short (usually four-bar) solos back and forth between the drums and the soloists, or between soloists.

transpose to shift an entire musical phrase to a higher or lower pitch. See also *sequence*.

traps see *drum kit*.

trap set see *drum kit*.

tremolo the speedy alternation of two notes some distance apart; on a piano, this action imitates a brass vibrato.

triad the standard three-note chord (e.g., C-E-G) that serves as the basis for tonal music.

trill the rapid alternation of two adjacent notes.

trio (1) the third, or C section of *march* or *march/ragtime form*, usually twice as long (32 bars), *modulating* to a new key, and offering contrast; (2) a group with three members.

triple meter a *meter* that groups beats into patterns of threes; every *measure*, or bar, of triple meter has three beats.

triplet a note divided into three equal parts.

tritone a dissonant *interval* made up of three *whole steps* (e.g., C to F-sharp). also known as flatted fifth.

trombone a low-pitched *brass instrument* that uses a *slide* to adjust the column of air. See also *valve trombone*.

trumpet the most common *brass instrument*; its vibrating tube is completely cylindrical until it reaches the end, where it flares into the instrument's *bell*.

tuba a large, low-pitched *brass instrument* with an intricate nest of tubing ending in an enormous bell; often used in early jazz groups as a bass instrument because of its powerful volume.

turnaround (or turnback) a faster, more complex series of chords used in the last two bars of a blues or the last A section of an A A B A form, leading back to the beginning of the chorus.

twelve-bar blues see *blues form*.

unison the "interval" formed by two different instruments performing the same pitch.

upbeat note or notes that precede the *downbeat*.

valve trombone a *trombone* that uses valves rather than a *slide* to change the length of the tube.

valves controls in *brass instruments* that shunt air into a passageway of tubing, altering a pitch.

vamp a short, repeated chord progression, usually used as the introduction to a performance.

variable intonation a tuning system that allows for certain pitches to fluctuate by microtones, thus creating *blue notes*.

variable layers contrasting parts played above the *foundation layers* in a piece.

vaudeville blues an early theatrical form of the blues featuring female singers, accompanied by a small band; also known as classic blues.

verse the introductory portion of a *popular song*, preceding the *chorus;* usually omitted by jazz musicians.

vibraphone (vibraharp) an amplified metallophone (metal xylophone) with tubes below each slab; a disc turning within each tube helps sustain and modify the sound.

vibrato a slight wobble in pitch produced naturally by the singing voice, often imitated by wind and string instruments.

voicing distributing the notes of a chord on a piano, or to different instruments in an arrangement.

walking bass   a bass line featuring four equal beats per bar, usually used as a rhythmic foundation in jazz.

whole note   the longest possible rhythmic note; in a four-beat *duple meter,* it would fill up an entire *measure.*

whole step   an interval made up of two half steps; the distance between *do* and *re.*

whole-tone chord   an *augmented chord* made up of *intervals* (major thirds) from the *whole-tone scale.*

whole-tone scale   a six-note *scale* made up entirely of *whole steps;* because it avoids the *intervals* of a perfect fourth or fifth (the intervals normally used to tune instruments), it has a peculiar, disorienting sound.

wind instruments   in jazz, instruments that are played by blowing air into a tube; also known in jazz as horns.

wire brushes   drumsticks—actually hollow handles with thin wire strands—used to strike or brush the drumheads.

work song   a type of folk song used during work to regulate physical activity or to engage the worker's attention.

Collecting Jazz Recordings

Trust Yourself

The process of collecting music or anything else tends to combine dedication (as in "I'm going to acquire every record Billie Holiday ever made") and serendipity (as in "While searching for Billie Holiday, I discovered a really obscure and wonderful singer named Teddy Grace"). This book—with its seventy-five Listening Guides and supplementary recommendations—should serve as a fairly comprehensive beginning. You are likely to find yourself either drawn to particular pieces and the styles and eras they represent, or acquiring a more capacious interest in confronting jazz whole, from early twentieth-century New Orleans traditionalism to early twenty-first-century international eclecticism.

Reading this book for a class almost certainly entails a few obligations, like papers and tests. But jazz is a blend of art and entertainment, and its first objective is to give pleasure. In pursuing it, spare yourself further obligations and trust your instincts: go with what you like. If Artie Shaw's "Star Dust" makes you want to look more deeply into bands of the Swing Era, you're not required to give equal time to the avant-garde. And if Albert Ayler's "Ghosts" blows your mind, you don't have to feign a love of soul jazz. Even those of us who are seemingly enamored of every facet of jazz are likely to roll our eyes at a facet or two. (On the other hand, everyone has to venerate Louis Armstrong; it's a law, punishable by loss of affect.)

In any case, your taste will change over time, and if you are lucky, that will mean an expansion rather than a diminishment in interest, curiosity, and receptiveness. There is something deeply creepy about middle-aged people who will listen to nothing but music that turned them on when they were teenagers. Listen to everything with empathy, but don't be intimidated into letting go of your bullshit detector—this applies to arts and to arts criticism. It applies even to this book.

Jazz criticism and reference books are a good way to expand your knowledge and find recommendations for new recordings. Monthly magazines like *Jazz Times, Jazziz,* and *Down Beat* (which began publishing during the Swing Era) are stocked with reviewers who are dedicated and opinionated listeners. After reading a few issues of a magazine and seeing the same bylines again and again, you will find yourself trusting some writers more than others—because their tastes prove similar to yours, and because you find their perspectives and styles of articulation companionable and persuasive. Obviously, you'll never agree with one critic all the time, but you will know whose passions and discontents ring true to you.

Unhappily, criticism has a larger role in introducing jazz recordings and reissues than it should, owing to jazz's low (almost nonexistent in many places) profile on radio and television. Record stores have listening apparatuses and just about every online music service allows you to sample tracks, but part of the fun of collecting jazz is occasionally taking a flyer because you like the cover design or have heard someone mention the artist's name or you recognize a few of the tunes or just want to hear something new.

It is now a sad reality that retail stores have disappeared from the music landscape in many areas. Most of us buy records online, as CDs or MP3s, sacrificing the pleasure of shuffling through bins and racks and coming across a gem we didn't know existed. Yet the advantages of online shopping are obvious, not the least of which is that we can buy a single track before investing in an album. In doing that, we are replicating the experience of our ancestors, who bought 78s: single discs consisting of a hit side and a flip side.

Almost all records made before 1948 were sold as single discs, so it is logical—especially when looking for music from that era—to sample a selection or two by an artist before springing for a collection of two dozen or so tracks. From the early 1950s until the middle 1980s, the industry was dominated by the Long Playing record (LP); many of those albums ought to be considered as integrated works. If a track may be compared to a short story or bagatelle, an album may be thought of as a novel or symphony. Works such as Miles Davis's *Sketches of Spain,* Duke Ellington's *Far East Suite,* and John Coltrane's *A Love Supreme,* among hundreds more, should be experienced in their entirety—no less than a Beethoven symphony or *Sgt. Pepper's Lonely Hearts Club Band.*

The album concept remained in force in the CD era, but its hold began to slacken, especially in jazz. Why? For one thing, the playing time got so long that it surpassed the average listener's attention span, and musical dullness spread. In introducing CDs, the recording industry elected to *double* the price of vinyl LPs, even though the digital audio quality was initially much inferior to analogue engineering and despite the fact that CDs were far less costly to manufacture. The record companies hoped to compensate for this shameless flimflam with semantic pomp and extended playing time. They even devised a laughably devious euphemism for those crappy plastic CD cases: "jewel boxes." In an exercise akin to price-fixing, they settled on an arbitrary CD playing time of about seventy-five minutes.

Extended play is a good thing for an opera, symphony, jazz suite, or anthology of short selections, but it isn't a virtue when it's turned into a rule. As the producers of jazz albums felt increasingly obliged to offer maximum-time discs (critics actually grumbled about discs that played under an hour), they achieved their goal by encouraging long individual tracks. The art of economy, the philosophy of less-is-more, the goal of improvising a perfect solo in one or two choruses, the showbiz adage of "Always leave them wanting more," gave way to long improvisations that were motivated not by the fever of inspiration but by the need to fill up the disc. Not surprisingly, a later generation of listeners preferred to download tracks rather than albums.

Meanwhile, the record labels began offering elaborate boxes, dumping material onto discs, including rejected takes, false starts, unedited session tapes, and random recording session chatter. One notorious idiot even restored to classic concert recordings longer applause interludes and the sounds of roadie labor, as a chair was pushed around or another mike brought to the stage. Some of these makeshift documentary recordings are extremely interesting, others are simply annoying. Gerry Mulligan, confronted with a boxed set of his "complete" sessions (the tracks arranged in the order they were recorded rather than as they were sequenced for the original album), was appalled: "Do you know how much time we spent arranging the tunes so they would be fun to listen to? They've turned it into homework."

Special editions are for specialist interests. For one artist, you may be satisfied with a greatest-hits type collection; for another, you may want everything the artist ever released; for yet another, you may want the released stuff plus those newly excavated alternate takes and false starts. Bigger is not necessarily better. Some classics have been rendered virtually unlistenable by the addition of scraps from the cutting-room floor. To pick one of many examples, in 1959 Verve released the beloved album *Gerry Mulligan Meets Ben Webster.* In 1997, that same label issued *The Complete Gerry Mulligan Meets Ben Webster,* a two-disc CD set in which the original tracks are cluttered with twenty rejected takes—only a truly obsessed fan is likely to enjoy four consecutive versions of the same tune. One of Ellington's great late-period triumphs, the 1967 *. . . and His Mother Called Him Bill,* a tribute to Billy Strayhorn, ended with an unplanned Ellington piano rendition of a Strayhorn song, "Lotus Blossom," played quietly at the end of a session as the other musicians were packing up; it serves as an emotionally devastating *l'envoi.* A CD producer, noting that "Lotus Blossom" was played at the end of a middle session, mindlessly programmed it midway on the CD.

You need to examine an album's contents, even in the case of a genuine classic, before buying it. Are you getting the original work, or the original work with new tracks, and are the new tracks added at the end (a bonus that no one is likely to complain about) or scattered throughout? On the list below, we intended to include Bill Evans's 1961 album *Waltz for Debby,* recorded live at the Village Vanguard, and were saddened to find that the only versions presently in print are an admirable but expensive "complete" three-disc set of the Vanguard engagement, or a single-disc version with consecutive performances of the same tunes, destroying the concentrated beauty of the original LP.

In this book, we discuss the original version of Charles Mingus's "Boogie Stop Shuffle," which Mingus approved for release. That track is difficult to find now, because after Mingus's death a producer spliced back passages that Mingus had edited out. You may prefer the longer version, but we believe that the record label also ought to offer the album as the artist conceived it. On the other hand, we've included the false start to Charlie Parker's "Ko-Ko" because it offers a fascinating insight into how that masterpiece was created. We've used the second (or rejected) take of Jelly Roll Morton's "Dead Man Blues" because, despite the flawed trumpet solo, we think it a more effective performance than the one chosen for release in 1926. (The Morton album in the list below offers both takes.) The point is that there is a sensible way to program reissues; as sensibleness is often in short supply, the consumer is obliged to do some digging to learn exactly what is being offered.

One way to check recording information is by consulting a discography—a book or site that lists all of an artist's recording sessions (and surviving concert performances) chronologically, with the recording dates, band personnel, and catalog numbers. A discography for all of jazz, collating tens of thousands of sessions, may be very expensive, but dozens of individual jazz artists are represented by free online discographies (check the indispensable website www.jazzdisco.org). Ellington recorded several performances of "Mood Indigo," and if you are looking for a particular one, you need to know the label (he recorded five versions in 1930 alone, for Victor, OKeh, and Brunswick), the present owner of the labels (Victor and OKeh now belong to Sony,

Brunswick to Polygram), the full date, and the matrix or catalog number to be certain of getting the desired take.

For the most part, however, buying jazz records is a straightforward business. Reliable mail-order companies often have people who can answer questions, as retail stores once did. The best and easiest way to get advice is to solicit it from the large and passionate circle of fellow jazz enthusiasts. A few decades ago, this would have presented a challenge—many jazz lovers, especially in small towns, were totally isolated. Yet cyberspace is rich in jazz sites (the best known include allaboutjazz.com, jerryjazzmusician.com, and jazzcorner.com) and chat groups. The population of dedicated jazz fans may be small, and at times cranky, but it is also ardent and helpful—most jazz lovers love to be in touch with other jazz lovers. It's them against the world.

Go for Broke

Meanwhile, here is a list of 100 albums by 100 artists. Two things make this discography unusual and potentially useful beyond the recommendation of a lot of good records. First, it is not a 100-best list. No artist is represented by more than a single work as a leader—a serious library of recorded jazz would include many recordings by central figures like Ellington and Miles Davis, whose influence and achievement represent artistic growth over decades. In fact, by sticking to our rule, which favors variety over prominent individuals and acknowledged masterworks, we were obliged to exclude some of our favorite records, some of which appear in the text proper—as Listening Guides or supplementary recommendations.

With this list, we offer a way to a look at the jazz map from several perspectives; all these albums are excellent, and each one may lead you—through sidemen, arrangers, songs—to others, in an ever-expanding web that touches on most of the major jazz avenues and side streets that make up the jazz world of the past century. (Admittedly, some areas are underrepresented, most conspicuously foreign jazz.) Each entry represents a way to explore a part of jazz and, with it, your own emotional and intellectual responses to it.

In keeping with that idea, the second unusual aspect of this list is that it's alphabetical rather than chronological. The idea here is to distract you from the customary tendency—encouraged by our largely chronological text—to pigeonhole musical works according to the eras that produced them. It is one thing, for example, to study 1950s jazz and listen to Art Blakey as an example of hard bop, and another to encounter him on his own ground, possibly in tandem with Bix Beiderbecke and Arthur Blythe, who are connected to him on this list only through the juxtapositions of alphabetical serendipity.

Not that you need to start at number one and work down the list. Start anywhere you like. The point is to create a fourth narrative for jazz, one that is unique to your experience. The first three narratives, discussed in the book, concern (1) artistic progression, (2) fusions with other musical forms, and (3) historicist responses to jazz's past. The fourth narrative is as random as life, and may well provide the most rewards. Still, we do include with each entry the years in which it was recorded, so that if you find yourself favoring a particular period, you can pursue it by reading the list from the right rather than the left.

Note that this list includes no catch-all collections, like Martin Williams's celebrated *Smithsonian Collection of Classic Jazz* or *Ken Burns's Jazz: The Story of American Music*. In fact, there are no boxed sets, no items with more than two discs. Our selections, especially in cases where the same music is available in various formats from multiple labels, were influenced by audio quality, price, and availability. They are intended to encourage you to investigate the market on your own. For example, if you search for our single-disc Dizzy Gillespie compilation of his 1940s RCA recordings, you will discover that a superior two-disc edition exists for those who would rather get the complete works.

Some of these albums survey entire careers, while others are classic LPs. Some capture the early work that established an artist's reputation, while others exemplify autumnal maturity (see, for example, Ornette Coleman, Stan Getz, Sonny Rollins). We suggest you not worry about duplicating tracks here and there. The Ellington and Monk CDs are almost certain to make you want to hear more Ellington and Monk, yet even though this may lead you to albums from which some of these tracks were taken, the compilations are pleasingly conceived in their own right—there is an art to editing.

Finally, all these items were available in one form or another in the final months of 2008. (A few, like Lee Konitz's *Motion* and Roy Eldridge's *Uptown,* no longer exist as domestic CDs, but can be purchased as MP3s from iTunes.) By the time you read this, it is certain that some of these recordings will *not* be readily available, while others, left off the list, will be back in catalog. The record business has never been more volatile than it is now, when technology and changes in ownership have brought it to a point of crisis.

At this moment, the entire Black Saint catalog of loft jazz from the 1970s and 1980s is out of print but has recently been purchased by a company that will rerelease it, beginning in 2009. Also missing is the Commodore catalog of 1930s and 1940s swing and Dixieland classics, and no one knows when or how it will reemerge. We were astonished that we could not find—as CDs or MP3s—suitable anthologies or classic albums by Jack Teagarden, Randy Weston, Henry Threadgill, Anthony Braxton, and, incredibly, the prewar Lester Young (though his major solos are collected on the Count Basie, Billie Holiday, and Jimmy Rushing discs). Yet record company execs complain when jazz fans trade and download favorite recordings! Every jazz lover is a sleuth. Your sleuthing may as well begin here.

1. Muhal Richard Abrams: *Blu Blu Blu* (Black Saint), 1990
2. Cannonball Adderley: *Mercy, Mercy, Mercy!* (Capitol), 1966
3. Gene Ammons and Sonny Stitt: *Boss Tenors* (Polygram), 1961
4. Louis Armstrong: *The Complete Hot Five & Hot Seven Recordings, vol. 3* (Columbia), 1928
5. Albert Ayler: *Spiritual Unity* (ESP-Disk), 1964
6. Count Basie: *One O'Clock Jump: The Very Best of Count Basie* (Sony), 1936–42
7. Mildred Bailey: *The Rockin' Chair Lady* (Verve), 1931–50
8. Sidney Bechet: *The Legendary Sidney Bechet* (RCA), 1932–41
9. Bix Beiderbecke: *At the Jazz Band Ball* (ASV Living Era), 1924–28
10. Art Blakey: *Mosaic* (Blue Note), 1961
11. Arthur Blythe: *Focus* (Savant), 2002
12. Lester Bowie: *The Great Pretender* (ECM), 1981
13. Clifford Brown and Max Roach: *Clifford Brown and Max Roach* (Polygram), 1954

14. Dave Brubeck: *Time Out* (Columbia), 1959
15. Jaki Byard and Roland Kirk: *The Jaki Byard Experience* (Prestige), 1968
16. Don Byron: *Tuskegee Experiments* (Nonesuch), 1992
17. Benny Carter: *Further Definitions* (Impulse!), 1961
18. James Carter: *Chasin' the Gypsy* (Atlantic), 2000
19. Bill Charlap: *Live at the Village Vanguard* (Blue Note), 2007
20. Charlie Christian: *The Benny Goodman Sextet Featuring Charlie Christian* (Sony), 1939–41
21. Nat King Cole: *After Midnight: The Complete Session* (Blue Note), 1956
22. Ornette Coleman: *Sound Grammar* (Sound Grammar), 2006
23. John Coltrane: *A Love Supreme* (Impulse!), 1964
24. Chick Corea: *Now He Sings, Now He Sobs* (Blue Note), 1968
25. Sonny Criss and Horace Tapscott: *Sonny's Dream* (Prestige OJC), 1968
26. Bing Crosby: *Jazz Singer* (Retrieval), 1931–41
27. Miles Davis: *Kind of Blue* (Columbia), 1959
28. Eric Dolphy: *Out There* (Prestige), 1960
29. Roy Eldridge: *Roy Eldridge with the Gene Krupa Orchestra Featuring Anita O'Day Uptown* (Sony), 1941–49
30. Duke Ellington: *The Essential Duke Ellington* (Sony), 1927–60
31. Bill Evans: *The Paris Concert, Edition One* (Blue Note), 1979
32. Gil Evans: *Out of the Cool* (Impulse!), 1960
33. Ella Fitzgerald: *Something to Live For* (Verve), 1937–66
34. Erroll Garner: *Concert by the Sea* (Sony), 1955
34. Stan Getz and Kenny Barron: *People Time* (Polygram), 1992
35. Dizzy Gillespie: *A Night in Tunisia: The Very Best of Dizzy Gillespie* (RCA), 1946–49
36. Benny Goodman: *Carnegie Hall Jazz Concert* (Sony), 1938
37. Dexter Gordon: *Go!* (Blue Note), 1962
38. Herbie Hancock: *Maiden Voyage* (Blue Note), 1965
39. Roy Hargrove: *Habana* (Polygram), 1997
40. Johnny Hartman: *John Coltrane and Johnny Hartman* (Impulse!), 1963
41. Coleman Hawkins: *Ken Burns Jazz Collection* (Polygram), 1926–63
42. Roy Haynes: *Roy Haynes Trio Featuring Danilo Perez and John Pattitucci* (Polygram), 2000
43. Fletcher Henderson: *Ken Burns Jazz Collection* (Sony), 1924–40
44. Woody Herman: *Blowin' Up a Storm: The Columbia Years* (Sony), 1945–47
45. Andrew Hill: *Point of Departure* (Blue Note), 1964
46. Billie Holiday: *Lady Day: The Best of Billie Holiday* (Sony), 1935–42
47. Dave Holland: *Conference of the Birds* (ECM), 1972
48. Keith Jarrett: *Whisper Not* (ECM), 1999
49. Stan Kenton: *Contemporary Concepts* (Blue Note), 1955
50. Lee Konitz: *Motion* (Verve), 1961
51. George Lewis: *Jazz in the Classic New Orleans Tradition* (Riverside OJC), 1950
52. Abbey Lincoln: *You Gotta Pay the Band* (Polygram), 1991
53. Joe Lovano: *Joyous Encounter* (Blue Note), 2005
54. Jimmie Lunceford: *Rhythm Is Our Business* (ASV Living Era), 1933–40
55. Rudresh Mahanthappa: *Kinsmen* (PI), 2008
56. Wynton Marsalis: *Standards & Ballads* (Sony), 1983–97

57. John McLaughlin: *Live at the Royal Festival Hall* (Polygram), 1989
58. Brad Mehldau: *Live* (Nonesuch), 2008
59. Charles Mingus: *The Black Saint & the Sinner Lady* (Impulse!), 1963
60. Roscoe Mitchell: *Sound* (Delmark), 1966
61. Modern Jazz Quartet: *Django* (Prestige), 1953–54
62. Thelonious Monk: *The Best of the Blue Note Years* (Blue Note), 1947–52
63. Wes Montgomery: *Smokin' at the Half Note* (Verve), 1965
64. Jason Moran: *Modernistic* (Blue Note), 2002
65. Lee Morgan: *The Sidewinder* (Blue Note), 1963
66. Jelly Roll Morton: *Birth of the Hot* (RCA Bluebird), 1926–27
67. Gerry Mulligan: *The Concert Jazz Band at the Village Vanguard* (Verve), 1960
68. David Murray: *Shakill's Warrior* (Sony), 1991
69. Fats Navarro and Tadd Dameron: *The Complete Blue Note and Capitol Recordings* (Blue Note), 1947–49
70. Oliver Nelson: *The Blues and the Abstract Truth* (Impulse!), 1961
71. King Oliver: *Off the Record: The Complete Jazz Band Recordings* (Archeophone), 1923
72. Charlie Parker: *Best of the Complete Savoy and Dial Studio Recordings* (Savoy), 1944–48
73. Bud Powell: *Jazz Giant* (Verve), 1949–50
74. Joshua Redman: *Back East* (Nonesuch), 2007
75. Django Reinhardt: *The Best of Django Reinhardt* (Blue Note), 1936–48
76. Sam Rivers: *Fuchsia Swing Song* (Blue Note), 1964
77. Sonny Rollins: *Road Shows, vol. 1* (Doxy), 1980–2007
78. Jimmy Rushing: *Mr. Five by Five* (Pearl), 1929–42
79. George Russell: *Ezz-Thetics* (Riverside), 1961
80. John Scofield and Pat Metheny: *I Can See Your House from Here* (Blue Note), 1994
81. Artie Shaw: *Begin the Beguine* (RCA), 1938–41
82. Archie Shepp: *Fire Music* (Impulse!), 1965
83. Wayne Shorter: *Footprints Live!* (Verve), 2002
84. Horace Silver: *Song for My Father* (Blue Note), 1964
85. Bessie Smith: *The Essential Bessie Smith* (Sony), 1923–33
86. Jimmy Smith: *The Sermon* (Blue Note), 1958
87. Art Tatum: *Piano Starts Here* (Columbia), 1933–49
88. Cecil Taylor: *Unit Structures* (Blue Note), 1966
89. Lennie Tristano: *The New Tristano* (Atlantic), 1955–62
90. Joe Turner: *The Boss of the Blues* (Atlantic/Collectables), 1956
91. Sarah Vaughan: *Sarah Vaughan with Clifford Brown* (Polygram), 1954
92. Fats Waller: *The Very Best of Fats Waller* (RCA), 1929–42
93. David S. Ware: *Go See the World* (Columbia), 1998
94. Dinah Washington: *The Essential Dinah Washington* (Polygram), 1952–59
95. Weather Report: *Heavy Weather* (Sony), 1977
96. Chick Webb: *Stompin' at the Savoy* (ASV Living Era), 1934–39
97. Ben Webster and Oscar Peterson: *Ben Webster Meets Oscar Peterson* (Verve), 1959
98. Cassandra Wilson: *Belly of the Sun* (Blue Note), 2002
99. World Saxophone Quartet: *Revue* (Black Saint), 1980
100. Lester Young and Teddy Wilson: *Pres and Teddy* (Verve), 1956

Jazz on Film

In 1981, a British researcher, David Meeker, published his second edition of *Jazz in the Movies*, listing 3,724 feature films, short subjects, television shows, and documentaries with jazz content, however little it might be. That was thirty years ago, and even then his work had dozens of unavoidable lapses. Hardly a year goes by when significant jazz footage, unknown to the most zealous collectors, isn't discovered—often from long forgotten television programs languishing in European broadcasting archives. Here is an introductory guide to jazz-related movies, divided into four categories: feature films with jazz as the subject; feature films with jazz scores; documentaries and performance films; and television series. Most of these films have been available on one or more home video formats over the years, usually on DVD. Those that are not presently in catalog may be found in libraries or are likely to be reissued.

Feature Films with Jazz Stories

Jazz has had a rather twisted relationship with Hollywood dating back to the silent era, when jazz, blues, and ragtime themes were often used to indicate wayward flappers, dissolute roués, and other lost souls. During the Swing Era, Hollywood imported jazz orchestras to suggest optimism and good times. As bandleaders achieved national recognition, it was good business to banner them on movie marquees. After the war, jazz usually signified the denizens of urban blight. Some of the movies listed here are unintentionally hilarious, but they all have savory musical moments.

The Benny Goodman Story (1955, Valentine Davis): Cliché-ridden idiocy at every turn and a stupefying lead performance, but worthy music makes it endurable.

Bird (1988, Clint Eastwood): A powerful, partly factual and partly imagined telling of the Charlie Parker story with much music and an eye-popping studio recreation of New York's 52nd Street.

Birth of the Blues (1941, Victor Schertzinger): One of several films reflecting the historicist New Orleans revival, with Bing Crosby, Jack Teagarden, and a game Mary Martin inventing jazz as only Hollywood Caucasians could.

Black Orpheus (1959, Marcel Camus): A visually and musically thrilling version of the Orpheus legend told against the Brazilian Carnival and introducing several of the sambas that helped to launch bossa nova.

Blues in the Night (1941, Anatol Litvack): A Warner Bros. gangster film from the perspective of white jazz musicians, inspired by authentic Negro "misery"; this is a revealing curio, briskly directed, with a cameo appearance by Jimmie Lunceford's band.

Cabin in the Sky (1942, Vincente Minelli): A brilliant all-black musical with production numbers featuring Ethel Waters, Duke Ellington, Lena Horne, Eddie "Rochester" Anderson, the wickedly cool tap dancer John Bubbles, and a funny cameo by Louis Armstrong.

The Connection (1961, Shirley Clarke): The garrulous junkies waiting for their connection, in this film version of Jack Gelber's play, include the Freddie Redd Quartet, playing a celebrated score and featuring saxophonist Jackie McLean.

The Gig (1985, Frank Gilroy): A smart, realistic comedy about a group of white professionals who play jazz for fun, until they get a gig at a Catskills resort working with a pro.

The Glenn Miller Story (1953, Anthony Mann): A nostalgic fabrication in which Miller explains his radical musical ideas: "To me, music is more than just one instrument. It's a whole orchestra playing together!" Louis Armstrong and Gene Krupa drop by.

Hollywood Hotel (1937, Busby Berkeley): This is the way Hollywood packaged swing for the masses, salvaged by Benny Goodman's integrated quartet at its absolute peak.

Jazzman (1983, Karen Shakhnazarov): Hard to find, but keep an eye out for this superb Russian film about musicians risking their freedom to play hot jazz in the Soviet Union of the 1920s.

A Man Called Adam (1966, Leo Penn): Sammy Davis Jr. plays an overwrought trumpet player in an overwrought film made memorable by Louis Armstrong, in a straight acting role, and a musical score by Benny Carter.

Murder at the Vanities (1934, Mitchell Leisen): A backstage murder mystery immortalized by Duke Ellington playing his take on Liszt (classical musicians mow his band down with machine guns) and the production number "Sweet Marijuana"—those were the days.

New Orleans (1947, Arthur Lubin): More New Orleans revivalism, purportedly from the black perspective, as Louis Armstrong leads his people in an exodus from Storyville and Billie Holiday shows up as a maid who sings as she dusts.

Orchestra Wives (1942, Archie Mayo): Underrated, surprisingly well-written story in which Glenn Miller's band hits the road (look sharp for Bobby Hackett), and the great Nicholas Brothers steal his thunder with acrobatic jazz dancing.

Passing Through (1977, Larry Clark): Difficult to see, this stunning student film, with a musical score by Horace Tapscott along with records by Charlie Parker and Eric Dolphy, captures the dilemma of the Los Angeles jazz avant-garde struggling to survive.

Pennies from Heaven (1936, Norman Z. McLeod): A Depression fable that may strike a relevant note today, with Bing Crosby in excellent voice and Louis Armstrong making his first feature film appearance performing "A Skeleton in the Closet."

Paris Blues (1961, Martin Ritt): Not much plot animates this soap opera, but when Paul Newman and Sidney Poitier shut up, Duke Ellington's all-star orchestra takes over, including sequences featuring Louis Armstrong.

Pete Kelly's Blues (1955, Jack Webb): A splendidly photographed and scored saga of Kansas City in the 1920s, in which a white jazz band battles racketeers while Ella Fitzgerald operates a speakeasy, Peggy Lee goes insane, and Lee Marvin plays clarinet.

A Song Is Born (1948, Howard Hawks): A remake of the comedy *Ball of Fire* in which cloistered professors, led by Danny Kaye, investigate jazz with the help of Benny Goodman, Louis Armstrong, Lionel Hampton, Tommy Dorsey, and others.

Ray (2004, Taylor Hackford): Jamie Foxx's uncanny imitation of Ray Charles traces his career from swing to gospel-infused R & B to his unique amalgamation of jazz, R & B pop, and rock—interrupted by narcotics, sex, and other domestic interludes.

Round Midnight (1986, Bertrand Tavernier): Dexter Gordon's performance, in a role based on the lives of Bud Powell and Lester Young, is astonishing; Bobby Hutcherson, Herbie Hancock, Wayne Shorter, and others also appear.

Stormy Weather (1943, Andrew L. Stone): This all-black musical loosely touches on the early years of jazz, including James Reese Europe, but is best savored for performances by Bill Robinson, Lena Horne, Fats Waller, Cab Calloway, and the Nicholas Brothers.

Sweet Love, Bitter (1966, Herbert Danska): Melodrama of a black genius, thinly based on Charlie Parker (he's called Eagle), as experienced by his concerned white friend; score by Mal Waldron, alto saxophone solos by Charles McPherson.

Sweet Smell of Success (1957, Alexander Mackendrick): A dark, caustic classic that involves an incestuous columnist framing a jazz musician for marijuana use; Elmer Bernstein's score is complemented by the on-screen Chico Hamilton Quintet.

Tap (1989, Nick Castle): The modest story is an excuse to gather several of the greatest jazz or tap dancers assembled in a Hollywood film, including star Gregory Hines, Sandman Sims, Bunny Briggs, Sammy Davis Jr., and the young Savion Glover.

The Tic Code (2000, Gary Winick): A young boy suffering from Tourette's syndrome learns to express himself through jazz, with Gregory Hines as a jazz star who learned to cover-up his own TS and a score by pianist Michael Wolff.

Feature Films with Jazz Scores

Hollywood soundtracks often employed jazz or jazzy touches, but not until the 1950s did composers start using jazz as the governing style for film scores. Not surprisingly, the plots of most of these films concern junkies, sexual deviants, and murderers. In the late 1950s and 1960s, genuine jazz composers were also hired. Here are a few benchmarks in chronological order.

A Streetcar Named Desire (1951): Often cited as the first film to use a jazz-style score for a nonjazz-themed story, fittingly set in New Orleans, and composed by Alex North.

The Man with the Golden Arm (1955): Elmer Bernstein's score is mostly pseudo-jazz, but it conveys a kick as the basic blues theme comes up during the opening credits. Frank Sinatra is the junkie who wants to play drums with the on-screen Shorty Rogers band.

Elevator to the Gallows (*Ascenseur pour l'echafaud,* 1957): For Louis Malle's first thriller, one of the most piquant and influential film scores of all time was entirely improvised by Miles Davis, during an all-night session.

I Want to Live! (1958): Director Robert Wise hired former big-band composer Johnny Mandel to write the first true jazz score in a Hollywood feature—a brilliant achievement, underscored by on-screen performances by an all-star Gerry Mulligan band.

Touch of Evil (1958): The prolific Henry Mancini is best known for his movie ballads, like "Moon River" (from *Breakfast at Tiffany's*), but he used ingenious jazz scoring in several 1950s works, including this Orson Welles classic and the TV series *Peter Gunn*.

Anatomy of a Murder (1959): Director Otto Preminger made a counterintuitive decision in hiring Duke Ellington to score a film about a Midwestern trial lawyer; Ellington wrote a superb score, and appears on-screen as the local pianist, Pie Eye.

Odds Against Tomorrow (1959): Robert Wise's race-conscious heist film is luminously scored by the Modern Jazz Quartet's John Lewis, including his tender ballad "Skating in Central Park"—Bill Evans and Jim Hall play in the soundtrack orchestra.

Shadows (1961): Charles Mingus never completed his score for John Cassavetes's film about racial conflict in New York, so the director created a soundtrack out of Mingus's bass solos.

Mickey One (1961): Arthur Penn's surreal showbiz fantasy boasts an Eddie Sauter score with improvised solos by Stan Getz—a musical sequel to their renowned album *Focus*.

The Cincinnati Kid (1965): Lalo Schifrin, the former pianist for Dizzy Gillespie, wrote more than 200 film scores; this one uses Ray Charles on the title song and various New Orleans traditionalists—Cab Calloway has an acting role.

In the Heat of the Night (1967): One of the best of Quincy Jones's many scores employs Ray Charles on the title song, and bassist Ray Brown and flutist Roland Kirk throughout.

The Young Girls of Rochefort (1968): Michel Legrand, a French jazz pianist and songwriter, scored several New Wave classics by Jean Luc Godard, Agnes Varda, and Jacques Demy—his swinging take on the MGM musical in this Demy film is irresistible.

The Gauntlet (1977): Clint Eastwood used jazz in most of his films, never more memorably than in this Jerry Fielding score, with expansive solos by trumpeter Jon Faddis and alto saxophonist Art Pepper.

Naked Lunch (1991): For David Cronenberg's adaptation of William Burroughs's novel, Howard Shore wrote a suitably mind-bending score constructed around improvisations by the Ornette Coleman Trio.

Documentaries and Performance Films

Although the market for jazz documentaries is small, the field has attracted dozens of filmmakers. Many of their films were made initially for television, a few had theatrical releases, some were conceived for educational purposes, and others went directly to home video. Note that the following list, the tip of a rapidly expanding iceberg, excludes all but a few short subjects: many early jazz bands were filmed for one-reelers by Vitaphone and other movie companies. Anthologies of these films occasionally appear (see *The Best of Jazz and Blues* below), and individual shorts are often included as extras on DVDs of classic movies—especially by Warner Bros. Also worth noting are cartoons of the 1930s and 1940s. Warner Bros. (Looney Tunes and Merrie Melodies), Disney, and other studios frequently used jazz—none as cannily as Fleischer Studio, which produced the great Betty Boop series: "Snow-White," "I Heard," "I'll Be Glad When You're Dead You Rascal You," and "The Old Man of the Mountain" (1932–33) are among the best in the risqué Betty series, using on-screen and traced (rotoscoped) images of Cab Calloway, Don Redman, and Louis Armstrong.

"After Hours" and "Jazz Dance" (1961/1954): The former was created as a television pilot but never broadcast, probably because of inane narration and a terrible singer. But Roy Eldridge and especially Coleman Hawkins *kill*.

Art Blakey: The Jazz Messenger (1987): A documentary of the drummer whose band became a graduate school for young musicians, by Dick Fontaine and Pat Hartley.

The Art Ensemble of Chicago (1981): A live performance at Chicago's Jazz Showcase.

Artie Shaw: Time Is All You've Got (1985): Brigitte Berman's Oscar-winning life of a great clarinetist and bandleader who gave up music because he hated being a celebrity.

Barry Harris: The Spirit of Bebop (2000): Interviews, performances, classic footage.

Benny Carter: Symphony in Riffs (1989): Harrison Engle's life of a musician for all seasons.

The Best of Jazz & Blues (2001): An indispensable Kino Video compilation of short films from 1929–41, including Bessie Smith's *St. Louis Blues* and others featuring Duke Ellington, Louis Armstrong, Fats Waller, Cab Calloway, and more.

Billie Holiday: The Long Night of Lady Day (1984): Though hard to find, this BBC film by John Jeremy remains the best biographical portrait of the singer.

Bix: Ain't None of Them Play Like Him Yet (1981): Brigitte Berman's detailed biographical portrait of Bix Beiderbecke.

Buena Vista Social Club (1999): Wim Wenders's multiple-prize-winning and hugely popular study of Cuban music as seen through some of its aging masters.

Celebrating Bird: The Triumph of Charlie Parker (1987): Gary Giddins's biographical portrait includes Parker's 1952 television performance (with Dizzy Gillespie) of "Hot House."

Ella Fitzgerald: Something to Live For (1999): Charlotte Zwering's PBS documentary, narrated by Tony Bennett, traces the First Lady of Song's career from her discovery at the Apollo Theater.

Erroll Garner in Performance (1964): Two sets initially broadcast by the BBC.

Fred Anderson, Timeless (2005): The avant-garde saxophonist leading his trio in concert in Chicago.

A Great Day in Harlem (1995): Jean Bach's Oscar-nominated documentary, centered on a celebrated 1958 photograph, is a treasure brimming with anecdotes; it's improved on a two-disc DVD with hours of added footage.

Imagine the Sound (1981): Ron Mann's beautifully photographed film includes uninterrupted performances by Cecil Taylor, Bill Dixon, Paul Bley, and Archie Shepp.

Jammin' the Blues (1941): The best ten minutes of jazz ever filmed—a Vitaphone short with Lester Young and other swing greats (including drummers Jo Jones and Sid Catlett)—can be found as an extra on the DVD of *Blues in the Night* (see above).

Jazz '34 (1996): Robert Altman's superior companion piece to his film *Kansas City* focuses on music, as such modernists as Joshua Redman, James Carter, and Geri Allen revisit 1930s swing.

The Jazz Master Class Series (2007): Seven double-disc sets explore the lives and artistry of Barry Harris, Jimmy and Percy Heath, Hank Jones, Cecil Taylor, Clark Terry, Toots Thielemans, and Phil Woods though extensive interviews and master class sessions with student musicians.

Jazz on a Summer's Day (1958): The first great music video, exquisitely photographed by Bert Stern at the 1958 Newport Jazz Festival, capturing classic performances by Louis Armstrong, Anita O'Day, Mahalia Jackson, Gerry Mulligan, and others.

Jazz (2001): Ken Burns's PBS epic, written by Geoffrey C. Ward, is the most ambitious film ever made about jazz (nineteen hours long, more than 2,000 film clips); criticized for cutting the story off in the 1960s, it remains a remarkable, matchless achievement.

John Hammond: From Bessie Smith to Bruce Springsteen (1990): Hart Perry's Peabody-winning film, written by Gary Giddins, traces the life of jazz's most influential talent scout and record producer.

Last Date: Eric Dolphy (1991): Hans Hylkema's life of the great and tragic saxophonist and flutist.

Last of the Blue Devils (1979): Bruce Ricker's expansive look at the history and ongoing influence of Kansas City jazz, focusing on Jay McShann, Count Basie, and Big Joe Turner.

Norman Granz Presents Improvisation (2007): Long-suppressed material from the 1940s and 1950s, including Jazz at the Philharmonic sequences and previously unknown footage of Charlie Parker and Coleman Hawkins.

Ornette: Made in America (1985): Shirley Clarke's study of Ornette Coleman, with recreations of his early years and extensive interviews with Coleman.

The Miles Davis Story (2001): A lively documentary by Mike Dibb with interviews of more than a dozen of Davis's associates.

Mingus (1968): A controversial, riveting film by Thomas Reichman, capturing Mingus at home, on the bandstand, and in the process of being evicted from his studio.

Satchmo (1989): Gary Giddins's award-winning PBS documentary on Louis Armstrong, based on his book, with much rare footage.

Sonny Rollins: Saxophone Colossus (1986): Robert Mugge's film features archival footage and interviews but is best remembered for the concert footage in which Rollins suddenly leaps from a precipice, finishing his solo lying on the ground with a sprained ankle.

The Sound of Jazz (1957): The best hour of jazz ever broadcast on American television (on a Sunday afternoon), with an all-star cast, including a legendary Billie Holiday blues with Lester Young, Coleman Hawkins, Ben Webster, Gerry Mulligan, and Roy Eldridge.

Thelonious Monk: Straight, No Chaser (1988): Peerless concert footage shot by Charlotte Zwerin is edited, with many interviews, into a gripping portrait of an enigmatic genius on tour.

Television Series

Jazz Casual: In the 1960s, critic Ralph J. Gleason produced twenty-eight half-hour shows, all issued on DVD. They include performances by and interviews with John Coltrane, Sonny Rollins, Louis Armstrong, Dizzy Gillespie, Carmen McRae, Jimmy Rushing, the Modern Jazz Quartet, and Dave Brubeck.

Jazz Icons: A magnificent, ongoing series of concert performances, shot live or in the studio for European television between the late 1950s and the early 1970s; these broadcasts were largely unknown here, and include first-class work by such figures as Dizzy Gillespie, Louis Armstrong, Sonny Rollins, Art Blakey, Bill Evans, Thelonious Monk, Buddy Rich, Dexter Gordon, Sarah Vaughan, Dave Brubeck, Wes Montgomery, Charles Mingus, Roland Kirk, and Nina Simone.

Jazz Scene USA: A short-lived 1962 series, shot in California, with two half-hour segments on each DVD, including shows with Cannonball Adderley, Jimmy Smith, Teddy Edwards, and Stan Kenton.

Selected Readings

In these pages, we have done our best to provide a basic outline of jazz history. Anyone interested in doing further research in jazz will encounter a vast and uneven literature—some of it decades old, some of it recently published. This selected bibliography is an attempt to provide you with a guide to the most relevant and interesting books on the subject. A few older volumes may be difficult to find in a bookstore, but are likely to be held by public libraries.

We begin with discographies, reference books, and works covering the entire range of jazz history. Thereafter, the list is organized by chapter. Note that the earlier chapters are more complete: anyone wishing to explore more contemporary forms of the music will have to rely on databases providing links to the broader periodical literature.

Discography

Bruyninckx, Walter. *90 Years of Recorded Jazz and Blues* (CD-ROM). Mechelen, 2007.

Jazz Discography Project: www.jazzdiscog.org.

Rust, Brian. *Jazz Records, 1917–1942.* New Rochelle, N.Y.: Arlington House, 1978.

Reference

Chilton, John. *Who's Who of Jazz: Storyville to Swing Street.* Philadelphia: Chilton, 1972.

Feather, Leonard. *The Encyclopedia of Jazz.* New York: Bonanza, 1960.

Kernfeld, Barry, ed. *The New Grove Dictionary of Jazz.* New York: Macmillan, 1988.

General

Balliett, Whitney. *American Musicians: Fifty-six Portraits in Jazz.* New York: Oxford University Press, 1986.

———. *American Singers: Twenty-Seven Portraits in Song.* New York: Oxford University Press, 1988.

Feather, Leonard G. *The Encyclopedia of Jazz.* New York: Da Capo Press, 1984 (originally Horizon, 1960).

———, and Ira Gitler. *The Biographical Encyclopedia of Jazz.* New York: Oxford University Press, 1999.

Gabbard, Krin, ed. *Jazz Among the Discourses.* Durham, N.C.: Duke University Press, 1995.

Gennari, John. *Blowin' Hot and Cool: Jazz and Its Critics.* Chicago: University of Chicago Press, 2006.

Giddins, Gary. *Riding on a Blue Note: Jazz & American Pop.* New York: Oxford University Press, 1981.

———. *Visions of Jazz: The First Century.* New York: Oxford University Press, 1998.

———. *Weather Bird: Jazz at the Dawn of Its Second Century.* New York: Oxford University Press, 2004.

Gioia, Ted. *The History of Jazz.* New York: Oxford University Press, 1997.

Gottlieb, Robert, ed. *Reading Jazz: A Gathering of Autobiography, Reportage, and Criticism from 1919 to Now.* New York: Pantheon, 1996.

Hinton, Milt, and David G. Berger. *Bass Line: The Stories and Photographs of Milt Hinton.* Philadelphia: Temple University Press, 1988.

Hobsbawm, Eric. *The Jazz Scene.* Rev. ed. New York: Pantheon, 1993.

Hodeir, André. *Jazz: Its Evolution and Essence.* Trans. David Noakes. New York: Grove Press, 1956.

Kart, Larry. *Jazz in Search of Itself.* New Haven: Yale University Press, 2004.

Kirchner, Bill, ed. *The Oxford Companion to Jazz.* New York: Oxford University Press, 2000.

Morgenstern, Dan. *Living with Jazz.* New York: Pantheon, 2004.

Murray, Albert. *Stomping the Blues.* New York: McGraw-Hill, 1976.

O'Meally, Robert, ed. *The Jazz Cadence of American Culture.* New York: Columbia University Press, 1998.

Shapiro, Nat, and Nat Hentoff. *Hear Me Talkin' to Ya: The Story of Jazz as Told by the Men Who Made It.* New York: Rinehart, 1955.

Stokes, W. Royal. *The Jazz Scene: An Informal History from New Orleans to 1990.* New York: Oxford University Press, 1991.

Walser, Robert, ed. *Keeping Time: Readings in Jazz History.* New York: Oxford University Press, 1999.

Ward, Geoffrey C., and Ken Burns. *Jazz: A History of America's Music.* New York: Knopf, 2000.

Williams, Martin. *Jazz Heritage.* New York: Oxford University Press, 1985.

———, ed. *Jazz Panorama: From the Pages of the "Jazz Review."* New York: Da Capo Press, 1979 (reprint of Crowell-Collier, 1962).

———. *The Jazz Tradition.* 2nd rev. ed. New York: Oxford University Press, 1993.

———. *Where's the Melody? A Listener's Introduction to Jazz.* New York: Pantheon, 1969.

Chapter 3

Albertson, Chris. *Bessie.* New York: Stein and Day, 1972.

Badger, Reid. *A Life in Ragtime: A Biography of James Reese Europe.* New York: Oxford University Press, 1995.

Bebey, Francis. *African Music: A People's Art.* Westport, Conn.: Hill, 1999.

Berlin, Edward A. *King of Ragtime: Scott Joplin and His Era.* New York: Oxford University Press, 1994.

Blesh, Rudi, and Harriet Janis. *They All Played Ragtime.* New York: Oak, 1971.

Bushell, Garvin. *Jazz from the Beginning.* As told to Mark Tucker. Ann Arbor: University of Michigan Press, 1988.

Chernoff, John Miller. *African Rhythm and African Sensibility.* Chicago: University of Chicago Press, 1979.

DeVeaux, Scott. *Jazz in America: Who's Listening?* Carson, Calif.: Seven Locks Press, 1995.

———, and William Howland Kenney, eds. *The Music of James Scott.* Washington, D.C.: Smithsonian Institution Press, 1992.

Emerson, Ken. *Doo-Dah! Stephen Foster and the Rise of American Popular Culture.* New York: Da Capo Press, 1998.

Erenberg, Lewis A. *Steppin' Out: New York Nightlife and the Transformation of American Culture, 1890–1930.* Chicago: University of Chicago Press, 1981.

Gioia, Ted. *Delta Blues: The Life and Times of the Mississippi Masters Who Revolutionized American Music.* New York: Norton, 2008.

Handy, W. C. *Father of the Blues: An Autobiography.* New York: Macmillan, 1941.

Jones, LeRoi (Amiri Baraka). *Blues People: Negro Music in White America.* New York: Morrow, 1963.

Lott, Eric. *Love and Theft: Blackface, Minstrelsy, and the American Working Class.* New York: Oxford University Press, 1993.

Nelson, Scott Reynolds. *Steel Driving Man: John Henry, the Untold Story of an American Legend.* New York: Oxford University Press, 2006.

Wald, Elijah. *Escaping the Delta: Robert Johnson and the Invention of the Blues.* New York: Amistad, 2004.

Waldo, Terry. *This Is Ragtime.* New York: Da Capo Press, 1991.

Chapter 4

Bechet, Sidney. *Treat It Gentle.* New York: Hill and Wang, 1960.

Charters, Samuel. *A Trumpet Around the Corner: The Story of New Orleans Jazz.* Oxford: University of Mississippi Press, 2008.

Chilton John. *Sidney Bechet: The Wizard of Jazz.* Basingstoke, Eng.: Macmillan, 1997.

Foster, Pops. *Pops Foster: The Autobiography of a New Orleans Jazzman.* Berkeley and Los Angeles: University of California Press, 1971.

Gushee, Lawrence. *Pioneers of Jazz: The Story of the Creole Band.* New York: Oxford University Press, 2005.

Lomax, Alan. *Mr. Jelly Roll: The Fortunes of Jelly Roll Morton, New Orleans Creole and "Inventor of Jazz."* New York: Duell, Sloan and Pearce, 1950.

Marquis, Donald. *In Search of Buddy Bolden, First Man of Jazz.* Baton Rouge: Louisiana State University Press, 1978.

Schuller, Gunther. *Early Jazz: Its Roots and Musical Development.* New York: Oxford University Press, 1968.

Turner, Frederick. *Remembering Song: Encounters with the New Orleans Tradition.* New York: Viking Press, 1982.

Williams, Martin. *Jazz Masters of New Orleans.* New York: Da Capo Press, 1978 (reprint of Macmillan, 1967).

Chapter 5

Appel, Alfred. *Jazz Modernism: From Ellington and Armstrong to Matisse and Joyce.* New York: Knopf, 2002.

Brooks, Tim. *Lost Sounds: Black and the Birth of the Recording Industry, 1890–1919.* Urbana: University of Illinois Press, 2004.

Brown, Scott E. *James P. Johnson: A Case of Mistaken Identity.* Metuchen, N.J.: Scarecrow Press, 1986.

Charters, Samuel B., and Leonard Kunstadt. *Jazz: A History of the New York Scene.* Garden City, N.Y.: Doubleday, 1962.

DeLong, Thomas A. *Pops: Paul Whiteman, King of Jazz.* Piscataway, N.J.: New Century, 1983.

Giddins, Gary. *Bing Crosby: A Pocketful of Dreams.* Boston: Little, Brown, 2001.

Hadlock, Richard. *Jazz Masters of the Twenties.* New York: Macmillan, 1965.

Haskins, James. *The Cotton Club: A Pictorial and Social History of the Most Famous Symbol of the Jazz Era.* New York: Random House, 1977.

Jasen, David A., and Gene Jones. *Spreadin' Rhythm Around: Black Popular Songwriters, 1880–1930.* New York: Schirmer, 1998.

Kenney, William H. *Chicago Jazz: A Cultural History, 1904–1930.* New York: Oxford University Press, 1993.

Tucker, Mark. *Ellington: The Early Years.* Urbana: University of Illinois Press, 1991.

Chapter 6

Armstrong, Louis. *Satchmo: My Life in New Orleans.* New York: Da Capo Press, 1986 (reprint of Prentice-Hall, 1954).

Bergreen, Laurence. *Louis Armstrong: An Extravagant Life.* New York: Broadway, 1997.

Berrett, Joshua, ed. *The Louis Armstrong Companion.* New York: Schirmer, 1999.

Brothers, Thomas. *Louis Armstrong in His Own Words: Selected Writings.* New York: Oxford University Press, 1999.

———. *Louis Armstrong's New Orleans.* New York: Norton, 2006.

Cogswell, Michael. *Louis Armstrong: The Offstage Story of Satchmo.* Portland, Ore.: Collector's Press, 2003.

Dance, Stanley. *The World of Earl Hines.* New York: Scribner, 1977.

Dickerson, James. *Just for a Thrill: Lil Hardin Armstrong, First Lady of Jazz.* New York: Cooper Square Press, 2002.

Giddins, Gary. *Satchmo.* Rev. ed. New York: Da Capo Press, 2001.

Jones, Max, and John Chilton. *Louis: The Story of Louis Armstrong, 1900–1971.* Boston: Little, Brown, 1971.

Kennedy, Rick. *Jelly Roll, Bix, and Hoagie: Gennett Studios and the Birth of Recorded Jazz.* Bloomington: Indiana University Press, 1994.

Lion, Jean Pierre. *Bix: The Definitive Biography of a Jazz Legend.* New York: Continuum, 2005.

Mezzrow, Mezz, and Bernard Wolfe. *Really the Blues.* Garden City, N.Y.: Anchor, 1972.

Von Eschen, Penny. *Satchmo Blows Up the World: Jazz Ambassadors Play the Cold War.* Cambridge: Harvard University Press, 2004.

Chapter 7

Barnet, Charlie. *Those Swinging Years: The Autobiography of Charlie Barnet.* With Stanley Dance. Baton Rouge: Louisiana State University Press, 1984.

Calloway, Cab, and Bryant Rollins. *Of Minnie the Moocher and Me.* New York: Crowell, 1976.

Collier, James Lincoln. *Benny Goodman and the Swing Era.* New York: Oxford University Press, 1989.

Dance, Stanley. *The World of Swing.* New York: Da Capo Press, 2001.

Erenberg, Lewis. *Swingin' the Dream: Big Band Jazz and the Rebirth of American Culture.* Chicago: University of Chicago Press, 1998.

Hampton, Lionel, and James Haskins. *Hamp: An Autobiography.* New York: Warner, 1989.

Levinson, Peter. *Tommy Dorsey: Living in a Great Big Way.* New York: Da Capo Press, 2006.

Magee, Jeffrey. *The Uncrowned King of Swing: Fletcher Henderson and Big Band Jazz.* New York: Oxford University Press, 2008.

McCarthy, Albert. *Big Band Jazz.* New York: Berkley, 1977.

Schuller, Gunther. *The Swing Era: The Development of Jazz, 1930–1945.* New York: Oxford University Press, 1989.

Shaw, Artie. *The Trouble with Cinderella: An Outline of Identity.* New York: Da Capo Press, 1979.

Simon, George T. *The Big Bands.* New York: Schirmer, 1981.

Stowe, David. *Swing Changes: Big-Band Jazz in New Deal America.* Cambridge: Harvard University Press, 1994.

Chapter 8

Basie, Count. *Good Morning Blues: The Autobiography of Count Basie.* With Albert Murray. New York: Random House, 1985.

Dahl, Linda. *Morning Glory: A Biography of Mary Lou Williams.* New York: Pantheon, 1999.

———. *Stormy Weather: The Music and Lives of a Century of Jazzwomen.* New York: Pantheon, 1984.

Dance, Stanley. *The World of Count Basie.* New York: Scribner, 1980.

———. *The World of Duke Ellington.* New York: Scribner, 1970.

Driggs, Frank, and Chuck Haddix. *Kansas City Jazz: From Ragtime to Bebop-A History.* New York: Oxford University Press, 2005.

Ellington, Duke. *Music Is My Mistress.* Garden City, N.Y.: Doubleday, 1973.

Ellington, Mercer, and Stanley Dance. *Duke Ellington in Person: An Intimate Memoir.* Boston: Houghton Mifflin, 1978.

Hajdu, David. *Lush Life: A Biography of Billy Strayhorn.* New York: Farrar, Straus and Giroux, 1996.

Hammond, John. *John Hammond on Record: An Autobiography.* With Irving Townsend. New York: Penguin, 1977.

Hasse, John Edward. *Beyond Category: The Life and Genius of Duke Ellington.* New York: Simon and Schuster, 1993.

Kirk, Andy. *Twenty Years on Wheels.* As told to Amy Lee. Ann Arbor: University of Michigan Press, 1989.

Pearson, Nathan W. *Goin' to Kansas City.* Urbana: University of Illinois Press, 1994.

Russell, Ross. *Jazz Style in Kansas City and the Southwest.* Berkeley and Los Angeles: University of California Press, 1971.

Tucker, Mark, ed. *The Duke Ellington Reader.* New York: Oxford University Press, 1993.

Tucker, Sherrie. *Swing Shift: "All-Girl" Bands of the 1940s.* Durham, N.C.: Duke University Press, 2000.

Van de Leur, Walter. *Something to Live For: The Music of Billy Strayhorn.* New York: Oxford University Press, 2002.

Chapter 9

Berger, Morroe, Edward Berger, and James Patrick. *Benny Carter: A Life in American Music,* vols. 1 and 2. Metuchen, N.J.: Scarecrow Press, 1982.

Büchmann-Möller, Frank. *Someone to Watch Over Me: The Life and Music of Ben Webster.* Ann Arbor: University of Michigan Press, 2006.

Chilton, John. *Roy Eldridge: Little Jazz Giant.* New York: Continuum, 2003.

———. *The Song of the Hawk: The Life and Recordings of Coleman Hawkins.* London: Quartet, 1990.

Clarke, Donald. *Wishing on the Moon: The Life and Times of Billie Holiday.* New York: Viking Press, 1994.

Cohodas, Nadine. *Queen: The Life and Music of Dinah Washington.* New York: Pantheon, 2004.

Daniels, Douglas Henry. *Lester Leaps In: The Life and Times of Lester "Pres" Young.* Boston: Beacon Press, 2002.

Friedwald, Will. *Jazz Singing: America's Great Voices from Bessie Smith to Bebop and Beyond.* New York: Da Capo Press, 1990.

Gourse, Leslie, ed. *The Billie Holiday Companion: Seven Decades of Commentary.* New York: Schirmer, 1997.

Holiday, Billie. *Lady Sings the Blues.* With William Dufty. London: Abacus, 1975.

Nicholson, Stuart. *Ella Fitzgerald: A Biography of the First Lady of Jazz.* New York: Scribner, 2004.

O'Meally, Robert. *Lady Day: The Many Faces of Billie Holiday.* New York: Da Capo Press, 1991.

Porter, Lewis, ed. *A Lester Young Reader.* Washington, D.C.: Smithsonian Institution Press, 1991.

Stewart, Rex. *Boy Meets Horn.* Ann Arbor: University of Michigan Press, 1991.

———. *Jazz Masters of the Thirties.* New York: Macmillan, 1972.

Chapter 10

Burke, Patrick. *Come In and Hear the Truth: Jazz and Race on 52nd Street.* Chicago: University of Chicago Press, 2008.

Crowther, Bruce. *Gene Krupa: His Life and Times.* New York: Universe, 1987.

Dregni, Michael. *Django: The Life and Music of a Gypsy Legend.* New York: Oxford University Press, 2004.

Korall, Burt. *Drummin' Men: The Heartbeat of Jazz—The Swing Years.* New York: Schirmer, 1990.

Lester, James. *Too Marvelous for Words: The Life & Genius of Art Tatum.* New York: Oxford University Press, 1994.

Sallis, James, ed. *The Guitar in Jazz: An Anthology.* Lincoln: University of Nebraska Press, 1996.

Shaw, Arnold. *52nd Street: The Street of Jazz.* New York: Da Capo Press, 1991.

Shipton, Alyn. *Fats Waller: His Life and Times.* New York: Universe, 1988.

Waller, Maurice, and Anthony Calabrese. *Fats Waller.* New York: Schirmer, 1977.

Chapter 11

DeVeaux, Scott. *The Birth of Bebop: A Social and Musical History.* Berkeley and Los Angeles: University of California Press, 1997.

Feather, Leonard. *Inside Jazz.* New York: Da Capo Press, 1977. Reprint of *Inside Be-Bop* (New York: Robbins, 1949).

Giddins, Gary. *Celebrating Bird: The Triumph of Charlie Parker.* New York: Morrow, 1987.

Gillespie, Dizzy. *To Be or Not . . . to Bop: Memoirs.* With Al Fraser. Garden City, N.Y.: Doubleday, 1979.

Gitler, Ira. *The Masters of Bebop: A Listener's Guide.* New York: Da Capo Press, 2001.

———. *Swing to Bop: An Oral History of the Transition in Jazz in the 1940s.* New York: Oxford University Press, 1985.

Groves, Alan, and Alyn Shipton. *The Glass Enclosure: The Life of Bud Powell.* New York: Continuum, 2001.

Korall, Burt. *Drummin' Men: The Heartbeat of Jazz—The Bebop Years.* New York: Oxford University Press, 2002.

Owens, Thomas. *Bebop: The Music and the Players.* New York: Oxford University Press, 1995.

Paudras, Francis. *Dance of the Infidels: A Portrait of Bud Powell.* New York: Da Capo Press, 1998.

Reisner, Robert George. *Bird: The Legend of Charlie Parker.* New York: Da Capo Pres, 1977.

Shipton, Alyn. *Groovin' High: The Life of Dizzy Gillespie.* New York: Oxford University Press, 1999.

Woideck, Carl, ed. *The Charlie Parker Companion: Six Decades of Commentary.* New York: Schirmer, 1998.

———. *Charlie Parker: His Music and Life.* Ann Arbor: University of Michigan Press, 1996.

Chapter 12

Bryant, Clora, ed. *Central Avenue Sounds: Jazz in Los Angeles.* Berkeley and Los Angeles: University of California Press, 1998.

Cook, Richard. *Blue Note Records: The Biography.* Boston: Justin, Charles, 2003.

Gioia, Ted. *West Coast Jazz: Modern Jazz in California, 1945–1960.* New York: Oxford University Press, 1992.

Goldberg, Joe. *Jazz Masters of the Fifties.* New York: Macmillan, 1965.

Goldsher, Alan. *Hard Bop Academy: The Sidemen of Art Blakey and the Jazz Messengers.* Milwaukee: Hal Leonard, 2002.

Hamilton, Andy. *Lee Konitz: Conversations on the Improviser's Art.* Ann Arbor: University of Michigan Press, 2007.

Klinkowitz, Jerome. *Listen: Gerry Mulligan—An Aural Narrative in Jazz.* New York: Schirmer, 1991.

Maggin, Donald L. *Stan Getz: A Life in Jazz.* New York: Morrow, 2003.

Nisenson, Eric. *Open Sky: Sonny Rollins and His World of Improvisation.* New York: Da Capo Press, 2000.

Pepper, Art, and Laurie Pepper. *Straight Life: The Story of Art Pepper.* New York: Schirmer, 1979.

Rosenthal, David H. *Hard Bop: Jazz and Black Music, 1955–1965.* New York: Oxford University Press, 1992.

Silver, Horace. *Let's Get to the Nitty Gritty: The Autobiography of Horace Silver.* Phil Pastras, ed. Berkeley and Los Angeles: University of California Press, 2006.

Chapter 13

Crease, Stephanie Stein. *Gil Evans: Out of the Cool—His Life and Music.* Chicago: A Cappella, 2002.

De Wilde, Laurent. *Monk.* Trans. Jonathan Dickinson. New York: Marlowe, 1997.

Easton, Carol. *Straight Ahead: The Story of Stan Kenton.* New York: Da Capo Press, 1981.

Fitterling, Thomas. *Thelonious Monk: His Life and Music.* Berkeley, Calif.: Berkeley Hills, 1997.

Mingus, Charles. *Beneath the Underdog: His World as Composed by Mingus.* New York: Vintage, 1971.

Priestly, Brian. *Mingus: A Critical Biography.* New York: Da Capo Press, 1982.

Russell, George. *Lydian Chromatic Concept of Tonal Organization.* New York: Choice, 1959.

Solis, Gabriel. *Monk's Music: Thelonious Monk and Jazz History in the Making.* Berkeley and Los Angeles: University of California Press, 2008.

Van der Bliek, Rob, ed. *The Thelonious Monk Reader.* New York: Oxford University Press, 2001.

Chapter 14

Carner, Gary, ed. *The Miles Davis Companion: Four Decades of Commentary.* New York: Schirmer, 1997.

Carr, Ian. *Miles Davis: A Critical Biography.* London: Paladin, 1982.

Chambers, Jack. *Milestones: The Music and Times of Miles Davis.* Toronto: University of Toronto Press, 1985.

Davis, Miles. *Miles: The Autobiography.* With Quincy Troupe. New York: Simon and Schuster, 1989.

Early, Gerald, ed. *Miles Davis and American Culture.* St. Louis: Missouri Historical Society Press, 2001.

Kahn, Ashley. *Kind of Blue: The Making of the Miles Davis Masterpiece.* Boston: Da Capo Press, 2000.

———. *A Love Supreme: The Story of John Coltrane's Signature Album.* New York: Penguin, 2002.

Kirchner, Bill, ed. *A Miles Davis Reader.* Washington, D.C.: Smithsonian Institution Press, 1991.

Pettinger, Peter. *Bill Evans: How My Heart Sings.* New Haven: Yale University Press, 1998.

Porter, Lewis. *John Coltrane: His Life and Music.* Ann Arbor: University of Michigan Press, 1998.

Szwed, John. *So What: The Life of Miles Davis.* New York: Simon and Schuster, 2002.

Chapter 15

Anderson, Iain. *This Is Our Music: Free Jazz, the Sixties, and American Culture.* Philadelphia: University of Pennsylvania Press, 2007.

Giddins, Gary. *Rhythm-a-ning: Jazz Tradition and Innovation in the '80s.* New York: Oxford University Press, 1985.

Jones, LeRoi (Amiri Baraka). *Black Music.* New York: Morrow, 1967.

Jost, Ekkehard. *Free Jazz.* Graz: Universal Edition, 1974.

Lewis, George. *A Power Stronger Than Itself: The AACM and American Experimental Music.* Chicago: University of Chicago Press, 2008.

Litweiler, John. *The Freedom Principle: Jazz After 1958.* New York: Morrow, 1984.

———. *Ornette Coleman: A Harmolodic Life.* New York: Morrow, 1992.

Mandel, Howard. *Miles, Ornette, Cecil: Jazz Beyond Jazz.* New York: Routledge, 2008.

Radano, Ronald M. *New Cultural Figurations: Anthony Braxton's Cultural Critique.* Chicago: University of Chicago Press, 1993.

Spellman, A. B. *Four Lives in the Bebop Business.* New York: Pantheon, 1966.

Such, David. *Avant-Garde Musicians: Performing "Out There."* Iowa City: University of Iowa Press, 1993.

Szwed, John. *Space Is the Place: The Lives and Times of Sun Ra.* New York: Pantheon, 1997.

Williams, Martin. *Jazz Masters in Transition, 1957–69.* New York: Macmillan, 1970.

Wilmer, Valerie. *As Serious as Your Life: The Story of the New Jazz.* Westport, Conn.: Hill, 1980.

Chapter 16

Castro, Ruy. *Bossa Nova: The Story of the Brazilian Music That Seduced the World.* Chicago: A Capella, 2000.

Charles, Ray, and David Ritz. *Brother Ray: Ray Charles's Own Story.* New York: Dial Press, 1978.

Chilton, John. *Let the Good Times Roll: The Story of Louis Jordan and His Music.* Ann Arbor: University of Michigan Press, 1994.

Epstein, Daniel Mark. *Nat King Cole.* Boston: Northeastern University Press, 1999.

Fernandez, Raoul A. *From Afro-Cuban Rhythms to Latin Jazz.* Berkeley and Los Angeles: University of California Press, 2006.

Friedwald, Will. *Sinatra! The Song Is You—A Singer's Art.* New York: Da Capo Press, 1995.

Gourse, Leslie. *Sassy: The Life of Sarah Vaughan.* New York: Scribner, 1993.

Petkov, Steven, and Leonard Mustazza, eds. *The Frank Sinatra Reader.* New York: Oxford University Press, 1997.

Roberts, John Storm. *Latin Jazz: The First of the Fusions, 1880s to Today.* New York: Schirmer, 1999.

Sublette, Ned. *Cuba and Its Music: From the First Drums to the Mambo.* Chicago: Chicago Review Press, 2004.

Washburne, Christopher. *Sounding Salsa: Performing Latin Music in New York City.* Philadelphia: Temple University Press, 2008.

Wexler, Jerry, and David Ritz. *Rhythm and the Blues: A Life in American Music.* New York: Knopf, 1993.

Chapter 17

Coryell, Julie, and Laura Friedman. *Jazz-Rock Fusion: The People, the Music.* Milwaukee: Hal Leonard, 2000.

Freeman, Phil. *Running the Voodoo Down: The Electric Music of Miles Davis.* San Francisco: Backbeat, 2005.

Mercer, Michelle. *Footprints: The Life and Works of Wayne Shorter.* New York: Tarcher, 2004.

Milkowski, Bill. *Jaco: The Extraordinary and Tragic Life of Jaco Pastorius.* New York: Backbeat, 1995.

Nicholson, Stuart. *Jazz-Rock: A History.* New York: Schirmer, 1998.

Pond, Steven. *Head Hunters: The Making of Jazz's First Platinum Album.* Ann Arbor: University of Michigan Press, 2005.

Tingen, Paul. *Miles Beyond: The Electric Explorations of Miles Davis, 1967–1991.* New York: Billboard, 2001.

Chapter 18

Berry, Jason, Jonathan Foose, and Tad Jones. *Up from the Cradle of Jazz: New Orleans Music Since World War II.* Athens: University of Georgia Press, 1986.

Bethell, Tom. *George Lewis: A Jazzman from New Orleans.* Berkeley and Los Angeles: University of California Press, 1977.

Gabbard, Krin. *Jammin' at the Margins: Jazz and the American Cinema.* Chicago: University of Chicago Press, 1996.

Gennari, John. *Blowin' Hot and Cold: Jazz and Its Critics.* Chicago: University of Chicago Press, 2006.

Hazeldine, Mike, and Bill Russell. *Bill Russell's American Music.* New Orleans: Jazzology, 1993.

Lock, Graham. *Forces of Motion: The Music and Thoughts of Anthony Braxton.* New York: Da Capo Press, 1988.

Marsalis, Wynton, and Frank Stewart. *Sweet Swing Blues on the Road.* New York: Norton, 1994.

Ramsey, Frederic Jr., and Charles Edward Smith, eds. *Jazzmen.* New York: Harcourt, Brace, 1939.

Wein, George, and Nate Chinen: *Myself Among Others: A Life in Music.* New York: Da Capo Press, 2004.

Chapter 19

Carver, Reginald, and Lenny Bernstein. *Jazz Profiles: The Spirit of the Nineties.* New York: Billboard, 1998.

Mandel, Howard. *Future Jazz.* New York: Oxford University Press, 1999.

Nicholson, Stuart. *Is Jazz Dead? (Or Has It Moved to a New Address).* New York: Routledge, 2005.

Stokes, W. Royal. *Living the Jazz Life: Conversations with Forty Musicians About Their Careers in Jazz.* New York: Oxford University Press, 2000.

End Notes

Chapter 1 Musical Elements and Instruments

8. "You got to be in the sun": Sidney Bechet, *Treat It Gentle* (Hill and Wang, 1960), p. 2.

Chapter 3 The Roots of Jazz

53. Jazz is an "art form": Robert Walser, ed., *Keeping Time* (Oxford University Press, 1999), p. 333.

55. The "mulatto" nature: Albert Murray, *The Omni-Americans: Black Experience and American Culture* (Vintage, 1970), p. 22.

55. The blasting of a railroad tunnel: Scott Reynolds Nelson, *Steel Drivin' Man: John Henry—The Untold Tale of an American Legend* (Oxford University Press, 2006).

56. "The Buzzard Lope" is a spiritual dance: Mark Knowles, *Tap Roots: The Early History of Tap Dancing* (McFarland, 2002), p. 320.

58. African American society had shifted: Lawrence Levine, *Black Culture and Black Consciousness* (Oxford University Press, 1978), pp. 222–23.

59. "I wasn't making money": liner notes to *Long Way from Home: The Blues of Fred McDowell* (Milestone MSP 93003, 1966).

63. "They were led by a long-legged chocolate boy": W. C. Handy, *Father of the Blues: An Autobiography* (Collier, 1941), pp. 80–81.

66. "distort a sentimental, simple": Eileen Southern, *The Music of Black Americans*, 2nd ed. (Norton, 1983), p. 108.

67. "We get our dances": Lewis A. Erenberg, *Steppin' Out: New York Nightlife and the Transformation of American Culture* (Greenwood Press, 1981), pp. 163–64.

67. "When a good orchestra": ibid., p. 153.

69. "a town without its brass band": Raoul Camus, "Band," in *The New Grove Dictionary of American Music*, ed. H. Wiley Hitchcock and Stanley Sadie (Macmillan, 1986), vol. 1, p. 133.

74. "Sweatman was my idol": Garvin Bushell (as told to Mark Tucker), *Jazz from the Beginning* (University of Michigan Press, 1988), p. 18.

Chapter 4 New Orleans

81. A consequence of a large African population: Jerah Johnson, *Congo Square in New Orleans* (Louisiana Landmarks Society, 1995), p. 43.

83. The jazz guitarist Danny Barker: Alan Lomax, *Mister Jelly Roll* (Duell, Sloan and Pearce, 1950), p. 61.

86. "Everybody got up quick": *Down Beat*, December 15, 1940.

86. "He was one of the sweetest trumpet players": Donald M. Marquis, *In Search of Buddy Bolden* (Louisiana State University Press, 1978), p. 100.

87. "You never had to figure": Nat Shapiro and Nat Hentoff, *Hear Me Talkin' to Ya: The Story of Jazz as Told by the Men Who Made It* (Rinehart, 1955), pp. 66–67.

89. "He played practically the same way": Sidney Bechet, *Treat It Gentle* (Twayne, 1960), p. 84.

97. "Even if a tune": Lomax, *Mister Jelly Roll*, p. 63.

100. "I was sitting at the piano": Shapiro and Hentoff, *Hear Me Talkin' to Ya*, pp. 45–46.

104. "He was standing there": Richard Merryman, *Louis Armstrong—A Self-Portrait* (Eakins Press, 1971), pp. 48–49.

105. "I wish to set down": Ralph de Toledano, ed., *Frontiers of Jazz* (Durrell, 1947, trans. and rev.), p. 122.

Chapter 5 New York in the 1920s

114. "Negroes playing it": *San Francisco Examiner*, April 11, 1928, p. 6.

121. "[Fletcher's] was the band": Duke Ellington, *Music Is My Mistress* (Doubleday, 1973), p. 49.

127. J. A. Rogers celebrated jazz: Alain Locke, *The New Negro* (Albert and Charles Boni, 1925), pp. 216–24.

Chapter 6 Louis Armstrong and the First Great Soloists

139. "had the potential capacity": Gunther Schuller, *Early Jazz* (Oxford University Press, 1968), p. 89.

142. "She never envied no one": Louis Armstrong, *Satchmo: My Life in New Orleans* (Prentice-Hall, 1954), p. 9.

Chapter 7 Swing Bands

171. "We arrived in one town": Nat Shapiro and Nat Hentoff, *Hear Me Talkin' to Ya: The Story of Jazz as Told by the Men Who Made It* (Rinehart, 1955), pp. 328–30.

171. By 1939, two-thirds of the public: Russell B. Nye, *The Unembarrassed Muse: The Popular Arts in America* (Dial, 1970), p. 384.

172. "the abandon of a crowd": David W. Stowe, *Swing Changes: Big-Band Jazz in New Deal America* (Harvard University Press, 1994), p. 24.

173. "fancy wall decorations all over": Clyde Bernhardt, *I Remember: Eighty Years of Black Entertainment, Big Bands, and the Blues* (University of Pennsylvania Press, 1986), pp. 149–50.

173. "For the dancer, you know what will please him": Howard Spring, *American Music* 1997 (15:2), p. 191.

173. "to observe the Lindy Hop": ibid., p. 210.

174. "If you were on the first floor": Count Basie (with Albert Murray), *Good Morning Blues: The Autobiography of Count Basie* (Random House, 1985), p. 120.

174. "a lot of kids playing": Dickie Wells, quoted in Jeffrey Magee, *The Uncrowned King of Swing: Fletcher Henderson and Big Band Jazz* (Oxford University Press, 2005), p. 171.

178. "get a Harlem book": James Maher, transcript from *Ken Burns's Jazz* (http://www.pbs.org/jazz/about/pdfs/Maher.pdf).

179. "These were our songs": ibid.

179. "I have always been Mr. Showmanship": Lionel Hampton and James Haskins, *Hamp: An Autobiography* (Warner, 1989), p. 36.

182. "There was no white pianist": John Hammond, *John Hammond on Record: An Autobiography* (Penguin, 1977), pp. 68, 32–33.

182. "Hammond in action": Stowe, *Swing Changes*, p. 57.

182. "vapid and without the slightest": John Hammond, "The Tragedy of Duke Ellington," in *The Ellington Reader*, ed. Mark Tucker (Oxford University Press, 1993), p. 120.

183. "one of the foremost jazz conservatories": Artie Shaw, *The Trouble with Cinderella: An Outline of Identity* (Farrar, Straus, and Young, 1952), pp. 196–97, 203.

183. "I was actually living": ibid., p. 228.

184. "They won't even let me play": Richard M. Sudhalter, *Lost Chords: White Musicians and Their Contribution to Jazz, 1915–1945* (Oxford University Press, 1999), p. 581.

187. "Until I met Jimmie": Sy Oliver, quoted in Alyn Shipton, *A New History of Jazz* (Continuum, 2001), p. 299.

187. "They would come out and play a dance routine": Eddie Durham, National Endowment for the Arts/Smithsonian Institution Jazz Oral History Project.

191. One musician remembers: Albert McCarthy, *Big Band Jazz: The Definitive History of the Origins, Progress, Influence and Decline of Big Jazz Bands* (Berkley, 1974), p. 211.

192. "The only difference": Cab Calloway and Bryant Rollins, *Of Minnie the Moocher and Me* (Crowell, 1976), p. 42.

Chapter 8 Count Basie and Duke Ellington

197. "the colored patrons": Dave Dexter, quoted in Frank Driggs, *Kansas City Jazz: From Ragtime to Bebop—A History* (Oxford University Press, 2005), pp. 130–31.

200. Sometimes they were paid: Linda Dahl, *Morning Glory: A Biography of Mary Lou Williams* (Pantheon, 1999), p. 85.

201. "She'd be sitting": Andy Kirk (as told to Amy Lee), *Twenty Years on Wheels* (University of Michigan Press, 1989), p. 73.

201. "I listened to how a pianist": Dahl, *Morning Glory*, pp. 87, 77.

203. While touring with the Count Basie band: Billie Holiday (with William Dufty), *Lady Sings the Blues* (Abacus, 1975), p. 56.

203. "What does a jacket": Anita O'Day (with George Eells), *High Times, Hard Times* (Putnam, 1981), pp. 101–2.

204. "I had never heard": Count Basie (with Albert Murray), *Good Morning Blues: The Autobiography of Count Basie* (Random House, 1985), pp. 4–5.

204. "Whenever we wanted to do something": Driggs, *Kansas City Jazz*, p. 121.

204. The band finally dissolved: Nathan W. Pearson Jr., *Goin' to Kansas City* (University of Illinois Press, 1987), p. 75.

204. This tiny, L-shaped salon was so small: Basie, *Good Morning Blues*, p. 164.

205. "I don't think we had": ibid.

205. "It wasn't unusual": Nat Shapiro and Nat Hentoff, *Hear Me Talkin' to Ya: The Story of Jazz as Told by the Men Who Made It* (Rinehart, 1955), p. 291.

205. "revival meetings": Gene Ramey, National Endowment for the Arts/Smithsonian Institution Jazz Oral History Project.

206. "the poor, the black": Pearson, *Goin' to Kansas City*, p. 84.

206. "might as well have been": Roy Wilkins, quoted in Douglas Henry Daniels, *Lester Leaps In: The Life and Times of Lester "Pres" Young* (Beacon Press, 2002), p. 182.

206. "just like you were mixing": Stanley Dance, *The World of Count Basie* (Scribner, 1980), p. 103.

208. "did not aspire to live": Gerald Early, *Tuxedo Junction: Essays on American Culture* (Ecco Press, 1989), p. 279.

208. "I don't think I even knew": Basie, *Good Morning Blues*, p. 137.

208. "By the time you read this": ibid., p. 180.

208. "It was like the Blue Devils": ibid., p. 199.

210. "You know, don't you": Albert McCarthy, *Big Band Jazz: The Definitive History of the Origins, Progress, Influence and Decline of Big Jazz Bands* (Berkley, 1974), p. 207.

211. "Negro folk music": Richard Boyer, "The Hot Bach," in *The Ellington Reader*, ed. Mark Tucker (Oxford University Press, 1993), p. 218.

211. "beyond category": Edward Kennedy Ellington, *Music Is My Mistress* (Doubleday, 1973), p. 237.

212. "I'm supposed to remember": Dizzy Gillespie (with Al Fraser), *To Be, or Not . . . to Bop* (Doubleday, 1979), p. 184.

212. "There's always a mental picture": Boyer, "The Hot Bach," p. 233.

212. "Each member of his band": Billy Strayhorn, "The Ellington Effect," in *The Ellington Reader*, p. 270.

213. "at the height of his creative powers": Irving Townsend, "When Duke Records," in *The Ellington Reader*, p. 320.

213. "You can't write music right": Boyer, "The Hot Bach," p. 228.

214. "a sort of majestic folk quality": ibid., p. 231.

214. "Those were my two ways of being": Stanley Dance, *The World of Duke Ellington* (Scribner, 1970), p. 106.

214. "Duke merely lifts a finger": *Down Beat*, November 5, 1952, p. 18.

216. "It's a primitive instinct": Archie Bell, "The Ellington Orchestra in Cleveland," in *The Ellington Reader*, p. 53.

216. "This band has no boss": Boyer, "The Hot Bach," p. 217.

216. "It was a happy day": Duke Ellington, "We, Too, Sing 'America,'" in *The Ellington Reader*, p. 146.

217. "Where in the white community": Ralph Ellison, "Homage to Duke Ellington on his Birthday," in *The Ellington Reader*, pp. 96–97.

217. "take Uncle Tom out of the theater": Ellington, *Music Is My Mistress*, p. 175.

217. "I guess serious is a confusing word": "Why Duke Ellington Avoided Music Schools," in *The Ellington Reader*, p. 253.

217. Playing by ear: Mercer Ellington, in Dance, *The World of Duke Ellington*, p. 39.

217. "I don't feel the pop tunes": Boyer, "The Hot Bach," p. 231.

221. "That was the last thing": David Hajdu, *Lush Life: A Biography of Billy Strayhorn* (Farrar, Straus and Giroux, 1996), p. 253.

222. "His greatest virtue, I think": ibid., p. 257.

Chapter 9 Swing Era Soloists

229. "the man for whom Adolphe Sax": Jon Hendricks on the album *Lambert, Hendricks, & Bavan at Newport '63* (RCA-Victor, 1964).

229. "People always say I invented the jazz tenor": Hawkins on the album *Coleman Hawkins: A Documentary* (Riverside Records, 1956).

233. "so-called Southwest tenor style": Martin Williams, *The Jazz Tradition* (Oxford University Press, rev. ed., 1993), p. 75.

234. "During his early period": Rex Stewart, *Jazz Masters of the 30's* (Macmillan, 1972), p. 128.

235. "Man, this cat ain't playing harsh": Gary Giddins, *Visions of Jazz* (Oxford University Press, 1998), p. 191.

236. "I'm looking for something soft": Francois Postif, "Lester Paris 59," in *Jazz Hot* (Paris), April 1959.

237. "Zoot and I worked in a club in Hollywood": Giddins, *Visions of Jazz*, p. 331.

240. "it's most improbable that anyone will ever know": Duke Ellington on the album *The Afro Eurasian Eclipse* (Fantasy Records, 1976).

Chapter 11 Bebop

279. "entirely separate and apart": Charlie Parker, "No Bop Roots in Jazz: Parker," *Down Beat*, September 9, 1942, p. 12.

280. "Everybody would get up there": Trummy Young, National Endowment for the Arts/Smithsonian Institution Jazz Oral History Project.

281. "Man, is that cat crazy?": Nat Shapiro and Nat Hentoff, *Hear Me Talkin' to Ya: The Story of Jazz as Told by the Men Who Made It* (Rinehart, 1955), p. 356.

282. "Stop that crazy boppin'": ibid., p. 351.

283. "That's what I've been hearing": Ira Gitler, *Jazz Masters of the Forties* (Collier, 1974), p. 20.

283. "With bop, you had to know": Scott DeVeaux, "Conversation with Howard McGhee," *Black Perspective in Music* 25 (September 1987), p. 73; italics added.

284. "Bird couldn't play much": Gene Ramey, National Endowment for the Arts/Smithsonian Institution Jazz Oral History Project.

285. "real advanced New York style": Leonard Feather, *Inside Be-Bop* (Robbins, 1949), p. 15.

285. "I worked hard": Dizzy Gillespie (with Al Fraser), *To Be, or Not . . . to Bop* (Doubleday, 1979), p. 218.

286. "head and hands": Miles Davis (with Quincy Troupe), *Miles: The Autobiography* (Simon and Schuster, 1989), p. 64.

287. "Charlie Parker brought the rhythm": Gillespie (with Fraser), *To Be, or Not*, p. 232.

287. "As we walked in": Marshall Stearns, *The Story of Jazz* (Oxford University Press, 1956), pp. 224–25.

288. "I had never heard": DeVeaux, interview with Howard McGhee, December 20, 1980.

288. "Naming-day at Savoy": Douglass Parker, in *The Bebop Revolution in Words and Music*, ed. David Oliphant (University of Texas Press, 1994), p. 165.

293. "The one was jazz": Teddy Reig (with Edward Berger), *Reminiscing in Tempo: The Life and Times of a Jazz Hustler* (Scarecrow Press, 1990).

295. "All we wanted to do": Davis (with Troupe), *Miles*, p. 114.

296. "I listened to bebop after school": Imanu Amiri Baraka, *The Autobiography of LeRoi Jones/Amiri Baraka* (Freundlich, 1984), pp. 57–58, 60.

297. "He had to stop and think": Gitler, *Jazz Masters*, p. 125.

298. "one with the music itself": ibid., p. 110.

301. "When Pres appeared": ibid., p. 205.

302. "There'd be a lot of cats on the stand": ibid., p. 209.

305. "Since I've been over here": Dan Morgenstern, *Living with Jazz* (Pantheon, 2004), p. 375.

305. "There was no such thing": Gillespie (with Fraser), *To Be, or Not*, p. 343.

306. "nervous jazz": Whitney Balliett, "Pandemonium Pays Off," in *Collected Works: A Journal of Jazz, 1954–2000* (St. Martin's Press, 2000), p. 8.

306. "They rarely move from their seats": ibid.

Chapter 12 The 1950s: Cool Jazz and Hard Bop

310. "gave up jazz": Hugues Panassie and Madeleine Gautier, *Guide to Jazz* (Houghton Mifflin, 1956), p. 210.

311. "One countered racial provocation": Ralph Ellison, *The Collected Essays of Ralph Ellison* (Modern Library, 1995), p. 631.

313. "Diz and Bird play a lot of real fast notes": Miles Davis (with Quincy Troupe), *Miles: The Autobiography* (Simon and Schuster, 1989), pp. 219–20.

319. "We had a hard time": author interview, Gary Giddins, *Visions of Jazz* (Oxford University Press, 1998), p. 384.

322. "We used to jam together": Giddins, *Visions of Jazz,* p. 331.

Chapter 13 Jazz Composition in the 1950s

346. "I say play your way": Grover Sales, "I Wanted to Make It Better: Monk at the Blackhawk," in *Jazz: A Quarterly of American Music* 5 (Winter 1960).

347. "I used to have a phobia": Nat Hentoff, *The Jazz Life* (London: P. Davies, 1962), p. 203.

348. "I always had to be alert": Nat Hentoff, liner notes to *Giant Steps* (Atlantic Records, 1959).

353. "I am Charles Mingus": *Mingus,* a film by Thomas Reichman, 1968.

365. "It's not like when you base stuff on chords": Miles Davis (with Quincy Troupe), *Miles: The Autobiography* (Simon and Schuster, 1989), p. 225.

365. "The challenge here": ibid.

365. "I thought that Kind of Blue": Eric Nisenson, *The Making of "Kind of Blue"* (St. Martin's Press, 2000), p. 177.

368. "Such men must be guarded": Leonard Feather, "The Jazz Workshop," in *Down Beat Jazz Record Reviews,* vol. 2 (Maher, 1958), p. 169.

Chapter 14 The Modality of Miles Davis and John Coltrane

372. "My ultimate culture hero": William C. Banfield, *Black Notes* (Scarecrow Press, 2004), p. 148.

383. "It took that long": Ralph J. Gleason, liner notes to *Coltrane's Sound* (Atlantic Records, 1960).

387. "He gets a very personal sound": Ian Carr, Digby Fairweather, and Brian Priestley, *Jazz: The Essential Companion* (London: Grafton, 1987), p. 510.

388. "the turning point": ibid., p. 182.

389. "musical nonsense": John Tynan, "Take Five," *Down Beat,* November 23, 1961.

393. "The main thing a musician would like to do": John Coltrane, liner notes to *Crescent* (Impulse Records, 1964).

Chapter 15 The Avant-Garde

410. "Musicians tell me, if what I'm doing": Ornette Coleman at World Jazz Scene, Great Quotes of and About Musicians, http://www.worldjazzscene.com/quotes.html.

410. "Bebop is like playing scrabble": Duke Ellington, *Look Magazine,* August 10, 1954.

410. "It's like not having anything to do with what's": Charles Mingus, quoted in Gary Giddins, *Visions of Jazz* (Oxford University Press, 1998), p. 445.

412. "You can always reach into the human sound": Ornette Coleman, quoted in Nat Hentoff, liner notes to Coleman's *Something Else!!!!* (Contemporary Records, 1958).

412. Hale Smith . . . observed: interview with Gary Giddins, 1978.

412. "Jazz is the only music in which": Ornette Coleman, quoted in Wilfrid Mellers, *Music in a New Found Land* (Hillstone, 1975), p. 346.

418. "The eyes are really not to be used": Cecil Taylor, quoted in Gary Giddins, *Riding on a Blue Note* (Oxford University Press, 1981), pp. 281–82.

418. "We had a magical dialogue": Andrew Cyrille, quoted in *Cecil Taylor,* an interview by Ted Panken, 2005.

424. "screaming the word 'FUCK'": Ted Joans, review of Albert Ayler in *Coda Magazine* (Canada), 1971.

424. "coonish churchified chuckle tunes": Leroi Jones (Amiri Imamu Baraka), *Black Music* (Morrow, 1968), p. 126.

424. "Salvation Army band on LSD": Dan Morgenstern, "Concert Review: Newport '67," *Down Beat,* August 10, 1967.

430. "We were not in the business of showcasing standards": Muhal Richard Abrams, quoted in Giddins, *Riding on a Blue Note,* p. 194.

430. "Until I had the first meeting": Joseph Jarman, quoted in J. B. Figi, liner notes to Jarman's *Song For* (Delmark Records, 1967).

437. "exhibits a disciplined disregard": unsigned statement, Vision Festival website, http://www.visionfestival.org/literature.php.

Chapter 16 Fusion I (to 1960): R & B, Singers, and Latin Jazz

439. "Jazz is an octopus": Dexter Gordon, quoted in Gary Giddins, *Visions of Jazz* (Oxford University Press, 1998), p. 330.

446. "When finally I got enough money": Jimmy Smith, quoted in Leonard Feather, liner notes to *The Sounds of Jimmy Smith* (Blue Note Records, 1957).

451. "Every song he sings is understandable": Duke Ellington, *Music Is My Mistress* (Doubleday, 1973), p. 239.

458. "If you can't manage to put tinges": Jelly Roll Morton, in *The Complete Library of Congress Recordings,* 1938 (released in 2005 by Rounder Records).

462. "It was similar to a nuclear weapon": Dizzy Gillespie, in *Routes of Rhythm,* PBS series (telecast 1997).

462. "If I had let it go": Dizzy Gillespie (with Al Fraser), *To Be, or Not . . . to Bop* (Doubleday, 1979), p. 321.

465. "I truly believe jazz ended up influencing": Chico O'Farrill, quoted in Giddins, *Visions of Jazz,* p. 325.

469. "There was a noticeable difference": Charlie Byrd, quoted in John Litweiler, liner notes to *Jazz Samba: Stan Getz: Charlie Byrd* (Verve Records, 1996).

Chapter 17 Fusion II: Jazz, Rock, and Beyond

478. "an unprecedented share": Eric Hobsbawm, *The Jazz Scene* (Pantheon, 1993), p. xxviii.

479. "I had discovered that my strength": James Brown (with Bruce Tucker), *James Brown: The Godfather of Soul* (Thunder's Mouth, 1997), p. 158.

480. "Everybody was dropping acid": *Down Beat*, May 1984, p. 16.

481. "They would play my music": Stuart Nicholson, *Jazz Rock: A History* (Schirmer, 1998), p. 79.

481. "walking eye candy": Michael Henderson, quoted in *Jazziz*, February 2004, p. 37.

481. "the $1.50 drums and the harmonicas": Miles Davis (with Quincy Troupe): *Miles: The Autobiography* (Simon and Schuster, 1989), p. 288.

483. "He'd go out and play": *Down Beat*, March 28, 1974, p. 15.

483. "nobody stepped on anybody's feet": Joe Zawinul, liner notes to *Forecast: Tomorrow* (Columbia, 2006).

483. "If you stop calling me a jazz man": Clive Davis, *Clive: Inside the Record Business* (Morrow, 1975), p. 260.

483. "It was loose and light at the same time": Davis (with Troupe), *Miles*, p. 299.

485. "It was like group therapy": *Down Beat*, October 21, 1976, p. 14.

485. "More than my experience with Miles": *Down Beat*, September 1988, p. 19.

485. "to be the fastest guitarist": Nicholson, *Jazz Rock*, p. 203.

486. "To me," he later said: *Down Beat*, June 15, 1978, p. 21.

486. "We were a black band": *Down Beat*, April 1988, p. 17.

487. "Jaco . . . brought the white kids in": ibid.

490. "We jazz listeners tend": Herbie Hancock, in *Down Beat*, September 8, 1977, p. 56.

490. "I can get toys in a toy shop": *Down Beat*, August 2005, p. 43.

491. "I looked at myself in the mirror": *Down Beat*, October 24, 1974, p. 44.

491. "I decided that it was now time": *Time*, July 8, 1974.

492. "I don't even think this is well-done funk": *Down Beat*, May 17, 1979, p. 33.

493. "The main reason I joined the band": *Down Beat*, October 24, 1974, p. 17.

493. "You don't usually see": *Down Beat*, August 2005, p. 43.

493. "It was the wrong piano": *Jazz Times*, June 2001, p. 73.

493. "I was trying to get rid of all": *Down Beat*, September 2003, p. 50.

494. "play a different blues": *Jazz Times*, June 2001, p. 73.

497. He was born a displaced person: *Jazziz*, April 2005, p. 36.

501. "all these rich people in fur coats": *Electronic Musician*, September 2005, pp. 85–86ff.

501. "that more danceable element": *Down Beat*, November 2000, p. 28.

501. "I can hit three notes on any of my keyboards": *Electronic Musician*, September 2005, pp. 85–86ff.

501. "I'm at a point now": *Guitar Player*, June 1998, p. 40.

504. "Groove Collective has the energy": *Rolling Stone*, June 16, 1994, p. 21.

506. "in what looked like a leftover": Martin Williams, *Jazz In Its Time* (Oxford University Press, 1989), pp. 48–49.

506. "Wow," he said, "if Miles": Paul Tingen, *Miles Beyond: The Electric Explorations of Miles Davis, 1967–1991* (Billboard, 2001), p. 232.

507. "As soon as Miles walked into the studio": ibid., p. 235.

Chapter 18 Historicism: Jazz on Jazz

530. "The thing I'm trying to do": Gary Giddins, *Rhythm-a-ning* (Oxford University Press, 1985), p. 99.

Chapter 19 Jazz Today

544. "We're like the anti young lions": Greg Osby, press release, 1999.

544–45. "The hard part is actually trying to unlearn": Jason Moran, press release, 2007.

Part Opener Photo Credits

Part Opener 1

Jam session: Photo by Charles Peterson, courtesy of Don Peterson. Ma Rainey: Frank Driggs Collection. Henderson/Webb poster: Frank Driggs Collection. Cab Calloway: Frank Driggs Collection. Cecil Taylor: Frank Driggs Collection. Thelonious Monk / Charlie Rouse: © Paul Hoeffler / Frank Driggs Collection. Horace Silver Band: Photo by Carole Reiff / ©Carole Reiff Archive. Wynton Marsalis: ©Herman Leonard Photography LLC/CTSIMAGES.COM.

Part Opener 2

All photos from the Frank Driggs Collection.

Part Opener 3

Savoy Ballroom: Frank Driggs Collection. Fats Waller: Frank Driggs Collection. Roy Eldridge: Timme Rosenkrantz / Duncan Schiedt Collection. Original Blue Devils: Duncan Schiedt Collection. Benny Goodman band: Duncan Schiedt Collection. Mary Lou Williams: Frank Driggs Collection. Ella Fitzgerald: ©Herman Leonard Photography LLC/CTSIMAGES.COM. Dancers: Frank Driggs Collection. Rosie the Riveter: The Granger Collection, New York.

Part Opener 4

Charlie Parker / Dizzy Gillespie: ©Herman Leonard Photography LLC/CTSIMAGES.COM. John Lewis / Dizzy Gillespie: Frank Driggs Collection. Oscar Pettiford: Frank Driggs Collection. Bebop at Royal Roost: ©Herman Leonard Photography LLC/CTSIMAGES.COM. Spotlight Club: Frank Driggs Collection. Woody Herman: ©Herman Leonard Photography LLC/CTSIMAGES.COM. Gerry Mulligan: Frank Driggs Collection. Gil Evans: Frank Driggs Collection. Civil rights activists: © Bettmann/CORBIS.

Part Opener 5:

Nat King Cole / Billy Eckstine: ©Herman Leonard Photography LLC/CTSIMAGES.COM. Gunther Schuller / Ornette Coleman: Photo by Carole Reiff / ©Carole Reiff Archive. Sonny Rollins: ©Herman Leonard Photography LLC/CTSIMAGES.COM. Miles Davis: ©Herman Leonard Photography LLC/CTSIMAGES.COM. John and Alice Coltrane: ©Chuck Stewart. Coltrane memorial service: Neal Boenzi / The New York Times / Redux. Louis Jordan: Frank Driggs Collection. David Murray / Butch Morris: ©Chuck Stewart. Berlin Wall: AP Photo / Lionel Cironneau.

Music Credits

Leon Berry and Andy Razaf: "Christopher Columbus," lyric by Andy Razaf. music by Leon Berry. © 1936 (renewed), Edwin H. Morris & Company, a division of MPL Music Publishing, Inc. All Rights Reserved. Reprinted by permission.
Walter Donaldson: "Changes," by Walter Donaldson. © 1927, renewed 1983, Donaldson Publishing Co. LLC (ASCAP).
Fred Longshaw and Jack Gee: "Reckless Blues," by Fred Longshaw and Jack Gee, as performed by Bessie Smith. Reprinted by permission of C.R. Publishing Company.
Big Joe Turner and Pete Johnson: "It's All Right, Baby," by Big Joe Turner and Pete Johnson, from *From Spirituals to Swing: The Legendary 1938-1939* Carnegie Hall Concerts.

Charles Warfield and Clarence Williams: "Baby, Won't You Please Come Home?" by Charles Warfield and Clarence Williams, as performed by Sarah Vaughan.

Every effort has been made to contact the copyright holder of each of the selections. Rights holders of any selections not credited should contact Permissions Department, W.W. Norton & Company, Inc., 500 Fifth Avenue, New York, NY 10110, in order for a correction to be made in the next reprinting.

Index

Page numbers in *italics* indicate illustrations.